The IDG Books Bible Advantage

The *Word 97 Bible* is part of the Bible series brought to you by IDG Books Worldwide. We designed Bibles to meet your growing need for quick access to the most complete and accurate computer information available.

Bibles work the way you do: They focus on accomplishing specific tasks — not learning random functions. These books are not long-winded manuals or dry reference tomes. In Bibles, expert authors tell you exactly what you can do with your software and how to do it. Easy to follow, step-by-step sections; comprehensive coverage; and convenient access in language and design — it's all here.

The authors of Bibles are uniquely qualified to give you expert advice as well as insightful tips and techniques not found anywhere else. Our authors maintain close contact with end users through feedback from articles, training sessions, e-mail exchanges, user group participation, and consulting work. Because our authors know the realities of daily computer use and are directly tied to the reader, our Bibles have a strategic advantage.

Bible authors have the experience to approach a topic in the most efficient manner, and we know that you, the reader, will benefit from a "one-on-one" relationship with the author. Our research shows that readers make computer book purchases because they want expert advice on a product. Readers want to benefit from the author's experience, so the author's voice is always present in a Bible series book.

In addition, the author is free to include or recommend useful software in a Bible. The software that accompanies a Bible is not intended to be casual filler but is linked to the content, theme, or procedures of the book. We know that you will benefit from the included software.

You will find what you need in this book whether you read it from cover to cover, section by section, or simply one topic at a time. As a computer user, you deserve a comprehensive resource of answers. We at IDG Books Worldwide are proud to deliver that resource with the *Word 97 Bible*.

Brenda McLaughlin
Senior Vice President and Group Publisher
Internet: YouTellUs@idgbooks.com

Word 97 Bible

Word 97 Bible

by Brent Heslop and David Angell

IDG Books Worldwide, Inc.
An International Data Group Company

Foster City, CA ✦ Chicago, IL ✦ Indianapolis, IN ✦ Southlake, TX

Word 97 Bible

Published by

IDG Books Worldwide, Inc.

An International Data Group Company

919 E. Hillsdale Blvd.

Suite 400

Foster City, CA 94404

Library of Congress Catalog Card No.: 96-78771

ISBN: 0-7645-3038-0

Printed in the United States of America

10 9 8 7 6 5 4 3 2 1

1E/RQ/QR/2X/FC

Distributed in the United States by IDG Books Worldwide, Inc.

Distributed by Macmillan Canada for Canada; by Transworld Publishers Limited in the United Kingdom and Europe; by WoodsLane Pty. Ltd. for Australia; by WoodsLane Enterprises Ltd. for New Zealand; by Longman Singapore Publishers Ltd. for Singapore, Malaysia, Thailand, and Indonesia; by Simron Pty. Ltd. for South Africa; by Toppan Company Ltd. for Japan; by Distribuidora Cuspide for Argentina; by Livraria Cultura for Brazil; by Ediciencia S.A. for Ecuador; by Addison-Wesley Publishing Company for Korea; by Ediciones ZETA S.C.R. Ltda. for Peru; by WS Computer Publishing Company, Inc., for the Philippines; by Unalis Corporation for Taiwan; by Contemporanea de Ediciones for Venezuela. Authorized Sales Agent: Anthony Rudkin Associates for the Middle East and North Africa.

For general information on IDG Books Worldwide's books in the U.S., please call our Consumer Customer Service department at 800-762-2974. For reseller information, including discounts and premium sales, please call our Reseller Customer Service department at 800-434-3422.

For information on where to purchase IDG Books Worldwide's books outside the U.S., please contact our International Sales department at 415-655-3172 or fax 415-655-3295.

For information on foreign language translations, please contact our Foreign & Subsidiary Rights department at 415-655-3021 or fax 415-655-3281.

For sales inquiries and special prices for bulk quantities, please contact our Sales department at 415-655-3200 or write to the address above.

For information on using IDG Books Worldwide's books in the classroom or for ordering examination copies, please contact our Educational Sales department at 800-434-2086 or fax 817-251-8174.

For press review copies, author interviews, or other publicity information, please contact our Public Relations department at 415-655-3000 or fax 415-655-3299.

For authorization to photocopy items for corporate, personal, or educational use, please contact Copyright Clearance Center, 222 Rosewood Drive, Danvers, MA 01923, or fax 508-750-4470.

is a trademark under exclusive license to IDG Books Worldwide, Inc., from International Data Group, Inc.

About the Authors

Brent Heslop
Brent Heslop is an avid Word user. He has coauthored more than 15 books and written numerous magazine articles using Word. He also works as a consultant and teaches HTML publishing and interactive programming classes at the University of Santa Cruz Extension. His books include *Word for Windows 95 Bible*, *HTML Publishing on the Internet* (Windows and Macintosh editions) and the *Webheads Guide to Netscape*. Brent lives in Silicon Valley with his lovely wife, Kim, and their devoted dog, Cassius.

David Angell
David Angell (david@angell.com) is a computer industry writer and consultant. He has used Word as his word-processing workbench since the early days of Word for MS-DOS. David has authored and coauthored 14 books. His books include *Word for Windows 95 Bible*, *ISDN For Dummies* (both IDG books), and *The Internet Business Companion*. He is also a principal in angell.com (www.angell.com), an Internet and ISDN consulting and technical communications firm. He lives in Boston with his wife, Joanne, and a growing intranet.

Virginia Andersen
Virginia Andersen is a freelance author and writer specializing in personal-computer-based applications. She has written textbooks and instructor's manuals and written or contributed to more than 20 books on topics such as Microsoft Office, Word, Access, Borland's dBASE and Paradox, Corel's WordPerfect, and Lotus 1-2-3. She taught information systems and mathematics for the University of Southern California graduate school for more than 10 years. She lives in Southern California with her husband, 3 computers, 49 rose bushes, and 2 cats.

Winston Steward
Winston Steward is the author of *Every Family's Guide to Computers* and a coauthor of *CorelDraw! SECRETS* and the *Windows Sources Office 97 SuperGuide*. He is currently writing a book on Microsoft Publisher and lives in Los Angeles with his wife, Barbara, and two children.

ABOUT IDG BOOKS WORLDWIDE

Welcome to the world of IDG Books Worldwide.

IDG Books Worldwide, Inc., is a subsidiary of International Data Group, the world's largest publisher of computer-related information and the leading global provider of information services on information technology. IDG was founded more than 25 years ago and now employs more than 8,500 people worldwide. IDG publishes more than 275 computer publications in over 75 countries (see listing below). More than 60 million people read one or more IDG publications each month.

Launched in 1990, IDG Books Worldwide is today the #1 publisher of best-selling computer books in the United States. We are proud to have received eight awards from the Computer Press Association in recognition of editorial excellence and three from *Computer Currents'* First Annual Readers' Choice Awards. Our best-selling *...For Dummies®* series has more than 30 million copies in print with translations in 30 languages. IDG Books Worldwide, through a joint venture with IDG's Hi-Tech Beijing, became the first U.S. publisher to publish a computer book in the People's Republic of China. In record time, IDG Books Worldwide has become the first choice for millions of readers around the world who want to learn how to better manage their businesses.

Our mission is simple: Every one of our books is designed to bring extra value and skill-building instructions to the reader. Our books are written by experts who understand and care about our readers. The knowledge base of our editorial staff comes from years of experience in publishing, education, and journalism — experience we use to produce books for the '90s. In short, we care about books, so we attract the best people. We devote special attention to details such as audience, interior design, use of icons, and illustrations. And because we use an efficient process of authoring, editing, and desktop publishing our books electronically, we can spend more time ensuring superior content and spend less time on the technicalities of making books.

You can count on our commitment to deliver high-quality books at competitive prices on topics you want to read about. At IDG Books Worldwide, we continue in the IDG tradition of delivering quality for more than 25 years. You'll find no better book on a subject than one from IDG Books Worldwide.

John J. Kilcullen

John Kilcullen
President and CEO
IDG Books Worldwide, Inc.

*Eighth Annual
Computer Press
Awards ≥1992*

*Ninth Annual
Computer Press
Awards ≥1993*

*Tenth Annual
Computer Press
Awards ≥1994*

*Eleventh Annual
Computer Press
Awards ≥1995*

To Kim Merry and Joanne Angell, our good karma.

—B.H. and D.A.

Credits

Acknowledgments

We owe a debt of thanks to numerous people who helped us make this book a reality. First, we want to thank Gregory Croy at IDG Books and our agent, Matt Wagner, at Waterside Productions, who gave us the opportunity to work on this Bible.

We feel extremely fortunate to have had Kerrie Klein and Nancy Albright as our development editors for this book. We especially want to thank Kerrie. She was a joy to work with, always going the extra mile to help us meet our deadlines by working weekends, helping us troubleshoot problems, and spending numerous early mornings and late nights ensuring that this project went smoothly through production. It is rare to find such a skilled and dedicated editor. We are truly grateful.

We are also grateful to our copy editor, Kelly Oliver, who made numerous helpful comments as she assisted us in polishing our prose. Thanks also to our tech editors, Paul and Mary Summitt, for bringing their expertise to this project.

One person whom we especially want to acknowledge and thank is Virginia Andersen. Virginia helped us by writing numerous chapters under a tight schedule. As well as being a pleasure to work with, Virginia wrote well, beat her deadlines, and was always willing to help us meet our deadlines. We really can't thank Virginia enough for all her help. Winston Steward was also a great help writing this book. Winston spent countless late-night hours writing and revising chapters. His cheerful attitude and enthusiasm made working together on this book a pleasure. Winston would like to thank MegaImage computers in Pomona, CA for loaning him a laptop computer to use.

We also want to thank the individuals and companies that gave us permission to use their graphic images to enhance the examples in this book. Thanks to Mary Douglas at PhotoDisk; Tammy Wing at Image Club Graphics, Inc.; Nick Scheer at Bettmann Archive; and Lori Reese at Archive Photos, a division of Archive Holdings, Inc.

A special thanks to Rich White at Best Internet Communications and Bob Berger at InterNex Information Services, who helped us speed up the delivery of files by letting us set up and use FTP sites during this project.

Lastly, we want to thank Dawn Merry, who jumped in to assist us by reviewing chapters, taking screen shots, and helping with many other tasks that might otherwise have stood in the way of meeting our deadlines.

(The publisher would like to give special thanks to Patrick J. McGovern, who made this book possible.)

Preface

Welcome to *Word 97 Bible*. As part of the IDG Bible series, this book emphasizes "handiness" by giving you complete coverage of Word 97 in an easy-to-use format. In this book, you will find all the information that you need to successfully use Word, whether you're a new user or someone who has just upgraded from an earlier version of Word.

To make it as easy as possible to find, understand, and implement information, throughout the text, you will find the major tasks clearly delineated at the heads of sections with supporting material following. You also will find notes, tips, and cautions that annotate the tasks being discussed. This guide is designed to facilitate your access to Word 97 and get you quickly on your way to enjoying and getting the most out of this truly exciting and powerful new product.

The Audience for This Book

This book is both a tutorial for beginners as well as a complete reference for more experienced Word users. If you're upgrading to Word 97, you will find that this book fully integrates the new features with those that remain the same, so you can learn about new features in the context of features with which you are already familiar.

The Structure of This Book

This book matches the way you work with Word 97. Organized into seven parts, it starts with the fundamentals and builds on them as you progress through the book. Each chapter stands on its own, however, and points you to any information in this book that you may need before reading the chapter. You can use this guide as a hands-on tutorial or as a handy reference to find out quickly how to accomplish any Word 97 task.

Part I: The First Word: The Fundamentals

Part I is comprised of six chapters that cover the fundamentals of using Word to produce simple documents.

Chapter 1: "Getting Started with Word for Windows 97," explains the basics of working in the Word 97 environment. It covers such fundamentals as starting and exiting, working with menus and toolbars, understanding Word 97's features, using the Intellimouse in Word 97, using different views for your documents, working with Help, and more.

Chapter 2: "Typing, Navigating, and Editing Documents," tells you how to perform essential word processing tasks, such as entering text; creating paragraphs; navigating a document; selecting text; deleting, copying, and moving text; inserting special characters in your documents; and a great deal more.

Chapter 3: "Finding and Replacing Text and Formatting," covers searching documents for specific text or formatting and replacing them.

Chapter 4: "Proofing Documents," describes Word 97's tools for checking your spelling and grammar in documents, including proofing with AutoCorrect.

Chapter 5: "Printing Documents," contains all the information you need to manage the printing of your documents.

Chapter 6: "Managing Documents and Surviving Crashes," tells you how to open, save, back up, and manage your document files. It also explains how to recover documents after a power outage or system crash.

Part II: The Newfashioned Word: Formatting Documents

Part II includes six chapters that cover formatting features and techniques for adding finishing touches to your documents.

Chapter 7: "Character Formatting and Fonts," covers formatting characters in your document. It explains such character formatting as boldfacing, italicizing, underlining, using superscripts and subscripts, changing case, and more. This chapter also explains how to change fonts and use them effectively in your documents.

Chapter 8: "Paragraph Formatting," explains formatting paragraphs, which are the core building blocks of a Word 97 document. This chapter tells you how to align paragraphs, adjust line spacing, set tabs, set indents, add borders and shading, and create numbered and bulleted lists.

Chapter 9: "Sections, Columns, and Page Formatting," covers formatting your documents into sections, with each section formatted differently. It also explains formatting documents into newspaper-style columns and formatting pages in your document, such as how to set margins.

Chapter 10: "Working with Wizards and Templates," explains how to use Wizards, which are built-in programs supplied with Word 97 and the ValuPack that let you create documents by answering a series of questions. This chapter also covers working with templates, which are frameworks of formatting that define a document's appearance.

Chapter 11: "Styles and AutoFormatting," covers using styles to automatically apply multiple formatting options to a paragraph simultaneously. This chapter also explains using Word 97's AutoFormatting to automatically apply formatting to your entire document.

Chapter 12: "Working with Tables," tells you how to create sophisticated tables in your Word documents to better present your information. You can use tables to create columns of numbers or arrange side-by-side text or pictures.

Part III: The Fine Arts: Graphics and Links to Other Applications

The four chapters in Part III cover working with graphics. They also explain how to work with other Windows applications in conjunction with Word.

Chapter 13: "Illustrating Documents with Graphics," explains how to use Word's powerful new graphics features to add graphics to your documents. It also explains using WordArt to add shaped text with special effects to your pages.

Chapter 14: "Positioning Text and Graphics with Text Boxes," covers how to lay out your documents by using text boxes for positioning text and pictures.

Chapter 15: "Linking Information from Other Applications," tells you how to bring information from other Windows applications into your Word 97 documents, such as an Excel spreadsheet or chart.

Chapter 16: "Working with Microsoft Graph 97 Chart and Microsoft Equation 3.0," describes working with two of Word 97's support applications that you can use to create spreadsheets and charts and to enter mathematical symbols in your documents.

Part IV: Spreading the Word: Publishing Web Documents and Working with Workgroups

Part IV covers using Word to create and publish HTML documents on the World Wide Web and explains how to share your Word documents as well as tracking annotations and revisions.

Chapter 17: "Creating Basic HTML Documents with Word 97," explains how the World Wide Web is revolutionizing publishing and how you can use Word to create your own Web (HTML) documents with graphics and links.

Chapter 18: "Advanced HTML Publishing with Word," jumps into more advanced Web publishing techniques, such as how to use Word to create images with transparent backgrounds and use an image map to create clickable images. It also explains how to create and process an HTML form and publish your HTML documents.

Chapter 19: "Sharing Documents and Working with Workgroups," delves into using Word 97 with Exchange and Office 97's new Outlook program to share documents via a fax or e-mail. It also explains how to share and revise documents in a workgroup environment.

Part V: The Great Plays: Mail Merge, Forms, Outlines, and Long Documents

Part V covers, in five chapters, working with Word's powerful mail merge, forms, and long documents features.

Chapter 20: "Creating Form Letters, Envelopes, Labels, and Catalogs," tells you how to create and print form letters, envelopes, labels, and lists by merging information from a database.

Chapter 21: "Creating Forms," covers using Word 97's powerful form features to create your own forms and tie them directly to a database.

Chapter 22: "Getting Organized with Outlines and Master Documents," describes how to use outlines to organize your thoughts and documents. It also explains using Word 97's Master Document feature to create a single, large document from many subdocuments for consistent formatting.

Chapter 23: "Working with Long Documents," covers several features suitable for working with long documents, including annotations, bookmarks, captions, cross-references, and footnotes.

Chapter 24: "Creating Tables of Contents and Indexes," explains how to create a table of contents and index for your long documents.

Part VI: The Perfect Word: Customizing Word

Part VI includes three chapters that cover techniques for customizing Word to tailor it to the way you work.

Chapter 25: "Customizing Menus, Options, Toolbars, and Keys" explains how to tailor Word 97 to go beyond its default settings. You learn how to add commands to menus and buttons to toolbars, create new toolbars, and specify your own shortcut keys.

Chapter 26: "Using Field Codes," describes how to master field codes, which are sets of instructions to automate Word 97 tasks.

Chapter 27: "Working with Macros," tells you to how to work with macros, which are sets of commands that you can automatically execute by choosing a single menu item or button.

Part VII: Appendixes

Part VII includes the appendixes, which explain how to install Word 97 and what's new in Word 97.

Appendix A: "Installing Word 97," tells you how to install Word 97 as part of Office 97. It also explains how to install and remove specific components of Word 97, as well as how to remove and reinstall Word 97.

Appendix B: "What's New in Word 97," surveys the new and improved features in Word 97, including Word's improved interface, automatic formatting, easier document management, new networking features, and much more. It also examines the programs contained in the ValuPack that ships with Word 97.

Appendix C, "A Word HTML Reference," is a reference to common HTML tags that Word 97 supports. You can insert any of HTML tags manually to create or edit a Web page.

The Conventions in This Book

The conventions used in this book enable you to quickly follow any of several learning paths through the material on your way to becoming a skilled Word user. You can, of course, read the book from cover to cover for complete coverage of all of Word's features. You may want to start learning by following the instructions that are presented as Steps within various sections of each chapter. The text is also sprinkled with information that is directed to the longtime Word user who is looking for ways to become more effective and productive. To help you identify supplementary, noteworthy, or new text, look for the following icons:

Note Marks a special point or supplementary information about a feature or task.

Tip Marks a tip that saves you time and helps you work more efficiently.

Caution Marks a warning about a particular procedure to which you should pay particular attention.

New Marks a new or enhanced capability that is accessible to Word 97 users.

To assist you in reading and learning the material in this book, the following formatting conventions are used throughout:

Text you are asked to type appears in **bold.**

New words and phrases that may require definition and explanation appear in *italics.* Text that carries emphasis and single characters that may be easy to lose in the text also appear in *italics.*

On-screen messages and prompts appear in a `special typeface`.

Menu commands are indicated in chronological order by using the following command arrow: File⇨Open.

Keyboard shortcut keys look like this: Alt+Tab.

Feedback, Please!

We would appreciate your feedback. After you've had a chance to use the book, take a moment to complete the IDG Books Worldwide Registration Card in the back of the book. Please send us your comments by e-mail at either of the following addresses:

Brent Heslop
bheslop@bookware.com

David Angell
dangell@angell.com

Contents at a Glance

Table of Contents

Part I: The Fundamentals   1

Chapter 1: Getting Started with Word for Windows 97 3

Part II: Formatting Documents   177

Chapter 7: Character Formatting and Fonts 179

Part III: Graphics and Links to Other Applications   397

Chapter 22: Getting Organized with Outlines and Master Documents 685

Chapter 23: Working with Long Documents 715

Part VI: Customizing Word 777

Chapter 25: Customizing Menus, Options, Toolbars, and Keys 779

Chapter 26: Using Field Codes 817

The First Word: The Fundamentals

Getting Started with Word for Windows 97

Word 97 and Office 97 bring new ways to create and open Word documents. Word 97 and Office 97 are integrated to give you greater flexibility and let you take a document-centric approach rather than an application-centric approach. This chapter gives you an overview of Word and explains the purpose of Word's tools. Primarily, this chapter teaches you the fundamentals that you need to start working with Word quickly and to increase your productivity. It also explains how to use Word's new Help features.

Starting Word and Opening Documents

Microsoft Word 97, Microsoft Office 97, and Windows 95 give you a variety of ways to start Word and open documents. Learning the different methods you can use to launch Word increases your flexibility with Word. For example, both Office and Word let you choose from a wide selection of predefined document templates and Wizards to simplify the creation of standard documents such as memos, letters, faxes, newsletters, reports, and so on. You've probably discovered that Windows 95 lets you create a shortcut icon to quickly start Word from your desktop. If you plan to work on the same document for several days, you can modify the properties of the shortcut icon so that Word automatically starts and loads the last document you worked on each time you start Windows.

Starting Word manually from the taskbar

In Windows 95, the most common method of starting Word is from the Start menu in the taskbar. The Start menu is the equivalent of Windows 3.*x*'s Program Manager, and the taskbar is the equivalent of the Task list. A button appears in the taskbar for each active program. After you start Windows and log in, click the Start menu button and choose Microsoft Word from the Programs menu. When Word starts, a depressed button appears in the taskbar, indicating that Word is active. If you have already created a Word document, you can also start Word by clicking Start and choosing the Word document from the Documents menu. Using Windows NT, you start Word by double-clicking the Microsoft Word icon in the Microsoft Office program group.

Using the Word program file and great shortcuts

Several other options exist for starting Word, but they require that you know how to locate the Winword program file or a shortcut. A *shortcut* is a link to a Windows 95 program or device. Shortcuts are powerful additions to Windows 95 that let you use different names to refer to programs and devices. Shortcuts are similar to aliases used on the Macintosh and to shadow programs used with OS/2. A shortcut lets you create a reference to Word so that you can start Word or any program from the desktop or any drive or folder. Shortcut files end with the extension .lnk, which stands for link. A shortcut file icon looks similar to the program file, except that a small, curved arrow appears in the icon's lower-left corner.

You can locate program and shortcut files by double-clicking the My Computer icon on the desktop. You can also choose Windows Explorer from the Start menu's Programs submenu, and then navigate the folders to display the Winword.exe file icon. Unlike the Windows File Manager, Explorer lets you view files as unique icons. When using Microsoft Office, the default path for Winword is C:\Program Files\Microsoft Office\Winword.exe.

Knowing the path name, you can choose Start⇨Run, enter the path and program names in the Open text box, and then click the OK button to start Word. This method also works with shortcut files; for example, you can replace Winword.exe with Winword.lnk to reference a link to the Winword program. Simply dragging the Word program file to the desktop or another folder automatically creates a short-cut icon. Double-click the shortcut icon to start Word. All these methods display the Microsoft Word window in full-screen size, as shown in Figure 1-1.

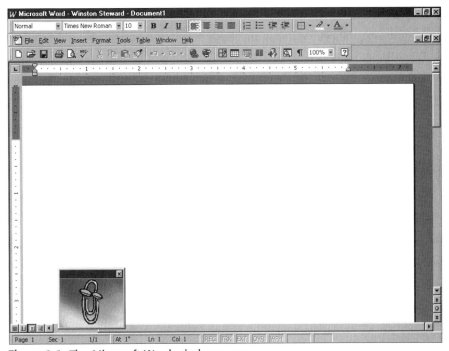

Figure 1-1: The Microsoft Word window.

Using the Office Shortcut Bar

If you chose to install the Microsoft Office Shortcut Bar, you can start Word by clicking the Start a New Document button or the Open a Document button in the Office Shortcut Bar. When you choose the Start a New Document button, a dialog box appears with tabs that indicate the different types of documents you can create. Figure 1-2 shows the New document dialog box. To start Word, click the tab that indicates the type of document you want to create. Click the Word template or Wizard that you want to use as the basis for your document.

If the Office Shortcut Bar doesn't automatically appear after installing Office 97 and the Office Shortcut Bar, you can add it to the Start or Programs menu so it will appear the next time you start Windows 95 as follows:

1. Click the Start button, and then point to Settings.

2. Choose the Taskbar option, and then click the Start Menu Programs tab.

3. Click <u>A</u>dd, and in the <u>C</u>ommand-line text box, for example, type **"C:\MSOffice\Microsoft Office Shortcut Bar.lnk"** (be sure to include the quotation marks). Or click <u>B</u>rowse to find it yourself.

4. Click the Next button.

5. Type the name that you want to see on the menu, and then choose the Finish button.

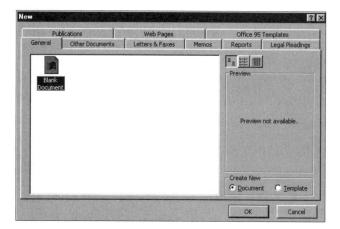

Figure 1-2: The New document dialog box.

Starting Word automatically

If you want Word to run whenever you start Windows 95, add Winword to the StartUp folder in the Start menu. To add Word to the StartUp folder using Windows 95:

1. Click the Start menu button, and then point to <u>S</u>ettings.

2. Click <u>T</u>askbar, and then click the Start Menu Programs tab.

3. Click <u>A</u>dd, and then enter the path for the Winword program in the <u>C</u>ommand-line text box; for example, type **C:\Program Files\Microsoft Office\Winword.exe**. If you like, use the B<u>r</u>owse button to locate the Winword program icon. Click Next.

4. Click the Start Up folder in the <u>S</u>elect folder to place shortcut in box and click Next.

5. Type **Microsoft Word**, and then click Finish or press Enter. Click OK to close the Taskbar P<u>r</u>operties dialog box.

Opening documents automatically

By editing the properties of the shortcut, you can open a specified document at the time you start Word. Clicking the right mouse button on a Word shortcut displays a pop-up menu that includes a Properties option. Clicking Properties and then clicking the Shortcut tab for the Word shortcut displays a property sheet that contains settings for configuring how Word starts. For example, adding a document filename after the program name in the Target text box causes the document to load automatically when the shortcut is used. To start Word and open a document named Letter.doc that is stored in a folder named Docs on the C drive, you type **"C:\Program Files\Microsoft Office\Winword.exe" "C:\Docs\Letter.doc"** in the Target text box.

You also can modify a property sheet to start Word and load multiple docu-ments by separating the path names with a space. To load two documents named Letter.doc and Resume.doc in the Docs folder, type **"C:\Program Files\Microsoft Office\Winword.exe" "C:\Docs\Letter.doc" "C:\Docs\Resume.doc"** in the Target text box.

Tip   Here's a shortcut you can use to return to the last place you were working in a specific document. After the document name, enter **/mGoBack**. You can use this shortcut only for the last document in your command line. The /m (macro) switch is one of the startup switches we talk about in the next section. GoBack is a command macro that is the equivalent of pressing Shift+F5. By pressing Shift+F5, you can return to any of the last three locations at which you have worked in a document.

Controlling Word using startup switches

A startup switch lets you control how Word starts. A *switch* is a command-line parameter that is added after the Winword program. As in the preceding section's example, you click the right mouse button on a Word shortcut to display the pop--up menu, and then you choose the Properties option. Click Properties to display the property sheet for the Word shortcut. You add the switch to the end of the Target settings command line. For example, you can modify the command line to include the /n switch by entering **"C:\Program Files\Microsoft Office\Winword" "/n"**. The /n switch instructs Word to start without a default document. The following sections explain the switches you can use to control how Word starts. You can include more than one switch by adding a space between each switch.

Any of the Word switches that work with Windows 95 work the same way with Windows NT.

Opening the last document loaded

The last four documents you worked on appear in the File menu. You can load any one of them by choosing it from Word's File menu. You can start and automatically load the last document you worked on in Word by using the /m switch with the Word macro that specifies the last document loaded (File1).

The Word program includes macros to load any of the last four files you used. *Macros* are sequences of actions that are stored in named files and executed as commands. The macros used to load the last four documents are named File1 through File4. Word also lists these macros as commands in the File menu. You can run any macro when you start Word simply by adding the macro name after the /m switch. Be sure that you don't add a space between the /m and the macro name. For more information on using macros, see Chapter 27. To start Word with the last document:

1. Click the Word shortcut icon.

2. Click the right mouse button on the Word shortcut icon. Click Properties; the Properties dialog box appears.

3. Click the Shortcut tab, and type **"C:\Program Files\Microsoft Office\ Winword.exe" "/mFile1"** (see Figure 1-3) in the Target text box. The /mFile1 switch instructs Word to open the last file you were working on in the program. If you want to return to where you were last working in the document, add the GoBack macro by adding **/mGoBack** to the end of the command line (`"C:\Program Files\Microsoft Office\Winword.exe" "/mFile1" "/mGoBack"`).

4. Click the OK button or press Enter.

Figure 1-3: Adding the /mFile1 switch opens the last document loaded.

Note You can choose to display up to nine of the files last opened, rather than four, by first choosing Tools⇨Options and clicking the General tab. The Entries box across from the Recently Used File List option displays the number of recently used filenames in the File menu. To display the last seven files, enter **7** in the Entries box.

Starting without a default document

Typically, Word starts with a blank document named Document1, but you can start Word without loading the default blank document. Using this startup option displays Word faster than loading it with a document.

To start Word without loading a default document:

1. Click the Word shortcut icon.
2. Click the right mouse button on the Word shortcut icon. Click Properties; the Properties dialog box appears.
3. Click the Shortcut tab, and type **"C:\Program Files\Microsoft Office\ Winword.exe**" "**/n**" in the Target text box. The /n switch instructs Word not to open a default document.
4. Click the OK button or press Enter.

Opening a document as a template

Word can save you a lot of work by creating a template from an existing document. A *template* is a file that stores formatting and other settings for a document. To start Word and open a document as a template that you can modify, add the /t switch followed by the name of the document that you want to open as a template. For example, by using the Letter Wizard, you create a letter document and modify it. You can open the document as a template and remove text that you don't want to use in future letters, and then save it as a new template. To open a document named Letter.doc in a folder named Docs on the C drive as a template, click the Start button, choose Run, and type **"C:\Program Files\Microsoft Office\ Winword**" "**/t**" "**C:\Docs\Letter.doc**". After modifying the template, save it in the template folder as a template and use it for future letters.

Starting with a Word add-in

Word is extremely flexible for working with add-in programs. Add-ins are typically programs written in the C programming language. You might use an add-in program to add custom commands on toolbars and menus and assign the shortcuts to keys, similar to the way you add a macro. For example, The ValuPack folder included with your Office 97 package contains powerful add-in programs that add commands to Word so that you can create and edit documents in the HyperText Markup Language (HTML). HTML documents can be published on the World Wide Web.

Most add-in programs automatically install themselves into Word. If you want to load an add-in program automatically each time you start Word, you can place it in the Startup folder. You can also use the /l add-in switch to start an add-in you specify. For example, "C:\Winword\Winword" "/l" "C:\Winword\ Wordaddin.wll" loads the add-in program Wordaddin.wll, when you start Word.

Please note that in all these shortcuts in which you type in a command line, you have to first click Start and open the Run dialog box to begin typing.

Starting without preset defaults

In some rare cases, you may need to start Word without loading the preset defaults that Word normally uses. If you try to start Word after installing an add-in program that is incompatible with Word, try adding the /a switch after the program name (for example, `"C:\Program Files\Microsoft Office\Winword.exe" "/a"`). The /a switch is used to start Word and exclude the typical startup commands, including the Normal template that is used by the default Document1. The /a startup switch may give you access to Word when other options fail. Keep in mind that this switch prevents setting files from being modified, so any changes you make to Word, such as changing settings in the Options dialog box (Tools⇨Options), will not take effect the next time you start Word.

The Word Environment

Initially, Word displays a new document that is based on the Normal template (Normal.dot) in full-screen size. When you start Word with the default document, Word's Normal template determines the initial settings. This template, which you can customize and use as a basis for creating other templates, is Word's main workhorse template.

A window displayed in full-screen size is called a *maximized* window, and clicking the document's own Maximize button displays your document as "windowed." When your document is windowed, you can display two documents at a time on your screen; you can move them around to compare and edit them simultaneously. The three buttons on the upper-right of the screen either minimize, "window" or restore, or exit your document, respectively. The Restore button returns your document to its previous "windowed" state. Figure 1-4 labels the main components of the Word screen. The title bar at the top of the screen displays the program name (Microsoft Word) and the document filename (Document1). The Document1 filename is the default filename assigned to a new document. The Word Control menu now appears represented as the letter "W" located in the upper-left corner of the title bar. The Control menu provides a menu of commands for manipulating the Word program window. The Document Control menu now appears as a small Word document icon located directly below the Word Control menu. The Document Control menu provides a menu of commands for manipulating the document window. It's likely that you will use the controls that appear at the opposite side to control the Word program window and the document windows.

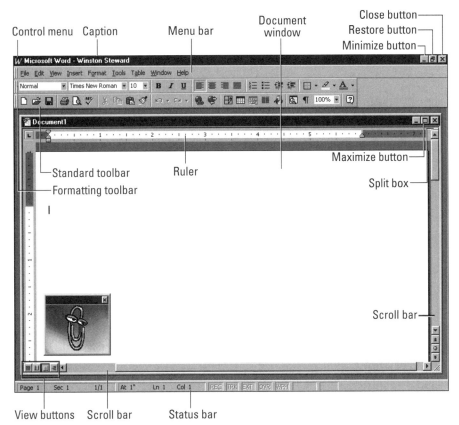

Figure 1-4: The parts of the Word screen.

The document window

The text area of the document window occupies the bulk of the screen. You create, edit, format, and view your document files in the document window. The blinking vertical bar is called the *insertion point.* It indicates where text is to be entered into a document. You also use the insertion point to specify the point from which you want to select or edit text. The mouse pointer appears in the shape of an I-beam when it is in a document window's text area.

The Word menu bar

Directly below the title bar is the *menu bar.* The menu bar contains pull-down menus that organize families of commands for working with documents. Word's menus arrange together the commands that carry out similar actions. The File menu contains a group of commands that manipulate your document files, as shown in Figure 1-5. Choosing a command tells Word what to do; for example, the File menu contains commands that you use to open, print, and save your documents.

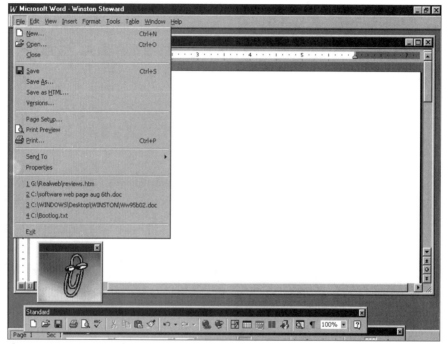

Figure 1-5: The menu bar with the File menu displayed.

By opening each menu and looking at its contents, you can get a good overview of Word's main features. To get an idea of what each command does, select Help from the menu bar and scroll down to What's This? Your cursor becomes an arrow-question mark. Click any feature on the screen—a dialog box, command, or toolbar—and you'll receive a brief description of its function. Pressing Shift+F1 also converts your cursor to the "What's This" icon. Additionally, clicking Office Assistant opens an inquiry dialog box. Type any question or feature you'd like help with. Pressing Alt+H opens the Help dialog box. .

Dialog boxes and control settings

A command in a menu or a button followed by an ellipsis (...) displays a dialog box after you choose that command or button. For example, choosing the Format⇨Font command displays the dialog box with control settings, as shown in

Figure 1-6. Notice that some controls are already set or have text entered. These settings are Word's default settings, which you can change. Control settings vary, depending on the type of information Word needs to activate a feature. A label identifies each control setting. Related control settings are usually grouped together and placed inside a box with a group label. One control setting is always active in a dialog box. You can tell which control is active because it either has a dotted rectangle around the label or the setting appears highlighted.

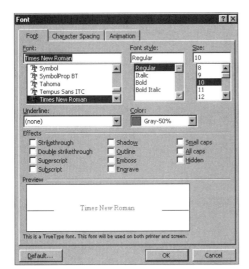

Figure 1-6: The Font dialog box.

Notice that in each label, with the exception of the OK, Cancel, and Close buttons, one letter is underlined. You press the underlined letter in conjunction with the Alt key to activate the control setting. Using the keyboard, press Tab to move in order through the control settings and buttons—from upper left to lower right in the dialog box. By pressing Shift+Tab, you move through the options and controls in the opposite direction. By clicking the setting, use the mouse to choose a control setting.

If a label for a setting, group of settings, or button is dimmed, then that item is not available. When a control setting is available, it is black. You must choose the OK button to save your setting changes, or choose the Cancel button (or press Esc) to cancel the command before choosing another command or typing text in a document. If you try to do something outside some dialog boxes, Word beeps to remind you that you must first close the dialog box.

Many dialog boxes use a file folder metaphor to let you choose from sets of related options. You can organize and reference each set of options by clicking a tab. For example, notice the tab labeled Character Spacing back in Figure 1-6. Clicking this tab or pressing Alt+R displays the Font Character Spacing options, as shown in Figure 1-7. Clicking the Font tab or pressing Alt+N redisplays the Font options.

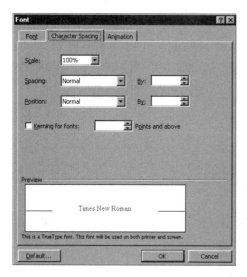

Figure 1-7: The Font Character Spacing tab.

Dialog box control settings allow you to converse with Word by specifying how you want the program to affect your text. Word provides different types of control settings, including the tab, option button, check box, text box, list box, and command button, as shown in Figure 1-8. Table 1-1 describes each of these settings.

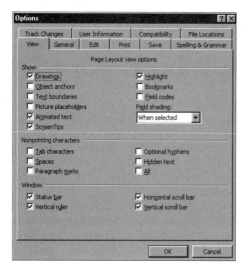

Figure 1-8: A dialog box showing the various Word control settings.

Table 1-1
Dialog Box Control Settings

Control Setting	Action
Tab	Separates groups of options. Clicking the tab or pressing Alt and the underscored character displays the additional options.
Option button	(A round button, sometimes referred to as a radio button.) Selects a single option from multiple options in a group. Displays a dot in the center when selected.
Check box	Displays a check mark when the setting is selected. Check boxes often are clustered in groups, but, unlike option boxes, choosing one doesn't prohibit you from choosing others.
Text box	Used to enter text, such as a filename or measurement specification. When you move the mouse pointer to a text box, the pointer changes to an I-beam, indicating that you can insert text. When you select a text box, the highlighted text is replaced with the new text you type.
List box	Displays a scrolling list of alternatives. Includes a text box with a list of options displayed under the text box. The drop-down list box has a down arrow displayed to the right of the text box. When you choose the down arrow, a list of available options appears. Word often uses drop-down list boxes to save space in dialog boxes. If the list is longer than the list box, a scroll bar appears at the right side of the list box. Many list boxes allow you either to type your own entry or choose an option from the list. Some list boxes, however, require you to choose from the options in the list.
Command button	Instructs Word to perform the appropriate task or display additional information. For example, the OK button saves your control setting changes and exits the dialog box. If the name on the command button is followed by an ellipsis (...), choosing this button either opens another dialog box related to that command and closes the first dialog box, or opens a dialog box related to that command while leaving the first dialog box open. When the second dialog box is closed, you can continue to select options in the first dialog box. The active command button has a dotted rectangle around its label.
? button	Calls up Office Assistant's What would you like to do? dialog box. Type in any words pertinent to the topic in question..

Note When you perform certain options, you may find it confusing that the Cancel button changes to a Close button. When Word completes an action that cannot be canceled, the Cancel button changes to the Close button. The Close button closes the dialog box without reversing any completed changes. Choosing the Cancel button discards the options you have selected, closes the dialog box, and returns you to your document. The keyboard equivalent to the Cancel and Close buttons is Esc. Double-clicking the Control menu icon in the upper-left corner closes the dialog box.

Toolbars

The Standard and Formatting toolbars are displayed just below the menu bar by default. Unless you've gone out of your way to choose a different Office Assistant, you should also notice "Clipit," one of several fully animated characters on hand to answer any questions. The Standard and Formatting toolbars enable you to access several of the most commonly used commands with the mouse, without having to choose commands from the menus. For example, to print a document, click the printer icon instead of choosing the File⇨Print command. This action immediately prints the document without displaying the Print dialog box. To display the Tip of the Day, click the Office Assistant and select Tips (or press Alt+T). To make Word display the Tip of the Day at startup, click Office Assistant, select Options, and then click the appropriate check box.

Additional toolbars are available for different features. To display a list of available toolbars, choose View⇨Toolbar. This displays the Customize dialog box, as shown in Figures 1-9, 1-10, and 1-11. The options in this dialog box let you show or hide any of Word 97's thirteen toolbars, edit their tools and features, and change the way toolbars look on the screen. .

Figure 1-9: The Customize dialog box.

A few Word critics have pointed out that some buttons on Word's toolbars are designed more for marketing dog-and-pony shows than for day-to-day use. For example, you are much more apt to use the Find and Replace commands on a day-to-day basis than to insert columns or Microsoft Excel worksheets. You can customize a toolbar by adding commands or macros to it, or by replacing the commands that appear on the toolbar with commands of your own choosing. You can create a customized toolbar for each type of document that you regularly produce. For example, you can create a toolbar with buttons to access a command you use often, such as creating a Search and Replace button to replace the chart or columns buttons that are less often used. Chapter 3 includes simple instructions for adding frequently used editing commands to the standard toolbar. For more information about customizing the toolbar, see Chapter 25.

If you let your mouse "float" over any toolbar button momentarily, its name appears. To find out more about a toolbar button's function, press Shift+F1 and click any item you need help with. You can also select the question mark on the right of the Standard toolbar or click Office Assistant. Type the name of the button in the resulting dialog box, and Office Assistant tells you what you need to know.

How to display and hide toolbars

A quick way to choose a toolbar is to display a pop-up toolbar menu by clicking the right mouse button anywhere on a toolbar. Choosing toolbars from the Toolbars shortcut menu is equivalent to using the View⇨Toolbars command.

How to move and resize toolbars

The Standard and Formatting toolbars are normally anchored just below the menu bar. When you display other toolbars, they either appear stacked in the order you display them or they float on-screen like small windows. Some, like the Drawing toolbar, anchor themselves to the bottom of the screen, above the status line. To rearrange a floating toolbar, just drag the toolbar to the position where you want it displayed. You can also change an anchored toolbar to a floating toolbar, and vice versa, by double-clicking in the background area of the toolbar. On the left side of most anchored toolbars is a "drag bar" that allows you to reposition it anywhere you want along its horizontal axis. Quickly dragging a floating toolbar by this handle to the left of the screen anchors it vertically to the left margin bar. Double-clicking anchors it as a normal toolbar above your document. Figure 1-10 displays all toolbars as floating toolbars. To anchor a floating toolbar, drag it just below the menu bar, or double-click in the background of the toolbar or title bar.

If you use large toolbar buttons, you may need to resize the toolbars to see all the buttons. To resize a floating toolbar, move the mouse pointer to the border of the toolbar that you want to resize. The pointer changes to a two-headed arrow. Drag the two-headed arrow in the direction you want the toolbar enlarged. Figure 1-11 shows samples of resized toolbars.

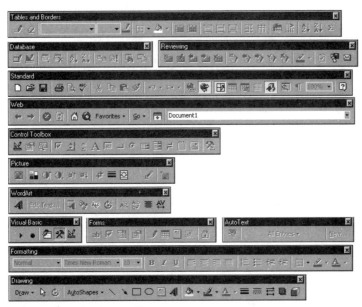

Figure 1-10: Floating toolbars.

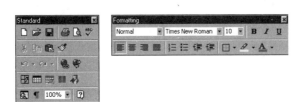

Figure 1-11: Resized floating toolbars.

The Standard toolbar

The Standard toolbar includes frequently and infrequently used commands for working with Word. Table 1-2 describes the default buttons that appear on the Standard toolbar.

Table 1-2
The Standard Toolbar Buttons

Button	Name	Action
	New	Opens a new document based on current default settings.
	Open	Opens an existing document or template. Word displays the Open dialog box, where you can locate and open the file you want.
	Save	Saves the active document or template with its current name. If you have not named the document, Word displays the Save As dialog box so that you can do so.
	Print	Prints all pages of the active document.
	Print Preview	Displays the layout of a document as it will appear when printed.
	Spelling	Checks the spelling of the entire document, or, if you have selected text, checks the spelling of the selection. Word displays the Spelling dialog box when it does not find a word in the dictionary.
	Cut	Removes selected text and graphics from the document and stores them on the Clipboard.
	Copy	Copies selected text and graphics and stores them on the Clipboard.
	Paste	Inserts the contents of the Clipboard at the insertion point or over the selection.
	Format Painter	Copies character formatting to other selected text.
	Undo	Reverses your last action. You can undo up to 100 commands. Clicking the down arrow attached to the Undo button lets you choose from a list of the most recently changed operations.
	Redo	Repeats the last change you made to a document. Clicking the down arrow attached to the Redo button lets you choose from a list of the most recently changed operations.
	Insert Hyperlink	Opens a dialog box that enables you to insert a URL in your document. You can create a link to a file on your own computer, the Internet, or an office-wide network.

(continued)

Table 1-2 *(continued)*

Button	Name	Action
	Web Toolbar	Opens the Web toolbar, which provides single-click access to your Web home page, Microsoft Internet Explorer, or a list of your favorite Web sites.
	Tables and Borders	Opens the Tables and Borders toolbar.
	Insert Table	Inserts a table. To select the number of rows and columns you want, drag over or past the sample table that is displayed. The sample expands as you drag the pointer.
	Insert Microsoft Excel Worksheet	Inserts a Microsoft Excel worksheet into your document.
	Columns	Formats the current section of your document with one or more newspaper-style columns. To select the number of columns, drag over or past the sample columns that are displayed. The number of sample columns expands as you drag the pointer.
	Drawing	Displays the Drawing toolbar.
	Document Map	Opens a separate window to the left of your document that shows an outline of its headings. Jump to any heading in your document by clicking it in the Document Map.
¶	Show/Hide	Makes normally invisible, nonprinting characters, such as tabs and paragraph marks, visible for easier editing.
100% ▾	Zoom Control	Determines how large or small documents appear. Your choices include 200%, 150%, 100%, 75%, 25%, 10%, Page Width, Whole Page, and Two Pages. The default is 100%. You can type in any integer value from 10 to 200 percent.
	Help	Displays Office Assistant's Search dialog box.

The Formatting toolbar

The controls displayed on the Formatting toolbar affect the appearance of characters and paragraphs in your document. As you move the insertion point through the text in your document, the Formatting toolbar reflects the formatting applied to your text. Table 1-3 lists the buttons on the Formatting toolbar.

Table 1-3
The Formatting Toolbar Buttons

Button/List box	Name	Action
Normal ▾	Style	Determines the style to apply to a selected paragraph or paragraphs. A style is a collection of character and paragraph formatting instructions that are commonly used together. Word comes with several styles and also allows you to create your own. By default, Word displays the Normal style in the Style list box.
Times New Roman ▾	Font	Displays the Font list box for choosing different typefaces. The default font is Times New Roman.
10 ▾	Font Size	Displays a Font Size (Points) list box for controlling the size of characters. A point is 1/72 inch. In addition to using the drop-down list box, you can directly enter any point size between 1 and 1,638. The default is 10 points.
B	Bold	Boldfaces text.
I	Italics	Italicizes text.
U	Underline	Underlines words and spaces.
▤	Align Left	Aligns the current paragraph along the left indent. Align Left is the default setting.
▤	Center	Centers the current paragraph between indents.
▤	Align Right	Aligns the current paragraph along the right indent.
▤	Justify	Aligns the paragraph between the left and right indents.
▤	Numbered List	Numbers the selected paragraphs sequentially by inserting an Arabic numeral (1, 2, 3, and so on) in front of each paragraph and aligning paragraph text 1/4 inch to the right of the numbers.
▤	Bulleted List	Places a bullet in front of each selected paragraph and aligns the paragraphs 1/4 inch to the right of the bullets.
▤	Decrease Indent	Moves selected paragraphs left to the previous default tab stop. The default is 1/2 inch.

(continued)

Button/List box	Name	Action
	Increase Indent	Moves selected paragraphs right to the next tab stop. The default is 1/2 inch.
	Borders	Displays the Borders toolbar, which you can use to add borders and shading to selected paragraphs, table cells, graphics, and frames.
	Highlight	Highlights words and spaces, using a color you specify.
	Font Color	Allows you to quickly change the color of the current font.

Table 1-3 (continued)

The Office Assistant

By now, you've probably met the little paper clip icon that pops up on the lower right of the screen when Word 97 starts. Perhaps you've discovered that the Office Assistant can be moved around the screen, and that by clicking it, you can get help on any topic. Office Assistant is your best bet for getting help with Word 97. Gone are the days when Windows Help was a vague and general overview, renowned for leaving out whatever it is *you* really needed to know. Office Assistant is intelligent and specific, and it can get to the heart of a matter quickly. If you're not happy with the Clipit icon, right-click it, select Choose Assistant, and pick from nine others, including The Bard himself. Right-clicking also gives you access to the Tip of the Day. Clicking the Close box (the one with the X in it) closes Office Assistant, and clicking the question mark on the Standard toolbar brings it back. Under the Help menu, Contents and Index, Microsoft on the Web, and the "What's This?" tool are always available, even with the Office Assistant turned off.

The Ruler

Word's horizontal Ruler (see Figure 1-12) shows and adjusts the margin indent and tab settings of paragraphs. The Ruler is displayed across the top of the document window to give you quick access to the mouse so that you can change paragraph indents, adjust margins, change the width of newspaper-style columns, change the width of table columns, and set tab stops. To display and hide the Ruler, choose the View⇨Ruler command. The measure, which by default is in inches, displays the available text area width, indent markers, and tab settings. The Ruler displays applied settings as you move the insertion point through your document. The zero point on the Ruler aligns with the left boundary of the first paragraph of the selection.

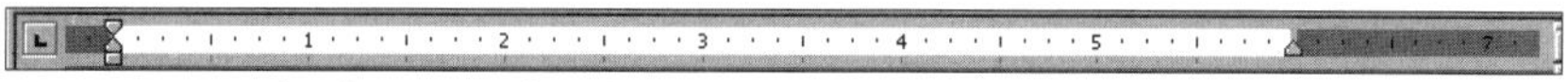

Figure 1-12: The horizontal Ruler.

This Ruler lets you adjust settings for selected paragraphs or the paragraph that contains the insertion point. To use the Ruler to change settings for one or more paragraphs, move the insertion point into the paragraph, or select the paragraphs you want to change and drag a marker on the ruler. Set tabs by clicking the ruler at various points along the horizontal Ruler bar. Word also includes a vertical Ruler, which appears only when your document is displayed in Page View mode. (Changing to Page View mode is explained later in this chapter.)

The scroll bars

At the far right side of the screen, you can see the vertical scroll bar, which is part of the document window. Clicking the arrow buttons located at the top and bottom of the vertical scroll bar scrolls the document in the direction of the respective arrow, one line at a time. The box within the scroll bar is called a *scroll box*. Its position in the scroll bar indicates the position of the insertion point relative to the size of your document. By dragging the scroll box with the mouse, you can move up or down your document. As you scroll through your document by using the scroll box, a box appears to the left of the scroll bar, showing you the current page number.

Three additional buttons appear at the bottom of the vertical scroll bar. The double-headed up arrow moves you to the top of the previous page, and the double-headed down arrow moves you to the bottom of the next page. The middle button, (the one with the circle on it) is the Browse by Objects button. Clicking it allows you to browse your document by moving from picture to picture, for example, or table to table, footnote to footnote, and so on. It's a real timesaver when you have a long document and you only want to review editorial comments, headings and footers, and so on. While using Browse by Object, the double arrows turn blue, and clicking them takes you to the next or previous object in your chosen category. The horizontal scroll bar also contains buttons that allow you to switch quickly between the four most common document views, and so on. Word's different document views are explained later in this chapter.

The status bar

At the bottom of the Word program window is the status bar, as shown in Figure 1-13. It displays information regarding the status of the document and the task you're currently performing. For example, when you save a document, the status bar displays a dotted line that reflects the amount of the file that has been saved.

Figure 1-13: The parts of the status bar.

The first section of the status bar gives you information about your location in a document based on the position of the insertion point. This section shows the current page number, the section number, and the current page number followed by a slash and the total number of pages in the document. *Sections* are specially formatted parts of a document. The next portion of the status bar displays the precise location of the insertion point. It shows the distance (in inches) from the top edge of the page to the insertion point, followed by the insertion point's line and column number. A *column* is the character position within the line of text. Tabs and spaces are counted as characters.

The last section of the status bar displays the current time according to your computer's clock. The last items in this section indicate when certain Word features or modes are active. For example, when you press the Insert key, OVR (overtype) is displayed. When you press Insert again, the OVR indicator is dimmed. Double-clicking a mode indicator also turns the mode on or off. For example, double-clicking OVR switches you to overtype mode. In overtype mode, each character you type replaces the character that lies to the right of the insertion point. When OVR is dimmed, insert mode is active. In insert mode, Word moves the existing text to the right to make room for the new text. The following list identifies the status bar mode indicators:

REC   Records macros

TRK   Track changes in your text

EXT   Extends selections

OVR   Overtypes text

WPH   Provides online Help for WordPerfect users

By default, the status bar is displayed. However, you can hide it so that you can view more of your document. To turn off the status bar from the keyboard, choose the Tools➪Options command. In the Options dialog box, select the View tab and click the Status Bar check box located in the Window options. To turn the status bar back on, choose the Tools➪Options command and again click the Status Bar check box in the View tab.

The style area

A *style* is a collection of formats, such as font, indent, and line spacing, that is given a special name. The vertical pane along the left edge of the document window can display the style name for each paragraph visible in the window. Figure 1-14 shows a 1/2-inch style area. To display and hide the style area, follow these steps:

1. Choose View⇨Normal. The style area is available only in Normal and Outline views.

2. Choose Tools⇨Options.

3. Enter a width or click the up arrow to specify a width greater than zero in the Style Area Width box under Window. For example, enter **0.5"**.

4. Click the OK button, or press Enter.

5. To hide the style area, drag the style area boundary to the left until the style names disappear.

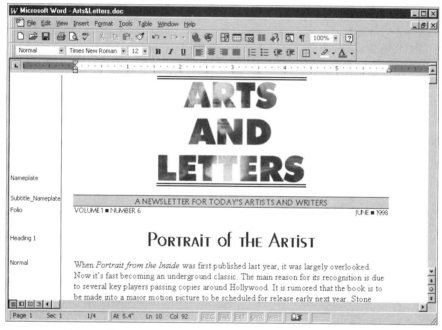

Figure 1-14: The style area.

Using the Mouse and the Keyboard

You can use the mouse or the keyboard to display and choose commands from Word's menus. Whether you use the keyboard or the mouse, a number of commands require that you first select the part of your document on which you want the command to act. These commands appear dimmed in a menu until you make a selection. For example, you can't choose the Edit⇨Cut command until you select the item that you want to remove from your document.

Choosing some commands displays a bullet or check mark next to a command name, which indicates that the command is currently in effect. If more information is needed to complete a command, Word displays a dialog box. You select options in the dialog box to control how the command is carried out. If you choose a command or feature that has not been installed, Word tells you that it cannot locate the command or feature.

Using the mouse

The mouse is an indispensable tool in Word's graphical point-and-shoot environment of buttons and icons. Simply by pointing to a button or icon with the mouse pointer and clicking a mouse button, you can execute a command. Mouse use has its own special lingo. Table 1-4 lists basic terms used throughout this book to define mouse operations. Working with the mouse quickly becomes second nature. As you become proficient with Word, you can use the mouse to integrate various keyboard shortcuts and perform many tasks more quickly.

Table 1-4 Mouse Function Terms	
Term	**Meaning**
Click	Quickly press and release the left mouse button while the mouse pointer is on an object, such as a menu command, icon, or button.
Right-click	Quickly press and release the right mouse button while the mouse pointer is on an object, such as a menu command, icon, or button.
Double-click	Quickly click the left mouse button twice while the mouse pointer is on an object, such as a menu command, icon, or button.
Drag	Move the mouse pointer to an object on-screen. Press and hold the left mouse button while moving the mouse, and then release the button.
Point	Move the mouse pointer directly to a specific location on-screen, such as a menu command, icon, or button.

When you move the mouse pointer to different parts of your screen, or perform certain commands, the pointer shape changes. The mouse pointer's shape indicates the kind of action being performed. For example, it appears as an arrow when you select commands from a menu, an hourglass when Word is processing a command, or an I-beam when the pointer is in a text entry area. Table 1-5 describes where the mouse pointer changes shape and explains the action indicated by the different mouse pointer shapes.

Table 1-5
The Mouse Pointers

Pointer	Description
I I	Appears in the text area. This insertion point is also called the I-beam pointer. In italic text, this pointer slants to make positioning and selecting easier. You use this pointer to indicate where you want to begin typing.
↖	Appears in menus, inactive windows, scroll bars, ribbon, ruler, or toolbar. You can choose a menu and command, click a button, or drag a tab stop marker.
↖	Appears in the selection bar or the style name bar along the window's left edge. You can select a line, paragraph, or the entire document. This pointer also appears in table selection bars.
⧖	Appears when Word is performing a task that takes a few seconds.
÷	Appears after you choose the Split command in a Control menu or when the mouse pointer is on the split box in the vertical scroll bar.
⊹∥⊹	Appears when the pointer is on the style name area split line. Drag the pointer to change the width of the style name area, which displays more or less of each style name.
↔	Appears in Outline view when positioned on a selection symbol. It indicates that you can drag the heading. It also appears when positioned over a frame, indicating that you can drag the frame to a new position. Appears after you choose the Move or Size command from the Control menu. You can move the window to a new position or drag a window border.
↔	Appears in Outline view as you drag a heading left or right to a new level in the outline. It also appears when positioned on the left or right side of a frame, embedded object, or picture, indicating that you can size the frame by dragging the handle. Appears in a window border. It indicates that you can change the size of a window horizontally.
↕	Appears in Outline view as you drag a heading up or down to a new position. It also appears when positioned over the top or bottom side of a frame, embedded object, or picture, indicating that you can size the frame by dragging the handle. Appears in a window border. It indicates that you can change the size of a window vertically.
↗ ↖	Appears when positioned over the corner of a frame, embedded object, or picture, indicating that you can resize the picture by dragging the handle. Appears in a window border. It indicates that you can change the size of a window diagonally.
↓	Appears when the pointer is over a column in a table. Click to select the column.

(continued)

Table 1-3 *(continued)*		
Button/List box	**Name**	**Action**
▯		Appears when you select text or a graphic and press a mouse button to drag the selection to a new location, where you can drop or insert it. A small plus sign also appears as part of the pointer when you press Ctrl to copy text to a new location.
▯		Appears in the Help window, indicating that an option or term definition is available.
+		Appears in print preview when margins are displayed and the pointer is over an object you can drag, such as a margin or page break.

Using the keyboard

To choose a command from a menu by using the keyboard, press the Alt key while pressing the underlined letter in the menu that you want to open, and then press the underlined letter in the command that you want to execute. For example, press Alt+F, and then press S to execute the File⇨Save command. You can also use the up- and down-arrow keys to highlight a command within an open menu. Press Enter to execute the highlighted command. Pressing Alt alone places you in the menu bar. You can then use the right or left arrow to highlight a menu name, and then press Enter to open the menu. Alt is a toggle key. Any time you want to exit a menu without selecting a command, press Alt again. You can also press Esc to exit a menu without selecting a command and return to your document.

You can choose a number of commands by pressing the shortcut keys listed on the menu to the right of the command. Shortcut keys let you execute a command without having to open a menu. For example, to save a document, press Ctrl+S. Word provides many shortcut keys so that you can use the keyboard while you work. You can press Ctrl+B to apply bold formatting to selected text. If a keyboard shortcut is available for a command, it is usually listed to the right of the command in the menu. Some keys also are assigned to Word commands that are not listed in menus. For example, you can execute the File⇨Exit command directly from the keyboard by pressing Alt+F4.

Tip   For a list of the shortcut keys for different tasks, click the Office Assistant icon and type **Shortcut Keys**. You can also open the Help menu, select Contents and Index, and type **Shortcut Keys**.

Right-click for shortcut menus

When you point to or select certain items in Word, such as a paragraph, graphic, or table, you can display a shortcut menu. Shortcut menus contain commands related to the item you're working with. They appear in the document window exactly where you're working. For example, Figure 1-15 shows the shortcut menu for working with text in a document. To display a shortcut menu, position the insertion point on the text or item you want to work with, and then click the right mouse button, or press Shift+F10. When the shortcut menu appears, choose a command. To close a shortcut menu without choosing a command, click anywhere outside the shortcut menu, or press Esc.

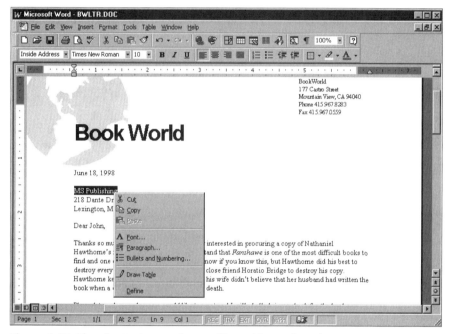

Figure 1-15: The shortcut menu for working with text in a document.

How to undo commands

As you work, it helps to keep the Undo command in mind. The Undo command is located in the Edit menu. It cancels the most recent commands or actions you complete. Word keeps track of the editing and formatting changes that you make. If you don't like the results of a command or accidentally delete text, choose Undo. The fastest way to undo an action is to click the Undo button on the Standard toolbar, or press Ctrl+Z. Some actions, such as saving a document, can't be reversed. In this case, Undo changes to Can't Undo and appears dimmed on the menu, indicating that it is unavailable. You can also redo an action that you've undone.

How to repeat commands

The Repeat command in the Edit menu repeats the last command or action you completed. It's often easier to choose Repeat than to choose the same command several times, particularly when the previous command involved a complex formatting change that you applied by using the Format⇨Font or Format⇨ Paragraph command. You can select other text and then choose Repeat to apply the same formatting in one step. The Repeat command also duplicates typing. Choose Repeat when you type a long paragraph and want to include the same text else-where in your document. Ctrl+Y and the F4 key are both keyboard shortcuts for the Repeat command.

Working with Word's Document Views

Word lets you view your documents from a number of different perspectives. Changing views in Word doesn't change the document; it only changes your view of the document. Think of Word's different views as similar to looking at an object through a magnifying glass. As you change the angle or the distance of the magnifying glass, the object appears to change.

Changing views

You can easily change to any view by using the View menu. You can also use the buttons on the horizontal scroll bar to change views (see Figure 1-16). With the buttons, you are limited to switching between Normal view, Page Layout view, Outline view, and Online Layout view. If you want to use Full Screen view, you must use the menus. To change views:

1. Choose View (Alt+V) to display the View drop-down menu.

2. Select the view in which you want to display your document.

 Figure 1-16: The View buttons on the horizontal scroll bar.

Normal view

Normal view is the default view. The benefit of working in Normal view is relative speed. It is not a true WYSIWYG (What You See Is What You Get) view because you cannot see headers and footers, footnotes, and annotations without issuing a command from the View menu, but you can see the formatting and layout elements of the document.

You can use two methods to customize Normal view to speed up text entry. The tradeoff is that you don't see the text in the actual font you are using or any images in the document. This view of a document was called Draft view in previous versions of Word. Customizing the Normal view to work with a draft font causes all character formatting to appear only as an underline, and, remember, headers, footers, and annotations don't appear. To really speed up text entry, display graphics as placeholders so that you don't have to wait for Word to redraw the screen. To customize Normal view to speed up Word's response time when entering text:

1. Choose View⇨Normal.

2. Choose Tools⇨Options.

3. Select the Draft Font and Picture Placeholders in the View tab.

4. Choose the OK button, or press Enter.

Page Layout view

Page Layout view is the most accurate of all the views available in Word. It is also the slowest. Depending on how fast your computer and graphics card work, scrolling and screen refreshing can slow down drastically when you include graphics in a document and use Page Layout view. The main benefit of Page Layout view is that it is true WYSIWYG. It enables you to see all the elements of your document on the page. You'll likely find it most efficient to work in the faster Normal view and switch to Page Layout view to see how the page will look when printed.

Tip   Page Layout view shows the vertical ruler along the left side of the document. You can change the left and right margins in Page Layout view by using the horizontal ruler, and you can change the top and bottom margins by using the vertical ruler.

Outline view

Outline view is a specialized view that you can use to organize a document. In Outline view, you can collapse and expand portions of the document so that you see only the headings of your choice. You can quickly and easily move and copy large portions of the document in Outline view. The real key to using this view efficiently is to also use Heading styles, as these styles are immediately recognized by Word in Outline view.

Online Layout view

To view your document in Online Layout view, click the second button from the left of the four View buttons right above the status bar. Online Layout view optimizes viewing for an online document, enlarges fonts, and wraps text around a window (rather than letting it run off the edge of the screen). It automatically opens running Document Map, which is a strip of text on the left side of the screen that shows your document's headings. Click a heading, and you'll jump to that portion of the document. Online Layout view removes the View buttons from the bottom of the screen; to leave the view, you must use the View menu options on the menu bar.

Full Screen view

Wish you could hide all of Word's menus, toolbars, and Rulers and have the whole screen for writing? Use the Full Screen view. When you select View⇨Full Screen, only the document and a small one-button toolbar appear. The one-button toolbar appears in the lower-right area of the screen. Like all toolbars, you can close it by clicking once on the control button in the upper-left corner. When you do, nothing is displayed on-screen except the document. To return to the previous view, click once on the button, or press Esc.

The menus and toolbars are still available in Full Screen view, so you can customize the Word screen to suit your needs. The main menu is hidden, not inactive, which means that you can still press menu shortcut keys to display menu options. For example, you could press Alt+V to display the View menu and display or hide rulers and toolbars. You can also click or drag the mouse near the top of the screen to display the pull-down menus. Of course, you can always press the right mouse button to display a shortcut menu.

Not only can you display menu options in Full Screen view, but you can also display the scroll bars and status bar. To display the scroll bars and the status bar, choose the Tools⇨Options command, and select the View tab. If you choose Normal Page view, and then choose Full Screen view in the View menu, the View tab lets you define a style area to show the styles used in your document.

Zoom

Zooming changes the magnification of the document (see Figure 1-17). In addition, you can select Page Width, Whole Page, or Many Pages. Choosing View⇨Zoom displays the Zoom dialog box. See Table 1-6 for explanations of these options. The Zoom Control in the Standard toolbar lets you choose a preset percentage or enter a percentage. Your choices include 500%, 200%, 150%, 100%, 75%, 50%, 25%, 10%. The default is 100%. If you're in Normal view, only the Page Width option appears. If you're in Page Layout view, you can choose Page Width, Whole Page, and Two Pages.

Tip   The Zoom Control in the Standard toolbar lets you change your view faster than by changing the settings found in the Zoom dialog box. As with the Percent option, you can highlight and change the % number in the Zoom Control box to any number that you want. For example, entering **41%** displays your document in 41% of its actual size.

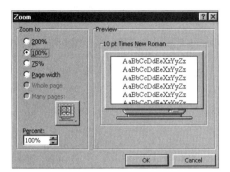

Figure 1-17: The Zoom dialog box.

Table 1-6
The Zoom Options

Option	What It Displays
Percentages	Accesses preset percentage and page options. Your choices include 200%, 100%, and 75%. The default is 100%. You can also type in any integer between 10 and 200 percent.
Page Width	Fits the page on-screen within the left and right margins.
Whole Page	Fits the page on-screen, showing all margins. This option is available only when the document is in Page Layout view.
Many Pages	Displays two or more pages. To select the number of pages, click the icon of the monitor that appears just below the Many Pages option, and then drag to select the number of pages you want to view. You can view up to four columns of documents that can be up to nine documents wide. This option is available only when the document is in Page Layout view.
Percent	Magnifies the page from 10% to 200%. You can enter any number in the Percent box.
Preview	Estimates the appearance of your text with the selected options applied. Also displays the font and font size of the text.

Getting Help

There are four main methods for obtaining help with Word 97. The Office Assistant, which incorporates "IntelliSense" Technology, is often the least frustrating way to get a good answer to a question. There's the What's This icon, which quickly identifies toolbar buttons and dialog boxes with a descriptive sentence or two. You can open Windows' traditional Help files by selecting the Help menu and then either clicking Contents and Index or selecting any of the Microsoft on the Web addresses for new features and upgrades.

The Office Assistant

If the Office Assistant animations seem a tad frivolous, give them a chance. Try them for help first. They are actually rather shrewd guides, providing tutorials and demonstrations of skills, rather than didactic prattle.

The Office Assistant is, by default, always on the screen. Click its icon to receive help on any subject. Right-click Office Assistant to see the Tip of the Day, to see Office Assistant animations, or to choose a different Office Assistant. Right-click and select Options to alter the situations in which Office Assistant will offer help. If Office Assistant has been turned off (by clicking the Close box in the Assistant's upper-right corner), select H̲elp on the menu bar, and then click Microsoft Word Help to bring the Assistant back. Figure 1-18 shows the various Office Assistants you can choose from. Although the animations and characters are different, the advice offered is the same. In previous versions of Word, the Answer Wizard performed many of the same functions as Office Assistant.

Figure 1-18: Office Assistants you can choose from.

The menu bar's Windows Help system

Recent iterations of Windows brought major improvements to Word's Help system. Help is now much more direct and context-sensitive. The Word toolbar now has an automatic link to the Microsoft Network, which features downloadable FAQ sheets, add-ons and patches, and Word forums for the expert and the beginner.

From the menu bar, click the word Help (not the question mark on the Standard toolbar or on Office Assistant). Select Microsoft on the Web to see a generous menu of Microsoft Internet Help links. You'll also notice that Word has included streamlined Help features for WordPerfect users. If you don't want to use Office Assistant and you'd rather use the Windows 95-style Help menus, go to Help on the menu bar and select Microsoft Word Help Topics. The first time you choose this item, Word displays an animated icon of a pen writing in a book and displays the message "Loading Word List." The Help Topics window then appears, as shown in Figure 1-19.

Figure 1-19: The Help Topics: Microsoft Word window.

The Help Topics window includes three tabs: Contents, Index, and Find. The tab that was last displayed appears. Three buttons appear at the lower-right corner. The Open button lets you display the topic you have selected in the window. The Print button in the lower-right corner appears grayed when it's unavailable and dark when you can print Help information. The Cancel button lets you cancel any Help selections. You can move the Help window anywhere on-screen by moving the mouse pointer to the Help window's title bar, holding down the mouse button, and dragging the mouse. When you position the Help window where you want it, release the mouse button.

Browsing the Help Contents

The Contents tab displays a table of contents for Help topics, as shown earlier in Figure 1-19. The book icons that appear in the Contents tab are referred to as *chapters*. Click the book icon next to the topic for which you need help, and page icons appear for the related topics. Some chapter topics will display additional chapter topics, enabling you to narrow your choice to a specific procedure that appears as a page icon.

As you browse through Help Topics, two types of Help can be displayed: the standard topic page and the Word Help window. Certain topics display a topic page that lists solutions available for tasks. For example, clicking the page icon labeled "Getting assistance while you work," which is under the Getting Help chapter, displays the screen shown in Figure 1-20. Move the mouse over one of the callouts, and the bar in the callout changes from dark maroon to bright red. Click the red bar to display a pop-up window for additional information about the topic.

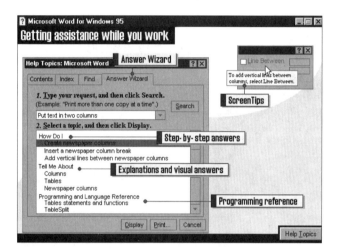

Figure 1-20: Getting assistance while you work.

Some topic pages include examples that you can choose. Choosing Fast Formatting Techniques from the Formatting chapter displays an online example of three formatting techniques. Choosing a specific procedure displays the Word Help window that contains step-by-step instructions you can follow while you're working on a document. To view the instructions while you work, choose the Options button, point to the Keep Help on Top item, and choose On Top. If the window covers your document, you can move or resize the Help window. Click the Close button to close the Word Help window.

The Microsoft Word Help window contains three buttons: Help Topics, Back, and Options. Help Topics displays the Help Topics window. Back returns to the previous Word Help window. The Options button displays six items that let you annotate or customize how the Help window is displayed. You can also display the Options shortcut menu by right-clicking in the Microsoft Word Help window. Table 1-6 explains each of the options.

Table 1-6 The Help Options Menu	
Option	**Action**
Annotate	Adds text to a Help procedure. To see your annotations, choose the help topic, and, after adding your text, select Annotate again.
Copy	Copies the selected contents of the window to the Clipboard. If text isn't selected, all the contents of the window are copied.
Print	Prints the contents of the window.
Font	Displays a submenu of small, medium, and large fonts.
Keep Help on Top	Displays a submenu that lets you choose whether to keep the Help window.
Use System Colors	Determines whether the window displays using only system colors. Choosing this item replaces the yellow background with a white background. For the color change to take effect, Help must be restarted.

Definitions, jumps, and shortcuts

To make following steps even easier, the Microsoft Word Help window provides *definitions, jumps,* and *shortcut buttons.* A definition has a green dotted underline. A jump appears with a solid underline. Clicking a jump moves to the underlined topic. Shortcut buttons appear as an arrow, as shown in Figure 1-21.

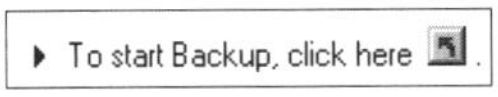

▸ To start Backup, click here 🖼️ .

Figure 1-21: A shortcut button displays additional related information.

Clicking a shortcut button displays related information or steps in the Help window. The mouse pointer becomes a pointing hand when it's on a definition, jump, or a shortcut button. When you want to obtain the definition of a term, hold down the left mouse button to display a definition window. Using the keyboard, press Tab to move the highlight to the definition, jump, or shortcut button. Then press Enter to display the related Help or definition window. Press Enter again to remove the definition window.

To display additional information or steps pertaining to a topic, click with the pointer on the shortcut button, or press Tab to highlight the topic you want, and then press Enter. To move back, choose the Back button at the top of the Help window.

Locating Help topics with the Help Index

The Index tab lets you enter the first few letters of a topic to match available index entries. It allows you to quickly move around within the Help files to find information. To use the index to get help, click the Index tab and enter the first letters of the topic for which you want information. A list of matching indexed entries appears in the lower window. Double-click the topic you want. For a shortcut to display Help with the Index tab selected, double-click the Help button on the Standard toolbar.

Searching for words and phrases in Help Topics

The Find tab lets you search for particular words and phrases in Help Topics. To search through Word's help information, click the Find tab and choose the Next button. Word creates a database for you to use to locate topics. After the topic list is created, you can type the word or words you want to search for, or select matching words to narrow your search. Also displayed is a list of topics that is similar to the listing available in the Index tab. If you make a mistake or want to remove text, click the Clear button. Clicking the Options button displays the Find Options dialog box, shown in Figure 1-22. This dialog box lets you set the criteria for your search.

Figure 1-22: The Find Options dialog box.

Getting context-sensitive Help

Context-sensitive means that the Help window displays information directly tied to what you are working on. Click the word Help on the menu bar and scroll down to an arrow with a question mark by it. It's labeled "What's This?" Clicking it turns your mouse into the arrow-question mark cursor. Use this cursor to obtain a brief description of any command or item on the screen.(The keyboard equivalent to clicking the Help button is Shift+F1. It brings up the same cursor.) This method gives you more latitude in obtaining help with specific areas of the screen, such as window features. For example, pressing Shift+F1, moving the question mark pointer, and clicking the window title bar displays information about the title bar. When you're working in a dialog box, choose the Help button, or press Fl with the pointer placed on the feature for which you want help. Otherwise, when you press F1, Word displays the Inquiry dialog box for Office Assistant.

How to quit Help

To close the Help window while you're working in Word, click the Close button (the X button) in the upper right of the Help title bar. You can also double-click the Control menu icon in the upper-left corner of the window.

Getting help from Microsoft on the Web

Word includes an option to automatically connect to an entire menu of online Help sites to by clicking Help on the menu bar and scrolling down to Microsoft on the Web. Here you have access to the entire wealth of the Internet in getting assistance with Word 97 and your document itself. Click Microsoft on the Web, and select an option from the submenu—these options connect you to a particular Internet site. You can load these through any Internet browser, such as Microsoft Internet Explorer or Netscape Navigator.

Help for WordPerfect users

Word goes out of its way to ease the transition for users switching from WordPerfect to Word. There is a separate Help dialog box for WordPerfect users, and you can even turn on an option that automatically tells you how to use a Word feature when you press a WordPerfect keystroke combination.

If you're a WordPerfect user who is new to both Word and Windows, choose Help⇨WordPerfect Help to display the Help for WordPerfect Users dialog box. Figure 1-23 shows the Help for WordPerfect Users dialog box. In the Command Keys list, select the WordPerfect command you want to find out about. If there is an ellipsis after the selected item, double-click the item, or choose Help Text to display a submenu of related items. When the selection bar is on a command, the right half of the dialog box displays information about how to access the feature in Word. If an arrow is next to the item, you can choose the Demo button to have Word demonstrate the feature.

Tip   A shortcut for displaying the Help for WordPerfect Users dialog box is to double-click WPH on the status bar.

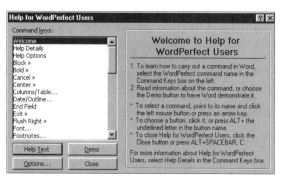

Figure 1-23: The Help for WordPerfect Users dialog box.

Word formatting and WordPerfect Reveal Codes

The main conceptual difference between Word and WordPerfect is how formatting is applied. Word is a paragraph-oriented system and does not use codes in the same way as WordPerfect. You can view the paragraph and character formatting for specific text by pressing Shift+F1 or Help⇨What's This. A question mark attaches itself to your mouse pointer. Click the text you want to inspect to display a bubble that gives you information about the para-graph and font formatting for that text. The question mark remains attached to your mouse pointer until you click the Help button again or press Esc.

You can also display various nonprinting characters in your document. Choose Tools⇨Options, and select the View tab. In the Non Printing Characters group, click in the All check box to display all nonprinting characters, or select the check boxes for the specific nonprinting characters you want to view.

Word fields and WordPerfect codes

Fields are powerful tools. Word uses fields for any type of information that must be updated or compiled. You can create fields from scratch, or, in many cases, you can insert a field simply by using the Word feature. They store the variable infor-mation for merge documents, tables of contents, and indexes. Fields also can be used to link data between documents and different applications. Word has more than 60 fields in nine categories.

Fields are as integral to Word as Reveal Codes are to WordPerfect. For example, automatic page numbers are inserted as codes in WordPerfect and as fields in Word. Often, you don't have to know you're inserting a field; you use a standard Word feature to automate the process of creating the field. Using the page num-bering example, you choose Insert⇨Page Numbers, make your selections in the Page Numbers dialog box, and Word takes care of creating the field. This is the briefest of introductions to fields and is meant only to give you an idea of the importance of fields in Word. For an in-depth discussion of fields, see Chapter 26.

Getting additional help

In addition to comprehensive online documentation, Word provides demonstrations and Wizards that give you step-by-step instructions for creating specific types of documents. Microsoft FastTips gives recorded or faxed answers to common technical questions. You can also order notes and articles from the Microsoft Knowledge Base by fax or mail. For free access to Microsoft FastTips, 24 hours a day, seven days a week, use a touch tone telephone to call 800-936-4100. You can request a catalog of Word documents, listen to recorded answers to common technical questions, and find out how to order items by fax.

If you've tried the Help system, the documentation, and the fax line, but still can't find an answer to your Word question or problem, call 206-462-9673 (Microsoft Word's tech support line), Monday through Friday from 6 a.m. to 6 p.m. Pacific time. If you're in Canada, call 905-568-7200, Monday through Friday from 8 a.m. to 8 p.m. Eastern time.

About Microsoft Word

Choosing Help⇨About Microsoft Word displays a dialog box that includes information about Word's version number, the product's license, and system information about your computer and Windows settings. You will most likely need this information when you call for technical support.

Creating a Document

Recall, when you first open Word, a new, blank document called Document1 appears. To begin working, just start typing. By default, this new document is based on the Normal template. A template, as mentioned earlier in this chapter, is a blueprint or pattern for all documents of a certain type, such as a letter, memo, or report. The standard, stripped-down Normal template includes minimal formatting options. Table 1-7 lists Word's Normal template default settings. You can choose from a list of predefined templates in addition to the default template.

Tip   If you make changes to the Normal.dot template that you later regret, you can change back to the default Normal.dot template by deleting the Normal.dot file. Word creates a new Normal.dot automatically the next time you start the program.

To create a New document with Word's Normal template:

1. Click the New button on the Standard toolbar, or choose the File⇨New command (Ctrl+N).

   When you choose the New command, the New dialog box appears with the Normal template selected (see Figure 1-24).

2. Click OK, or press Enter.

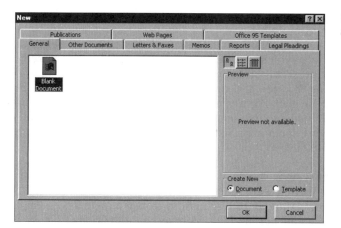

Figure 1-24: The New dialog box.

Table 1-7
Word's Normal Template (Normal.dot) Default Settings

Option	Default Setting
Paper size	Letter (81/2 inches x 11 inches)
Left and right margins	1.25 inches
Top and bottom document margins	1 inch
Line spacing	Single
Justification	Align left
Tabs	0.5 inch
Font	Times New Roman
Point size	10 points
View	Normal

Creating a document with a Wizard

Word provides a collection of Wizards for automatically creating letters, memos, resumes, newsletters, and other common documents. Wizards use templates and include step-by-step instructions to walk you through creating a document. They prompt you to fill in information, which is then inserted into the document.

To create a new document using a Wizard:

1. Choose File➪New (Ctrl+N). The New dialog box appears with the blank document (Normal template) selected. If you're using Office 95, you can also choose the Start a New Document button on the Office Shortcut toolbar.

2. Choose the tab indicating the type of document you want to create, and select the Wizard you want from the list. For example, if you want to create a letter, choose the Letters & Faxes tab.

3. Double-click the Letter Wizard. A Wizard dialog box appears. Figure 1-25 shows a sample Letter Wizard dialog box.

4. Answer the questions in the dialog boxes, and follow the instructions on-screen. Word sets up the basic formatting and layout of your document.

5. To move to the next step, choose the Next button; to return to the previous step, choose the Back button.

6. To create the document and close the Wizard, choose the Finish button. Word displays the new document on-screen. Text from the Wizard is included in the new document.

To have Word display Help as you work with a Wizard document, choose the Display Help as I work option before you choose the Finish button in the last dialog box.

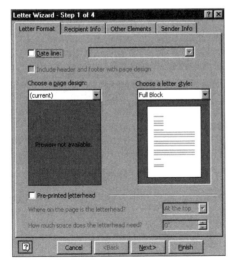

Figure 1-25: A Letter Wizard dialog box.

Starting with a template

Word includes a number of preconstructed templates for creating documents such as letters, resumes, memos, and so on. To create a new document and select one of Word's templates, choose the File⇨New command. This operation displays the New dialog box with tabs organizing templates and Wizards by document types. Select a tab for the type of document you want to create, and choose a template or Wizard icon from the list. Make sure the Document radio button in the lower-right corner is selected, and then click OK. Word displays either the new document with the specified template's layout and formatting or the Wizard's on-screen instructions for creating the document.

Saving a Document

Until you save a document to disk, the document exists only in the computer's memory. In saving a new document, you must name the file and specify where you want it to be saved. Word 97 can store files in the same file format as Word for Windows 6. This means that you can easily edit existing Word files without having to convert the file from one format to another. This capability also enables you to exchange files with others who are using version 6. Using the Microsoft Word Converter, Word 97 documents can be opened in earlier versions of Word, including Macintosh formats.

Windows 95, Windows NT, and Word 97 bring a major benefit to saving files. No longer are you limited by DOS's 11-character limitation on filenames. Now, you can save files with filenames up to 255 characters in length. Keep in mind, though, that the longer the filename that you use, the larger the window that you will need to display the full filename. So, it's probably best to be concise, but not cryptic.

If you plan on sharing files with users who may be using an older version of Windows, you may want to let them know how Windows stores files so that the files can be used with systems following the old MS-DOS filename conventions. When you save a file with a long filename, and view it by using another system or from the DOS prompt, the filename is truncated, so that a file with the name `Mydocument1.doc` appears as `Mydocum~1.doc`. The tilde 1 is used to indicate that the file is the first file beginning with the characters Mydocum. If another is created using the same first eight characters the next file is truncated as `Mydocum~2.doc`, and so on until you reach the number 10, in which case the file appears as `Mydocu~10.doc`. This naming scheme ensures that short filenames are unique even when the first eight characters of the long filenames are the same.

To save a document with a filename you want:

1. Click the Save button, or choose File⇨Save (Ctrl+S). The Save As dialog box appears.

By default, the Filename text box lists the first sentence of the document in the text box.

2. Enter a name up to 255 characters for the file.

   A Word 97 document filename can contain letters, numbers, and spaces, as well as these symbols: ! @ # $ % & ( ) [ ] _ { }. Word automatically adds the filename extension .doc to your filename unless you assign it a different extension.

3. Choose OK, or press Enter, to save your document. If you try to save a document with the name of a previously existing file, Word displays a dialog box asking you to confirm that you want to replace the existing document. Choose No to type a different name for the document, or choose Yes to replace, or overwrite, the existing document.

Tip   If you click the Look in Favorites icon, Favorites becomes the current folder. If you plan on using the document frequently, this folder is an excellent place to store the file. The Office Shortcut toolbar lets you display all the files stored in the Favorites folder as icons. To display the Favorites toolbar, make sure that the Office Shortcut toolbar is displayed and click the right mouse button with the pointer on the background of the toolbar. This shows the different toolbars you can display. Choose Favorite, and the Office Shortcut toolbar changes to display the Favorites toolbar. Click the icon representing the document you want to load on the Favorites toolbar. This action starts Word and automatically loads the file.

The save options: fast save or full save

The Save As dialog box includes an Options button. Clicking the Options button is the same as choosing the Tools⇨Options menu and clicking the Save tab. The Save tab displays different options for saving a file. The two most important save options are Allow Fast Saves and Always Create Backup Copy.

These two options are mutually exclusive. If you select the Always Create Backup Copy check box, the Allow Fast Saves check box is cleared because backup copies can be created only with full saves. The Allow Fast Saves check box instructs Word to save only the changes to a document. This is faster than a full save, in which Word saves the complete, revised document. Fast saves cannot be performed over a network. A full save requires less disk space than a fast save. In your day-to-day work, fast saves are fine. But, if you plan on making a file available to another user or on converting the file to a different format full saves are the choice. If you are working with a large document, you are wise to save the file before performing memory-intensive operations, such as creating an index.

Exiting Word

Word creates numerous different files during the course of its operation, many of which are stored in memory until you quit the program. Some of these files are temporary files that are deleted when you exit Word. If you don't exit properly, some of these files may not close properly, which can result in wasted space and hard disk problems down the road. Simply turning off the power switch also destroys any unsaved data. Use one of the following five methods to correctly exit Word:

✦ Choose the File⇨Exit command.

✦ Press Alt+F4.

✦ Click the Close button in the right corner of the Word program title bar.

✦ Double-click the Control menu icon in the left corner of the Word program title bar.

✦ Right-click in the Microsoft Word button in the taskbar, and choose Close from the pop-up menu. This method enables you to close Word while you're using another application.

When you use one of these techniques to exit Word, the program lets you know whether you have unsaved data by displaying a dialog box, as shown in Figure 1-26. This dialog box gives you the chance to save your work or cancel the Exit command.

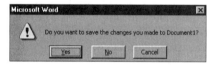

Figure 1-26: The Word dialog box asks whether you want to save your files.

Summary

This chapter gave you several ways to save time by showing the many different ways you can automatically start Word. For example, you can now:

✦ Use shortcut icons to start word from the desktop or any folder in Windows 95.

✦ Modify the Word shortcut icon in Windows 95 or the Word program icon in Windows NT, and add a switch to specify how Word starts.

✦ Automatically load the last document you were working on when you start Word.

✦ Start Word each time you start Windows by using the StartUp option in the Start menu in Windows 95 and the Startup program group in Windows NT.

✦ Use the Microsoft Office 97 Shortcut bar and Word's File⇨ New command (Ctrl+N) to quickly create documents using Wizards and templates.

In addition, this chapter gave you an overview of the Word environment and explained how to work with Word's Help features, including Office Assistant. If you have trouble with a button or if a pointer appears and you're uncertain how it works, use this chapter as a reference.

Where to go next...

✦ If you're new to word processing or are working with Word for the first time, we recommend that you read Chapter 2.

✦ One of the fastest ways to get started creating documents is to use Word's Wizards and predefined templates. To get started fast, check out Chapter 10.

✦ This chapter included a taste of customizing Word to get started quickly; for a full course on customizing Word, check out Chapter 25. This chapter includes numerous nifty ways you can customize Word's menus and toolbars.

✦   ✦   ✦

Typing, Navigating, and Editing Documents

CHAPTER

2

Most of the time you spend working with Word, you are probably typing, navigating, or editing text. At first glance, these tasks may seem elementary, but numerous timesaving keystrokes and commands are at your fingertips, just waiting to be discovered. This chapter unveils methods you can use to speed up entering text and navigating and editing a document. You will learn how to insert date, time, and special symbols and characters. Last but not least, this chapter explains how to use two of Word's powerful tools, AutoCorrect and AutoText, to automatically insert and correct text as you type.

Typing and Editing Text

When you first create a document by using the Normal.dot template, the insertion point rests at the top of the document, ready for you to begin typing. To add text to a document, just start typing. If you're new to word processing, you will most likely be fighting the urge to press Enter at the end of each line. The only time you need to press Enter is when you want Word to create a new paragraph. By default, Word will automatically wrap your text to the next line when the text reaches the right margin. If the wrap occurs within a word, Word takes the entire word and places it on the next line.

Don't try to correct mistakes and apply formatting as you type. For now, relax. Word makes correcting text and applying formatting to text simple. In fact, Word includes AutoText, AutoFormat, and AutoCorrect features that will automatically enter text, apply formatting, and correct mistakes for you on-the-fly as you type. AutoText is covered later in this chapter. For information on AutoFormat, see Chapter 11. Using Word's new AutoCorrect spelling feature is explained in Chapter 4.

Displaying nonprinting characters

If you're new to Word, you may have trouble understanding how Word displays and handles text. This is largely because your text includes nonprinting characters that affect how text is displayed. One of the most revealing commands is the Show/Hide button (the paragraph button) in the Standard toolbar. Show/Hide displays *nonprinting characters,* characters that can be displayed on-screen but don't print. Toggled on, Word shows the invisible characters you include in a document, such as paragraph marks, spaces, and tabs. Table 2-1 lists common nonprinting characters and explains how you can insert them into your documents.

Displaying nonprinting characters is a good idea because you can see at a glance whether you have typed an extra space or pressed Enter accidentally. If you don't see the nonprinting characters in your document, click the Show/Hide button on the Standard toolbar. You can change which nonprinting characters appear by changing the settings in the View tab of the Options dialog box (Tools⇨Options). By default, the All check box is selected in the Nonprinting Character group.

Table 2-1
Common Nonprinting Characters

Nonprinting Character	Character Name	How to Create It
Options	Hidden text	This text appears only when you use the Hidden option in the Effects group, which is located in the Font tab of the Font dialog box (Format⇨Font). See Chapter 7 for information on working with hidden text.
↵	Line break or new line	Press Shift+Enter.
¬	Optional hyphen	When you choose the Tools⇨Hyphenation command, Word inserts optional hyphens in your document. Word allows you to use three types of hyphens, as explained in Chapter 3.

Nonprinting Character	Character Name	How to Create It
¶	Paragraph mark	Press Enter.
.	Space	Press the spacebar.
→	Tab	Press Tab. See Chapter 8 for information on working with tabs.

To specify which nonprinting characters are displayed:

1. Choose Tools⇨Options.

2. Select the View tab in the Options dialog box (see Figure 2-1).

3. In the Nonprinting characters group, select or clear the check box for the character you want to display or hide.

4. Click OK.

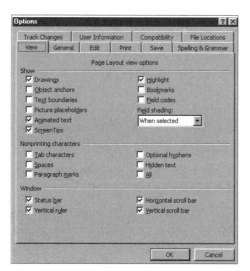

Figure 2-1: The View tab.

Inserting and overtyping text

When you insert text into a line, Word moves the existing text to the right to make room for the new text. If you want to type over existing text, switch to Overtype mode by double-clicking OVR on the status bar at the bottom of the Word window or by pressing Insert. To switch back to Insert mode, double-click OVR or press Insert again.

Beginning a new paragraph

To start a paragraph, position the insertion point where you want the new paragraph and press Enter. The program inserts a paragraph mark and moves the insertion point down to the first line of the new paragraph.

In Word, a paragraph is any amount of text and graphics that ends with a paragraph mark. Even when you have not typed any text and press Enter, Word creates a paragraph mark. Paragraphs are central to working with text and graphics in Word. They have meaning beyond a simple grammatical definition because many types of formatting are applied to paragraphs as a whole. Here are some guidelines for working with paragraphs in Word:

✦ Don't delete or separate a paragraph mark unless you want to lose the formatting for the paragraph's text and merge it with the next paragraph. A paragraph's format (such as alignment, indents, and tab settings) is stored in the paragraph mark, not in the text itself.

✦ If you accidentally delete a paragraph mark, restore it by clicking the Undo button on the Standard toolbar or by pressing Ctrl+Z.

✦ Set your basic paragraph formats once; when you press Enter to start a new paragraph, Word carries over the preceding paragraph's formatting to the new paragraph. For more information on formatting paragraphs, see Chapter 8.

Adding a new line

Word automatically wraps text to the next line when the text reaches the right margin. In some situations, such as when typing a list, you might start a new line before reaching the margin to keep the line within the paragraph. New lines (called *line breaks*) are extremely helpful for keeping the format of several short lines the same, because the one paragraph mark that ends the list controls all of the new lines.

To start a new line anywhere within a paragraph, position the insertion point where you want to start the new line, and press Shift+Enter. Word inserts a line break character and moves the insertion point to the beginning of the next line. Line breaks appear as a curved arrow when you display nonprinting characters.

Aligning text

Don't press the spacebar to align text. The spacebar method works on a typewriter because the type is *monospaced,* which means that every letter takes up the same amount of space. This method doesn't work with Word because Windows uses *proportional fonts*. When you use a proportional font, letters occupy different amounts of horizontal space. For example, in a proportional font, an *i* occupies a much narrower space than an *M*.

Align text by using Word's tabs and indents or other formatting options. This way, you ensure that the text is aligned properly, and Word can automatically readjust the paragraph when you add or delete text.

Inserting the date and time

By using the Insert⇨Date and Time command, you can quickly insert the date and time in a variety of different formats (see Figure 2-2). The date and time entry is tied to your computer's clock, so it uses the current date and time.

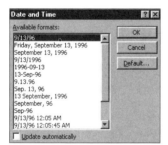

Figure 2-2: The Date and Time dialog box.

To insert the date or time in a document:

1. Position the insertion point where you want to insert the date or time.

2. Choose Insert⇨Date and Time. The Date and Time dialog box appears, as shown in Figure 2-2. Selecting the Update automatically check box in the Date and Time dialog box creates a dynamic link to your computer's clock, which updates the time or date entry.

3. Double-click the date or time format you want in the Available formats list, or select the entry, and then choose OK.

If your computer's clock is not set, double-click the time displayed in the Windows 95 status bar or, use the Date/Time utility in the Control panel to change the settings.

You can easily add buttons to include the Insert date and Insert time commands on a toolbar. To do this, choose Tools⇨Customize Commands, and select Insert from the Categories window. Now drag the Insert Date (the daily calendar) icon to a toolbar. To add the time button, drag the Insert Time (the clock) icon to the toolbar. For more information on customizing toolbars, see Chapter 25.

Splitting a document window for easier editing

Word lets you view different parts of a document at the same time by splitting the window into two panes. Figure 2-3 shows a split document window. Splitting a document window can make navigating and editing long documents easier. Changes you make in one pane are reflected in the other. You also can work in a different view in each pane: the document can be in Outline view in one pane and Normal view in another.

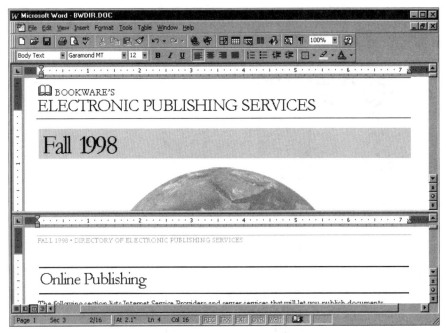

Figure 2-3: A split document window.

The easiest way to split a document window is to double-click the split box at the top of the vertical scroll bar. When the mouse pointer is on the split box, it appears as an up-and-down arrow divided by two short lines. The document window is split evenly into two panes with the split box at the top of the split. To adjust the size of the panes, drag the split box up or down. Notice that each pane has its own scroll bar and ruler. To switch between panes, click in the pane you want to activate. To remove the split, double-click the split box.

You can also split a document window with the keyboard by choosing Window⇨Split or pressing Alt+Ctrl+S. Then use the up or down arrow to position the horizontal gray line where you want the split, and press Enter. After you split the window, the Split command in the Window menu changes to Remove Split. To remove the split, choose Window⇨Remove Split. Press F6 to move between panes.

You can easily add a button to a toolbar to split the current window quickly. To do this, choose Tools⇨Customize, and select Window and Help in the Categories window. Drag the Split Window (window divided with a dotted line) icon to a toolbar. You can now divide the window by clicking the Split Window button.

Navigating a Document

The insertion point shows where the text you type will appear. As you type, Word scrolls the document to keep the insertion point visible in the window. If you want to insert text in another part of your document, you must move the insertion point to that location and then insert the text. The following sections explain how to navigate your way around a document.

Commands for moving the insertion point and scrolling are also used in conjunction with keyboard commands for selecting text and graphics, as explained later in this chapter.

Moving the insertion point

Keep in mind that scrolling doesn't move the insertion point. When you're ready to type text into a new location of your document, point and click with the mouse to position the insertion point at the new location. Otherwise, as soon as you resume typing, Word will move back to the location of the insertion point and insert the new text there.

To move the insertion point to another page with the mouse, drag the scroll bar until you reach the desired location. A page reference appears for the current location in the scroll bar. After displaying the page you want, click the location where you want to position the insertion point. The insertion point always stays within the margins. When you click outside the right margin or after the final paragraph mark of your document, the insertion point moves to the text closest to where you clicked. When you click outside the left margin, you select a line. You can also use the keyboard to move the insertion point. Table 2-2 shows the keyboard options for moving the insertion point around in a document.

Table 2-2
Keyboard Commands for Moving the
Insertion Point and Scrolling

To Move	Press
One character to the left	Left-arrow key
One character to the right	Right-arrow key
One line up	Up-arrow key
One line down	Down-arrow key
One word to the left	Ctrl+left-arrow key
One word to the right	Ctrl+right-arrow key
To the end of a line	End
To the beginning of a line	Home
To the beginning of the current paragraph	Ctrl+up-arrow key
To the beginning of the preceding paragraph	Ctrl+up-arrow key twice
To the beginning of the next paragraph	Ctrl+down-arrow key
Up one screen	Page Up
Down one screen	Page Down
To the bottom of the screen	Ctrl+Page Down
To the top of the screen	Ctrl+Page Up
To the top of the previous page	Alt+Ctrl+Page Up
To the top of the next page	Alt+Ctrl+Page Down
To the end of the document	Ctrl+End
To the beginning of the document	Ctrl+Home
To the preceding insertion point location	Shift+F5 or Alt+Ctrl+Z

Scrolling through a document

The scroll bars at the right and bottom edges of the window let you scroll vertically or horizontally through the active document. To scroll quickly, drag the scroll box. To scroll up or down one line at a time, click the up or down arrow. If the scroll bars are not displayed, you can display them by choosing Tools⇨Options, selecting the View tab, and then selecting the Vertical Scrollbar and Horizontal Scrollbar check boxes. Table 2-3 lists methods of scrolling with the mouse or keyboard.

	Table 2-3 **Methods of Scrolling by Using the Mouse or Keyboard**	
Method	*Mouse Action*	*Key*
Scroll up one line	Click the up-arrow key	Up arrow
Scroll up one screen	Click above the scroll box in the scroll bar	Page Up
Move to any specific location horizontally or vertically	Drag the scroll box	Not available
Scroll down one line	Click the down-arrow key	Down arrow
Scroll down one screen	Click below the scroll box in the scroll bar	Page Down
Move to the same position on previous page in Page Layout view	Click the double-up-arrow key	Not available
Move to the same position on the next page in Page Layout view	Click the double-down-arrow key	Not available
Scroll into the left margin, beyond the text area	Shift+click the left-arrow key	Not available
Scroll left	Click the left-arrow key	Left arrow
Scroll right	Click the right-arrow key	Right arrow

Word scroll bars do not merely scroll through one page of your document, but move from the beginning end of the entire document, as you move the vertical scroll button downward.. The horizontal scroll box represents the portion of the screen displayed. The scroll box in the vertical scroll bar shows the current position in the document. Word 97 introduces the Select Browse Object button (discussed later), on the bottom of the scroll bar. In Word 97, clicking the scroll box displays the current page. The real benefit of the current page feature is that it also works when dragging the scroll box. As you scroll through the document, a box displays the current page number where you will be when you release the mouse button. Figure 2-4 shows the current page reference displayed when scrolling.

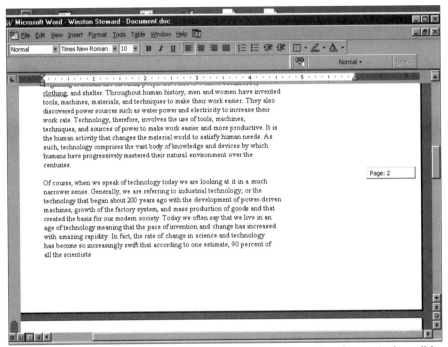

Figure 2-4: A page reference appears when you scroll by using the vertical scroll bar.

Returning to the location of your last edit

When you work on a large document, finding the exact location where you performed your last edit can be tedious. Word makes it easy by remembering the last three locations where you either entered or edited text. To return to the location of your last edit, press Shift+F5. Word moves the insertion point to where you last edited the document. The next two times you press Shift+F5, Word moves to the previous last two locations where you entered or edited text. For bigger jobs, use the Browse by Object option on the toolbar. Click the button with the circle on it between the two arrows on the bottom right of the toolbar. Select the picture of a pen, and the text bar above the pen reads "Browse by edits." Providing you have used the Review toolbar to mark your edits, clicking the scroll arrows now moves you to each edit found in your document.

Navigating by using the Go To dialog box

The Edit⇨Go To command lets you move the insertion point anywhere in your document. By choosing Edit⇨Go To, pressing Ctrl+G or F5, or double-clicking in either of the first two sections of the status bar at the bottom of the Word window, you can display the Go To tab. This box contains the G̲o to what list that shows where you can move in the document (see Figure 2-5). You can go to just about any location: sections, lines, footnotes, annotations, graphics, tables, and so on. The Find and Replace tabs and dialog boxes are located beneath the Go To tab. They'll be covered in Chapter 3.

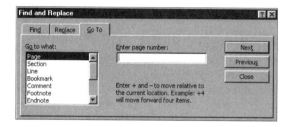

Figure 2-5: The Find and Replace dialog box.

To use the Go To tab, choose what you're looking for from the G̲o to What list box. If you simply want to go to the next item, choose Next̲; to go to a specific occurrence of the item you selected, type a number in the E̲nter box. The E̲nter box changes its name in relation to the category you choose. For example, when you choose the Line option, the E̲nter box name changes to E̲nter line number.

The Go To tab also lets you move forward or backward a specific number of occurrences for most options listed in the G̲o to what list. Select the item you want, and enter a plus or minus sign in the E̲nter box followed by the number of occurrences of the selected item that you want to move. For example, to move forward seven pages, choose Page in the G̲o to what box, and type **+7** in the E̲nter page number text box. To move back seven pages, choose Page in the G̲o to what box, and type **-7** in the E̲nter page number text box.

With the G̲o To command, you can also specify a percentage of an item selected in the G̲o to what list box. For example, to move to a location 50 percent from the beginning of the document, select the Page item in the G̲o to what list, type **50%** in the E̲nter box, and click the Go T̲o button.

You can also combine options by using their initials. For example, to go to line 33 on page 72, select the page item and type **p72l33** in the E̲nter page number box. Then click the Go T̲o button.

The E̲dit⇨F̲ind command also lets you move to specific text quickly, as explained in Chapter 3.

Selecting Text and Graphics

Before moving, copying, deleting, or otherwise changing text or a graphic, you must first select the item. The general rule is to select first and then do. This rule applies to nearly every action you perform in Word. You can select with the mouse or the keyboard. The program highlights selected text or graphics. To cancel most selections, click outside the selection, or use the arrow keys to move the insertion point.

Selecting text and graphics by using the mouse

You can select words, sentences, and areas of text by double-clicking, dragging, or pressing a key as you click. To select lines, paragraphs, or an entire document, use the *selection bar,* the invisible area along the left edge of the text area. You can quickly identify the selection bar by moving the mouse pointer to the left side of your document. When the pointer is in the selection bar, the pointer changes from an insertion point to a right-pointing arrow. Table 2-4 describes the different ways to select text and graphics with the mouse.

Table 2-4	
Mouse Options for Making Selections	
To Select	***Do This***
A word	Double-click the word.
A graphic	Click the graphic.
A line of text	Click in the selection bar to the left of the line.
Multiple lines of text	Click and drag in the selection bar in the direction of the lines you want to select.
A sentence	Hold down Ctrl, and click in the sentence you want to select.
A paragraph	Double-click in the selection bar to the left of the paragraph.
Multiple paragraphs	Drag in the selection bar in the direction of the paragraphs you want to select.
Any item or amount of text	Click where you want the selection to begin. Then hold down Shift, and click where you want the selection to end.
An entire document	Triple-click in the selection bar.
A vertical block of text	Hold down Alt, click the mouse button (except within a table), and drag.

If you begin selecting in the middle of a word and drag to include part of the second word, Word selects both words, as well as the spaces after the words. To turn off automatic word selection, choose Tools⇨Options, and select the Edit tab. Under Editing Options, clear the When Selecting, Automatically Select Entire Word check box.

You can select text and graphics quickly by positioning the insertion point at the beginning of the text or graphic you want to select, holding down the Shift key, and clicking where you want the selection to end.

Selecting text and graphics with the keyboard

If you know the key combination to move the insertion point, you can select the text by using that key combination while holding down the Shift key. For example, Ctrl+Right arrow moves the insertion point to the next word, and Ctrl+Shift+right arrow selects the text from the insertion point to the beginning of the next word. Table 2-5 describes the ways to select text or graphics with the keyboard.

Table 2-5
Keyboard Options for Making Selections

To Select	Press
One character to the right	Shift+right-arrow key
One character to the left	Shift+left-arrow key
To the end of a word	Ctrl+Shift+right-arrow key
To the beginning of a word	Ctrl+Shift+left-arrow key
To the end of a line	Shift+End
To the beginning of a line	Shift+Home
One line down	Shift+down-arrow key
One line up	Shift+up-arrow key
To the end of a paragraph	Ctrl+Shift+down-arrow key
To the beginning of a paragraph	Ctrl+Shift+up-arrow key
One screen down	Shift+Page Down
One screen up	Shift+Page Up
To the end of a document	Ctrl+Shift+End
To the beginning of a document	Ctrl+Shift+Home
To include the whole document	Ctrl+A or Ctrl+5 (on the numeric keypad)

Using the Extend Selection mode

The F8 key is called the Extend Selection key. This key is a great way to select text in Word. It allows you to take your finger off the Shift key while selecting text. For example, normally, to select a single character of text, you must press Shift and an arrow key. If you press F8, Word, in essence, holds down the Shift key for you while selecting text. To turn off Extend Selection, press the Esc key. While in Extend Selection mode, use the text selection keys listed in Table 2-6. Don't forget to press the Esc key when you're finished selecting, or you could end up accidentally selecting much more text than you intended. (Refer back to Table 2-2 for keyboard positioning commands.) To start and stop an extended selection:

1. Move the insertion point to the beginning of the text you want to select.

2. Press F8 (Extend Selection). You are now in Extend Selection mode.

3. Press one of the keys listed in Table 2-6.

4. Press Esc to exit Extend Selection mode. When out of Extend Selection mode, press any arrow key to deselect the selected text.

Table 2-6
Selecting Text Options in the Extend Selection Mode

To Select	Press
Next or previous character	Left-arrow or right-arrow key
Up or down one line at the same location	Up-arrow or down-arrow key
End of line	End
Beginning of line	Home
Top of the previous screen	Page Up
Bottom of the next screen	Page Down
Beginning of the document	Ctrl+Home
End of the document	Ctrl+End

You also can use Extend Selection mode to select specific units of text, such as a word, a sentence, or a paragraph. For example, pressing the F8 key twice selects the word where the insertion point is. Table 2-7 lists the F8 options for selecting specific units of text. Before pressing F8, make sure that the insertion point is on the unit of text that you want to select. To shrink a selection and make it smaller than the current selection, press Shift+F8 as many times as needed to decrease the selection.

Table 2-7
Options for Selecting Specific Units of Text by Using the F8 Key

To Select	Press F8
Word	2 times
Sentence	3 times
Paragraph	4 times
Section	5 times
Document	6 times

You can also use the Go To command in conjunction with the Extend Selection mode to select text. To select text with F8 and the Go To command:

1. Move the insertion point to the beginning of the text you want to select.

2. Press F8 (Extend Selection).

3. Press F5 (Go To).

4. Select the item you want to move to in the Go to what list, and enter the number or other identifier that represents the end of your selection; for example, select line and then enter **+21** to select the next 21 lines.

5. Choose the Go To button.

6. Choose Close to remove the Go To dialog box.

Deleting Text and Graphics

Word lets you delete text and graphics quickly. If you plan to replace text, select the text and start typing. As soon as you press a key, Word replaces the selected text with the new text. If you don't want selections replaced as you type, choose Tools⇨Options, select the Edit tab, and clear the Typing replaces selection check box. Table 2-8 describes Word's keyboard deletion options. Word also lets you delete any selected text or graphics by using the Edit⇨Clear command, which works in the same way as pressing the Delete key.

Table 2-8 Deletion Options	
To Delete	**Press**
Selected text	Backspace or Delete
Characters before the insertion point	Backspace
Characters after the insertion point	Delete
A word before the insertion point	Ctrl+Backspace
A word after the insertion point	Ctrl+Delete

Undoing Actions

When you make a mistake in Word, you can undo the action or command. For example, if you accidentally delete a word, you can easily bring it back. If you decide to go through with the action or command after all, you can redo it. Word gives you three methods to undo or redo the most recent action: clicking the Undo button or the Redo button on the Standard toolbar, choosing Undo or Redo from the Edit menu, or pressing the shortcut keys Ctrl+Z (undo) or Ctrl+Y (redo).

To undo or redo multiple actions, first click the arrow beside either the Undo or Redo button to display a list of actions. Figure 2-6 shows a list of previous actions that appears after you click the Undo button. Then click or drag to select the actions that you want to undo or redo. Undo and redo actions are performed in sequential order of the original actions. You can't undo certain actions, such as saving a document, after you've executed them.

Figure 2-6: Clicking the Undo button displays a list of previously executed actions.

Moving and Copying Text and Graphics

At the heart of word processing is the capability to manipulate text. After you rapidly fire off your ideas, Word makes it easy to delete, copy, or move text. The following sections explain the essential tools for manipulating text and graphics in a document.

Using the Clipboard

Cutting differs from deleting because the text that is cut is stored in the Clipboard. The *Clipboard* is a temporary storage area for cut or copied selections. When you cut or copy a selection, you can *paste* (insert) it anywhere in your document. *Cutting* removes the original selection from the document. *Copying* makes a copy of the selected text or graphic and leaves the original selection unchanged. After you paste a selection that you copied or cut, it remains on the Clipboard, so you can continue pasting the text into new locations as many times as you want. When you cut or copy another selection, the first one is replaced. If you accidentally replace text or a graphic stored on the Clipboard, click the Undo button on the Standard toolbar, or press Ctrl+Z to retrieve it.

When you quit Word after cutting or copying large amounts of text or graphics to the Clipboard, the program may display a dialog box asking whether you want to save the Clipboard contents. Save the Clipboard if you plan to use its contents with another application; if you don't, choose No to clear the Clipboard. You can display the Clipboard's contents by clicking the Clipboard Viewer icon in the Accessories menu (Start⇨Program⇨Accessories⇨Clipboard Viewer). To close the Clipboard, choose File⇨Exit. The following sections explain how to use Word's versatile copy and move features.

You can permanently store text and graphics for use over and over again with the AutoText command, as explained later in this chapter.

Smart cutting and pasting

When you cut or paste text, Word adjusts the spaces remaining in the sentence. For example, if you paste a word in front of a period, Word removes any spaces between the word and the period. If you don't want to use the Smart Cut and Paste feature, choose Tools⇨Options, select the Edit tab, and clear the Use Smart Cut and Paste check box.

Drag-and-drop editing

Drag-and-drop editing with the mouse is an easy way to move or copy a selection. This feature is especially convenient for copying or moving text a short distance or between two documents appearing on-screen at the same time. Drag-and-drop editing also lets you scroll through a document to copy or move text and graphics long distances, such as numerous pages. To scroll through a document when performing a drag-and-drop operation, drag the selected item beneath the horizontal ruler or above the horizontal scroll bar.

The drag-and-drop editing feature lets you select text in the document window and drag and drop the selected text on the desktop. This creates a document scrap that can be dragged into another document or the existing document. By default, text is copied rather than moved from the current document. To move text from your document to the desktop, press the Shift key when you drag the selected text. On the desktop, the first part of the selected text appears after the icon label Document Scrap. Double-click the Document Scrap icon, and Word displays the document as it does any Word document.

A shortcut menu is also available for dragging text to the desktop. Using the right mouse button to drag selected text to the desktop displays a shortcut menu, which helps you decide how to handle the scrap. Four options appear on the shortcut menu to let you choose whether to copy the selection, move the selection, create a document shortcut (a link) to the selected text in the original document, or cancel the drag-and-drop operation. The shortcut menu works only when dragging from a document to the desktop. Dragging a scrap document from the desktop to a document copies the selection to the document and works the same no matter which mouse button you use. If you want to delete a Document Scrap, right-click the icon, and choose Delete from the shortcut menu.

If you are unable to use the drag-and-drop feature, choose Tools⇨Options, and select the Edit tab. Under Editing Options, select the Drag-And-Drop Text Editing check box.

One quick way to gather several pieces of text and graphics for pasting is to use a second document window or drag and drop selections on the desktop to create scrap documents. To open and work with a new document window, Choose File⇨New and then Window⇨Arrange All. Use drag-and-drop editing to move or copy text and graphics between document windows. To move or copy text and graphics by using drag-and-drop editing between windows:

1. Select the text and graphics that you want to move.

2. Do one of the following:

   • To move a selection, point to the selection, and hold down the mouse button until you see the drag-and-drop pointer.

   • To copy a selection, hold down the Ctrl key, point to the selection, and hold down the mouse button until you see the drag-and-drop pointer.

3. Drag the pointer to the new location. Note that the object will be inserted at the insertion point and not at the pointer.

4. Release the mouse button to drop the text into place. Click Undo on the Standard toolbar if you accidentally activate the drag-and-drop pointer and move text.

Using the Cut, Copy, and Paste buttons

Use the Cut, Copy, and Paste buttons on the Standard toolbar to move or copy text or graphics within a document, among different documents, or among most applications. To move or copy text and graphics with the Standard toolbar:

1. Select the text or graphic that you want to move or copy.

2. Do one of the following:

   • To move the selection, click the Cut button on the Standard toolbar.

   • To copy the selection, click the Copy button on the Standard toolbar. Word places the text on the Clipboard.

3. Position the insertion point at the new location. If the new location is in another document or application, open or switch to that document or application. If the new location is in a Word document that is already open, choose the document from the Window menu.

Moving and copying with commands and keyboard shortcuts

You can also use commands and keyboard shortcuts to copy and move selections. To copy a selection, choose Edit⇨Copy, move the insertion point to where you want to insert the copied selection, and choose Edit⇨Paste. To move a selection, choose Edit⇨Cut, move the insertion point to where you want to insert the cut selection, and choose Edit⇨Paste. Word's shortcut keys make copying and moving selections with the keyboard much faster. Table 2-9 describes these keyboard shortcuts.

Take special care when editing a hyperlink text or image. If you want to edit the appearance of hyperlink text or image and you click it to begin editing, you'll most likely just launch the linked document. Use Shift and the keyboard to select hyperlinks instead of using the mouse.

Table 2-9
Keyboard Shortcuts for Copying and Moving Selections

To Do This	Press
Copy selected text and graphics to the Clipboard	Ctrl+C
Move selected text and graphics to the Clipboard	Ctrl+X
Paste Clipboard contents in a document	Ctrl+V
Move a paragraph up	Alt+Shift+up-arrow key
Move a paragraph down	Alt+Shift+down-arrow key

You may find it helpful to use mnemonics to remember the shortcut commands for cutting, copying, and pasting. For example, you might think of X as looking like scissors, that C stands for copying, and of V as the insert text symbol in proofreading marks. One editor says that she uses the mnemonic, " 'V' is for vomit, spewing something forth," in order to remember the shortcut for pasting. Also, notice the sequence of these three keys on your keyboard, X, then C, and then V. They mirror the toolbar's sequence Cut, Copy, and Paste, which are the commands these keys correspond to.

Moving and copying with the shortcut menu

As if all these methods weren't enough, Word also includes a shortcut menu that lets you cut, copy, or paste text with a simple right-click of the mouse in the document area. Remember that, unless you have selected text, the menu item appears dimmed. You can mix and match keyboard and mouse methods to perform copy and move operations. For example, you can press Ctrl+C and then right-click and choose Paste from the shortcut menu.

Using the Spike for multiple cut and paste operations

When you want to remove several items from one or more documents and insert them as a group elsewhere, use the Spike. The Spike is a multiple cut-and-paste tool that collects, in order, each item you delete; the first item you cut appears at the top of the Spike entry; the second item follows it, and so on. Word distinguishes each item with a paragraph mark. When you insert the contents of the Spike, you can choose either to clear the Spike or save the items to use again. The Spike lets you cut and paste data to and from multiple documents. To Move selections by using the Spike:

1. Select the text or graphic that you want to move to the Spike.

2. Press Ctrl+F3. Word removes the selected text or graphic and adds it to the Spike.

3. Repeat Steps 1 and 2 for each item you want to collect in the Spike.

4. Position the insertion point where you want to insert the contents of the Spike.

5. Do one of the following:

   • To paste the text and keep the contents of the Spike after you paste it, either choose Edit⇨AutoText and choose the Insert button or type **spike** and press F3.

   • To paste the text and clear the contents of the Spike, press Ctrl+Shift+F3.

You cannot copy text to the Spike. The Spike only works with the cut command; however, it's easy to get around this limitation. You can copy the contents of the Spike to the same or to another location without emptying the Spike by typing **spike** in your document and pressing F3. This method treats the Spike as an AutoText entry. Working with AutoText is explained later in this chapter.

Before you add a new set of items to the Spike, you may need to clear it. To clear the contents of the Spike, choose Insert⇨AutoText, and then AutoText again. Scroll through the list of AutoText entries and select Spike from the list of AutoText names. The contents of the Spike appears in the Preview area at the bottom of the AutoText dialog box. Choose Delete to remove the contents from the Spike.

Pasting text into other documents

The formatting that Word applies to pasted text depends on whether the text you copy includes a section break and whether the document to which you copy is empty. A section break contains all the formatting for the section that precedes it. Section formatting includes margins, number of columns, line numbers, page size and orientation, and headers and footers. Each document has at least one section. The last paragraph mark in a Word document functions like a section break: it contains all section formatting for the last section of a document. If you include the last paragraph mark when you copy or move text, one of the following happens:

✦ If you include a section break when you copy or move text, you create a new section when you paste the text into another document. The formatting in the copied or moved section break is applied to all the text that precedes it, up to an existing section break or to the beginning of the document.

✦ If the document into which you paste the text is empty, Word applies the section formatting of the document from which the text was copied. For example, any headers or footers in the document from which you copied the text become part of the document into which you paste the text.

✦ If the document into which you paste the text is not empty, the text takes on the section formatting of that document. For example, headers and footers copied with the section break are discarded; Word retains the headers and footers of the document into which you paste the text.

✦ When you copy text without including either a section break or the final paragraph mark, the section formatting is not copied. The text takes on the section formatting of the document into which it is pasted.

Controlling how text is inserted by using Paste Special

One of the most overlooked editing commands is Paste Special. Paste Special can save you a lot of time by giving you options that are not available with the standard Paste command. If you are inserting text that has special formatting, you can control whether to insert the text with or without formatting. Many times, people cut and paste formatted text into a document and wonder why the text appears different from the existing text. The best way to make text match the current paragraphs text is to use Edit⇨Paste Special, and choose the Unformatted Text option. If you want to retain the formatting of the original text, choose Formatted Text (RTF). RTF stands for Rich Text Format and instructs Word to retain the text's basic format.

When you paste material into your document from another Word document or another application, such as Microsoft Excel, use the Edit⇨Paste Special command to link the pasted item to its original file. The item in your Word document is updated when you make changes to the original. For more information about exchanging information with other applications, see Chapter 15.

Inserting Symbols and Special Characters

In addition to the letters, numbers, and punctuation marks shown on the keyboard, numerous fonts include many other special characters, such as bullets, copyright and trademark symbols, curly quotes, foreign characters, and em and en dashes. (Em dashes are used to interrupt or highlight a thought in a sentence, and en dashes are used to represent the word "to" or "through" between words.)

You can insert these characters by using the Symbol command or by pressing a unique key combination. Word includes several shortcut keys for symbols and lets you assign symbols that you use frequently to custom shortcut key combinations. You can also use the Windows Character Map applet (an applet is a small application that performs a specific task, for example, the Calculator in Windows) to insert symbols and special characters. Inserting characters by using the Windows Character Map applet is explained later in this chapter.

Word includes an Equation Editor that lets you insert mathematical symbols or create equations. See Chapter 16 for more information.

Using the Symbol command

When you choose Insert⇨Symbol, the Symbol dialog box (see Figure 2-7) displays the symbols available for the font you're using. All fonts based on the ANSI character set that you have installed in Windows use the (normal text) entry in the Font drop-down list in the Symbol dialog box. Table 2-10 lists the ANSI character set. Fonts that don't comply with the ANSI character set are listed by name on the Font drop-down list in the Symbol dialog box. The Symbol dialog box remains open until you choose Cancel or Close, allowing you to scroll through a document and insert symbols repeatedly without having to choose the Symbol command each time. When you're using AutoCorrect and you type certain characters, they automatically change into symbols. For example, typing a "c" that has parentheses on both sizes automatically changes into ©. To give you more symbol creation abilities, the Symbol dialog box contains a link to AutoCorrect.

Symbols and special characters in non-ANSI fonts, such as those of the Symbol font, are protected if you insert them via the Symbol dialog box. Otherwise, when you change the font of a symbol, you might also change the symbol itself. For example, selecting the entire document and choosing an ANSI font that contains a Wingdings symbol doesn't change the Wingdings character to the ANSI font character. To change a protected character, you must delete it, choose the font that you want to use, and insert the symbol again. To insert symbols by using the Symbol dialog box:

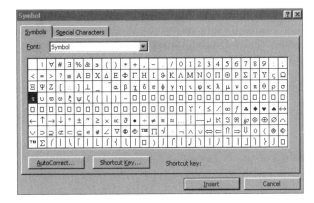

Figure 2-7: The Symbol dialog box.

1. Position the insertion point where you want to insert the symbol.

2. Choose Insert⇨Symbol.

3. To see an enlarged version of the symbol in the dialog box, click the symbol itself, or press Tab to move the symbol area and then use the arrow keys to move to the symbol.

4. Double-click with the highlight on the symbol you want, and press Enter. Word inserts the character in the point size of the text that precedes the insertion point.

5. To insert another symbol, position the insertion point in the document and repeat Step 4. If you are using the keyboard, press Ctrl+Tab to move between the Symbol dialog box and your document.

6. After you finish inserting symbols, choose Close.

Entering a character code

Every character in a character set has a unique three-number code. When you select a symbol from the Symbol dialog box, the status bar displays the character code. For fonts that are ANSI-based, these codes are standardized. In order to insert a symbol based on its ANSI code, press Alt+0 and the code number with the numeric keypad; for example, pressing Alt+0153 inserts the trademark symbol ™ at the insertion point. Table 2-10 lists the ANSI character set.

Don't confuse character codes with the shortcut keys that Word assigns to commonly used characters. If a shortcut key is assigned to a symbol, that key appears after the Shortcut Key label in the Symbol dialog box.

To insert a symbol by typing the ANSI character code:

1. Position the insertion point where you want to insert the symbol.

2. Make sure that Num Lock is activated.

3. Hold down Alt, and press 0 (zero) on the numeric keypad followed by the appropriate ANSI character code.

The AutoCorrect command lets you insert any symbol as you type, as explained later in this chapter.

Table 2-10
The ANSI Character Set

Code	Character
130	,
131	ƒ
132	„
133	…
134	†
135	‡
136	ˆ
137	‰
138	Š
139	‹
140	Œ
145	'
146	'
147	"
148	"
150	–
151	-

Code	Character
161	¡
162	¢
163	£
164	¤
165	¥
166	¦
167	§
168	¨
169	©
170	ª
171	«
172	¬
173	-
174	®
175	¯
176	°
177	±
178	2
179	3
180	´
181	µ
182	¶
183	·
184	¸
185	1
186	º
187	»
188	¼
189	½

(continued)

Table 2-10 *(continued)*

Code	Character
190	¾
191	¿
192	À
193	Á
194	Â
195	Ã
196	Ä
197	Å
198	Æ
199	Ç
200	È
201	É
202	Ê
203	Ë
204	Ì
205	Í
206	Î
207	Ï
208	Ð
209	Ñ
210	Ò
211	Ó
212	Ô
213	Õ
214	Ö
215	×
216	Ø
217	Ù
218	Ú

Code	Character
219	Û
220	Ü
221	Ý
222	(
223	ß
224	à
225	á
226	â
227	ã
228	ä
229	å
230	æ
231	ç
232	è
233	é
234	ê
235	è
236	ì
237	í
238	î
239	ï
240	ð
241	ñ
242	ò
243	ó
244	ô
245	õ
246	ö
247	÷
248	ø
249	ù

(continued)

Table 2-10 *(continued)*	
Code	**Character**
250	ú
251	û
252	ü
253	y
254	þ
255	ÿ

Using the Symbol dialog box and shortcut keys

The Special Characters tab (see Figure 2-8) in the Symbol dialog box (Insert⇔Symbol) includes a collection of frequently used symbols and special characters. These special characters have been assigned to shortcut keys so that you can insert them quickly. For example, you can insert the copyright symbol © directly in your document and avoid displaying the Symbol dialog box by pressing Alt+Ctrl+C. Table 2-11 lists some of Word's default shortcut keys for special characters.

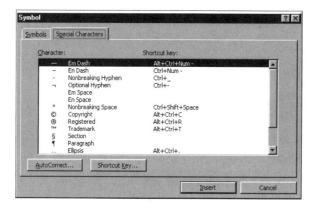

Figure 2-8: The Special Characters tab.

To insert a special character from the Special Characters tab:

1. Position the insertion point where you want to insert the special character.

2. Choose Insert⇔Symbol.

3. Select the Special Characters tab.

4. Double-click the special character in the listing, or highlight the entry, and choose Insert.

5. To insert another special character, position the insertion point in the document, and repeat Step 4.

6. When you finish inserting symbols, choose Close.

Table 2-11	
Shortcut Keys for Common Special Characters	
Character	*Shortcut Key*
Em dash	Alt+Ctrl+ –– (minus sign on numeric keypad)
En dash	Ctrl+ – (minus sign on numeric keypad)
Nonbreaking hyphen	Ctrl+_
Optional hyphen	Ctrl+-(not the numeric keypad)
Nonbreaking space	Ctrl+Shift+spacebar
Copyright	Alt+Ctrl+C
Registered	Alt+Ctrl+R
Trademark	Alt+Ctrl+T
Ellipsis	Alt+Ctrl+.

Using shortcut keys to insert a symbol

If you frequently insert a particular symbol, you can assign it a custom shortcut key. You can then insert the symbol by pressing the shortcut key rather than by using the Symbol command. If the symbol is a non-ANSI font, inserting it with a shortcut key is advantageous because the shortcut key inserts the symbol as a protected character. To assign a symbol to a shortcut key:

1. Choose Insert⇨Symbol.

2. Select the Symbols or Special Character tab containing the character you want.

3. Select the symbol or character you want.

4. Choose the Shortcut Key button. The Customize dialog box appears with the Keyboard tab already selected, and the chosen symbol displayed (see Figure 2-9).

5. In the Press <u>N</u>ew Shortcut Key box, type the key combination you want to use for the symbol or character, and click the Assign button.

6. Repeat Steps 3 through 5 for each symbol you want to assign to a key combination.

7. When you finish assigning symbols to keys, choose the Close button in the Customize dialog box, and choose Close in the Symbol dialog box.

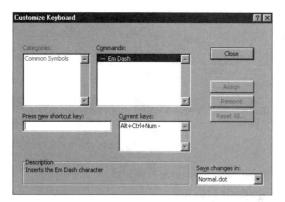

Figure 2-9: The Customize Keyboard dialog box.

You can automatically insert any symbols with the AutoCorrect command, as explained later in this chapter.

Inserting characters using the Character Map applet

The Character Map applet works similar to the Insert Symbol dialog box. One feature that the Character Map applet includes that isn't available in the Symbol dialog box is a box that displays the keyboard equivalent for the selected character. Check and see if Character Map is installed; click Start and go to Accessories. If Character Map is installed, you'll see it there. If the Character Map applet isn't installed on your computer, you can perform the following steps to install it:

1. Click the Start button, point to Settings, and then click Control Panel.

2. Double-click the Add/Remove Programs icon.

3. Click the Windows Setup tab.

4. Click Accessories, and then click the Details button.

5. Click the Character Map check box, and choose OK.

6. Choose OK in the Add/Remove Program dialog box. The applet is added to the Accessories menu.

After you install the applet, you can use the Character Map applet to insert a special character into a document:

1. Click Start, point to Accessories, and choose Character Map.

2. Click the Font box, and then select a font. The map displays the characters for the selected font.

3. Double-click each character that you want to appear in your document. The character(s) appear in the Characters To Copy box. As with using the symbol dialog box, holding down the mouse button magnifies the selected character.

4. Choose the Copy button.

5. In your document, choose Edit↪Paste, and press Ctrl+V. The character(s) are inserted in your document.

6. Select the character(s), and then change them to the same font you used in Character Map.

AutoCorrect and AutoText

Both the AutoCorrect and AutoText commands let you insert frequently used boilerplate text and graphics quickly. With AutoCorrect, Word inserts your previously created entries automatically as you type. For example, when you type **(r)** and press the Spacebar, Word inserts the Registered symbol ®. You can also use AutoCorrect to correct misspelled words or insert a symbol not available on the keyboard. For example, it can automatically replace "teh" with "the." AutoText entries are inserted after you choose the AutoText command or type the entry name and use a shortcut key.

Working with AutoCorrect

When you store an AutoCorrect entry, Word saves it with its original formatting if the selection contains fields, symbols, paragraph marks, imported graphics, or objects other than text. If the selection contains only text, Word stores the entry as plain text (without formatting). Each time you type the name of an AutoCorrect entry followed by a space, Word inserts the entry. Suppose you create an entry called "idg" for the company name "International Data Group." Whenever you type **idg** followed by a space, Word replaces "idg" with "International Data Group." Word's AutoCorrect feature can understand that, if you add an *apostrophe s* to the entry, AutoCorrect changes the text to the correct possessive form. For example, if you enter "idg's," AutoCorrect changes the entry to a possessive form. "idg's Style Guide" is automatically changed to "International Data Group's Style Guide." AutoCorrect also lets you replace text with symbols automatically, as explained earlier. To undo an AutoCorrect entry, click the Undo button on the Standard toolbar, or press Ctrl+Z.

Creating AutoCorrect entries

You can create an AutoCorrect entry in two ways: by entering text in the Auto-Correct dialog box or by selecting a block of text or graphics before choosing the Tools⇨AutoCorrect command. The length of an AutoCorrect entry is limited only by available memory. Word comes with a set of predefined AutoCorrect entries. To use AutoCorrect for commonly misspelled words or other typing errors, enter the incorrect version and then the correct version in the AutoCorrect dialog box. After entering or selecting an AutoCorrect entry, you must give it a unique name. Here are guidelines for naming an AutoCorrect entry:

✦ An AutoCorrect name can be as long as 31 characters and must not contain spaces.

✦ Don't use a common word to name an AutoCorrect entry unless you alter the word. For example, don't name an entry "address"; instead precede it with an asterisk or other character to make it unique, such as "*address." When you don't make the word unique, Word inserts the AutoCorrect entry whenever you type the word.

The AutoCorrect dialog box also includes five helpful check box settings to make your text more appealing and your typing easier. You can select or clear these options by clicking in the setting's check box. By default, Word changes straight quotes on a keyboard to the more professional looking curly quotes. You can keep Word from changing straight quotes to curly quotes by choosing Tools⇨Auto-Correct and then selecting the AutoFormat As You Type tab. Click in the Straight Quotes with 'Smart Quotes' check box. AutoCorrect also includes these features:

✦ Correct TWo INitial CApitals corrects a common mistake in typing, where an extra capital is typed. This setting doesn't affect any acronyms typed in all caps. The default is selected (checked).

✦ Capitalize First Letter of Sentence capitalizes the first letter to save you from pressing the Shift key. The default is cleared (unchecked). By the way, pressing Shift + F3 at the end of a word will capitalize that word. Pressing it again turns the word into all caps.

✦ Capitalize Names of Days setting capitalizes the names of days. The default is selected (checked).

✦ Correct accidental usage of cAPS LOCK Key automatically fixes words typed after accidentally pressing the Caps Lock key. The default is selected (checked).

✦ Replace Text as You Type lets you enter text that the feature will replace automatically. The default is selected (checked).

Changing or deleting AutoCorrect entries

You can rename, change, or delete any AutoCorrect entries. The method you use to change an entry depends on whether the entry is created from a formatted selection or entered as plain text in the dialog box. To rename, change, and delete an AutoCorrect entry:

1. Choose Tools⇨AutoCorrect.

2. Do one of the following:

   • To change the name of an AutoCorrect entry with formatting, select the AutoCorrect entry name under Replace, and click the Delete button. Type a new name in the Replace box, and click the Add button.

   • To change the contents of an AutoCorrect entry stored as plain text, select the entry under With. Type the new entry, and click the Replace button. Click Yes when Word displays a dialog box asking whether you want to redefine the existing entry.

   • To delete an AutoCorrect entry, select the entry you want to remove, and click the Delete button.

3. Choose OK.

In addition to changing an AutoCorrect text entry, you can easily replace an existing AutoCorrect text entry. To do this, insert the existing entry in your document, make your changes, and select the revised entry. Choose Tools⇨Auto-Correct, type the existing AutoCorrect name in the Replace box, and click the Replace button. When Word displays a message asking whether you want to redefine the entry, choose Yes. Click the OK button to replace the entry and close the AutoCorrect dialog box.

When you change the capitalization after Word makes an auto correction, Word notes the change and doesn't continue to change additional references.

There are three tabs under the AutoCorrect tab. AutoFormat As You Type allows you to type 1/2 and have it appear as $^{1}/_{2}$. Similarly, 1st is transformed into 1st, and typing http//www.insiders.com instantly creates an active hyperlink to that site (if it exists!). All AutoFormat As You Type features are turned on by default. Click the appropriate check box to remove any of them.

The next tab is the AutoText menu, exactly the same menu you would see if you had selected Insert from the menu bar, pointed towards AutoText, and then selected AutoText from the resulting submenu. The final tab is AutoFormat, which instantly gives your document the look of a business letter, letter to a government official, and so on. This topic is covered thoroughly in Chapter 12.

Turning off AutoCorrect

To turn off the AutoCorrect command when you don't want to use it, choose Tools⇨AutoCorrect. Clear the Replace Text as You Type check box, and choose OK.

Saving time with AutoText

AutoText provides a quick and easy way to store and insert frequently used text and graphics. When you create an AutoText entry, you can insert it by using the Standard toolbar, the AutoText dialog box, or a keyboard shortcut. Word also lets you manage AutoText entries so that you can keep them up to date by deleting, renaming, and editing them.

Creating AutoText entries

The first step in creating an AutoText entry is selecting the text or graphics from a document that you want to save as an entry. You should then open the AutoText toolbar by right-clicking any toolbar and selecting AutoText. Now select New from the from options on the AutoText toolbar. Word creates an AutoText entry and gives it a default name by using the first few words of the entry, including any spaces. Either accept this name or change it by typing over it. Label your AutoText entries with names that are short and easy to remember so that you can quickly insert them with the keyboard shortcut.

Word saves AutoText entries exactly as they are formatted when you store them. However, if you want an AutoText entry to match the formatting of surrounding text, you can specify that it should be inserted without the formatting, as explained later.

To create an AutoText entry:

1. Select the text or graphics that you want to store as an AutoText entry. To store formatting with the entry, include the paragraph mark with the selection.

2. Use the AutoText toolbar as mentioned, or select Insert from the menu bar, and select AutoText. The AutoText dialog box appears (see Figure 2-10). By default, the first words and any punctuation appear in the Name text box.

3. Accept the default name, or type a new name in the Name box. An AutoText name can have up to 32 characters, including spaces. But keep it as short as possible and make it easy to remember.

4. Do one of the following:

   • If you want the AutoText entry available in any document, the Look in scrolling list should read "All Active Templates." This list displays only the Normal document template (the Normal.dot template) and the template that is attached to the current document, if different from the Normal template. For more information about templates and copying AutoText entries among them, see Chapters 11 and 12.

• If the document you're currently working on is based on another template, you may want to save it to the template so that it is only available to documents based on that template. To change the template, choose the template from the Make AutoText entry available to list.

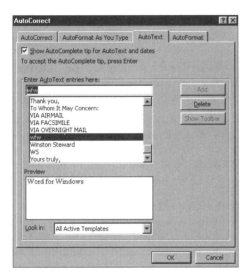

Figure 2-10: The AutoText tab of the AutoCorrect dialog box.

5. Click the Add button.

Beware of using curly quotes in your AutoText entry name. When you include curly quotes, you can only insert the AutoText entry with the Edit⇨AutoText command.

If you store a phrase that you intend to insert into a sentence, select one blank space after the phrase when you create the AutoText entry. Then, when you insert the phrase in a sentence, the blank space you usually insert after typing a word is already there. You can add punctuation, such as a period, when a phrase is usually inserted at the end of a sentence.

Inserting AutoText entries

You can insert an AutoText entry in one of three ways: by using the AutoText button on the toolbar, by choosing Insert⇨AutoText, or by using the F3 keyboard shortcut. When you want to insert the AutoText entry quickly with its original formatting, use the AutoText button or the keyboard. Use the AutoText dialog box when you don't remember the name of the AutoText entry, when you want to preview its contents, or when you want to insert it as plain text when it is saved as formatted text. To insert an AutoText entry by using the AutoText dialog box:

1. Position the insertion point where you want to insert the AutoText entry.

2. Choose Insert⇨AutoText or click the "Hand on Calculator" drop-down menu on the AutoText toolbar.

3. In the Enter AutoText entries here box, type or select an AutoText name.

To insert an AutoText entry using the keyboard shortcut:

1. Position the insertion point where you want to insert the AutoText entry. Make sure that the insertion point is at the beginning of a line or surrounded by spaces if you are inserting within text.

2. Type the name of the entry or just enough letters to uniquely identify the name of an AutoText entry. For example, if you have entries named "number" and "name," type **nu**. If you type too few characters to specify a particular entry, Word displays a message in the status bar. Type a few additional characters to specify which entry you want.

To insert an AutoText entry using the AutoText toolbar:

1. Position the insertion point where you want to insert the AutoText entry. Again, you need to be near a blank space or at the beginning of a line.

2. Click the scroll down menu on the middle of the AutoText toolbar. It will say "All Entries" or show the name of a style or template you are using. Simply scroll down, find the one you want to insert, and press enter. You'll see it in your text. If you are using a style that does not permit certain AutoText entries, use the Style command on the Format menu to allow the current template or style to be more flexible about AutoText availability.

If you use a specific AutoText entry frequently, you can assign it to a toolbar button, menu, or key combination. For more information on customizing toolbars, see Chapter 25.

Managing AutoText entries

Over time, you may need to change your collection of AutoText entries. By using the AutoText command, you can delete an entry, change the contents of an Auto-Text entry, or rename an AutoText entry.

Use the Style command in the Format menu to manage AutoText entries across templates as just mentioned, including moving them between document templates as well as renaming and deleting them. See Chapter 11 for more information on styles.

Editing an AutoText entry

If you only want to make changes to an AutoText entry, you can change the exist-ing AutoText entry's contents and then resave the entry instead of creating a new entry from scratch. To edit an AutoText entry:

1. Insert the AutoText entry in a document.

2. Make your changes.

3. Select the entire revised entry. To store paragraph formatting with the entry, include the paragraph mark with the selection.

4. Click the "Hand on Calculator" drop-down menu on the AutoText toolbar, or select Insert⇨AutoText, and then AutoText again.

5. In the Enter AutoText Entries Here box, type or select the original name of the AutoText entry, and then click the Add button. When Word displays a mes-sage asking whether you want to redefine the AutoText entry, choose Yes.

Deleting an AutoText entry

To quickly remove an AutoText entry that you no longer need, open the AutoText dialog box by choosing Insert⇨AutoText, then AutoText again. In the Enter AutoText Entries Here box, type or select the AutoText entry name that you want to remove, and click the Delete button.

Renaming an AutoText entry

After you work with AutoText entries, you may want to rename an entry to make it easier to insert. To rename an AutoText entry, you must insert it into a document, save it as a new entry, and delete the old entry. Changing the name of an entry changes its location in the AutoText dialog box because AutoText entries are listed in alphabetical order in the Name list box.

Printing AutoText entries

To help you manage your AutoText entries, you can print the names and contents of AutoText entries attached to the current document. Entries are printed in alphabetical order by AutoText name. Entries stored in the current template are printed first, entries stored in Normal.dot are printed next, and entries stored in add-in templates are printed last. AutoText entries are printed with their original formatting. To print a list of AutoText entries:

1. Choose File⇨Print, or press Ctrl+P.

2. In the Print What drop-down list, select AutoText Entries.

3. Click the OK button.

Summary

As you've learned in this chapter, Word gives you a number of ways to work with text. Some of the timesaving navigation and editing techniques explained include:

✦ Displaying and using the GoTo dialog box (F5) to quickly move to a specific location in a document.

✦ Using the mouse and the selection bar and the Extend mode key (F8) to select text.

✦ Pressing the right-mouse button to display the shortcut menu for cutting, copying, and pasting selected text.

✦ Editing by using drag and drop.

✦ Cutting and pasting multiple selections of text by using the Spike.

✦ Inserting special characters and symbols by using the Symbol dialog box.

✦ Using AutoCorrect and AutoText to speed up and automatically correct frequently typed words and phrases.

Where to go next...

✦ For more information on working with graphics, see Chapters 13 and 14.

✦ For information on working with Word's Outline features, check out Chapter 22.

✦ For more information about formatting text on the fly by using AutoFormat, go to Chapter 11.

✦ For information about how to use the Microsoft Equation 3.0 to insert mathematical formulas and expressions in your document, see Chapter 16.

✦   ✦   ✦

Finding and Replacing Text and Formatting

T his chapter explains how to use the Find and Replace commands, two of Word's most powerful navigation and editing tools. The Find command lets you move to a specific point in your document quickly, and the Replace command lets you search for and replace text, with or without formatting. You also can search for nonprinting characters, such as spaces, paragraph marks, or tabs. Word enables you to search an entire document, including annotations, footnotes, endnotes, headers, and footers. You can limit searches to the part of the document before or after the insertion point. Word also includes wildcard characters and several special characters, called operators, to refine your searches.

Finding Text Using the Find Command

The Find command lets you search a document for words, phrases, punctuation, and formatting; you can then make changes to them, if needed. To display the Find and Replace dialog box with the Find tab selected, choose Edit⇨Find, press Ctrl+F, or click the Select Browse Object button in the vertical scroll bar and click the Find icon (it has binoculars on it), as shown in Figure 3-1. To see all the options you have available, click the More button. Figure 3-2 shows the Find dialog box. The Find Next button in the Find and Replace dialog box is dimmed until you enter text in the Find what text box. In the Find what text box, enter the text that is the subject of your search. (The last seven Find what text box entries are available for reuse when you choose the down-arrow button and select the entry.)

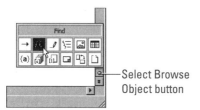

Figure 3-1: The Find icon selected in the Select Browse Object menu.

Select Browse Object button

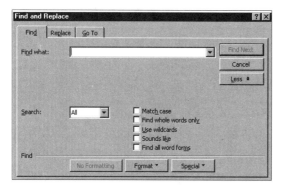

Figure 3-2: The Find and Replace dialog box with the Find tab selected.

Entering more than 41 characters causes the beginning text to scroll out of view. To view the text scrolled out of view, use the arrow, Home, or End keys. Standard text-editing keys work in the Find what text box. For example, you can use the Backspace or Delete key to erase text. You can enter up to 255 characters in the Find what text box.

The Find command is a fast way to move to specific text. Entering a sequence of unique characters to mark text makes using the Find command an easy way to return to that part of your document. For example, you may want to use two asterisks to mark text that you want to revise later. You can then use the Find command to quickly move to any text marked with two asterisks. The Edit⇨Go To command also enables you to move directly to a specific line, page, section, table, and a variety of other places. For more information on navigating documents using the Go To command, see Chapter 2.

Before activating the Edit⇨Find command, you can cut or copy text to the Clipboard, and then paste it in the Find What text box by pressing Ctrl+V.

Tip   Unfortunately, the Find command doesn't appear on the Standard toolbar, but it should. Do yourself a favor and add the Find command to the Standard toolbar. To do this, choose Tools⇨Customize, and then click the Commands tab. Select the Edit option in the Categories list box. Scroll down to Find in the Commands list box. Drag the Find icon (the one with binoculars on it) to the Standard toolbar, and then choose Close to close the Customize dialog box. You can now begin a search for specific text by clicking the Find button in the toolbar. If you're using a stan-dard VGA (640 × 480) screen, you may want to add the Find button to another toolbar to make sure it shows on-screen. For more information on customizing toolbars, see Chapter 25.

Searching for whole words

Selecting the Find whole words only check box restricts the search to entire words that match your search text. Focusing your search this way saves time. For example, suppose that you're searching for the word "ate." By choosing the Find whole words only check box, you instruct Word to find only the word "ate" and to skip words such as "congratulate," "irritate," "late," and "substantiate."

Searching by case

By default, the Find command locates each occurrence of your search text regard-less of whether characters are uppercase or lowercase. Choosing the Match case check box instructs Word to find only text that matches the uppercase and lower-case letters of your search text. As in using the Find whole words only check box, selecting the Match case check box focuses your search to save time.

Specifying the direction and extent of a search

The Search list setting controls the direction of your search beginning at the insertion point. The All setting searches the entire document, including annota-tions, footnotes, endnotes, headers, and footers. The default direction is All, meaning Word searches from the insertion point to the end of your document or selected text, and then it begins at the top of your document and ends where you started the search.

You can also confine searches to a selection of text. Selecting a block of text before issuing the Find command confines the search to that selection.

The Search list also includes two other search options: Up and Down. Selecting Up or Down limits the search to the main document and excludes annotations, foot-notes, endnotes, headers, and footers. Choosing Up instructs Word to search from the insertion point to the beginning of the document. When Word reaches the beginning of the document, it displays a dialog box asking whether you want to continue the search to the opposite end of the document. If you're using the Office Assistant, the Assistant informs you that Word has finished searching the document.

You can easily search your entire document by using the Up or Down options without displaying the dialog box that asks whether you want to continue by moving the insertion point to the top or bottom of your document before searching. To move the insertion point with the Find and Replace dialog box open, click outside the dialog box or press Ctrl+Tab. Then press Ctrl+Home to move the insertion point to the top of the document, or press Ctrl+End to move the insertion point to the bottom of the document.

Continuing a search

After entering text and setting any controls in the Find and Replace dialog box, choose the Find Next button to continue the search. Word either finds and highlights the first occurrence of your search text or displays the dialog box informing you that the text was not found (see Figure 3-3). If Word locates your search text, you can make changes to the text or continue searching for the next occurrence. You don't have to close the Find and Replace dialog box to make changes to your document; just click outside the dialog box or press Ctrl+Tab. Then continue to use the Find and Replace dialog box by choosing the Find Next button to move to the next occurrence.

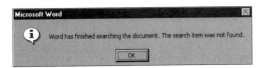

Figure 3-3: The dialog box telling you the search item was not found.

If you select Up or Down in the Search box, Word displays a dialog box when it reaches the top or bottom of the document (depending on the Search setting you selected). This dialog box asks whether you want to continue the search from the opposite end of the document to complete the search of the entire document. If you are searching a selected block of text, Word asks whether you want to search the remainder of the document.

If you want to continue searching for the text in the Find what text box without using the Find and Replace dialog box, click the Cancel button or press Esc to close the dialog box. Then press Shift+F4 to move to the next occurrence of search text. The found text is highlighted. To replace it, just type your text. To move to the next occurrence of search text without making any changes, press Shift+F4. To search a document for text using the Find and Replace dialog box:

1. Choose Edit⇨Find. The Find and Replace dialog box appears with the Find tab selected.

2. Enter the text you want to search for in the Find what text box. The Find Next button changes from dimmed to regular text, and the button appears with a border, indicating that you can choose it.

3. Make sure that the All option is selected in the Search list.

4. Choose Find Next. Word begins the search and highlights the first occurrence of the search text.

5. Do one of the following:

   • To make changes to the selected text, click outside the Find and Replace dialog box or press Ctrl+Tab. After you make your changes, choose Find Next to continue the search.

   • To leave the selected text unchanged and continue the search, choose the Find Next button.

6. When Word reaches the end of your document, a dialog box or the Office Assistant informs you that Word has finished searching the document. If you're not using the Office Assistant, a dialog box appears; choose OK to close the dialog box. Word returns you to the Find and Replace dialog box.

Finding and Replacing Text

The Edit⇨Replace command, like the Find command, also finds text that you specify. However, Edit⇨Replace enables you to automatically replace each occurrence of search text with replacement text. For example, by using the Edit⇨ Replace command, you can search for Intel 586 and replace each occurrence with Pentium. You can instruct Word to search for and replace each occurrence one-by-one or all at once.

To display the Find and Replace dialog box with the Replace tab selected, as shown in Figure 3-4, choose the Edit⇨Replace command, press Ctrl+H, or click the Replace tab in the Find and Replace dialog box. The settings in the Replace tab are the same as the Find tab with the exception of the Replace with text box and the Replace and Replace All buttons.

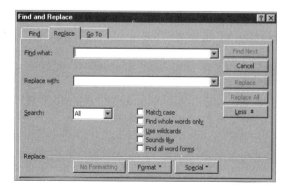

Figure 3-4: The Find and Replace dialog box with the Replace tab selected.

Unlike the Find command, the Replace command defaults to search down to the end of the document. You also can search up to the top of your document or search the entire document (All) by changing the Search setting. After you enter the search text in the Find what text box, choose the Replace with text box and enter the replacement text. Choosing Cancel or pressing Esc cancels the current replace session, leaving any changes made during the replacement session intact.

The Replace tab in the Find and Replace dialog box gives you options for searching for text or replacing text in one of three ways:

✦ Choosing the Find Next button finds the next occurrence of the search text.

✦ Choosing the Replace button replaces each occurrence on a one-by-one basis. This method lets you confirm whether you want to make the replacement or choose the Find Next button to move to the next occurrence without making any changes.

✦ Choosing the Replace All button instructs Word to replace all occurrences of the search text with the replacement text. When the replacement session is completed, a dialog box and the status bar display the number of changes made.

Caution   Be careful using the Replace All button. If you notice that the number of changes is large, check your document. If text was changed but you didn't mean to change it, choose the Edit⇨Undo Replace All command or press Ctrl+Z after the replace session. Remember that you can undo your previous commands by using the Undo button on the Standard toolbar. To search and replace text in a document:

1. Choose Edit⇨Replace. The Find and Replace dialog box appears with the Replace tab selected.

2. Enter the text you want to search for in the Find what text box.

3. Make sure the All option is selected in the Search list box. If you want to limit the search to text before or after the insertion point, choose the Up or Down option in the Search list box.

4. In the Replace with text box, enter the replacement text.

5. Do one of the following:

   • To confirm each replacement, choose Find Next. Then choose Replace to replace the text or Find Next to skip to the next occurrence.

   • To change all occurrences of the search text without confirmation, choose Replace All. You can use the Replace All anytime during the replace session.

6. If you chose the Replace All button, when the replace session is completed, a dialog box informs you that the document has been checked in the direction that you specified and tells you how many replacements were made. If you

chose either the Up or Down option, Word asks whether you want to continue searching from the opposite direction. If you want to continue the search, choose Yes. Choose No to close the dialog box and return to the Find and Replace dialog box. If you have searched the entire document or you chose the All option and you're not using the Office Assistant, a dialog box appears informing you that Word has searched the entire document; click OK to close the dialog box. If you're using the Office Assistant, a message appears informing you that Word has searched the entire document.

7. Choose Close in the Find and Replace dialog box to end the replace session.

Finding and replacing word forms

The Find and Replace dialog box includes a check box labeled Find all word forms. *Word forms* refers to the different grammatical versions of a word. For example, when you perform a search and replace operation with the Find all word forms check box selected, the replace operation does its best to change the tense of the verb to be grammatically correct for the current sentence. When you enter the word "locate" in the Find what text box and the word "search" in the Replace with text box, Word replaces each form of the word "locate" to the proper tense of the word "search." The word "locate" is replaced with "search"; "locates" is replaced with "searches"; "locate" is replaced with "searched"; and "locating" is replaced with "searching."

Be careful when using this feature; the changes are not always grammatically correct. Using the previous example, the sentence "Locating this book has not been easy" is changed to "Searching this book has not been easy." In most cases, it's safest to use the Replace button to verify the changes rather than use the Replace All button after selecting the Find all word forms check box. If you use this option and choose Replace All, a dialog box appears informing you that Replace All is not recommended with Find all word forms; the dialog box asks you to confirm whether or not you want to continue the Replace All operation.

Replacing special characters

Besides searching for and replacing text, you can search for and replace Word's special characters, such as paragraph and tab marks. The procedure is similar to that used for text, except that you use the Special menu button or enter the code representing the character in the Find what and Replace with text boxes. For example, entering ^p indicates a paragraph mark. Table 3-1 lists the special characters available in the Special menu and the respective codes that appear in the Find what or Replace with text boxes. Notice that some codes are available for only the Find what text box. Figure 3-5 shows the menu options for the Find what (shown first) and Replace with (shown second) text boxes.

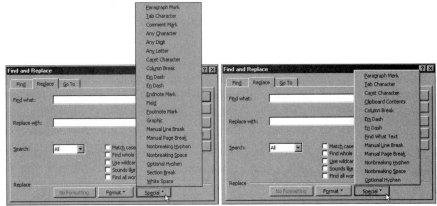

Figure 3-5: The Special menu options for the Find what and Replace with text boxes.

Use the lowercase letter when entering the code for a special character. If you enter an uppercase letter and try to execute the Find or Replace command, Word displays a message box informing you that the uppercase character is not a valid special character.

If you are replacing a symbol or a special character, you can always copy and paste it in the Find what or Replace with text box. If you know the shortcut key or ANSI code for a symbol, you can insert it directly into the Find what and Replace with text boxes. For example, to insert the copyright symbol ©, press the shortcut key Alt+Ctrl+C or the ANSI character code Alt+0169. Remember that you must use the numeric keypad to enter the ANSI character code. For more information on working with symbol shortcut keys and ANSI codes, see Chapter 2.

Tip   You might want to turn on the Show/Hide button before you search for and replace special marks so that you can see the nonprinting characters Word locates. To turn on the Show/Hide button, click the Show/Hide button on the Standard toolbar.

To find and replace special characters:

1. Choose Edit⊷Replace. The Find and Replace dialog box appears with the Replace tab selected.

2. Click inside the Find what text box.

3. Choose the Special button, and select the special character or item you want to find and any text for which you want to search.

4. Position the insertion point in the Replace with text box.

5. Click the Special button, and select the special character or item you want to add to the Replace with text box. You can add more than one special character to the text box. Of course, you can also add text before or after a special character in the Replace with text box.

6. Make sure that the All option is selected in the Search box. If you want to limit the search to text before or after the insertion point, choose the Up or Down option in the Search box.

7. Do one of the following:

   • To confirm each replacement on a one-by-one basis, choose Find Next. Then choose Replace to replace the text, or choose Find Next to skip to the next occurrence.

   • To change all occurrences of the search text without confirmation, choose Replace All.

8. When the replace session for the entire document is completed, either a dialog box appears or the Office Assistant informs you how many replacements were made. If the Office Assistant isn't open, the dialog box appears; click the OK button or press Enter to close the dialog box.

9. Choose Close in the Find and Replace dialog box to end the replace session.

Table 3-1
Characters in the Special Menu

Special Character	Code	Available
Paragraph Mark	^p	Always
Tab Character	^t	Always
Comment Mark	^a	Find Only
Any Character	^?	Find Only
Any Digit	^#	Find Only
Any Letter	^$	Find Only
Caret Character	^^	Always
Clipboard Contents	^c	Replace Only
Column Break	^n	Always
Em Dash	^+	Always
En Dash	^=	Always

(continued)

Table 3-1 *(continued)*		
Special Character	**Code**	**Available**
Endnote Mark	^e	Find Only
Field	^d	Find Only
Find What Text	^&	Replace Only
Footnote Mark	^f	Find Only
Graphic	^g	Find Only
Manual Line Break	^l	Always
Manual Page Break	^m	Always
Nonbreaking Hyphen	^~	Always
Nonbreaking Space	^s	Always
Optional Hyphen	^-	Always
Section Break	^b	Find Only
White Space	^w	Find Only

Automatically adding text to replacement text

The Find What Text option is added to the Special list when the insertion point is in the Replace with text box. Clicking the Special button and choosing the Find What Text option inserts ^& in the Replace with text box. This instructs Word to include the text in the Find what text box as part of the replacement text. Using ^& gives you an easy way to add text before and/or after existing text. For example, say the Find what text box contains "July 19" and you want to replace the text with "Sunday, July 19, 1998." In the Replace with text box, you can enter "Sunday, ^&, 1998."

Making a replacement using the Clipboard

When you choose the Replace with text box, the Clipboard Contents option is added to the Special list. Clipboard Contents lets you insert graphics and other non-text elements that you have stored on the Clipboard in conjunction with the Replace command. This option is helpful for inserting replacement elements such as text containing different formats, blocks of text larger than 255 characters, tables, or pictures. You can also use Clipboard Contents to insert text with mixed formatting, such as an italicized word and a word that contains a single underlined letter. For more information on working with the Clipboard, see Chapter 2.

To use the Clipboard with the Replace command:

1. Select the text or graphics you want to place on the Clipboard.

2. Choose Edit⇨Copy (Ctrl+C) or Edit⇨Cut (Ctrl+X). Word copies or cuts the selection on the Clipboard.

3. Choose Edit⇨Replace. The Find and Replace dialog box appears with the Replace tab selected.

4. In the Find what text box, enter the text you want to locate.

5. In the Replace with text box, enter ^c or choose Special⇨Clipboard Contents. No other text can be entered in the Replace with text box if you choose Clipboard Contents.

6. Make sure that the All option is selected in the Search box. If you want to limit the search to text before or after the insertion point, choose the Up or Down option in the Search box.

7. Do one of the following:

   • To confirm each replacement on a one-by-one basis, choose Find Next. Then choose Replace to replace the search text, or Choose Find Next to skip to the next occurrence.

   • To change all occurrences of the search text without confirmation, choose Replace All.

8. If you chose the Replace All button, when the replace session is completed, a dialog box informs you that the document has been checked in the direction you specified and tells you how many replacements were made. (If you are using the Office Assistant, it will tell you the document has been checked— you won't get a dialog box.) If you chose either the Up or Down option, Word asks whether you want to continue searching from the opposite direction. If you want to continue the search, choose Yes. Choose No to close the dialog box and return to the Find and Replace dialog box. If you have searched the entire document or you chose the All option and are not using the Office Assistant, choose OK to close the dialog box.

9. Choose Close in the Find and Replace dialog box to end the replace session.

Finding and Replacing Formatting

Word can find and replace any kind of formatting, including character and paragraph formatting, styles, and even the language you assign to specific text for proofing. You can specify formatting three ways in the Find and Replace dialog boxes: using formatting dialog boxes, using buttons on the Formatting toolbar, or using shortcut key combinations.

Formatting dialog boxes become available when you choose the F<u>o</u>rmat button and select a formatting option from the F<u>o</u>rmat menu. Figure 3-6 shows the F<u>o</u>rmat menu. The options in this menu display dialog boxes similar to those you use to create the formatting. For example, choosing the <u>F</u>ont option in the F<u>o</u>rmat menu displays the same options as in the Find Font dialog box (see Figure 3-7), which appears when you choose the F<u>o</u>rmat⇨<u>F</u>ont command. After the dialog box is displayed, you can choose the formatting for which you want to search. For more information on working with the Font dialog box, see Chapter 7. For information on working with the Paragraph dialog box, see Chapter 8.

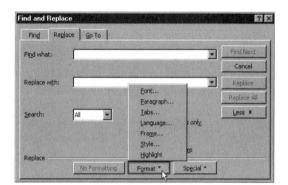

Figure 3-6: The Format menu.

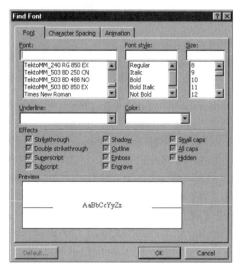

Figure 3-7: The Find Font dialog box.

Even without using the formatting dialog boxes, you can still perform search and replace operations for basic character formatting by using the Formatting toolbar or shortcut key combinations. Table 3-2 gives the key combinations to enter in the Find what and Replace with text boxes for common character formats.

The most convenient way to enter common formatting in the Find what and Replace with text boxes is to choose the formatting option directly from the Formatting toolbar (see Figure 3-8). For example, with the insertion point in the Find what text box, you can choose a font from the font list and the Bold button for boldface. When you choose a style format such as bold, italic, or underline, you can choose to exclude a style format from the search. For example, clicking twice on the Italic button in the Formatting toolbar displays Not Italic and instructs Word to find only matching text that is not italicized.

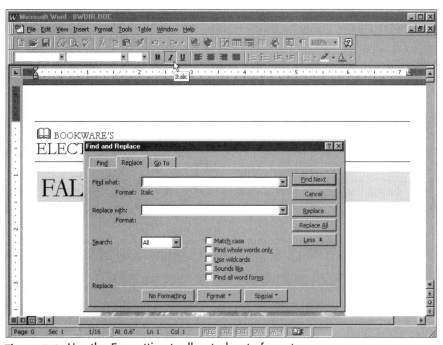

Figure 3-8: Use the Formatting toolbar to locate formats.

Table 3-2
Shortcut Keys for Locating Character Formats

Character Format	Key Combination
Boldface	Ctrl+B
Hidden	Ctrl+Shift+H
Italic	Ctrl+I
Remove character formatting	Ctrl+spacebar
Subscript	Ctrl+=
Superscript	Ctrl+Shift++(plus sign)
Underline	Ctrl+U
Word underline	Ctrl+Shift+W

Be sure to clear the character formats or fonts from the Find what and Replace with text boxes after performing a find operation or a find and replace operation. If one or more character formats and a font name appear below a text box, press Ctrl+ spacebar, or choose the No Formatting button to remove them. To find and replace underlined text with italic text:

1. Choose Edit⇨Replace. The Find and Replace dialog box appears with the Replace tab selected.

2. Choose the Find what text box. Press Ctrl+U (the key combination for underlined characters), or choose the Underline button on the Standard toolbar.

3. Choose the Replace with text box. Press Ctrl+I (the key combination for italicized characters), or choose the Italic button on the Standard toolbar.

4. Make sure the All option is selected in the Search box.

5. Do one of the following:

   • To confirm each replacement, choose Find Next. Then choose Replace to replace the search text, or choose Find Next to skip to the next occurrence.

   • To replace each occurrence of search text on a one-by-one basis without confirming each replacement, choose Replace.

   • To change all occurrences of the search text without confirmation, choose Replace All.

6. If you chose the Replace All button, when the replace session is completed, a dialog box or an Office Assistant message appears that informs you that the document has been checked in the direction you specified and tells you how many replacements were made. If you chose either the Up or Down option, the Office Assistant displays a message or a dialog box appears that asks whether you want to continue searching from the opposite direction. If you want to continue the search, choose Yes. Choose No to close the dialog box and return to the Find and Replace dialog box. If you have searched the entire document or you chose the All option and are not using the Office Assistant, choose OK to close the dialog box.

7. Choose Close in the Find and Replace dialog box to end the replace session.

Note   If you want the replacement text to include different formats, such as one word in italics and one in normal text, see the section "Making a replacement using the Clipboard" earlier in this chapter.

To replace fonts using the mouse and the Formatting toolbar:

1. Choose Edit⇨Replace. The Find and Replace dialog box appears with the Replace tab selected.

2. With the insertion point in the Find what text box, click the font list box on the Formatting toolbar, and then select the font you want to find. You can add other formatting options by clicking the appropriate buttons.

3. Choose the Replace with text box, and then click the font list box on the Formatting toolbar and select the font you want to use to replace the existing font you selected in the Find what text box. You can add other formatting options by clicking the appropriate buttons.

4. Make sure that the All option is selected in the Search list box. If you want to limit the search to text before or after the insertion point, choose either the Up or Down option in the Search box.

5. Do one of the following:

   • To confirm each replacement on a one-by-one basis, choose Find Next. Then choose Replace to replace the search text or Find Next to skip to the next occurrence.

   • To change all occurrences of the search text without confirmation, choose Replace All.

6. If you chose the Replace All button, when the replace session is completed, a dialog box informs you that the document has been checked in the direction you specified and tells you how many replacements were made. If you chose either the Up or Down option, Word asks whether you want to continue searching from the opposite direction. If you want to continue the search,

choose <u>Y</u>es. Choose <u>N</u>o to close the dialog box and return to the Find and Replace dialog box. If you have searched the entire document or you chose the All option and you're not using the Office Assistant, choose OK to close the dialog box.

7. Choose Close in the Find and Replace dialog box to end the replace session.

Refining Searches

Word lets you refine your searches using wildcard characters and operators. The question mark and asterisk are wildcard characters that are used to represent characters in the search text. The question mark matches any single character; the asterisk matches any group of characters, commonly called a *text string*. Word looks past the asterisk to see whether the search is limited by any other characters. For example, searching for "wo*d" finds text such as "word," "world," and "worshipped."

To use these wildcard characters, select the <u>U</u>se wildcards check box in the Find and Replace dialog box. These wildcards are handy for finding words that you don't know how to spell. For example, if you are not sure how to spell "receive," you can enter "rec??ve." Word locates any word that begins with "rec" followed by any two characters, followed by "ve." Another method of searching for words that you aren't sure how to spell is to use the Sounds li<u>k</u>e check box. Selecting this option instructs Word to consult a list of words that sound like each other, for example, similar names such as "Cathy" and "Kathy" and British spellings such as "colour" for "color."

Caution Just as parentheses are used in math to specify equations to be performed first, Word uses parentheses to indicate the order of evaluation and to group expressions. An expression is any combination of characters and operators that specifies a pattern. An operator is a symbol that controls the search. Using operators allows you to create specific search criteria. For example, you can find all words that start with a particular prefix and end with a specific suffix, such as all words that start with "dis" and end with "ed." Using this search criteria, Word might find words such as "disinterested," "disinherited," "displaced," and "distinguished."

To use operators, you must select the <u>U</u>se wildcards check box. When you select this check box, the Spe<u>c</u>ial menu changes to include a list of operators at the top of the menu (see Figure 3-9). Table 3-3 lists search operators and describes how each operator affects a search. To search for or replace text with a character that serves as an operator, precede the character with a backslash (\) in the Fi<u>n</u>d what or Replace w<u>i</u>th text box. For example, to find a question mark, type \? in the Fi<u>n</u>d what text box. You only need to precede the character that serves as an operator with a backslash if <u>U</u>se wildcards is selected.

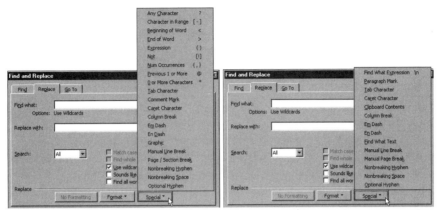

Figure 3-9: The Special menu for the Find what and Replace with text boxes after selecting the Use wildcards check box.

Tip   One other operator that you can use in the Replace with box is \n. This operator rearranges expressions in the Find what box in the order given in the Replace With box. If you typed **(Windows) (for) (Word)** in the Find what text box and **\3 \2 \1** in the Replace with text box, the text would change from "Windows for Word" to "WordforWindows" (without spaces).

Table 3-3
Search Operators

To Find	Operator	Examples
Any single character	?	d?g finds "dig," "dog," and "dug."
Any string of characters	*	des*t finds "descent," "desert," "dessert," and "destruct."
One of the specified characters	[]	b[aeiou]t finds "bat," "bet," "bit," and "but."
Any single character in this range	[-]	[a-m]end finds "bend," "fend," "lend," and "mend." (The range must be in ascending order.)
Any single character except the characters inside the brackets	[!]	t[!ae]ll finds "till" and "toll," but not "tall" and "tell."
Any single character except characters in the range inside the brackets	[!a-z]	m[!o-z]st finds "mast" and "mist," but not "most" or "must."
Exactly *n* occurrences of the previous character	{n}	to{2} finds "too," but not "to."

(continued)

Table 3-3 *(continued)*		
To Find	*Operator*	*Examples*
At least *n* occurrences of the previous character	{*n,*}	*{4,} finds four or more asterisks.
From *n* to *n* occurrences of the previous character	{*n,n*}	10{2,3} finds "100" and "1000," but not "10."
One or more occurrences of the previous character	@	^p@^t finds one or more paragraph break marks followed by a tab mark.
The beginning of a word	<	<tele finds "telemarketing," "telephone," and "television."
The end of a word	>	tion> finds "aggravation," "inspiration," and "institution."

Summary

This chapter has given you several ways to save time when trying to locate and replace text and formatting. To control searches in order to quickly find or find and replace text, you can do the following:

✦ Limit the search to a portion of your document.

✦ Specify the formatting for text that you want to find or replace.

✦ Instruct Word to automatically replace different word forms, such as nouns and verbs.

✦ Search and replace special characters, including nonprinting characters.

✦ Replace text with multiple formats or text and graphics by using the Clipboard.

✦ Use pattern matching and operators to refine your search.

Where to go next...

✦ For more information on formatting characters, see Chapter 7. Chapter 8 explains how to apply formatting to paragraphs. Chapter 9 includes information on sections and page formatting.

✦ Chapter 4 tells you how to use Word's proofing tools, including how to check spelling and grammar and how to use the Thesarus.

✦ If you're anxious to see what your printed document looks like, skip to Chapter 5.

✦   ✦   ✦

Proofing Documents

People occasionally make errors in spelling or in grammatical syntax when writing a new document either because they focus on the ideas and concepts they are writing about or because of simple typographical errors. Careful reading of a finished document can catch most or all such errors, but that takes time. Instead, you can use the spell checker that Word provides, which compares all words in the document to those words in a dictionary that you specify. The Word grammar checker detects possible errors in word usage. The automatic checking features catch the misspelled words and other errors immediately so that you can correct them as you go.

Correcting Spelling Errors

Word's main dictionary contains most common words. When Word finds a word that is not in the dictionary, that word is displayed in the Spelling and Grammar dialog box (see Figure 4-1), which offers you choices on how to handle the word. Word also displays instances of repeated words. In all cases, you can see the errors Word selects in the context of the sentence.

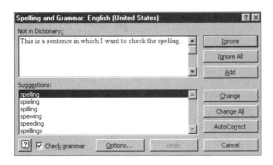

Figure 4-1: The Spelling and Grammar dialog box showing a spelling error.

The Spelling and Grammar dialog box handles both spelling and grammatical errors and makes suggestions for correcting both. (More on grammar checking later.)

You can check the spelling of an entire document, a selection of text, or a single word. To use the Spelling tool, however, it must be installed. If the Spelling and Grammar option does not appear on the Tools menu, run Word's Setup program again and install the spelling and grammar checker. To run the spell checker from the menu:

1. Select the word or text that you want to check. To check the entire document, make sure that nothing is selected.

2. Choose Tools⇨Spelling and Grammar. The Spelling and Grammar checking begins, and the Spelling and Grammar dialog box appears when Word finds the first error.

You can begin a spell check quickly by pressing F7.

During a spell check, Word stops automatically each time it finds what it considers an error and then the Spelling and Grammar dialog box opens showing the error highlighted in red. Table 4-1 describes the dialog box options that appear when Word finds a spelling error. If you have turned on the grammar checker, Word also stops when it finds a grammar error.

Checking spelling quickly with the Spelling and Grammar button

The Spelling and Grammar button is on the Standard toolbar, which appears by default the first time you open Word (see Figure 4-2). If you choose not to display the Standard toolbar, you can still add the Spelling and Grammar button to any toolbars you do choose to display. (For more on customizing the toolbars, see Chapter 25.)

Figure 4-2: The Spelling and Grammar button on the Standard toolbar.

Using the Spelling and Grammar button is a quick way to begin a spelling check. If you want to check the spelling of a single word, just select that word and then click the Spelling and Grammar button. The same is true of a paragraph or any other selection of text. If you want to check the spelling of the entire document, make sure that nothing is selected when you click the Spelling and Grammar button.

Spell checking while you type

Word 97 can automatically check your spelling as you type if you want it to. Word will either call the misspellings to your attention immediately or keep track of them for later. This saves time after you complete the document because Word already knows where all the possible errors occur and you can move to them quickly.

Possible errors are flagged with wavy red underlines so that they are easy to spot. After you edit the word, the red line disappears. If you would rather correct all the errors at once after you complete the last golden paragraph, you can hide the red lines while you work by checking the Hide spelling errors in this document option in the Spelling & Grammar tab of the Options dialog box. The next section gives you more information about setting the Spelling options.

Table 4-1
Spelling Error Options

Option	Action
Not in Dictionary:	Displays the error in context.
Suggestions:	Displays a list of suggested corrections if you have selected the Always suggest corrections option via the Options button.
Ignore	Continues the spell check without changing the selection. Word will display any additional instances of the same error.
Ignore All	Continues the spell check without changing the selection. Word does not display additional instances of the same error during the current session (which means this option applies to all open documents, not just the active document).
Add	Adds the selected word to the active dictionary. To see the name of the active dictionary, click the Options button.
Change/Delete	Accepts the suggestion in the Suggestions box. You can also edit the error in place instead of choosing one of the suggestions, and then click Change. If the error is a repeated word, this button changes to Delete, which removes the repeated word.
Change All/Delete All	Changes all instances of the selection in the current document (unlike Ignore All) to whatever you select in the Suggestions box or type in the text. If the error is a repeated word, this button changes to Delete All.
AutoCorrect	Adds the error and its correction to the AutoCorrect list.
Options	Opens the Spelling & Grammar tab of the Options dialog box where you can specify various spelling options. (You'll read more about this later.)

(continued)

	Table 4-1 *(continued)*
Option	**Action**
<u>U</u>ndo	Undoes the last action made during the current spell check session. Clicking this button a second time undoes the second-to last action, and so on. This button is not available until you make at least one change.
Cancel/Close	When you first open the Spelling and Grammar dialog box, the Cancel button is displayed. When you make the first change, the Cancel button changes to the Close button. Clicking either button closes the dialog box, saving any changes you have made.

To correct the error immediately, right-click the offending word to open a context-sensitive shortcut menu (see Figure 4-3). The menu offers suggestions for correcting the error, as well as the choice to ignore it. Then add the word to your dictionary or open the Spelling and Grammar dialog box for further options.

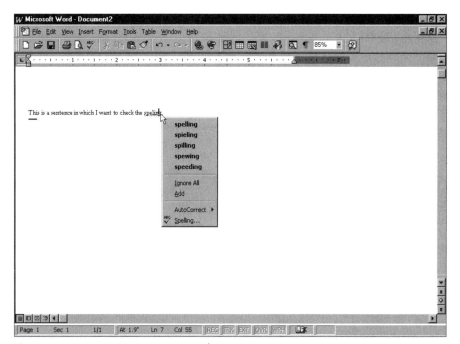

Figure 4-3: A spell check shortcut menu.

The status bar also displays three icons at the right end that indicate the current spelling and grammar status of your document. One icon means that spell and grammar checking is underway. A second, an open book with an X, indicates that checking is complete and errors were found. If the icon shows an open book with a check mark, checking is complete and Word found no errors.

You can use the status bar icons to navigate through the spelling errors by double-clicking the icon showing a book with an X. The shortcut menu of suggestions automatically opens when the next error is highlighted. After all the errors are attended to, the icon changes to the book with the check mark. Double-clicking this icon brings up the message that the spell and grammar check is complete.

If you are not sure about the spelling of a single word and want Word 97 to help you spell it correctly, you can find the correct spelling by using wildcards to take the place of the characters you don't know. The asterisk (*) wildcard represents any number of characters, and the question mark (?) wildcard takes the place of a single character. For example, if you're not sure about the spelling of "embarrass-ment," you can type **emba*a*ment**, select it, and click the Spelling and Grammar button. Word will show you the correct spelling. If you type **emba*ment**, Word will show you three words that fit that pattern.

Finding duplicated words

Whenever Word finds an instance of a repeated word during a spell check, it highlights the second instance of the word in red and stops until you make a decision. In some instances, you may want to keep double words. In most cases, however, repeated words are an error. You can delete the second instance of the word, if that is appropriate.

Skipping selected text

Sometimes you may want to skip parts of your document during a spell check. Memos and letters, for example, have headings and address blocks that contain names and other text that slow down the spell check. Word provides a way for you to skip text while checking your document. To skip selected text during a spell check:

1. Select the text you want to skip.
2. Choose Tools⇨Language⇨Set Language. This opens the Language dialog box (see Figure 4-4).

Figure 4-4: The Language dialog box.

3. Scroll up the list and select the top selection (no proofing).

4. Click OK.

Checking spelling in other languages

With Word, you can run spell checks for text written in languages other than English. However, you must buy and install a language dictionary for each language you want to check. Call Microsoft Customer Service for more information about this option.

Tip You can receive free Microsoft Word for Windows support by calling 206-462-9673, 6 a.m. to 6 p.m. Pacific time, Monday through Friday, excluding holidays. However, you have to pay for the long distance charges. Microsoft also has support services available on the Internet and on CompuServe. You can also purchase from third parties special supplemental dictionaries, such as for the medical or legal professions.

To check selected text in another language:

1. Select the text you want to format in the other language.

2. Choose Tools➪Language➪Set Language. This opens the Language dialog box as before.

3. Select the language from the Mark selected text as list.

4. Click OK.

You can create a style that includes a language format and the appropriate dictionary for each language that you use. See Chapter 11 for more on styles in Word.

Setting other spelling options

Customizing, fine-tuning, and many dictionary handling options are found in the Spelling & Grammar tab of the Options dialog box. The choices in this dialog box are very important if you write or edit many different styles of documents. To customize spelling options:

1. Choose Tools⇨Options. The Options dialog box appears.
2. Click the Spelling & Grammar tab to display the Spelling & Grammar Options dialog box (see Figure 4-5).

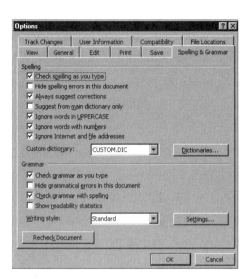

Figure 4-5: The Spelling & Grammar tab of the Options dialog box.

3. Select the options you want (see Table 4-2).

Note If you are working in the Spelling and Grammar dialog box, click the Options button to display the Spelling & Grammar tab of the Options dialog box.

Table 4-2 **Spelling Options**	
Option	*Action*
Check spelling as you type	Checks for spelling errors as you type the words. Misspelled words appear underlined with a wavy red line.
Hide spelling errors in this document	Shows or hides wavy red underline, indicating a possible spelling error.
Always suggest corrections	Shows suggested replacements for all words found during the spell check.

(continued)

Table 4-2 *(continued)*	
Option	*Action*
Suggest from <u>m</u>ain dictionary only	Shows suggestions from only the main dictionary, not from other open custom dictionaries.
Ignore words in <u>U</u>PPERCASE	Skips words with all uppercase characters.
Ignore words with num<u>b</u>ers	Skips words that contain numbers.
Ignore Internet and <u>fi</u>le addresses	Skips Internet and e-mail address and file names.
<u>D</u>ictionaries	Opens the Custom Dictionaries dialog box where you can create a new dictionary, add an existing one to the list, edit or remove an existing dictionary, or apply a different language format to your document.

Using Custom Dictionaries

When you install the spelling option in Word, it includes a dictionary known as the *main dictionary* (the filename for the main English (US) dictionary is Mssp2_en.lex) that Word always uses during a spell check. Besides using this standard dictionary, you can create specialized dictionaries. For example, if you frequently create docu-ments that contain industry-specific words and acronyms, you can create a custom dictionary and add those special words and terms to that dictionary. The spell checker won't highlight those words or terms unless they are not spelled correctly in the document.

A *custom dictionary* is just a list of words that you don't want to add to the main dictionary but do want the spell checker to skip in some situations. Word automat-ically starts its own custom dictionary when you first run spell checking for your document. Any Change all and Ignore all selections are added to that dictionary. Word uses any additional custom dictionaries you activate (up to ten) in conjunc-tion with the main dictionary to perform the spell check.

To activate a custom dictionary:

1. Choose <u>T</u>ools⇨<u>O</u>ptions. The Options dialog box appears.

2. Click the Spelling & Grammar tab to display the Spelling & Grammar Options dialog box.

3. Click the <u>D</u>ictionaries button to display the Custom Dictionaries dialog box (see Figure 4-6).

4. Select the check box next to each dictionary you want to use. Clear the check boxes of those you no longer want to use.

5. Click OK.

Figure 4-6: The Custom Dictionaries dialog box.

The Custom Dictionaries dialog box contains all the options you need to create and modify Word dictionaries. Table 4-3 describes the custom dictionary options.

	Table 4-3 **Custom Dictionary Options**
Option	**Action**
New	Opens a dialog box that lets you create a new custom dictionary.
Edit	Opens the selected custom dictionary where you can add, delete, or edit the words in the list.
Add	You can have custom dictionaries that do not appear on the Custom Dictionary list in the Spelling & Grammar Options dialog box because clicking the Remove button removes a dictionary from the list but does not delete the dictionary file. The Add button opens a dialog box in which you can select existing dictionary files to add to the Custom dictionary list. You can also use the advanced find feature to locate the dictionary in another folder.
Remove	Removes the selected dictionary from the Custom dictionary list. (You must first clear the check box to use this option on a dictionary.) Selecting this option does not physically delete the custom dictionary from your disk; rather, it simply removes it from the list so that it no longer appears when you open the Spelling & Grammar Options dialog box. Do not remove the first dictionary (Custom.dic) in the list; it is used by the other Microsoft applications.
Language	Applies language formatting of your choice to a custom dictionary. Select the custom dictionary, select the language, and click OK. Word then uses that dictionary when checking text formatted in that language.

Changing the custom dictionary list

Activating and deactivating tells Word which of the custom dictionaries in the list to use in spell checking. If the dictionary you want exists but is not on the list, you can add it to the list. If you want an entirely new list of words in a custom dictionary, you can create a new one and then add it to the list. When you remove a dictionary from the list, it still exists on your disk. To delete the dictionary, you must use the normal file management process.

To add a custom dictionary to the list, simply open the Spelling & Grammar Options dialog box, choose Dictionaries, and then click the Add button. Word displays the Add Custom Dictionary dialog box with a list of the dictionary files in the current folder. You can switch drives and directories to find the dictionary you want to add. Then be sure to activate the new dictionary by selecting the check box in the Custom Dictionaries dialog box.

Because you can have no more than ten dictionaries on the list at once, you may need to take off the ones you don't use. To remove a custom dictionary from the list, open the Spelling & Grammar Options dialog box and choose Dictionaries. Then select the custom dictionary you want to take off the list and click the Remove button. The name is no longer on the list, but you can add it back later, if necessary.

Creating a new custom dictionary

A custom dictionary is just a list of words each on its own line in a document with the .dic extension.

To create a custom dictionary:

1. Open the Spelling & Grammar Options dialog box as before and click the Dictionaries button to display the Custom Dictionaries dialog box.

2. Click the New button to open the Create Custom Dictionary dialog box (see Figure 4-7).

3. Enter a name for the new custom dictionary.

4. Click Save. A blank document window opens, ready for you to enter the word list.

5. Enter the word list, each word on a separate line, and then click the Save button.

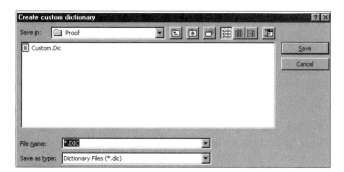

Figure 4-7: The Create Custom Dictionary dialog box.

The name you entered in Step 3 now appears in the Custom dictionary list. You must activate it before Word will use it for spell checking.

Besides creating custom dictionaries, you can create an *exclude dictionary* to specify the preferred spelling of certain words. An exclude dictionary contains words that you want selected even if they appear to be spelled correctly. For example, some words are spelled slightly differently in England than they are in America (such as "colour" versus "color"), and you may want to review these types of words in some cases. You can also use the exclude dictionary to spot words you habitually spell wrong. For example, if you often type "that" when you intend to type "than," you can add "that" to the exclude dictionary and Word will ask for your approval of each instance. The downside of the exclude dictionary is that because it is saved with the same name as the main dictionary but with a different extension, Word always uses it with the main dictionary. You have to rename the exclude dictionary if you don't want Word to use it.

To create an exclude dictionary:

1. Open a new document.

2. Type the words that you want listed in the exclude dictionary. Press Enter after you type each word so that it is on a line of its own.

3. Choose File⇨Save As.

4. Switch to the `\Windows\MsApps\Proof` folder.

5. The exclude dictionary must have the same filename as the main dictionary except for the extension. Therefore, name the exclude dictionary `Mssp2_en.exc`.

6. Select Text Only in the Save as type box at the bottom of the dialog box.

7. Click Save.

Adding new words to a dictionary

You have two ways to add words to a custom dictionary: during spell checking and by editing the dictionary directly. When you run a spell check, one of the options in the Spelling and Grammar dialog box is the Add button. Just click the Add button while the word is highlighted to add the word to the activated custom dictionaries.

If you want to add several words at once to your dictionary, use the Edit option in the Custom Dictionaries dialog box to open the word list. Be sure each word is on a separate line. You cannot edit Word's Custom.dic dictionary.

Using the Word Grammar Tool

Word's grammar checker identifies sentences that contain possible grammatical or style errors and suggests corrections. The grammar checker by default also runs a spell checker at the same time it checks the grammar. You can turn this spell checker off via the Options button in the Spelling and Grammar dialog box.

The grammar checker has four style levels: standard, formal, technical, and casual. You can further customize each of these styles to observe or ignore certain grammar or style rules. You can also create up to three custom grammar styles that contain rules you specify. To run the grammar checker from the menu:

1. Select the sentence or other text that you want to check. Don't select anything if you want to check the entire document.

2. Choose Tools⇔Spelling and Grammar to begin the grammar check. (No dialog box is displayed; the process begins immediately.)

3. As each possible error is caught, it is displayed in the Spelling and Grammar dialog box with the offending words displayed in the upper box highlighted in green (see Figure 4-8). Select the appropriate option. See Table 4-4 for an explanation of the various grammar options in the Spelling and Grammar dialog box.

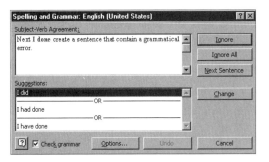

Figure 4-8: The Spelling and Grammar dialog box showing a grammar error.

Table 4-4 **Grammar Options**	
Option	**Action**
Suggestions	Displays one or more suggested corrections, if any, for the selection in the upper box.
Ignore	Ignores the selection and proceeds to the next selection, if any. If you edit the document, this button changes to Undo Edit.
Undo Edit	Reverses the editing just made to the document and changes back to Ignore.
Ignore All	Ignores the current selection and any remaining similar errors in the document.
Next sentence	Moves to the next sentence that contains a grammar or spelling error. Clicking this button accepts whatever changes you made to the current selection and ignores any remaining suggestions.
Change	Makes the correction.
Options	Displays the Spelling & Grammar Options dialog box.
Undo	Undoes the last actions made during the current grammar check session one at a time. Clicking this button a second time undoes the second most recent action, and so on.
Cancel/Close	Closes the dialog box. The Cancel button becomes the Close button after you make at least one change.

If you are using the Office Assistant, an explanation of the grammar error is automatically displayed (see Figure 4-9). If the Office Assistant is not active, you can click the Office Assistant button (the one with the question mark) in the lower-left corner of the dialog box to see the explanation.

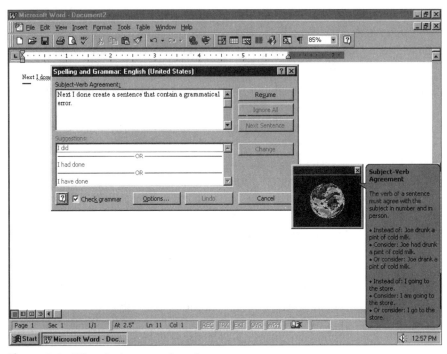

Figure 4-9: Office Assistant explanation.

Changing grammar options

You can specify what level of rules to include in the grammar check and choose to display the readability statistics after the checking is complete. You can also choose whether to include a spell check with the grammar check.

To check grammar without checking spelling:

1. Choose Tools➪Options. This displays the Options dialog box.

2. Click the Spelling & Grammar tab to display the Spelling & Grammar Options dialog box as before.

3. Select the options you want (see Table 4-5).

Table 4-5 **Grammar Options**	
Option	**Action**
Check grammar as you type	Checks grammar and marks possible errors as you enter text by underlining with wavy green lines.
Hide grammatical errors in this document	Hides the wavy green lines. If cleared, the lines are visible under sentences containing possible errors but do not print.
Check grammar with spelling	Combines spelling and grammar checks in the same pass.
Show readability statistics	Specifies whether readability statistics are displayed after a complete grammar check (more about this later).
Writing style	Displays a list of available writing styles from which to choose. Standard observes all the rules in the grammar checker. Technical uses rules appropriate for technical documents. Casual relaxes many of the rules. Formal applies rules suitable for formal documents. You can also define and save your own custom styles.
Check Document	Checks the spelling and grammar. If you have run it once already, the button changes to Recheck Document.
Recheck Document	Resets the internal Ignore All list and reruns the spelling and grammar checks.

Creating new grammar and style rules

Besides selecting what rules you want to use from the grammar options, you also can customize any style listed. For example, if you select technical as the style, you can then modify the rules that this style uses. To select grammar rules:

1. Choose Tools⇨Options to open the Options dialog box.

2. Click the Spelling & Grammar tab to display the Spelling & Grammar Options dialog box.

3. Click the Settings button to open the Grammar Settings dialog box (see Figure 4-10).

4. Select the options you want (see Table 4-6). Word automatically selects a set of grammar and style rules appropriate for the writing style you specify.

Figure 4-10: The Grammar Settings dialog box.

To create your own custom style, check the grammar and style options you want to include and save the style with one of the custom names.

Table 4-6
Grammar Settings Options

Option	Action
Writing style	Displays the list of available writing styles. Changing the style revises the list of rules checked in the Grammar and style options list.
Grammar and style options	Displays a list of grammar options and rules that you can select.
(Require) Comma before last list item	List of options includes always, never, and don't check (default).
(Require) Punctuation with quotes	List of options includes inside, outside, and don't check (default).
(Require) Spaces between sentences	List of options includes 1, 2, and don't check (default).
Reset All	Restores all the default settings for the selected writing style.

If you want an explanation of a rule, right-click the rule and click the What's This? box or select the rule and click the Help button on the Standard toolbar. To create your own custom style, check the grammar and style options you want to include and save the style with one of the custom names.

Viewing Document Statistics and Readability Estimates

When you perform a grammar check on the entire document, a Readability Statistics dialog box (see Figure 4-11) is displayed when the grammar check finishes (unless you opted not to display the statistics in the Spelling & Grammar Options dialog box). Document statistics in this dialog box include the number of characters, words, sentences, and paragraphs in the document. They also show the average number of sentences per paragraph, words per sentence, and characters per word.

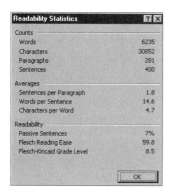

Figure 4-11: The Readability Statistics dialog box.

The readability level of a document is often measured in terms of a grade level. Various algorithms have been developed to estimate reading ease. The Readability Statistics dialog box includes the results of three of these commonly accepted estimates.

The readability estimates consist of the following:

✦ **Passive Sentences.** Percentage of sentences written in the passive voice. Active voice is considered more readable, so a high number here means higher difficulty.

✦ **Flesch Reading Ease.** Readability based on the average number of syllables per word and the average number of words per sentence. Standard writing averages 60 to 70. The higher the score, the more people can readily understand the document.

✦ **Flesch-Kincaid Grade Level**. Readability based on the average number of syllables per word and the average number of words per sentence. This score indicates a grade school level. Standard writing level is approximately seventh- to eighth-grade level.

Browsing in the Thesaurus

A thesaurus is the tool you use when you want to find a *synonym* (a word that means essentially the same as the word it replaces). Word's Thesaurus also displays antonyms for some words. (An *antonym* is a word that means the opposite of the selected word.)

Note   If the Thesaurus command does not appear on the Language submenu of the Tools menu, the Thesaurus feature was not installed. You need to run the Office Setup program again if you want to use the Thesaurus.

As mentioned, an antonym is a word that means the opposite of the selected word. The Word Thesaurus finds primarily synonyms rather than antonyms, but it displays a list of antonyms for some words. The same is true of related words. If a selected word has an antonym or related words, the entries "Antonyms" or "Related Words" appears in the Meanings box in the Thesaurus dialog box.

To use the Thesaurus to find synonyms:

1. Select (or type) the word for which you want a synonym.

2. Choose Tools➪Language➪Thesaurus. This displays the Thesaurus dialog box (see Figure 4-12).

3. Select the options you want (see Table 4-7).

Figure 4-12: The Thesaurus dialog box.

Table 4-7
Thesaurus Dialog Box Options

Option	Action
Looked Up/Not Found	Displays the currently selected word. Clicking the down arrow displays the list of words you have looked up while the Thesaurus dialog box is open. If you want to return to a previous word, click the down arrow and select that word. If the word is not in the Thesaurus, the box is labeled Not Found and displays the selected word.

Option	Action
Meanings	Many words have more than one meaning. Select the meaning that is closest to what you want from this list. If the Thesaurus contains an antonym for the word in the Looked Up box, the word Antonym also appears in this list. Click it to see a list of antonyms in the Replace with Antonym box.
Alphabetical List	If the word is not in the Thesaurus, the Meanings button changes to Alphabetical List and a list of words alphabetically similar to the word is displayed.
Replace with Synonym	Displays the suggested synonym to replace the original selection. Additional synonyms, if any, are displayed in a list below the suggested synonym. If you have selected to see antonyms, this button changes to Replace with Antonym.
Replace with Related Word	Displays a list of words related to the selected word in the text when Related Words is selected from the Meanings list.
Replace	Processes the specified replacement and closes the dialog box.
Look Up	Looks up synonyms for the word in any of the lists.
Previous	Returns to the word most recently looked up.
Cancel	Closes the Thesaurus dialog box without making any changes to your document.

You can also open the Thesaurus quickly by pressing Shift+F7.

Proofing with AutoCorrect

Word offers two similar features that you can use to insert text and graphics: Auto-Correct and AutoText. With AutoCorrect, Word automatically corrects or inserts the text or graphics as you type. With AutoText, you insert the text or graphics later. See Chapter 13 for more information on using these features to insert text and graphics.

Because AutoCorrect inserts text automatically as you type, you can use it to automatically correct your most common typing and spelling errors, which are contained in a table along with their corrections. You can also use AutoCorrect to correct capitalization and punctuation. You can easily add entries directly to the AutoCorrect table or during a spell check. You can also specify exceptions to the capitalization and initial caps rules you have selected.

Depending on the options you select, AutoCorrect can do the following automatically:

✦ Correct words in which you inadvertently type two initial caps instead of one.

✦ Capitalize the first word of a sentence if you do not.

✦ Capitalize the names of days of the week if you do not.

✦ Correct accidental use of the Caps Lock key.

✦ Replace specific text as you type.

To add entries to AutoCorrect during a spell check:

1. Run the spell checker.

2. When Word finds an error and you select a correct spelling in the Spelling and Grammar dialog box, click the AutoCorrect button.

To add entries to AutoCorrect directly:

1. Choose Tools⇨AutoCorrect. This displays the AutoCorrect dialog box (see Figure 4-13).

2. In the Replace box, type the word you commonly misspell.

3. In the With box, type the correct spelling of that word.

4. Click the Add button.

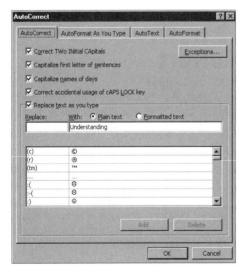

Figure 4-13: The AutoCorrect dialog box.

To specify exceptions to the AutoCorrect rules:

1. In the AutoCorrect dialog box, click the Exceptions button. The AutoCorrect Exceptions dialog box appears (see Figure 4-14).

2. Click the First Letter tab or the INitial CAps tab to enter exceptions to those rules.

3. Click OK twice to return to your document.

Figure 4-14: The AutoCorrect Exceptions dialog box.

Hyphenating Your Document

Hyphenation allows you to fit more text on a page. It tightens justified paragraphs and reduces the ragged appearance of unjustified text. Word offers four methods of hyphenation:

✦ Automatically hyphenate

✦ Manually hyphenate

✦ Insert optional hyphens

✦ Insert nonbreaking hyphens

The hyphenation options are available through the Language option on the Tools menu.

Using automatic hyphenation

Automatic hyphenation inserts *optional* hyphens. An optional hyphen is one that Word uses only when a word or phrase appears at the end of a line. If, due to editing, the word or phrase moves to a different position, the optional hyphen doesn't print.

Note Normally, optional hyphens are not visible in your document. You can view optional hyphens by choosing Tools➪Options, and clicking the View tab. Under Nonprinting Characters, select the Optional Hyphens check box.

To select automatic hyphenation:

1. Choose Tools➪Language➪Hyphenation to open the Hyphenation dialog box (see Figure 4-15).

2. Select the Automatically hyphenate document check box.

3. If you do not want to Hyphenate words in CAPS, leave that check box blank.

4. Set a value in the Hyphenation zone. The value you enter here is the distance in inches between the end of the last complete word in a line of text and the margin. Word uses this measurement to determine whether a word should be hyphenated. Large numbers decrease the number of hyphens; low numbers reduce the raggedness of the right margin.

5. If you don't want consecutive lines to have hyphens, set a limit in the Limit consecutive hyphens to box.

6. Click OK.

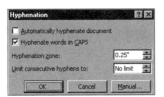 **Figure 4-15:** The Hyphenation dialog box.

If you don't want certain paragraphs to be hyphenated automatically, select the paragraphs, and choose Format➪Paragraph. In the Paragraph dialog box, select the Line and Page Breaks tab, and select the Don't hyphenate check box.

Hyphenating manually

Manual hyphenation gives you more control over what is hyphenated and how it is hyphenated. You can select which parts of the document are hyphenated and where a hyphen appears in specific words. To select manual hyphenation:

1. Select the text you want to hyphenate manually. If you want to manually hyphenate the entire document, don't select anything.

2. Choose Tools⇨Language⇨Hyphenation to open the Hyphenation dialog box as before.

3. Click the Manual button. Word immediately begins scanning the selection or the document for words to be hyphenated. When such a word is located, Word displays the Manual Hyphenation dialog box (see Figure 4-16).

4. To hyphenate the word at a different point than the one suggested in the Hyphenate at box, click where you want the hyphen inserted.

5. To accept the suggestion, choose Yes.

6. To skip the word and move on, choose No.

7. To stop hyphenation, choose Cancel.

Figure 4-16: The Manual Hyphenation dialog box.

Inserting nonbreaking or optional hyphens

Use nonbreaking hyphens to hyphenate phrases or terms that you don't want to wrap to another line (for example, 02-12-98). The entire phrase or term wraps to the next line instead of breaking. To insert a nonbreaking hyphen:

1. Position the insertion point where you want the nonbreaking hyphen.

2. Press Ctrl+Shift+- (hyphen).

Use an optional hyphen when you want to break specific lines of text. For example, if a lengthy word wraps to the next line, leaving a large amount of white space, you can insert an optional hyphen in that word so that the first part of it appears on the first line. If the word later moves to a different position because of editing, the optional hyphen will not print.

To insert an optional hyphen:

1. Position the insertion where you want the optional hyphen to appear.

2. Press Ctrl+- (hyphen).

Summary

Using the automatic spelling and grammar checking and correcting tools makes it quick and easy to improve the quality of your documents. Word 97 provides a standard dictionary that you can customize with your own special terms. You can document statistics to quickly estimate the reading level of the resulting document. Here are some other highlights from this chapter:

✦ Word 97 quickly scans the entire document and picks out words that are apparently misspelled or repeated and often suggests a correction.

✦ You can create a custom dictionary that contains words and acronyms that are specific to your work.

✦ Word's grammar checker finds errors in syntax or style and offers alternatives. You have the choice of asking for an explanation of the rule violation, accepting the suggested change, or ignoring the apparent violation.

✦ Word's Thesaurus helps you create more interesting documents by suggesting synonyms and antonyms for selected words.

Where to go next...

✦ For exciting ideas for creating interesting documents, see Chapter 7.

✦ To create a special document style that you can save and use over and over, read Chapter 11.

✦   ✦   ✦

Printing
Documents

◆ ◆ ◆ ◆

In This Chapter

Printing all or part of a document

Selecting the right printer

Previewing a document before printing

Selecting printing options

Printing several documents

Printing to a file

Printing envelopes and labels

◆ ◆ ◆ ◆

Most of the documents you create with Word are probably destined to be printed for distribution. You have learned in previous chapters how to create a well-written, well-formatted document. Now you are ready to print it. For those letters and other documents that are to be mailed, you also learn in this chapter how to print envelopes and mailing labels.

Quick Printing with Word

With one click of a button, you can print your Word document: just click the Print button in the Standard toolbar, and the document goes directly to the printer. You can tell Word exactly what you want printed by using the File⇨Print command to display the Print dialog box, shown in Figure 5-1. The Print dialog box lets you print the entire document, only selected text, or a range of pages. It also enables you to specify how many copies of the document to print. Other options available in the Print dialog box are explained later in this chapter.

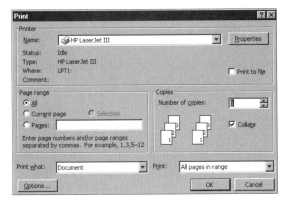

Figure 5-1: The Print dialog box.

Always save your document before printing. By saving your document just before printing it, you ensure that you can return to your document without losing any changes if a printing problem occurs.

Printing part of the text

You have two choices when you want to print part of a document in Word. You can print specific pages or only a selection. A *selection* means that you select the text before you begin the print process. If you do not select any text before opening the Print dialog box, the Selection option is not available. When you select text to print, nothing else in the document (such as headers, footers, and footnotes) will print.

To print a portion of a document:

1. Select the text you want to print. If you want to print one whole page of your document, move the insertion point to the page you want to print.

2. Choose the File⇨Print command, or press the Ctrl+P shortcut key.

3. Do one of the following:

   • To print selected text, choose the Selection option.

   • To print only the page that is displayed in the document window, select the Current page option.

   • To print a page other than the current page, enter the page number in the Pages box.

   • To print specific pages, enter the page numbers separated by commas in the Pages box. For example **3,7,21** prints pages three, seven, and 21. The page numbers must be in numerical order.

   • To print a range of pages, enter the number of the first page that you want to print, a dash, and the last page you want to print in the Pages text box. For example, **25-30** prints pages 25 through 30.

   • To print a mixture of specific pages and contiguous pages, combine the two previous actions. For example, enter **3,7,21,25-30** to print them all at once.

   • To print only the odd or even pages, choose either Odd Pages or Even Pages from the Print list box.

4. Choose OK.

Choosing the Right Printer

You may have trouble when you try to print a document that has been formatted for a printer other than the one you're using. Problems can occur because different printers have different capabilities. If you create a document by using an HP LaserJet III as the printer, for example, and print it on a PostScript printer, the page breaks, and word-wrapping formatting may change.

If you use more than one printer, make sure that the selected printer matches the type of printer you'll be printing the new document on before you begin a new document. If you open the File menu and the Print command is not available, you probably need to select the printer.

Note Installing a printer is a function of Windows, not Word. When you install one or more printers in Windows, any Windows software application can use the installed printers, generally without any other action on your part.

To select a printer:

1. Choose File➪Print. The Print dialog box appears.

2. Click the Printer Name drop-down arrow.

3. Select an installed printer from the list. If you want to install a new printer, refer to the Microsoft Windows guide. In most cases, you will need to have your Windows disks handy to install a new printer.

To check the formatting of a document created by using a different printer, view the document in Print Preview (see the following section). You can change any significant formatting errors before printing the document.

Problems can also occur when you open a document created on a system that was using fonts that are unavailable on your current printer. Word will substitute a similar available font, but you can also specify a substitution font. For information on specifying substitution fonts, see Chapter 7.

Using Print Preview Before Printing

Print Preview is a significant tool in Word (see Figure 5-2). By using the Print Preview toolbar, you can view your document in a variety of ways. Figure 5-3 shows the Print Preview toolbar, and Table 5-1 describes each of the Print Preview toolbar's buttons.

To preview a document in Print Preview:

1. Choose File⇨Print Preview or click the Print Preview button on the Standard toolbar.

2. To close Print Preview, choose the Close Preview button.

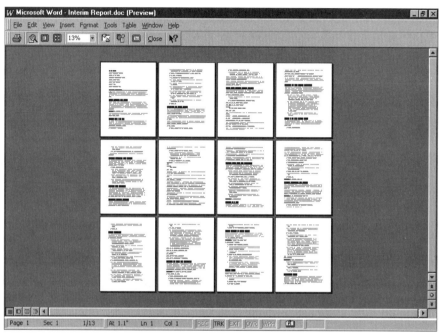

Figure 5-2: The Print Preview showing 12 pages.

Table 5-1
The Print Preview Toolbar Buttons

Button Name	Action
Print	Prints the document by using default print options (also indicates the current printer).
Magnifier	Enlarges or reduces the document view.
One Page	Displays the document in single-page view.
Multiple Pages	Views one or more pages of a document.
Zoom Control	Selects different magnifications, from 10 to 500 percent (also includes the Page Width, Whole Page, and Two Pages options).

Button Name	Action
View Ruler	Displays or hides the horizontal and vertical rulers.
Shrink to Fit	Shrinks your document to fit on one or less pages if the last page of your document contains only a few lines of text.
Full Screen	Removes title bar and toolbars to show a full screen display of the document in Print Preview.
Close Preview	Closes Print Preview and returns to your document.
Context Sensitive Help	Provides context-sensitive Help for Print Preview options.

Figure 5-3: The Print Preview toolbar.

You can move around a document in Print Preview the same way as in a document window, using the arrow keys, the scroll arrows, and the PgUp and PgDn keys. If you are viewing multiple pages, the PgUp and PgDn keys move through the document one page at a time.

Changing the Print Preview appearance

Print Preview gives you several options for viewing documents. You can show the page width, display the whole page, or magnify a part of a page. Print Preview also lets you display up to 24 pages in three rows at one time. You can also configure how the pages are displayed. For example, if your document consists of 12 pages, you can display two rows of six pages or three rows of all four pages. The following list describes ways to change your view of a document in Print Preview:

✦ To display only the width of a page, one whole page, or two pages, click the Zoom Control down arrow to the right of the magnification percentage in the Print Preview toolbar. Choose the Page Width, Whole Page, or Two Pages option. Alternatively, to display a single page, choose the One Page button on the Print Preview toolbar.

✦ To display more than two pages, click the Multiple Pages button (to the left of the magnification percentage). A drop-down box appears, showing six pages arranged in two rows. Place the mouse pointer inside the drop-down box, and click and drag. You can drag past the boundaries of this box down and to the right to increase the number of pages displayed to a maximum of 24. For example, if your display shows two rows of three pages and you want to see one row of four pages, drag the mouse right to highlight the pages you want to display and release the mouse button.

✦ To reduce or enlarge the previewed document, change the Zoom Control percentage, or click the Magnifier button and click in your document.

Editing in the Print Preview mode

You can edit your document directly in Print Preview, which can save time by avoiding those annoying little errors that seem to appear on every other printed page. You can also perform edits with one or more pages displayed in Print Preview, but if you are viewing multiple pages, you may find that the text is too small to see clearly. To edit in Print Preview mode:

1. Choose File⇨Print Preview.

2. Click the One Page button, if a whole page is not displayed. (Word often displays a whole page by default, depending on previous Print Preview settings.)

3. To begin editing, click in your document, and then make your changes.

If the text is too small to read, change to Page Width or increase the magnification percentage.

Adjusting margins in Print Preview

You can change any margins in Print Preview by using the rulers (Print Preview displays a horizontal ruler and a vertical ruler). Remember that margin changes in Print Preview apply to the entire document, not just a portion of it. If you want to apply margin changes to specific portions of the document, you must use File⇨Page Setup instead. To change a document's margins in Print Preview:

1. Choose File⇨Print Preview.

2. If the rulers are not displayed, click the View Ruler button to display them. The horizontal ruler shows the width of the entire page. The vertical ruler shows the height of the entire page. The margin areas are displayed in gray on the rulers; the text areas are displayed in white.

3. Position the mouse pointer in the margin boundary, the spot where the white portion of the ruler meets the gray portion. The mouse pointer changes to a double-headed arrow.

4. Press and hold the left mouse button. A dashed line appears through the page, indicating the margin position. Drag to adjust the selected margin, and release the mouse button. You can repeat this step for each of the remaining margins, if desired.

Shrinking your document

If only a few lines of your document appear on the last page, try choosing the Shrink to Fit button in the Print Preview toolbar. This shrinks (changes your font size and the spacing between lines) so that the lines will not spill over. When you choose the Shrink to Fit button, Word calculates the changes that are needed. The status bar reflects the repagination process for each of Word's attempts to shrink your document. If you are working with a long document, Word can shrink your font and spacing so that the document shrinks more than one page. If choosing the Shrink to Fit button shrinks the font point size and line spacing too much, press Ctrl+Z to undo the changes.

Choosing Printing Options

Word gives you a variety of printing options. The Print dialog box also offers choices of what to print—relating to the current document. The Print what list includes document itself (the default), document properties, comments, a list of styles used in the document, AutoText entries, and shortcut key assignments.

The Print tab of the Options dialog box offers more options, as described in Table 5-2. To choose print options:

1. Choose File⇨Print. The Print dialog box appears.

2. Choose the Options button to open the Print options dialog box, as shown in Figure 5-4. You can also open this dialog box by choosing Tools⇨Options, but the first method goes directly to the Print tab.

3. Select the options you want to use. The Print tab printing options are described in Table 5-2.

4. Choose OK to return to the Print dialog box.

Figure 5-4: The Print tab in the Print options dialog box.

Table 5-2
Print Options

Name	Action
Draft output	Specifies to print the document without formatting or graphics. The result of Draft output depends on your printer.
Update fields	Updates all the fields in your document before printing. Chapter 26 covers fields.
Update links	Updates all the links in your document before printing. You'll see more on linking information in Chapter 15.
Allow A4/Letter paper resizing	Automatically adjusts documents from another country's standard paper size (for example, A4) to letter. Affects printout only, not the document.
Background printing	Prints in the background so that you can continue with your work. However, this option uses memory and slows the program's overall performance.
Print PostScript over text	Prints PostScript code such as a watermark in a converted Word for Mac document on top of text rather than underneath. Affects only documents containing PRINT field codes.
Reverse print order	Prints the first page last (useful for early laser printers). Not used when printing envelopes.
Document properties	Prints document summary information on a separate page along with printing your document. Properties include the author, subject, print date, number of pages, number of words, and characters.
Field codes	Prints the field codes rather than the results of a field code.
Comments	Prints a list of comments on a separate page at the end of your document. The list includes page number headings indicating where each comment occurs.
Hidden text	Prints any hidden text, such as table of contents entries, in the location where hidden text appears in your document.
Drawing objects	Prints drawing objects you created. Clear to print only a blank box in place of a drawing. Speeds up printing of a draft document.
Print data only for forms	Prints the data entered into an online form without printing the form itself. Chapter 21 covers creating forms.
Default tray	Selects the print tray. (To set different paper sources for different sections of the document, choose File⇨Page Setup to open the Page Setup dialog box, and select the Paper Source tab. See Chapter 9 for more on this topic.)

Printing More than One Document

Printing multiple documents is different than printing a single document because you do not open them first. Instead of using the File⇨Print command, you use the File⇨Open command to locate the files you want to print and then select the files from the list in the Open dialog box. At this point, you can print the selected files. To print multiple files:

1. Choose File⇨Open. The Open dialog box (see Figure 5-5) appears with a list of the files in the current folder. If the files you want are not listed, you will need to use Word's Find feature to look for them. You can find more information on searching for documents in Chapter 6.

2. To select the documents to print, do one of the following:

   • To select adjacent files in the list, click the first filename, press and hold the Shift key, and then click the last file you want to select. You can also click the first filename and drag to the last name.

   • To select nonadjacent files, press and hold down the Ctrl key as you click the names of the files that you want to print.

   • To select a group of adjacent files and then skip to include nonadjacent files, combine the actions above as necessary.

3. Right-click one of the selected filenames, and select Print from the shortcut menu. The Print dialog box appears for you to choose your printing options.

4. Select any printing options you want, and choose OK. The files print in the order they appeared in the Open list. The selected options apply to all the documents.

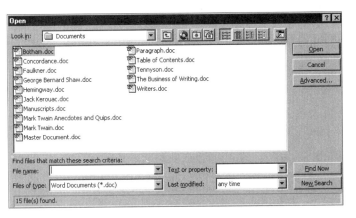

Figure 5-5: The Open dialog box.

Printing to a File

Printing to a file means that you instruct Word to send printing instructions with the document to a file rather than to the printer. You may want to do this if you are working on a portable computer that is not connected to a printer or if you want to print the file later with a different printer. Printing to a file is also helpful when you want to send a document to another person who is not using Word. By printing to a file, that person can print the file without Word from DOS or Windows.

The important thing to remember about this procedure is that you need to first select the printer that will ultimately print the file; otherwise, you will undoubtedly encounter significant formatting problems when the file prints. Also, if you print to a floppy disk, you may have to divide the document if it is too large to fit on one disk. To print to a file:

1. Choose File⇨Print, or press Ctrl+P. The Print dialog box appears.

2. Click the Printer Name drop-down arrow.

3. Select the printer name from the list.

4. Select the Print to file check box, and then choose OK. The Print to File dialog box (see Figure 5-6) appears.

5. Type a filename in the File name box. Word automatically adds the `.prn` extension to the filename.

6. Choose Printer Files (.prn) as the Save as type.

7. If necessary, select the drive and directory where you want to save the file.

8. Choose OK.

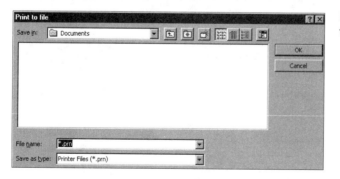

Figure 5-6: The Print to File dialog box.

Printing Envelopes and Labels

Word makes printing envelopes an easy task. You can print mailing and return addresses directly on an envelope. You can also print addresses on a mailing label or on a sheet of mailing labels. To print mailing labels for multiple addresses such as for form letters, see Chapter 20.

Word 97 offers two new Wizards to help you create and print envelopes and labels. With these Wizards, you can create a single envelope label or multiple envelopes and labels for form letters. See Chapter 10 for information on using the Envelope Wizard and Labels Wizard.

Word automatically locates the mailing address in the document, or you can select it. The return address is entered automatically from information entered in the User Information tab of the Options dialog box. You can change this information for every envelope by changing the information in the User Information tab of the Options dialog box (see Figure 5-7).

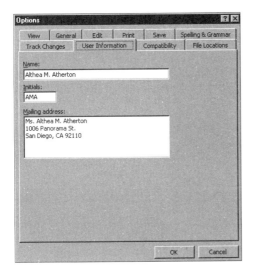

Figure 5-7: The User Information tab of the Options dialog box.

You can also change the default return address for any envelope or label when you create it by using the Envelopes and Labels dialog box. Changing the return address in the Envelopes and Labels dialog box affects only the current envelope. The next time you bring up the Envelopes and Labels dialog box, the default return address appears. To change your default return address:

1. Choose Tools⇨Options. The Options dialog box appears.

2. Select the User Information tab.

3. Choose the Mailing address text box, and then enter your name and/or company name and return address. You can also enter your name and initials.

4. Choose OK.

Printing envelopes

You can print a return address and delivery address directly on an envelope, or you can add the envelope to a document and print it later with the letter itself. Word provides predefined envelope styles and sizes, or you can customize your own envelope formatting. To create and print an envelope:

1. Select the mailing address in the document. If the address is a contiguous block of three to five short lines near the beginning of the letter, Word will automatically select the address for you when you choose the Tools⇨Envelopes and Labels command.

2. Choose Tools⇨Envelopes and Labels. The Envelopes and Labels dialog box (see Figure 5-8) appears.

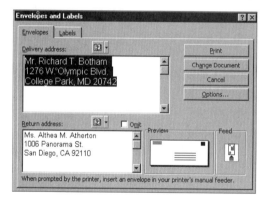

Figure 5-8: The Envelopes and Labels dialog box.

3. Select the Envelopes tab. Check that the mailing address is correct. If it is not, you can correct it for the current envelope.

4. If you want to omit the return address from printing on your envelope, select the Omit check box. Use this option if your envelopes are preprinted with your return address.

5. Choose the Options button and click the Envelope Options tab to open the Envelope Options dialog box (see Figure 5-9).

6. Do any of the following in the Envelope Options dialog box:

- To change the envelope size, choose an envelope size from the Envelope size drop-down list. If you want to define your own custom size, choose the Custom option from the list, which displays the Envelope Size dialog box (see Figure 5-10). Enter the Width and Height measurements, or use the increase or decrease button, and then click OK.

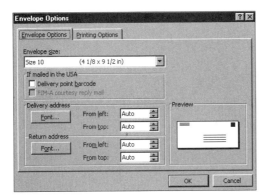

Figure 5-9: The Envelope Options dialog box.

Figure 5-10: Envelope Size dialog box.

- To change the Font size for either the Delivery address or Return address, choose the appropriate Font button. The Font dialog box appears. For more information on working with fonts, see Chapter 7.

- To change the position of the Delivery address on the envelope, use the From left and From top settings. You can see how the changes look in the Preview box in the Envelope Options dialog box.

- To change the position of the Return address on the envelope, use the From left and From top settings. Watch the effects in the Preview box in the Envelope Options dialog box.

7. Choose the OK button to return to the Envelopes and Labels dialog box.

8. Do one of the following:

- To print the envelope now, insert the envelope in the printer, and click the Print button. You can check to see how to insert the envelope in your printer by choosing the Options button and then selecting the Printing

Options tab. Figure 5-11 shows the Printing Options tab in the Envelope Options dialog box. Word shows the recommended envelope feed method as the highlighted option in the Feed method group.

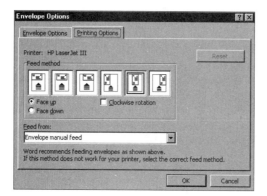

- To add the envelope to the document, click the Add to Document button. (If you select this option, the envelope is added to the beginning of the document, and Word inserts a section break directly after the envelope information, as shown in Figure 5-12. The envelope information becomes page 0, so you will have to print page 0 to print the envelope later.) If an envelope is already attached to the document, the Change Document button will be available. Choose this button to replace the old envelope with the new one.

Including barcodes with addresses

There are two types of postal barcodes. POSTNET codes are simply ZIP codes translated into barcode language that the United States Postal Service's computers can read. Facing Identification Marks (FIMs) are used in the U.S. on courtesy reply mail to identify the front of the envelope during presorting. Figure 5-13 shows these two types of barcodes on an envelope—one just above the addressee and one near the stamp area. Adding barcodes to your mail can speed up the delivery of your mail as well as lower your postage costs if you're doing mass mailings that qualify.

To add a POSTNET barcode:

1. Choose Tools⇨Envelopes and Labels.
2. Choose the Options button and click the Envelope Options tab.

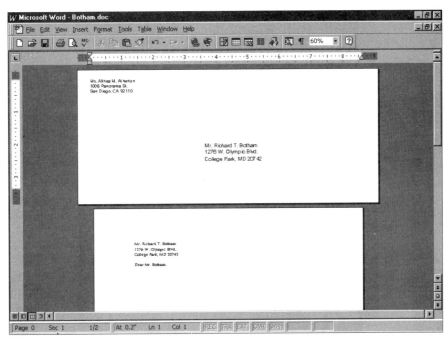

Figure 5-12: An envelope added to a document.

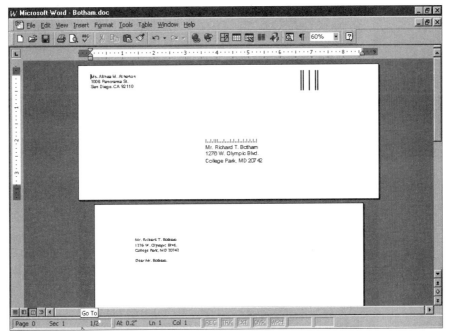

Figure 5-13: The two types of barcodes on an envelope.

3. Select Delivery point barcode in the If mailed in the USA group. Notice that the FIM-A box becomes available. That's because you can't have an FIM-A bar without a POSTNET code. However, you can use POSTNET codes on standard mail that doesn't need a FIM-A mark.

4. If you're creating courtesy reply mail, check the FIM-A courtesy reply mail box.

5. Choose OK. Then choose Change Document, if necessary.

Adding graphics for special effects

Word lets you add graphics or some form of logo to your envelope. This makes your envelopes look professional without paying for printed stationary. Figure 5-14 shows a graphic added to the return address of an envelope. Once created and added to the envelope design, the graphic can be saved as AutoText and used repeatedly. See Chapter 3 for more information about AutoText.

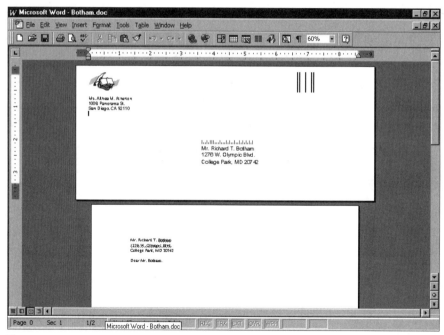

Figure 5-14: An envelope with a graphic added.

To add graphics to an envelope:

1. Select the mailing address in the document.

2. Choose Tools⇨Envelopes and Labels. The Envelopes and Labels dialog box appears. Be sure the Envelopes tab is selected. Modify the mailing and return addresses, if necessary.

3. Choose the Add to Document button (or the Change Document button, if appropriate).

4. Choose the Page Layout View button in the status bar.

5. Create the graphic by using Word's drawing tools, or insert a graphic by choosing Insert⇨Picture. You might also use WordArt to create a special text image. See Chapter 13 for more information on working with Word's graphics tools.

6. Position and resize the item on the envelope. If you choose an item of clip art or create a drawing by using Word's drawing tools, you can just drag it to a new position and drag the sizing handles to resize. Otherwise, you must insert a frame to position the item. For more information on working with graphics and frames, see Chapter 14.

Printing labels

Word lets you print a single label or a full page of the same label with either your outgoing or return address. To print mailing labels for multiple addresses, see Chapter 20.

To print a single label or the same address on a sheet of labels:

1. Choose Tools⇨Envelopes and Labels. The Envelopes and Labels dialog box appears.

2. Select the Labels tab (see Figure 5-15).

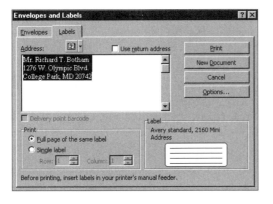

Figure 5-15: The Labels tab in the Envelopes and Labels dialog box.

3. Do one of the following:

   - To change the address, choose the <u>A</u>ddress box, and enter new address text.

   - To print your return address on a label instead of the delivery address, select the Use <u>r</u>eturn address box. Again, you can accept what appears, modify it, or enter a new return address.

4. Do one of the following:

   - To print a full page of identical labels, use the <u>F</u>ull page of the same label print option, which is selected by default.

   - To print a single label, select the Si<u>n</u>gle label print option. You must specify the row and column number position of where you want the label to print. For example, the Avery Address 5160 label sheet has three columns and ten rows of labels. To print a label in the second row, fourth column, enter **2** in the Ro<u>w</u> text box, and then enter **4** in the <u>C</u>olumn text box. You can also use the increase (or decrease) buttons to set the values in the Ro<u>w</u> and <u>C</u>olumn text boxes.

   - To select the type of label you want to print, choose the <u>O</u>ptions button to open the Label Options dialog box (see Figure 5-16). Choose Dot <u>m</u>atrix or <u>L</u>aser and ink jet (the default) printer and the desired paper tray. Open Label <u>p</u>roducts to select the manufacturer of the labels you're using. You can choose from four options here: Avery standard, A4 and A5 sizes, MACD standard, and Other. Other allows you to use HP, Inmac, RAJ, and UNISTAT labels.

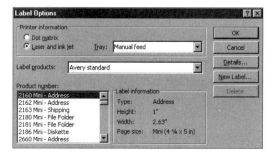

Figure 5-16: The Label Options dialog box.

5. Select the Product n<u>u</u>mber for the type of label you're using. When you have made your selections, choose OK to return to the Envelopes and Labels dialog box.

6. To print the label (or labels), insert a sheet of labels in the printer, and click the <u>P</u>rint button.

7. To save the settings you used to create your labels for future use, click the New <u>D</u>ocument button.

Customizing labels

If none of the predefined labels match your requirements, create your own. Word offers you two ways to create custom labels: start with one of the predefined labels and make changes to the specifications, or start from scratch. To see the specifications of a predefined label, choose Details. The information dialog box appears with the name of the selected label type in the title bar, as shown in Figure 5-17. The information will vary with the label type. To start a new label design, choose New Label. The information dialog box is the same as when you choose Details.

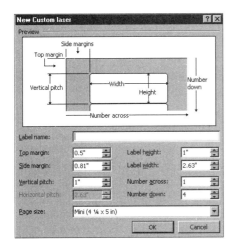

Figure 5-17: The New Custom Laser information dialog box.

In addition to the illustrated label layout, the box shows the exact label specifications. The Top margin and Side margin settings tell Word how close the first label should be to the upper and left edges of the page. The Horizontal pitch and Vertical pitch settings let you specify the space between the beginning of one label and the beginning of the next. Labels often have a space between one label and the next or between adjacent labels in the same row. To set the label's height and width, use the Label height and Label width settings. Number across and Number down instruct Word as to how many labels to place on each row and how many rows are in a column. When you make changes, notice that the Preview box adjusts the picture of the label to show you the current size and location of your label. If you have made changes to a predefined label layout, it becomes a custom label and Word asks you to name it.

After you have created and named a custom label, the name (followed by "- custom") appears at the top of the Product number list. To remove the custom label design, select it on the list and choose Delete. Word asks for confirmation before deleting the label.

To make sure that your labels print correctly, you can choose to create a New Document that contains the labels as they will print. This allows you to preview how the labels will print. You also can save the document and print it later. It is a good idea to print a sheet of labels on plain paper to check the layout rather than risk an expensive sheet of labels.

Summary

Printing is the final step in producing your document whether it is a book, a letter, an envelope, or a mailing label. This chapter covers the following highlights:

✦ Any number of copies of a complete document or only a few pages can be printed to a selected printer by using standard or customized printing options.

✦ The Print Preview gives you a preview of how a single page or multiple pages will look when printed.

✦ You print envelopes and mailing labels with choices of size, feed method, added bar codes, and, in the case of labels, the label layout.

Where to go next...

✦ To add interesting illustrations and frames to your document, see Chapters 13 and 14.

✦ To see how to print those personalized form letters and envelopes, turn to Chapter 20.

✦   ✦   ✦

Managing Documents and Surviving Crashes

✦ ✦ ✦ ✦

CHAPTER 6

In This Chapter

Managing documents in Word

Opening files

Saving files

Making backup files

Adding document protection

Finding documents in Word

Solving problems with document files and surviving system crashes

✦ ✦ ✦ ✦

So far, you have learned the main techniques for creating, editing, and printing Word documents. All these activities are in the foreground of word processing. In the background are operations that are also important, such as document management, distribution, and protection, all of which you learn about in this chapter. You also gain some valuable insight into file recovery and abnormal retrieval.

Managing Documents in Word

When you turn your documents over to Word, you can be sure that you will be able to create, store, and retrieve your documents at any time. All you need to learn are a few file management principles to use the powerful tools that Word provides.

Word considers a document as a file, so when you create and save a new document, you are actually creating a file. The three basic file activities you are concerned with are creating, modifying, and deleting.

After you've created a file, you can open and close it as often as necessary. You can even make changes and save the modified document with a new name so that you still have both versions.

Word also gives you the power to protect files so that other people cannot make changes to them. In addition, an AutoRecover feature can protect your files in case of an abnormal shutdown, such as a power failure. You can choose to create back-up copies of any file that you save.

Chapter 2 showed you how to create and save a document and explained the long filename rules. Chapter 19 explains how to share documents via e-mail and collaborate with others using Word in a workgroup environment. Chapter 23 explains working with long documents.

Opening Files

After you create and save a document, the file exists on your disk. You can preview the contents of a file or print the file without opening it. If you want to use Word to make changes to the file or save a copy of it with a different name, you need to open the file. Word provides several methods for opening files. The easiest way is to click the Open button on the Standard toolbar. Another is to choose the Open command from the File menu. Both of these take you to the Open dialog box where you can locate the file you want to open. (This dialog box is discussed in the next section.) If you've worked on the file recently, it may be listed at the bottom of the File menu. In this case, you need only to click its name to open it. The default number of files listed is four, but Word can list up to nine filenames at the bottom of the File menu. To change the number of files listed at the bottom of the File menu:

1. Choose Tools⇨Options.

2. Click the General tab (see Figure 6-1).

3. In the entries box opposite Recently used file list, type or select the number of documents (up to nine) that you want to appear at the bottom of the File menu. If you don't want any recently used files to appear, disable the option.

4. Click OK, or press Enter.

A fourth method of opening a recently accessed document file is through Windows. Without opening Word, first, choose Document from the Start menu and click the document file you want. Windows then starts Word and opens the selected document.

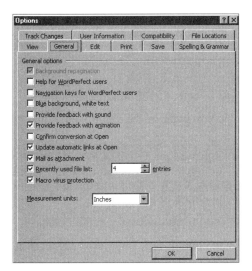

Figure 6-1: The General tab in the Options dialog box.

Opening a file

If the file you want to open is not listed on the File menu, you must use the Open dialog box (see Figure 6-2) to locate and open your document. Use this dialog box to browse through drives and directories and select the file you want to open. The Open dialog box displays a list of all the Word files in the current drive or folder. You can look in a different drive or folder for the document you want. The dialog box buttons allow you to move to the next higher folder and change the way you view the listed items. As you learned in Chapter 1, you can display the list with details, properties, or even a preview of the document. Other buttons access the Win-dows Favorites folder to create links to your files or look for a file in that folder.

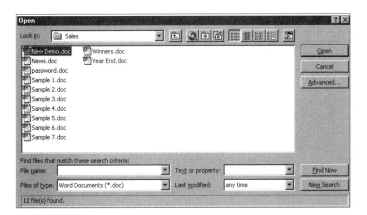

Figure 6-2: The Open dialog box.

To open a file:

1. Choose File⇨Open. Alternatively, click the Open button on the Standard toolbar. The Open dialog box appears with a list of Word files in the current drive.

2. Click the Look in down arrow to select a different drive.

3. If you see the name of the file you want in the list, select it, and click the Open button.

4. If the file you want is in a different folder, type the folder (and subfolder) name in the File name box, and click the Find Now button. The names of all Word files in that folder appear in the list. The number of files found is displayed at the bottom of the dialog box.

5. Click the Preview button to see the contents of the document.

6. When you decide this is the document you want, click Open, or press Enter.

You can open more than one file at a time from the list of files displayed in the File Open dialog box. See the section "Managing Documents with Open" later in this chapter for more information on opening several documents at once.

Note If you don't see the file you want in the list of files after you select the correct drive and folder, the file may not be a Word document. To change the file type, click the down arrow to the right of the Files of type box (at the bottom of the Open dialog box). The top choice in the list is All Files. Select this option to see all files in the current folder regardless of their type. All files now show their file extension so that you can tell what type they are. You can also tell the file type by the accompanying icon.

Creating a new folder

Before you begin creating your own new files, create one or more document folders to use for storing your files. You can create a folder by using the File Locations tab of the Options dialog box in Word. You can create folders based on any filing system that appeals to you: topic, date, document type, and so on. For example, you may decide to create one folder to store letters, another for memos, and yet another for other documents. Alternatively, you can use the Windows Explorer to create new folders.

To create a new file folder using Word, open the File Locations tab of the Options dialog box and make changes to the location for the file type documents. The new folder becomes a subfolder of the current folder. So, if you want them on the same level, move up one level before creating the new folder. To create a new folder:

1. Choose Tools⇨Options, and click the File Locations tab (see Figure 6-3).

2. Select Documents under the File types heading.

3. Click the <u>M</u>odify button to open the Modify Location dialog box (see Figure 6-4).

4. To create a subfolder of the current folder, click the Create New Folder button to open the New Folder dialog box (see Figure 6-5).

5. Enter the name for your new folder in the <u>N</u>ame box, and click OK. The Modify Folder dialog box reappears, where you can immediately assign the new folder as the default as described in the next paragraph.

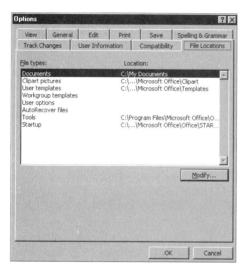

Figure 6-3: The File Locations tab in the Options dialog box.

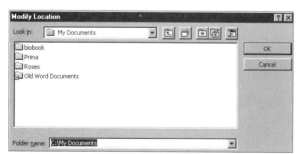

Figure 6-4: The Modify Location dialog box.

Figure 6-5: The New Folder dialog box.

Changing the default folder

Word uses the My Documents folder as the default folder for new documents if you do not specify another. In other words, when you type the name of your file in the Open or Save As dialog box, Word looks for the existing file or saves the new file in the My Documents folder. If you want to keep your documents in one or more different folders (and you should), you also need to pick that different folder name from the list before opening or saving. Once you create your own folders, you can specify the one you use most often as the default folder that Word uses for file management. To change the default folder:

1. If you have left the Modify Location dialog box, return to it by using the previous steps.

2. Click the Folder name down arrow, and choose the new folder name from the list.

3. Click OK or press Enter to return to the File Locations tab of the Options dialog box.

4. If you want to change the default locations of any other file types, select the appropriate file type and click the Modify button.

5. When you have finished, click the OK button.

Saving Files

Word has many ways to help you save and protect your files. The options determine how and when you save your documents. To see what the options are, choose Tools⇨Options. Then click the Save tab (see Figure 6-6). Table 6-1 explains these options.

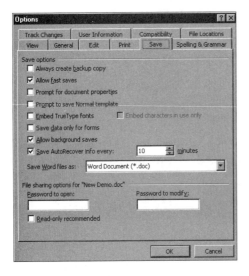

Figure 6-6: The Save tab in the Options dialog box.

Table 6-1
Save Options

Option	Action
Always create backup copy	Creates a complete backup copy of the previous version of the file. Each time you open the file, Word updates the backup.
Allow fast saves	Adds the changes you make to the file instead of updating the entire file. This option is quicker than doing a full save, but your files can become substantially larger. This option is an alternative to the Always create backup copy option. You cannot use both.
Prompt for document properties	When saving a document for the first time, Word will display a prompt for document properties (including a title, a subject, an author, and key words), which is added to the Word file. You can use the properties to search for a file and keep track of details about a file.
Prompt to save Normal template	Displays a prompt when you close Word that asks whether you want to save changes made to the Normal template file (Normal.dot file). The prompt appears only if you made such changes (margin settings, AutoText items, and so on).
Embed TrueType fonts	Embeds any TrueType fonts in the document so that other users who open the document can view it with its original fonts, whether or not they have TrueType fonts.
Embed characters in use only	Embeds only the TrueType fonts you used in the document. Decreases file size. Available only when Embed TrueType fonts is checked.
Save data only for forms	Applies to data entered in a form on the monitor. Enabling this option saves the data as a single tab-delimited record in Text Only format so that you can use it in a database.
Allow background saves	Saves documents in background without disrupting your work. Status bar shows a pulsating disk icon during background saves.
Save AutoRecover info every x minutes	Automatically saves a copy of the active document at the specified interval.
Save Word files as:	Select a file format to use as default.
Password to open	Requires that the user know the password to open the document.
Password to modify	Requires others to know the password in order to save changes to the original document. If not, they must save the modified document as a new file.
Read-only recommended	Recommends to others who open the document that they open the document as read-only. The file can be opened normally, however, if the user wants.

Saving a File with a New Name

Although saving a file with a different name uses extra disk space, there are several reasons for doing just that. For example:

✦ You want to track modifications made by others.

✦ You want to save a copy in a different folder than the original.

✦ You want to make changes to the original document but also keep the original intact so you can compare the different versions.

✦ You want to save the file in a different format so another application can use it.

When applied to an open document, the Save As command from the File menu can create a copy of the current document and allow you to change the name, select a new location, and select a different file format. You can also create a new folder by clicking the Create New Folder button in the Save As dialog box. To save a document with a new name:

1. Choose File⇨Save As. The Save As dialog box (see Figure 6-7) appears.

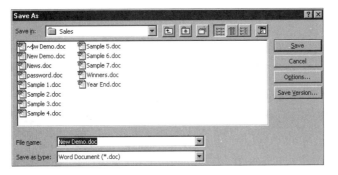

Figure 6-7: The Save As dialog box.

2. Type the new name in the File name box.

3. Select the appropriate drive from the Save in drop-down list if you want to save the new file in a different location.

4. To save the document with a different file format, click the down arrow to the right of the Save as type box, and select the desired format.

5. Click Save, or press Enter.

When you use the File⇨Save As command to save an existing document with a new name, Word creates a copy of that document and makes it the new current document. Word automatically closes the original and stores it in its original folder. Any changes made to the original but not saved are contained in the new file but not in the original. Therefore, if you want to be sure the original file has all the changes, save it before using the File⇨Save As command. If you want to continue working on the original, you have to open it again.

Using AutoRecover

Word's AutoRecover feature protects you in case of a power failure or if you inadvertently turn off your computer without saving your work. The AutoRecover feature creates and updates a *copy* of the current file. It doesn't save the current file itself. Therefore, you must always decide whether to save any changes you make to the original file. You cannot rely on the AutoRecover feature to do this for you. This is in contrast to some other applications, in which an automatic save actually saves your work periodically and you cannot unsave the changes.

When you close Word normally, that temporary copy is deleted. If Word is not closed normally (as in the case of a power failure), however, the temporary copy is saved. The next time you open Word, any saved temporary files are automatically open as recovered files. You must still choose whether to save the previous changes to the original document.

The AutoRecover feature is set to save the open files every ten minutes by default when Word is first installed. This means that you cannot lose more than ten minutes worth of work because of a power failure or inadvertent shutdown. You can change the interval between automatic saves to a value between 1 and 120 minutes anytime you want. You also can turn off the AutoRecover feature, but there isn't any solid reason to disable this power-ful and friendly safety feature. To save automatically as you work:

1. Choose Tools⇨Options.
2. Click the Save tab.
3. Select the Save AutoRecover info every option.
4. Select or type the number of minutes you want between automatic saves in the minutes box.
5. Click OK, or press Enter.

Creating Backup Files

If you choose to have backup files, Word creates a duplicate of the document you are opening and gives it the same filename, but with a .bak extension. When you update the file and save your updates, you will have two files: the current document and the backup, which is one version old. This option requires a full save, so when you select it, Word clears the Allow fast saves check box. You cannot have both.

The only disadvantage of this option is that each file you save in Word will have a complete backup copy, so you may double the amount of disk space required by your files. Many Word users decide to turn this option off as they gain confidence in their file handling abilities. To create backup files:

1. Choose Tools⇨Options.

2. Click the Save tab.

3. Select the Always create backup copy option.

4. Click OK, or press Enter.

Adding File Protection

You can add any of three levels of protection for your Word documents. You can:

✦ Create a password so that no one else can open the protected document without it.

✦ Create a password so that others can open the document but must save any changes to a new document.

✦ Recommend that the file be opened as read-only.

Passwords can contain up to 15 characters, including characters, numbers, symbols, and spaces. As you enter the password, Word displays an asterisk for each character you type without revealing the characters you are entering. Passwords are case-sensitive, so you must type the password exactly as you created it by using the correct upper- and lowercase letters.

You can also create a password for a document that you intend to circulate for review and comments that allows others to add only annotations and marked revisions. To protect your documents:

1. Choose Tools⇨Options.

2. Click the Save tab.

3. In the File-sharing options part of the tab, type the password in the appropriate box or enable the Read-only recommended option.

4. Click OK, or press Enter.

Note If you decide to add a password to your document, make sure that you keep it somewhere in case you forget it. If you forget your password, you cannot open the document.

When you are preparing a document for routing electronically to others for review, you can assign a password that prevents any changes except revisions and annotations. Use the Protect Document command on the Tools menu to assign a routing password. See Chapter 19 for more information on routing documents.

Creating a Document Summary

You can certainly work with documents without entering any additional summary information beyond the filename, but when you are trying to find an elusive document, summary information can be quite useful. You can create a search based on the author, any of the key words, the subject, or even a longer title than the document name itself.

To enter summary information for a new or existing document, open the file in the View window, and then choose File⇨Properties. The Properties dialog box opens where you can enter or view several categories of document properties. Choose the Summary tab to enter or modify summary information (see Figure 6-8).

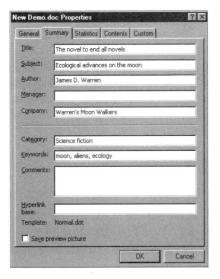

Figure 6-8: The Summary tab of the Properties dialog box.

The author name is automatically filled in from the previously created document. Enter any additional information that may help identify the document in a search, such as a longer title, the main subject, and any other key words or comments tht may help you remember what the document contains.

You can also view statistics about the current document by clicking the Statistics tab in the Properties dialog box. The new Word 97 statistics counts not only characters but also counts characters combined with spaces to give you a more accurate estimate of the space required to print the document.

Summary information is tedious to create and easy to ignore. When you are searching for that lost document, however, you'll be glad you took the time to enter the summary information completely. If you want to be reminded to create a summary for a new document, select Prompt for document properties on the Save tab of the Options menu.

To automatically create a summary of an existing document, use the new Word 97 AutoSummarize feature available from the Tools menu. You have a choice of four ways to view the document summary and also specify the amount of detail you want in the summary. When you choose AutoSummarize from the Tools menu, Word takes a few moments (depending on the length of your document) to read it through and prepare a summary. Then the AutoSummarize dialog box (see Figure 6-9) is displayed where you can select how you want to view the results. The four options are:

✦ Highlight key points

✦ Insert an executive summary or abstract at top of document

✦ Create a new document and put the summary there

✦ Hide everything but the summary without leaving the original document

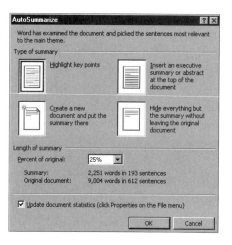

Figure 6-9: The AutoSummarize dialog box.

An example of each option is shown in the dialog box. Be sure to have the Show Highlight options selected in the View tab of the Options dialog box if you want the summary elements highlighted. The second option is useful for condensing the subject matter for an introductory section of the document. The third option is handy for creating a summary to be included in a separate document.

You set the length of the summary to specify the amount of detail you want in it. Click Percent of original to display a drop-down list of options: 10 (or 20) sentences, 100 (or 500) words or less, 10%, 25%, 50%, or 75% of original. As you change the length of summary, the number of words and sentences in the Summary line change accordingly. The final option in the AutoSummarize dialog box automatically updates your document statistics with the number of words, sentences, and so on. Choose OK when finished. Figure 6-10 shows a document with a 19% summary highlighted in the text.

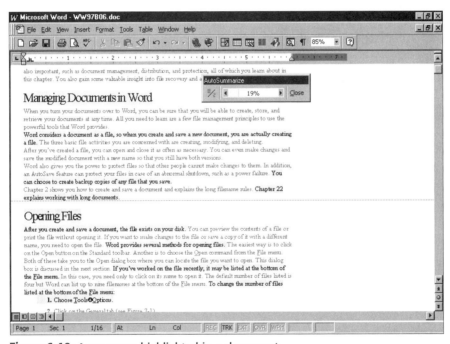

Figure 6-10: A summary highlighted in a document.

The AutoSummarize toolbar that appears when you have chosen to highlight the key words contains tools to change the view of the summary from highlighting the summary elements to hiding the original document and displaying only the summary elements. The scaling bar lets you change the level of detail in your summary by dragging the vertical line. You can see the percent or original change as you drag the line. Chose Close when you have finished reviewing the summary elements, and you are returned to your original document.

Finding Files

Sometimes it seems impossible to locate that file you created six months ago but need to review now. Searching every folder in the hopes of finding the file is tedious. Fortunately, Word provides a feature for just such occasions. This feature is part of the Open dialog box.

The Find Files feature works by searching for a filename (or a portion of a filename) or specific words or phrases in the document. You can also create a search based on any of the summary properties that you previously entered for files you saved.

When you first open the Open dialog box, you are confronted with a list of files in the current folder (see Figure 6-11). If you want to locate a file that isn't on the list, you need to conduct a search.

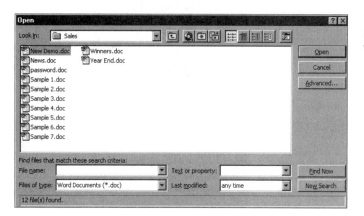

Figure 6-11: The Open dialog box with features for finding files.

Searching by filename

If you know the file's name (or even part of it) and the folder the file is in, you can locate it easily with the options in the Open dialog box.

To change to another drive, click the Look in down arrow, and select the desired drive from the list. To change to another folder, click the File name down arrow, and choose from the list of previously accessed folders and saved searches. The list of files in the dialog box changes to include the files in the selected folder. You can also find the document by typing all or the first few characters of the document name in the File name box, and choosing Find Now.

If you type the complete name, only that filename will appear in the file list. If you type only two or three characters of the name, all file names that begin with those characters appear. For example, if you type **sam** as the filename, only the Sample files appear in the list as shown in Figure 6-12. (The search text string is not case-sensitive by default.) The first of the list is selected. To search for documents by filename and drive:

1. Choose File➪Open to display the Open dialog box as before.

2. Enter the filename in the File name box. You can click the down arrow to the right of the Files of type box to select a different file type.

3. To start the search, click Find Now. The Open dialog box displays a list of files that meet the criteria you entered.

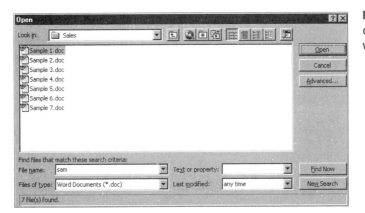

Figure 6-12: The list of files beginning with "sam."

Searching by text or date of last modification

If you don't know the document name, you can search for a file based on a text string in the file. For example, if you have a printout of the file you need to find, you can check the printout for a distinguishing word or phrase, and enter it in the Text or property box. Word will search for that text string in any document file in the current folder, and list all the documents that include the text string, as well as those that meet any other criteria you set.

Another type of search finds files based on the date they were last modified. For example, you want to open all documents that were modified last month so that you can be sure they are current. Click the Last modified down arrow, choose last month from the list, and choose Find Now.

Searching by using advanced search criteria

You may need to be more specific with your search criteria to find the file you need. For example, you may need to combine two or more criteria based on document properties, such as key words, number of pages, template used, or level of security. These searches are called *advanced searches*. To start an advanced search, click the Advanced button in the Open dialog box.

An advanced search criterion consists of three parts: the property of the document, a condition, and a value. The file property you use in a search can be its name, contents, author, or any of the other summary properties. Next, specify a condition for the criterion, such as includes, begins with, ends with, or is (exactly). Then enter a value with which to compare the property. Putting it all together, you specify a document property, set the condition, and finally enter a value. Figure 6-13 shows the criterion we entered earlier as it appears in the Advanced Find dialog box: "Files of type is *WordDocuments" (*.doc)* and File name **includes** *sam.*"

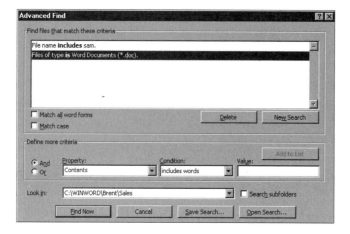

Figure 6-13: The Advanced Find dialog box.

Using advanced searches, you can combine search criteria with And or Or operators. An And combination requires that both criteria must be met; Or will find a file that meets any of the criteria.

If you don't know the exact spelling of the value you are looking for, you can use special wild card characters and search operators when you specify summary information in search criteria. Table 6-2 explains these special characters.

Table 6-2
Special Search Characters and Operators

Character	Action
? (question mark)	Matches a single character.
* (asterisk)	Matches any number of characters.
" " (quotation marks)	Matches all characters within the quotation marks.
\ (backslash)	Means the next character should be treated as a normal character instead of a special character. Used with a question mark or asterisk, for example.
, (comma)	Logical OR operator connecting two criteria and indicating that the document must match at least one of the criteria.
& (ampersand) or space	Logical AND operator connecting two criteria and indicating that the document must match all of the criteria.
~ (tilde)	Logical NOT indicating the document must not match this criterion.

To search for documents by using advanced search criteria:

1. Choose File⇨Open to display the Open dialog box.

2. Click the Advanced button to open the Advanced Find dialog box.

3. Click the Property down arrow and choose from the list of 90 properties. (These properties are from all five tabs of the Document Properties dialog box.) Figure 6-14 shows a partial list of the available document properties.

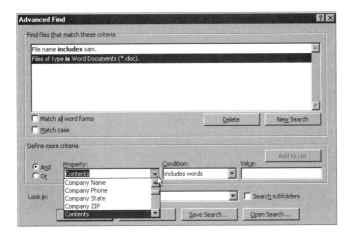

Figure 6-14: The Property list in the Advanced Find dialog box.

4. Click the Condition down arrow, and select the condition you want from the list. The list on conditions differs with different choices from the Property list.

5. Enter the value to search for in the Value box.

6. Choose Add to List to add the new criterion to the list.

7. When you have created all the criteria you want, click Find Now to return to the Open dialog box where Word displays all files that match the criteria you set.

To create a new advanced search similar to one you've already created, you can modify the existing search and save it with a different name. You can delete any of the criteria from the list by selecting the criterion to delete and choosing Delete. To delete the entire list and start over, choose New Search.

Notice that the Look in box shows the current folder. If you check Search Subfolders, Word will also search all the subfolders of the current folder.

Note The more criteria you specify, the longer it takes to find your files. Also, if you specify incorrect criteria, you probably won't find your files. For example, if you specify but misspell a key word, Word will not find the file. It is usually better to specify fewer criteria to choose from a long file list than to specify too many criteria and risk not finding any matches in a much shorter list.

Saving advanced search criteria

If you think you may want to use a set of search criteria again, you can save it by choosing Save Search in the Advanced Find dialog box. The Save Search dialog box appears where you can save a set of search criteria with a descriptive name. Then, when you need to use it again, choose Open Search in the Find Files dialog box, and select the search name from the list in the Open Search dialog box (see Figure 6-15). You can also change saved search criteria rather than create new criteria, or you can delete the search criteria. When you click Find Now, Word immediately begins a search based on the saved criteria.

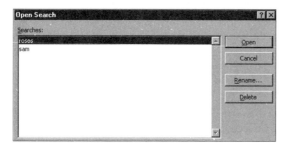

Figure 6-15: The Open Search dialog box.

Previewing a Document

After you think you've found the document you need, you can make sure by previewing the document before opening it. The Open dialog box contains a Preview button that opens a pane to display the document. Although the pane is small, word-wrapping and a vertical scroll bar let you view the entire document. To preview documents:

1. Choose File⇨Open to display the Open dialog box.

2. To see a preview of a listed document, select the document, and click the Preview button. A preview of the file appears in the right pane of the file list area, and you can use the scroll bar to the right of the previewed document to scroll through it.

3. To see the information about a file, select the file, and click either the Details or Properties button. Details displays the file name, size, type, and date it was last modified (see Figure 6-16). Properties displays the title of the file, the author, the template, and other summary and statistics properties.

4. To open the selected file, click the Open button.

5. To close the Open dialog box without opening a file, click the Cancel button.

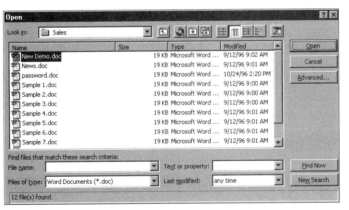

Figure 6-16:
Previewing document details.

Managing Documents with Open

You have already seen how to open and preview a file. The Open dialog box allows you to perform many other file management operations on one or more files without leaving Word. To do these things, you first need to find the files you want to manage and list them in the Open dialog box. After the documents are in the Open dialog box, you can work with them by using the shortcut menu. To manage documents with Open:

1. Choose File➪Open to display the Open dialog box.

2. Select the file with which you want to work. (If the file you want to work with isn't listed, follow the steps above to search for documents by filename, folder, and drive, or with advanced find.)

3. Right-click the filename, and select the appropriate command from the shortcut menu (see Figure 6-17). Table 6-3 lists the commands and the actions carried out.

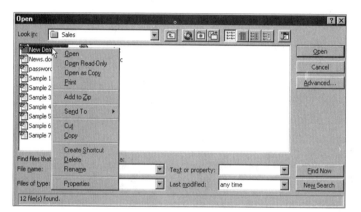

Figure 6-17: The Open shortcut menu.

Table 6-3
Open Shortcut Menu Options

Command	Action
Open	Opens the selected file.
Open Read Only	Opens the selected files as read-only. You cannot save changes to this file.
Open as Copy	Opens a copy of the selected file.
Print	Opens the Print dialog box, where you can select the options you want before printing the selected file.
Add to Zip	Opens WINZIP and adds the document to a compressed archive.

Command	Action
Send To	Copies the file to a disk or the e-mail system.
Cut	Removes the document to the Clipboard.
Copy	Copies the document to the Clipboard.
Create Shortcut	Creates a shortcut to the document that you can later move to the desktop or another folder.
Delete	Deletes the selected file after you confirm that you want to send it to the Recycle Bin.
Rename	Highlights the file name for editing.
Properties	Opens the Properties dialog box, where you can view any of the general, summary, or statistics properties. You may also edit summary properties or change the file attributes.

You can use many of the commands in the Open shortcut menu to manage groups of multiple files. First, select all the files on which you want to perform the same operation, and then select the command. To select multiple files:

1. Choose File⇨Open to display the Open dialog box.

2. To select multiple adjacent files, click the first file, press and hold the Shift key, and click the last file in the series. The two files you clicked on and all the files in between are selected. (You can also go from last to first.)

3. To select multiple nonadjacent files, click the first file you want to select, press Ctrl, and click additional files one at a time to select them as well. To deselect a selected file, press Ctrl and click the file.

4. After the group is selected, right-click any one of the filenames to open the shortcut menu.

Most of the shortcut menu commands apply to all the selected files. Delete asks for confirmation that you want to send all the selected items to the Recycle Bin. Properties applies only to the first file in the selected group.

When you delete a file, Windows 95 doesn't actually erase it from the disk. Instead, the file is sent to the Windows 95 Recycle Bin. You can recover the file anytime until you empty the bin. To recover a file, minimize the active windows until you can see the Recycle Bin icon. Double-click the icon to open the Recycle Bin dialog box. Select the file you want to recover, and choose File⇨Recover. Windows 95 places the file back in its original folder.

Solving Problems and Surviving Crashes

Inevitably, one day you're going to lose a file. The power could go out, a sector on your hard disk could go bad and corrupt a file, or you may accidentally overwrite a file. You cannot recover all files, but, luckily, Word is fairly adept at recovering files.

An ounce of prevention is worth a pound of cure. Taking the necessary precautions, you can ensure that if you have a power outage or overwrite a file, all is not lost. As we mentioned earlier in the chapter, The Allow fast saves option instructs Word to save only the changes to a document. This takes less time than a full save, in which Word saves the complete document. Ironically, full saves require less disk space than fast saves. Fast saves are larger than full saves because, when using fast saves, Word keeps track of all your changes to a document by appending the changes to the end of your document file. Using full saves preserves the document without keeping track of your changes. Documents saved automatically are stored in a special format and location until you save them.

On the flip side of the coin, you can select the Always create backup copy check box on the Save tab (Tools⇨Options). Word clears the Allow fast saves check box because only full saves can create backup copies. Word can save backup copies only when it performs a full save.

How Word stores and manages document files

To help you understand how to solve problems and survive a crash, you may find it helpful to know just how Word handles your files. When you select the save AutoRecover info every feature to save documents at a specified interval, Word saves a temporary copy of the document at the interval you specify. You still need to use the File⇨Save command to save the document when you finish working on it. When you first start Word, it saves your document in a temporary file that begins with a tilde (~) and ends with a .tmp extension in the Temp folder in the Windows folder. If you want to find out or change where your temporary files are stored, choose Tools⇨Options and click the File Locations tab. Click AutoRecover files in the File types list box. Select this entry, and choose Modify to change this location.

If you are working with a file that you have saved, another temporary file is stored in the folder where you saved your document. While you're editing the file the name of the file appears with an initial tilde followed by a dollar sign; for example a file named Proposal appears as **~$Proposal.doc**. When you close the file or exit Word, Word prompts you to first save or discard your changes to the file and the temporary file is deleted.

Word keeps track of your changes in a special auto save document file that ends with the extension .asd. This file is hidden, but is referenced inside the document file.

If there is a power outage or a system crash, Word creates a document named AutoRecover save of *filename*.doc, where *filename* is the name of the file on which you were working.

Recovering document files after a system crash

Our experience has been that using the Allow fast saves option is very reliable. When you restart Word after a power outage, Word opens all automatically saved documents so that you can recover them. Word displays the word "(Recovered)" in the title bar of the window for the file. Use the File⇨Save command to save these documents. Any recovered documents that were not saved are deleted when you quit the Word session.

Note The last changes made to the file may not be available depending on when the last automatic save was done and the time of the crash.

Recovering backup files after a system crash

As mentioned earlier in this chapter, you can also choose to use a backup file method to save files. Again, using the backup file method, Word saves full versions of your file and renames the previous version with Backup of *filename*.bak. If a problem, such as a power failure, occurs, open the file ending with the .bak extension to restore the latest version. You still will be missing any changes since the last save operation, but at least you will have saved most of your file. Remember, the biggest drawback to saving files by using the backup method is that backup versions take up space on your hard disk.

Peripheral devices and problems with files

If you open a document and it doesn't appear the way you think it should, there are a couple of ways you can troubleshoot the problems with the document. You can trace some problems back to how Windows was set up. For example, if fonts don't appear, you may simply have installed and/or selected the wrong printer. Make sure that the printer you are printing to is the same as the printer selected in the Print dialog box. To display and change the printer, choose File⇨Print and choose the printer you want to use from the Printer name drop-down list. In cases where fonts or document files don't appear correctly, you may want to reinstall your printer by opening the Printer folder in My Computer and double-clicking the Add Printer icon. If problems persist, check with the manufacturer of your printer to see whether a new printer driver is available.

An incorrect or old version of a display driver can cause the screen to become distorted or display stray characters on the screen. It's also possible that your display driver can cause Word to display a General Protection Fault error message. If you try to start Word and either of these two problems occur, try changing to a standard VGA driver and then reinstall your display driver software. If the problem persists, you may want to check with the manufacturer of your video card to see if a new version of the Windows driver is available.

What to do when a file will not open

If you try to open a document file that has been corrupted, the Office Assistant displays a message informing you that the file cannot be opened and prompts you to check to make sure that the file ends with a .doc extension. In some rare cases, your computer may hang (stop responding) when you try to open a damaged file. Word 97 includes a special file converter for recovering text from a damaged document file. If a file is corrupted Word, automatically displays the Convert File list box, as shown in Figure 6-18. You can use this file converter manually to recover text stored in the file by doing the following.

1. Choose Tools⇨Options, and click the General tab.

2. Click the Confirm conversion at open check box, so a check mark appears in the box, and choose OK.

3. Choose File⇨Open. The Open dialog box appears.

4. Click the Files of type down arrow, and select the Recover Text from Any File *.* item. If you don't see Recover Text from Any File *.* in the Files of type box, you need to install the file converter.

5. Choose Open or double-click on the file.

Figure 6-18: The Convert File dialog box includes a file converter to recover text from any file.

If this fails, you can try to open the file in NotePad, and cut and paste text into a Word for Windows document. If the file format is not recognized, try to open the file in a different format. For example, you may want to try to open the file as a text file (.txt) and save the document in Word format.

If a file opens but it has become corrupted and contains control characters or other characters that you don't want in the final document, another trick is to use the Edit⇨Paste Special command and choose the unformatted text option to copy text from a file to a new Word document. This eliminates any control characters that Word may have difficulty displaying. Another way to remove control characters is to cut and paste text to the Notepad text editor, and then paste the text back in Word. The Notepad editor is a true text editor, so it automatically strips any control characters from the file.

What to do when Word will not save your file

One of the most frustrating problems is when Word displays a message informing you that it cannot save a file on which you have been working. This message may also state that your drive is full. This is especially aggravating when you know for a fact that you have lots of disk drive space. The most common reason for this message is that the Temp folder is full. The solution is easy: go to the temp directory, delete any old temp files, return to Word, and try to save the file. A dialog box appears informing you that it cannot delete any files that are currently in use. Temporary files begin with a tilde (~) and end with the .tmp extension. It is possible that temporary files will cause Word to report that the drive is full when in fact it is not.

In some cases, Word may display an "Unrecoverable Disk Error" message. This message appears when Word cannot open a temporary file it needs to save the file in the current folder. If you are saving the file on a floppy disk, make sure you have the original file that you loaded the document from in the drive. You cannot change floppy disks in the middle of a session to save a file to a different disk. Instead, save the file, change the floppy disk, and choose the File⇨Save As command. It is a much safer practice to first exit Word and copy the file from Windows. If Word continues to display the error message, the disk may have limited space or be damaged. You may want to try another floppy disk. Finally, if the file is located on a network drive, you may not have permission to the folder on a network drive in which it is stored.

What to do if Word states the file is in use

When you run Word from a network, the program files and the main folder in which they are located are marked as read-only. You can share individual files, but you must have enabled sharing. To do this, in the Control Panel, double-click the Network icon, and choose the File and Print Sharing button. This displays a dialog box. To share your files, click the "I want to be able to give others access to my files" option. Otherwise, a message box appears, asking whether you want to make a copy of the file when more than one user tries to access Word. If the problem persists, contact your network administrator and make sure that you have Read and Write permissions for the folder in which Word stores the temporary files.

Macro viruses: What to do if Word starts acting strange

If Word doesn't work like it's supposed to, it's possible that your Word document may have contracted a new type of virus, known as a *macro virus*. A macro virus distributes itself through Word documents containing macros. The Prank macro virus (also known as the Concept virus) was one of the first macro viruses that received a considerable amount of media coverage. The Prank virus made it so that you could only save documents as templates. After you open a document containing a macro virus, the virus can be passed to other documents; thereafter, any document you save in Word can contain a copy of the macro virus. The Prank macro virus was soon followed by the Nuclear and DMV macro viruses. Microsoft released a macro virus protection tool to combat these existing macro viruses. Word 97 automatically checks for these macro viruses, but it is likely that other macro viruses are bound to raise their ugly heads in the future. A document infected with a macro virus can infect any version of Word that supports macros. For example, an infected Word for Windows 95 document can be opened by Word 6 for the Macintosh and infect that machine, making this type of virus a "platform independent" virus.

On its own, Word cannot determine whether the instructions in the macro are desired or not. It really is close to impossible to determine whether a macro is a macro virus or a regular macro. Each new macro virus will need to be evaluated and treated on a case-by-case basis. Most virus protection software companies are now including macro virus killers in their latest releases. If you think you have a macro virus, check **http://www.microsoft.com/msoffice** for macro virus updates. You can also get information on new macro viruses at Symantec's Anti Virus Center by starting your Web browser and entering the following URL: **http://www. symantec.com/avcenter/**. Another excellent source of macro virus information is McAfee Associates at the URL **http://www.mcafee.com/**. More importantly, McAfee Associates will let you download a trial version of their virus protection program that you can use to eliminate any virus. The version will time out in 30 days.

Using a disk editor to retrieve files

If your files are scattered into different clusters on your hard disk, some helpful techie will likely tell you that you can use a disk editor to recover the file. Although this is possible to reconstruct a fragmented file, it is comparable to a carpenter telling you that you can rebuild your house after it's been hit by a tornado. Our experience has been that it just isn't worth the amount of work required to recover the file using a disk editor. If you decide to use a disk editor, be sure to use a reliable disk editor, such as Norton Utilities available from Symantec. Also, make sure you back up your hard disk first so that you can restore your disk to its original format in case of an emergency.

Summary

Windows 95, Windows NT, and Word 97 bring several new features to managing documents in Word. This chapter has taken you on a tour of Word's file management features from finding, opening, and saving files to recovering from a system crash. Some of the more salient points covered in this chapter include the following:

✦ When you manage documents in Word, you are actually managing files. Word lets you create new documents and save the files in any folder in the system, even one you created as your personal folder.

✦ When you want to locate a file, you can search for it by name, by a text string within the document, or by the date of last modification. Use the Open dialog box to locate the desired file. If the document is difficult to find, you can use any of the advanced find techniques provided by Word.

✦ Word restores AutoRecover files when using the Allow fast saves to protect you from losing work caused by a power failure or a system crash. You can also restore your work after a system crash or a power failure from a backup file.

✦ When Word isn't displaying your document correctly, you can check your printer and video drivers. If you are unable to open a Word document file, use Word's converter to recover the text from a corrupted Word document file. You can also save a file even if Word erroneously reports that you are out of disk space. If Word starts acting strange, you can check to find out if Word has contracted a macro virus and squash the bug with a virus protection program.

Where to go next...

For information on embedding objects that are created by others in your Word 97 document, look in Chapter 15.

The next part of this book introduces you to the myriad of formatting options that you have at your fingertips, beginning with explaining the possibilities for formatting characters and working with fonts. Knowing how to format characters and use different fonts brings a more professional look to your documents and prepares you for formatting documents created using wizards and templates.

✦   ✦   ✦

The Newfashioned Word: Formatting Documents

Character Formatting and Fonts

So far you have learned how to work with text to express yourself with words. Now it's time to enhance your message with character formatting and fonts. Basic character formatting lets you apply boldface, italic, and underlines to your text. Beyond the basics, Word includes a variety of character formatting options to make your documents look professional.

Applying Character Formats

Word includes a rich collection of character formatting options. You can easily apply formats to any selected text, from a single character to an entire document. You can change the format of selected text by choosing a formatting command, or you can choose character formats before entering the text. If you choose a formatting command without first selecting text, Word begins applying the format at the insertion point. Text you type from that point forward has the new format until you turn off the formatting option. Word has three ways to change character formats:

> ◆ The Formatting toolbar lets you apply the three most common character formats by clicking the Bold, Italic, and Underline buttons (see Figure 7-1). If you do not see the Formatting toolbar on your screen, choose View⇨Toolbars, or right-click any blank toolbar space. Select the Formatting check box and choose OK. Word lets you add buttons that apply character formatting options to the Formatting toolbar. For information on customizing toolbars, see Chapter 25.

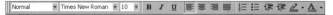

Figure 7-1: The Formatting toolbar provides easy access to Word's commonly used formatting commands.

✦ The Font dialog box (see Figure 7-2) enables you to apply one or multiple character formats at one time. In the Font dialog box, you can choose options from the Font tab or Character Spacing tab. Display the Font dialog box by pressing Ctrl+D or by displaying the shortcut menu (click the right mouse button in the document window, or press Shift+F10) and choosing the Font option. You can also access the Font dialog box by choosing Format⇨Font.

Figure 7-2: The Font dialog box.

✦ Shortcut keys let you apply a format as you enter text. For example, pressing Ctrl+B inserts boldface text beginning at the insertion point, and pressing Ctrl+I inserts italic text beginning at the insertion point. Pressing the shortcut keys again turns the format off. You can use shortcut keys to format selected text. Word provides an extensive collection of shortcut keys for applying most of Word's character formats. We describe these keys in the rest of this chapter.

When you apply character formats in a document, they affect only the current document. However, Word lets you save changes you made in the Font dialog box as default settings, which Word uses when you open a new document based on the current template. For example, if you're using the Normal template, which is the default template, the character formatting changes are saved to the Normal template. Additionally, you can create character styles, which can be attached to document templates, to apply a collection of character formats at one time. Chapter 11 explains working with character styles.

Note Word lets you find and replace character formatting by using the Find or Replace command from the Edit menu. The Font dialog box used for applying character formatting also appears when you want to find and replace character formatting. See Chapter 3 for more information on working with the Find or Replace command.

Boldfacing text

Boldfacing makes characters heavier in their stroke weight. Boldface text is commonly used for headers or headlines or to bring out an important word or phrase in a paragraph. Different fonts offer different boldface options. The Bold button on the Formatting toolbar and the Ctrl+B shortcut key apply the standard bold member of a font family. If the font you're using offers other boldface options, use the Font style, the Font setting in the Font dialog box, or the Font drop-down list on the Formatting toolbar. To format text in boldface by using the Formatting toolbar or shortcut keys:

1. Select the text you want to boldface, or, for new text you want to type, position the insertion point where you want boldfacing to begin.

2. Click the Bold button on the Formatting toolbar, or press Ctrl+B. Any selected text appears in boldface.

3. If you didn't select any text before clicking the Bold button or pressing Ctrl+B, enter the text that you want to insert in boldface. Then click the Bold button, press Ctrl+B, or press Ctrl+spacebar to return to regular text.

Italicizing text

An italic format is a script version of a font style that slants the character. Use italics instead of underlining or boldfacing to emphasize a word or a phrase. But be careful not to overuse italics; otherwise, they lose their effect. The Italic button on the Formatting toolbar and the Ctrl+I shortcut key apply the standard italic member of a font family. If the font you're using offers other italic options, use the Font style or Font setting in the Font dialog box or the Font drop-down list on the Formatting toolbar. To italicize text:

1. Select the text that you want to italicize, or, for new type, position the insertion point where you want italicized text to begin.

2. Click the Italic button on the Formatting toolbar, or press Ctrl+I. Any selected text appears in italics.

3. If you didn't select text before clicking the Italic button or pressing Ctrl+I, enter the text you want to be italicized. Then click the Italic button, press Ctrl+I, or press Ctrl+spacebar to return to regular text.

Underlining text

Word lets you format text with four types of underlining: single, words only, double, and dotted. Table 7-2 describes these underlining options. Choosing the Underline button on the Formatting toolbar formats all selected text or any text at the insertion point, including spaces, with a single underline. To use any of the other underlining options, use the Font dialog box or use shortcut keys to apply three of the four underlining options, as listed in Table 7-1. To underline text:

1. Select the text that you want to underline, or position the insertion point where you want underlining to begin.

2. Do one of the following:

   • Click the Underline button on the Formatting toolbar.

   • Press one of the shortcut keys in Table 7-1.

   • Choose Format➪Font, press Ctrl+D, or choose Font from the shortcut menu, and choose an underline option (see Table 7-2) from the Underline drop-down list. Then choose OK.

3. If you didn't select text before clicking the Underline button, pressing the shortcut keys, or choosing an underline option in the Font dialog box, enter the text that you want underlined. To return to regular text, click the Underline button, press the shortcut key, press Ctrl+spacebar, or choose None from the Underline drop-down list in the Font dialog box. Then choose OK.

Table 7-1	
Underlining Shortcut Keys	
Shortcut Keys	*Underline Action*
Ctrl+U	Single underline
Ctrl+Shift+W	Words only
Ctrl+Shift+D	Double underline

You can add buttons for underlining words only and for double underlining by choosing Tools➪Customize to display the Customize dialog box. Then click the Command Tab, and under Categories, scroll down and select Format. Now move right to the Commands menu, and then scroll down and drag the Double underline and/or Words only underline buttons to the toolbar.

Note   You can also access the Customize dialog box by right-clicking any blank toolbar space and selecting Customize.

Table 7-2
Underlining Options in the Font Dialog Box

Option	Description
(none)	Normal text. Used to stop or remove underlining.
Single	Single underline. The space between words is underlined.
Words only	Single underline. The space between words is not underlined.
Double	Double underline. The space between words is double-underlined.
Dotted	Single broken underline. The space between the words is underlined.
Thick	Produces a thick line
Dash	Produces a dashed underline
Dot dash	Produces an alternating dot-dash line
Dot dot dash	Produces a line that alternates between two dots and a dash
Wave	Produces a wavy line

Using superscripts and subscripts

The superscript and subscript formats let you change the location of characters above or below the normal line of text. Superscripts and subscripts are commonly used in mathematical and scientific formulas. For example, the number 2 is formatted in superscript in the equation $E=MC^2$ or in subscript for H_2O. You can select superscripts or subscripts and make their point size smaller.

You can add buttons for superscript and subscript to a toolbar by choosing Tools⇔Customize to display the Customize dialog box. Then click the Command Tab, and under Categories, scroll down and select Format. Now move right, to the Commands menu, scroll down and drag the Superscript and/or Subscript button to the toolbar.

To format text as superscript or subscript:

1. Select the text to be formatted as either superscript or subscript.

2. Do one of the following:

   • Press Ctrl+Shift+= to format text as a superscript, or press Ctrl+= to format text as a subscript.

   • Choose Format⇔Font, press Ctrl+D, or choose Font from the shortcut menu to display the Font dialog box. Then select the Superscript or Subscript check box in the Effects group, and choose OK.

3. If you didn't select any text, enter the text that you want in the superscript or subscript format. To return to regular text, press Ctrl+Shift+= or Ctrl+=

to toggle superscript and subscript, respectively. Or you can press Ctrl+ spacebar. You can also display the Font dialog box, clear the Superscript or Subscript check box in the Effects group, and choose OK.

Note Word also includes a powerful equation editor for creating and working with mathematical formulas. For information on the Equation Editor, see Chapter 16.

You can also format text as superscript or subscript by using the Character Spacing tab in the Fonts dialog box:

1. Select the text that you want to format in superscript or subscript.

2. Choose Format⇨Font, press Ctrl+D, or choose Font from the shortcut menu to display the Font dialog box. Choose the Character Spacing tab (see Figure 7-3).

3. Choose Raised or Lowered from the Position box.

4. Choose the By box and enter the value you want, or click the up-arrow button to change the default three-point setting.

5. Choose OK.

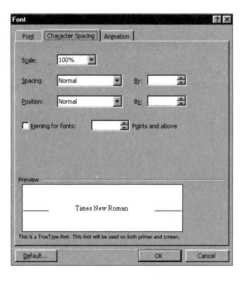

Figure 7-3: The Character Spacing tab.

Underlining superscript or subscript text

To place an underline beneath superscript, select the superscript text—not the surrounding text—before underlining. If you apply underlining to selected text that includes superscripts, Word underlines the text, including the superscript, below the base line of the text. When underlining is applied to text that contains subscripts, the underlining is automatically placed underneath the subscript characters, just below the baseline of regular text.

Spacing superscript and subscript text

In calculating where superscripts and subscripts appear in relation to normal text, Word begins with the text baseline. The baseline is an imaginary horizontal line directly beneath a line of text. By default, Word raises superscript three points above the baseline and lowers subscript three points below the baseline. You can change the vertical position of superscript or subscript in the Font dialog box by using the Character Spacing tab (see Figure 7-3). Position control indicates where superscript and subscript text appears raised or lowered in relation to the baseline.

Note If you specify the superscript or subscript position in the Position box and the characters appear clipped, use the Paragraph command on the Format menu to increase the line spacing, as explained in Chapter 8.

All Caps and Small Caps

Word's All Caps format changes selected lowercase characters to uppercase characters. If you want to add All Caps as you type, simply press the Caps Lock key. The Small Caps format changes lowercase characters to uppercase characters and reduces their size. Neither of these formatting options affect uppercase letters, numbers, punctuation, or nonalphabetic characters. When you remove All Caps or Small Caps formatting, the text becomes lowercase.

You can add buttons for Small Caps and All Caps by choosing Tools⇨Customize to display the Customize dialog box. Then click the Command Tab, and under Categories, scroll down and select Format. Move to the Commands menu, and then scroll down and drag the Small Caps or All Caps buttons to the toolbar.

To format text as small caps or all caps:

1. Select the text that you want to format, or position the insertion point where you want to begin to type all capital letters or small capital letters.

2. Do one of the following:

   - Press Ctrl+Shift+K for Small Caps, or press Ctrl+Shift+A for All Caps.

   - Choose Format⇨Font, press Ctrl+D, or choose Font from the shortcut menu to display the Font dialog box. Then select Small caps or All caps from the Effects group, and choose OK.

3. If you didn't select text, enter the text that you want in small caps or all caps format. To return to regular text, press Ctrl+spacebar; or choose the Font dialog box, clear the Small Caps or All Caps check box, and choose OK.

Note The Change Case command also lets you change case formatting, as explained later in this chapter.

Note   To remove any button from any toolbar, open the Customize dialog box as discussed earlier and drag a button away from the toolbar area. You'll notice that your mouse becomes a cursor holding a button. When you've dragged the button about an inch or so away from the toolbar, let up on the mouse button. You'll find the button is gone. This feature works no matter which Tab of the Customize dialog box is exposed.

Colorizing your text

Here's a Word feature that Ted Turner would love: colorized text. If you're using a color monitor, Word lets you choose from 16 different colors to display text. you can use different colors for text to add emphasis to a displayed document. For example, you can format an urgent item in red. If you have a color printer, colored text also prints in color. Of course, if your printer doesn't print in color, colored text prints in black. The default Auto setting in the Color control in the Font dialog box displays text in the color that you've chosen for window text. (Choose this color in the Color options of the Windows Control Panel.) To colorize your text:

1. Select the text that you want to appear in a different color, or position the insertion point where you want colorized text to begin.

2. Choose Format⇨Font, press Ctrl+D, or choose Font from the shortcut menu, and then select a color option from the Color box and choose OK.

3. If you didn't select any text, enter the text that you want to appear in the color you chose. To return to regular text, press Ctrl+spacebar; or display the Font dialog box, and change the Color setting to Auto or Black. Then choose OK.

Striking through text

Select the Strikethrough check box in the Font dialog box's Effect group to add a line through selected text. If you are using Strikethrough to mark revisions, select Tools⇨Revisions, and employ Word's Revision Tools. See Chapter 19 for more information on working with Word's revision features. To strikethrough text:

1. Select the text that you want to format with strikethrough, or, for new text, position the insertion point where you want strikethrough to begin.

2. Choose Format⇨Font, press Ctrl+D, or choose Font from the shortcut menu to display the Font dialog box.

3. Select Strikethrough from the Effects group, and choose OK. Any selected text appears in strikethrough format.

4. If you didn't select text, enter the text that you want to appear in the strike-through format. To return to regular text, press Ctrl+spacebar; or display the Font dialog box, clear the Strikethrough check box, and choose OK.

Note Strikethrough text that originates from the Tools⇨Track Changes command or from the Reviewing Toolbar cannot be removed by using the Font dialog box.

Creating text with a shadow

Select the Shadow check box in the Font dialog box's Effects group to add a gray "drop shadow" through selected text. You cannot change the shadow's color or position. The effect is subtle and not loud. To create text with a shadow (see Figure 7-4):

1. Select the text that you want to format with a shadow, or, for new text, position the insertion point where you want the shadow effect to begin.

2. Choose Format⇨Font, press Ctrl+D, or choose Font from the shortcut menu to display the Font dialog box.

3. Select Shadow from the Effects group, and choose OK. Any selected text appears in shadow format.

4. If you didn't select text, enter the text that you want to appear in the shadow format. To return to regular text, press Ctrl+spacebar; or display the Font dialog box, clear the Shadow check box, and choose OK.

Creating text with an outline effect

Select the Outline check box in the Font dialog box's Effects group to turn the selected text white, and the text's formatted color is used to create a thin outline around each letter of text (see Figure 7-4). You cannot change the thickness of the outline, and the "fill color" of the text will always be white while using this effect. To create outlined text:

1. Select the text that you want to outline, or, for new text, position the insertion point where you want the outline effect to begin.

2. Choose Format⇨Font, press Ctrl+D, or choose Font from the shortcut menu to display the Font dialog box.

3. Select Outline from the Effects group, and choose OK. Any selected text appears outlined.

4. If you didn't select text, enter the text that you want to outlined. To return to regular text, press Ctrl+spacebar; or display the Font dialog box, clear the Outline check box, and choose OK.

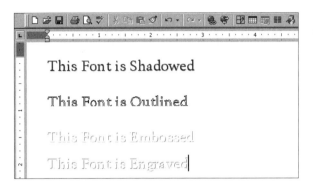

Figure 7-4: Text with special effects applied.

Creating embossed or engraved text

Select the Emboss check box in the Font dialog box's Effects group to make the text appear slightly "raised." The amount of embossing effect is preset and cannot be changed. Similarly, selecting the Engrave check box in the Font's dialog box's Effects group makes the text appear "carved in," or engraved, into the page (refer to Figure 7-4).The engraved effect's depth is preset and cannot be altered. To create embossed or engraved text:

1. Select the text that you want to format with embossing or engraving. Or, for new text, position the insertion point where you want the effect to begin.

2. Choose Format⇨Font, press Ctrl+D, or choose Font from the shortcut menu to display the Font dialog box.

3. Select Emboss or Engrave from the Effects group, and choose OK. Any selected text appears in your chosen effect's format.

4. If you didn't select text, enter the text that you want to appear embossed or engraved. To return to regular text, press Ctrl+spacebar or display the Font dialog box, clear the Emboss or Engrave check box, and choose OK.

Note   You cannot mix shadowed, embossed, or engraved text. Only one at a time may be applied to your selected text.

Using Text Animation

The third tab under the Fonts dialog box is Animation (see Figure 7-5). You can give your text a blinking background, make your text sparkle, or create a "light show" or "marching ants" around its parameter. These special effects are not printable, but in small doses, are rather fun on your screen. The effect increases in size as you increase the font size, so the Las Vegas Lights animation applied to a 72-point font is quite splashy (see Figure 7-6). To apply text animations to your text:

1. Select the text that you want to format an animation, or, for new text, position the insertion point where you want the effect to begin.

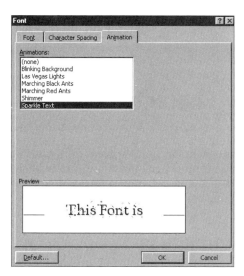

Figure 7-5: The Animation tab.

"Romance of the Rose" was born, appeared to be in as perfect a state of revolution as if the Huguenots had just made a second Rochelle of it. Many citizens, seeing the women flying toward the High Street, leaving their children crying at the open doors, hastened to don the cuirass, and, supporting their somewhat uncertain courage with a musket or a partizan, directed their steps toward the hostelry of the Franc-Meunier, before which was gathered, increasing every minute, a compact group, vociferous and full of curiosity.

In those times panics were common, and few days passed without some city or other enregistering in its archives an event of this kind. There were nobles who made war against each other; there was the king, who made war against the cardinal; there was Spain, which made war against the king. Then, in addition to these, concealed or public, secret or patent wars, there were, moreover, robbers, mendicants, Huguenots, wolves, and scoundrels who made war upon everybody. The citizens always took up arms readily

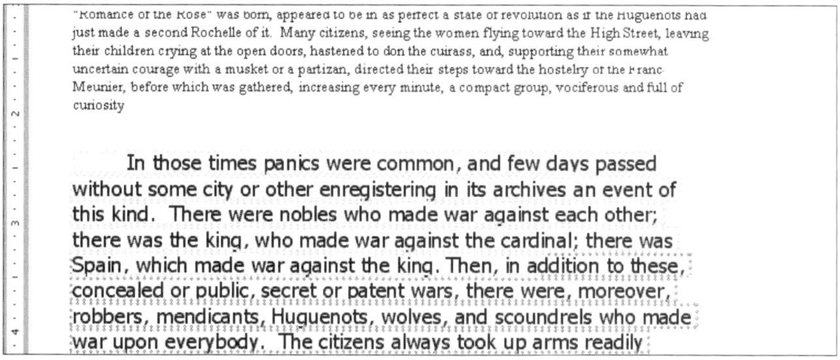

Figure 7-6: Text with "Las Vegas Lights" animation. I guess you just had to be there.

2. Choose Format➪Font, press Ctrl+D, or choose Font from the shortcut menu to display the Font dialog box.

3. Click the tab labeled Animation and select any of the five animations that appeal to you. You cannot mix animations. Check the Preview box for a quick peek at how the effect looks when applied to your text selection, and choose OK. Any selected text appears in your chosen animation's format (see Figure 7-6).

4. If you didn't select text, enter the text that you want to appear animated. To return to regular text, press Ctrl+spacebar; or display the Font dialog box, click the Animation tab, select (none) in the Animations list box, and choose OK.

Using Word's Handy Character Formatting Tools

Beyond applying character formats, Word includes some handy tools to efficiently work with character formats. These tools let you display the character formats applied to a selection of text, repeat or copy character formats, and undo character formats. The following sections explain the use of these tools.

Displaying character formatting

Word lets you view the character formatting applied to any existing text. This feature is helpful when you want to know what formatting is applied to a paragraph before you begin copying the formatting. To see which formats are applied to a given section of text, choose Help⇨What's This.

When the pointer becomes an arrow and a question mark, click the text you want to check. Word displays information about the paragraph and font formatting, as shown in Figure 7-7. The Font Formatting information shows formats applied with paragraph and character styles and formats applied directly with formatting commands. (Chapter 11 explains working with paragraph and character styles.) When you finish checking text formatting, select Help⇨What's This? or press Esc to return to your text.

Word also lets you view common formats applied to text by selecting the text (or positioning the insertion point in the text) and looking at the settings on the Formatting toolbar or in the Font dialog box. If the selected text has different fonts or different font sizes, the Font and Font Size lists on the Formatting toolbar or in the Font dialog box appear blank. For example, if the selection includes both 12-point and 10-point text, the Font Size box on the toolbar is blank. However, you can still change the selected text, even though a control is blank.

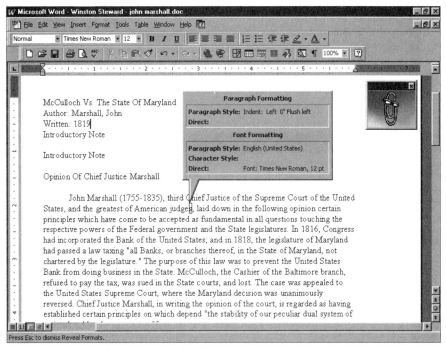

Figure 7-7: A sample formatting display.

Repeating character formatting

The Repeat command from the Edit menu lets you copy formatting immediately after you have formatted characters. This method repeats only the most recent format. If you use the Font dialog box to apply several formatting choices at once, the Repeat command repeats all those choices because you made them as a single action. But if you use the Repeat command after making several formatting choices by using shortcut keys or the Formatting toolbar, the command repeats only the most recent choice. To copy character formatting with the Repeat command, select the text you want to format, and then choose Edit⇨Repeat or press Ctrl+Y or F4.

Copying character formatting

The Format Painter is a handy feature that lets you copy multiple character formats in a section of text, regardless of how the formats were applied. After you apply the formats to one section of text, you can copy the formatting to other selected text by using the Format Painter button on the Standard toolbar or by using shortcut keys. To copy character formatting:

1. Select the text that has the formatting that you want to copy.

2. Do one of the following:

   • To copy character formatting to another location, click the Format Painter button on the Standard toolbar. The mouse pointer changes to a paintbrush with an I-beam pointer. Select the text you want to format. When you release the mouse button, the format is copied, and the pointer changes back to the I-beam.

   • To copy the character formatting to several locations, double-click the Format Painter button, select the text that you want to format, and release the mouse button. Then select additional text anywhere in the document. When you finish copying character formatting, click the Format Painter button, or press Esc to return to the I-beam pointer.

   • To copy character formatting by using shortcut keys, press Ctrl+Shift+C to copy the selected text's formatting. Select the text that you want to format, and press Ctrl+Shift+V.

Undoing character formatting

Word's formatting commands, buttons, and shortcut keys act as toggle switches for turning a formatting feature on or off. For example, selecting text and clicking the Bold button boldfaces the text. Selecting the same text and clicking the Bold button removes the boldface formatting from the text.

Also, by pressing Ctrl+spacebar, you can quickly remove any character formatting and return to the regular text format (as defined in your Normal style). Word removes any character formats that you applied by using the Formatting toolbar, shortcut key combinations, or the Font dialog box. However, Word does not remove any character formats that are part of the paragraph style. For information on styles, see Chapter 11.

If you mistakenly format the wrong text, reverse the action by using the Undo command. Word lets you undo the most recent action or command by using one of three methods: click the Undo button on the Standard toolbar, choose Undo from the Edit menu, or use the shortcut keys Ctrl+Z or F4. To undo multiple actions, first click the arrow beside the Undo button to display a list of actions that have occurred, and then select the actions that you want to undo. The actions are undone in the order in which they took place.

Highlighting Text

In the world of paper-based documents, one tool we all have used heavily at one time or another is a highlighter pen. These handy pens let you highlight text in a document with just about any color—although yellow is the classic color. Word includes this handy tool in digital form. Using Word's highlighter pen button on the toolbar, you can highlight any text or graphic. You can choose from a wide variety of colors. To highlight text:

1. Click the Highlight button on the Formatting toolbar. The mouse pointer changes to a highlight marker pen.

2. Click the arrow button next to the Highlight button to select a highlighting color. If you use the same highlighting color again, you don't need to select the color again.

3. Select the text you want to highlight. If you change your mind, you can click the selected text to remove highlighting.

4. Select the next item in the document that you want to highlight.

5. When you're done highlighting text, press Esc, or click the Highlight button again (see Figure 7-8).

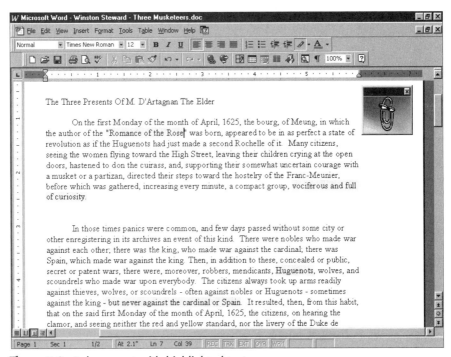

Figure 7-8: A document with highlighted text.

Note Highlighting parts of a document works best when the recipients of your document review the document online. If you highlight parts of a document that you are going to print on a black-and-white printer, run a test print of highlighted text to make sure the results are legible.

You can choose other highlighting colors by opening the Reviews toolbar to display several highlighting options. Also, select Options from the Tools menu and click the arrow next to Highlight Color, select the color you want, and click OK.

Note The current color you select for the highlighting pen always appears in the square under the highlighting marker pen in the Highlight button.

You can remove highlighting by clicking the Highlight button, clicking the arrow next to the Highlight button, and selecting None. You can then select highlighted text to remove the highlighting.

To search an entire document for highlighting and replace it on a one-by-one basis or all at once, you can use Word's Replace command. When you remove highlighting, the text is not removed, only the highlight is deleted. To use the Replace command:

1. Click the beginning of the document, and choose Edit⇨Replace. The Replace dialog box appears.

2. Click the Format button, and select Highlight from the list.

3. Do one of the following

   • To find the first occurrence of highlighted text, click the Find Next button, and then click the Replace button; or click the Find Next button to continue to the next occurrence without replacing the highlight.

   • To replace all occurrences of highlighted text, click Replace All to remove all the highlights in a document.

4. After Word finishes searching your document, a message box appears. Click OK, and then click Close to close the Replace dialog box.

Note You can move quickly between all the highlighted portions of your document without having to open the Find dialog box. Click the Select Browse Object button at the bottom-right of the screen (the button with the circle in it between the arrows.) You'll see a menu fly out, allowing you to select which item to use as your scrolling points. Select Browse by Edits. This means that when you use the scroll but-tons, each click of a scroll button will take you to the next (or previous) instance of highlighted text, rather than scrolling from page to page.

You can control whether the highlighting appears in your document from the View tab in the Options dialog box. Choose Tools⇨Options, and click the View tab. Clicking the Highlight check box (removing the x) hides the highlighting from your document.

Changing Character Spacing

The normal spacing between letters in a word is suitable for most situations. However, sometimes you may need to adjust the space between letters. For example, in a newsletter headline using a large character size, you may need to adjust the space between a certain pair of characters, or you may need to tighten the space between all characters in a sentence to fit the text into a tight space, such as a two-column newsletter. *Character spacing* increases or decreases the amount of space equally between characters in selected text by the amount you specify. *Kerning*, on the other hand, reduces or expands the spacing between certain letter pairs to improve the appearance of these character pairs. To make changes to either kind of spacing, display the Font dialog box by pressing Ctrl+D; or choose Font from the shortcut menu, and then choose the Character Spacing tab.

Note You can save changes made in the Character Spacing tab as defaults for the template of your current document, as explained later in this chapter.

Expanding and condensing character spacing

The Spacing control in the Character Spacing tab defines how much space appears between characters. This control changes the spacing between characters by the same amount for all characters in a selection. The default is Normal. Choosing Expanded expands all the spacing between characters of your selected text. Choosing Condensed condenses all the spacing between characters of your selected text. Figure 7-9 shows a sample of expanded and condensed text. By default, Word uses one point for expanded spacing and condensed spacing. You can customize spacing for the Normal, Expanded, or Condensed options by typing a number between 0.25 and 14 in the By box, by choosing the By text box and clicking the up- or down-arrow buttons, or by pressing the up- or down-arrow keys.

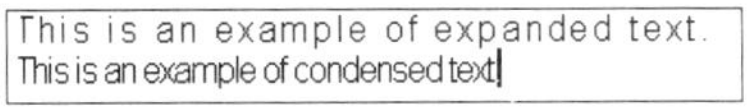

This is an example of expanded text.
This is an example of condensed text

Figure 7-9: Expanded and condensed text.

Adjusting spaces between character pairs

Word lets you automatically kern a proportionally spaced TrueType or PostScript Type 1 font above a minimum size, which varies depending on the font. In a proportionally spaced font, the width of each character varies; for example, *i* and *w* have different widths. If you select the Kerning for fonts option in the Character Spacing tab, Word adjusts the kerning for TrueType or PostScript Type 1 fonts above the font size you specify. In the Points and above box, you can specify the point size to be *at* or *above* automatic kerning.

In addition, Word offers a limited kerning feature to increase or decrease the space between two individual letters. Kerning is most noticeable when you use large font sizes, such as in a headline, because the spacing allocated to some characters becomes too large when certain characters are paired with other characters. For example, when you have a capital *T* followed by a lowercase *o,* you can use kerning to nestle the *o* under the top of the *T.* To adjust spaces between character pairs:

1. Select the character pair that you want to change.

2. Do one of the following:

   • Press Ctrl+Shift+] to increase kerning.

   • Press Ctrl+Shift+[to decrease kerning.

   • To turn Kerning on or off, press Ctrl+D or choose Font from the shortcut menu, select the Character Spacing tab, and select Kerning for fonts. The current point size appears in the Points and above box. Choose OK to close the Fonts dialog box.

Changing the Case of Characters

The Change Case command lets you automatically change selected characters from uppercase to lowercase, or vice versa. Format⭢Change Case displays the Change Case dialog box (see Figure 7-10). Table 7-3 describes the available options in the Change Case dialog box. You can only choose one option at a time. The Change Case command does not affect letters using the Small Caps format; you must remove this format to make the letters lowercase. To change the case of characters:

1. Select the text that you want to change.

2. Do one of the following:

   • Press Shift+F3 to toggle through one of three options: Sentence case, lowercase, or UPPERCASE. Each time you press Shift+F3, Word changes to the next case option.

   • Choose Format⭢Change Case, choose one of the options listed in Table 7-3, and choose OK.

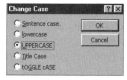

Figure 7-10: The Change Case dialog box.

Table 7-3 Change Case Dialog Box Options	
Option	**Action**
Sentence case	Changes the first character of the sentence to uppercase and all other characters to lowercase.
lowercase	Changes all characters to lowercase.
UPPERCASE	Changes all characters to uppercase.
Title Case	Changes the first character of each word to uppercase and all other characters to lowercase.
tOGGLE cASE	Switches uppercase to lowercase and lowercase to uppercase.

Changing Fonts and Font Sizes

When you create or open a new document by using the Normal template, Word reverts to a default Times New Roman, 10-point font. The current font name and size appears in the Formatting toolbar. Word lets you choose from any of the fonts installed on your system to change the appearance of text. The last six fonts that you used appear at the top of your font list and are separated by a line (see Figure 7-11). All your installed fonts are listed alphabetically below the line. The following sections explain the different types of fonts available for use with Word, how to change from one font to another, and how to change the size of a font.

You can change Word's default font and font size, as explained later in this chapter.

Figure 7-11: The Font list box displays the last six fonts used above the line.

The fonts listed in the Font list box

The two font standards for Windows are TrueType and PostScript Type 1. Both are *scalable* fonts, which are also called *outline* fonts. Scalable fonts are device-independent, meaning they can be printed to any printer supported by Windows.

A scalable font uses a single font file to display and print the font to give you true WYSIWYG (*What You See Is What You Get*). Windows comes with a basic collection of TrueType fonts and two symbol fonts (Symbol and Wingdings). The Symbol font character set includes the Greek alphabet, the four standard card suit symbols, and a variety of other mathematical, logical, chemical, and business symbols. The Wingdings font character set includes many unique symbols not found in other character sets, such as computer pictograms, astrological signs, and clock faces.

Note   Because Word is a Windows application, it lets Windows do most of the font management work. Windows 95 includes a Font Control Panel to install and manage TrueType fonts. To install and manage Adobe Type 1 fonts, you need the Adobe Type Manager.

The fonts and font sizes you can use in your documents depend on the fonts available from your printer and the fonts installed on your system. The Font list box on the Formatting toolbar and the Font list box in the Font dialog box list the installed fonts.

Microsoft breaks fonts into two major divisions: TrueType (Microsoft's font standard) and every other type of font. TrueType fonts have a TrueType symbol (refer back to Figure 7-11) to the left of the font name in the Font list. PostScript Type 1 fonts are lumped with other font formats and are identified by a printer icon. Any printer fonts that you have displayed in the Fonts list come from the printer driver you're using to print documents.

Some fonts listed, such as Modern, Roman, and Script, don't have a TrueType symbol or a printer icon next to them. These are *Vector fonts*. Vector fonts are also known as *stroke* or *plotter fonts* because they were designed for plotters. Plotters create fonts by drawing line segments between various points. While Vector fonts can be printed on most printers, you won't likely want to use these fonts over the available TrueType fonts.

Although Windows works with PostScript Type 1 fonts using the Adobe Type Manager, Word doesn't display a helpful icon to identify PostScript Type 1 fonts. This is the result of the ongoing "font wars" between Microsoft and Adobe. Unfortunately, if you're using PostScript Type 1 fonts, you're the victim of this war.

About font names included in the Font list box

Font names often have a direct relationship to the names of their designer, places, or even events in history. Some font names also include the name of the licenser. For example, font names licensed from International Typeface Corporation, a leading source for hundreds of font designs licensed to many font foundries, have the letters ITC before the name. In addition, many font vendors also add a code in the name to identify the font as theirs. For example, Bitstream adds a BT to the end of the font name, AGFA Compugraphic adds ATT to their font names, and Monotype adds MT to many of their font names. Font names in your font lists are often abbreviated names from the actual names of the fonts.

About font styles listed in the Font dialog box

A *font style* is a variation of a font's design. For the Times New Roman font, there are different variations of the font's standard design, such as bold, italic, and bold italic. Each of these variations is a separate font style, and together they make up a *font family*. Commonly, the italic, bold, and bold italic members of a font family do not appear in Word's Font list because Word uses the related format button on the Formatting toolbar for these font family members. In most cases, only the regular font name and any members of the font family other than italic, bold, and bold italic, such as expanded or condensed, appear in the font list.

The Font dialog box's Font style control list displays all the variations in a font style. Different fonts have different styles associated with them. Within most font families, the standard font is usually referred to as *regular, roman,* or *medium.* Some font families are more extensive than others; for example, they might include several different weights and widths of a font, such as condensed, extra thin, expanded, extra bold, and so on. Different font designs use different descriptive terms for a font's weight, and no standardization of font style terms exists.

Changing a font

Word provides three methods to change fonts: using the Font dialog box, the Font list on the Formatting toolbar, or shortcut keys. The easiest way to choose a font is to use the Formatting toolbar or shortcut keys. To change a font:

1. Select the text that you want to change to a different font, or, before you begin typing, position the insertion point where you want the new font to begin.

2. Do one of the following:

   • Click the down arrow to the right of the Font list box on the Formatting toolbar, and select the font you want.

   • Press Ctrl+Shift+F, and press the down-arrow key to display the list of fonts. Select the font from the list by using the up- or down-arrow key, and press Enter.

3. If you didn't select text before choosing your font, any text you begin typing *now* will be in the font you just selected.

Note   Pressing Ctrl+Shift+Q automatically chooses the TrueType Symbol font.

Changing the size of a font

The standard measuring unit for fonts is called a *point*. There are 72 points in an inch. A font's point size is measured from the top of the highest ascender to the bottom of the lowest descender. Commonly used point sizes from eight to 72 points appear in the Fonts list box, but you can enter any point size from one point to 1,638 points. Different fonts in the same point size can appear noticeably different in size because of the relationship between the font's x-height and the ascenders and descenders (see Figure 7-12). The term *x-height* refers to the height of a font's lowercase x. Because the letter x sits squarely on the baseline with no ascenders or descenders, it provides a point of reference for the height measurement for a font. Table 7-4 lists shortcut keys for changing font sizes.

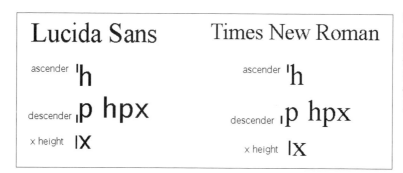

Figure 7-12: A font's point size is measured from the top of the highest ascender to the bottom of the lowest descender.

To change a font size:

1. Select the text that you want to change to a different font size, or, before you begin typing, position the insertion point where you want the new font size to begin.

2. Do one of the following:

   • Click the down arrow to the right of the Font size list box on the Formatting toolbar, and select the font size you want.

   • Press Ctrl+Shift+P, and enter the font size you want; or press the down-arrow key to display the list of font sizes. Select the font size from the list by using the up- or down-arrow keys, and press Enter.

   • Press one of the shortcut keys in Table 7-4.

3. If you didn't select text before choosing your font size, enter the text that you want to appear in the font size you selected. Then choose a different font size to end the task.

Key	Action
Ctrl+Shift+>	Increases the font to the next larger point size available in the Font size list box.
Ctrl+Shift+<	Decreases the font to the next smaller point size available in the Font size list box.
Ctrl+[	Increases the font size by one point.
Ctrl+]	Decreases the font size by one point.

Table 7-4
Shortcut Keys for Changing Font Sizes

Changing Default Character Formatting

When you begin typing in a new document, Word uses the font, font size, and other formats that are preset for Normal style (the default text style). You can change the character formats for Normal style. If you change the default character format, Word uses the new formats in all new documents that you create using the current document's template. For example, you may want to change Word's default font size of 10 points to a 12-point font to make reading the text a little easier.

The default font formats you choose affect most text in the document. To change the text formats for specific elements, such as body text, topic headings, bulleted lists, and headers and footers, you modify the built-in styles. For example, to change the font and size of header text, you must modify the formats of the built-in header style. For more information about modifying styles, see Chapter 11. To change the defaults on character formatting itself:

1. Press Ctrl+D or display the shortcut menu, and then choose Font to display the Font dialog box.

2. Do any of the following:

    • To set a new default font, type or select a font name in the Font box.

    • To set a new default font size, type or select the new size in the Size box.

    • To make any changes to the effects applied to the default text, select the font effect you want in the Effects section.

3. Choose the Default button.

4. Choose the <u>Y</u>es button when Word displays a dialog box asking you to confirm that you want to change the default font for the current template. Word immediately applies the new formats in the current document. This changes the default font for all documents you create using the Normal style template.

Note To change the default formatting quickly, select text that has the formats you want, display the Font dialog box, and choose the <u>D</u>efault button.

Hiding Text in Your Document

Any document text, such as notes, comments, or any kind of information that you don't want displayed or printed, can be formatted as hidden text. Hiding text does not make the text private (anyone using the file in Word can still display the hidden text), so be careful not to hide any skeletons. Adding hidden text does not affect text formatting. Hidden text is displayed with a dotted underline. If you print hidden text, the underline is not printed. To hide text:

1. Select the text that you want to hide, or position the insertion point where you want to enter hidden text.

2. Do one of the following:

   • Press Ctrl+Shift+H.

   • Choose F<u>o</u>rmat⇨<u>F</u>ont, press Ctrl+D, or choose Font from the shortcut menu, and then select H<u>i</u>dden from the Effects group. Then choose OK.

3. If you didn't select any text, enter the text that you want to be in hidden format. To return to regular text, press Ctrl+Shift+H, press Ctrl+spacebar, or display the Font dialog box, and then clear the <u>H</u>idden check box. Then choose OK.

Word also uses the hidden text format to hide entries for tables of contents, index entries, and annotation marks. See Chapter for more information on creating tables of contents and indexes and Chapter 19 for more information on annotations.

Caution You can format any character as hidden text, even a page break or paragraph mark, but doing so affects page numbering. Be sure to display hidden text if you intend to print hidden text or hide hidden text if you don't want hidden text printed. Otherwise, page breaks and page numbering may appear in odd places because no text is visible.

You can toggle hidden text on and off by using the keyboard shortcut Ctrl+Shift+H, but the text must be selected. You see hidden text in normal, outline, page layout, and master document views only if you choose to display hidden text. To see hidden text in any view except Print Preview, click the Show/Hide button on the Standard toolbar or press Ctrl+Shift+*. To specify not to display hidden text when you click the Show/Hide button, choose Tools⇨Options. Then, in the View tab, clear the All check box under Nonprinting characters, and select any other settings you want to display (except the Hidden text check box).

If you want to display hidden text in Print Preview or print hidden text, choose File⇨Print⇨Options to display the Options dialog box. Select the Hidden text check box in the Include with document group.

Using Fonts with Shared Documents

Word supports TrueType font embedding so that you can include TrueType fonts in your document files. This feature lets you share your document files with other users or send a document out to be professionally printed at a service bureau. There are three types of font embedding: *print/preview, editable,* and *installable.* The type of embedding affects the way you can use the font on another system. If the TrueType font you're using supports font embedding and you choose to embed the font in the document, when other users open the document file on their systems, the embedded TrueType fonts will display and print, even if the fonts are not installed on their computers.

Some font vendors don't build the capability of font embedding into their fonts. If an application doesn't support font embedding, Windows uses an internal font mapping system to substitute an available font for the unavailable TrueType font. The following sections explain each type of TrueType font embedding and Windows font substitution. Here's how to accomplish this:

1. Make sure the document in which you want to embed the fonts is the active document.

2. Choose File⇨Save As.

3. Enter the name of the document in the File Name text box. If you need to, change the drive and directory using the Drives and Directories list boxes.

4. Choose the Options button to display the Options dialog box with the Save tab selected.

5. Select Embed TrueType Fonts. If this option is dimmed, you cannot embed the TrueType fonts.

6. Choose OK to close the Options dialog box.

7. Choose OK to save the file with the embedded TrueType file, and close the Save As dialog box.

Note   The way in which fonts are embedded in a document is determined by the font foundry and is not evident until you open the document on a system that does not contain the particular fonts, such as PostScript fonts. Remember, you cannot embed some fonts.

Print/preview font embedding

Using a font with print/preview embedding temporarily installs the embedded fonts when you open the document on a computer not equipped with the embedded fonts. You can then preview the document on the screen and print it with the correct fonts. However, you cannot modify the document. Windows doesn't share these temporary fonts with other documents or applications. Instead, the temporary fonts are deleted when you close the document. Most TrueType font foundries support print/preview font embedding.

Editable font embedding

Editable fonts go beyond print/preview font embedding. They store enough font information in the file so that you can modify your text, save changes to the original filename, and print the document. This gives you more flexibility to start a document on one computer and then complete and print it on another. However, you cannot save the file with a different filename. If you cut or copy text to the Clipboard and paste it into another document, Windows applies one of the fonts installed on the computer—not the embedded font—to the pasted text. Like print/preview embedding, opening the file on a computer that does not have the required fonts causes the embedded fonts to be temporarily installed in the file. When you close the document, the temporary fonts are deleted.

Installable font embedding

Installable fonts offer all the flexibility of editable fonts, but they go one step further. When you open a document with embedded fonts, Word checks to see whether the fonts are installed there. If the fonts cannot be found, Word asks if you want to permanently install the fonts. When you share a document containing installable TrueType fonts, it's as though the user already has the fonts installed. The person can access the font in any other Windows application, add it to his or her documents, and share it with someone else. The font remains installed even after the user closes the shared document.

When you select the option to save a document with installable fonts, the document file increases in size, because the font files are literally embedded in the document. For example, if you create a document by using the Lucida Fax font from the Microsoft TrueType font pack, the document file increases in size by approximately 50K because of the embedded font file.

Substituting unavailable fonts

Again, a common problem when switching printers or sharing documents with other users is that fonts may be used on one configuration or system that are not on another. If the fonts used to format a document are not available, Word tries to substitute a similar available font to display and print the document. For example, if you format text with the Helvetica font available on a PostScript printer and then switch to a LaserJet printer, Word substitutes the Arial font. The substituted font is not actually applied to the text. If you select text that is formatted with the unavailable font, the name of that font is displayed in the Font box on the Formatting toolbar and in the Font dialog box. However, the font is not included in the list of available fonts. You can apply the font by entering the font name in the Font box. The original font will be used whenever you print the document from a system on which that font is available.

Word tries to match missing fonts with similar fonts, but Word's choice may not be your choice. Not only can you view the names of the fonts that are missing from a document and the fonts that Word is using as substitutes, you can also specify which fonts Word should use as substitutions. Word also lets you permanently change the font formatting to use the substituted fonts. If no font substitution is necessary, Word displays the message "No font substitution is necessary." All fonts used in this document are available. Choose the OK button to continue. To substitute unavailable fonts:

1. Open the document containing fonts that you need to substitute.

2. Choose Tools⇨Options. The Options dialog box appears.

3. Select the Compatibility tab.

4. Choose the Font Substitution button. Word displays the Font Substitution dialog box (see Figure 7-13).

5. Select the missing font in the Missing document font box.

6. Select the font that you want to substitute for the missing font in the Substituted font list box.

7. To replace the missing fonts with substituted fonts, choose the Convert Permanently button, and choose OK when Word asks you whether you want to permanently convert all of the missing fonts to their current substitutes.

8. Choose OK to close the Font Substitution dialog box.

9. Choose OK to close the Options dialog box.

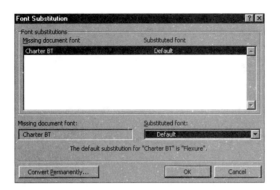

Figure 7-13: The Font Substitution dialog box.

Managing Fonts in Windows 95

The two scalable font formats that dominate in Windows are TrueType and Adobe PostScript Type 1 fonts. You can use both scalable font formats simultaneously in Windows; even your Word documents can use any mixture of the two font formats. PostScript fonts have long been the standard in the professional desktop publishing industry and offer a richer library of available fonts. PostScript fonts are a good choice if you plan to send documents to service bureaus to create higher resolution output than the 300 to 600 dpi of laser printers. The number of TrueType fonts available, however, is more than enough for most Word users, and the number of available TrueType font designs continues to grow.

Word takes advantage of a new Windows 95 feature called *font smoothing*. The font smoothing feature improves the readability of fonts on your screen. It reduces the jagged effect that fonts get on the low resolutions of PC monitors. Font smoothing involves the addition of gray pixels between a font's pixels to make the font appear less jagged.

You install and manage TrueType fonts by using the Fonts Control Panel in Windows 95. The Fonts Control Panel makes TrueType fonts available to Word and any other Windows applications. To install and work with Adobe PostScript Type 1 fonts, you need to use the Adobe Type Manager (ATM). TrueType and PostScript fonts are device-independent, meaning that they can be printed to any printer supported by Windows.

Caution   Make sure that you use ATM Version 3.0 or later with Windows 95.

Fonts in Windows 95 are stored in the Fonts subfolder in the Windows folder. You can access the Font Control Panel (Figure 7-14) by double-clicking the My Computer icon on the Desktop and double-clicking the Control Panel and Fonts folders. The icons with the double *T*s indicate the font is a TrueType font.

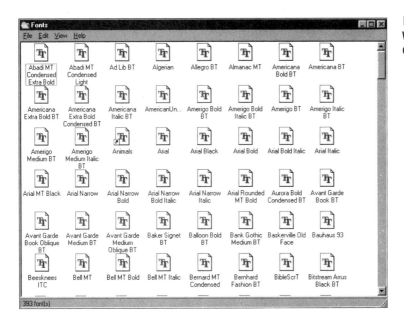

Figure 7-14: The Windows 95 Fonts Control Panel.

To add TrueType fonts by using the Font Control Panel, drag the font icons from the floppy drive window to the Windows 95 Fonts folder. You can also install a new font by choosing File⇨Install New Font in the Font Control Panel. Deleting fonts is just as easy. To delete a font, simply select the font and press Delete or choose File⇨Delete.

Double-click any font icon to display a window with sample text and other information about the font (see Figure 7-15). The typeface name, file size, version, and vendor appear at the top of the window area followed by the alphanumeric characters of the font. The remaining part of the window displays the font in several sizes. You can also change how fonts are listed in the Fonts Control Panel by choosing one of the options listed in Table 7-5 from the View menu.

Tip   Choose View⇨Toolbars to display a toolbar that lets you use a button for the Large Icons, List, List Fonts By Similarity, and Details views.

Figure 7-15: A font sample.

Table 7-5
The View Options in the Fonts Control Panel

Menu Item	How It Displays Font Files
<u>L</u>arge Icons	Displays the default of large icons for each font on your system.
<u>L</u>ist	Lists font files using small icons and as an alphabetical listing. This is the best way if you're using a lot of fonts.
List Fonts By <u>S</u>imilarity	Organizes fonts in the list according to their similarity. All the fonts in the family are listed together, as well as any other fonts that are similar.
Details	Displays the list of fonts by font name, filename, file size, and last date modified.
Hide Variations	Displays only font families rather than all the members of the font family.

Summary

Character formatting is the basic form of formatting in Word. Character formatting includes such essentials as boldfacing, italicizing, and underlining; but it also includes working with different fonts. Word lets you format your text by using the handy Formatting toolbar, the Font dialog box, or shortcut keys. In this chapter, you learned about formatting characters and working with fonts, including how to:

✦ Use the Formatting toolbar and Font dialog box to perform a variety of character formatting tasks. To display the Font dialog box, press Ctrl+D, or choose F<u>o</u>rmat⇨<u>F</u>ont.

✦ Display character formatting by pressing Shift+F1 and clicking the text you want to check. You can also simply move the insertion point to the text and read the Formatting toolbar.

✦ Use the highlighter pen to highlight text by clicking the Highlight button and selecting text.

✦ Change fonts and font sizes by using the Formatting toolbar's Fonts and Font Size drop-down lists or by using the Fonts dialog box. You can also press Ctrl+Shift+[to increase the font size by one point, and press Ctrl+Shift+] to decrease the font size by one point.

✦ Change the default character formatting from the Font dialog box by choosing your setting and then choosing the <u>D</u>efault button.

Where to go next...

✦ If you want to find out more about character formatting by using Word's character styles, check out Chapter 11.

✦ If you want to find out how to enter different character symbols, see Chapter 2.

✦ ✦ ✦

Paragraph Formatting

Paragraphs, the basic building blocks of any document, have special meanings in Word. They can be any amount of text and graphics, or any other item followed by a paragraph mark. Paragraph marks store the formatting applied to each paragraph. In this chapter, you learn the fundamentals of paragraph formatting in Word.

Applying Paragraph Formatting

You insert a paragraph mark each time you press Enter. If you don't see paragraph marks on your screen, click the Show/Hide button on the Standard toolbar, or press Ctrl+Shift+* to display them.

Word applies formats only to the current paragraph or paragraphs you select. You can format paragraphs in two ways: by applying a style or using direct formatting. A style is a collection of character and paragraph formatting commands saved as an item, which you can easily apply by selecting the style name from a list. Direct formatting applies a format, one at a time. You can apply them by using buttons on the Formatting toolbar (Figure 8-1) or settings in the Paragraph dialog box (Figure 8-2) or by pressing shortcut keys.

Figure 8-1: The Formatting toolbar.

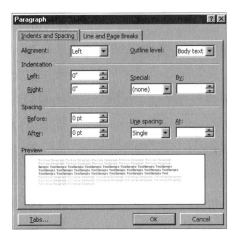

Figure 8-2: The Paragraph dialog box.

Changing the formatting of a paragraph lets you change the alignment and spacing of the lines of your paragraph. To change the formatting, move the insertion point anywhere in the paragraph, or select the paragraphs that you want to change, and apply the formats you want. When you press Enter to start a new paragraph, Word carries over the preceding paragraph's formatting. You can format a paragraph before you begin typing or after you finish typing.

Checking a paragraph's formatting

The formats applied to the current paragraph appear in the settings on the Formatting toolbar, the horizontal Ruler, and in the Paragraph dialog box. If you select several paragraphs that have different formats, dialog box settings may appear blank or dimmed. Word can't indicate different formats at the same time. On the Ruler, dimmed indent and tab markers show the settings for the first paragraph in the selection.

Word lets you display information about any paragraph formats that are applied to a paragraph. To check the formatting of a paragraph, choose Help➪What's This. When the pointer becomes a question mark, click the text you want to check. Word displays information about the paragraph formatting and font formatting, as shown in Figure 8-3. This method works for only one paragraph at a time.

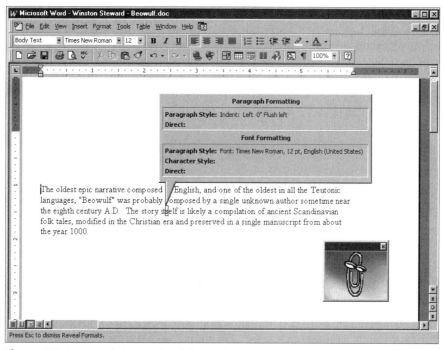

Figure 8-3: Paragraph formatting information.

Duplicating paragraph formats

The easiest way to duplicate paragraph formatting is to carry the formatting forward by pressing Enter. This way, the current paragraph ends and a new one begins using the same formatting as the preceding paragraph. You can also duplicate formatting by using the Format Painter, which duplicates all the formatting of the selected text. Other ways to duplicate formatting are to use Edit⇨Repeat, press Ctrl+Y, or press F4. Remember that these commands duplicate only the last action.

Because formats are stored in the paragraph mark, you can copy just the mark. To do so, select the paragraph mark of the paragraph that you want to change, and then paste the copied paragraph mark. This applies the paragraph formats to the paragraph. To duplicate paragraph formatting:

1. Select the paragraph containing the formats that you want to copy.

2. Do one of the following:

- Click the Format Painter button on the Standard toolbar. The pointer changes to a combination insertion point and paintbrush. Drag the format pointer over a paragraph mark to copy a single paragraph's format or drag the pointer across the paragraphs with the formatting you want to copy, and then release the mouse button.

- Press Ctrl+Shift+C to copy the formatting. Select the text with the format you want to change, and press Ctrl+Shift+V.

Note You can duplicate paragraph formatting by using styles. Chapter 11 explains creating and using styles.

Removing paragraph formats

You can use a shortcut to remove paragraph formatting. Press Ctrl+Q to remove any direct paragraph formatting, leaving only the paragraph style formatting. This doesn't change any direct character formatting applied to the paragraph's text. Pressing Ctrl+Shift+N applies the default Normal style formatting to the paragraph.

Most paragraph formatting commands and buttons act as toggle switches that let you turn the formatting on or off. For example, with the insertion point in a paragraph, you can convert it to a bulleted item by clicking the Bullets button on the Formatting toolbar. With the insertion point in the same paragraph, clicking the Bullets button again removes the bullet format of the paragraph.

If you cut and paste text from a Word document or from another applications and have difficulty reformatting the paragraph, cut the text and select Edit➪Paste Special. Then choose Unformatted Text. All the formatting commands are removed.

Using line breaks

Word lets you create multiple lines that use one paragraph format. Instead of pressing Enter to go to the next line, press Shift+Enter. Word inserts a *line break* but not a paragraph mark. This feature is also referred to as a *soft return*. This allows you to break lines but keep them in the same paragraph. After you finish entering line breaks, press Enter in the usual way to end that paragraph and begin the following one.

Aligning Paragraphs

Word lets you align paragraphs four ways within your document's margin: left-aligned, right-aligned, center-aligned, and justified. By default, Word aligns text flush with the left margin, leaving a ragged right edge (left-aligned). Figure 8-4 shows the four different paragraph alignments. Word lets you align paragraphs by using the Paragraph dialog box, clicking the align buttons on the Formatting toolbar, or using shortcut keys. To align paragraphs:

1. Position the insertion point in a paragraph, or select the paragraphs you want to align.

2. Do one of the following:

   • Click the alignment button on the Formatting toolbar for the justification you want (see Table 8-1).

   • Press one of the shortcut keys in Table 8-1.

   • Choose Format⇨Paragraph, or choose Paragraph from the shortcut menu (Shift + F10) to display the Paragraph dialog box. Choose the alignment option from the Alignment list in the Indents and Spacing tab, and choose OK.

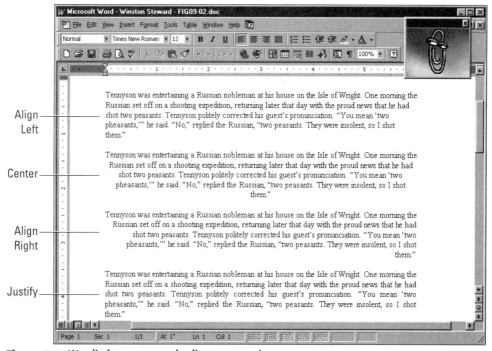

Figure 8-4: Word's four paragraph alignment options.

Note Before centering or aligning a paragraph relative to the left and right margins, make sure that the paragraph is not indented. Paragraphs are aligned to the margins if no indentations are set for them. If paragraphs are indented, they align to the indentation. Working with indents is explained later in this chapter.

Table 8-1
Paragraph Alignment Buttons and Shortcut Keys

Alignment Type	Button	Shortcut Keys	Description
Align Left		Ctrl+L	Text aligns with the left margin. The right margin is ragged. This is the default setting.
Center		Ctrl+E	Text is centered between margins.
Align Right		Ctrl+R	Text aligns with the right margin. The left margin is ragged.
Justifiy		Ctrl+J	Text aligns with both the left and right margins by adding extra spaces between words.

Adjusting Line and Paragraph Spacing

You can adjust the spacing between lines in a paragraph as well as spacing between paragraphs. Adjusting spacing between paragraphs lets you control the white space around paragraphs that contain oversized graphics or fonts. Using paragraph spacing lets you manage the layout of your documents more precisely than pressing Enter to create paragraph marks for spacing.

Spacing between lines in a document is called *leading* (pronounced "ledding"). Word lets you control the leading to improve the readability of the text in paragraphs. For example, if your text is in long lines, you may need more spacing so that the eye doesn't lose its place when moving from the right margin back to the left. Or, if you're using a font style with small letters, your text may require less spacing between the lines than lines containing larger fonts.

Adjusting paragraph spacing

Instead of pressing Enter or adding blank lines before or after a paragraph, use the Format⇨Paragraph command. Using the Paragraph dialog box lets you make precise adjustments to paragraph spacing, as well as keep any spacing changes with a paragraph if you copy, move, or delete the paragraph. To adjust paragraph spacing:

1. Position the insertion point in a paragraph, or select the paragraphs you want to affect.

2. Choose Format⇨Paragraph, or choose Paragraph from the shortcut menu. Select the Indents and Spacing tab if it isn't already selected.

3. Do one of the following:

- To add line spacing before the selected text, type a number in the Spacing Before box, or click the up or down arrow, which increases or decreases the spacing amount in half-line increments. The Preview section of the Paragraph dialog box shows the effect of your selected spacing.

- To add line spacing after the selected text, type a number in the Spacing After box, or click the up or down arrow, which increases or decreases the spacing amount in half-line increments. You can use measurements other than points to specify spacing. To add a quarter-inch of spacing, type **.25** in the Before or After box. To add spacing of two centimeters, type **2 cm**, and to add spacing of one pica, type **1 pi**. The Preview section of the Paragraph dialog box shows the effect of your selected spacing.

4. Choose OK.

Note   If a paragraph has spacing before it and it falls at the top of a page, Word ignores the spacing so that the top margins of your document always remain even. However, if the paragraph is the first paragraph in a document or a formatted section, Word always observes this spacing. Word also observes the spacing before a paragraph that follows a hard page break. Chapter 9 explains working with sections and hard page breaks.

Adjusting line spacing

Word's line spacing feature begins with automatic spacing and enables you to increase spacing, reduce spacing, permit extra spacing for a large character or superscript on the line, or control the spacing exactly. Spacing is measured by lines. Normal text has single spacing of one line, but you can choose from several line options or specify line spacing based on points. Table 8-2 describes Word's line-spacing options. You can apply line spacing by using the Paragraph dialog box or shortcut keys. The Paragraph dialog box, (refer to Figure 8-2) offers the most options for line spacing. To adjust spacing between lines:

1. Position the insertion point in a paragraph, or select the paragraphs you want to affect.

2. Do one of the following:

- Choose Format⇨Paragraph, or choose Paragraph from the shortcut menu. The Paragraph dialog box appears (refer to Figure 8-2). Select the Indents and Spacing tab, if it isn't already selected. Choose in the Line Spacing box one of the options listed in Table 8-2. To specify your own line spacing, type the spacing amount in the At box; for example, enter **1.25** for an extra quarter line of space between lines, or click the up or down arrow to increase or decrease the amount. Choose OK.

- Press one of the shortcut key combinations in Table 8-3.

Table 8-2
Line Spacing Options

Option	Spacing
Single	Single-line spacing. (Line height automatically adjusts to accommodate the size of the font and any graphics or formulas that have been inserted into a line.)
1.5 Lines	Line-and-one-half spacing (extra half line of space between lines).
Double	Double-spacing (extra full line of space between lines).
At Least	At least the amount of spacing you specify in the At box. (Word adds extra spacing, if necessary, for tall characters, big graphics, or superscript/subscript text.)
Exactly	The exact amount of spacing you specify in the At box. All lines are exactly the same height, regardless of the size of the characters in the line. Word does not add extra spacing. Some text may be cut off if enough space is not available.
Multiple	Multiples of single-line spacing, such as triple (3) or quadruple (4).

Table 8-3
Line Spacing Options Shortcut Keys

Press	To Do This
Ctrl+I	Single-spacing
Ctrl+5	1.5 line spacing
Ctrl+2	Double-spacing
Ctrl+0 (zero)	Add or remove 12 points of space before a paragraph

Setting Tabs

You can set your own tab stops or use the default left-aligned tab stops that occur every 1/2-inch. Setting the tab stops includes selecting the type of tab (left, centered, right, decimal, or bar) and specifying the location of the tab stop. When you set a custom tab, all preset tabs to the left of the custom tab are cleared. There's an advantage to using tabs rather than spacing; after the tabs are in your document, you can move or change the tab stops, and then the selected text moves or realigns with the stops. Keep in mind that tabs belong to paragraphs. If you set tab stops as you type text and press Enter, the tab settings carry forward to the next paragraph.

You can set tabs by using the Ruler or the Tabs dialog box. You can display the Tabs dialog box by choosing Format⇨Tab or the Tabs button in the Paragraph dialog box (Format⇨Paragraph). Table 8-4 describes the tab options available in Word, and Figure 8-5 shows how left-aligned, center-aligned, right-aligned, and decimal tab settings affect a paragraph. Figure 8-6 shows columns that are aligned by using the bar tab.

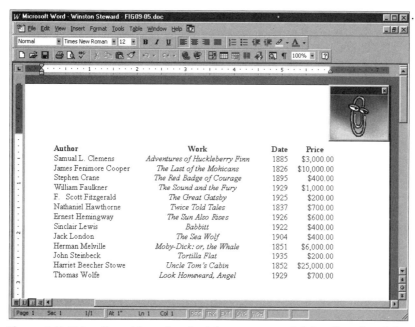

Author	Work	Date	Price
Samuel L. Clemens	Adventures of Huckleberry Finn	1885	$3,000.00
James Fenimore Cooper	The Last of the Mohicans	1826	$10,000.00
Stephen Crane	The Red Badge of Courage	1895	$400.00
William Faulkner	The Sound and the Fury	1929	$1,000.00
F. Scott Fitzgerald	The Great Gatsby	1925	$200.00
Nathaniel Hawthorne	Twice Told Tales	1837	$700.00
Ernest Hemingway	The Sun Also Rises	1926	$600.00
Sinclair Lewis	Babbitt	1922	$400.00
Jack London	The Sea Wolf	1904	$400.00
Herman Melville	Moby-Dick: or, the Whale	1851	$6,000.00
John Steinbeck	Tortilla Flat	1935	$200.00
Harriet Beecher Stowe	Uncle Tom's Cabin	1852	$25,000.00
Thomas Wolfe	Look Homeward, Angel	1929	$700.00

Figure 8-5: Tabs aligned by using the left-, center-, and right-aligned and decimal tab settings.

Work with new lines rather than paragraphs when you want to use tabs to line up short text in columns. That way, you can line up information quickly without having to select paragraphs. Remember, line breaks let you insert a line without creating a new paragraph. Press Shift+Enter to insert a new line. New lines limit the amount of information that Word has to store with the document file because the same formatting is not repeated in multiple paragraph marks. If you add tabs later using new lines, the tab applies to all the lines before the next paragraph mark. If you want to line up large columns of text, use Word's powerful table feature, which is explained in Chapter 12.

Table 8-4
Tab Options

Type of Tab	Ruler Tab Indicator	Action
Left-aligned	∟	Begins tabbed text at tab stop. The default tab setting.
Center-aligned	⊥	Centers text on tab stop.
Right-aligned	⅃	Ends tabbed text at tab stop.
Decimal	⊥·	Centers text over decimal point for list of numbers.
Bar	❘	Runs a vertical line through a selected paragraph at the tab stop.

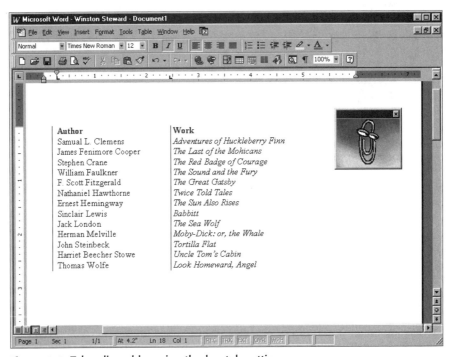

Figure 8-6: Tabs aligned by using the bar tab setting.

Setting tabs by using the Ruler

A convenient way to set tabs is to use the Ruler (see Figure 8-7). If your Ruler is not displayed, choose View⇨Ruler to display it. At the left of the Ruler is the Tab Alignment button, which lets you quickly change tab styles. Using the mouse and the Ruler, you can set, move, and remove the left-aligned, center-aligned, right-aligned, or decimal tabs up to one-sixteenth of an inch in precision. Bar tabs are not available from the Ruler, nor are they reflected on the Ruler. The Ruler displays Word's default tab stops (set every 1/2-inch, unless you change the interval) as tiny vertical lines along the bottom of the Ruler. When you set your own tab stops, all default tab stops to the left are removed from the Ruler. To set tabs by using the Ruler:

1. Position the insertion point in a paragraph, or select the paragraphs you want to affect.

2. Click the Tab Alignment button at the far left of the Ruler until the symbol is selected for the tab style you want to use (see Table 8-4).

3. Position the pointer just below the mark on the Ruler where you want the tab stop to appear. Click the left mouse button to place the tab stop on the Ruler. The tab stop marker appears for the style of tab selected.

4. Do one of the following:

   • Repeat Step 3 to add more tab stops of the same style.

   • Repeat Steps 2 and 3 to add other types of tab stops to the Ruler.

Figure 8-7: The Ruler with tab stops.

Changing or clearing a tab stop by using the Ruler

To change a tab marker on the Ruler, make sure that you position the insertion point in the paragraph, or select the text you want to affect. Then position the mouse pointer on the tab marker, hold down the left mouse button to select the marker, and drag the tab marker to the new position.

To clear a tab stop quickly with the mouse and Ruler, position the insertion point in the paragraph or select the text you want to affect, position the mouse pointer on the tab marker you want to clear, and drag the tab marker off the Ruler and onto the document.

Setting tabs using the Tabs dialog box

Using the Tabs dialog box (see Figure 8-8) to set tabs offers some advantages over using the Ruler and mouse. You can precisely set each tab's position by typing decimal numbers (in inches), and you can add dotted, dashed, or underlined tab leaders. A *tab leader* links related but separate items across a page, such as entrees and prices in a menu or chapters and page numbers in a table of contents (see Figure 8-9). You can also set bar tabs, which you cannot do with the Ruler. To set tabs by using the Tabs dialog box:

1. Position the insertion point in a paragraph, or select the paragraphs you want to affect.

2. Choose Format⇨Tabs. The Tabs dialog box appears.

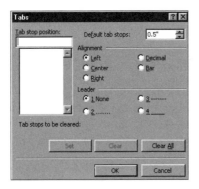

Figure 8-8: The Tabs dialog box.

3. Type the position of the tab stop that you want to set, using decimal numbers, in the Tab stop position box.

4. From the Alignment group, select the tab style you want: Left, Center, Right, Decimal, or Bar.

5. If you want a leader, select the tab leader style you want in the Leader list: 1 None for no leader (the default), 2 for a dotted leader, 3 for a dashed leader, or 4 for an underlined leader.

6. Choose the Set button to set the tab stop. The Tab stop position list box displays your tab stops after you set them.

7. Repeat Steps 3 through 6 to set additional tab stops.

8. Choose OK to close the Tabs dialog box.

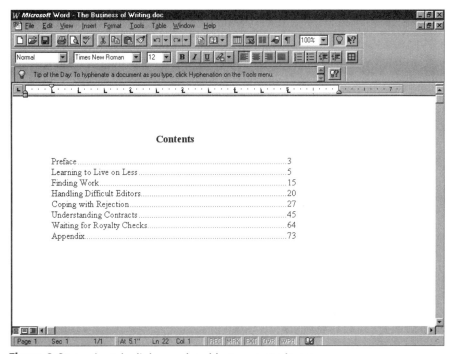

Figure 8-9: Leader tabs link up related but separate items.

Changing and clearing tabs by using the Tabs dialog box

To change existing tab stops from the Tabs dialog box (Format⇨Tabs), select the tab stop you want to change in the Tab stop position list box. Select the new formatting options for the selected tab stop in the Alignment and Leader boxes, and choose the Set button.

The Tabs dialog box lets you clear tab stops individually or as a group. You can clear tabs by using the Tabs dialog box, whether you set the tabs by using this dialog box or the Ruler. To clear tabs:

1. Position the insertion point in a paragraph, or select the paragraphs you want to affect.

2. Choose Format⇨Tabs to display the Tabs dialog box.

3. Do one of the following:

- Choose the Clear Δll button to clear all the tab stop settings.

- Select the tab you want to delete from the Ţab Stop Position list, and choose the Clear button. Repeat this process to clear additional tab stops. As you select tab stops to clear and choose the Clear button, the tab stops that are removed are listed in the Tab stops to be cleared area at the bottom of the Tabs dialog box.

4. Choose OK.

Changing Words default tab stops

By default, Word has preset tabs every 1/2-inch. When you set a custom tab, all preset tabs to the left of the custom tab are cleared. Use the Tabs dialog box to change the default tab stop interval if you routinely use the preset tabs and do not like the default tab setting. Any custom tab stops you may have set for existing paragraphs are not affected. To change the default tab stops, display the Tabs dialog box. In the Deḟault tab stops box, type a new default tab interval, or click the up or down arrow to change the number in the box. Choose OK.

Setting Indents

Indenting lets you set off a paragraph from other text. Figure 8-10 shows paragraphs formatted with different indents. Do not confuse the page margins with paragraph indents. Margins specify the overall width of the text and the area between the text and the edge of the page, whereas changing an indent moves the paragraph's text in or out from the left and right margins. You can indent paragraphs in the following ways:

✦ Indent paragraphs from the left, right, or both margins to set the paragraphs off from other text.

✦ Use negative indents to run text into the left or right margin.

✦ Indent only the first line of a paragraph, which is commonly used as a substitute for pressing Tab at the beginning of each new paragraph.

✦ Create a *hanging indent,* which "hangs" the first line of a paragraph to the left of the rest of the paragraph. Every line is indented except the first line. Hanging indents are often used when creating bulleted and numbered lists.

✦ Create *nested indents,* which are indentations within indentations.

Word provides several ways to create indents. You can indent paragraphs by using the Formatting toolbar, the Ruler, shortcut keys, or the Paragraph dialog box. Indenting by using the Formatting toolbar and shortcut keys depends on tab stop settings. If you haven't changed Word's default 1/2-inch tab stops, then using the Formatting toolbar or shortcut keys lets you create indents at 1/2-inch intervals.

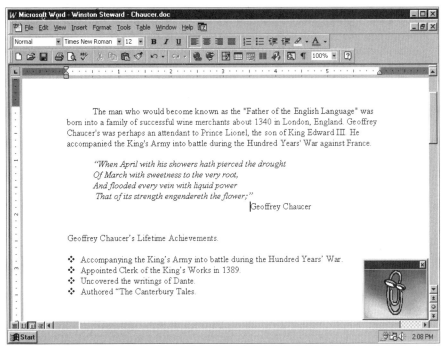

Figure 8-10: Examples of indented paragraphs.

Note Although you can use hanging indents to create a bulleted or numbered list, using Word's bullets and numbering features lets you create these lists automatically, which includes adding the bullets and numbers. Working with bulleted and numbered lists is explained later in this chapter.

Setting indents by using the Formatting toolbar

The Formatting toolbar includes two buttons for indenting paragraphs to the next tab stop: the Decrease Indent and the Increase Indent buttons. Use these buttons to create left indents only. You cannot create first-line or hanging indents. To indent or remove indents from paragraphs by using the Formatting toolbar, position the insertion point in a paragraph or select the paragraphs you want to indent. Click the Increase Indent button to indent to the next tab stop. Click the Decrease Indent button to unindent to the previous tab stop. You can click the Indent button as many times as you want to continue moving the left indentation to the right.

Setting indents by using the Ruler

You can create indents of any kind by using the Ruler. The Ruler contains triangular markers, called *indent markers,* at the left and right margins. Table 8-5 shows and describes each of the indent markers. You can drag them left and right on the Ruler to set indents. The top triangle at the left margin represents the first-line indent. The bottom triangle represents the left indent. Both the top and bottom triangles move independently. You use the square below the bottom triangle to move the first-line and left-paragraph indents at the same time. The triangle at the right margin represents the paragraph's right indent.

Table 8-5
Indent Markers on the Ruler

Drag	*To Set*
▽	First-line indent
⬘	Left indent
▽⬘	First-line and left indents
△	Right indent

To set indentations by using the Ruler:

1. Position the insertion point in a paragraph, or select the paragraphs you want to affect.

2. Do one of the following:

   • To set a first line indent, drag the First Line Indent marker to the position where you want the indentation.

   • To set a left indent, drag the square below the Left Indent marker to the Ruler position where you want the indentation. (Notice that the top triangle moves also.)

   • To set a right indent, drag the Right Indent marker to the position where you want the indentation.

   • To set a hanging indent with the first line at the left margin, drag the Left Indent marker to a new position on the Ruler.

Note When you drag the left or First Line Indent to the left of the left margin, the Ruler automatically scrolls to the left. If you want to scroll into the left margin on the Ruler without moving the indent markers, hold down the Shift key while you click the left scroll arrow on the horizontal scroll bar.

Setting indents by using keyboard shortcuts

You can create indents by using keyboard shortcuts. Keyboard shortcuts rely on existing tab settings to determine the position of indents. To create indents by using keyboard shortcuts, position the insertion point in a paragraph, or select the paragraphs you want to indent. Then press one of the keyboard shortcuts listed in Table 8-6.

	Table 8-6
	Keyboard Shortcuts for Indenting Paragraphs

Keyboard Shortcut	Indention Type
Ctrl+M	Moves the left indent to the next tab stop.
Ctrl+Shift+M	Moves the left indent to the preceding tab stop.
Ctrl+T	Creates a hanging indent.
Ctrl+Shift+T	Moves the left indent to the previous tab stop. The first line remains in its current position.

Setting indents by using the Paragraph dialog box

You can use the Paragraph dialog box (shown earlier in Figure 8-2) to set any type of indent. An advantage of using the Paragraph dialog box is that you can enter precise measurements instead of eyeing text alignments with Ruler measurements. You can create indents in measurements other than decimal inches. To create a six-point left indent, for example, type **6 pt** in the Left indentation box. To create a left indent of two centimeters, type **2 cm**. And to create a left indent of one pica, type **1 pi** (six picas per inch; 12 points per pica). To set indentations by using the Paragraph dialog box:

1. Position the insertion point in a paragraph, or select the paragraphs you want to effect.

2. Choose Format⇨Paragraph, or choose Paragraph from the shortcut menu (Shift+F10). The Paragraph dialog box opens. Select the Indents and Spacing tab, if it isn't already selected.

3. Do one of the following:

   • To create a paragraph indent, type or select a value in the Left or Right Indentation text box. The Preview box lets you see the effect of your choice. The Indentation list in the Paragraph dialog box lists three options: Left, Right, and Special. Table 8-7 describes these indentation options.

- To create a first-line or hanging indent, select First Line or Hanging from the Special list box. Type or select a value in the By text box to indent the first line or create a hanging indent. Type the amount you want the first line of the paragraph to extend to the left of the rest of the paragraph.

4. Choose OK.

Table 8-7 Indention Options	
Option	**Action**
Left	Indents selected text from the left margin. If the amount to indent is positive, the paragraph is indented inside the left margin; if the amount to indent is negative, the paragraph is indented outside the left margin (sometimes called *outdenting*).
Right	Indents selected text from the right margin. If the amount to indent is positive, the paragraph is indented inside the right margin; if the amount to indent is negative, the paragraph is indented outside the right margin.
Special	Indents the first line(s) of selected text from left indent (or left margin, if no indent is made). Click the down arrow to select First Line or Hanging. First Line indents inside the left indent; Hanging Indent indents outside the left indent. The default indent is 1/2-inch. Change the indent by typing a new number or by using the up- or down-arrow key. Hanging indents are frequently used with tabs to create lists.

Bordering and Shading Paragraphs and Pages

A border can be a box surrounding a paragraph on all sides or a line that sets a paragraph off on one or more sides. Shading fills a paragraph (with or without borders) with a background pattern. Boxes and lines can be solid black, and shading can be gray; or, if you have a color monitor, they can be different colors. If you have a color printer, you can also print colored lines, boxes, and shading. Figure 8-11 shows samples of different types of borders and shading applied to paragraphs.

Borders, like all forms of paragraph formatting, belong to the paragraphs where they are applied. They carry forward when you press Enter at the end of a paragraph. If a group of paragraphs is formatted with a box around them and you press Enter at the end of the last paragraph, your new paragraph falls within the same box as the previous paragraph. To create a new paragraph outside the border, move the insertion point outside the border before you press Enter. If you're at the end of a document and have nowhere to go outside the border, create a new paragraph and remove the border.

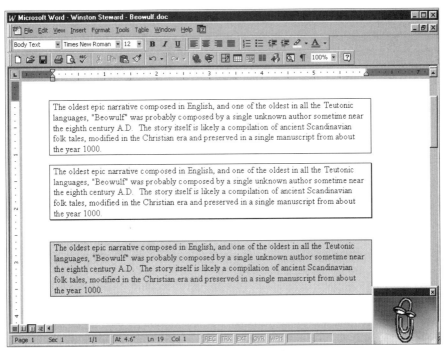

Figure 8-11: Border and shading samples.

The width of a paragraph border (box or line) or shading is determined by the paragraph indent. If no indent exists, the page margins determine the width of a box or line. To place several paragraphs in a single box or have the same background shading, make sure that all the paragraphs have the same indents. If you select and box or shade several paragraphs that have different indents, each paragraph appears in its own separate box or shading (instead of all appearing together). To make paragraphs with different indents appear within a single box or background shade, you must create a table and put each paragraph in a row by itself and then format a box around the table. For information about creating tables and adding borders to a table, see Chapter 12.

Note Sometimes the screen inaccurately shows text extending beyond borders or shading. This situation results from screen fonts and screen resolutions that differ from the printer's fonts and resolution. Your printed text does format within the border or shading, even though it doesn't display correctly.

Borders can also be applied to a page. The same border and shading options for paragraphs can also be applied to an entire page. Tools for creating paragraph borders and page borders are located in the same dialog box.

Adding borders by using the Borders toolbar

Word includes a Tables and Borders toolbar for applying borders and shading. Figure 8-12 shows the Tables and Borders toolbar. Creating tables is covered in Chapter 12 of this book. To add boxes or lines to paragraphs by using the Tables and Borders toolbar:

1. Click the Tables and Borders button on the Formatting toolbar or choose <u>V</u>iew⇨<u>T</u>oolbars and select the Tables and Borders toolbar. You can also right-click a blank portion of any toolbar and select Tables and Borders.

Figure 8-12: The Tables and Borders toolbar.

2. Position the insertion point in a paragraph, or select the paragraphs that you want to enclose. Remember, if you create a box for more than one paragraph, the box encloses the paragraphs as a group (unless they have different indents) with no borders between them.

3. Click the Line style box down arrow, and choose a line style.

4. Choose the border you want to add by clicking one of the buttons in Table 8-8.

Table 8-8
Border Type Buttons in the Borders Toolbar

Button	Action
	Adds a box border.
	Adds a border along the top.
	Adds a border along the bottom.
	Adds a border along the left edge.
	Adds a border along the right edge.
	Adds inside borders.
	Adds a border only on the inside.
	Adds a border vertically inside.
	Adds a border horizontally inside.
	Removes all borders.

Adding borders using the Borders and Shading dialog box

You can also add borders by using the Borders and Shading dialog box (see Figure 8-13). Table 8-9 explains the options in the Border tab. The Borders and Shading dialog box provides additional options that are not available if you use the Borders toolbar. These extra features include specifying colors and changing the distance from a box line to the surrounded text. You can also specify a shadow or 3D border option. Special options for placing a border on an entire page are found here also. To add a border by using the Borders and Shading dialog box:

1. Position the insertion point in a paragraph, or select the paragraphs that you want to enclose. Remember, if you create a box for more than one paragraph, the box encloses the paragraphs as a group (unless they have different indents) with no borders between them.

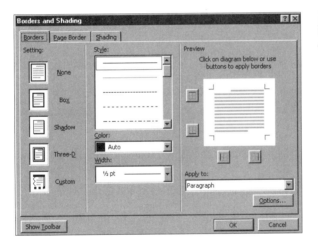

Figure 8-13: The Borders tab in the Borders and Shading dialog box.

2. Choose Format⇨Borders and Shading. The Borders and Shading dialog box appears. Select the Borders tab if it is not already selected. If you plan to apply a border to a page or group of pages (rather than paragraphs), click the Page Border tab in the Borders and Shading dialog box and choose the Apply To group.

3. Do one of the following:

   • To create a line by using the mouse, click the side of the paragraph in the Preview box where you want the line. (If a style has already been selected from the Style group, a line with that style will be inserted.) You can continue inserting lines with this approach.

Then select a line from the Style group to insert lines at all the selected locations. A line with the currently selected style will be inserted.

If multiple paragraphs are selected, you can create a line between them by clicking the horizontal line between paragraphs in the Preview box.

- To create a line, in the Preview box, click the side of the paragraph where you want the line.

4. To set the spacing (other than the default) between a box and the text, specify the distance in the From Text box.

5. To apply color to all your boxes and lines, choose a color from the Color list.

6. Choose OK.

Table 8-9	
The Borders and Page Borders Tab Options	
Option	**Effect**
None	No box. Use this option to remove an existing box. This option is often used with the Shading options to create a shaded box with no border.
Box	A box with identical lines on all four sides.
Shadow	A box with a drop shadow on the bottom-right corner.
3-D	Creates a border with a 3-D effect.
Custom	Selected when any effect above is combined with non-boxed border options.
Apply to:	The specified effect can be applied to the Whole Document, This Section, This Section-First Page Only, or This Section-All Except First Page. By choosing the Page Border tab, you can apply the border to the entire document or section
None	No line. Use this option to remove individual lines.
Style	A line or box in the selected line style. Options listed show exact point size and a sample display.
Width	Allows selection of various line widths, ranging from $1/4$ pts. to 6 pts.
Color	A line or box in the selected color. Sixteen colors and gray shades are available. If you select the Auto option, the default color for text is used. This is usually black, but you can change it in the Windows Control Panel.

Fitting a border within margins

If you're creating a border for unindented paragraphs, the border extends outside the margins by the amount of space used to create the line. In most cases, you'll want the borders to fall within or exactly at the margins. To make a border fit within the margins, you must indent the paragraph on both the left and right sides by the width of the border. Although you can use the Ruler, using the Paragraph Borders and Shading dialog box lets you be more precise. To make borders fall on the margins by using the Paragraph Borders and Shading dialog box:

1. Position the insertion point in a paragraph, or select the paragraphs you want to effect.

2. Choose Format⇨Borders and Shading.

3. On the Borders tab, note the width of the border line in the Width control.

4. Click the Options button. The Borders and Shading Options dialog box appears. Note the spacing specified in the From text boxes.

5. Click OK or Cancel twice to close both dialog boxes.

6. Choose Format⇨Paragraph. Then choose the Indents and Spacing tab if it isn't already selected.

7. In the Left and Right boxes in the Indentation group, type the number of points equal to the combined width of the border and the spacing specified in the From Text box. For example, if your border is three points thick and your From Text entry is one point, enter four points in the Left and Right boxes.

8. Choose OK.

Removing or changing borders

You can remove borders all at once or line by line. You can remove or change a border by using the Borders toolbar or the Borders and Shading dialog box. To remove or change borders by using the Borders toolbar:

1. Position the insertion point in a paragraph, or select the paragraphs you want to affect.

2. Display the Tables and Borders toolbar by clicking the Borders button on the Formatting toolbar.

3. Do one of the following:

   • Click the Outside Borders button and choose no borders.

   • Choose a new line style.

   • Click the buttons for the boxes or borders you want to add.

To remove or change borders by using the Borders and Shading dialog box:

1. Position the insertion point in a paragraph, or select the paragraphs you want to affect.

2. Choose Format⇨Borders and Shading, and select the Borders tab, if it isn't already selected. Select the Page Border tab if you are removing borders applied to an entire page or group of pages.

   • To remove a box border, select the None option in the Presets group.

   • To remove individual border lines, select Setting⇨None.

   • To change a line, select the line you want from the Style scroll box.

3. Choose OK.

Adding shading

Word's shading comes in various percentages of black (grays) and different colors, as well as patterns. For each shade or pattern, you can select a foreground or background color. Colors are converted to shades of gray or patterns on a black-and-white printer. You can use shading with borders so that a paragraph is surrounded by a line and filled with shading, or you can use shading alone so that no border goes around the shaded paragraph.

Working with shading requires playing with different configurations to see what is most readable. As a rule, the smaller the font size, the lighter you make the paragraph shading. Applying bold to text may also help. To change the color of the text with a background shading, use the Font dialog box (Format⇨Font) to change the text color. See Chapter 7 for information on how to work with the Font dialog box.

Word lets you apply shading by using the Shading tab on the Borders and Shading dialog box (see Figure 8-14) or by using the Borders toolbar. To shade paragraphs by using the Borders toolbar, position the insertion point in a paragraph or select the paragraphs you want to affect. Click the Borders button on the Formatting toolbar to display the Borders toolbar. Then, from the Shading box, choose the shading or pattern you want. Table 8-10 describes each of the Shading options in the Shading tab of the Borders and Shading dialog box.

To shade paragraphs by using the Borders and Shading dialog box:

1. Position the insertion point in a paragraph, or select the paragraphs you want to affect.

2. Choose Format⇨Borders and Shading.

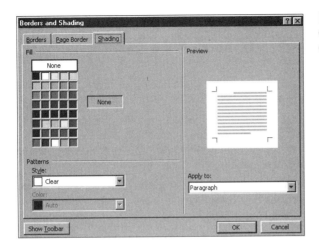

Figure 8-14: The Shading tab on the Borders and Shading dialog box.

3. Select the Shading tab.

4. Select the shading pattern you want. Style options include Clear (uses the back-ground color), Solid (uses the foreground color), percentages, and striped and checkered patterns such as Dk Horizontal (for dark horizontal stripes) and Lt Grid (for a grid made of light cross-hatching). You can also apply light and dark trellises.

5. Select a color from the Color list to color a percentage pattern or a pattern background. The result of your selection then appears in the Preview box.

6. Choose OK.

Removing shading

You can remove shading by using the Borders and Shading dialog box or the Borders toolbar. To remove shading:

1. Select the paragraph or paragraphs from which you want to remove shading.

2. Do one of the following:

   • Choose Format⇨Borders and Shading, and choose the Shading tab. Choose None from the Fill group, and choose OK.

   • Click arrow next to the Paint Bucket on the Tables and Borders toolbar to display fill color options. Choose None from the menu.

	Table 8-10
	Shading Options in the Shading Tab

Shading Option	Action
Apply to:	Enables shading by using the custom shading options.
Style	Shades in the selected custom darkness or pattern. Options include increasing degrees of shading and various patterns. Clear applies the selected background color; Solid (100%) applies the selected foreground color.
Color	Specifies the foreground color for the selected shading pattern. Auto selects the best color, which is usually black. Select from 40 colors, including black and white.
Fill palette	Specifies the background color for the selected shading pattern. Auto selects the best color, which is usually white. Select from 40 colors, including black and white. For no shading in the selected text, choose None.

Creating Bulleted or Numbered Lists

Bulleted lists help distinguish a series of important items or points from the rest of the text in a document. Numbered lists are often used for step-by-step instructions. Word provides flexible, easy-to-use methods for creating bulleted or numbered lists with a variety of bullets or numbering formats. You can type the text for the bulleted or numbered list and then apply the list formatting to the text, or you can place the insertion point in a blank line, apply the bulleted or numbered list format to that line, and type the list. Either way, after you select a bulleted or numbered list format, Word sets a 1/2-inch hanging indent and adds the bullet or number in front of each paragraph, in the selected text, or in each new paragraph you type.

You can add another bulleted or numbered item anywhere in a list by placing the insertion point where you want to add the new item and then pressing Enter to begin a new paragraph. Word automatically adds a bullet or number to the beginning of the new paragraph and formats the paragraph with a hanging indent to match the other paragraphs in the list.

Note   You can create a numbered or bulleted list automatically as you type. At the beginning of a new paragraph, type a number or an asterisk followed by a space or tab. When you press Enter to add the next list item, Word automatically inserts the next number or bullet. To finish the list, press Enter followed by Backspace.

Creating bulleted lists

Word offers seven standard bullet shapes: round, square, diamond, arrow, 3-D box, cloverleaf, and checkmark. If you want to use a heart, pointing hand, or some other symbol as your bullet, you can select the bullet from any of your installed fonts. You can create a bulleted list by using the Bullets and Numbering dialog box (see Figure 8-15) or by using the Formatting toolbar.

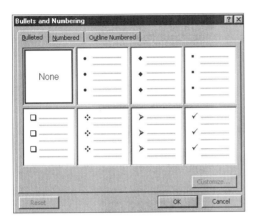

Figure 8-15: The Bulleted tab in the Bullets and Numbering dialog box.

With the Formatting toolbar, you can easily create a bulleted list by clicking the Bulleted List button. Word uses the bulleted list formatting options you selected in the Bullets and Numbering dialog box. By default, Word uses a round bullet and a 1/4-inch hanging indent to format lists with the Bulleted List button.

When you work with a bulleted list, menu items are added to the shortcut menu (see Figure 8-16). These items let you increase or decrease the list's indent amount and open the Bullets and Numbering dialog box.

Figure 8-16: The shortcut menu changes when the insertion point is in a bulleted list.

To create a bulleted list:

1. Type the list at the left margin without using the Tab key to indent the text, and select it, or place the insertion point on a blank line.

2. Do one of the following:

   • Choose Format⇨Bullets and Numbering, or choose Bullets and Numbering from the shortcut menu. Choose the Bulleted tab if it is not already selected. Select the bulleted list format you want from the predefined choices. The choices include a round, square, or diamond bullet; a 3-D box; a two-tone arrow; a cloverleaf pattern; and a check. If you prefer a bulleted list with no hanging indent, select Customize, and in the Text position area, change the Indent at amount to zero.

   • Choose the Bulleted List button from the toolbar.

3. Press Enter to add a bulleted, blank line to the end of the bulleted list.

4. Click the Bullets button on the Formatting toolbar.

Tip   You can quickly convert a bulleted list to a numbered list by selecting the bulleted list and then clicking the Numbering button on the Formatting toolbar.

Customizing a bulleted list

To customize an existing bulleted list or to make your own specifications for the formatting of a new bulleted list, use the Customize button from the Bullets and Numbering dialog box. The Customize Bulleted List dialog box opens (see Figure 8-17). Clicking Font lets you choose a character from any of your installed fonts to use as a bullet and specify the bullet's point size, color, and Character Spacing options. Beneath Font is the Animation tab, which allows you to add an animation effect to your bullet. Clicking Bullet lets you select a different symbol from the current Font. From here, you can also specify the size of the hanging indent, and how much space appears between the bullet character and the text in the bulleted item. You can customize a bulleted list format only by using menu commands; there is no toolbar shortcut. If your custom bulleted list format is the most recently specified format, the Bulleted List button will apply your custom format.

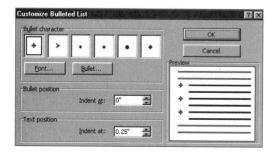

Figure 8-17: The Customize Bulleted List dialog box.

If you customize or reformat an existing bulleted list that contains subordinate (unbulleted) paragraphs, the subordinate paragraphs have bullets added to them. To create a custom bulleted list:

1. Select the bulleted list with the format you want to customize.

2. Choose Format⇨Bullets and Numbering, or choose Bullets and Numbering from the shortcut menu.

3. Choose the Bulleted tab to display the bulleted list options, if that tab is not already up front.

4. Choose the Customize button. The Customize Bulleted List dialog box appears (refer to Figure 8-17).

5. Select the bullet character you want to use by clicking it or using the arrow keys. Using the bullet button to select a custom bullet character is explained later in this chapter.

6. Set any of the controls listed in Table 8-11.

7. Choose OK. The Customize Bulleted List dialog box closes, and the Bullets and Numbering dialog box appears.

8. Choose OK. The Bullets and Numbering dialog box closes, and the new bullet format is applied to the bulleted list.

Table 8-11
Custom Bulleted List Option

Option	Action
Bullet character	Allows you to choose a bullet type from the preset bullet list.
Font button	Opens the standard Font dialog box, allowing you to edit a bullet selection as you would any Windows font.
Bullet button	Allows the selection of a bullet from any character found in the current font.
Bullet position: Indent at	Sets the size of the hanging indent.
Text position: Indent at	Sets the distance between the bullet and the text in the bulleted paragraph.

Selecting a custom bullet character

Word allows you to select any character from any of your installed fonts to use as the bullet character in a bulleted list. For example, you can choose symbols from the Symbol or Wingdings fonts that come with Windows. To select a custom bullet character:

1. Open the Bullets and Numbering dialog box. Select the Bulleted tab, if it isn't already selected.

2. Choose the Customize button. The Customize Bulleted List dialog box opens.

3. Choose the Bullet button. The Symbol dialog box opens.

4. Use the Font list box to select the font displayed in the Symbol dialog box.

5. Select the bullet character you want from the Symbol dialog box by clicking the character or using the arrow keys.

6. Choose OK. The Symbol dialog box closes, and the bullet character you selected appears in the Bullet Character group in the Customize Bulleted List dialog box.

7. Choose OK to close the Customize Bulleted List dialog box.

Creating numbered lists

Numbered lists are created in a similar manner as bulleted lists except that they are numbered sequentially rather than bulleted. Each paragraph you add to a numbered list is numbered sequentially after the number of the preceding paragraph. If you add a paragraph in the middle of a numbered list or rearrange the order of paragraphs in a numbered list, Word automatically renumbers all the paragraphs in the list so that they retain their sequence. The Numbered tab in the Bullets and Numbering dialog box (see Figure 8-18) offers seven standard numbering formats and enables you to customize them. You can create a numbered list in two ways: by using the Bullets and Numbering dialog box or by using the Numbering button on the Formatting toolbar. To create numbered lists:

1. Type your list, and then select it.

Figure 8-18: The Numbered tab in the Bullets and Numbering dialog box.

2. Do one of the following:

- Choose Format⇨Bullets and Numbering, or choose Bullets and Numbering from the shortcut menu. Select the Numbered tab if it isn't already. Select the numbering style you want from the predefined choices. Your choices include Arabic numbers, Roman numerals, and letters, with either periods, parentheses, or double parentheses to separate the numbers from the list text. If you prefer a numbered list with no hanging indent, click the Customize button and decrease the Indent At amount to zero.

- Choose the Numbered List button from the toolbar; each new paragraph is formatted as part of the numbered list.

3. Press Enter to add a numbered, blank line to the end of the numbered list.

4. Click the Numbering button on the Formatting toolbar.

Tip   You can quickly convert a numbered list to a bulleted list by selecting the numbered list and then clicking the Bullets button on the Formatting toolbar.

Customizing numbered lists

You can customize an existing numbered list or make your own specifications for the number format by using the Customize button in the Bullets and Numbering dialog box. The Customize button in the Numbered tab displays the Customize Numbered List dialog box (see Figure 8-19). Table 8-12 explains the Numbered List options in the Customize Numbered List dialog box.

If you customize or reformat an existing numbered list that contains unnumbered paragraphs, the subordinate paragraphs will have numbers added to them. To create a custom numbered list:

1. Select the numbered list whose format you want to customize.

2. Choose Format⇨Bullets and Numbering. Select the Numbered tab if it isn't already selected.

3. Choose the Customize button. The Customize Numbered List dialog box appears.

4. Choose any combination of the numbered list options in Table 8-12.

5. Choose OK in the Customize Numbered List dialog box.

6. Choose OK in the Bullets and Numbering dialog box.

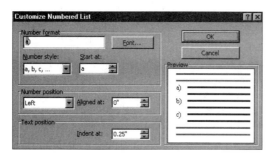

Figure 8-19: The Customize Numbered List dialog box.

Table 8-12
Numbered List Options

Option	Action
Number format text box	Types the characters, if any, that you want to come before each number. If you want each number enclosed in parentheses, for example, type ([the opening parenthesis] here.
Number style	Specifies the numbering style you want. Available choices include Arabic numerals, uppercase and lowercase Roman numerals, uppercase and lowercase alphabet letters, and word series (1st, One, and First). You can also choose no numbers at all.
Font button	Specifies the special font or font attributes (such as bold, italic, and underline), and lets you set the point size for the numbers. A standard Font dialog box appears.
Start at	Indicates the starting number for your list. If you're doing a series of lists, the starting number may be something other than 1.
Number position list box	Chooses the alignment of the number within the space used for the indent. Word offers you the choice of left- right- or center-justification.
Aligned at	Sets the amount of space between the number and the text in the numbered paragraph.
Indent at	Sets the size of the hanging indent.

Adding unbulleted or unnumbered paragraphs to a list

Sometimes the topic of a bulleted list or numbered item cannot be conveniently discussed in a single paragraph. If you require more than one paragraph to describe a single topic in a bulleted list, you want only the first paragraph for that topic to have a bullet. The remaining subordinate paragraphs for that topic do not need bullets, although they do need the same hanging indent as the bulleted paragraphs in the list. You can change a bulleted or numbered paragraph to a subordinate paragraph by using the shortcut menu or the Formatting toolbar. To change a bulleted or numbered list item to a subordinate paragraph:

1. Position the insertion point in a bulleted or numbered item, or select bulleted or numbered list items from which you want to remove the bullets or numbers.

2. Choose the Bullets or Numbering button on the Formatting toolbar.

Ending a bulleted or numbered list

Like other paragraph formatting, the bulleted or numbered list format carries forward each time you press Enter to begin a new paragraph. If you create a bulleted list by pressing Enter, you'll need to end the bullet or numbered list formatting. You can end a bulleted or numbered list by using the Bulleted List buttons in the Formatting toolbar. To end a bulleted or numbered list:

1. Select the list from which you want to remove bullets or numbering.

2. Click the Bullets or Numbering button.

Creating outline numbered lists

Outline numbered lists are similar to numbered and bulleted lists, but the number or bullet of each paragraph in the multilevel list changes according to its indention level. Outline numbered lists let you mix numbered and bulleted paragraphs based on indentation level. You can create multilevel lists up to a maximum of nine levels. You may use an outline numbered list format if you want your list to have numbered items that contain indented, bulleted subparagraphs. Many types of technical or legal documents require each paragraph and indentation level to be numbered sequentially. Multilevel lists are created by using the Outline Numbered tab in the Bullets and Numbering dialog box (see Figure 8-20). Although you can customize the numbering formats for the various indentation levels of a multilevel list, you cannot have more than one multilevel list format in use in the same document.

Note Don't confuse multilevel lists with the outline view and outlining features described in Chapter 22. In the outline view and heading numbering, only paragraphs that have one of the nine heading styles are numbered. In an outline numbered list, only paragraphs that have a body text style (such as Normal) can be part of the list.

Figure 8-20: The Outline Numbered tab in the Bullets and Numbering dialog box.

To create an outline numbered list:

1. Type your list, and use indents to indicate the different levels. Don't indent the first-level item. Use one indent to indicate a second level item, and so on. Use the Increase Indent or Decrease Indent buttons on the Formatting toolbar (or the shortcuts Shift+Alt+right-arrow key and Shift+Alt+left-arrow key) to set the indentation level of each paragraph in the list.

2. Select the list.

3. Choose Format⇨Bullets and Numbering, and choose the Outline Numbered tab.

4. Select the multilevel numbering style you want from the predefined choices. Your choices include combinations of numbered and lettered paragraphs, technical, and legal numbering styles. If you prefer an outline numbered list with no hanging indent, clear the Hanging Indent option in the Customize Bulleted List dialog box.

5. Choose OK.

Customizing outline numbered lists

To add a new item to the outline numbered list at any indentation level, position the insertion point where you want to add the item and press Enter to add a new paragraph to the list. Finally, use the paragraph indenting commands to indent the paragraph to the desired level. Word automatically formats the new paragraph as part of the outline numbered list and renumbers the paragraphs in the list so that all the numbers remain sequential. Word lets you customize an outline numbered list format by choosing the Customize button on the Outline Numbered tab, which displays the Customize Outline Numbered List dialog box (see Figure 8-21). You can see additional options by clicking on the Mҁore button. Table 8-13 describes each of the available options in the Customize Outline Numbered List dialog box. To create a custom outline numbered list format:

1. Select the outline numbered list whose format you want to customize.

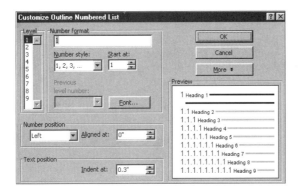

Figure 8-21: The Customize Outline Numbered List dialog box.

2. Choose the Format⇨Bullets and Numbering command. Choose the Outline Numbered tab if it isn't selected already.

3. Choose the Customize button.

4. Use the Level list box to select the indentation level for which you want to adjust the formatting. You must customize each indentation level separately.

5. For each indentation level you customize, set the options in Table 8-13 in any combination.

6. Choose OK to close the Customize Outline Numbered List dialog box.

7. Choose OK to close the Bullets and Numbering dialog box.

Paragraphs and Pagination

Word automatically creates page breaks as you write. You can control how paragraphs are positioned relative to these page breaks. For example, you may want to prevent page breaks within boxed or shaded paragraphs. To control paragraph positions relative to page breaks, you use the Line and Page Breaks tab on the Paragraph dialog box (see Figure 8-22). Table 8-14 describes the options in the Line and Page Breaks group.

Table 8-13
Options in the Customize Outline Numbered List Dialog Box

Option	Description
Level list box	Determines the level you want to modify
Number format	Characters, if any, that you want to come before each number or bullet at this indentation level.
Number style	Numbering or bullet style you want. Available choices include a combination of the numbering choices available for numbered lists and the bullet choices available for bulleted lists, or no number or bullet at all.
Follow number with	Characters, if any, that you want to come after each number or bullet at this indentation level.
Font button	Special font or font attributes (such as bold, italic, and underline), or the point size for the numbers or bullets used at this indentation level.
Start at	Starting number for paragraphs at the selected level of indentation.
Restart numbering after higher list level	Whether the numbering of indented paragraphs includes nothing from the previous level, the number only, or the number and position from the preceding indented paragraphs. This control is not available if level 1 is selected in the Level list box.
Number position list box	Allows choice of Left, Right, or Centered position of the number or bullet within the indent space. Allows the typing of a number to set the size of the hanging indent.
Aligned at	Specifies size of the hanging indent.
Indent at	Determines the amount of space between the number and the text in the numbered paragraph.
Link level to style	Links the selected numbering level with a particular text style. Defaults to (no style).
Legal style numbering	Converts Roman numerals (IV,V) to Arabic numerals (4,5).
ListNum field list name	Allows you to assign a name to the special parameter (ListNum) needed to create lists with multiple outline numbers on a line.

Figure 8-22: The Line and Page Breaks tab in the Paragraph dialog box.

Table 8-14
Pagination Options in the Line and Page Breaks Tab

Option	Action
Widow/Orphan control	Specifies not to let a single line from a paragraph appear by itself at the top or bottom of a page. This option is on by default. A *widow* is the final line of a paragraph that jumps to the top of the next page, because it doesn't fit on the current page. An *orphan* is a single line of a paragraph appearing at the end of a page, with the remainder of the paragraph appearing on the next page.
Keep lines together	Instructs Word not to split the paragraph into separate pages. Useful for working with lists.
Keep with next	Instructs Word to keep paragraph with next paragraph. This is useful for working with captions and lists.
Page break before	Specifies to place the paragraph on top of the next page. This is useful for working with figures, tables, and graphics.
Suppress line numbers	If your document displays line numbers, checking here will remove line numbers for the selected text.
Don't hyphenate	Excludes the selected paragraph from automatic hyphenation.

Summary

Mastering Word's paragraph fundamentals is essential to creating just about any document in Word. Even when you work with graphics in Word, basic paragraph formatting is used. Because of the importance of paragraphs, Word provides a number of ways to apply paragraph formats. In this chapter, you learned the key elements of formatting paragraphs, including how to:

✦ Apply paragraph formatting by using the Formatting toolbar or choosing Format➪Paragraph to display the Paragraph dialog box.

✦ Remove paragraph formatting by pressing Ctrl+Q or pressing Ctrl+Shift+N to apply the default Normal style to the paragraph.

✦ Align paragraphs by using the following shortcut keys: Ctrl+L for left-align, Ctrl+R for right-align, Ctrl+E for center-align, or Ctrl+J for justified text. You can also use an alignment button on the Formatting toolbar.

✦ Set tabs using the Ruler by clicking the Tab Alignment button at the far-left end of the Ruler to choose the tab style you want and then clicking the Ruler at the point you want to insert the tab. You can also use the Tabs dialog box (Format➪Tabs) to set tabs.

✦ Add borders and shading to paragraphs by clicking the Border button on the Formatting toolbar to display the Border toolbar or choosing Format➪Borders and Shading to display the Borders and Shading dialog box.

✦ Create bulleted and numbered lists by using the Bullets and Numbering buttons on the Formatting toolbar.

Where to go next...

✦ If you want to create a collection of paragraph formats and include them in a style, check out Chapter 11.

✦ If you want to move on to the next level of formatting in Word, which is section and page formatting, go to Chapter 9.

✦   ✦   ✦

Sections, Columns, and Page Formatting

The last two chapters introduced you to the most basic parts of a document: characters and paragraphs. This chapter moves to the next level of formatting so that you can format individual sections of a document. Working with sections is essential if you want to create a page with multiple columns, the format used for most newsletters. This chapter also explains how to change the formatting of the page, such as margins, headers, footers, page numbers, and so on.

Formatting Sections of a Document

When you create a document by using the Normal template, Word treats the entire document as a single section. When you insert a section break, the document then has two sections. Word enables you to divide a document into any number of sections and format each section separately. Think of each section as its own document with its own formatting. Sections are especially important in creating desktop publishing documents, where you often need to have different formatting on the same page. For example, you may want one section to have two columns and another to have a single column. Sections are needed to include changes for any of the following types of formatting:

- ✦ Columns
- ✦ Headers and footers
- ✦ Page numbering
- ✦ Footnotes
- ✦ Margins
- ✦ Page orientation
- ✦ Paper size and paper source
- ✦ Vertical alignment

Inserting section breaks

Section breaks are always visible in Normal view. To see them in Page Layout view, click the Show/Hide button on the Standard toolbar. A section break appears as double-dotted lines containing the words Section Break followed by the type of break, as shown in Figure 9-1. A section break marks the point in your document where new formatting begins. You can insert a section break anywhere in your document. The text following the section break, along with its new formatting, can begin in your document at the cursor, on the next page, or on the next even- or odd-numbered page. To insert a section break:

1. Position the cursor where you want to start a new section.

2. Choose Insert⇨Break. The Break dialog box appears (see Figure 9-2).

3. Choose one of the options in the Section breaks group. See Table 9-1 for a description of each option.

4. Choose OK.

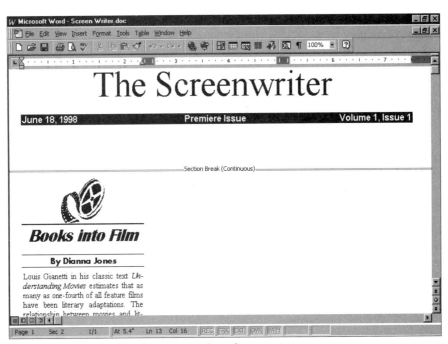

Figure 9-1: A section break appearing in a document.

Table 9-1	
Section Break Options	
Option	**Action**
<u>N</u>ext page	Inserts the section break at the top of the next page in the document.
Con<u>t</u>inuous	Inserts the section break at the insertion point without adding a page break.
<u>E</u>ven page	Inserts the section break at the next even-numbered page in the document (usually a left page). May leave an odd-numbered page blank.
<u>O</u>dd page	Inserts the section break at next odd-numbered page in the document (usually a right page). If the section break falls on an odd-numbered page, Word leaves the intervening even-numbered page blank.

Figure 9-2: The Break dialog box.

Copying section breaks

A section break mark stores section formatting for the preceding section, similar to the way a paragraph mark stores paragraph formatting. To quickly duplicate section formatting, copy and paste the section break. After you paste the section break, the preceding text takes on the formatting of the copied section break. See Chapter 2 for more information on copying, cutting, and pasting.

Tip Another way to duplicate section formatting is to copy and store a section break as an AutoText entry. That way, the section break with its special formatting is available in all new documents, and you can apply the break quickly and easily. See Chapter 2 for information on working with AutoText.

Removing section breaks

Just as removing a paragraph changes the format of a paragraph to the previous paragraph's format, removing a section break changes the formatting of a section to that of the previous section. In other words, removing a section mark merges the section so that it takes on the previous section's formatting. If you accidentally delete a section break marker, immediately click the Undo button or choose the Edit⇨Undo command (Ctrl+Z) to restore the break. To remove a section break, position the cursor on the section break and press Delete, or select the section break marker and choose Edit⇨Cut or the Cut button. To remove all the section breaks by using the Replace command:

1. Choose Edit⇨Replace, or press Ctrl+H. The Replace tab of the Find and Replace dialog box appears.

2. Place the insertion point in the Find what box.

3. Choose the Special button, and choose Section Break. (You may need to choose More to see the expanded dialog box.)

4. Make sure that the Replace with text box is empty, and click the Replace All button.

5. Click OK in response to the information box, and click Close to close the Find and Replace dialog box.

Protecting sections

If you are creating a form, you can protect a section of your document. Unfortunately this is the only way to protect a section of a document. Using a form lets you specify a password to protect a specific section of a document and leave some sections unprotected. This way, you can protect information that you don't want changed or that you want to selectively allow people to change. To password protect a section in a form:

1. Choose a form template, or choose File⇨New and choose Template in the Create New group.

2. Make sure the existing template has more than one section. If you are creating a new template, insert the section break for the section of the form you want to protect.

3. Choose Tools⇨Protect Document. The Protect Document dialog box appears.

4. Choose the Forms option button.

5. Choose the Sections button. The Section Protection dialog box appears showing all the sections selected. If the document doesn't have multiple sections, the Sections button appears dimmed.

6. Click the section you want to exclude from protection.

7. In the Password field, type the password you want to use to protect a document. A password can be up to 15 characters and can include letters, numbers, symbols, and spaces. As you type the password, Word displays an asterisk (*) for each character you type. The password is case-sensitive, so you must type uppercase and lowercase letters to gain access to the section.

Working with Columns

Word lets you create newspaper-style columns to make text more appealing and readable. *Newspaper columns* are also called *snaking columns* because text wraps continuously from the bottom of one column to the top of the next column. Figure 9-3 shows a document formatted with newspaper-style columns. Word gives you two methods of creating columns: choosing the Format⇨Columns command or the Columns button on the Standard toolbar.

Figure 9-3: Sample newsletter document with newspaper-style columns.

The first method opens a dialog box in which you can select the desired formatting. When you click the toolbar button, you can only select the number of evenly sized and spaced columns you want (up to six). Both methods automatically switch to Page Layout view.

You can include as many columns in a document as you have space for on your page. Additionally, you can include different numbers or styles of columns in different parts of your document, as long as you divide your document into sections. For example, you can create newsletters that have two or more sections with a different number of columns in each section.

Depending on which view you are in, columns appear differently on-screen. Normal view is faster for text entry but does not display columns side by side as they will appear when printed. In Normal view, the text appears in the same width as the column, but in one continuous column. To display columns side by side, change to Page Layout view. Print Preview will also display columns side by side.

Applying column formatting

Word enables you to apply column formatting to a selection, a section, multiple sections, or the entire document. As you'll recall, sections are divisions within a document that can be formatted independently. What you format as columns depends on the position of the insertion point or the text selection you make *before* you choose the Columns button or Format⇨Columns. When you format with the column commands, Word inserts a section break automatically if needed. Section breaks appear in your document as a double dotted line containing the words "Section Break," with the type of break in parentheses.

When you use the Columns dialog box to apply page formatting, the Apply to list displays the option to apply the formatting to — based on the position of the insertion point or your selection (see Figure 9-4). Table 9-2 explains the available options for applying column formatting to a document. The options shown in the Apply to list change depending on whether text is selected or whether your document contains multiple sections. Word displays the options available based on the location of the insertion point or your selection.

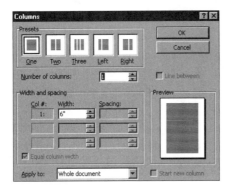

Figure 9-4: The Columns dialog box.

Note   You can save column formatting in a template that you can use as a basis for new documents. Chapter 10 explains how to work with document templates.

Table 9-2
Options for Affecting Column Formatting

To Affect	Action	Apply to List Option	Action
Entire document (single section)	Position the insertion point anywhere in the document.	Whole document	Sets the column formatting for the entire document. No section breaks inserted.
Current section	Position the insertion point inside the section.	This section	Sets column formatting for the current section — the section containing the insertion point. No section break is inserted. This option appears only if the current document is formatted with multiple sections.
Multiple sections (partial or all sections in a document)	Select the sections or the entire document.	Selected sections	Sets column formatting for multiple sections or the entire document containing multiple sections. No multiple-section section breaks are inserted. More than one section must be selected for this option to appear.
Text or graphic selection (within a single section)	Select the text or graphics.	Selected text	Sets column formatting for selected text. Appears only after you select text. Word inserts new-page section breaks at beginning and end of text.
From the insertion point forward	Position the insertion point where you want the page setup formatting to begin.	This point forward	Sets column formatting from the insertion point forward. Word inserts new page section break at the insertion point.

Calculating the number of columns

Word determines the number of columns available on a page based on three factors: the page width, the margin widths, the width of columns, and the spacing between columns. For example, on a wide landscape-oriented page, you have more room for columns than on a portrait-oriented page. Similarly, if your margins are narrow, there's room for more columns. Columns must be at least half an inch wide in Word. If you try to fit too many on a page, Word reverts to .5" columns, which means a maximum of 10 columns in portrait orientation or 16 columns in landscape. If you want more columns, change either your page margins or orientation or the spacing between your columns.

Creating equal-width columns

To create columns of equal width, use the Columns button on the Standard toolbar or choose the Format➪Columns command. The width of the columns depends on the number of columns you choose, your margins, and the amount of space you set between columns. For example, if you have one-inch left and right margins on a standard 8.5-inch paper width and you divide your text into three columns with one-quarter inch between them, you get three two-inch-wide columns. Remember, use Page Layout view to see your columns side by side. To create equal-width columns:

1. Position the insertion point in the section you want to format with columns, or select the text or sections you want to affect (see Table 9-2 for options).

2. Do one of the following:

   • On the Standard toolbar, point to the Columns button and drag the pointer in the drop-down palette down and to the right to select the number of columns you want. Figure 9-5 shows the column pull-down box with two columns selected.

   • Choose Format➪Columns. The Columns dialog box appears. In the Presets group, choose Two or Three columns. Or choose Number of columns, and type or choose the number of columns you want. Choose OK.

Figure 9-5: Inserting a table with the Columns button.

Creating unequal-width columns

Word lets you create columns of unequal width by using the Columns dialog box that appears when you choose Format⇨Columns. You *cannot* create columns of unequal width by using the Columns button. Using the Columns dialog box, you choose from two predefined unequal column widths or create your own custom columns. This dialog box also lets you specify the column widths and how much space you want between the columns to create columns of unequal widths.

The Columns dialog box offers two preset, unequal column width options. Both options include one wide and one narrow column; the wide column is twice as wide as the narrow column. The only difference is the position of two different columns. To choose one of these two preset unequal columns, from the Presets group in the Columns dialog box, choose Left if you want a narrow column on the left or choose Right if you want a narrow column on the right. To create custom columns of unequal width by using the Columns dialog box:

1. Position the insertion point in the section that you want to format with columns, or select the text or sections you want to affect.

2. Choose Format⇨Columns.

3. Choose Number of columns, and type or choose the number of columns you want.

4. Clear the Equal column width check box.

5. Choose Width, and type or choose the width you want for the column. The Columns dialog box has space for only three column numbers. If you chose a number greater than 3 in Step 3, a scroll bar appears to display the additional column numbers (see Figure 9-6).

6. Choose Spacing, and type or choose the spacing you want to the right of the selected column. Note that there is isn't any space to the right of the right-most column.

7. Choose OK.

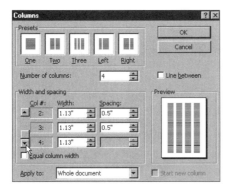

Figure 9-6: A scroll bar displays the additional column numbers.

Typing and editing text in columns

You type, edit, and format text in columns in the same manner as with any other text (see Chapter 3 for more information).

However, the following three options are available for navigating in column text:

✦ Click anywhere in a column of text.

✦ To move from one column to the top of the next column, press Alt+down arrow. To move to the top of the previous column, press Alt+up arrow.

✦ To move from one column to the bottom of the next column, press Ctrl+down arrow. If you want to move to the bottom of the previous column, press Ctrl+up arrow.

The selection bar that normally appears at the left margin of a page now appears at the left margin of each column in Page Layout view. When you move the mouse pointer into this area, it turns into an arrow you can use to select lines and paragraphs within a column (see Figure 9-7).

If text seems narrower than the columns, it may be because the text is indented. Use the ruler or choose Format⇨Paragraph to eliminate or change the indentation settings for selected text, as explained in Chapter 8.

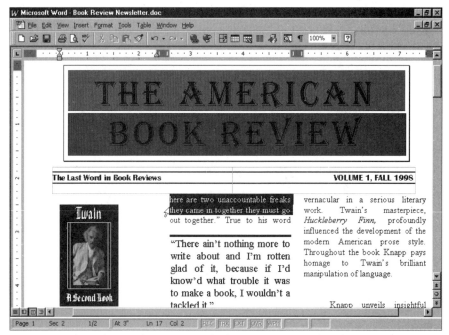

Figure 9-7: The selection bar exists at the left margin of each column in Page Layout view.

Adding a line between columns

Adding a vertical line between columns can add a visual element to help break up your page and make multicolumn text easier to read. Lines are the length of the longest column in the section. You also can add vertical lines on your page by choosing the Format⇨Borders and Shading command, as explained in Chapter 8. For columns, the Line between option in the Columns dialog box is a better choice because it creates lines of uniform length in the section, even if one column of text is shorter than the others. If you add a line by using the Line between option and the line doesn't display, make sure that you are in Page Layout view. The line doesn't appear in Normal view. To add a line between existing columns:

1. Position the insertion point in the section containing existing columns that you want to separate with vertical lines. You also can add a line between columns when you create columns.

2. Choose Format⇨Columns.

3. Choose the Line between option. To remove the lines, clear the Line between option.

4. Choose OK.

Changing the number of columns

If you want to change from equal-width to unequal-width columns, use the Columns dialog box. However, you can also change from unequal-width to equal-width columns by using the ruler. To change the number of equal-width columns or from unequal-width to equal-width columns:

1. Position the insertion point in the section you want to format with columns, or select the text or sections you want to affect.

2. Do one of the following:

   • On the Standard toolbar, point to the Columns button, and drag the pointer in the drop-down palette down and to the right to select the number of columns you want.

   • Choose Format⇨Columns. From the Presets group, choose One, Two, or Three. Or choose Number of columns, and enter or choose the number of columns you want. If you are changing from unequal-width to equal-width columns, choose Equal column width. Choose Left or Right from the Presets group if you want preset columns of unequal width. Or choose Number of columns, and type or choose the number of columns you want. If you're changing from equal-width to unequal-width columns, clear the Equal column width option.

3. Choose OK.

Changing column widths and spacing between columns

Word lets you change the width of columns or the space between columns in two ways: by using the ruler or the Columns dialog box. If your columns are currently equal-width and you want to change them to unequal-width, you must use the Columns dialog box. To change column widths and spacing by using the ruler:

1. Switch to Page Layout view and position the insertion point inside the section containing the columns you want to change. The gray column markers in the horizontal ruler indicate the spaces between columns. When columns are different widths, the gray area on the ruler contains a grid-like icon. Figure 9-8 shows how the ruler appears when columns are of unequal widths.

2. Move the mouse pointer to the column marker over the space that you want to change.

3. If your columns are of equal width, drag the edge of the marker away from the center to add the space between columns, or drag it toward the center to subtract the space between columns. If your columns are all the same width, changing the spacing for any one changes the spacing between all of them.

4. If columns are different widths, place the insertion point in the column (any except the leftmost) and drag either edge of the marker to change the spacing between two columns in either direction. Only that column and the one to the left change. Drag the grid icon instead to change the column width and keep the spacing unchanged.

To change column widths or spacing by using the Columns dialog box:

1. Position the insertion point inside the section containing the columns you want to change.

2. Choose Format⇨Columns.

3. Clear the Equal column width option if you are changing equal-width columns to unequal-width columns.

4. Choose Width, and type or choose the width you want for the columns to change the width of individual columns. Use the scroll bar to reach columns past the third. If your columns are all the same width, you can change only column number 1. All the other columns use the same measurements.

5. Choose Spacing, and type or choose the spacing you want between each column. If your columns are of equal width, the spacing between is also equal.

6. Choose OK.

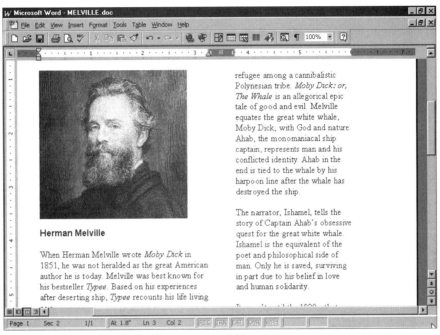

Figure 9-8: The ruler display for unequal-width columns.

Removing columns

The Columns button and the Columns dialog box let you remove columns easily. To remove columns, position the insertion point or select the sections where you want to remove columns. You can use the Columns button on the Standard toolbar to specify a single column. You can use the Columns dialog box by choosing Format⇨Columns. After the Columns dialog box is displayed, choose One in the Presets group and choose OK.

Breaking a column

When Word creates columns, it automatically breaks the columns to fit on the page. Sometimes the column may break inappropriately. For example, on a two- or three-column page, a column may end with a heading that should be at the top of the next column. By inserting a column break directly before the heading, you shift the heading to the top of the next column, keeping the heading and its following text together, as shown in Figure 9-9. To insert a column break:

1. Position the insertion point at the beginning of the line where you want the new column to start.

2. Do one of the following:

- Choose Insert⇨Break. The Break dialog box appears. Choose Column break, and choose OK.

- Press Ctrl+Shift+Enter.

If you want a column to start on a new page, insert a page break. To insert a page break, press Ctrl+Enter or format your document into columns. Positaon the insertion point where you want the break. Choose Insert⇨Break (the default selection is Page break), and choose OK. The column continues on a new page. To remove a break, position the insertion point at the beginning of the text where you created the break and press Backspace.

Figure 9-9: A column break inserted to specify where a column should end.

Balancing column lengths

On pages where the text in columns continues to the next page, Word automatically lines up the last line of text at the bottom of each column. But when a column's text runs out on a page, you may be left with two full-length columns and a third column that's only partially filled. You can balance column lengths so that the bottom of all the columns are within one line of each other. Figure 9-10 shows examples of unbalanced and balanced columns. To line up the length of multiple columns:

1. Position the insertion point at the end of the text in the last column of the section you want to balance.

2. Choose Insert⇨Break.

3. Choose Continuous in the Section breaks group.

4. Choose OK.

Figure 9-10: Unbalanced columns (left) and balanced columns (right).

If you want to add a page break after the balanced columns, place the insertion point after the continuous section break marker and choose Page break from the Break dialog box.

Formatting Your Pages

Page formatting encompasses formatting choices that affect the page, such as margins or headers and footers. Word enables you to apply page setup formatting options to a selection, a section, multiple sections, or the entire document. What you format depends on the positioning of the cursor or the selection you make *before* you execute the Page Setup command. When you use the Page Setup dialog box to apply page formatting, the Apply to list (see Figure 9-11) displays the option to apply the formatting, based on the position of the cursor or your selection. Table 9-3 describes the available options for applying page formatting to a document.

The default measurement Word uses is inches. As with most measurement entries in Word, you can specify centimeters (cm), points (pt), or picas (pi) by entering the two-letter code after entering a measurement value. After you close the dialog box, Word automatically converts your entries to inches. The default measurement unit can be specified in the General tab of the Options dialog box. In most cases, you should use the default inches measurements.

Note You can save page and section formatting as templates and use the templates as a basis for new documents. Chapter 10 explains how to work with document templates.

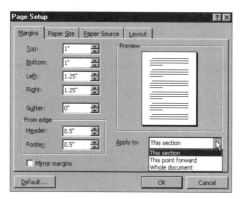

Figure 9-11: The Apply to list in the Page Setup dialog box.

Table 9-3
Options in the Page Setup Dialog Box

Option	Action
Whole document	Sets the page setup formatting for the entire document. No section breaks are inserted.
This section	Sets page setup formatting for the current section (the section containing the cursor). No section break is inserted. This option appears only if the current document is formatted with multiple sections.
Selected sections	Sets page setup formatting for multiple sections or the entire document containing multiple sections. No section breaks are inserted. At least part of more than one section must be selected for this option to appear.
Selected text	Sets the page setup formatting for selected text. Appears only after you select text. Word inserts new page section breaks at beginning and end of text.
This point forward	Sets the page setup formatting from the cursor forward. Word inserts new page section break at cursor.

Setting page margins

Margins are the borders on all four sides of a page within which the text of your document is confined. Figure 9-12 shows the margin areas of a document. Margins aren't necessarily blank; they can contain headers, footers, page numbers, footnotes, or even text and graphics. Different views give you different perspectives on your margins. In Normal view, you don't see the margins. In Page Layout view, you see the page as it will print, margins and all. Choose Page Layout view if you want to see headers, footers, page numbers, footnotes, and anything else that appears within the margins.

Word's default margins are 1 inch at the top and bottom and $1\frac{1}{4}$ inches on the left and right. You can use the Page Setup dialog box or the Ruler to change the margins for the entire document or for sections of the document. Print Preview mode also lets you change margin settings. Chapter 5 explains how to work in Print Preview mode.

Setting margins by using the Page Setup dialog box

Use the Margins tab in the Page Setup dialog box (File⇨Page Setup) to set margins; it gives you the greatest number of options for setting margins. Word lets you set the margins to precise measurements, establish facing pages (mirror margins) and gutters for binding, set varying margins for different sections of your document, and apply your margin settings to the current template. To set margins:

1. Position the cursor in the section for which you want to set the margins, or select the text or sections you want to affect (refer to Table 9-3 for a description of the options).

2. Choose File⇨Page Setup. The Page Setup dialog box appears.

3. Select the Margins tab (see Figure 9-13).

4. Choose the Top, Bottom, Left, or Right margin setting. For each setting, type the amount of the margin or use the increment/decrement arrows (or press the up- or down-arrow keys) to increase or decrease the margin setting by tenths of an inch. As you choose your margin settings, notice that the Preview box in the Page Setup dialog box shows you how your page or pages will look.

5. Choose OK after you are satisfied with the new margins.

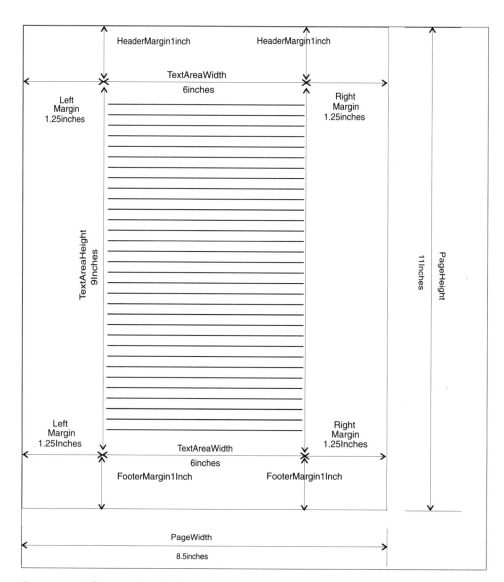

Figure 9-12: The margins of a document.

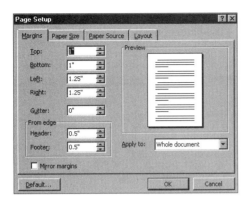

Figure 9-13: The Margins tab in the Page Setup dialog box.

Setting margins using the Ruler

A convenient way to set margins for your document or for a section is to use the Ruler and mouse. You must display the document in Page Layout or Print Preview view to change the margins on all four sides of your document. In Page Layout or Print Preview view, Word displays two Rulers: a horizontal Ruler, which appears at the top of your document and is used to set left and right (or inside and outside) margins; and a vertical Ruler, which appears at the left side of your document and is used to set top and bottom margins. Only the horizontal Ruler is available in Normal view. Figure 9-14 shows the horizontal and vertical Rulers as they appear in Page Layout view. On each Ruler as a gray or colored area and a white area. The gray or colored area indicates the margins; the white area indicates the text area. The edge between the gray area and the white area is the margin boundary. Rest the mouse pointer on the edge to display a ScreenTip describing the marker.

Note If only the horizontal Ruler appears in Page Layout view, choose Tools⇨Options, click the View tab, and choose the Vertical Ruler option in the Window group.

To change margins with a Ruler:

1. Position the cursor in the section where you want to set the margins.

2. Choose View⇨Page Layout. If your Rulers don't appear, choose View⇨Ruler to display them.

3. Position the pointer over the margin boundary that you want to change. The pointer turns into a two-headed arrow and a ScreenTip (if they are turned on) tells you which margin this marker will change.

4. Drag the margin boundary toward the edge of the page to make the margin smaller or toward the center of the page to make the margin wider. A dotted line appears, showing you where the new margin will be. Holding down the Alt key as you drag enables you to see margin measurements in the Ruler.

If you change your mind about changing a margin, press Esc before you release the mouse button or click the Undo button (or choose Edit➪Undo) after you release the mouse button.

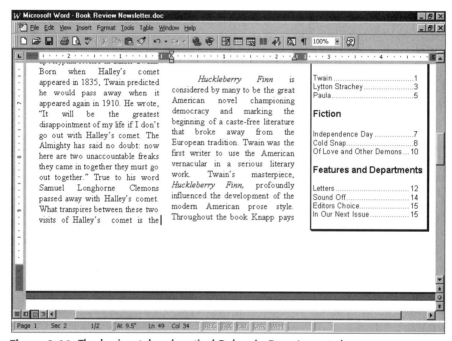

Figure 9-14: The horizontal and vertical Rulers in Page Layout view.

Creating facing pages and gutters

Facing pages in a document are the left and right pages of a double-sided document, as in a book. You create facing pages in Word with *mirror margins*. Using facing pages, you can have different headers and footers on each page and can position page numbers on opposite sides of the facing pages.

A *gutter* adds extra space to allow for the binding of a document. It doesn't change your document's margins, but it does reduce the printing area. Whether you're

working with normal pages that have left and right margins or facing pages that have inside and outside margins, Word enables you to add a gutter to leave extra space for binding. A gutter on normal pages adds space at the left edge of the page; a gutter on facing pages adds space at the inside edges of each page. To leave an extra $1/2$-inch for binding, for example, include a gutter of .5 inches. To create mirror margins and add a gutter:

1. Position the cursor in the section where you want to set the mirror margins and gutter, or select the text or sections you want to change.

2. Choose File⇨Page Setup.

3. Click the Margins tab.

4. Choose Mirror margins. The Preview shows two pages, and the Left and Right margin settings change to Inside and Outside. Type the amount of the margin, or use the increment and decrement arrows (or press the up- or down-arrow keys) to increase or decrease the margin settings by tenths of an inch. As you choose your margin settings, notice that the Preview box in the Page Setup dialog box shows you how your page or pages will look.

5. Choose Gutter, and type or select the amount by which you want to increase the inside margin. The Preview box shows a patterned area where the gutter appears. Figure 9-15 shows the Margins tab with mirror margins and a 1-inch gutter setting.

6. Choose OK.

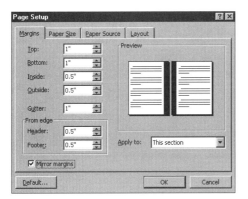

Figure 9-15: Preview box showing mirror margins and a gutter.

Changing paper size and orientation

Changing the paper size enables you to create documents other than the standard 8.5 x 11 inches. Word provides several predefined standard paper sizes such as legal, executive, and envelope. Word also gives you the option of defining your own custom paper size. In addition, you can change the orientation of a page from the default portrait to a landscape orientation. Landscape orientation is useful for presenting charts and tables, creating brochures, or creating certificates. Figure 9-16 shows a document in landscape orientation. To set paper size and orientation:

1. Position the cursor in the section for which you want to set the paper size and orientation, or select the text or sections you want to change.

2. Choose File⇨Page Setup.

3. Select the Paper Size tab (see Figure 9-17).

4. Do either of these:

   • Choose a predefined paper size from the Paper size list, or in the Width and Height boxes, type or choose the width and height of your custom paper size. The Custom size option appears in the Paper size box when you change the default measurement.

   • Choose Landscape from the Orientation group to change to a horizontal, sideways page. The default Portrait orientation is a vertical, upright page.

5. Choose OK.

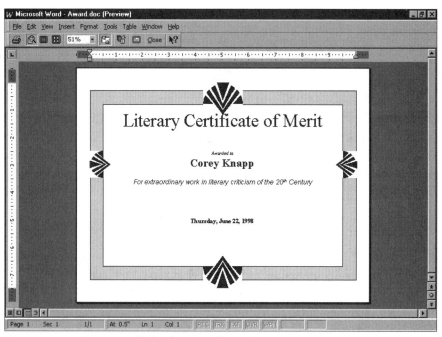

Figure 9-16: A document in landscape orientation.

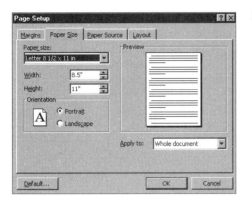

Figure 9-17: The Paper Size tab.

Specifying the paper source

Word enables you to specify where your printer finds the paper to print your document or specified sections, if your printer supports different paper storage options. Most laser printers, for example, have a default paper tray and a manual feed. You can specify that one section of your document be printed from the manual feed and the rest of the document be printed from paper in the default paper tray. Some printers have two paper trays, enabling you to specify that one section, such as the first page of a letter, print on letterhead from the first tray and the remaining pages print on plain paper from the second tray. To change the paper source:

1. Position the cursor in the section for which you want to set the paper source, or select the text or sections you want to affect.

2. Choose File➪Page Setup. The Page Setup dialog box appears.

3. Choose the Paper Source tab (see Figure 9-18). The Paper Source tab changes depending on the printer you're using.

4. Choose the paper source for the first page of your selection, section, or document from the First page list.

5. Choose the paper source for the remaining pages of your selection, section, or document from the Other pages list.

6. Choose OK.

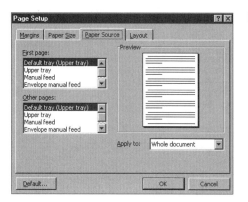

Figure 9-18: The Paper Source tab.

Changing page setup defaults

All new documents are based on a template. Unless you choose a different template, Word bases new documents on the Normal template. Because the default page formatting may not be what you want, Word lets you apply your own page formatting to the Normal template—or, in fact, any template the current document is based on. You also can change defaults for any option in the Page Setup dialog box directly from the Page Setup dialog box, or you can change page formatting for the Normal template (or any template) by modifying the template directly, as explained in Chapter 10. To change the default page setup settings:

1. Choose File➪Page Setup.

2. On any tab in the Page Setup dialog box, make the page setup selections you want.

3. Choose the Default button. Word asks you to confirm that all new documents based on the current template are affected by the change (see Figure 9-19).

4. Choose Yes.

Figure 9-19: Confirmation message for making page setup changes to the current template.

Changing pagination

Word starts a new page automatically when the current page is full. These page breaks are called *soft breaks*. By creating your own page breaks, you can manually control page breaks. As you edit and reformat, Word continually recalculates the amount of text on the page and adjusts soft page breaks accordingly. This process is called *background pagination*. When you are working with large documents, you can shut off background pagination to speed up editing.

Inserting hard page breaks

If you want to force a page to break at a particular place in your document, insert a *hard page break*. Word always starts text following a hard page break at the top of the next page. In Normal view, a soft page break appears as a dotted line, and a hard page break appears as a dotted line with the words *Page Break;* in Page Layout or Print Preview view, you see the page as it will print. You can insert a hard page break by using a command or a keyboard shortcut. After you insert a hard page break in Normal view, you can delete, move, copy, or paste it as you do any text. To insert a hard page break:

1. Position the cursor at the beginning of the text you want to start on a new page.

2. Do either of the following:

   • Choose Insert⇨Break, choose Page break, and choose OK.

   • Press Ctrl+Enter.

Note Hard page breaks take priority over paragraph pagination options. If you need to adjust paragraph breaks to match your page breaks, see Chapter 8.

Turning off background pagination

Word updates page breaks periodically as you work. This automatic pagination is called background pagination. Background pagination is always on in Print Preview and Page Layout view, but it's easy to turn it off for the other views (Normal, Outline, or Master Document). Turning off background pagination may slightly improve the performance of Word. Even if background pagination is turned off, Word paginates when you print your document, when you switch to Page Layout or Print Preview view, or when you compile an index or table of contents. To turn off background pagination:

1. Choose the View menu, and choose the Normal, Outline, or Master Document command.

2. Choose Tools⇨Options.

3. Select the General tab.

4. Clear the Background pagination option.

5. Choose OK.

Aligning text vertically on a page

Word provides three options for vertical alignment of text on a page: Top, Center, and Justified. These options determine how Word aligns a partial page of text between the top and bottom margins. This feature is useful for formatting single-page documents and title pages. If text fills each page, changing its vertical alignment doesn't make a difference. Figure 9-20 shows sample pages based on each of the vertically aligned text options. To vertically align text on the page:

1. Position the cursor inside the section containing the text you want to align.
2. Choose File➪Page Setup.
3. Select the Layout tab (see Figure 9-21).
4. Choose one of the options in the Vertical alignment list (see Table 9-4).
5. Choose OK.

If the section contains only one paragraph, the Justify option does not apply.

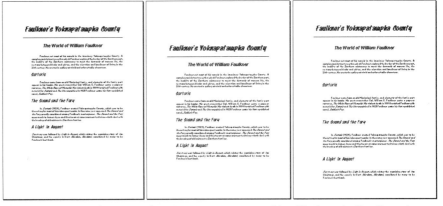

Figure 9-20: Sample pages showing top, center, and justified vertically-aligned text.

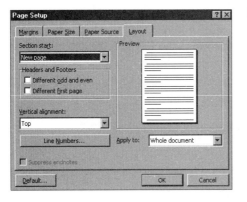

Figure 9-21: The Layout tab.

| Table 9-4 |
| Options in the Vertical Alignment List |

Option	Action
Top	Aligns the top of the first paragraph with the top margin. This is the default page alignment.
Center	Aligns the paragraphs in the center of the page, midway between the top and bottom margins.
Justified	Aligns the top of the first paragraph with the top margin, the bottom of the last paragraph with the bottom margin, and spaces the intervening paragraphs evenly between the top and bottom margins.

Inserting line numbers

Numbered lines are used frequently in legal documents to make referencing easier. Word lets you number some or all of the lines in a document. Word also has options for controlling how line numbers appear. Numbers can start at 1 or some other number, and they can appear on each line or only on some lines. They can be continuous, or they can restart at each section or page. You can specify the distance between text and the line numbers as well as suppress line numbers for selected paragraphs. Line numbers appear in the left margin of your page or to the left of text in columns, as shown in Figure 9-22.

To insert line numbers:

1. Position the cursor in the section where you want to set the line numbers. Or select the text or sections you want to affect.

2. Choose File⇨Page Setup. The Page Setup dialog box appears.

3. Select the Layout tab.

4. Choose the Line Numbers button. The Line Numbers dialog box appears (see Figure 9-23).

5. Choose Add line numbering.

6. If you want to change the default setting, do any of the following:

   • To change the starting number, choose Start at and type or select the starting line number.

   • To change the distance between the line numbers and text, choose From text and type the distance (be sure that your margins are wide enough to accommodate this distance).

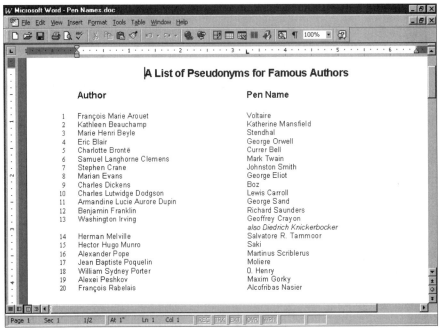

Figure 9-22: Line numbering in a document.

- To change the increment that lines are numbered, choose Count <u>b</u>y and type or select a new increment number.

- In the Numbering group, choose Restart each <u>p</u>age for numbering to start over on each page, choose Restart each <u>s</u>ection to start over in each section, or choose <u>C</u>ontinuous if you want line numbers continuous throughout the document.

7. Choose OK.

8. Choose OK again to close the Page Setup dialog box and return to your document. Notice that the line numbers in Figure 9-22 appear in the page margin as you can tell by the horizontal ruler. You may have to scroll your document right on the screen to see the line numbers.

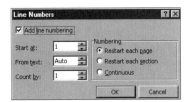

Figure 9-23: The Line Numbers dialog box.

Controlling line numbers

What if you don't want a particular line or section to be numbered? You can remove line numbers for a section or the entire document, or you can suppress line numbering for any selected group of paragraphs. To remove line numbers for a section or the entire document, position the cursor in the section or select the sections where you want to remove line numbers. In the Page Open dialog box (File⇨Page Setup), select the Layout tab and choose the Line Numbers button. In the Line Numbers dialog box, clear the Add line numbering option. Choose OK twice to return to your document. To suppress line numbers for paragraphs:

1. Select the paragraphs from which you want to remove line numbers.

2. Choose Format⇨Paragraph. The Paragraph dialog box appears.

3. Select the Line and Page Breaks tab (see Figure 9-24).

4. Check Suppress line numbers.

5. Choose OK.

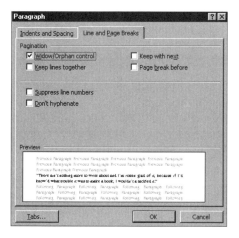

Figure 9-24: The Line and Page Breaks tab in the Paragraph dialog box.

Creating Headers and Footers

Headers and footers contain information repeated at the top or bottom of the pages of a document. The simplest header or footer is a page number. More elaborate headers or footers can contain just about anything, such as the date and time, fields, symbols, cross-references, frames, pictures, and objects. You format headers and footers like any other text in a document.

Headers and footers are placed within a page's top and bottom margins. The header and footer can be different on the first page of a document or section than it is on subsequent pages. Word also gives you the option of creating different headers and footers on even and odd pages. This feature is especially useful for chapter headers in books and manuscripts. Each section of a document's chapter, for example, can have its own header and footer identifying the topic discussed.

Inserting page numbers

Documents are easier to read and reference when the pages are numbered. There are two ways to insert page numbers: using the Insert⇨Page Numbers command or the View⇨Header and Footer command. The Insert⇨Page Numbers command inserts a page number header or footer automatically. Page numbers can appear at the top or bottom of the page and be aligned to the center or either side of the page. Word does not display page numbers in Normal view. To view page numbers, choose View⇨Page Layout or choose View⇨Header and Footer.

When you insert a page number, Word includes a Page field and frames the page number. That way, you can move the number anywhere within the header or footer. If you see {PAGE} instead of the page number, choose Tools⇨Options, click the View tab, and clear the Field codes check box. To insert page numbers:

1. Position the cursor in the section to which you want to add page numbers.

2. Choose Insert⇨Page Numbers. The Page Numbers dialog box appears (see Figure 9-25).

3. In the Position list, choose Bottom of page (Footer) to position your page number at the bottom of the page as a footer, or choose Top of page (Header) to position your page number at the top of the page as a header.

4. In the Alignment list, choose one of the options (Left, Center, Right, Inside, or Outside) to position the location of the page number. Inside positions the page numbers close to the inside edge of opposing pages. Outside positions the page numbers close to the outside edge of opposing pages. The Preview box shows your choice as it appears on the page.

5. Choose Show number of first page if you want a page number to appear on the first page of your document. Clear this option to prevent the page number from appearing on the first page.

6. Choose OK. Word automatically switches you to Page Layout view.

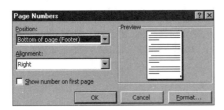

Figure 9-25: The Page Numbers dialog box.

Removing page numbers

To remove page numbers from headers or footers:

1. Position the cursor in the section from which you want to remove page numbers.

2. Choose View⇨Header and Footer. Word displays the document in Page Layout view and displays the Header and Footer toolbar. The header and footer areas are enclosed by a nonprinting dashed line. Text and graphics in the document are visible, but dimmed. If you need to switch to the footer or header, click the Switch Between Header and Footer button, shown later in this chapter in Table 9-5.

3. Select the page number.

4. Press Delete. Word removes the page numbers from the section of your document.

5. Choose the Close button on the Header and Footer toolbar or double-click text in your document.

Changing the position of a page number

The most flexible method of inserting a page number is to use the Insert⇨Page Numbers command. This displays the Page Numbers dialog box that lets you insert a framed page number field that you can drag to where you want the page number to appear. The Page Numbers dialog box also lets you change the position of a page number by choosing another position. This gives you more freedom for placing a page number on a page than does the Page Numbers button in the Header and Footer toolbar.

To move the page number, double-click the page number to activate the Header and Footer toolbar. You can also choose View⇨Headers and Footers, select the page number, drag it to a new position, and choose the Close button on the Header and Footer toolbar or double-click text in your document.

Formatting page numbers

Page numbers can appear in a variety of formats. They can appear as numbers, uppercase or lowercase letters, or uppercase or lowercase roman numerals. Using the Insert⇨Page Numbers command displays the Page Number dialog box, which includes a Format button that lets you easily change the format of the page numbers at the same time that you insert them. If you want to change the font or character formatting of a page number, select the page number and use the buttons on the Formatting toolbar or choose the Format⇨Font command. To format page numbers:

1. Position the cursor in the section containing the page number you want to change.

2. Choose Insert➪Page Numbers.

3. Choose the Format button. The Page Number Format dialog box appears.

4. In the Number format list box, choose the format you want (see Figure 9-26). Then choose the OK button to close the Page Number Format dialog box.

5. Choose the Close button to close the Page Numbers dialog box.

Note If your document is formatted with Word default heading styles (Heading 1 through Heading 9) and if you have applied heading numbering by choosing the Format➪Heading Numbering command and making a selection from the Heading Numbering dialog box, you can include chapter numbers in your header or footer. For more information on working with heading styles in headers and footers, see Chapter 11.

Figure 9-26: The Page Number Format dialog box.

Numbering pages for sections of a document

If you plan to divide a document into several sections, it's easiest to add page numbers before adding section breaks. If you decide to add page numbers and you have added section breaks, position the cursor in the first section of the document and insert page numbers. Even if your document contains more than a single section, page numbering applies by default to your entire document, and numbers are continuous throughout the document. You can start page numbering in any section at a number you specify. For example, you can have page numbering restart at 1 for each section. To change the starting page number in a section:

1. Position the cursor where you want to change the starting page number.

2. Choose Insert➪Page Numbers.

3. Choose the Format button.

4. Type or select a new starting page number in the Start at box in the Page numbering group. Then choose the OK button to close the Page Number Format dialog box.

5. Choose OK to close the Page Number dialog box, and return to your document.

If you select the Continuous section break option in the Break dialog box to create two or more sections, the new header or footer does not appear until the page following the page that contains the section break. A new header or footer doesn't take effect until after a page break. To make the new header or footer appear on the same page as the beginning of the new section, move the section break to the top of the page. Position the cursor at the top of the page that includes the current section break. Delete the old section break. Make sure that the cursor is still where you want the header or footer. Choose Insert⇨Break, and, in the Section breaks group, choose the Next page option. Word now applies the formatting, including the new header or footer, that followed the deleted section break to the current page.

If you are creating a long document that contains several sections, you can save time by using Word's Master Document feature. For more information on using Master Documents, see Chapter 22.

Including sections and total page numbers

When you insert a page number in a document, you are using a field. The page number is inserted as a {PAGE} field, which adds the page number in the header or footer of a document. In some cases, you will want to include the current section number and the total number of pages in a section or document using the {SECTION} field. The {NUMPAGES} field inserts the number of pages in the document, using the information that appears in the Document Statistics tab of the Document Properties dialog box (File⇨Properties). Using the {NUMPAGES} field along with the {PAGE} field lets you include the total number of pages in your page numbering. For example, you can include the total number of pages along with the current page number. A typical result using fields might display "Page 10 of 20." For more information on fields, see Chapter 26. To include section numbers or total page numbers:

1. Choose Insert⇨Field.

2. Do one of the following:

   - To include the total number of pages, highlight Document Information in the Categories list, and choose NumPages in the Field names list box.

   - To include the number of the current section, highlight Numbering in the Categories list, and choose Section in the Field names list box. This inserts the {SECTION} field and displays the number of the current section. The {SECTION} field inserts the section number on each page. For example, adding the {SECTION} field after the page field in the third section of the document lets you create an entry to show the page and section number (Page 2 of Section 3).

   - To include inserts showing the total number of pages in a section, highlight Numbering in the Categories list and choose SectionPages in the Field names list. The {SECTIONPAGES} field inserts the total number of pages in the section. For example, on page 3 in a section with a total of 25 pages, you can add a footer to read "Page 3 of 25."

Tip The brackets that surround fields are not the brackets on your keyboard. Besides using the Insert➪Field to insert a field, a more direct way of entering a field is to press Ctrl+F9. This displays the special brackets with a gray highlight for entering a field name. For example, to add the total number of pages, press Ctrl+F9 and enter **NUMPAGES** within the brackets. To display the result of the field code, press Alt+F9. If the Field code appears rather than the number, choose the Tools➪Options command, and check to make sure the Field Codes setting is not checked in the Show group on the View tab.

Adding header and footer text

When you add headers and footers, Word switches to Page Layout view, activates a pane where you enter your header text, and displays a special Header and Footer toolbar. When you are creating or editing headers or footers in Page Layout view, your document appears grayed. Headers and footers appear grayed when you're working on your document. To see both your document and its headers and footers, choose File➪Print Preview. Buttons on the Header and Footer toolbar aid you in creating your header or footer. Table 9-5 explains the function of the buttons on the Header and Footer toolbar.

Table 9-5
Buttons on the Header and Footer Toolbar

Button	Button Name	Description
Insert AutoText ▾	Insert AutoText	Displays drop-down list of AutoText entries.
[#]	Insert Page Number	Inserts a page number field.
[#]	Insert Number of Pages	Inserts total number of pages in document.
[#]	Format Page Number	Opens Page Number Format dialog box.
[date]	Insert Date	Inserts a date field. Uses whichever date format you last chose in using the Insert➪Date and Time command.
[clock]	Insert Time	Inserts a time field.
[setup]	Page Setup	Opens Page Setup dialog box.

Button	Button Name	Description
	Show/Hide Document Text	Toggles between displaying dimmed body text and graphics in the background or showing no text in background.
	Same as Previous	Links or unlinks a header from preceding section.
	Switch Between Header and Footer	Toggles between displaying header and footer.
	Show Previous	Shows header or footer for preceding section.
	Show Next	Shows header or footer for next section.
Close	Close	Closes the Header and Footer toolbar.

In addition to the buttons that let you insert the page number, date, and time fields, you can also use the new Word 97 AutoText button on the Header and Footer toolbar to insert pre-defined fields containing additional relevant information, such as the filename and author. Table 9-6 shows the list of available AutoText entries, most of which are acquired from the document properties.

Table 9-6
AutoText Entries for Headers and Footers

Entry	Example
-PAGE-	-1-
Author, Page #, Date	John Jones (left margin) Page 1 (centered) 6/15/98 (right margin)
Confidential, Page #, Date	Confidential (left) Page 1 (centered) 6/15/98 (right)
Created by	Created by John Jones
Created on	Created on 6/15/98 9:53 AM
Filename	Association Newsletter
Filename and path	C:\WINWORD\Jones\Association Newsletter
Last printed	Last printed 6/10/98 10:45 AM
Last saved by	Last saved by John Jones
Page X of Y	Page 5 of 26

To add a header or footer to your entire document:

1. Choose <u>V</u>iew⇨<u>H</u>eader and Footer. Word displays the document in Page Layout view and displays the Header and Footer toolbar (see Figure 9-27). The header and footer areas are enclosed by a nonprinting dashed line. Text and graphics in the document are dimmed. If you need to switch to the footer or header, click the Switch Between Header and Footer button (shown in Table 9-5).

2. Type the text for your header or footer within the dashed line that surrounds the header or footer area. Format the text as you do with any text. Use the Tab key and spacebar or the alignment buttons on the Formatting toolbar to position the text.

3. Use the Header and Footer toolbar buttons to insert the fields you want in the header or footer.

4. Choose <u>C</u>lose or double-click your document to close the Header and Footer toolbar and return to your document.

Tip To display and edit an existing header or footer quickly, double-click the dimmed header or footer in Page Layout view.

Another way to include the date or time in a header or footer is to insert a date or time field by using the <u>I</u>nsert⇨Date and <u>T</u>ime command. This command enables you to select a format for your date or time, as explained in Chapter 3.

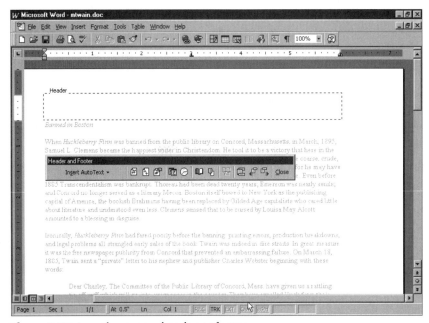

Figure 9-27: Inserting a new header or footer.

Hiding text while working with headers and footers

The document's text appears dimmed while you're working on headers and footers. If you want to hide the text completely, click the Show/Hide Document Text button on the Headers and Footers toolbar. Text is hidden only while you're working on the header or footer. To display the dimmed document text, click the Show/Hide Document Text button again.

Adding headers and footers to sections

Word applies the headers and footers to all sections in your document. If you divide a document into sections with existing headers or footers, the headers and footers are the same for all the sections. If you want a different header or footer in a section, you must go to that section, unlink the existing header or footer, and create the new header or footer.

The new header or footer applies to the current section and all following sections. Later, if you decide you want your new header or footer to be the same as the preceding header or footer, you can relink it. If you change one header or footer without unlinking it, all the headers and footers in all the sections change. If you want different headers and footers in different sections of your document, you first must divide your document into sections. To create a different header or footer for a section:

1. Position the cursor inside the section where you want to change the header or footer.

2. Choose View➪Header and Footer. Word selects the header for the current section. If you want to change the footer for that section, click the Switch Between Header and Footer button.

3. Click the Same as Previous button (refer to Table 9-5) to disconnect headers and footers in the current section from the preceding section.

4. To delete an existing header or footer, select the header or footer, and press Backspace or Delete.

5. Create the new header or footer you want for the current section. Word also inserts the same header or footer in all the following sections.

   To create a different header or footer in following sections, click the Show Next button to move to the next section, and repeat Steps 3 through 5 for each section.

6. Choose Close on the Header and Footer toolbar or double-click the document to close the Header and Footer toolbar and return to your document.

To relink a header or footer with the preceding header or footer:

1. Position the cursor inside the section containing the header or footer that you want to relink.

2. Choose View⟹Header and Footer. If you want to change the footer for that section, click the Switch Between Header and Footer button.

3. Click the Same as Previous button. Word displays a message box asking you whether you want to delete the header/footer and connect to the header/footer in the preceding section.

4. Choose the Yes button. The preceding header or footer is repeated in the current section.

5. Choose the Close button on the Header and Footer toolbar or double-click in the document to close the Header and Footer toolbar and return to your document.

Creating different first-page headers and footers

Many documents have a different header or footer on the first page (in fact, some have no header or footer on the first page). In Word, first-page headers and footers apply to sections; therefore, a different header or footer can appear at the beginning of each section in a document divided into sections.

You remove a first-page header or footer in the same way you create one: by navigating to the section, clicking the Page Setup button, selecting the Layout tab, and clearing the Different first page option in the Headers and Footers group. To create a different header or footer for the first page of a document or section:

1. Choose View⟹Header and Footer.

2. Click the Show Previous or Show Next button to locate the section in which you want a different first-page header or footer. If you want to change the footer for that section, click the Switch Between Header and Footer button.

3. Choose the Page Setup button on the Header and Footer toolbar, or choose the File⟹Page Setup commands. The Page Setup dialog box appears.

4. Select the Layout tab.

5. In the Headers and Footers group, choose Different first page.

6. Choose OK. The title First Page Header or First Page Footer appears at the top of the header and footer editing pane.

7. If you don't want header or footer text, leave the header or footer editing area blank. If you want a different header or footer on the first page of the section, enter the text for your header or footer.

8. Choose the Close button on the Header and Footer toolbar or double-click in the document to close the Header and Footer toolbar and return to your document.

Creating headers and footers for odd and even pages

Sometimes you want different headers and footers for the odd- and even-numbered pages in your document. In a document with facing pages (mirror margins), odd-numbered pages appear on the right side and even numbered pages appear on the left side. You may want left-aligned headers on even-numbered pages and right-aligned headers on odd-numbered pages so that headers always appear on the outside edges of your document. You can create different odd and even headers and footers for each section in your document. To create different headers and footers for odd and even pages:

1. Choose View⟹Header and Footer.

2. Click the Show Previous or Show Next button to locate the section in which you want different odd and even headers and footers. If you want to change the footer for that section, click the Switch Between Header and Footer button.

3. Click the Page Setup button on the Header and Footer dialog box, or choose File⟹Page Setup. The Page Setup dialog box appears.

4. Select the Layout tab.

5. Choose Different odd and even in the Headers and Footers group.

6. Choose OK. The header or footer area for the section you're in is titled "Even (or Odd) Page Header (or Footer)."

7. Enter the text and fields for the header or footer, and then click Show Next to create the alternate.

8. Choose the Close button on the Header and Footer toolbar or double-click in the document to close the Header and Footer toolbar and return to your document.

Positioning headers and footers

Depending on what you enter in a header and footer, you may want to change the position of the text in the header or footer or even its location on the page. For example, you may want to change their horizontal text alignment: you can center it between the left and right margins, align it with the left or right margin, or create a header that places text in the right or left margin outside the document text area. Additionally, you can change the vertical position: you can increase or decrease the distance from the top or bottom edge of the page. Word also lets you adjust the amount of space between the header or footer and the text in the main document.

The header and footer areas have two preset tab stops — one centered between the left and right margins and one right-aligned at the default right margin (6 inches). These tab stops make it easy to center a chapter title or place a page number flush with the right margin. The alignment buttons on the Formatting toolbar can also be used to align text in a header or footer.

If you want your headers or footers to run into the left or right margins, set a negative indent by using the Format⇨Paragraph command. For example, to create a header that starts in the left margin, enter **-1** in the Left box (located in the Indents and Spacing tab of the Paragraph dialog box). Most printers can't print all the way to the edge of the page; for example, HP LaserJet printers cannot print in the outermost $1/4$-inch of a page. If you specify a setting that invades the non-printing zone, that text will not print.

Headers and footers are printed in the top and bottom margins. You can also specify how much space is left on the page above a header or below a footer in the top or bottom margin. To change a header or footer's distance from the edge of the paper:

1. Choose View⇨Header and Footer.

2. Click the Show Previous or Show Next button to locate the section containing the header or footer you want to affect.

3. Click the Page Setup button or choose File⇨Page Setup to display the Page Setup dialog box.

4. Choose the Margins tab.

5. Do one of the following:

   • In the From edge group, choose the Header box, and type or select the distance that you want your header from the top edge of the page.

   • Choose Footer, and type or select the distance that you want your footer from the bottom edge of the page.

6. Choose OK to close the Page Setup dialog box.

7. Choose the Close button on the Header and Footer toolbar or double-click in the document to close the Header and Footer toolbar and return to your document.

If your header or footer is larger than your top or bottom margin, Word moves your document text so that there is room for the header or footer. The page margin is not changed. If you don't want Word to move your text, use Page Setup to make your header or footer smaller or move it closer to the edge of the page. If you want text to overlap a header or footer (when the header or footer is a graphic that you want to appear behind text), type a minus sign in front of your margin measurement. For example, if your header is 4 inches high and you want a top margin of 1 inch with the text overlapping the header, type **-1"** as your top margin.

The final adjustment you can make to the position of headers and footers is to set the amount of space between the header or footer and the document text. You can change the top and bottom margins in the Page Setup dialog box to increase the space, or you can drag the margin boundary marker (the line between gray and white) on the vertical Ruler. Using the second method, you can see the exact margin measurement if you hold down Alt while you drag the marker.

Creating a watermark

Here's a slick trick using a header or footer that lets you insert a watermark. A *watermark* is a background image that appears behind the text on a page. When you use a header or footer, the watermark appears behind the text on every page of your document. Before you insert an image as a watermark, you may want to use a graphics program, such as PaintShop Pro, to lighten the image so that it doesn't overshadow the text on your page. Figure 9-28 shows a watermark in Print Preview mode. For more information about inserting drawings, WordArt, and working with the Drawing toolbar, see Chapter 13. To add a watermark to every page of a document:

1. Choose View⇨Header and Footer.

2. Click the Drawing button in the Standard toolbar. The Drawing toolbar appears.

3. Click the Text Box button, and drag the marquee to create the size for the watermark.

4. Insert the picture, drawing, or WordArt object. If the image needs to be placed lower on the page, use the File⇨Page Setup command to change the location of the header and footer.

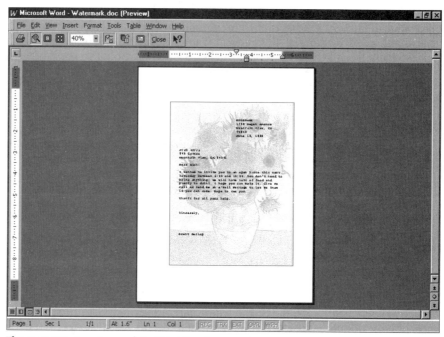

Figure 9-28: A watermark in Print Preview mode.

Formatting and editing headers and footers

Anything you can do to regular text, you can do to a header or footer. For example, you can change the font, reduce or enlarge the size of the text, insert graphics, draw pictures, include a table, add a line or box, and add shading. You also can add tabs, change the alignment or indents, or change line or paragraph spacing. Use any of Word's formatting techniques to make headers and footers look distinct from the text in your document, such as making the characters appear larger or in a different font. Draw a line beneath headers or above footers. Make headers and footers wider or narrower than the text with paragraph indents. Add borders or shading around headers and footers. You can use most of the commands in the Insert, Format, Tools, and Table menus to format headers and footers as well as use the ruler to set tabs and indents.

You must activate a header or footer to edit it. To activate a header or footer, use the same command you used to create it, or in the Page Layout view, double-click the header or footer. Once it is activated, you can edit the header or footer.

The Switch Between Header and Footer button enables you to move between headers and footers in the current section. If your document contains only one section, the headers and footers are the same throughout your document. If you edit one header or footer, they all change.

If your document contains multiple sections with different headers and footers, Word lets you edit the header and footer in one of two ways: you can activate headers and footers and, by using the Show Previous and Show Next buttons on the Header and Footer toolbar, move between sections. Or you can first locate in your document the header or footer you want to edit and activate it. To edit headers and footers:

1. Position the cursor in the section with the header or footer you want to edit.

2. Choose View⇨Header and Footer or in the Page Layout view, double-click the header or footer you want to edit. Word activates the header for the section containing the cursor.

3. To edit a footer rather than a header, click the Switch Between Header and Footer button, or press Page Down to scroll to the bottom of the page and click in the footer area.

4. To locate a header or footer in a different section of your document, click the Show Previous or the Show Next button.

5. After you locate the header and footer you want to edit, make the changes you want.

6. Choose the Close button on the Header and Footer toolbar or double-click in the document to close the Header and Footer toolbar and return to your document.

Tip   The Same as Previous button in the Header and Footer toolbar lets you replace the header or footer in the current section with the previous section's header or footer. The shortcut key for the Same as Previous button is Alt+Shift+R.

Deleting headers and footers

If you find that you don't need headers or footers, you can delete them from your entire document or on a section-by-section basis if your document has multiple sections. If the document consists of several sections and all headers or footers are connected, deleting a header or footer in any section deletes the header or footer for all sections. To delete a header or footer:

1. Position the cursor in the section with the header or footer you want to delete.

2. Choose View⇨Header and Footer command. Word activates the header for the section containing the cursor.

3. Select the header or footer you want to delete, and press Backspace or Delete. If you have different headers or footers in other sections of the document, click the Show Next or Show Previous button on the Header and Footer toolbar to find the next header or footer you want to delete.

4. Choose the Close button on the Header and Footer toolbar or double-click in the document to close the Header and Footer toolbar and return to your document.

Summary

Knowing how to create and work with sections and columns, and how to specify formats for the pages of your document gives you tremendous power. You can

✦ Create and change the formatting for new and existing documents.

✦ Create complex documents, such as reports, newsletters, and brochures.

Word 97 includes templates and Wizards that save you from having to create complex documents from scratch. Knowing how to format sections and columns and how to change the page setup is sure to simplify the process of modifying documents created with Word's templates and Wizards.

Where to go next...

✦ To start creating documents that include columns and sections, see the next chapter on working with Word's predefined templates and Wizards.

✦ When you work with columns and sections, it's sometimes helpful to check and change your margins in Print Preview mode. For information on working in Print Preview mode, see Chapter 5.

✦ For a refresher course on adding borders and shading to text in columns and other formatting tips, see Chapter 8.

✦ One of the more impressive tasks covered in this chapter is adding a watermark to every page of a document by inserting an image in a text box in a header or footer. For more information on creating and working with graphics and text boxes, see Chapters 13 and 14.

✦ This chapter explained adding page numbers in headers and footers. Page numbers are the result of inserting fields. For more information on working with fields, see Chapter 26.

✦ ✦ ✦

Working with Wizards and Templates

After working through the previous three chapters, you know a lot about Word's powerful formatting capabilities. Before you start creating a complicated document from scratch, though, you can save yourself a considerable amount of time by using one of Word's Wizards or templates. If you're using Word with Office 97, you can use the Binder to create compound documents, called binders. This chapter explains the different types of Wizards and templates that come with Word and the ready-made binders that come with Office 97. You'll also learn how to modify a document created by using Wizards, templates, and the Binder.

Conjuring Up Documents with Word's Wizards

Wizards are easy-to-use programs supplied with Word that enable you to create documents by answering a series of questions. Icons for Wizard files appear with a wand, and the files end with the .wiz extension. A Wizard creates a formatted document for you and prompts you to include items you may otherwise forget. When you choose the File⇨New command, Word displays the New dialog box, shown in Figure 10-1, that includes Wizards for different types of documents.

You can also use a Wizard to create a document by choosing the Start a New Document button in the Office toolbar. Word includes a wide spectrum of types of documents. For example, Figure 10-2 is an example of a calendar you can create by using the Calendar Wizard. Creating a complex document—such as an agenda, an award, a newsletter, or a resume—from scratch could take hours; by using Word's Wizards, these documents take only minutes. Table 10-1 lists the Wizards that are available in the different tabs. If some of these Wizards do not appear, install them by inserting the Office 97 or Word 97 CD in your CD-ROM drive and selecting Setup. (See Appendix A for more discussion on setting up additional Word components.)

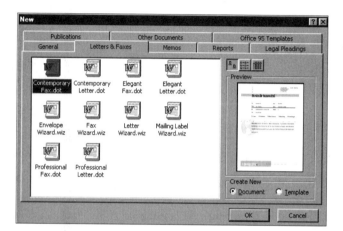

Figure 10-1: The tabs in the New dialog box let you choose from Word's Wizards.

Table 10-1
Wizards Supplied with Word

Tab	Name	Description
Publications	Newsletter	Classic or Modern newsletter
Legal Pleadings	Pleading	Legal pleading paper
Other Documents	Résumé	Entry-level, chronological, functional, and professional résumés
Other Documents	More	Provides link to Word 97 or Office 97 CD or Microsoft Word Web site for other Wizards and templates
Letters & Faxes	Fax	Fax cover sheet
Letters & Faxes	Letter	Allows stylizing of all components of a letter
Letters & Faxes	Label	Allows quick creation of several styles of mail label
Letters & Faxes	Envelope	Automatically addresses envelopes
Memos	Memo	Interoffice Memo
Web Pages	Web Page Wizard	Allows quick creation of Web pages

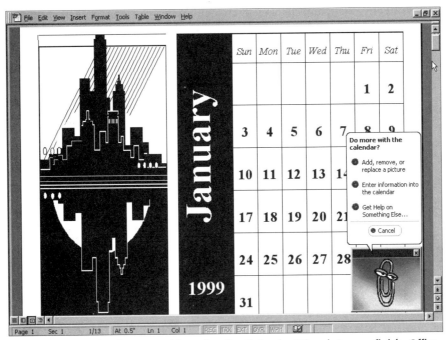

Figure 10-2: A calendar created by using the Calendar Wizard. As you finish, Office Assistant automatically appears with more options.

The Letters & Faxes tab will appear as the Letters tab if one of the following is true of your Word 97 installation: (1) you've installed Word 97 to run from the CD-ROM, or (2) this is the first time a version of Word has been installed on your computer (that is, you're not upgrading from a previous version).

Using a Letter Wizard

You use all Word's Wizards in much the same way. This section explains how to use the Letter Wizard to create a letter based on various page designs and styles, including personal, business, contemporary, or elegant. You can choose a block, modified, or semi-block style for your letter.

Adding your return address

The Letter Wizard can automatically place your return address at the top of the page. The Wizard refers to the User Information stored in Word to find the return address. To save time, make sure that this information is correct before opening the Wizard. To check your address in the User Information tab:

1. With any document displayed, choose Tools⇨Options to display the Options dialog box.

2. If necessary, select the User Information tab. The Options dialog box appears, as shown in Figure 10-3.

3. Verify that the Mailing address text box contains the return address you want to place at the top of your letters. If necessary, correct the address.

4. Choose OK, or press Enter to accept the address.

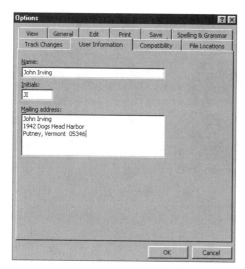

Figure 10-3: The Options dialog box with the User Information tab displayed.

Note   The User Information tab contains a text box for your name and a text box for your initials. The name and initials are not used by the Letter Wizard, but Word uses them at other times.

Starting the Letter Wizard

To create the letter, you open the Letter Wizard and make choices in a series of dialog boxes. To open a Wizard:

1. Choose File⇨New. The New dialog box appears.

2. Click the Letters & Faxes tab.

3. Double-click the Letter Wizard icon, or select the Letter Wizard icon, and choose OK.

The Office Assistant appears, asking if you would like to send one letter or send letters to a mailing list. Select Send One Letter to display the Letter Wizard dialog box, as shown in Figure 10-4. Selecting Send Letters to a Mailing List displays the Mail Merge Helper dialog box, from which you can match a data source with a document type appropriate for your project (see Figure 10-5). Mail Merge is covered thoroughly in Chapter 20. Word displays the Letter Wizard dialog box, as shown in Figure 10-4. This dialog box contains a miniature preview of a letter and asks you to choose a type of letter. As you make choices, the preview changes to show the current selection.

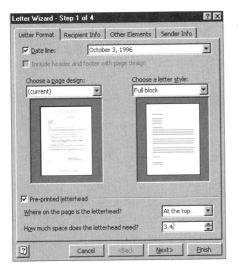

Figure 10-4: The first Letter Wizard dialog box.

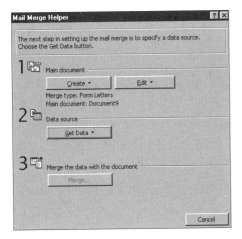

Figure 10-5: Selecting Send Letters to a Mailing List brings up the Mail Merge Helper dialog box.

Each Letter Wizard tab governs the appearance of your letter's Format, Recipient Info, Other Elements (such as a special Subject line), and Sender Info:

✦ Letter Format: Allows you to choose a page design, a letter style, and a date line style, and to create space for a preprinted letterhead. Selecting preprinted letterhead allows you to set aside space on your page for a return address and company logo. This space can be set aside anywhere on your page.

✦ Recipient Info: Allows you to type in the recipient's name or use the Address Book. You can also pick a Salutation style.

✦ Other Elements: Allows you to place a Reference, Subject, Attention, or Mail Instructions line in your document. You can also select who should receive courtesy copies (cc) of your document. A path to the Address Book is provided to select courtesy copy recipients..

✦ Sender Info: Allows you to type the sender's name or chose the Address Book and allows you to select a Complimentary closing. You can create a reference to Enclosures in your document, Job Title, and Company, and you can include the Writer/typist's initials.

Office Outlook's Address Book can be used to store address data used for Word mailings. It is mentioned in Chapter 20.

Addressing the letter

The Recipient Info tab is next to the Letter Format tab of Letter Wizard, and is shown in Figure 10-6. It contains the name and address you used in your most recent letter (it holds a dummy address or is blank if you haven't used the Letter Wizard before). In either case, you can delete the existing text and type the new recipient's name and address. If you have set up an Address Book with Office 97 by using Outlook or Microsoft Exchange, click the Address button and use an existing address from your Address Book.

The Other Elements tab contains special addressing components, such as mail instructions (CERTIFIED MAIL, CONFIDENTIAL). Components from the Other Elements tab are optional. You may skip this tab entirely and move to the Sender Info tab.

The Sender Info tab (see Figure 10-7) contains the address you entered earlier in the User Information dialog box. You can include options such as the typist's initials and references to enclosures. Any changes you make here do not affect the User Information data itself. After you've finished with this dialog box, choose Finish to move on.

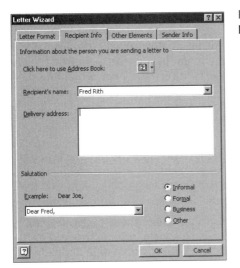

Figure 10-6: The Letter Wizard Recipient Info dialog box.

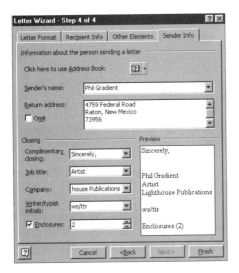

Figure 10-7: The Letter Wizard Sender Info dialog box lets you confirm the return address and include a number of options.

Choosing a letter style

You can choose a Professional, Contemporary, or Elegant style of a font for your letter. Professional uses Arial, a sans serif font; the Contemporary letter uses the serif font Times New Roman; and the Elegant uses a serif font, such as Garamond.

Which font the Wizard chooses for the Elegant letter style depends on what fonts are installed on your computer. In this case, choose Contemporary, and move through each tab to edit information in the four categories: Letter Format, Sender, Recipient, and Elements information. Even if you haven't yet reviewed the choices on each tab, clicking OK exits Letter Wizard entirely and begins building the letter based on your selections.

Finishing the letter

At this stage, you can choose what you want to do after the letter is created. You can

✦ Just display the letter.

✦ Create an envelope or mailing label. To automate these tasks, select Envelopes and Labels from the Tools menu. Of special note is the Add to Document option in the Envelope dialog box. With it, you can include envelope printing instructions right on your document, so that they always print out together. Envelopes and labels are covered in Chapter 20.

✦ Click Office Assistant and type **letter** or a more specific keyword related to your task. Even while inactive, Office Assistant keeps track of your letter-writing progress, and, if asked, helps you finish this step and move to the next one.

At any point, you can choose Finish, and Word displays the letter, as shown in Figure 10-8, so that you can tailor it to your needs.

As is the case for any of Word's Wizards, in each place where a name is mentioned, the prewritten letter shows **[NAME]** or **[Name]**. You can edit the letter to replace these markers with your own name in some places and the recipient's name in other places. To do so, highlight the entire marker, including the brackets, and type the name that should appear in the letter.

You can make any formatting changes that you prefer. However, think carefully before you change what the Wizard suggests. In general, Word's Wizards provide suitable character, paragraph, section, and page formats, so change them only if you have a good reason to do so. If you modify the letter quite extensively, you should generally include the points it covers. After you've made all the necessary changes, save the letter as you would save any other Word document, and print it.

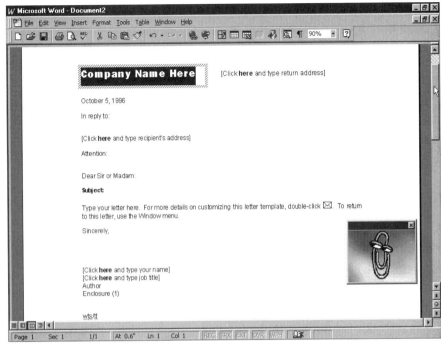

Figure 10-8: A business letter ready to edit. Some of Letter Wizard's options are already included in this example.

Creating Similar Letters

If you are using Word to create a product announcement or press release, you may need several similar but personalized cover letters. The following is a summary of the various ways that Word can help you create these letters:

✦ Using the Letter Wizard repeatedly.

When you use the Letter Wizard the first time, you make a series of choices. The Wizard remembers these choices and automatically uses them the next time you open it. So, after using the Letter Wizard to create one cover letter, you can create similar letters simply by changing the name and address for the recipient. This approach assumes that you haven't used the Letter Wizard for another type of letter between creating other cover letters. Of course, you have to do the same final editing to the prewritten letter each time.

✦ Creating a template from a Wizard letter.

In the "Creating a Template" section later in this chapter, you'll see how you can create a template from the edited version of the prewritten letter. Then you can use the template to quickly create cover letters for all the press releases you mail.

✦ Creating a form letter from a Wizard letter.

Using the edited version of the prewritten product announcement letter, you can create a form letter that includes information (such as the name, the address, and certain phrases) marked as fields so that you can personalize the letters. You create a data file containing the specific, personalized information that replaces the fields in each letter. Then, using Word's Mail Merge capability, you merge the form letter with the data file to print personalized letters to accompany your resumes. Chapter 20 explains how to perform mail merges with Word.

Using Word's Other Wizards

Word's Wizards all work in a similar fashion as the Letter Wizard. Each Wizard presents a series of dialog boxes in which you make choices and, in some cases, insert text. Just follow the instructions in each screen. Each Wizard remembers the choices you make. The first time you use a particular Wizard, you must work through quite a few steps. When you use the Wizard subsequently, however, you can usually accept your previous choices, so the process is fast and convenient.

You don't have to perform each step of a Wizard. After entering your information, you can click the Finish button to skip any subsequent questions. The Wizard uses the default settings for any options that you skip. Pictured in Figure 10-9 is the Résumé Wizard, which offers three styles and a flow chart to show you where you are in the creation process. Résumé Wizard offers quick choices for résumé type and address and heading appearances.

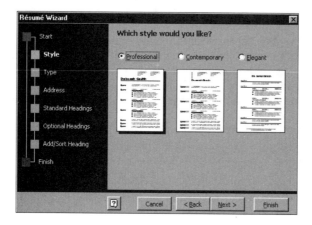

Figure 10-9: The Résumé Wizard dialog box.

Introducing Templates

Every Word document is based on a template. Think of a *template* as a framework boilerplate or a master pattern that defines a document's appearance and may define some of its contents. When you first create a document using the Normal template and start typing, text appears in the default font: Times New Roman, 10-point. The margins, meanwhile, are set to particular values for Word's Normal template. You don't have to use the Normal template. Word has numerous other templates, each suitable for a specific type of document. You can modify any of the supplied templates, including the Normal template, and you can create your own templates.

Many Word users make the mistake of ignoring templates; they always use the Normal template. By using templates, however, you can save time and effort, produce consistently formatted documents with ease, and ensure that all documents of the same type contain the required components. You can create templates suitable for all the types of documents you use, such as stationery (letters, memos, and faxes), forms and reports, proposals, and presentations.

What a template contains

A template can contain many components. A document uses these components when it is based on the template. Many templates contain only layout information. More sophisticated templates contain other components. The following explains each possible component of a template.

Layout information includes character formatting (refer to Chapter 7), paragraph formatting (Chapter 8), and section and page formatting (Chapter 9). Layout information also includes styles, which you learn more about in Chapter 11. When you base a document on a template, everything you type is initially formatted according to the layout information in that template. You can, however, change the formatting of individual parts of a document to override what its template specifies.

Boilerplate text in a template appears in every document based on that template. A template used for letters, for example, may include your return address as boilerplate text. A template used for proposals may include several paragraphs that summarize your organization's capabilities. A template can also include boilerplate graphics, such as your company logo. Each document based on a template initially includes all boilerplate text and graphics in that template. As with formats, you can delete or change any boilerplate text or graphics that you don't need in a particular document.

Field codes represent certain kinds of data. For example, a field code can represent the current date. Every document based on a template that contains that field code will replace the field code with the date that the document was created. Refer to Chapter 26 for more information about field codes.

You read about *AutoText entries* in Chapter 3. While you are typing or editing a document, you can access all the AutoText entries in the template on which that document is based.

A *macro* is a set of instructions that Word follows to accomplish a specific task. A template can contain macros that are available to all documents based on that template. Refer to Chapter 27 for information about macros.

Custom command settings simplify working with Word. When you first use Word, the menu bar includes nine menus, each containing certain commands; the toolbars contain predefined tools; and certain shortcut keys are available so that you can access specific features quickly. Chapter 25 explains how you can add menus to the menu bar, commands to existing menus, and buttons to toolbars. It also explains how you can add shortcut keys. You can place these custom features in specific templates.

Local and global templates

Local and *global* are two terms you will undoubtedly come across when working with templates. Local refers to something that applies in a restricted area; global refers to something that applies over a wide area. The switch on the wall of your kitchen is local: it controls only the light in your kitchen. In contrast, the main switch in the breaker box where electricity enters your home is global: it controls everything that uses electricity in your home.

Most Word templates are local. All the components in a local template affect, or are available to, only the documents based on that template or to which that template is attached. The Normal template, however, is global. Components of the Normal template may affect, or be available to, other documents based on another template.

If you want a certain template component, such as an AutoText entry, to be available to all documents, you should place it in the Normal template. Then you don't have to repeat that entry in other templates. However, if an AutoText entry is useful in only a particular type of document, you should create a suitable template and place the AutoText entry in it.

A local template always has priority over a global template. When a document is based on a local template, it looks for template components in its own template first. If it doesn't find a component there, it looks in the global Normal template.

Suppose that the Normal template has an AutoText entry named CoName, which contains the complete name of your organization. The Memo template also has an AutoText entry named CoName, but this entry contains an abbreviated version of your organization name. When you base a document on any template other than Memo, a reference to CoName provides the complete organization name. In contrast, when you work with a document based on the Memo template, a reference to CoName provides the abbreviated organization name.

By default, the Normal template is global and all other templates are local. As you will see later in this chapter, you can make any template act as a global template so that documents based on other templates can have access to its components.

Naming and Finding Templates

Template files end with the .dot filename extension. All templates you create must have this extension for Word to recognize them. The Word installation process creates a folder template as a subfolder of the folder that contains Word, and places the supplied templates in this folder. So, if you installed Word in a folder named Program Files\Microsoft Office, the templates are stored in the Program Files\Microsoft Office\Templates folder. If you're using Office 97, most Word templates are stored in subfolders under the Program Files\ Microsoft Office\Templates folder, but a few are stored in the Program Files\Microsoft Office\Templates folder itself. Any templates you create need to be saved in the main Templates folder.

Word allows you to create additional directories for templates. If you do so, you must use the File Locations tab of the (Tools⇨) Options dialog box to identify the folder that contains the template you want to use. Word looks for templates only in the folder specified in the Options dialog box. Chapter 25 covers other details of the Options dialog box.

Word's Predefined Templates

Word comes with numerous templates to simplify creating documents. As mentioned, the place where Word stores template files depends on whether you're using a stand-alone version of Word or Office 97. The default folder for Office 97 templates is Program Files\Microsoft Office\Templates, with additional templates stored in subfolders of the main Program Files\Microsoft Office\ Templates folder. Table 10-2 lists the templates that come with Word. Note that the templates marked with an asterisk are automatically installed; the others are available in the ValuPack folder of the word 97 or Office 97 CD-ROM.

Table 10-2
Templates Supplied with Word

Tab	Template Name	Description
General	Blank Document *	Default template (global)
Other Documents	Brochure *	Classic brochure: styles only
Other Documents	Contemporary Press Release	Styles and boilerplate text

(continued)

Table 10-2 *(continued)*		
Tab	**Template Name**	**Description**
Other Documents	Directory	Classic folder: styles only
Other Documents	Elegant Press Release	Classic press release: styles and boilerplate text
Other Documents	Manual	Classic manual: styles only
Publications	Newsletter *	Styles and boilerplate text
Other Documents	Professional Press Release *	Styles and boilerplate text
Other Documents	Thesis	Classic thesis: styles only
Other Documents	Contemporary Résumé *	Styles and boilerplate text
Other Documents	Elegant Résumé *	Styles and boilerplate text
Other Documents	Invoice	Styles, boilerplate text, and data-entry fields
Other Documents	Professional Résumé *	Styles and boilerplate text
Other Documents	Purchase Order	Styles, boilerplate text, and data-entry fields
Other Documents	Weekly Time Sheet	Styles, boilerplate text, and data-entry fields
Letters & Faxes	Contemporary Fax *	Fax cover sheet, Styles only
Letters & Faxes	Contemporary Letter *	Styles, boilerplate text, and field code
Letters & Faxes	Elegant Fax *	Fax cover sheet, styles only
Letters & Faxes	Elegant Letter *	Styles, boilerplate text, and field code
Letters & Faxes	Professional Fax *	Fax cover sheet: styles only
Letters & Faxes	Professional Letter *	Letter: styles, boilerplate text, and field code
Memos	Contemporary Memo *	Styles and boilerplate text
Memos	Elegant Memo	Styles and boilerplate text
Memos	Professional Memo *	Styles and boilerplate text
Reports	Contemporary Report *	Styles only
Reports	Elegant Report *	Styles only

Tab	Template Name	Description
Reports	Professional Report *	Styles only
Web Pages	Blank *	Styles and boilerplate text
Web Pages	More	Provides link to Word 97 or Office 97 CD or Microsoft Word Web site for other Web Pages templates

Adding New Templates

The Word 97 and Office 97 CD have many templates that may not automatically install them-selves to your `Program Files\Microsoft Office Templates` folder. Hence, some of the templates in Table 10-2 may not appear in your `Templates` folder. These templates are found in the ValuPack subfolder of the CD. To make sure all the templates included with Word 97 are available to you, select File⇨New, and click the Other Documents tab. Click the template called Other Templates and Wizards.doc and follow the on-screen instructions for installing new templates.

Previewing the Styles in a Template

You can preview how the styles in a template will affect the formatting of characters and paragraphs in an existing document. If you're thinking about using a template as the basis for a new document, you can look at the effect of that template on a sample document supplied with Word.

Using a sample document to preview a template

Suppose that you are about to write a letter and you're thinking of basing it on one of the letter templates supplied with Word. To see how your letter will look, access the Style Gallery dialog box, as described in the following steps. To preview a templates format:

1. Choose Format⇨Style Gallery to display the Style Gallery dialog box.

2. In the Template list box, choose the template you want to view. For example, select Elegant Letter to look at that template.

3. In the Preview section at the bottom left of the dialog box, choose Example. After a few seconds, you'll see the top part of an example letter with formatting based on the Elegant Letter template, as shown in Figure 10-10.

4. After you have finished looking at the example, choose OK or Cancel to remove the dialog box from the screen.

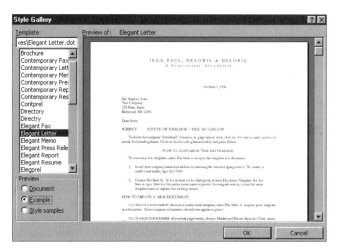

Figure 10-10: A letter based on the Elegant Letter template in the Style Gallery dialog box.

> **Note** If you consult Style Gallery at the beginning of a project, the Style Gallery's Preview of: area will remain blank—unless Example is checked.

Using a document to preview a template

Sometimes you have a document based on one template and want to see what it would look like if it was based on the character and paragraph styles in another template. To do so, open the document, and follow the steps in the preceding steps—but choose Document rather than Example in the Preview section at the bottom-left of the dialog box.

After you have looked at the document with the different formats, choose OK to copy the styles from the new template to your document, or choose Cancel to remove the dialog box without affecting your document. See Chapter 11 for more information about working with the Style Gallery dialog box.

Basing a New Document on a Template

As mentioned before, all Word documents are based on a template. By default, each document is based on the Normal template. You can choose any other template in the template folder as the basis of a new document. When you open a new document, Word copies all the boilerplate text from the selected template into the document. Styles defined in the template also are copied into the document. The template itself is attached to the document so that you have access to any AutoText entries and macros the template contains. If the template defines any custom command settings, these are available while you are working with the document.

To open a new document based on the Normal template, choose File⇨New, and double-click the Blank Page template icon in the General tab. You can also open a new document based on the Normal template by clicking the New button (the left-most button) in the Standard toolbar. The procedure for basing a new document on a template other than the Normal template is similar, except you choose the template you want to use before you choose OK. To create a document based on the Elegant Letter template:

1. Choose File⇨New to open the New dialog box.

2. Click the Letters & Faxes tab, and select Elegant Letter template icon.

3. Choose OK, or press Enter to open a new document based on the Elegant Letter template, as shown in Figure 10-11.

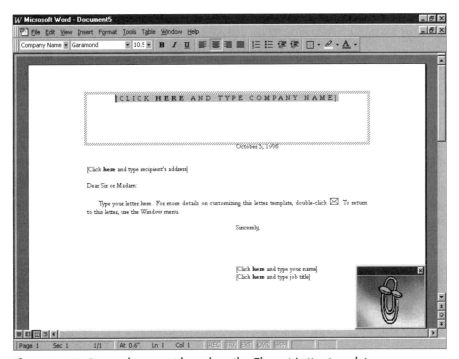

Figure 10-11: A new document based on the Elegant Letter template.

Tip   If you frequently use a specific template for new documents, it's a good idea to design a toolbar button for creating a document based on that template. Then, you can simply click the button to open the new document. Refer to Chapter 25 for information about creating toolbar buttons.

Creating a letter based on a template

The Elegant Letter template, like many of the supplied templates, contains styles that determine the overall appearance of the document and also boilerplate text. This template also contains a field code to automatically insert the date. When you open a new document, you'll see a copy of the template on which the document is based, not the template itself. Word displays the word **Document** in the title bar to remind you about this. Any changes you make on the screen apply only to the new document (the copy of the template), not to the template itself.

Changing boilerplate text

Most of the text you see in a new document based on the Elegant Letter template is boilerplate text. The text items in brackets are markers to show you where to put the text you want in your letter. Line by line, you select these markers, including the opening and closing brackets, and replace them with the appropriate text for your letter. The following steps describe the easiest way to replace an entire line of text. To replace the first return address marker in the Elegant Letter template:

1. Move the pointer into the space at the left end of the top line. When the pointer is in the correct position, its shape changes to a right pointing arrow.

2. Press the mouse button once to select the line of text.

3. Type the first character of your company name. As soon as you type the first letter of the name, the original text disappears and is replaced by the typed letter. Continue typing until the name is complete (see Figure 10-12).

Notice that the company name you type appears in the same font, size, and font style as the marker it replaces. This is because the Elegant Letter template defines a style for this line. You can see the name of this style, Inside Address, at the left end of the Formatting toolbar in Figure 10-12. For more information on styles, see Chapter 11.

Note Proceed in the same way to replace the boilerplate text in the next two lines. Replace [Street Address] with your street address and replace [City, State/Province, Zip/Postal Code] with your city, state or province, and ZIP or postal code.

As you will see later in this chapter, you can easily modify the template so that it contains your address, rather than markers, as boilerplate text. Then you won't have to type this information every time you write a letter.

The fourth line of text on your screen shows the date on which you are writing the letter. The next section, "Working with fields" explains this line. Moving down through the new document, you see three lines for the recipient's name and address. Replace these lines with the appropriate information, using the method already described.

Figure 10-12: The text you type replaces the company name placeholder.

Next, you see the greeting. You want to keep the word Dear (not in brackets), but you must replace [Recipient] with the name of the recipient, so you can't use the method previously described for replacing an entire line. Instead, perform the following steps:

1. Place the pointer just to the left of the opening bracket in the letter's greeting.

2. Press the mouse button, drag to the right until the entire word (including both brackets) is highlighted, and release the mouse button.

3. Type the recipient's name. The name you type replaces the original marker.

The template contains several other words and phrases enclosed in brackets. Replace [Type the body of your letter here] with what you want to say in the letter. Replace the other bracketed items with the appropriate text. Delete the items you don't need.

Working with fields

In the new document, the line below the return address contains the current date, as determined by the clock in your computer. If the wrong date is shown, your computer's clock is set incorrectly. You can change the clock by clicking the clock in the Windows 95 taskbar. This displays the properties dialog box for setting date and time.

Chapter 26 deals with fields in detail. For now, just understand that you can enter certain codes in a template or document and that these codes cause your computer to take certain actions. A frequently used example is the code that represents the current date. This code, which occurs in the Elegant Letter template, represents a field that causes Word to refer to the date setting in your computer clock and display it on the screen.

Saving a document based on a template

You already know how to save a new document: Choose File⇨Save, type a name for the document, and choose OK, or press Enter. If you have created a letter based on the Elegant Letter template, save the letter so that you can use it when you experiment with the steps described later in this chapter.

When you save a file, Word saves the boilerplate text copied from the template with any changes you made to it, and Word copies the styles defined in the template. Word also saves a record of the template to which the document is attached.

The next time you open the document, you see the text as it was when the document was saved. In addition, all the styles defined in the template are available, even those not used in the document. Word also attempts to reattach the document to the template to give you access to any AutoText entries, macros, or custom command settings that the template contains.

Of course, Word can reattach a document to its template only if the template is available. Suppose that you have a specialized template on one computer, and you create a document based on that template. After saving the document, you open the document on a computer that does not have access to the new template. The second computer displays the document, and you have access to the styles defined in the template because these styles are saved with the document. However, you do not have access to the other AutoText entries, macros, and customized command settings contained in the specialized template.

Note   Saving a document based on a template has no effect on the original template. The next time you open a new document based on the same template, you see a copy of the original template.

Creating a Template

The templates supplied with Word provide a good basis to get started with typical office documents. However, you will find that you need other templates. Some may be similar to those supplied with Word; others may be quite different. You can create a template by modifying an existing template or by converting a document to a template.

Using one template to create another template

Suppose that you like the general style of the Contemporary Letter template but would prefer to have the World graphic appear at the top of the page. You can easily modify the supplied template, and save the modified version for future use. To create a template by using an existing template, begin by opening the existing template as explained in the following steps:

1. Choose File⇨Open to display the Open dialog box.

2. In the Files of type list box at the bottom of the dialog box, choose Document Templates.

3. In the Look in list box, choose the folder that contains the template files from which you want to choose. Figure 10-13 shows the Templates folder.

4. Double-click the icon for the template you want to modify; in this case, open the Letters & Faxes folder and choose Contemporary Letter.dot. Choose OK, or press Enter.

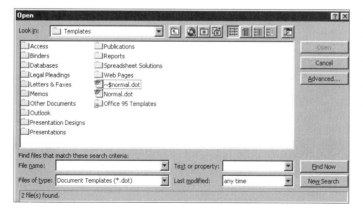

Figure 10-13: Letters & Faxes document templates displayed in the Open dialog box. Most templates are found in the subdirectories under the main Templates folder.

Note   You should save any modified template with a new name so that you still have access to the original template.

Word now displays the Contemporary Letter template. You can tell that the template—not a copy of it—is displayed because the title bar contains the name Contemporary Letter.dot.

Modifying a template

With the template displayed, you can use the editing procedures you learned in previous chapters to make your changes. You can easily replace the boilerplate text with your own text, such as your company name and address. To do so, delete the markers, and replace them with the text you want to use. Other changes you may want to make are to the alignment and choice of text and graphics. For example, Figure 10-14 shows the background shading and graphic dots removed and the image of the World moved from the middle to the top of the page in the Contemporary Letter template.

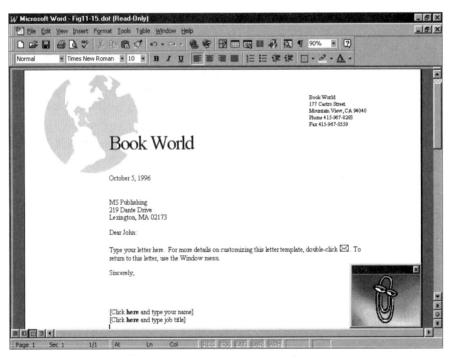

Figure 10-14: The modified Contemporary Letter template.

These are simple changes to the Contemporary Letter template. To make more extensive changes, you must modify the styles themselves. Chapter 11 explains modifying styles. You can also replace the graphics objects in templates, or add them to documents. For example, you may want to include your company logo in a letter, memo, or fax template. Refer to Chapters 13 and 14 for more information about working with graphics.

Saving a modified template

You should save a modified template with a new name. In this way, you retain the original template. After saving the modified template, the next time you create a new document, you will see the template you created in the list of available templates. To save a modified template:

1. Choose File⇨Save As to display the Save As dialog box, as shown in Figure 10-15. Word initially proposes to save the modified file with its original name.

2. Change to the folder where you want to save your template. Type a name for the new template. For example, you can type **My Letter**. Word automatically supplies the .dot extension.

3. Choose OK, or press Enter to save the template.

4. Choose File⇨Close to close the template.

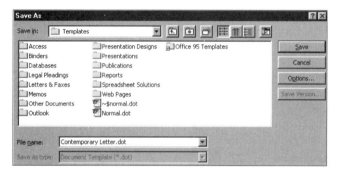

Figure 10-15: The Save As dialog box, ready to save the modified template.

Using a document to create a template

Instead of creating a new template by modifying an existing one, you can create a template from a document. You can use a document you created or one created by a Wizard. After creating a template based on a document, the next time you start a new document, the new template appears in the list of available templates. To create a template based on a document:

1. Create a document that contains all the boilerplate text, formatting, and other components you want in the template. If you are starting with an existing document, delete the items that are specific to the individual document, leaving only what is required in all the documents.

2. Choose File⇨Save As to open the Save As dialog box.

3. In the Save in list, choose the folder that contains your template files (Program Files\Microsoft Office\Templates).

4. In the Save as type list box, choose Document Template.

5. Replace the name in the File name text box with a name for the new template. Word automatically provides the `.dot` extension.

6. Choose OK, or press Enter to save the new template.

Working with Template Components

This chapter has focused on styles and boilerplate text in templates. As you know, a template may also contain AutoText entries, field codes, custom command settings, and macros. Every AutoText entry is stored in a template. When you learned to create AutoText entries in Chapter 3, you were working with documents based on the Normal template, so your entries were stored in that template. To create an AutoText entry, you begin by selecting text in a document, and then choose Insert➪AutoText➪AutoText to display the AutoCorrect dialog box, shown in Figure 10-16. Please note that AutoText appears as a tab under the AutoCorrect dialog box.

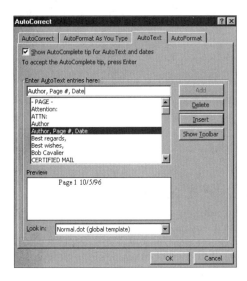

Figure 10-16: The AutoCorrect dialog box.

After naming the entry, you are ready to save it. Notice that the Look In text box initially contains All Documents (Normal.dot). If you choose Add, Word stores the new entry in the Normal template so that the entry is available in documents to which any template is attached. Choosing Insert Only inserts the AutoText entry into the current document. Only by selecting Add do you make it available to the currently selected template.

To store the new AutoText entry in the template attached to the active document, drop down the Look in list box. To store the AutoText entry in the template on which the active document is based, select that template in the list box, and choose Add.

Understanding field codes, custom command settings, and macros is helpful before you include them in templates. You can insert field codes in a template in the same way you insert them in a document. For information on inserting field codes in a document, see Chapter 26. Chapter 27 describes how to create macros and store them in templates.

Attaching a Different Template to a Document

After you create a document, it remains attached to its original template until you attach a different one. You may want to change the template attached to a document to modify the document's appearance. For example, after creating a letter based on the Contemporary Letter template, you may decide to give it a more sophisticated look. You can do so by attaching the Elegant Letter template to the letter. To attach a template to a document based on a different template:

1. Open the document to which you want to attach a different template.

2. Choose Tools⇨Templates and Add-ins to display the Templates and Add-ins dialog box, shown in Figure 10-17. The Document template text box at the top of the dialog box shows the name of the template to which the document is currently attached.

Figure 10-17: The Templates and Add-ins dialog box.

3. Enable the Automatically update document styles check box.

4. Choose the Attach button to display the Attach Template dialog box, which lists the available templates. Change to the folder containing the template you want to attach. Figure 10-18 shows the templates available in the Letters & Faxes folder.

Figure 10-18: The Attach Template dialog box.

5. Choose the name of the template you want to attach to the document. For example, you may choose Elegant Letter. Choose OK to return to the Templates and Add-ins dialog box. The Document template text box now shows the name of the template you want to attach to the document.

6. Choose OK, or press Enter to attach the new template to the document. After a few seconds, Word displays the document in the new format, as shown in Figure 10-19.

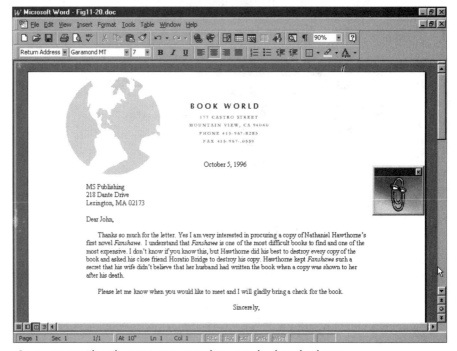

Figure 10-19: The Elegant Letter template attached to the letter.

Instead of following Steps 4 and 5, you can type the name of the new template in the Document template text box.

Attaching a different template to a document doesn't always reformat the document the way you may want. Some styles and formatting do not change automatically. In these cases, you will need to reapply the style for the new style to take effect. Attaching a document has the following effects on template components:

✦ Text in the document does not change although its appearance (font, size, and so on) may. The boilerplate text in the new template is not copied to the document. Any boilerplate text copied to the document from the original template remains unchanged.

✦ Graphics in the document do not change. Graphics in the new template are not copied to the document.

✦ The margin settings, page dimensions, and page orientation remain unchanged.

✦ Document styles and text formatting remain unchanged if the Automatically update document styles check box in the Templates and Add-ins dialog box is unchecked. If this check box is checked, document styles and text formatting defined in the new template are applied to the document. Each style in the document is replaced with a style of the same name in the new template. If the document uses a style that the new template does not have, the style in the document is unaffected.

✦ AutoText, macros, and custom command settings defined in the new template become available, replacing those defined in the original template.

Caution When you attach a new template to a document, the original template and new template must be compatible. In the example, you changed from one letter template to another, so everything worked well. If you had changed to an incompatible template, such as the Invoice template, you would see strange results because the Invoice template is not designed for letters.

Using Components from Different Templates

You have seen how documents based on any template can access components of the Normal template because the Normal template is always global. For this reason, you should keep widely used template components in the Normal template so that you don't have to repeat them in other templates. But what if you have components such as AutoText entries in one template and you want to use them in a document based on another template? You can accomplish this in several ways.

Attaching a template to a document

One way to use components from a template other than the one attached to your document is to attach that template to the document. Remember, though, that when you attach a new template to a document, the document is no longer attached to its original template. After changing the template in this way, your document has access to components in the new template, but not to those in the old template.

Changing a template from local to global

Another way to have access to components in a different template is to change that template from local to global. At the beginning of this chapter, you read that the Normal template is always global and that other templates are usually local. Word lets you make any template global so that a document attached to any other template can access the components. To provide global access to a template:

1. Choose File⇨Templates to open the Templates and Add-ins dialog box, shown in Figure 10-20. If you have not made any templates global, the Global templates and add-ins list box is empty.

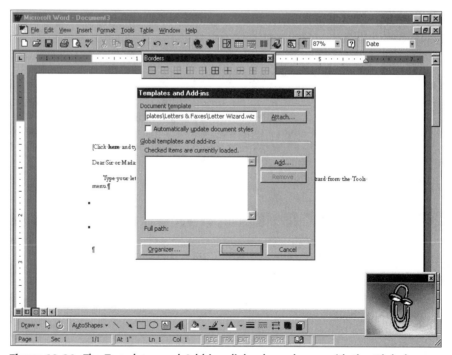

Figure 10-20: The Templates and Add-ins dialog box, shown with the Global Templates and add-ins box empty.

2. Choose A<u>d</u>d to display the Add Template dialog box, which contains a list of available templates, as shown in Figure 10-21.

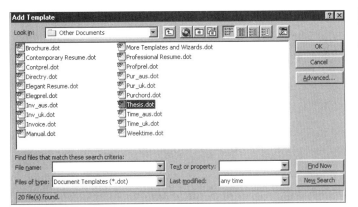

Figure 10-21: The Add Template dialog box.

3. Select the name of the template you want to make global, and choose OK to return to the Templates and Add-ins dialog box. The template is now listed in the <u>G</u>lobal templates and add-ins list box, as shown in Figure 10-22.

4. Choose OK or press Enter to return to your document.

Figure 10-22: The Templates and Add-ins dialog box with one template listed as global.

After you make a template global, you can use its AutoText entries, macros, and custom command settings—as well as those in the Normal template —in a document to which any template is attached.

Opening, closing, and removing global templates

Two things happen when you provide global access to a template. The template you choose is available to be opened as a global template, and that template is opened (that is, loaded into your computer's memory so that it can be used). You know that the template is available for use as a global template because it is included in the global templates list in the Templates and Add-ins dialog box. You know that it is open because the check box to the left of the template name is checked.

You can make any number of templates global. However, open global templates occupy memory, so don't open more global templates than you need. To close a global template, click the check box to the left of the template's name in the Templates and Add-ins dialog box. When you do so, the check mark disappears, but the template name remains in the list. You can easily reopen any template in the list by clicking the empty check box to the left of that template's name.

All open global templates remain open until you exit Word. The next time you open Word, all global templates are listed in the Global templates and add-ins list box, but they are not loaded or active. You must open the global templates you want to use in the current Word session. It's best to open only those templates to which you specifically need global access. Besides clicking in the check box to open a template, you can choose to delete a global template from the Global templates and add-ins list box. To unload and remove a template from the global list:

1. Choose File⇨Templates to open the Templates and Add-ins dialog box.

2. Select the name of the template you want to remove from the Global templates and add-ins list.

3. Choose Remove to immediately remove the selected template from the list.

4. Repeat Steps 2 and 3 to remove other templates.

5. Choose OK, or press Enter to close the dialog box.

Starting Word with global templates already open

The Word installation procedure automatically creates an empty folder named Startup as a subfolder of Winword (or whatever name you chose for your main Word folder). You can use the Startup folder for templates that you want to become active and global immediately when you start Word.

Suppose you have created a template called *main* that contains components you use frequently. You can use the Windows File Manager or DOS to copy this file to the Winword\Startup folder. You don't move *main* from the template folder; rather, you copy the template to the Startup folder. If you move the template file from the template folder, Word cannot access it as a template file. Now that the Startup folder contains a copy of Main.dot, it automatically becomes an open global template the next time you start Word.

Tip   You can copy more than one template file to the Startup folder. All templates in the Startup folder become global and open when you start Word.

Copying, deleting, and renaming template components

Word includes an Organizer dialog box that lets you copy components between templates and between a document and a template. You also can rename and delete template components with the Organizer dialog box.

Copying components between templates

The third way to use components from another template is to copy them from one template to another. Suppose that you have a document based on one template and you have made another template global so that you can access its components. Now you want access to the same document on another computer. Instead of making sure that the second computer has the same global template, it's often easier to copy the components of the global template you are using into the template on which the document is based. Then you copy one template to the other computer. To open the Organizer dialog box:

1. Open a document based on the template that contains the component you want to copy, or open the template itself.

2. Choose File⇨Templates to display the Templates and Add-ins dialog box.

3. Choose the Organizer button to display the Organizer dialog box with the Styles tab selected, as shown in Figure 10-23.

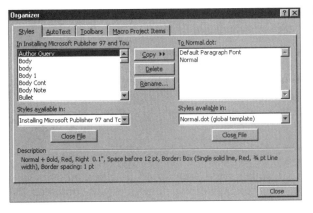

Figure 10-23: The Organizer dialog box with the Styles tab selected.

The Organizer dialog box is divided into four tabs: Styles, AutoText, Toolbars, and Macros. To illustrate how you can copy components between templates, look at the Styles tab. The dialog box contains two list boxes: each template's components. You list components of the template you want to copy *from* in the box on the left and components of the template you want to copy *to* in the box on the right.

The left list box initially lists the styles in the active document or template. You can drop down the Styles Available In list box, and choose to display styles in the active document, in the template attached to the active document, or in the Normal template. The right list box initially shows the styles in the Normal template. If the left list box does not list components of the template from which you want to copy, you must select the appropriate template. To select the template or document from which components will be copied:

1. In the Styles dialog box, choose the Close File button below the left list box. The items in the list disappear, and the Close File button is replaced with the Open File button.

2. Choose the Open File button to display the Open dialog box.

3. In the Open dialog box, select the document or template you want to use as a source of template components, and choose OK. Word displays a list of styles in the new document or template.

To change the right list box so that it contains the components of the template to which you want to copy components, use the previously outlined steps, but begin by choosing the Close File button beneath the right list box. The shortcut key for the Close File and Open File buttons below the left list box is F, whereas the shortcut key for the Close File and Open File buttons below the right list box is E. The Organizer dialog box now displays a list of styles in the document or dialog box from which you want to copy styles, and a list of the styles in the template to which you want to copy styles. Now you are ready to copy components. To copy one or more styles:

1. Select one or more style names in the list on the left.

2. Choose the Copy button to copy the selected styles to the list on the right. If the list on the right already contains any name you have selected to copy from the list on the left, Word asks you to confirm that you want to overwrite the existing style.

3. After you have finished copying styles, choose Close to close the Organizer dialog box.

The preceding procedure describes how to copy styles from one template to another. By selecting the appropriate Organizer dialog box tab, you can copy AutoText, toolbars, and macros between templates. If you copy a toolbar that contains a macro, you must also copy the macro itself.

Deleting template components

If you experiment extensively with templates, you will find eventually that some templates are quite large because they contain components that you don't use. To delete unwanted components from templates, select the appropriate tab in the

Organizer dialog box, display the template's components in either list box, select the component you want to delete, and choose the Delete button. When Word asks you to confirm, choose Yes or No.

Renaming template components

Working with predefined templates, you may find that you come across a component, such as a style, that you want to rename. For example, you may want to change the salutation style to greeting, or the signature style to the word name. The Organizer dialog box lets you rename template components as follows:

1. Select the appropriate tab in the Organizer dialog box. Select the component you want to rename.

2. Choose the Rename button to display the Rename dialog box, shown in Figure 10-24.

3. Type the new name for the template component, and choose OK. The Organizer dialog box reappears with the new name displayed.

Figure 10-24: The Rename dialog box.

Using Office's Ready-Made Binders

Office 97 brings new options for creating compound documents. The Binder gives you the ability to combine files from different applications into a single master document. The improved capability to create a compound document is made possible by an extension to OLE 2.0 called DocObjects. This extension lets you create a single document (object) by using several different applications. This object is saved in a file format called an Office Binder that ends with an .obt file extension. For more information on using the Binder and other applications, see Chapter 15.

Binders let a user group files from Word, Excel, PowerPoint, or any Office-compatible application into a document that can be edited, stored, printed, and distributed as a single file independent of the applications used to create it.

When you start Binder, a blank binder appears. Once you start the Binder, click New Binder on the File menu to start a new binder. You can also use the New Binder command to open one of the ready-made binders included with Office 97.

Basing a document on a ready-made binder

A binder acts as a "master copy" for a set of documents in a binder. You can add related documents and create a binder for a particular project. Office 97 ships with binders that you can modify easily. The binders include the following:

✦ Client Billing

✦ Meeting Organizer

✦ Proposal and Marketing Plan

✦ Report

To display the binders, choose the Start a New Document button in the Office toolbar, and select the Binders tab. If the binders mentioned above are not present, copy them over manually from the Office 97 CD. Files with the extension .obt are binders, and can be copied from the ValuPack subfolder of the Office 97 CD to the Program Files\Microsoft Office\Templates\Binders subfolder. They will now be available when you select the Binders tab from the Office toolbar. Figure 10-25 shows the New dialog box for Office 97 with the Binders tab selected. To create a new binder, double-click the binder icon that best matches the type of document you want to create.

The types of documents that make up the binder appear as icons in the left side of the window. You can hide or display the left pane of the Binder window by clicking the double arrow button to the left of the toolbars. Figure 10-26 shows a binder created by using the Proposal Binder Wizard that includes a cover letter, a price quote (Excel), a slide show (PowerPoint), referrals, details, and follow-up documents. Each document of a binder is referred to as a section. In the example shown in Figure 10-26, the cover letter section of the Proposal binder is shown. If you right-click the cover letter icon in the upper-left corner of the screen, a shortcut menu appears providing options for working with the cover letter section.

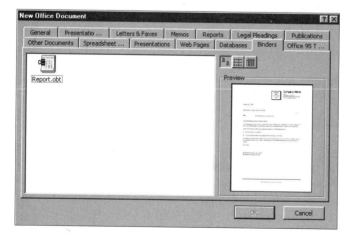

Figure 10-25: The New Office Document dialog box with the Binders tab selected.

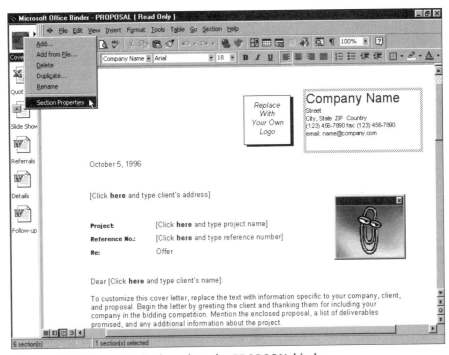

Figure 10-26: A new binder based on the PROPOSAL binder.

Editing a ready-made binder

You can add documents, called *sections*, to the binder by dragging existing documents into the left pane of the Binder window, or by choosing a command from the Section menu. To add a document or a selection (section) from Word or another application:

1. Open Word or the application that contains the section you want to add to the binder.

2. Do one of the following:

   • Select the part of the document you want to add, and drag and drop the selection into the left pane of the binder window. A pointer in the left border of the pane appears, indicating where the selection will be added.

   • Choose Section⇨Add. The Add Section dialog box appears. In this box, you can choose to add a blank section for an Excel Chart, an Excel Worksheet, a PowerPoint Presentation, or a Word Document. Choose the type of section you want to add.

   • Choose Section⇨Add from File. This displays the Add from File dialog box. Choose the file you want to add to the object, and click Add.

3. To save your binder, choose File⇨Save Binder. If you want to change the name of the binder, choose File⇨Save Binder As.

The Section menu lets you delete, move, or duplicate an existing binder section. Select the icon that represents the section you want to affect in the left pane of the binder, and choose the appropriate command. You can move a section by dragging and dropping the icon in the left pane. You can also use keyboard and mouse shortcuts. For example, you can copy a selection by pressing Ctrl and dragging the icon, or delete a section by pressing Delete with the section icon selected.

While working with a document opened in a binder, the menu bar at the top of the screen functions the same as it would with any Word document, with the following exceptions:

✦ Using File commands, such as Print, Save, and Properties, affects the entire binder, not the document you have open at the moment.

✦ The Section menu allows you to switch between documents that are saved with the binder, meaning those documents that appear as icons on the left side of the screen.

✦ The Section menu contains commands to print the open document itself, (rather than the entire binder), rename and rearrange the order of individual documents in the binder, and view the document in its native application.

✦ If you edit a document while it is open in a binder, use the command Save as File, (found in the Section menu) to save your work with that document apart from the binder.

✦ The Go menu allows access to Web sites and pages, so documents on the Internet can actually be part of your binder. Figure 10-27 shows the Add from File dialog box with the Search the Web icon available. With it, you can search Web sites from your Favorites list, or search with any Web browser installed on your computer.

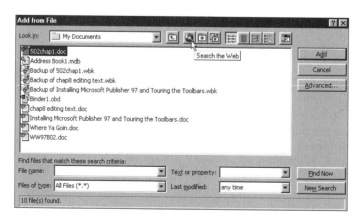

Figure 10-27: The Binder's Add from File dialog box found under the Section menu.

Note You can remove and reorganize sections in the binder templates, but, if you use an Office 97 binder template or Wizard, don't change a section that performs calculations and other automated tasks. For example, using the Client Billing Wizard and changing the Excel Invoice and TimeCard workbooks in the template may prevent the Excel formulas and macros from working correctly.

Summary

In this chapter, we explored ways to format entire documents quickly by using Word's Wizards, predefined templates, and binders. In this chapter, you learned how to

✦ Create documents using Word's Wizards. Select the Wizard you want to use by choosing the File⇨New command, clicking the tab in which the Wizard is located, and double-clicking the Wizard's icon. Or, you can choose the Start a New document button from the Office toolbar to open the New dialog box.

✦ Use Word's predefined styles in templates. This feature is one of the great, timesaving, formatting features available in Word 97.

✦ Create a template. You can create a new template by modifying an existing template, or by converting a document (created by you or a Wizard) to a template.

✦ Use components from different templates. You can accomplish this by attaching a new template to your document, changing a local template to a global template, or copying components between templates.

✦ Create compound documents using Office 97 Binder. Office 97 Binder comes with the ready-made binders that you can easily modify, including: Client Billing; Meeting Organizer; Proposal and Marketing Plan; and Report.

Where to go next...

The next chapter goes into greater depth on using styles. It shows how you can create and use your own styles to format paragraphs and add your styles to templates. Adding styles that you define to a template gives you greater control to create documents that match the specific formatting you want.

✦ To learn how to merge mailing addresses for letters you created by using Word's Wizards and templates, see Chapter 20.

✦ To learn how to replace existing graphics in documents you created by using Word's Wizards and templates, see Chapter 13.

✦ For more information on using graphics in documents, you may also want to check out Chapter 14, which explains positioning text and graphics by using frames.

✦ For more information on creating documents with the Binder, see Chapter 15. The Binder in Office 97 is a great way to create compound documents by using Word and other Office 97 applications.

✦   ✦   ✦

Styles and AutoFormatting

Perhaps the single most time-consuming task in creating a document is formatting it. Several significant issues are involved in formatting a document: its appearance, consistency of formatting throughout the document, adherence to your organization's guidelines, and so on. You can use styles to dramatically reduce the amount of time and effort needed in formatting. In this chapter, you learn how to master Word's powerful style features.

The Zen of Word's Styles

Simply put, a style is a collection of formats that you apply to the text in a document. Instead of applying the formats directly to the text, however, you give them a name (the style name), and you apply the style to the text. You derive two major benefits from this approach: applying formatting is simple and ensures uniformity, and reformatting is quick and easy.

When you apply style to text, all the text immediately becomes formatted with the formats defined in the style. Later, if you need to change some of the formatting, instead of searching for the text that you want to reformat, you just redefine the style with the new formats, and all the text that has that style applied to it changes instantly to match the new definition. Because direct formatting always overrides a style, anyone can make changes to the formatting, regardless of whether he or she is familiar with using styles.

Word uses two types of styles: paragraph and character. Paragraph styles format the entire paragraph at once, but character styles format only selected text. Paragraph styles can include any or all the following elements: font and font size, other character formatting, indentation, text alignment, pagination as it applies to a paragraph, line spacing, tab stops, borders, frame, numbering, and language.

Character styles include only character and language formatting. You can apply character styles to text within a paragraph that has been formatted with a paragraph style. If you select text that has been formatted with a character style, that style is displayed in the Style box in the Formatting toolbar; otherwise, the paragraph style is displayed.

You can use the Organizer button in the Style dialog box (Format⇨Style) and the Style Gallery dialog box (Format⇨Style Gallery) to copy styles from another document or template to the current one. The Organizer dialog box enables you to copy individual styles, and the Style Gallery dialog box copies all the styles from a document or template.

 Word 97 includes several style improvements and new style features that make creating and updating styles easier. These new features and improvements include:

✦ Improved automatic style updating that makes it easy for you to modify styles by automatically propagating style changes. You change a style in one location and Microsoft changes all other occurrences of the same style automatically.

✦ A new style preview feature that allows you to see the exact font, size, formatting, and justification of each style, making it easy for you to differentiate between styles.

✦ A new automatic style definition feature that lets Word automatically create styles as you format a document.

Styles and Templates

Styles and templates are closely related. A *template* is a special file that Word uses as a basis for creating a document. Every document created in Word is based on a template. Templates can contain text, styles, AutoText entries, macros, customized menus, customized keystroke assignments, and customized toolbars. So, for example, when you create a memo, instead of having to type the same headings and apply the same formats each time, you can just use a template that already contains these elements.

Word comes with templates for different types of documents, such as memos, reports, and business letters. You can use these templates just as they are, modify them, or create your own. If you don't choose any other template, Word uses the

Normal template. The Normal template is a general, all-purpose template that contains only a few basic definitions, such as the font and font size, margin settings, and line spacing.

When you use styles, rather than applying formatting directly to the paragraph or character, you assign a code name to your formatting. This code name is what is called the style. Then you apply the style to selected paragraphs or characters. Later, if you want to change the formatting of any of the applied styles, you simply change the style definition, and the same changes occur to all of the same styles throughout the entire document.

Word also comes with a set of styles that you can use immediately in a document, regardless of the template. You can modify the styles that come with Word or create entirely new ones. When you create a new style, you can save it in the current template so that it is available for you to use when you create another document based on that template.

If another template or document contains a style that you want to use, you don't have to recreate the style. You can use the Organizer to copy selected styles, or you can use the Style Gallery to copy all the styles from another template or document to the current document.

Styles that come with Word

Word comes with a set of predefined styles that you can use or modify in any document. When you begin a new document based on the Normal template, Word applies the Normal style to each paragraph unless you specify otherwise. The Style box on the Formatting toolbar initially contains only four paragraph styles (Heading 1, Heading 2, Heading 3, and Normal) and one character style (Default Paragraph Font) when you begin a document based on the Normal template (see Figure 11-1). These four styles are just a small sampling of all the styles available.

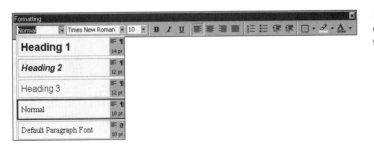

Figure 11-1: The Style drop-down list box on the Formatting toolbar.

If you want to see all the styles that come with Word and their definitions, choose Format⇨Style to open the Style dialog box (see Figure 11-2). Choose All Styles in the List drop-down menu at the bottom-left corner of the dialog box to make the styles that come with Word appear in the Styles box. You can see the preview and description of any style by selecting it from the Styles box. Paragraph styles are noted with a paragraph mark, and character styles are noted with a lowercase *a* to the left of the style name in the Styles list. You can apply any of these styles to the document text with the Apply button, or you can just modify them as you desire and apply them later.

Tip To see the complete list of styles in the Style box on the Formatting toolbar, first click somewhere in the document to deselect the Style box. Then press the Shift key and click the down arrow on the Style box. All the style names appear in the list.

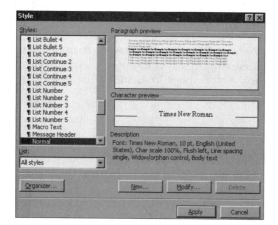

Figure 11-2: The Style dialog box.

Most of the styles that come with Word are available in all the templates that come with Word. Some templates have additional styles based on the type of document they create. You can create new styles and new templates as needed, or just use the existing ones. Although you can redefine the formatting for any of Word's built-in styles, you cannot delete them.

You can use Word's built-in Heading styles in Outline view to quickly reorganize a document by moving large blocks of text. You also can use them to compile a table of contents easily. Word also applies certain styles automatically, such as header and footer styles. Table 11-1 lists the styles that Word applies automatically when you use the appropriate command. As with all styles, you can change the definition of any of these styles as you want.

Table 11-1 **Styles That Word Automatically Applies**	
Style	*Applied To*
Annotation Text	Text entered in annotations
Annotation Reference	Annotation reference marks, which are the initials of the person entering the annotations
Caption	Text entered by using the Caption command
Footer	Text in footers
Footnote Text or Endnote Text	Text entered in a footnote or endnote
Footnote Reference or Endnote Reference	The footnote or endnote reference mark
Header	Text in headers
Index 1 - 9	Index entries
Line Number	Automatic line numbers from the Page Setup command
Macro Text	WordBasic macro text
Page Number	Automatic page numbers
TOC 1 - 9	Table of Content entries
Table of Authorities	Table of Authorities text
Table of Figures	Table of Figures text

Automatic formatting in Word

Word's AutoFormat feature allows you to format an entire document quickly and easily. Word scans each paragraph in the document and applies paragraph styles from the current template. After the entire document has been formatted, you have the option of accepting or rejecting each style that was applied. You can also use Word's AutoFormat feature as you type to automatically format lists, tables, headings, and bulleted items. Working with Word's AutoFormat feature is explained later in this chapter.

Creating new styles

Two methods are available in Word for creating a new style: using the Style command from the Format menu, and using existing text that contains the formats you want in the new style. The easier method is to use existing text that already contains the formatting you want. If you are creating a document according to specified formats, however, you may find it more efficient to create the styles by using the Style command from the Format menu. To create a new style from existing text:

1. Select the text that contains the formatting you want.

2. Click in the Style box on the Formatting toolbar. This selects the style name that is currently in the box.

3. Type a new name, and press Enter. Word adds the name you typed to the list of styles in that document.

You can create only paragraph styles by using the Style box, not character styles. This means that the new style will include any paragraph formatting as well as character formatting. For example, if you selected a paragraph that was justified, the new style will contain justification as a format.

Caution If the text you select to create the new style has conflicting formats (for example, the first word in the selection is bold but the rest of the selection is not), Word defines the style according to the first character of the selected text.

To create a new style using the Style dialog box:

1. Choose Format⇨Style to display the Style dialog box (refer to Figure 11-2).

2. Click the New button to display the New Style dialog box (see Figure 11-3).

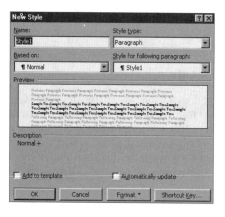

Figure 11-3: The New Style dialog box.

3. Type a name for the new style in the Name box.

4. Choose the type of style you want in the Style type box (Character or Paragraph).

5. If you want to base the new style on another style, choose the style from the Based on box. Otherwise, the new style is based on the current style. If you want a different style to follow the new style automatically, choose it from the Style for following paragraph box. (This topic is discussed more fully later in this chapter.)

6. Click the Format button to choose the different types of formats you want to add to the style. Click OK after you choose all the formats in order to return to the New Style dialog box.

7. If you want to be able to apply the style by using a keystroke, click the Shortcut Key button, and press a new shortcut key.

8. If you want to add the style to the current template, click in the Add to template check box. This makes the new style available to all new documents you create by using this template.

9. Click OK to create the new style.

Style-naming conventions

As with filenames, each style name in a document must be unique. However, you can give a style more than one name. This is an advantage if you commonly use many styles and you type the name of the style in the Style box on the Formatting toolbar. Then, if you forget the name of a style, you can scroll the list to find the longer descriptive name. When you give an additional name to a style (instead of changing the style name), the additional name is called an *alias*. You can add an alias to a style name by selecting the style name in the Style box on the Formatting toolbar and adding a comma and the alias after the existing style name. (When you first select a style in the Style box, the entire name becomes selected. To avoid replacing the existing name with the comma and the alias, click once again after the existing style name, and you will be able to enter the alias.)

Style names can be no longer than 253 characters, including aliases, spaces, and commas. Although you can use some special characters, it is best just to avoid them entirely.

Basing a new style on an existing style

When you create a new style based on existing text in Word, you can base the new style on an existing style. The style on which it is based is then known as the *base style*. The subtle concept of basing a new style on an existing style is important to understand for two reasons. The primary reason is that you can quickly change the formats in a group of styles by making the change in the base style. The other reason is to avoid unwanted errors that can be difficult to understand if you are unaware of the base style concept.

By default, a new style created from an existing paragraph is based on the style applied to that paragraph. You have the option of changing the base style or of using no base style at all. When you choose a base style (or use the default), the new style inherits many of the formats of the base style (font, font size, alignment, and line and paragraph spacing). Later, if you change the font in the new style, the base style remains unaffected.

If you change the font in the base style, however, the font changes in all the related styles. For example, you might use different styles for the different headings in your document, but all the headings use the same font. If all the heading styles are related to a base style and you decide to change the font for the headings in that document, you need only make the change in the base style. You can see how misunderstanding this subtle concept can cause you significant formatting problems.

Caution   Because many of Word's built-in styles are based on the Normal style, you should be careful about redefining the Normal style in any document. Changes you make to the Normal style may result in unwanted changes in parts of your document that use other styles based on the Normal style.

One way around this problem is to create base styles for the different elements of your document. You can create a base style for body text, for example, and then create a series of related styles that apply to indented text, double-spaced text, and so on. The trick then is not to apply the base style to any element of your document; rather, use it as a basis for creating the other styles. Later, if you need to make formatting changes that apply to all the text in the document (such as changing the font), you can just redefine the base style.

Applying styles

Word provides a variety of methods for applying styles to text. These methods include:

✦ The Style command from the Format menu

✦ The Formatting toolbar

✦ Shortcut keystrokes

✦ Automatically following one style with another

✦ Applying heading styles in Outline view

✦ Using the Edit➪Replace command to find and replace styles

✦ AutoFormatting

Some of these methods are more obvious than others. Automatically following one style with another or quickly applying the same style to several different items in your document may not be apparent at first, but you will find that they help reduce the tedium of formatting.

The following procedures describe the usual methods of applying a style. They are variations on a theme, so use whichever method appeals to you.

To apply a style by using Format⇨Style:

1. Choose the text to be formatted if you want to apply a character style. If you want to apply a paragraph style to a single paragraph, just position the insertion point somewhere in that paragraph.

2. Choose Format⇨Style to display the Style dialog box (refer to Figure 11-2).

3. Choose the style you want to apply from the list in the Styles box. If you don't see the style you want, click the down arrow to the right of the List box (in the bottom-right corner of the dialog box) to see more categories of styles. If there are character styles in the list, they appear in normal text, unlike paragraph styles, which are bold.

4. Click the Apply button.

Tip   Word enables you to format text directly, even though it has a style applied to it. This feature can be useful when you want to make a quick change or two to certain text but you don't need to redefine the style. Sometimes, however, you may want to reset the paragraph to the formats defined in the style. You can do this quickly by clicking in the paragraph and pressing Ctrl+Q.

To apply a style using the Formatting toolbar:

1. If the Formatting toolbar is not visible, choose View⇨Toolbars, and choose the Formatting menu item.

2. Select the text to be formatted. If you want to apply a paragraph format to a single paragraph, just position the insertion point somewhere in that paragraph.

3. Click the down arrow to the right of the Style box (refer to Figure 11-1). Paragraph styles are bold, and character styles are not.

4. Choose the style. Word applies it immediately to your selection.

To apply styles using shortcut keystrokes:

1. Select the text to be formatted. If you want to apply a paragraph format to a single paragraph, just position the insertion point somewhere in that paragraph.

2. Type the shortcut keystroke. (If the style doesn't have a shortcut keystroke defined, see the section "Modifying a style.")

Tip   If you want to apply a style to more than one selection, apply the style to the first selection, select the additional text or paragraph, and press Ctrl+Y or choose Edit⇨Repeat Style. Alternatively, you can use the F4 key, which is Word's Repeat key. In this way, you can apply the same style to a number of nonconsecutive selections throughout your document.

Automatically following one style with another

This method is best used in situations where one style naturally follows another, such as body text that follows a heading or a series of questions and answers where the questions have a different format than the answers do. When you define one style to follow another, Word applies the following style when you press Enter after having used the first style. For example, if you have a heading that is always followed by body text, you can define the heading style to have a body text style as the following style and define a shortcut keystroke to apply the heading style. Then, when you want to apply the heading style, you use the shortcut keystroke. When you press Enter after typing the heading, the next paragraph is formatted automatically with the body text style.

Applying heading styles in Outline view

You can use the heading styles that come with Word most efficiently in Word's Outline view, which Chapter 22 describes in detail. Briefly, the outlining tools let you easily apply heading styles and promote and demote heading levels. For example, if you have a level 2 heading that you think should be a level 1 heading, you can use the outlining tools to promote that heading to level 1. You also can collapse the text under the different heading levels in Outline view to better see the structure of your document and rearrange the headings as you desire.

Using the Replace command to find and replace styles

At some point, you may need to replace one style with another in your document. You accomplish this by doing the following:

1. Choose Edit⇨Replace (Ctrl+H). The Find and Replace dialog box appears. Select the Replace tab. If your Find and Replace dialog box doesn't appear the same as in Figure 11-4, click the More button.

2. After placing the text cursor in the Find what text box, click the Format button and then the Style option, to display the Find Style dialog box (see Figure 11-5).

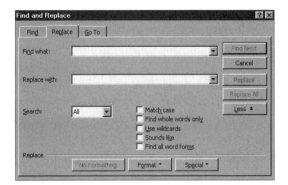

Figure 11-4: The Find and Replace dialog box.

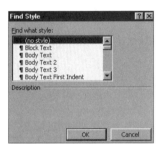

Figure 11-5: The Find Style dialog box.

3. Choose the style you want to replace in the Find what style list, and click the OK button in the Find Style dialog box. The style name now appears under the Find what text box in the Replace dialog box.

4. Place the text cursor in the Replace with text box, and, again, click the Format button to select the Style option from the pop-up list. This again will display the Find Style dialog box.

5. Choose the style you want to replace with in the Find what style list, and click the OK button in the Find Style dialog box. The style name appears in the Replace with text box in the Find and Replace dialog box. To change all instances at once, click the Replace All button. To choose specific instances, use the Find Next and Replace buttons.

Modifying a style

Modifying a style is the quickest way to change formatting in a document. When you modify a style, all the text that uses the style immediately becomes reformatted with the new formats. This is perhaps the single most compelling reason for using styles. You can modify a style by reformatting existing text that has the old style applied to it or by using Format⇨Style.

Using existing text to modify a style lets you see the new formatting applied to text in your document before you change the style. It's also a little quicker and easier.

To modify a style by using existing text:

1. Select the text or paragraph that has the style you want to modify. Be sure that the name of the style is displayed in the Style box on the Formatting toolbar.

2. Reformat the text as desired.

3. Click in the Style box on the Formatting toolbar to choose the style, and press Enter. The Modify Style dialog box appears (see Figure 11-6).

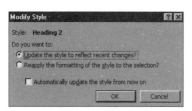

Figure 11-6: The Modify Style dialog box.

4. Choose the Update the style to reflect recent changes setting to change the style definition to match the formatting of the current selection.

The Reapply the formatting of the style to the selection setting in the Modify Style dialog box restores the formatting of the selection to that of the original style definition. The Automatically update the style from now on setting automatically changes the style definition to match the formatting of the current selection—without displaying the Modify Style dialog box. To turn off automatic updating, choose Format➪Style, select the style, click Modify, and then clear the Automatically update check box.

5. Click OK to redefine the style by using the selection as an example.

To modify a style by using Format➪Style:

1. Choose Format➪Style to open the Style dialog box (refer to Figure 11-2).

2. Choose the style you want to modify. If you don't see the style you want, click the down arrow to the right of the List box (in the bottom-right corner of the dialog box) to see more categories of styles.

3. Click the Modify button to open the Modify Style dialog box (see Figure 11-7).

4. Click the Format button. This opens a drop-down menu that lists the types of formatting you can change. For example, to change the font, choose Font to open the Font dialog box, where you can make your changes. When you make a change in a formatting dialog box and click OK, Word returns you to

the Modify Style dialog box so that you can pick another category of formatting if you want.

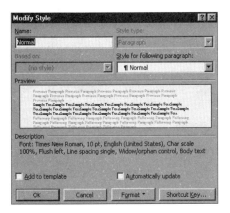

Figure 11-7: The Modify Style dialog box.

5. Make any other changes you want, such as assigning or changing a shortcut keystroke.

6. When you finish making your changes, click OK. This returns you to the Style dialog box.

7. To modify additional styles, repeat Steps 2 through 6. When you have finished, click the Close button. Word automatically updates all the text formatted with the modified style.

Copying styles

If you want to use a style that you know is in another document or template, you don't have to create the style again in the current document. Instead, you can use the Organizer. The Organizer enables you to copy styles, macros, toolbars, and AutoText from one document or template to another. The Organizer differs from the Style Gallery in that when you use the Organizer, you can copy individual styles, whereas the Style Gallery copies all the styles from a document or template. The Style Gallery, on the other hand, offers you a preview of the styles before you copy them.

Copying styles using the Organizer

The Organizer may take some practice at first. The Organizer dialog box is arranged to let you copy styles from one document or template to another document or template (see Figure 11-8). The dialog box consists of two list boxes side-by-side. You can choose a different document or template for each list box, and the box shows the styles in that document or template. You can choose individual styles in either list box and copy them to the other list box, thereby copying styles from one document or template to another. Below each list box is another box that displays the current document or template for that list box.

Note   One confusing aspect of this dialog box is that when you first open it, the Copy button points to the right, implying that you must copy styles from left to right. This is reinforced by the labels above the boxes. However, you can specify the direction of the copy by clicking any style name in the opposite box's list.

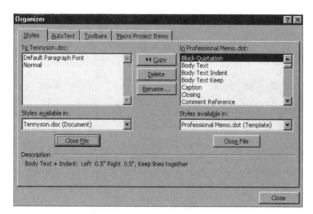

Figure 11-8: The Organizer dialog box.

One of the nicer features of the Organizer is that it lists the styles in both documents or templates and enables you to rename a style before you copy it. This is useful because when you copy a style into a document or template that already has a style with the same name, the incoming style overwrites the existing style, although there is a confirmation message that appears first. For this reason, you may want to take the time to be sure that all the styles you copy have names that aren't the same as in the document or template where you're copying them.

Note   Office 97 creates a Template folder when it's first installed. Template files are stored in this folder by default, so remember to switch to the Template folder in the Office 97 folder when you are searching for a template file. If you've created templates of your own, however, they may be stored in any folder you selected at the time you created the template. If the template you want doesn't appear in the list, choose a different folder.

To copy styles using the Organizer:

1. Choose Format⇨Style to open the Style dialog box (refer to Figure 11-2).

2. Click the Organizer button to open the Organizer dialog box (refer to Figure 11-8). Be sure that the Styles tab is selected. Although the Copy button points by default to the right, if you select a style in the list box on the right, the Copy button changes and points to the left.

By default, the styles listed in the box on the left are those in the template attached to the current document, and the box on the right shows the styles in the Normal template, but you can change either list box as you want (Steps 3 and 4).

3. To change the default document or template in either list box, click the Close File button below the list box. This clears the list box, and the Close File button changes to the Open File button.

4. Click the Open File button to display the Open dialog box (see Figure 11-9). You can choose a different template or document in this dialog box. After you choose the document or template, click OK to return to the Organizer dialog box.

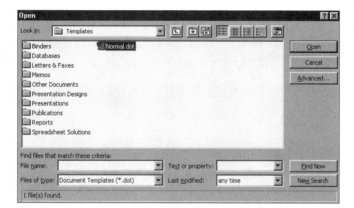

Figure 11-9: The Open dialog box.

Under both list boxes in the Organizer dialog box is a Styles available in box. These boxes display the document or template selected for the list boxes above. The Normal template is always an option in both of these boxes, so, if you want to select the Normal template, click the down arrow to the right and choose Normal.dot. (It's probably easiest to think of these two boxes as displays for the current document or template and a shortcut to choosing the Normal template.)

5. To select a style in a list box, click once on the style. To select multiple consecutive styles, click once on the first style, press the Shift key, and click once on the last style you want to select. To select multiple nonconsecutive styles, click once on the first style you want to select, press the Ctrl key, and click each additional style.

6. To copy selected styles from one list box to the other, click the Copy button. Remember, you can copy in either direction.

7. When you have finished copying your styles, click Close.

Note When you copy text that has a style applied to it from one document to another, you need to consider several factors. If the style name that is applied to the text you copy also exists in the second document but the formatting is different, the text will become formatted according to the style in the second document. If the style name doesn't exist in the second document, the style will be added to the list of styles in that document. If you don't want to add the style to the second document, take care not to include the paragraph mark in the selection of text you copy, because the paragraph mark carries the style.

Copying styles using the Style Gallery

You can use the Style Gallery to copy an entire set of styles (not individual ones) from a different template into the current document. The benefit of the Style Gallery is that you can preview the styles before you actually copy them. If a style from the template you choose has the same name as a style in the current document, the template style redefines and overwrites the current style. The Style Gallery copies all the styles from that template. If you want to copy selected styles, use the Organizer feature instead.

To use the Style Gallery to copy styles to your document:

1. Choose Format⇨Style Gallery to open the Style Gallery dialog box (see Figure 11-10).

2. Select the template you want from the list under the Template box.

3. To see the active document formatted with the styles from the selected template, choose the Document option under Preview.

4. To see a sample document formatted with the styles from the selected template, choose the Example option under Preview. For example, if you select one of the Memo templates and choose this option, a sample memo appears in the Preview of box.

5. To see a list of all the styles from the selected template with sample text that uses the styles, choose the Style samples option under Preview. This option lists the actual style names and applies the styles.

6. Click OK to copy the styles from the selected template to the active document.

Tip Step 2 in the preceding instructions directs you to select a template from the list of templates by clicking it. If you double-click instead, the styles from that template immediately are added to the current document and the dialog box closes. This is a shortcut you can use instead of selecting a style and then clicking the OK button. If you inadvertently double-click the template and you don't want the styles to be added to your document, click the Undo button on the Standard toolbar before you do anything else.

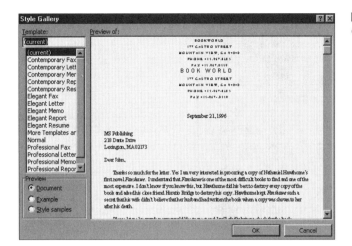

Figure 11-10: The Style Gallery dialog box.

Displaying style names in the Style Area

You can display the style names that you use as you work in Word. The only disadvantage to this is that you reduce the amount of screen space for your document. But if you work with styles to any degree, you probably will find it quite helpful to see the names of the styles as you work. The area where the style names are displayed is known as the *Style Area*. To display style names:

1. Make sure you are not in the Page Layout view in Word. Displaying the style names will not work in the Page Layout view. To check, be sure that Page Layout is not selected in the View menu.

2. Choose Tools⇨Options to open the Options dialog box (see Figure 11-11).

3. Be sure that the View tab is selected.

4. In the Style area width box in the lower-left portion of the View Options dialog box, enter a value or use the arrows to select a value. The style area width is an area on the left side of your document that can show the para-graph style names next to each paragraph. A good starting value is .5" width.

5. Click OK. The Style Area now appears to the left of your document (see Figure 11-12).

Tip   You can quickly display the Style dialog box by double-clicking anywhere in the Style Area (assuming it is visible).

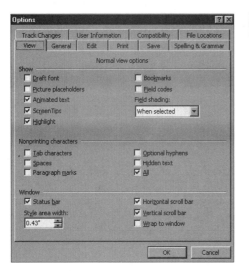

Figure 11-11: The Options dialog box with the View tab selected.

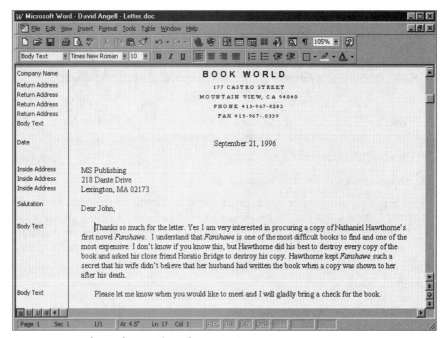

Figure 11-12: The Style Area in a document.

When you open a Style Area in your document, you can adjust the width by changing the value in the Options View dialog box. However, it's easier to use your mouse. The Style Area is separated from the text by a solid vertical line. If you carefully place the mouse pointer on this line, the pointer changes shape to show two opposing horizontal arrowheads. When the pointer has this shape, you can drag the line to the left or right, as you want. To close the Style Area quickly, just drag the line off the page to the left.

Renaming styles

You can rename a style a couple of ways. The easiest way is just to select the name that is currently displayed in the Style box on the Formatting toolbar and type a new name. The disadvantage to this approach is that the original style name still exists; so, if the number of styles in your document is a concern, use the following approach:

1. Choose Format⇨Style to open the Style dialog box.

2. Click the Organizer button to open the Organizer dialog box (refer to Figure 11-8). Be sure that the Styles tab is selected.

3. Select the style you want to rename from the list of styles in the box on the left. The styles displayed in this box are from the current document. If you want to rename a style from a different document or template, click the Close button below the list box. The list of styles are cleared from the list box, and the Close File button changes to the Open File button. Click the Open File button to display the Open dialog box, where you can select another document or template, and select the style you want to rename.

4. Click the Rename button to display the Rename dialog box (see Figure 11-13).

Figure 11-13: The Rename dialog box.

5. Type the new style name, and click OK to return to the Organizer dialog box.

6. Click the Close button to close the Organizer.

Deleting styles

As is always true of deleting anything, be careful about deleting styles. The style you delete may be in use in other parts of the document or in other documents based on the current template. If you delete a style that is being used, that text style will become the Normal style. If you really want to delete a style:

1. Choose Format⇨Style to open the Style dialog box (refer to Figure 11-2).

2. Select the style you want to delete from the list of styles in the box on the left. The styles displayed in this box are from the current document. To see other categories of styles, click the down arrow to the right of the List box at the bottom-left corner of the dialog box.

3. To delete selected styles, click the Delete button. Word asks you to confirm the deletion.

4. Click the Close button.

Note If the Delete button is dimmed, Word won't allow you to delete the style. For example if you select the Normal style, the Delete button is dimmed indicating the feature is disabled.

Printing a list of the styles in a document

Word lets you to print a list of the styles from the template used in the current document. When you print a list of the styles, Word prints the name of the style followed by all the formatting included in that style. This feature provides a handy way to check the makeup of all your styles currently available for the current document. To print a list of the styles in a document:

1. Choose File⇨Print or press Ctrl+P to open the Print dialog box (see Figure 11-14).

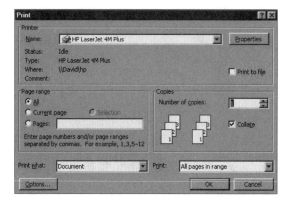

Figure 11-14: The Print dialog box.

2. Click in the Print what box to see a list of elements you can print.

3. Choose Styles from the list.

4. Click OK to print the styles.

Word's AutoFormat Tool

The automatic formatting feature in Word is called *AutoFormat*. This feature can save you a considerable amount of time and effort in your formatting tasks. When you use AutoFormat, Word analyzes each paragraph in the document to determine what kind of formatting should be applied: body text, bullets, heading styles, and so on. If you've already begun to format the document, Word uses the formatting you applied as a guide to which styles it applies. Any styles you applied are left unchanged.

When you use the AutoFormat feature, Word immediately begins the process of formatting the document. As soon as it finishes, you can review all the changes individually, reject them all at once, or accept them all at once. After the styles have been applied, it's a relatively easy matter to refine the document's appearance by changing the definition of a style or applying a different style to a particular paragraph (for example, change a Heading 2 style to a Heading 1). You also can change the overall design of the document by using the Style Gallery to copy styles from a different template.

Besides automatically applying styles to all the paragraphs in a document, the AutoFormat feature can

- ✦ Indent paragraphs when it finds tab characters or spaces at the beginning of a paragraph.
- ✦ Remove extra paragraph marks at the end of each line of body text.
- ✦ Replace straight quotation marks and apostrophes with "smart" (curly) quotes and apostrophes.
- ✦ Replace (C) with ©.
- ✦ Replace (R) with ®.
- ✦ Replace (TM) with ™.
- ✦ Replace asterisks, hyphens, or other characters typed as bullets with real bullets (•).
- ✦ Replace :-(with ☹ or :-) with ☺.

You can view all the AutoFormat options you can use in the AutoCorrect dialog box (see Figure 11-16). Remember that you can review each of these changes and accept or reject them. In addition, you can enable or disable different AutoFormat options in the AutoCorrect dialog box, although you should do this before using the AutoFormat feature.

Word also lets you automatically format text as you type by using the AutoFormat As You Type feature. Using this feature, Word automatically formats headings, numbered and bulleted lists, borders, and numbers as you type specific text and punctuation configurations.

Note Word also includes an AutoFormat Table feature (Table⇨Table AutoFormat). Working with table formatting is explained in Chapter 12.

Applying styles by using AutoFormat

You can use AutoFormat to apply styles to each paragraph in your document, or you can select the text you want to format.

To apply styles by using AutoFormat:

1. Select the text you want to format automatically. If you want to format the entire document automatically, don't select any text.

2. Choose Format⇨AutoFormat to display the AutoFormat dialog box (see Figure 11-15).

Figure 11-15: The AutoFormat dialog box.

3. To review and change AutoFormat options, click the Options button to open the AutoFormat tab in the AutoCorrect dialog box (see Figure 11-16). Enable the options you want, and click OK to return to the AutoFormat dialog box.

4. Click OK.

5. Choose the AutoFormat and review each change radio button. This option lets you double-check the formatting before it's actually applied. Choosing the AutoFormat now option automatically applies the formatting without your double-checking.

6. After Word has completed the automatic formatting process, another Auto-Format dialog box appears (see Figure 11-17). Now you can review, accept, or reject the changes made by the AutoFormat feature.

7. Click the Review Changes button. This opens the Review AutoFormat Changes dialog box (see Figure 11-18). Reviewing AutoFormat changes is explained in the next section. Clicking the Accept All button accepts all the changes without review, and clicking the Reject All button rejects all the changes without

review. To use styles from a different template, click the Style Gallery button to open the Style Gallery dialog box (refer to Figure 11-10).

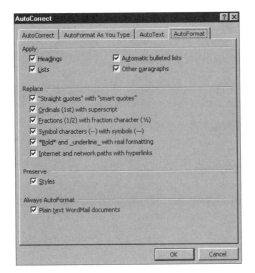

Figure 11-16: The AutoCorrect dialog box.

Figure 11-17: The second AutoFormat dialog box.

Figure 11-18: The Review AutoFormat Changes dialog box.

Reviewing AutoFormatting changes

As already described, when you use the AutoFormat feature to apply styles to your document, Word gives you the opportunity to accept or reject all the changes at once or to review each change. When you review the changes, Word uses temporary revision marks (and color on a color monitor) to indicate the changes. You can choose to hide the revision marks if you want to see the text as it appears with the changes. Table 11-2 lists the revision marks that Word uses.

Table 11-2
Revision Marks Used in AutoFormatting

Revision Mark	What It Means
Blue paragraph mark	Word applied a style to the paragraph
Red paragraph mark	Word deleted the paragraph mark
Strikethrough character	Word deleted the text
Underline	Word added the underlined text
Vertical line in the left margin	Word changed the formatting in that line

To review changes made by AutoFormat:

1. In the AutoFormat dialog box, click the Review Changes button. This opens the Review AutoFormat Changes dialog box (refer to Figure 11-18).

2. To review your changes, use any of the following three methods:

   • To move from change to change, use the Find next and the Find previous buttons (indicated by right-pointing and left-pointing arrows, respectively).

   • Scroll through the document. The dialog box remains open. (You can move the dialog box out of the way by dragging its title bar.) As you scroll, you can reject a change by selecting the particular paragraph and clicking the Reject button in the dialog box.

   • If you want to apply a different style while in the Review AutoFormat Changes dialog box, click in the paragraph you want changed and select the style you want from the Style drop-down box on the Formatting toolbar.

3. Each time you select a paragraph that has been changed, a description of the change appears in the Description box. To undo the change, click the Reject button. To undo the last rejected change, click the Undo Last button. To display the document without the revision marks, click the Hide Marks button.

Using the AutoFormat As You Type feature

Word also lets you automatically format text as you type by using the AutoFormat As You Type feature. This feature lets you automatically execute a limited number of formatting options as you type, including formatting headings, numbered and bulleted lists, borders, fractions, and ordinals. When you choose the AutoFormat As You Type option, Word automatically formats elements in your document based on the options you choose.

Table 11-3 explains what happens when you type a particular configuration of text and punctuation with the AutoFormat As You Type option active. To make any changes to the AutoFormat As You Type feature, choose Tools⇨AutoCorrect to display the AutoCorrect dialog box. Click the AutoFormat As You Type tab to display the settings (see Figure 11-19).

<table>
<tr><td colspan="2" align="center">Table 11-3
Using AutoFormat As You Type</td></tr>
<tr><td>*Option*</td><td>*Action*</td></tr>
<tr><td>Text that begins with a capital letter ends without punctuation, and is at least 20 percent shorter than the maximumline length</td><td>Makes the text a heading</td></tr>
<tr><td>Number followed by a space, a tab, or a period, and then text</td><td>Makes text a numbered list</td></tr>
<tr><td>Bullet followed by a space or tab and then text</td><td>Makes the text a bulleted list</td></tr>
<tr><td>Three or more dashes, underscores, or equal signs above a paragraph</td><td>Places a border above the paragraph: a thin line for dashes, a thick line for underscores, and a double line for equal signs</td></tr>
<tr><td>A fraction such as 1/2 or 1/4</td><td>Converts the entry to $^1/_2$ or $^1/_4$</td></tr>
<tr><td>Ordinal, such as 1st</td><td>Converts the entry to 1st</td></tr>
</table>

To stop a numbered list or bulleted list and return to normal paragraph formatting, press Enter twice. To do this, choose Tools⇨AutoCorrect, and select the AutoFormat As You Type tab to display the Automatic bulleted lists and Automatic numbered lists options, and then click the check boxes to remove the check marks.

Setting options for AutoFormat

You can select which options the AutoFormat feature uses. For example, you may not want to apply styles to your headings, or you may want to replace straight quotes with smart quotes. You can specify these options by choosing the Options button in the AutoFormat dialog box. You can also access these options by choosing Tools⇨AutoCorrect, and then choosing the AutoFormat tab. The AutoFormat tab appears with the AutoFormat option selected (refer to Figure 11-10). Table 11-4 explains each of the settings in the AutoFormat tab. Choosing the AutoFormat As You Type tab displays the settings for this option (see Figure 11-19). Table 11-5 describes each of the settings in the Auto Format As You Type tab.

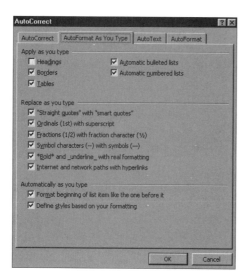

Figure 11-19: The AutoFormat As You Type settings in the AutoCorrect dialog box.

Table 11-4 AutoFormat Tab	
Apply Group Option	**What It Does**
Headings	Automatically applies Word's built-in styles (Heading 1 through Heading 9) to headings.
Lists	Automatically applies numbering and bullet styles to lists found in the document. If you select this option, Word first removes any manually inserted numbers or bullets.
Automatic Bulleted Lists	Automatically adds bullets to a list.
"Straight Quotes" with "Smart Quotes"	Changes the usual straight quotes and apostrophes to the curly ones.
Ordinals (1st) with Superscript	Replaces ordinals with superscript.
Fractions (1/2) with fraction character (1/2)	Replaces fraction entries into formatted fraction characters.
Symbol Characters with Symbols	Replaces typed characters that represent symbols with the actual symbols. For example, if you typed (R) in place of a registration symbol, this option replaces the text with ®.

Apply Group Option	What It Does
Bold and _underline_ with real formatting	Applies bold character formatting to words enclosed in asterisks and applies underline character formatting to words enclosed in underscore characters.
Internet and network paths and hyperlinks	Formats Internet and network paths as hyperlink fields so you can jump directly to an item by clicking the hyperlink.

Preserve Group Option	What It Does
Styles	Retains any styles you previously applied.

Always AutoFormat	What It Does
Plain text WordMail Documents	AutoFormats plain-text WordMail messages when you open them. This check box affects only WordMail messages; it does not affect pasted text or other text files.

Table 11-5
AutoFormat As You Type Tab

Apply Group Option	What It Does
Headings	Automatically applies Word's built-in styles (Heading 1 through Heading 9) to headings.
Borders	Automatically applies border styles as you type.
Tables	Creates a table when you type a series of hyphens and plus signs. For example, entering +—+—+ creates a two-column table.
Automatic Bulleted Lists	Automatically adds bullets to a list.
Automatic Numbered Lists	Automatically creates numbered lists as you type.

Replace as your type Group Option	What It Does
Straight Quotes with 'Smart Quotes'	Changes the usual straight quotes and apostrophes to the curly ones.
Ordinals (1st) with Superscript	Replaces ordinals with superscript.
Fractions (1/2) with fraction character (1/2)	Replaces fraction entries into formatted fraction characters.

(continued)

Table 11-5 *(continued)*	
Apply Group Option	**What It Does**
Symbol Characters with Symbols	Replaces typed characters that represent symbols with the actual symbols. For example, if you type (R) in place of a registration symbol, this option replaces the text with ®.
Bold and _underline_ with real formatting	Applies bold character formatting to words enclosed in asterisks and applies underline character formatting to words enclosed in underscore characters.
Internet and network paths and hyperlinks	Formats Internet and network paths as hyperlink fields so you can jump directly to an item by clicking the hyperlink.
Automatically as you type Group Options	**What It Does**
Format beginning of list item like the one before it.	Automatically repeats character formatting that you apply to the beginning of a list item.
Define styles based on your formatting	Creates new paragraph styles based on the formatting you apply in your documents. You can apply these styles in your document to save time and give your documents a consistent look.

Summary

Paragraphs may be the building blocks of Word, but it's styles that define the formats for any paragraph. Many of Word's formatting commands are simply premade styles. Word includes a sophisticated kit of style building tools to help you create styles for just about any type of formatting. Word's AutoFormat tool lets you apply your styles automatically to save time formatting so that you can concentrate on your document's content. This chapter explains working with both of these powerful features, including how to

✦ Master how styles work and their relationship to document templates, which are styles at the document level rather than the paragraph level.

✦ Apply styles by choosing the paragraph and choosing the style from the Style dialog box (Format➪Style) or the Styles list on the Formatting toolbar.

✦ Modify a style by selecting the paragraph that has the style you want to change, clicking in the Style box and pressing Enter, and choosing OK in the Reapply Style dialog box to redefine the style.

✦ Apply styles for an entire document by using the Format⇨AutoFormat command.

✦ Apply styles as you type by using the AutoFormat As You Type tab in the AutoCorrect dialog box.

Where to go next...

✦ If you want to know more about basic paragraph formatting that you can include in styles, check out Chapter 8.

✦ If you want to learn about applying document styles (templates), see Chapter 10.

✦   ✦   ✦

Working with Tables

A table gives you an efficient, concise way to present a lot of related data in a document. You can use a table to arrange columns of figures, lists of information, and even side-by-side paragraphs of different sizes. You also can place graphics objects together with text in tables. Tables in Word are easy to create and modify, and you can insert them anywhere in a Word document.

Understanding Tables

Tables are grid-like structures, similar to spreadsheets, and consist of cells arranged in rows and columns. A *cell* is the box where a row and a column meet. You can enter text, numbers, or even an image in a cell. Text wraps in a cell just as it does in a paragraph of regular text. Rows expand vertically to accommodate text that wraps in a cell. You can change the width of a cell as needed, but cells do not automatically widen as you enter text or graphics objects.

You can create a new table structure and enter text, or you can convert existing text to a table grid layout. After you create a table, you can format it in a variety of ways: merge and split cells; format some or all of the gridlines to print; add shading to selected cells; adjust column width and spacing; adjust row height; and add or delete rows and col-umns. You can even add formulas to perform calculations on table data.

If your table spans more than one page, you can specify whether page breaks are allowed to occur in a cell. You can also designate one or more rows as headings so that they appear at the top of the table on each new page.

Adding a Table to a Document

The basic method of adding a table is to insert the table grid into the document and then add the text. When you first insert a table, you select the number of columns and rows to match your data. The table initially occupies all the space between the margins, and each column is the same size. You can modify this after you add the text, see how much space you need, and judge how it looks in your document. Figure 12-1 shows an example of a table inserted into a document.

Class Report:
Graphic Art Design SFA425

Class size: 11

Instructor's Report:
Attendance was excellent. With adult education, one expects some absences due to work and family responsibilities. The teams worked well together and benefitted from the experience. The term projects were very innovative and original. Many students showed natural design talents. The computer laboratory was satisfactory although we could certainly use some new multimedia technology.

Class Performance:

NAME	Mid Term	Final	Term Project	Total Points	Grade
Baylor, L.	57	86	90	80.35%	C
Carlos, A.	71	81	95	84.10%	B
Denning, F.	83	95	98	93.20%	A
Farmer, I.	73	95	85	85.50%	B
Hayden, M.	65	89	100	87.40%	B
McGinnes, A	80	95	100	93.25%	A
Orbison, E.	87	95	95	93.00%	A
Quillan, P.	93	100	85	92.25%	A-
Sheridan, D.	73	89	90	85.40%	B
Slater, J.	83	100	88	90.95%	B+
Stanford, F.	89	95	90	91.50%	B+
			Class Average:------>	92.36%	

Respectfully submitted,
T. G. Alfredo, Instructor

Figure 12-1: A table inserted into a document.

The method you use to create the table depends on the complexity of the completed table. If your table is relatively simple, with evenly spaced rows and columns, it is easy to use the Insert Table button on the Standard toolbar or choose from the Table menu to create your table. If your table is more complex, with irregularly sized rows and columns, use the new Draw Table feature that is also available from the Table menu.

A table is limited to 63 columns when you insert from the Table menu, but it can include an unlimited number of rows. When you use the toolbar button, you can insert up to eight columns and 13 rows. You can always add or delete rows and columns later. To use the Insert Table button or the Table menu to create a table:

1. Position the insertion point where you want to insert the table.

2. Choose the Insert Table button on the Standard toolbar. This displays a drop-down grid, where you can drag to select the number of columns and rows you want to create (see Figure 12-2). Alternatively, choose Table➪Insert Table to display the Insert Table dialog box.

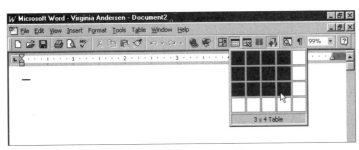

Figure 12-2: The Insert Table drop-down grid.

3. After you have dragged over to the number of columns and rows you want, release the mouse button to have Word insert the table. Alternatively, enter the number of rows and columns in the Insert Table dialog box, and choose OK.

4. If the gridlines do not appear, choose the Table➪Show Gridlines option. The option changes to Hide Gridlines. Figure 12-3 shows a sample table with the markers showing.

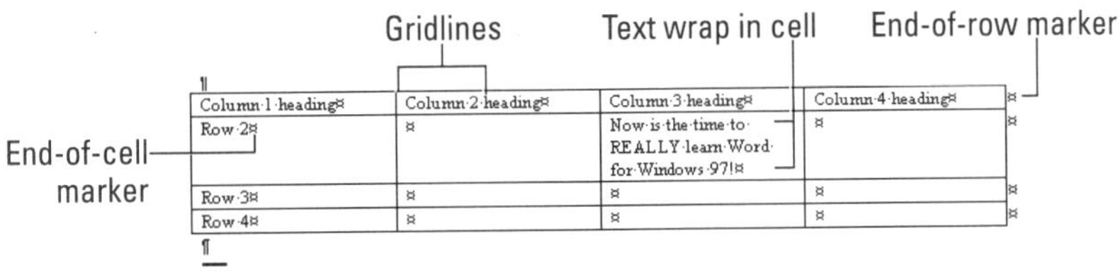

Figure 12-3: A sample table.

Tip   Although you can specify the number of rows when you first create a table, you may find it more efficient to begin with only one row. If you begin with a single row and start adding your text, you move from cell to cell by pressing Tab. When you press Tab in the last cell, a new row is added to the table. This method saves you the time of trying to count or predict how many rows your table will eventually have. The table creates itself as you type in your text. You should specify the number of columns when you create the table, however, because they are not quite so easy to add.

Drawing a table

The new Word 97 Draw Table feature helps you create a non-uniform table, one that contains cells of varying sizes. The rows don't need to contain the same number of columns. You can use Draw Table just as you would draw a table by hand with a pencil.

When you start Draw Table, the first thing you do is drag the table boundary where you want the table in the document. Then you draw the lines dividing the table into cells. After configuring the table, you can use the buttons on the Tables and Borders toolbar to customize your table with formatted lines and borders and with shading, and you can even change the orientation of the text in a cell.

To create a complex table with Draw Table:

1. Choose Draw Table from the Table menu or click the Tables and Borders button on the Standard toolbar. The new Tables and Borders floating toolbar appears. (Table 12-1 describes the Tables and Borders buttons.) The mouse pointer also changes to a pencil icon.

2. Click in the document where you want the upper left corner of the table, and then drag to the opposite corner and release the mouse button.

3. Use the pencil to draw row and column gridlines in the table. The lines need not span the table height or width.

4. If you want to remove a line, click the Eraser button on the Tables and Borders toolbar and drag it over the line.

After you have completed the table structure, you can begin adding text and graphics. You can also use the Tables and Borders toolbar to customize the appearance of selected cells or the entire table.

Table 12-1
Buttons on the Tables and Borders Toolbar

Button	Button Name	Description
	Draw Table	Toggles Draw Table feature on and off
	Eraser	Removes table lines
	Line Style	Displays drop-down list of line styles including solid, dotted and dashed
	Line Weight	Displays drop-down list of line weights from $1/4$ pt to 6 pts
	Border Color	Displays color palette for border lines
	Outside Border	Displays palette of border styles
	Shading Color	Displays color palette for background shading
	Merge Cells	Removes dividing lines between selected cells
	Split Cells	Displays Split Cells dialog box
	Align Top	Aligns text at the top of the cells
	Center Vertically	Centers text in the cells
	Align Bottom	Moves text to the bottom of the cells
	Distribute Rows Evenly	Moves inner horizontal cell boundaries to make selected rows all the same height
	Distribute Columns Evenly	Moves inner vertical cell boundaries to make selected columns all the same width
	Table AutoFormat	Opens Table AutoFormat dialog box
	Change Text Direction	Reorients text direction to one of three ways
	Sort Ascending	Sorts cell contents in ascending order
	Sort Descending	Sorts cell contents in descending order
	AutoSum	Automatically adds contents of all cells above or to the left of the current cell and places the total in the current cell

Moving Within a Table and Adding Text

You can use the mouse, the arrow keys, and the Tab key to move the insertion point within a table. The column marks in the ruler indicate the current position of the insertion point. When you create a table, the insertion point is positioned in the first cell so that you can begin entering text immediately.

Getting around in a table

Moving around in a table with the mouse is as simple as clicking the cell where you want to move. Table 12-2 shows the keystrokes used to move within a table.

Tip   If you have inserted a table in a new document and you want to add text above the table, place the insertion point at the beginning of the first cell, and press Enter.

Adding text to a table

Whether you are typing narrative text or entering numbers, you create new paragraphs in the cell by pressing Enter. To move to the next cell, press Tab. If you press Tab while the insertion point is in the last cell of the last row, Word creates a new row that has the same formatting as the preceding row.

Table 12-2
Using the Keyboard to Move Within a Table

Movement	Keystroke
Next cell	Tab or right-arrow key
Preceding cell	Shift+Tab or left-arrow key
Next row	Down-arrow key
Preceding row	Up-arrow key
First cell in a row	Alt+Home or Alt+7 (numeric keypad with Num Lock off)
Last cell in a row	Alt+End or Alt+1 (numeric keypad with Num Lock off)
Top cell in a column	Alt+PgUp or Alt+9 (numeric keypad with Num Lock off)
Bottom cell in a column	Alt+PgDn or Alt+3 (numeric keypad with Num Lock off)

There is no trick to entering text in a table. It's the same as entering text in a document. The only difference is that each cell has its own margins, so to speak. Thus, as the text fills a line, the text wraps in the cell. You can format text in a cell as you format any text in a document: select the appropriate text, and apply the formats.

Selecting Parts of a Table

You can use the mouse, the arrow keys, or the Tab key to select cells, rows, columns, or the entire table. You can also choose from the Table menu to select the row or column that contains the insertion point or select the entire table. After you make a selection, you can perform many operations on it.

As usual, Word offers many ways to perform the same operation, and selecting is no different. However, in Word, if you want to select multiple objects, they must be adjacent. In Word, unlike Excel, you cannot select nonadjacent cells, rows, or columns in a table.

Note There is a subtle difference between selecting text in a cell and selecting a cell itself. This difference is important when you want to print borders. If you select the text rather than the cell and use border formatting, the formatting applies only to the text and not to the cell gridlines. To select text in a cell, drag only over the text. To select a cell, include the end-of-cell marker.

Selecting with the mouse and the keyboard

If you are unfamiliar with tables, take a moment to drag the mouse pointer slowly through a single cell from right to left. As you approach the left gridline (but stay in the cell), the pointer changes from the familiar I-beam shape to an arrow pointing to the upper-right. When the pointer changes to the arrow, it is in the *selection bar* of the cell. If you drag the pointer to the left of the entire row outside the left gridline, the pointer also changes to an arrow pointing to the upper-right, but it is now in the selection bar of the entire row. Table 12-3 shows how to select the parts of a table with the mouse. Table 12-4 shows how to select parts of a table by using the keyboard.

Table 12-3
Using the Mouse to Select in a Table

To Select	*Do This*
Cell	Click in the cell's selection bar.
Row	Click in the row's selection bar, or double-click in a cell's selection bar.
Column	Position the pointer on the top gridline of the column until it changes to a down arrow, and click.

(continued)

Table 12-3 *(continued)*	
To Select	*Do This*
Multiple cells, rows, or columns	Drag across the cells, rows, or columns. Alternatively, click in the first cell, row, or column; press and hold the Shift key; and click in the last cell, row, or column. (This method may take a little practice, but it is quick and efficient for selecting cells, rows, and columns.) If you are selecting rows, be sure to include the end-of-row mark.
Entire table	Triple-click in any cell selection bar or choose Select All from the Edit menu.

Table 12-4 Using the Keyboard to Select in a Table	
To Select	*Do This*
Column	Press and hold Alt, and click anywhere in column.
Partial column	Place the insertion point in the cell from which you want to begin the selection, and press Alt+Shift+PgUp (if insertion point is in bottom cell of the range) or Alt+Shift+PgDn (if insertion point is in top cell).
Row	Place the insertion point in the first or last cell in the row. Press Alt+Shift+End (if the insertion point is in the first cell) or Alt+Shift+Home (if the insertion point is in the last cell).
Partial row	Place the insertion point in the cell from which you want to begin the selection, and then use the appropriate keystroke as above.
Entire table	Press Alt+5 (numeric keypad with Num Lock off).

To reduce the selection size to the previous size, press Shift+F8.

Tip   Another quick way to select a row, a column, or the entire table is to position the insertion point in a cell that is in the row or column you want to select (or anywhere in the table to select the entire table). Then choose Table⇨Select Row, Select Column, or Select Table.

Extending the selection

After you select a cell or a block of cells, you can include additional adjacent cells by entering the Extend Mode, rather than starting all over. To enter the Extend Mode, press F8. You will see EXT in bold letters in the status bar. To leave the Extend Mode, press Esc.

You can use the mouse to extend your selection simply by clicking the outmost cell in the new block of selected cells. Or you can use the keyboard by pressing Shift and one of the arrow keys. For example, if you select cell B3 and press Shift+right-arrow key, both B3 and C3 are selected. Then press Shift+up-arrow key, and a block of four cells is selected: B2, C2, B3, and C3.

Modifying a Table Layout

Modifying a table layout means altering the structure of the table. This includes copying, moving, inserting, and deleting rows, columns, and cells. It also includes merging and splitting cells, changing spacing and column width, changing row height, and splitting a table.

Inserting and deleting cells, rows, and columns

Before you can insert a cell, row, or column, you must select an existing cell, row, or column to tell Word where you want the new addition to appear. Then choose Table⇨Insert Cells (or Insert Rows or Insert Columns, depending on your selection).

If you selected a single cell, Word inserts a new cell at the location you specify in relation to the selected cell. A new column is inserted to the left of the selected column; a new row is inserted above the selected row. All inserted cells, rows, and columns adopt the same formatting as the selection.

If you want to insert multiple cells, rows, or columns, select the same number in the existing table that you want to insert. For example, to insert two columns, select cells in two columns. If you want to insert more rows or columns than currently exist in the table, you have to perform the task more than once.

Meanwhile, the Table menu changes, according to whether you first select a cell, row, or column. For example, if you select a row, the Table menu shows Insert Rows. If you select a column, the Table menu shows Insert Columns. The same is true of selecting a cell or cells, but that menu choice displays a dialog box so you can choose how to shift the existing cells. Similarly, the toolbar button changes with your selection: Insert Cells, Insert Rows, or Insert Columns.

Inserting cells

When you insert cells, you can choose whether to shift the existing cells to the right or down to make room for the new cells. If you choose to shift the existing cells to the right, an extra cell (or more, if you selected more than one cell initially) is added to the right end of that row and the contents move right with the cells. If you choose to shift the existing cells down, an extra row (or more, if you selected more than one cell initially), not just a cell, is added to the bottom of the table. The contents of the selected cell(s) move to the corresponding cell(s) in the new row. To add cells to a table:

1. Select a cell or cells adjacent to where you want the new cell or cells.

2. Choose the Insert Cells button on the Standard toolbar, or choose Table⇨Insert Cells. This displays the Insert Cells dialog box (see Figure 12-4).

3. Make the appropriate choice in the dialog box. (Shift cells down is the default.)

4. Choose OK to close the dialog box and insert the new cell or cells.

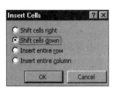

Figure 12-4: The Insert Cells dialog box.

You can also right-click a selected cell and choose Insert Cells from the shortcut menu. The Insert Cells dialog box appears as before.

Inserting rows and columns

You have to select an existing row or column before you can insert a new row or column. Word will insert the new row directly above the selected row. To insert multiple rows or columns, select the same number as you want to insert. If you just want to add a new row to the bottom of the table, you don't have to select any rows. Simply place the insertion point in the last cell in the last row, and press Tab. Word adds a new row to the end of the table with the same formatting as the row above it. To insert rows in a table:

1. Select the row or rows below where you want the new row or rows.

2. Choose the Insert Rows button on the Standard toolbar, or choose Table⇨Insert Rows. Word inserts the new row or rows.

When you insert a new column, Word inserts the new column to the left of the selected column. You may have up to 63 columns in a Word table. To insert columns in a table:

1. Select the column or columns to the right of where you want the new column or columns.

2. Choose the Insert Columns button on the Standard toolbar, or choose Table⇨Insert Columns. Word inserts the new column or columns.

If you want to add a column to the right of the last column with the mouse, carefully place the mouse pointer over the end-of-row marker at the end of the top row. The pointer changes to a down arrow. (You may have to click the Show/Hide button on the Standard toolbar to see the markers.) Click when it becomes the down arrow to select all the markers, and click the Insert Columns button on the Standard toolbar to add the new column.

Note You can also right-click a selected row or column and choose Insert Rows (or Insert Columns) from the shortcut menu. Word inserts a new row above the clicked row and the new column to the right of the clicked column.

Note The Insert Cells dialog box also gives you the opportunity to insert a new row or column. To do this, select the cell to the right or below where you want the new column or row, and choose the Insert Cells button on the Standard toolbar or Table⇨Insert Cells. This displays the Insert Cells dialog box. Select either Insert entire row or Insert entire column. This approach also applies to selecting multiple cells.

Deleting cells, rows, and columns

You can delete the contents of a cell or the cell itself. To delete the contents of a cell, select the contents, and press the Delete (or Del) key. To delete a cell, select the cell, and choose Table⇨Delete Cells to display the Delete Cells dialog box (see Figure 12-5). The choices are similar to those in the Insert Cells dialog box. After making the appropriate choice, choose OK. You can also display the Delete Cells dialog box by right-clicking in a cell and choosing Delete Cells from the Shortcut menu.

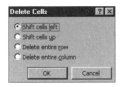

Figure 12-5: The Delete Cells dialog box.

Deleting rows and columns is the same as inserting rows and columns, except that you cannot use the toolbar button (it only inserts). You must choose Table⇨Delete Rows (or Columns). The Delete commands on the Table menu or Shortcut menu vary according to what is currently selected.

You can also delete a row or column by selecting it and choosing the Cut button on the Standard toolbar or Edit⇨Cut. The Shortcut menu also includes the editing Cut, Copy, and Paste commands. This method not only deletes the selection, but also places the selection on the Clipboard, so that you can paste it elsewhere if you want.

Note Remember that to delete an entire row, you must include the end-of-row marker in the selection. Otherwise, you delete only the contents of the row and not the row itself.

To delete an entire table, select all the rows and columns, and then choose Table⇨ Delete Rows (or Delete Columns). If you change your mind about the recent deletion, simply click the Undo Clear button.

Moving and copying cells, rows, and columns

You can move and copy the contents of a cell to another cell just as you move and copy any text or graphics. Select the contents of the cell, cut or copy, and paste elsewhere. You can also use the drag-and-drop method for moving cell contents. You have two options when moving or copying contents to a different location: add to the text already in the target location without changing it, and replace the existing text. To add to the existing text, do not include the end-of-cell markers in the selection. To replace the existing text, include the end-of-cell markers. To move and copy the contents of cells, rows, and columns:

1. Select the cells, rows, or columns you want to move or copy (do not include the end-of-cell or end-of-row marker).

2. Place the mouse pointer over the selection until the pointer becomes an arrow pointing to the upper-left.

3. To *move* the selection, click and drag. You can move the selection anywhere you want, including out of the table entirely. If you move it out of the table, the selection remains in the table format.

4. To *copy* the selection, press and hold Ctrl, and then click and drag. As in Step 3, you can copy the selection anywhere, including out of the table.

5. When dragging with the mouse, drop (release) the mouse button when you reach the location where you want the text placed.

If you want to move or copy a row from its original location in a table to a different location in the same table, include the end-of-row marker in the row selection. Otherwise, the drag-and-drop row selection will overwrite the row where you drop the selection and leave the selected row empty, instead of shifting the original row down. Also, be sure to drop the selection in the cell that is in the same column as the left-most cell selected. Otherwise, the entire selection is moved or copied offset to the right.

Column width, column spacing, and row height

Column width refers to the space within the column; *column spacing* refers to the amount of space between adjacent columns that is actually the right margin of the column. When you insert a table, Word divides the space between the margins by the number of columns you specify, so that each column is the same width. The default column spacing is set to .15 inch. Row height is set to Auto initially, which means a row expands to accommodate text that wraps. Several other row height options are available after you create the table.

Changing column width manually

You can change the width of columns in a table in several ways. One method is to drag a column's gridline in the table or one of the Move Table Column markers in the ruler (see Figure 12-6) to visually adjust the column's width. When you use this method, the columns to the right of the selected column automatically adjust proportionally so that the overall width of the table doesn't change. To display the horizontal ruler, choose View⇨Ruler.

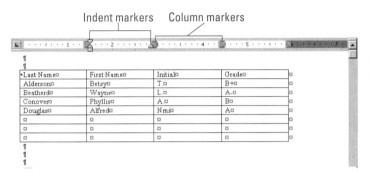

Indent markers   Column markers

Figure 12-6: Column markers on the ruler. (Notice the indent markers over the second column.)

To change column width manually:

1. Position the mouse pointer on the gridline to the right of the column you want to adjust. When the pointer is positioned correctly, it changes to two vertical lines with arrows on either side.

2. Drag the gridline to the right or left to adjust the column width. The column to the right adjusts automatically so that the overall width of the table does not change. If you do not want the column to adjust, press and hold Shift as you drag and the table width adjusts accordingly.

3. Release the mouse button.

Note If you press the Alt key as you drag a gridline to change a column width, the width measurements of all the columns are displayed in the ruler in place of the tick marks.

Changing column width using the Table menu

The advantage of using the Table menu to change the column width is that you can enter precise values for each column width. To change column width from the Table menu:

1. Select the column you want to adjust.

2. Choose Table⇨Cell Height and Width to display the Cell Height and Width dialog box.

3. Select the Column tab if it is not already selected (see Figure 12-7).

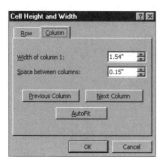

Figure 12-7: The Cell Height and Width dialog box showing the Column tab.

4. Enter a value for the column width and, if desired, the column spacing.

5. To move to another column, choose the Previous Column or Next Column button.

6. When you have finished, choose OK.

Changing column width automatically

Word provides two ways to allow automatic width adjustment of selected columns. One is an AutoFit option, in which Word resizes the selected columns according to their contents. The other is an automatic sizing option, in which Word proportionally resizes the selected columns regardless of their content.

The AutoFit option depends on the structure of the table. Word analyzes the table and resizes the selected columns according to their contents and the existing overall width of the table. If the table does not extend from margin to margin, the AutoFit option expands the width of the table to match the margins by changing the size of the selected columns. If the table is wider than the margins, Word reduces the width to match the margins.

The automatic sizing option is similar in that it also expands or reduces the width of the selected columns until the table extends from margin to margin. The difference is that it sizes the selected columns all the same width rather than according to their contents.

To change column width:

1. Select the columns you want to adjust.

2. Choose Table⇨Cell Height and Width to display the Cell Height and Width dialog box.

3. Select the Column tab if it is not already selected.

4. Choose the AutoFit button to let Word resize the columns. Or type **auto** in the Width of column box to activate automatic sizing.

5. Choose OK.

Another way to make selected columns all the same width is to select the columns you want to change as before and choose Table⊃Distribute Columns Evenly. This differs from typing auto in the Cell Height and Width dialog box in that the table remains the same size rather than expanding to fit the page margins. You can also click the Distribute Columns Evenly button on the Tables and Borders toolbar.

Changing column spacing

Column spacing refers to the amount of space between adjacent columns. The default amount of space is .15 inch. If you change the spacing between columns, the change applies to the entire table, not just to the selected columns. Increasing the amount of space between columns reduces the amount of space for your text in a column, because the overall width of the column (including column spacing) does not change.

You can achieve the same effect by using paragraph formatting to increase the right and left indents instead of changing the column spacing. The advantage to using paragraph formatting is that you can apply it to selected columns (or cells, for that matter) rather than to the entire table. To change column spacing:

1. Choose Table⊃Cell Height and Width to display the Cell Height and Width dialog box.

2. Select the Column tab if it is not already selected.

3. Enter a value in the Space between columns box.

4. Choose OK. You will notice that the cell markers have moved right to allow for the new column spacing.

Changing row height

When you create a table, the row height is set to Auto, which means the row will expand to fit text that wraps in any of the cells in the row. Therefore, the height of each row is large enough to accommodate the cell that contains the most data. Word changes row height automatically.

Word provides two other ways you can specify row height. You can set a minimum height and let the row expand if the contents of a cell exceed the minimum or specify a fixed row height, where the row will not change even if the cell contents exceed the height. Word will then display and print only the contents that fit in the limited space. To change row height:

1. Choose Table⇨Cell Height and Width to display the Cell Height and Width dialog box.

2. Select the Row tab if it is not already selected (see Figure 12-8).

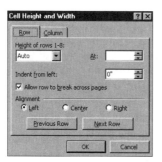

Figure 12-8: The Cell Height and Width dialog box showing the Row tab.

3. In the Height of rows box, select Auto, At least, or Exactly. At least lets you set a value that specifies the minimum row height, but the row will still expand as necessary. If you specify Exactly, the row will not expand beyond the value you enter in the At box.

4. Enter a value in the At box. (If the height was set to Auto, entering a value in the At box changes the height to At least.)

5. Choose OK.

You can change the height of an individual row by using the vertical ruler. (The document must be in page layout view to display the vertical ruler.) Rows are indicated by light gray lines in the vertical ruler. Dragging on one of these lines changes the row height to the At Least setting and allows you to visually select the height of the row. If you want to see the actual measurement as you drag, press and hold the Alt key. You may not reduce a row height to less than that needed for the existing text.

If you want the selected rows to show equal heights, choose Table⇨Distribute Rows Evenly or click the button on the Tables and Borders toolbar.

Splitting a table

Splitting a table allows you to enter ordinary text between rows in a table. You can split a table horizontally between rows but not vertically between columns. To split a table:

1. Position the insertion point in the row that you want for the top row of the lower table segment.

2. Choose Table⇨Split Table. Alternatively, you can press Ctrl+Enter, but this keyboard action adds a page break in your table split.

After splitting a table, you can move the table down and add plain text between the tables.

To reunite the split tables, click the Undo button on the Standard toolbar right away. Later, simply delete the text lines between the two tables to rejoin them.

Fine-Tuning a Table

After you've created your table, you can improve its visual appeal by changing the text format and appearance of the table, aligning text in the cells, creating column headings, formatting the gridlines to print, or adding shading to cells. Word also has an AutoFormat feature that you can use to select one of the preset table formats included with Word.

Formatting text in a table

Formatting table text is the same as formatting ordinary text. For character formatting, select the text and apply the formats. For paragraph formatting, place the insertion point in the paragraph and apply the formats. You can also apply styles to a table to automate the formatting. See Chapter 11 for more on styles. The table shortcut menu also has options for formatting paragraphs and changing text fonts.

Changing text orientation and alignment

Normally, the text you enter in a table cell reads from left to right and is aligned at the top of the cell. You may want some cells to read from the top down or from the bottom up. To change the text orientation, first select the cells you want to change, then choose Format⇨Text Direction or click the Change Text Direction button on the Tables and Borders toolbar. You have three choices of text orientation: horizontally from left to right, vertically reading down, and vertically reading up. These choices are represented in successive clicks of the menu option or the button. When you change the orientation, Word automatically switches to Page Layout view. You can see the new orientation only in Page Layout view.

With text oriented horizontally, you have a choice of aligning the text at the top of the cell, in the center or at the bottom. If the text is oriented vertically, either up or down, the alignment choices remain the same but align the text with respect to the direction of the text. For example, if your text reads from top to bottom, when you choose Align Top, the text will align with the right cell gridline; Align Bottom will move it to the left gridline. Figure 12-9 shows a table with text oriented and aligned in various combinations.

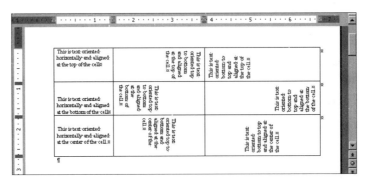

Figure 12-9: A table with realigned text.

Centering a table and aligning rows

If your table does not extend from margin to margin, you may want to center it horizontally or indent it so that it aligns with other text. To center or indent a table:

1. Select the table or rows you want to align.

2. Choose Table⇨Cell Height and Width to display the Cell Height and Width dialog box.

3. Select the Row tab if it is not already selected.

4. To indent the table, choose Left in the Alignment box, and enter a value in the Indent from left box. To center the table, choose Center. To align right, choose Right.

5. Choose OK.

Preventing page breaks

The Row tab of the Cell Height and Width dialog box has an option, Allow row to break across pages, which is on by default. If your table is less than a full page, you can ensure that it will all appear on one page by clearing this option.

Creating table headings

You can create headings that span several columns by merging several cells into one wide cell. You also can format headings to appear at the top of every page of a table that is longer than one page.

Merging and splitting cells

Merging cells refers to merging adjacent cells in a row or rows. With Word 97 you can now merge cells either horizontally so that they form fewer columns or vertically so that they form fewer rows. When you merge cells, Word converts the contents of each merged cell into paragraphs in the merged cell, that is, each one on a separate line in the new cell.

Splitting cells refers to dividing the selected cells horizontally (that is, so that they form additional columns). You can split selected cells whether or not they were previously merged. When you split a cell, all text that was in the cell now appears in the left-most cell. If you have added paragraphs in the cell, when you split it, the paragraphs will be divided among the new cells.

An additional option when splitting cells is to merge the cells before splitting. This allows you to reconfigure the table. For example, you want to change a 2 x 3 table to a 4 x 5 table of the same overall size. Word first merges the selected cells then splits the single cell into the number of rows and columns you specify.

When you split or merge cells, the overall width of the table does not change. To split and merge cells:

1. Select the cells you want to split or merge.

2. To merge the selected cells, choose Table⇨Merge Cells or click the Merge Cells button on the Tables and Borders toolbar. Word merges the cells containing text, creating a separate paragraph for each merged cell. If the selected cells for the merge are all blank, the resulting merged cell will have no paragraphs.

   Or, to split the selected cells, choose Table⇨Split Cells or click the Split Cells button on the Tables and Borders toolbar to display the Split Cells dialog box (see Figure 12-10). Enter the number of columns into which you want to split each selected cell. If any paragraphs existed in the cell you split, they are distributed among the new cells.

3. Choose OK.

Figure 12-10: The Split Cells dialog box.

The new Pencil and Eraser tools on the Tables and Borders toolbar offer quick and easy ways to split and merge cells. To split a cell, click the Pencil button and draw a line across or down the cell. You need not split the cell into equal parts—simply draw the line wherever you want to divide the cell.

Use the Eraser tool to merge cells by clicking the button and dragging the eraser icon over the line that divides the cells you want to merge.

Table headings on each page

You can create a table heading from the text appearing in the first row of the table. Word automatically repeats the table heading text only when the table is split by a soft page break (one that is inserted by the system). If you insert a hard page break in the table, the heading is not repeated automatically. However, you can add the headings manually. To add column headings for each page:

1. Select one or more cells in the top row whose text you want to use as table headings on each page.

2. Choose T\underline{a}ble⇨\underline{H}eadings. (This option is available only when the cursor is in the first row of the table or you have selected cells including one in the first row. If the first row is a header row, you can use this to add the second row to the header.)

Note If you change a table heading on the first page, table headings on all other pages change as well.

Borders and shading

The gridlines that appear on the screen while you are creating a table are used for designing only and do not print. However, you can print borders for the whole table or for selected cells in a table. You can also shade selected cells in a table. To quickly apply preset border and shading formats to a table, use the AutoFormat feature. Figure 12-11 shows an example of a table with border and shading formats applied.

Last Name	First Name	Initial	Grade
Alderson	Betsy	T.	B+
Beatherd	Wayne	L.	A-
Conover	Phyllis	A.	B
Douglas	Alfred	Nmi	A

Figure 12-11: One example of border formatting and shading in a table.

To apply custom border and shading formatting, choose F\underline{o}rmat⇨\underline{B}orders and Shading. From this, you can select a variety of colors, line thicknesses, and fill patterns, and apply the formatting to selected cells rather than the entire table. The Background option in the Format menu displays a palette of colors you can apply to the table background. You can also use five buttons on the Tables and Borders toolbar to customize your table appearance. Chapter 8 covers border formatting.

Note When you choose from the Format menu or the toolbar buttons, any border or shading format you select is applied only to your selection. Thus, if the insertion point is in a paragraph in a cell but the cell itself isn't selected, the formatting applies only to the paragraph, not to the cell. In this case, the formatted border appears only around the paragraph text and does not extend to the cell gridlines.

When you use AutoFormat, the selection applies to the entire table. To use the AutoFormat feature:

1. Position the insertion point inside the table.

2. Choose Table⇨Table AutoFormat to display the Table AutoFormat dialog box (see Figure 12-12). Alternatively, you can right-click anywhere in the table and choose Table AutoFormat from the shortcut menu.

3. In the Formats box, select a format. A preview of the selected format appears in the Preview box to the right.

4. In the Formats to apply area, select the elements you want to apply to the table. As you enable or disable each element, the preview changes to reflect your choices.

5. In the Apply special formats to area, select the parts of the table you want formatted.

6. Choose OK.

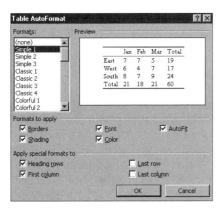

Figure 12-12: The Table AutoFormat dialog box.

Using Tabs in Tables

One of the nicer features of tables is that they usually give you an alternative to using tabs to line up multiple columns of text or numbers. Instead of having to contend with figuring out tab settings for multiple columns, a table is far easier to use. However, if you need to use tabs even in a table, refer to Chapter 8 for more information about setting tabs.

In ordinary text, you enter a tab in your text by pressing the Tab key. But pressing Tab in a table moves the insertion point to the next cell. To enter a tab in a table cell, you press Ctrl+Tab instead, and the insertion point moves to the next tab stop in the cell.

If your table consists of text, you probably won't have to worry about creating custom tab stops or entering tabs in the cells. Even if you want to add bullets or numbers to text in a cell, you can use the Bullet or Numbering button on the Formatting toolbar. Word will insert the bullets or numbers and automatically apply a hanging indent to the text.

If you do need to insert a custom tab stop for a cell, there are a few things to keep in mind. First, you can enter a tab stop for many cells at once by selecting the cells before entering the tab stop in the ruler. Second, if you select cells in multiple columns, you *must* enter the tab stop in the ruler above the leftmost column that has a selected cell. (For example, if you select cells in the second, third, and fourth columns in the table, you must enter the tab stop in the ruler over the second column.) This is the *active column* and is indicated by the indentation markers in the ruler above it (see to Figure 12-13). Word will not allow you to enter a tab stop in the ruler over any other column, whether it is selected or not.

Left, center, and right tabs work the same in tables as they do in ordinary text, except you must press Ctrl+Tab to move the insertion point to a tab stop in the cell. Decimal tabs, however, work differently in tables, because decimal tabs are most commonly used in tables that contain columns of numbers.

When you enter a decimal tab in the ruler over a selected column, the decimal tab takes effect immediately. There is no need to press Ctrl+Tab when you enter data in these cells. As with ordinary text, decimal tabs align numbers on the decimal point (or other specified character). Any number that does not contain a decimal point aligns right. Text in cells also aligns on the decimal tab.

If you have alignment problems with your decimal tabs, the quickest and easiest way to correct the problem is to select the table, choose Format⇨Tabs, and choose Clear All. This removes all tab stops for the table from the ruler. You can easily reapply the tab stops that you want.

After you've entered decimal tabs for a table, adjusting a column of numbers is simple. Select the column (or multiple columns), and drag the tab marker in the ruler to the left or right. The column aligns under the tab.

Adding Graphics Objects

Tables are useful when you must position text and graphics together. A common method is to create a one-row table with two columns and then copy and paste the graphics object into one of the two cells. Type the text in the other cell, and use paragraph formatting to add spacing before the text to make it appear vertically-centered on the graphics object.

Figure 12-13 consists of a table with one row and three columns, for a total of three cells. One graphic image is in the left cell, with text in the second and third cells. The text in the third cell is a bulleted list with another graphics image below the text. The row height increased to allow for the added graphics.

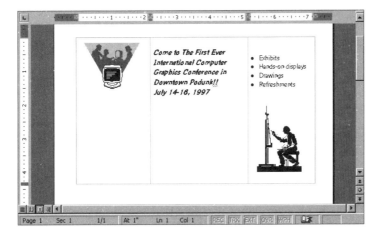

Figure 12-13: Example of text and graphic objects in a table.

Converting Existing Text to a Table and Vice Versa

You may decide that you need to convert text in your document to a table format or that you no longer want your information in a table layout. To convert the text quickly, select it, click the Table button on the Standard toolbar, and drag across the drop-down grid to the desired table dimensions. One problem with this method, however, is that Word will probably not arrange the table to your liking. If this is the case, you need to undo the conversion and use the Table menu instead. To convert text to a table by using the Table menu:

1. Select the text you want to convert to a table.

2. Choose Table⇨Convert Text to Table to open the Convert Text to Table dialog box (see Figure 12-14).

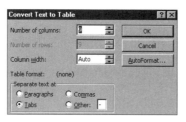

Figure 12-14: The Convert Text to Table dialog box.

3. Choose the number of columns, the number of rows (if the row option is not dimmed), and the desired column width.

4. Choose how Word should separate the text for the columns and rows in the Separate text at area of the dialog box.

5. If you want to choose a custom format now, choose AutoFormat and select a design from the Table AutoFormat dialog box as before.

6. Choose OK.

Note   Sometimes, creating the exact table you want from existing text is a challenge. For example, selecting the text of the six numbered steps in the previous numbered list and clicking the Table button creates a six-row, one-column table, with each step taking up an entire row. If, however, you want to create a one-row, six-column table with each step in a column of its own, follow Steps 1 through 4, choosing six columns in Step 3 and choosing Paragraph as the Separate text at option in Step 4.

Converting table text to ordinary text is the opposite of converting ordinary text to a table format. You can convert all or part of a table, but you must convert entire rows if you want to convert only part of a table. To convert table text to ordinary text:

1. Select the entire table or only the rows you want to convert.

2. Choose Table⇨Convert Table To Text to open the Convert Table To Text dialog box (see Figure 12-15).

Figure 12-15: The Convert Table To Text dialog box.

3. Select how you want to separate the text. (Tabs are best for columns of numbers; paragraph marks are best for straight text.)

4. Choose OK. Figure 12-16 shows a table converted to text.

Last Name	First Name	Initial	Grade
Alderson	Betsy	T.	B+
Beatherd	Wayne	L.	A-
Conover	Phyllis	A.	B
Douglas	Alfred	Nmi	A

Figure 12-16: Table converted to text.

Sorting Table Data and Numbering Cells

Sorting and numbering cells is easy in a Word table. You can sort by the contents of any column—alphabetically, numerically, or by date and in ascending or descending order. Adding numbers to table cells (such as the first cell in each row) or to every cell in the table is just as simple.

Sorting in a table

Word enables you to sort up to three columns at one time. When you sort the information in a table, Word arranges the rows according to the criteria you set. In special situations, you may need to sort a single column in a table without reordering the other columns, or you may want to specify a case-sensitive sort. To sort rows:

1. Select the rows you want to sort, if only part of the table.

2. Choose Table⇨Sort to open the Sort dialog box (see Figure 12-17).

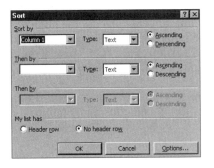

Figure 12-17: The Sort dialog box.

3. In the first Sort by box, select the first column you want to sort from the drop-down list.

4. Under Type, select Number, Text, or Date. (Word automatically selects a data type that matches the content of the column.)

5. Select Ascending or Descending order for the sort.

6. To sort with more criteria, repeat Steps 3 through 5, by using the Then by boxes. Word sorts the table by the criteria first in the Sort by section, then in the first Then by section, and finally in the second Then by section.

7. If the first row of the table is a header row that you don't want to include in the sort, select the Header row option under My list has. If not, select No header row.

8. Choose OK.

You can quickly sort table data by the value in a single column with the Tables and Borders toolbar. Select the column you want to sort by and click the Sort Ascending or Sort Descending button. The top row is assumed to be a header row and is not included in the sort.

Note   You can sort tabular text not in a table structure, either by paragraphs or fields. In this case, the word *fields* refers to columns of numbers or text that are not in a table but are separated by tabs or other characters. As long as each line has the same number of separators, Word will sort the selection correctly. Choose the Options button to specify other separation characters for columns of numbers and to specify other sort options for text. If you select text that is not in a table for sorting, the Table menu shows Sort Text instead of Sort.

Numbering cells in a table

To number cells in a table, select the cells you want numbered, and choose the Numbering button on the Formatting toolbar. Word numbers the selected cells from left to right, beginning in the first row. If you want to number only the first cell in each row, select only the first column in the table. Word numbers all the selected cells whether or not they have text. The cell numbers adjust automatically if you sort or otherwise change the order of the table. If cells contain more than one paragraph, Word numbers each paragraph separately.

If you do not see the Formatting toolbar or you want to use custom number formats, choose Format⇨Bullets and Numbering and click the Numbered tab for your numbering choices (see Figure 12-18).

To remove numbering from the table, select the cells that have numbers, and click the Number button on the Formatting toolbar.

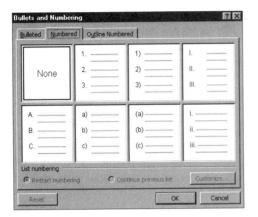

Figure 12-18: The Numbered tab of the Bullets and Numbering dialog box.

Special Uses for Tables

If you use tables for columns of numbers, you can add, subtract, multiply, and divide numbers in cells. You can also calculate averages, percentages, and minimum and maximum values. If you must perform complex calculations in a table, you can create the table in Excel and link or embed the table in your Word document so that you can update it in Excel (see Chapter 15).

You can also use a table as a simple database for storing such information as a list of names and addresses for use in sending form letters.

Calculating in a table

When you use table data to perform calculations, Word uses a code to refer to the cells, rows, and columns. Letters refer to columns, and numbers refer to rows, so a letter-number combination indicates a specific cell. For example, the first column in a table is column A, the second column is B, and so on. The first row is row 1, the second row is 2, and so on. Thus, the cell in the second column and third row is cell B3.

The cell placement of the insertion point at the beginning of the process is critical (unless you enter your own formulas) because it determines which numbers Word calculates. For example, if you place the insertion point at the bottom of column C, Word assumes you want to calculate using the data in that column. If you place the insertion point in an ambiguous cell (such as the lower-right cell), Word doesn't know whether you want to calculate to the left or above the formula so it takes a chance and uses the values in the column above. If you enter your own formula, however, you not only can select a Word function but can also enter specific cell addresses in the formula.

Word provides a quick way to calculate the sum of values in a row or column of a table. After placing the insertion point in an empty cell at the end of a row or at the bottom of a column, click the AutoSum button on the Tables and Borders toolbar. If you click in the lower right cell, Word sums the values in the column above by default. If there is only one cell in the above or left of the cell containing the insertion point, you will see a syntax error message. You cannot sum just one value.

If you want to create a more complex formula, use the F*o*rmula option on the T*a*ble menu. Word generally suggests a formula when you begin a calculation. If Word doesn't suggest a formula, it places an equal sign in the Formula box. All Word formulas begin with an equal sign, so you can enter whatever formula you want after the equal sign.

If Word does suggest a function through its built-in analysis of the surrounding cell data, you can still select a different formula or enter one of your own. Word stores additional formulas in the Paste F*u*nction box, which is part of the Formula dialog box. Additional functions include averaging, counting, rounding, and many more.

You can enter your own simple formula with specific cell references. For example, to add the third and fourth cells in the second column, you type **=B3+B4**. To divide the first cell in the table by the cell in the third column, fourth row, you type **=A1/C4**.

You must separate specific cell references by a comma. For example, if you want the average of the values in cells A1, B3, and D5, type **=average(a1,b3,d5)** in the Formula box. You must separate ranges of cells by a colon. If you want the average of the values in all the cells from A1 to C5, type **=average(a1:c5)**. To calculate in a table:

1. Position the insertion point in the cell where you want the answer to appear.

2. Choose T*a*ble⇨F*o*rmula to open the Formula dialog box (see Figure 12-19).

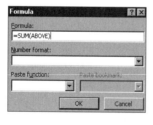

Figure 12-19: The Formula dialog box.

3. If the suggested formula in the Formula box is not acceptable, select another one from the Paste Function box, or enter one of your own.

4. Select a number format if you want (see Table 12-5).

5. Choose OK.

If the format you want to apply to your result is not in Table 12-5, you can create your own. For example, to display the result with a single decimal place rather than none or two, you can type **0.0** directly in the Number Format box. Or, if you want to display leading zeros for two-digit numbers, type **000.00**.

Table 12-5
Number Formats in the Formula Dialog Box

Format Code	Meaning
#,##0	The pound signs represent number placeholders so that numbers with four or more digits have a comma separator and no decimal places. The zero ensures that the formatted number displays at least 0, even if the number is less than 1. For example, 4321223 is displayed as 4,321,223, and .22 is displayed as 0.
#,##0.00	This is the same format as the preceding one, except the formatted number always shows two decimal places. For example, 4321223 is displayed as 4,321,223.00, and .22 is displayed as 0.22.
$#,##0.00; ($#,##0.00)	This is a two-part format: the first part of the format is for positive numbers, and the second part is for negative numbers. For example, 4321223 is displayed as $4,321,223.00, and .22 is displayed as $0.22. However, the number-12345.6 is displayed with parentheses, as ($12,345.60).
0	This format ensures that at least one positive digit is displayed. For example, .002 is displayed as 0, and 12345.09 is displayed as 12345.
0%	This formats a number as a percentage. For example, 104 is displayed as 104%.
0.00	This format ensures that at least one digit is displayed as a positive number with two decimal places. For example, 123 isdisplayed as 123.00, and .0987 is displayed as 0.09.
0.00%	This formats the number as a percentage with two decimal places. For example, 104 is displayed as 104.00%, and .79 is displayed as 0.79%.

Figure 12-20 shows a table to which a custom formula is being added to compute the Total Points for the first student by combining the points earned for the exams and the term project. The formula is then replicated for each student, altering the cell addresses accordingly. The formula for computing the class average used the Word AVERAGE function: **=AVERAGE(ABOVE)**. After computing the total points, it is helpful to sort the table in descending order of Total Points to be able to assign grades. Then return to alphabetic order by name for the final report.

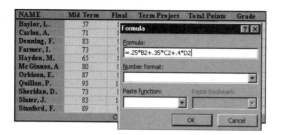

Figure 12-20: Adding a formula to a table.

If you change the value in any of the fields included in a formula, the calculated value must be updated. To update with the new values, move to the cell containing the formula and press F9. You can also right-click the number (not the cell), and choose Update Field from the shortcut menu.

Unfortunately, you can't copy the formula from the first cell to the other cells and expect the cell references to be changed accordingly. For that kind of help, you need to use Excel.

Using Excel to create a table

You can create a table in Excel, copy it, and paste it in your Word document. Several options are available when you do this. For more on this topic, see Chapter 15.

Using a table as a database

A table is an efficient way to store lists of names and addresses. You can sort, edit, and retrieve information easily in a table. If your table consists of names and addresses, you can define the table as a database and use it in a mail merge operation. For more information on using a table as a data source in a mail merge, see Chapter 20.

Creating Forms

When you need to collect the data, forms are essential. A *form* is simply an arrangement of empty places where you fill in data. In Word, forms are really document templates. Word gives you the ability to generate *fill-in forms* that you can print or *online forms* for use at the computer. You can carry away and complete the hard copy of fill-in forms as the data is located or becomes available. The online forms are displayed on the screen for data entry. When you create an online form, you can add message dialog boxes with text boxes for data entry. They may also display prompts that indicate the type of information that is expected in each cell of the table.

Creating a fill-in form

A fill-in form is little more than a blank table with a few labels. You create a fill-in form the same way you create a table, but you save it as a template file (with the .dot file extension) instead of a document file. The table should have one cell for each form label and one cell for each fill-in blank. You can arrange the labels and blanks any way you like and merge cells to give more room for some entries. You can even insert more than one table in the form.

Figure 12-21 shows an example of a fill-in form made out of three tables. The top table, the letter head, contains only one row with three cells. The second table was inserted below a line of general text and contained at first six rows and four columns. Several cells were merged to create longer spaces for the customer information. The third table contains the product orders and payment information. Again, some cells were merged to form the lower-left box.

Figure 12-22 shows an online form similar to the fill-in form of Figure 12-21. Each of the blanks in the customer information table includes a fill-in field with a prompt. The Total column contains a formula that computes the product of the quantity and the unit price. The totals in the four cells at the bottom-left of the form also contain formulas.

To create a fill-in form:

1. Choose File⇨New, and select the Blank Document template.

2. Select Template, and choose OK.

3. Choose the Insert Table button on the Standard toolbar, and drag the drop-down grid to include as many columns and rows as necessary.

4. Type the text of the labels adjacent to or above the blanks as desired.

5. Adjust cell height and width to match expected data, and merge cells as needed.

6. Choose File⇨Save As.

7. Type the name of the file in the File name box with a .dot extension.

8. Choose OK.

Templates are usually saved in the Microsoft Office\Templates folder. When you start a new document, you can select the template name from the list.

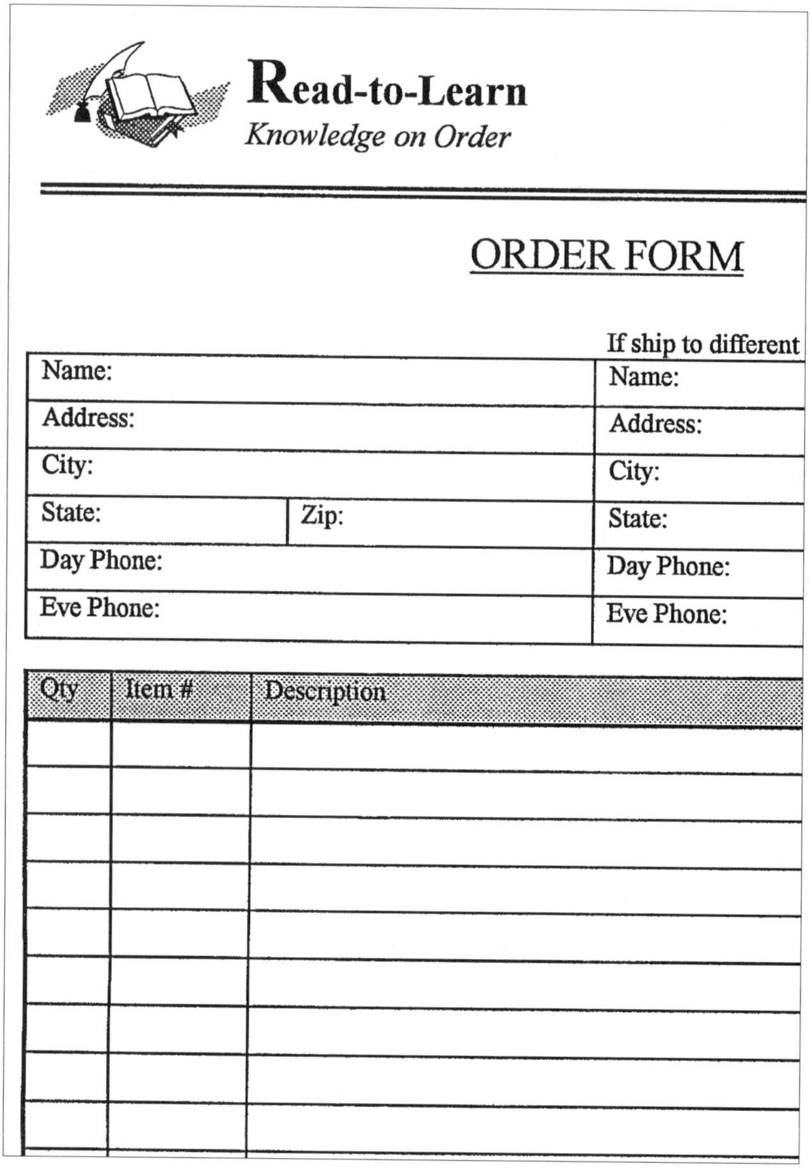

Read-to-Learn
Knowledge on Order

ORDER FORM

If ship to different

Name:	Name:
Address:	Address:
City:	City:
State: / Zip:	State:
Day Phone:	Day Phone:
Eve Phone:	Eve Phone:

Qty	Item #	Description

Figure 12-21: An example of a fill-in form.

Read-to-Learn
Knowledge on Order

1-800-555-6342 Voice
1-800-555-5900 FAX

SHIPPING LIST

June 17, 1998
Shipped to:

Name:			
Address:			
City:	State:	Zip:	

	Qty	Item #	Description	Unit Price	Total
1.					
2.					
3.					
4.					
5.					
6.					
7.					
8.					
9.					
10.					
11.					
12.					
13.					
14.					
15.					
16.					
17.					
18.					
19.					
20.					

Subtotal-->	$0.00
Tax------->	$0.00
S&H------>	$0.00
TOTAL-->	$0.00

Paid: Date:_____
    Check #:_____

   MC ___   VISA ___   Money Order ___

Figure 12-22: An example of an online form.

Creating an online form

The online form also includes one or more tables that contain a cell for each label and for each field. You begin creating an online form the same way you create a fill-in form, by specifying the dimensions of the table and typing the labels. Then, because this is an interactive form, insert a fill-in type field in each of the blanks where you want to type information. As you insert each field, you can add a prompt that appears in a message dialog box for data entry.

After completing the online form, save the file as a template with the .dot file extension and enter any summary information.

To create an online form:

1. Create a new template as before, and insert a table containing the desired number of rows and columns.

2. Type labels in the desired cells.

3. Place the insertion point in the first cell where you want to enter data when you fill in the form.

4. Choose Field from the Insert menu to display the Field dialog box (see Figure 12-23).

Figure 12-23: The Field dialog box.

5. Scroll down the list of Field Names, and select Fill-in. The FILLIN field type appears in the Field codes box.

6. Place the insertion point in the Field codes box (after the space following FILLIN), and type a prompt message enclosed in quotation marks (see Figure 12-24).

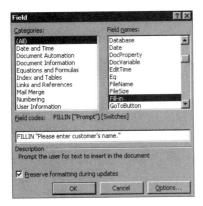

Figure 12-24: Adding a prompt message to the fill-in field.

7. Choose OK. The prompt message appears on the screen in a data-entry dialog box (see Figure 12-25).

Figure 12-25: The data-entry message dialog box.

8. Choose OK to close the dialog box.

9. Repeat Steps 3 through 8 until you have added a fill-in field for each blank cell.

10. Save the file as a template with the .dot extension.

Using an online form

Once you have created an online form and saved it as a document template, you can create a new document using that template. The first data-entry dialog box appears for entering data in the first cell of the table. If you added a prompt to the field code for that field, the message appears in the dialog box. If you don't want to enter data in the field, choose Cancel to move to the next field without entering data. The next data-entry dialog box automatically displays; here you can type the data. To enter data in an online form:

1. Choose File⇨New.

2. Choose the name of the online form template from the General tab of the New dialog box, and choose OK. (You may have to look in another folder for it.) The data-entry dialog box for the first field appears.

3. Type the data in the text box and choose OK or choose Cancel to move to the next field.

4. Fill in the rest of the blank fields.

5. Choose File➪Save As, and save the new document.

You can also open an existing document that was created with the online form template and update information. Click in the field and press F9 to update the data. The prompts appear in the data-entry dialog boxes as before.

Summary

In this chapter, you have seen some of the ways tables can enhance your documents. Tables include a lot of information in a small space. By following the examples in this chapter, you should be able to take advantage of Word's valuable table features. The following points were covered in this chapter:

✦ The new Draw Table feature provides all the tools you need to create and customize tables to place in your documents.

✦ To move around in the table, enter text in the cells, and select blocks of cells, you can use either the mouse, the arrow keys, or various keystroke combinations.

✦ After the table is inserted in the document, you can change the row height, column width or spacing and move or copy cells, rows and, columns. You can also split a cell into two or more cells or merge two or more cells into one.

✦ For data collection, Word provides two types of forms: fill-in forms that are intended to be printed and online forms that provide an interactive form for data entry at the computer.

Where to go next...

✦ For information on how to enhance your Word 97 tables with graphics and frames, see Chapters 13 and 14.

✦ For more help on using data from Excel in a Word table, see Chapter 15.

✦   ✦   ✦

Fine Arts: Graphics and Links to Other Applications

Illustrating Documents with Graphics

Adding graphics or pictures to illustrate your documents makes them more appealing. Pictures that you insert in your documents can come from numerous sources, such as stand-alone graphics programs, scanned art, and clip art. In Word, you can add graphics to your document by importing a graphic from another application, cutting and pasting a picture using the Clipboard, and creating your own graphics from scratch by using Word's powerful drawing tools. Word also includes the WordArt application, which lets you add impressive special text effects to your document. This chapter takes you on a guided tour, explaining how to use Word's graphic tools to add and work with graphics in your documents.

Working with Bitmap and Vector Graphics

Graphic formats fall into two camps: bitmap and vector. *Bitmap graphics* are composed of small dots, called *pixels*. Each pixel is represented by one or more bits in the computer's memory that define color and intensity. A bitmap graphic is stored at a fixed resolution that is determined by the number and layout of the pixels. You can easily edit an image at that fixed resolution, but, if you enlarge a graphic, you distort it and lose image quality.

Images containing subtle colors or a great deal of detail, such as shadings, work best as bitmap graphics. Microsoft Image Composer that comes with Microsoft FrontPage 97, Adobe Photoshop, and PaintShop Pro from JASC are examples of programs that create bitmapped pictures.

Vector graphics, in contrast, comprise a set of drawing instructions that describe the dimension and shape of every line, circle, arc, or rectangle. The resolution of a vector image is not fixed: the resolution of your output device determines the quality of a vector image's appearance. You can enlarge, reduce, and otherwise edit vector graphics affecting resolution or image quality. Vector graphics are best for line art. With Word, you can create vector images directly in your documents.

Bitmap graphics require more disk space than vector graphics because they must contain information about each pixel displayed on-screen. Vector graphics are stored as commands that create images. Sometimes vector graphics take longer to *render* (convert from vector outlines to fully formed graphics) because your processor must draw them; small bitmaps are simply loaded directly into memory.

Graphics file formats supported by Word

Word is compatible with most popular graphics programs. You can insert into Word documents any pictures or objects created with any of the programs or formats listed in Table 13-1.

<table>
<tr><th colspan="3">Table 13-1
Graphics File Formats Compatible with Word</th></tr>
<tr><th>Program Format</th><th>File Extension</th><th>Graphics Type</th></tr>
<tr><td>AutoCAD</td><td>DXF</td><td>Vector</td></tr>
<tr><td>AutoCAD Plot files</td><td>PLT</td><td>Vector</td></tr>
<tr><td>CompuServe Graphics Interchange Format</td><td>GIF</td><td>Bitmap</td></tr>
<tr><td>Computer Graphics Metafile</td><td>CGM</td><td>Bitmap/Vector</td></tr>
<tr><td>CorelDRAW!</td><td>CDR</td><td>Vector</td></tr>
<tr><td>Encapsulated PostScript</td><td>EPS</td><td>Bitmap/Vector</td></tr>
<tr><td>JPEG Interchange Format</td><td>JPG</td><td>Bitmap</td></tr>
<tr><td>Kodak Photo CD</td><td>PCD</td><td>Bitmap</td></tr>
<tr><td>Macintosh PICT</td><td>PCT</td><td>Vector</td></tr>
<tr><td>Micrografx Designer and Micrografx Draw</td><td>DRW</td><td>Vector</td></tr>
<tr><td>PC Paintbrush</td><td>PCX</td><td>Bitmap</td></tr>
<tr><td>Portable Network Graphics</td><td>PNG</td><td>Bitmap</td></tr>
<tr><td>Tagged Image File Format</td><td>TIF</td><td>Bitmap</td></tr>
<tr><td>Targa</td><td>TGA</td><td>Bitmap</td></tr>
<tr><td>Windows Bitmap/Windows Paint</td><td>DIB BMP RLE</td><td>Bitmap</td></tr>
</table>

Program Format	File Extension	Graphics Type
Windows Metafile	WMF	Bitmap/Vector
Windows Enhanced Metafile	EMF	Bitmap/Vector
WordPerfect Graphics	WPG	Bitmap/Vector

Word typically uses import filters to place pictures into a document. However, some programs, such as CorelDRAW!, include OLE support to let you insert pictures as objects. If you chose the Complete Setup option when you installed Word, all the graphics import filters were added to your system. If you chose a Custom installation, you may not have installed all the filters. To see which filters are installed, choose Insert⇨Picture⇨From File, and check the Files of type list. If you need to install an additional graphics filter, you will need to run Setup again to install it. For help with installing filters, see the section on installing individual Word components in Appendix B.

If the graphics filter you need to import a graphic is not shipped with Word, you must open the file in an image editing program. Then you can select the graphic, copy it, and paste it into your document. The graphic becomes a Windows metafile (.wmf). Another alternative is to see whether you can open the file in another application and save it in a format listed in Table 13-1. Many image editing programs, such as PaintShop Pro, let you save files in a different format.

Where to get graphic images

You may have wondered where people find professional images for desktop publishing. Numerous sites on the World Wide Web archive non-royalty images of varying quality that are free for downloading. Be careful when you use an image from personal Web sites, because verifying whether the image is royalty free or being published illegally is difficult. Different commercial online services, such as CompuServe and America Online, have forums for graphic files and utilities. Many of the images used in this book came from two services available on CompuServe. Bettman and Archive have thousands of images available that you can search for using keywords. To connect to Bettman using CompuServe, enter **Go Bettman**; to connect to Archive, enter **Go Archive**. You can then search for and view the image files and decide which ones you want to download. If you want to use the picture for commercial use, you need to pay a nominal licensing fee, which is explained when you first log on to the company's forum.

Numerous companies exist that sell royalty-free digital photos and clip art. But beware: many more companies sell cheap, low-quality digital photos and clip art. We have used pictures and clip art from PhotoDisk and Image Club in this book. Both of these companies have high-quality images that are reasonably priced. Both PhotoDisk and Adobe represent other companies that sell quality images. For example, Photo Disk also sells CMCD images that we have found to be quite unique and of very high quality. You can get a starter CD-ROM from PhotoDisk for under $40. To contact PhotoDisk, call 800-528-3472. Image Club was recently purchased by Adobe, the premier font and graphics company. Image Club currently sells fine art images from Planet Art and other high quality graphics companies. To receive a catalog from Image Club, call 800-661-9410. You can visit Image Club online via the World Wide Web site at `http://www.imageclub.com/`. You may also want to check application packages for clip art.

Many companies bundle fonts and clip art with their applications to draw customers. Corel is well-known for its massive clip art collection. Corel has also made an impressive entry offering a huge library of digital photos. Corel sells two indexed catalogs and CDs that contain thumbnails of available photo images, each selling for under $30. You can contact Corel by calling 800-772-6735.

Inserting pictures in documents

Word is extremely flexible in the ways you can insert a picture in your document. For example, you can place it in the text directly or insert it in a text box or a table. Different techniques offer different advantages. Inserting a picture in a text box, which you can position anywhere in your document, enables you to have text and images stored in containers that you can easily move anywhere on a page. Inserting a picture in a cell of a table lets you position the picture next to text in an adjacent cell.

When you insert a picture in your Word document, the image appears where the insertion point is located. When you use text boxes, the image moves with the text when you add or delete text preceding or following the picture. For details on working with text boxes to position pictures independently of text, see Chapter 14.

You can insert a picture in your document in one of three ways:

✦ Use the Insert⇨Picture command and choose either the Clip Art or From File submenu.

✦ Use the Insert⇨Object command to insert a picture that you plan to link to a graphics program. After you insert a linked picture, you can later edit it with the program that created it.

✦ Open the program used to create pictures, and copy (or cut) a picture to the Windows Clipboard. Then use the Edit⇨Paste command to paste the picture into your Word document.

You can automatically include a caption with each picture you insert by choosing the Insert⇨Caption command and choosing the AutoCaption button. Chapter 23 covers how to insert a caption.

Note To view, draw, and modify pictures and drawing objects, you need to work in Page Layout view.

Inserting clip art and pictures

Choosing Insert⇨Picture⇨Clip Art displays a message box informing you that you can insert clip art from the CD-ROM that shipped with Word. You can make it so the dialog box no longer appears by clicking in the Don't remind me again check box. After clicking OK to close the message box, the Microsoft Clip Gallery 3.0 dialog box appears (shown in Figure 13-1). Click the Clip Art tab if it isn't already selected.

When you display the Clip Art tab, a button with the Internet Explorer logo on it appears in the lower-right corner (Figure 13-1). If you have an Internet connection and a Web browser, such as Microsoft Internet Explorer or Netscape Navigator, and you click this button, your browser starts and connects to a special Microsoft site, Clip Gallery Live, that lets you import additional clip art.

Figure 13-1: The Microsoft Clip Gallery 3.0 dialog box.

Microsoft Office and Word 97 come with a clip art library of pictures. Office stores the clip art in the folder Microsoft Office\Clipart. The clip art is categorized by topic. Click the category to display a preview of the related clip art files you can choose from. When you see a clip art image you want, either select the image and click the Insert button or double-click the image.

To insert a picture from a file into your document:

1. Position the insertion point where you want to insert the picture.

2. Choose Insert⇨Picture⇨From File. The Insert Picture dialog box appears.

3. From the File name list, select the picture file that you want to insert. (You can use the Files of type list to restrict the File name list to a particular file type.) If your picture file is not in the current drive, select the drive containing your file from the Look in list. From the Look in list, select the folder that contains your file. If you want help finding your file, choose the Find Now button to locate your file. Chapter 6 explains working with Find Now.

4. If not already selected, click in the Float over text check box to place the picture in the drawing layer so you can position it precisely on the page or in front of or behind text or other objects. To insert the picture directly in the text at the insertion point, clear the Float over text check box.

5. Choose Insert.

Tip You can reduce the size of a document file by choosing to link the file instead of inserting the picture in your document. To link to the file, select the picture, click the Link to file check box, and then clear the Save with document check box.

Word 97 lets you acquire a picture directly from a scanner. To scan a picture from Word, select Insert⇨Picture⇨From Scanner. The program you use to acquire scanned images appears. After scanning the image, it will appear in Microsoft Photo Editor. When you finish editing the picture, choose File⇨Exit and Return to Document command on the Photo Editor File menu. The image is inserted in your document.

Note If Microsoft Photo Editor is not installed, run the Setup program again and install it. For more information, on setting up components with Word 97, see Appendix B.

Inserting picture objects in documents

A *picture object* is a picture that you can edit in a Word document. A picture object is not linked to a file outside the document. In fact, the Word document contains all the data that defines a picture object. You can insert several types of picture objects, including Microsoft Word pictures or WordArt images. Different programs include support for objects. For example, if CorelDRAW! is on your computer and you installed the CorelDRAW! import filter when you installed Word, you can insert any CorelDRAW! object.

To insert picture objects in Word, choose the Insert⇨Object command, which displays the Object dialog box (shown in Figure 13-2). From the Object type list in the Create New tab, select your graphics program of choice. Of course, you must then draw your picture. For example, if you select Microsoft Word Picture, Word displays the Microsoft Word Picture screen in Figure 13-3. (Notice the Drawing toolbar displayed at the bottom of the screen.) You can now create your picture by using Word's built-in drawing program. We explain how to work with the Word drawing tools later in this chapter.

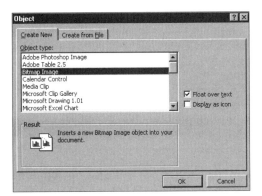

Figure 13-2: The Create New tab in the Object dialog box.

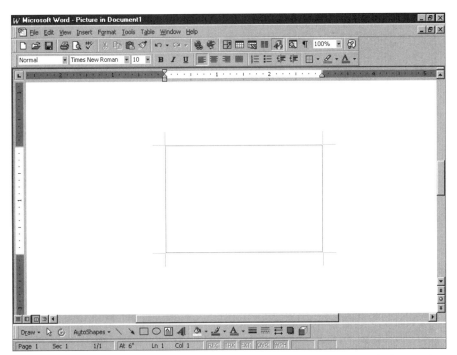

Figure 13-3: When you insert a picture object by using Microsoft Word Picture, the Drawing toolbar appears at the bottom of the screen.

Selecting the Create from File tab (see Figure 13-4) lets you insert an existing graphics file as an object. In most cases, you will want to leave the Float over text check box selected. This places the object in the drawing layer, so you can position it in front of or behind text and other objects using commands on the Draw menu. Clearing the Float over text check box places the object in-line with the current paragraph.

If you choose the Create from File tab, you can select the file you want to add as an object, so that you can edit it later with the program to which the file is associated. To edit the object, double-click the picture. The picture is loaded in the associated program. To return to your Word document, click outside of the picture. The Create from File tab includes the Link to file option, which lets you link a picture to its original file (we'll explain linking files later in the "Linking Graphics" section). The Display as icon option (in both tabs) lets you display a picture as an icon, saving room in your document. An icon displays on-screen or when it is printed. You can double-click an icon to see its contents.

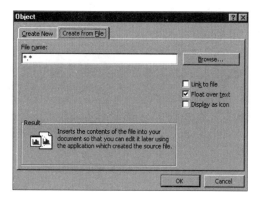

Figure 13-4: The Create from File tab in the Object dialog box.

To insert a picture object into your document:

1. Position the insertion point where you want to insert the picture object.

2. Choose Insert⇨Object. The Object dialog box appears.

3. Do one of the following:

   • To create a new picture, select the Create New tab. From the Object type list, select the type of picture object you want to insert. If you want to display an icon rather than the picture, choose the Display as icon option. Choose OK. The program you use to create the picture starts.

   • To insert an existing file, select the Create from File tab. In the File name list box, type or select the filename of the picture you want to insert. If you need to navigate to another drive or directory, click the Browse button. If you want to display an icon rather than the picture, choose the Display as icon option. Choose OK.

4. Return to your Word document from the graphics program. How you return depends on the graphics program. In Microsoft Photo Editor, for example, choose the File⇨Exit and Return to Document command.

Linking graphics

If you're using a graphic created in another Word-compatible program, you can choose Link to file in the Insert Picture dialog box (Insert➪Picture➪From File) or in the Create from File tab in the Object dialog box (Insert➪Object). If you created a link to your graphic's original program, you can tell Word via the Insert Picture dialog box to keep only the link in your document, not the entire file. To do so, clear the Save with document check box *after* checking the Link to file check box.

If you use this method, you minimize your document's file size because Word does not store a copy of the whole picture in your document. This method also has two disadvantages. First, Word takes longer to display the picture. Worse, if you move a graphic without re-establishing the link, or if the program that created the image is not available, the graphic disappears from your document and is replaced by a generic image consisting of a square, a circle, and a rectangle.

If you're just editing text, you can specify that Word not display the document's graphics. This speeds up working in Word because pictures don't have to be redrawn as you move around your document. To replace graphics with picture placeholders, display the View tab in the Options dialog box (Tools➪Options), and choose Picture placeholders.

To link a picture file to a Word document:

1. Position the insertion point where you want the picture to appear.

2. Choose Insert➪Picture➪From File, and select the picture file you want to insert.

3. Choose the Link to file option and clear the Save with document option.

4. Choose Insert. If you move or edit the original picture file, you can update the link by positioning the insertion point on the picture placeholder and pressing F9.

Selecting pictures

As with text, in order to perform a formatting command, you need to select the graphic first. To select a picture, simply click it. When you select a picture, sizing handles appear on the picture's corners and sides—eight in all. You can use a mouse to move the selection handles and thereby resize the picture. You can format a selected picture with picture-formatting commands. To format a picture select it, right-click the mouse, and choose Format Picture.

Copying pictures into documents

One of the easiest ways to insert a picture into Word that you created with a graphics program is to use the Clipboard. Choosing the Edit⇨Paste Special command lets you paste a graphic as a link. By linking a picture to the original file, you can update the picture if you later make changes to the original. To copy a picture into your document:

1. Start your graphics program and open the file containing the picture you want to copy to your Word document.

2. Select the picture.

3. Choose Edit⇨Copy in your graphics program.

4. Switch to your Word document.

5. Position the insertion point where you want to insert the picture.

6. Do one of the following:

   • Choose Edit⇨Paste.

   • To link the picture to the original file, choose Edit⇨Paste Special. Choose Paste link from the Paste Special dialog box, which is shown in Figure 13-5. From the As list, select the format for your picture (the formats depend on the type of picture copied). Choose the Display as icon option if you want to display an icon rather than the picture in your text to keep the document size smaller. To display and edit the picture, double-click the icon.

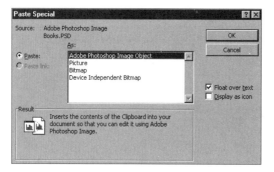

Figure 13-5: The Paste Special dialog box.

If you paste the picture as an object, you can edit it later. If you paste the graphic as a picture, it may take up less space. Read the Result box at the bottom of the Paste Special dialog box to help decide how to paste your picture. Different text appears in the Result box for each of the different formats in the As list. For more information about how to work with links, refer to Chapter 15.

Resizing and cropping pictures

After you insert a picture, you can scale or stretch it to a smaller or larger size by a percentage: proportionally or nonproportionally. You also can size a picture to the exact desired width and height, or you can crop away parts of a picture that you don't want to display.

Resizing is useful when you need a picture to be a certain size. Cropping is effective when you want to zoom in on one part of a picture. You can resize and crop pictures using either the mouse or a dialog box.

You can't add shading to a graphic or the white space that you add to the graphic with the cropping tool. However, you can place the graphic inside a text box, enlarge the text box, and shade the portion of the text box that doesn't contain the graphic.

Resizing and cropping a picture using the mouse

After you select a picture, you can use the mouse to move the selection handles and thereby resize or crop the picture. With the corner handles, you can scale or crop from two sides (for example, top and left) at the same time. As a result, when you use a corner handle to resize a picture, the picture remains proportional. The side handles enable scaling and cropping from just one side. When you use a side handle to resize, the picture's proportions change. Whenever you drag a handle, the opposite handle stays anchored to its current position.

Using the mouse to resize or crop a picture lets you see how your picture looks while you're making your changes. Cropping a picture in Word doesn't change the inserted picture, so you can later restore the cropped portion of the picture. As you crop the picture, you can see your picture's dimensions: Word displays the exact size of the image in the status bar. Figure 13-6 shows the Picture toolbar and a picture that has been reduced and then cropped.

To resize and crop a picture using the mouse:

1. Select the picture you want to resize or crop. If the Picture toolbar isn't already displayed, right-click and choose Show Picture Toolbar.

2. Do one of the following:

   • To crop the picture, click the Crop button in the Picture toolbar. The mouse pointer changes shape to two overlapping corner angles. Move the pointer on a handle and drag the bounding box to display only the portion of the picture you want to appear. Release the mouse button when only a portion of the picture you want showing is left. If you're cropping, you add a blank border after you pass the picture's original edges.

• To resize the picture, move the mouse pointer over a selection handle. The pointer turns into a two-headed arrow. Table 13-2 lists the mouse and key combinations for resizing your image proportionally. Dragging a handle toward the picture's center makes the picture smaller. The diagonal sizing handles increase or decrease the size of the graphic without changing its proportion. The middle sizing handles on the left and right of the box widen or narrow the image. The middle sizing handles on the top and bottom make the graphic taller or shorter. Release the mouse button when the picture is the desired size.

Figure 13-6: A picture that has been reduced and cropped.

Tip   If you want to perform multiple operations on a picture or drawing double-click the button in the Picture or Drawing toolbar. The button remains active until you click another button or begin typing.

Table 13-2
Mouse and Key Combinations for
Resizing Your Image Proportionally

Keep Proportional	Key and mouse operation
From a corner	Shift and drag a corner sizing handle.
Vertically, horizontally, or diagonally from the center outward	Ctrl and drag any sizing handle
From the center outward	Ctrl+Shift and drag a corner sizing handle
To temporarily override the settings for the grid	Alt and drag any sizing handle

Resizing and cropping using the Picture dialog box

Though convenient, using the sizing handles is not nearly as precise as using the Picture dialog box to resize or crop a picture. Choosing the Format Picture button or the Format⇨Picture command displays the Picture tab in the Format Picture dialog box (see Figure 13-7). The Picture dialog box contains five active tabs that enable you to enter exact measurements for not only resizing or cropping the image, but the placement of the image as well. The boxes includes up and down arrows you can use to increase or decrease the measurement. In the Crop from boxes, located on the Picture tab, you can specify Left, Right, Top, and Bottom crop amounts (to 1/100 inch). Negative crop amounts add white space around the image. The Size tab enables you to control the Scale to 1/100 inch by specifying Width and Height in percentages. You can control the overall image size by changing the Width and Height boxes in the Size area, also located on the Size tab. If you change the proportions, the related boxes automatically change.

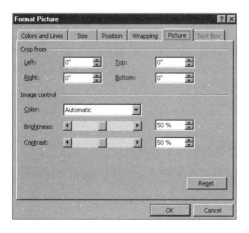

Figure 13-7: The Picture tab in the Format Picture dialog box.

If you want to identify a picture's dimensions, select the picture and choose Format⇨Picture. The entries in the size tab indicates the picture's current dimensions.

Resetting a picture to its original dimensions

The percent you enter in the Scale boxes is always a percent of the original size; therefore, you can easily reset your picture to its original dimensions, even after scaling the picture by using the mouse. The Original size is also noted on the Size tab. To reset a picture to its original dimensions, select the picture, choose the Reset Picture button, or choose the Format⇨Picture command and then choose the Reset button. You must choose the Reset button on the Picture and Size tabs. This will not reset any information you may have changed on the Position or Wrapping tabs. To resize or crop a picture using the Format Picture dialog box:

1. Select the picture.

2. Choose Format⇨Picture. The Format Picture dialog box appears.

3. Do one of the following:

    - If you want to crop the picture, choose the Picture tab. In the Crop from section in the dialog box, enter the crop amount in the Left, Right, Top, or Bottom box, or click the up or down arrows to increase or decrease the crop amount. For example, to crop $1/4$-inch off the bottom of the picture, type **.25** in the Bottom box. To crop $1/4$-inch off the right side, type **.25** in the Right box.

    - If you want to scale your picture by a percentage, choose the Size tab and use the Scale section in the dialog box. In the Width or Height box (or both), enter the percentage by which you want to scale the picture. For example, to scale the picture to half its original size, type **.50** in the Width and the Height boxes. Typing the identical scaling amount keeps the scaled picture proportional. If you type different scales in the Width and Height boxes, the picture is distorted.

    - If you want to make your picture an exact size, use the Size and rotate section located on the Size tab. Enter the dimensions for your picture in the Width and Height boxes. If you want to return the picture to its original dimensions, remember the original dimensions are listed in the Original size box at the bottom of the Size tab.

4. Choose OK.

Adding borders and shadows to pictures

You can add a border to around a picture or a drawing in one of three ways:

✦ Use the Lines button in the Drawing or Picture toolbar.

✦ Choose the Format⇨Borders and Shading command.

✦ Choose Format Picture from the shortcut menu and click the Borders and
Shading tab in the Picture Borders dialog box (shown in Figure 13-8).

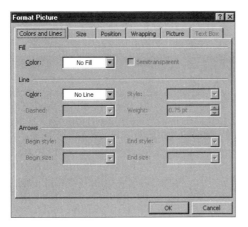

Figure 13-8 The Colors and Lines tab
in the Format Picture dialog box.

The fastest way to add a border to a picture is to click the line style button on the
Drawing or Picture toolbar. You can then select your line color using the line color
button. The line color box includes two additional options: More Line Colors and
Patterned lines. If you choose the More Line Colors option, you can select colors
from a standard or a custom palette. The Patterned line styles box includes a
variety of line patterns, as shown in Figure 13-9. If you want, you can choose to
have a dashed line surround the image by clicking the Dashed line button and
selecting one of the many dashed line patterns.

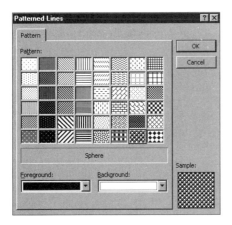

Figure 13-9: The Patterned
Lines dialog box.

If you want to add a single line to one side of a picture, draw a line using the Line
button in the Drawing toolbar. If you insert a picture in a text box, you can use the
Tables and Borders toolbar to add a single line to any side of an image.

To give your picture more definition, you can use the Shadow button in the Drawing Toolbar to add a shadow to any sides of the box. You can display a Shadow Settings toolbar by clicking the Shadow button in the Drawing Toolbar and choosing the Shadow Settings option. To quickly apply a drop-shadow, choose the Shadow On/Off button. Figure 13-10 shows an image with a drop shadow created using the Shadow Settings toolbar.

Displaying and hiding pictures

In previous versions of Word, images were inserted as inline images by default. Word 97 inserts images as floating images. If you clear the Float over text check box when inserting an image, the graphic is added inline right next to your text. Including a large number of inline pictures in your documents slows down Word's performance. Word lets you hide inline pictures and display picture placeholders to speed up working with a document. For example, you can display the pictures while you're inserting and formatting them; you then hide them while you work on the text in your document. A picture placeholder appears as a box outlined by thin lines (Figure 13-11). You can select and work with hidden pictures as though they are displayed.

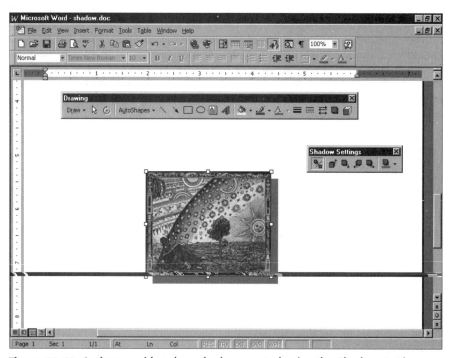

Figure 13-10: An image with a drop shadow created using the Shadow Settings toolbar.

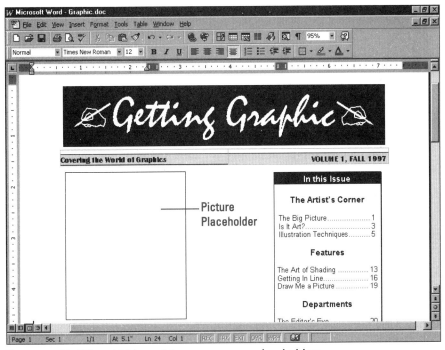

Figure 13-11: When hidden, pictures appear as placeholders.

To speed up scrolling by hiding pictures:

1. Choose Tools⇨Options.

2. Select the View tab.

3. Choose the Picture placeholders check box in the Show group. To display pictures, clear the Picture placeholders check box in the Show group.

4. Choose OK.

If you want to really improve your scrolling speed and you don't need to see any of your pictures, choose Tools⇨Options, click the View tab and clear the Drawings check box. Turning off this option improves scrolling speed by not displaying drawing objects, such as AutoShapes, or floating graphics. To display drawings, choose Tools⇨Options, click the View tab, and select the Drawings check box.

Editing and converting pictures

To edit a picture that was inserted as a linked file or an object, you must have the program that was used to create the picture on your system. If you try to edit the picture and the program is not available, Word places the image in a Microsoft

Word Picture window. If you choose Edit⇨Edit Picture to edit a picture with Microsoft Word Picture, Word converts the picture to an object. As a result, the next time you select that picture for editing, the Edit⇨Picture Object command appears rather than the Edit⇨Edit Picture command. To edit a picture:

1. Do one of the following:

   • Double-click the picture you want to edit.

   • Select the picture, and then choose Edit⇨Edit Picture, Edit⇨ Picture Object or Edit⇨ Clip Object. (Word displays the appropriate command, which depends on the type of picture selected and whether the object is linked.) Either the program used to create the picture or Microsoft Word Picture appears on your screen.

2. Edit your picture. In Microsoft Word Picture, you can replace the picture or enhance it by using tools on the Drawing toolbar.

3. Do one of the following:

   • Choose File⇨Update, and then File⇨Close & Return to. If you're using a program that supports OLE 2.0 or higher, simply click outside the picture in your document.

   • Close the Microsoft Word Picture window. If you choose Exit, you exit Microsoft Word completely.

Note If nothing happens when you double-click my embedded object, a likely reason is that program you used to create the embedded object is not on your computer or the embedded object has been ungrouped and converted to a drawing object. If you have converted your picture to a drawing object, you can't edit it in its original program. You must create a new object in the original program and then embed the new object.

Converting pictures to Word Picture format

Word lets you convert a picture object from its original format to Microsoft Word Picture format. For example, you can convert a clip art file from a CorelDRAW! (CDR) format to a Microsoft Word picture. Once converted, you can edit the Microsoft Word picture by using Word's drawing tools. Word also lets you preserve your picture's original format, so you can specify that the picture be *activated in* but not *converted to* a different format. To activate or convert a picture object in a different format:

1. Select the picture object you want to convert.

2. Choose Edit⇨Object, and choose Convert from the submenu. The name of this command varies, depending on the type of picture selected and whether the object is linked. The Convert dialog box appears (shown in Figure 13-12). The format of your picture is displayed as Current Type.

3. Do one of the following:

- To permanently convert the picture object, choose Convert to, and select the picture's target format. Choose Display as icon if you want to display your converted picture as an icon.

- To temporarily activate a picture without converting to a different format, choose Activate as, and select the target format.

4. In the Object type box, select the application whose file format you want to convert the picture object to and choose OK.

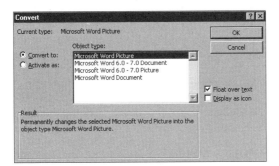

Figure 13-12: The Convert dialog box.

Editing pictures from other programs

You can use Word to edit drawings imported from other Windows drawing programs. First, make sure that Microsoft Word is selected as the Picture editor in the Edit tab of the Tools⇨Options dialog box, the default box. (If you're comfortable using some other drawing program, though, select it.) Then, double-click the graphic to edit it.

If you want, you can change the image so that you can edit it in Microsoft Word only. Import the image as an object by choosing Insert⇨Object and selecting the Create from File tab. After inserting the object into your document select it, and choose Edit⇨Picture Object⇨Convert. Select Microsoft Word from the Convert list. This action permanently converts the object to a Microsoft Word picture that can be edited from Word only.

Drawing in Word

Word's drawing features are built directly into Word. Using Word, you can create vector images, called *objects*, which you can print on any printer supported by Windows. A Word drawing can comprise many objects, such as lines and circles.

These objects, which you draw, appear directly on the page. You then can move them anywhere on the page—even beneath the text.

When you use Word's drawing tools, you work directly on a page in your document in Word's Page Layout view. Like floating images the objects you create are location-independent, so that you can move a drawing by simply dragging it. This section explains how to work with Word's Drawing toolbar to create graphics directly on the page.

Using the Drawing toolbar

You create a drawing in Word by using the Drawing toolbar. To display the Drawing toolbar, click the Drawing button on the Standard toolbar or click the right mouse button with the pointer anywhere on the background of the toolbar and choose Drawing. You also can display a Drawing toolbar by choosing View➪Toolbars and selecting Drawing from the Toolbars list. Figure 13-13 shows a floating Drawing toolbar. If you move the mouse pointer over a button, Word displays a description for the current button in the status bar. Table 13-3 lists detailed descriptions of these buttons.

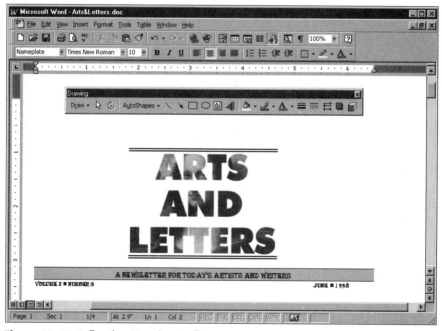

Figure 13-13: A floating Drawing toolbar.

Table 13-3
Word's Drawing Toolbar

Button	Name	Function
Draw ▾	Draw	Opens a drop-down menu that enables you to Group, Ungroup and/or Regroup objects or pictures; you can Order your selected objects or pictures, Bring to Front, Send to Back, Bring Forward, Send Backward, Bring in Front of Text, or Send Behind Text; you can set your Grid parameters, Nudge, Align or Distribute, and Rotate or Flip your pictures and objects in every direction; you can Edit Points of a line drawn in a curve, freeform or a scribble; you can change the shapes of AutoShape objects with the Change Autoshape option; and/or you can Set AutoShape Defaults.
▯	Select Objects	Draws a marquee around objects in the drawing.
⟳	Free Rotate	Rotates selected object or picture in any increment in either direction.
AutoShapes ▾	AutoShapes	Opens a drop down menu of drawing options; Lines, Basic Shapes, Block Arrows, Flowchart, Stars and Banners, and Callouts.
╲	Line	Draws straight lines. When you hold down Shift, draws straight lines at 15-degree angles from its starting point.
↖	Arrow	Draws a basic arrow. When you hold down Shift, draws straight arrows at 15-degree angles from its starting point.
▭	Rectangle	Draws rectangles. When you hold down Shift, draws squares.
◯	Oval	Draws Ovals. When you hold down Shift, draws circles.
▤	Text Box	Inserts a text box.
◢	Insert WordArt	Opens the WordArt Gallery dialog box, allowing you to insert WordArt.
◔ ▾	Fill Color	Fills a selected shape with color. If no shape is selected, sets the default fill color. Also enables you to select Fill Effects.
✎ ▾	Line Color	Colors a selected line (or the line around a selected shape). If no shape is selected, sets the default line color. Also enables you to use Patterned Lines.
A ▾	Font Color	Changes the color of the selected text. If no text is selected, sets the default text color.

(continued)

Button	Name	Function
<div>≡</div>	Line Style	Changes the width and style of a selected line. More Lines opens the Format AutoShape dialog box, where you have additional line style options.
<div>⋮⋮⋮</div>	Dash Style	Changes the style of a selected line to one of eight dashed options.
<div>⇄</div>	Arrow Style	Changes the style of a selected line to one of several preset arrow options. More Arrows opens the Format AutoShape dialog box, where you have additional arrow and line options.
<div>▣</div>	Shadow	Adds or changes the shadow of a selected object or picture. Shadow Settings displays the Shadow Settings toolbar, which allows you to turn Shadow On/Off, Nudge Shadow Up, Down, Left and/or Right, and give you control over the Shadow Color.
<div>◪</div>	3-D	Adds or changes a 3-D effect of a selected object or picture. 3-D Settings displays the 3-D Settings toolbar that allows you to turn 3-D On/Off. Tilt Up, Down, Left and/or Right, gives you control over the Depth, Direction, Lighting, Surface, and 3-D Color.

Table 13-3 (continued)

Drawing lines and shapes

To create a line or shape, choose the drawing button you want (your mouse pointer becomes a crosshair), click the page where you want the shape to begin and drag the pointer to where you want the shape to end. When you release the mouse button, the shape appears with small square handles at the ends or corners of the shape. The handles indicate that the shape is *active*. You can delete an active shape by pressing Delete or Backspace. The object you draw appears in the layer above the text, and it appears on top of any other objects you've drawn. You can change the layer position of an object, as explained in the "Layering drawing objects" section later in this chapter.

Choosing line styles, line colors, and fill colors

An object that you draw appears on-screen in the default line style, line color, and fill color. You can choose a different width of a line by choosing a line from the Line Style palette shown in Figure 13-14. With your line selected, you can specify a different fill or line color by using the Fill Color palette or Line Color palette. For example, if you want all your lines to be drawn in red, choose the Line Color button and select the color red from the color palette. You can select an object and change its color, fill, or line style at any time. Your most recent choices become the defaults used for the next drawing.

Figure 13-14: The Line Style palette.

Saving time with AutoShapes

One of the best additions to Word's drawing toolbar is the AutoShapes button. Using AutoShapes, you can easily select a shape from one of six submenus of predefined shapes, including Lines, Basic Shapes, Block Arrows, Flowchart, Stars and banners, and Callouts. Figure 13-15 shows each of the available AutoShapes submenus. To add a shape, make sure that the line and fill colors you want to use are selected, and then choose the shape you want from the AutoShapes submenu. Once inserted, the shapes can be resized, rotated, flipped, colored, and combined with other shapes to create more complex shapes.

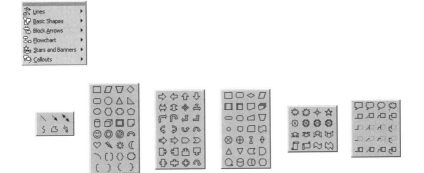

Figure 13-15: The AutoShape submenus.

Drawing lines

The Line button lets you draw straight lines. Pressing Shift as you draw constrains the line; you can create straight horizontal, vertical, or diagonal lines (at 30-, 45-, and 60-degree angles) only. If you don't press the Shift key when drawing a line, the line may print at an angle. Hold down Ctrl to draw a line from the center outward, instead of drawing from one end to the other (in other words, the line extends in two directions). If you're creating a shape with the Freeform button, click and drag to draw the first part of the shape. After you complete the drawing, double-click or press Esc.

After you draw a line or shape, the crosshair turns back into an I-beam for typing text. If you want to draw additional lines or shapes, double-click the Drawing button. The crosshair remains so that you can draw additional lines or shapes. The crosshair changes back to an I-beam when you click the page or choose another button from the Drawing toolbar.

You can press the Esc key to cancel a line or shape before it's completed. To draw lines and shapes:

1. Display the Drawing toolbar, and choose your Line Style, Line Color, and Fill Color settings.

2. Click the Line button and move the mouse arrow to the page where the pointer turns into a crosshair. Double-click the Line button if you want to draw more than one line.

3. Click and hold down the left mouse button while you drag the crosshair in any direction to draw a line. When you release the mouse button, the line is completed. If you want to draw a perfectly horizontal or vertical line, or a 30-, 45-, or 60-degree line, press the Shift key before you click the mouse to draw. Then hold down Shift until you release the mouse button to complete your drawing.

Drawing lines with arrowheads

Word gives you a number of options for adding arrows to your document. The fastest way to add a arrow is to click the Arrows button. You can also choose AutoShapes⇨Lines for some simple lines with arrowheads. The Line Style button lets you add arrowheads at either or both ends of straight or freeform lines. Word 97 lets you add an arrowhead to arcs or other shapes. The Arrow Styles button displays a variety of arrowheads. Select More Arrows from the Arrow Styles menu to display the Format AutoShape dialog box (Figure 13-16) to get more control over your lines and arrowhead styles. To draw a line with custom arrows:

1. Draw a line or use the arrow button on the Drawing toolbar to draw a standard arrow.

2. While the line is selected, click the Arrow Style button on the toolbar.

3. Make any of the selections in the menu. Keep in mind that these options affect only the head of the arrow:

   • Select the arrowhead style you want (open or closed, one or the other, or both ends).

- Select More Arrows. The Format AutoShape dialog box appears. Click the End style to chose a different arrowhead and choose End size to change the size of the arrowhead.

4. Choose OK.

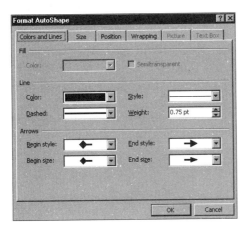

Figure 13-16: The Format AutoShape dialog box gives you control over the size and style of an arrowhead.

Drawing curves and freeform shapes

The AutoShapes submenus give you a wide assortment of predefined shapes. Choosing AutoShapes⇨Lines lets you draw a curve, freeform line, scribble, straight line, or polygon. A completed freeform or polygon comprises any combination of line segments connected by nodes (see Figure 13-17). When you select a line or shape, the line or shape appears in the selected line color or style. To fill a closed polygon, click the fill button. To keep your straight-line segments perfectly vertical, horizontal, or at a set angle, hold down the Shift key as you draw.

To draw a freeform shape or polygon:

1. Display the Drawing toolbar, and choose AutoShapes⇨Lines.

2. Choose the Freeform button. The mouse pointer changes to a crosshair.

3. To draw your shape, click the left mouse button to start the shape, move the crosshair to the end of the first line segment, and click again. Continue moving the crosshair and clicking to define each line segment.

4. Do one of the following to finish your freeform shape or polygon:

   ✦ For an open shape or a line, double-click the mouse when you finish drawing or press Esc.

   ✦ For a closed shape, click the beginning point of your shape.

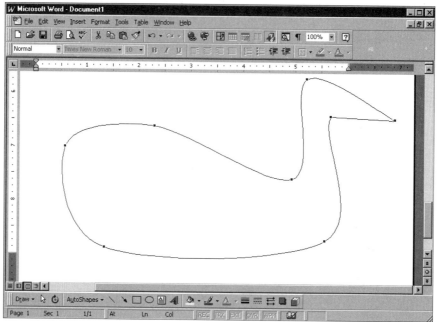

Figure 13-17: A freeform shape or polygon comprises line segments connected by nodes.

Drawing basic shapes

Choosing A<u>u</u>toShapes⇨<u>B</u>asic Shapes let you quickly add rectangles, squares, ellipses (ovals), or circles. The shapes you draw with these tools can be empty or filled, bordered or not, and in color or in blacks and grays. Figure 13-18 shows sample shapes created with the Basic Shapes option.

You can create your own circles and rectangles using the Rectangle and Circle buttons on the Drawing toolbar. If you hold down the Shift key as you draw after choosing the Rectangle button, you can draw a perfect square. If you hold down the Shift key as you draw after choosing the Ellipse button, you can draw a perfect circle. Hold down the Ctrl key to draw a rectangle, square, ellipse, or circle from the center outward. Use the Shift and Ctrl keys together to draw a perfect square or circle from the center outward. To draw from the center outward, hold down the Ctrl key as you draw.

Figure 13-18: Some sample basic shapes created using the Basic Shapes submenu.

Drawing shadowed lines and shapes

Word lets you add several different shadow options to any line or shape. New to Word 97 are the Shadow Settings and 3-D buttons that let you add drop shadows and give an interesting three-dimensional effect to lines, rectangles, and ovals. Figure 13-19 shows the 3-D menu on the Drawing toolbar.

Figure 13-19: The 3-D menu on the Drawing Toolbar.

Drop-shadows can be applied to arcs in the same manner they are applied to lines and other shapes. Select Shadow Settings to use the Shadow Settings toolbar. From this toolbar, you can turn shadows on/off, nudge them in all directions, and/or create a custom shadow color. Figure 13-20 shows the Shadow Settings toolbar and a drop-shadow added to an image.

Figure 13-20: A drop-shadow added to an image using the Shadow Settings toolbar.

To create a drop-shadow:

1. Select the drawing or line you want to shadow.
2. Choose the Shadow button on the Drawing toolbar.
3. Choose a Shadow option.

Editing drawing objects

Changing an object is a process similar to drawing an object. For example, you follow the same steps to *change* the color of a line as when you first selected the color of a line: select the object and change the line color using the Drawing toolbar.

Selecting drawing objects

You must select an object before you can format or change it. Remember that in a Word drawing, each line or shape is considered a separate object. To select any individual object, you can simply point to it and click the left mouse button.

When you want to select a group of objects, click the Select Objects button. By clicking and dragging this button, you can *completely* enclose all the objects you want to select. Make sure that no part of any object you want to select is outside the area your selecting. If an object such as a square or circle is unfilled, you must click its edge to select it (you can't select an unfilled object by clicking in its center).

As shown in Figure 13-21, selection handles appear at each corner or end of any selected object. When you click a location to draw a new object or when you click a different button on the Drawing toolbar, any selected object is deselected.

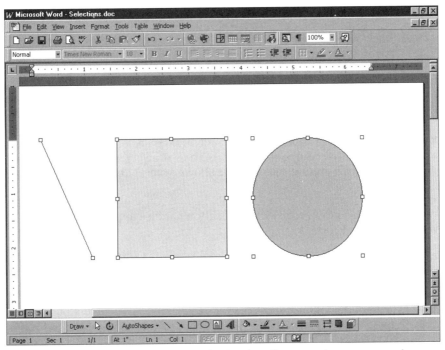

Figure 13-21: Selected objects have selection handles at each corner or end.

To select and deselect drawing objects:

1. Move the mouse pointer over the object you want to select. A four-headed selection arrow appears next to the mouse pointer.

2. Do one of the following:

   - To select one object, click the object.

   - To select several objects one by one, click the first object, hold down the Shift key, and click the other objects you want to select. Release the Shift key when you're finished.

   - To select several objects all at once, click the Select Options button. Position the pointer somewhere outside all the objects you want to select. Click and drag to draw a dotted-line marquee around all the objects you want to select. Release the mouse button. The marquee disappears, and all the objects inside the marquee are selected.

   - To deselect a single object from a group of selected objects, hold down the Shift key, and click the object you want to deselect.

   - To deselect all objects, click outside the selected objects.

Grouping and ungrouping objects

Word lets you group individual drawing objects into a single object to make editing the objects easier. By grouping multiple objects together, you can work with the drawing as a whole, moving or resizing it as a single object. Grouping objects makes it easier to move and resize picture objects. If you later need to separate objects, you can ungroup them.

You can even group groups, as well as individual objects. For example, you may want to separate the components of a complex drawing into several smaller groups for easier handling. Figure 13-22 shows several objects before and after being grouped.

When you click a group to select it, selection handles appear just as they do when you select a single object.

To group and ungroup objects:

1. Select the objects that you want to group or ungroup.

2. Do one of the following:
   - Choose Draw⇨Group from the Drawing toolbar.
   - Move the pointer to any selected object, click the right mouse button to display the shortcut menu, choose the Grouping item, and then select Group.

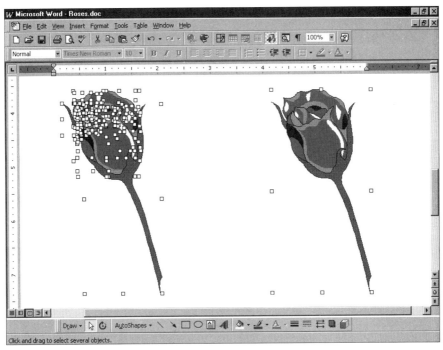

Figure 13-22: Objects before and after being grouped.

3. To change any individual part of a group, Choose Draw⇨Ungroup from the Drawing toolbar or the Ungroup option from Grouping in the shortcut menu. After making changes you can Regroup your image from either the Drawing toolbar or the shortcut menu.

Resizing lines and shapes

You resize an object by dragging its selection handles. (When a line is selected, it has selection handles at each end. When a shape is selected, square selection handles appear at the corners and sides.) To set precise measurements for a line or a shape use the Format AutoShape dialog box, as shown in Figure 13-23. To display the AutoShape dialog box, choose the Format⇨AutoShape command or double-click the selected line or shape. The following rules apply to resizing a line or shape:

✦ If you drag a side handle, you resize only from that side.

✦ If you drag a corner handle, you can resize from two directions at once.

✦ If you hold the Shift key as you drag a corner handle on a shape, the object retains its proportions (a square stays square, a circle stays round, and a freeform retains the same shape). Hold the Shift key as you resize a straight line to keep it at a horizontal, a vertical, or a 30-, 45-, or 60-degree angle.

✦ If you hold the Ctrl key as you resize, you resize from the center outward.

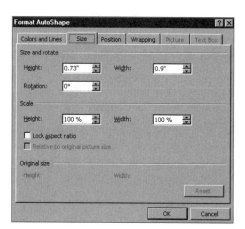

Figure 13-23: The Format AutoShape dialog box.

Editing curves and freeform shapes

Curve and freeform shapes appear with handles so you can choose to change the shape. To manipulate the contours of a curve or freeform shape, select the shape, right-click, and choose Edit Point from the shortcut menu. Right-click again, and the Edit Points shortcut menu appears. This shortcut menu lists options to edit the points of the object. Using this menu, you can move, delete, and add nodes. Alternatively, you can choose the Draw⇨Edit Points on the Drawing toolbar.

The Edit Points option lets you drag any line endpoint in a freeform shape to a new position. If you select a freeform shape and choose Draw⇨Edit Points from the Drawing toolbar, you find that the shape is composed of small lines connected by movable handles, called *nodes*. To change the shape, drag any one of these nodes.

You can reshape a freeform shape or polygon in two ways. When a freeform shape is selected, you can drag any one of the eight handles, reshaping and resizing as needed. Once in Edit Points, you also can reshape a freeform shape by dragging the nodes that connect its segments.

You can add or delete nodes to reshape a freeform or polygon object. Adding a node between existing nodes gives you another node with which to smooth a curve. Deleting a node joins the line segments on both sides of the deleted node.

You can group arcs with lines and freeform shapes, but you cannot connect them.

To reshape a freeform or polygon object:

1. Select the freehand or polygon object to display the nodes linking the individual line segments, and then choose Draw⇨Edit Points from the Drawing toolbar.

2. Move the pointer to a node. When the pointer turns into a crosshair, hold down the mouse button and drag the node to a new location. Release the mouse button when the node reaches the desired destination. Repeat to move other nodes.

3. Click in the background to return to editing your document.

To add or delete a node to a freeform or polygon shape:

1. Select the freehand or polygon object, and choose Draw⇨Edit Points from the Drawing toolbar, or right-click and choose Edit Points from the shortcut menu. The nodes linking the individual line segments appear.

2. Do one of the following:

   • To add a node, move the mouse pointer to the place on the line where you want a new node, hold down the Ctrl key, and click the mouse button.

   • To remove a node, point to the node, hold down the Ctrl key, and click the mouse button.

Rotating and flipping lines, shapes, and objects

The Draw⇨Rotate or Flip command and Free Rotate button on the Drawing toolbar let you rotate a selected line or shape or entire picture object. You can also rotate a single selected object or a group of selected objects. When you rotate a callout, the text remains right-side up. If you want to rotate text, you can insert your text as WordArt and choose the Free Rotate button on the WordArt toolbar or add a text box and choose the Change Text Direction button on the Text Box toolbar. WordArt is covered later in this chapter, for more information on using text boxes, see Chapter 14. Figure 13-24 shows rotated and flipped objects.

To rotate or flip an object:

1. Select an object you want to rotate or flip.

2. Do one of the following:

   • To rotate an object, choose the Free Rotate button.

   • To flip an object from right to left, choose Draw⇨Rotate or Flip⇨Flip Horizontal.

   • To flip an object from top to bottom, choose Draw⇨Rotate or Flip⇨Flip Vertical.

3. If you want to shrink or enlarge the boundaries of the picture to fit the rotated or flipped contents, click the Reset Picture button on the Picture toolbar.

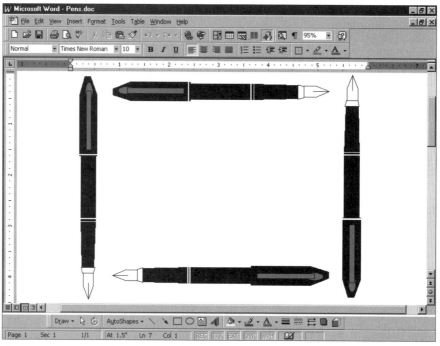

Figure 13-24: Rotated and flipped objects.

Removing lines and shapes

You can easily remove a shape or group of shapes from your drawing. Just select the objects you want to delete, and press Delete. If you accidentally delete an object, choose the Edit⇨Undo command before doing anything else. You also can remove an object by selecting it and cutting it (choose Edit⇨Cut).

Moving and copying lines and shapes

You can move any line, shape, or group of lines and shapes from one part of your drawing to another or from one part of your document to another. The quickest way to move an object is to drag it to a new position on the page. When you drag to the edge of the screen, the page automatically scrolls. In this way, you can move objects beyond the area of the page that's displayed. To move longer distances or to move objects between documents, use Word's Cut, Copy, and Paste commands. After an object is cut or copied, you can paste it as many times as you want. To move and copy an object:

1. Select an object you want to move.

2. Do one of the following:

   • To move an object with the mouse, position the mouse pointer over the object, but not over a selection handle. Drag the object to its new location. Release the mouse button when the object reaches the desired destination. If you hold down the Shift key as you drag, you move an object in a straight line.

   • To move an object by using the Cut and Paste commands, choose Edit⇨Cut (Ctrl+X) or click the object with the right mouse button and choose the Cut command from the shortcut menu; you can also choose the Cut button on the Standard toolbar. Position the insertion point where you want to move the object. Choose Edit⇨Paste (Ctrl+V), or click the screen with the right mouse button, and choose the Paste command from the shortcut menu. You can also choose the Paste button on the Standard toolbar.

   • To copy an object by using the mouse, hold down Ctrl as you drag the object.

   • To copy an object using Copy and Paste commands, choose Edit⇨Copy (Ctrl+C) or click the object with the right mouse button and choose the Copy command from the shortcut menu; or choose the Copy button on the Standard toolbar. Position the insertion point where you want to move the object. You cannot paste a drawing object into a location unless text is already there. Now Choose Edit⇨Paste (Ctrl+V) or click the screen with the right mouse button and choose the Paste command from the shortcut menu; you can also choose the Paste button on the Standard toolbar.

Positioning objects

Choosing the Format⇨AutoShape command and clicking the Position tab displays options that let you specify how far an object should be positioned from the margins, a column, a paragraph, or the edges of the page.

A drawing object is always *anchored* to the nearest paragraph. When you move an object by dragging it, the object shifts its anchor to the paragraph nearest the new location unless you lock the anchor. In that case, the object stays with the paragraph when the paragraph moves. Anchors provide another way for you to move objects: you can drag an object's anchor (which, when displayed, appears in the margin) to a new paragraph and the object moves to that paragraph. Drawings always appear on the same page as the anchor paragraphs. If you delete the paragraph to which a drawing is anchored, the drawing is also deleted.

To display anchors, choose the Show/Hide button on the Standard toolbar, or choose Tools⇨Options and, in the View tab, select the Object anchors check box. When you select a drawing object, the anchor is displayed. To specify an exact position for objects:

1. Select the object(s).

2. Choose the Format➪AutoShape command. The Format AutoShape dialog box appears.

3. Select the Position tab.

4. Type or select the distance you want the object to be positioned from the margin, column, or page in the Horizontal and From box.

5. Type or select the distance you want the object to be positioned from the margin, paragraph, or page in the Vertical and From box.

6. Choose OK.

To lock an object's anchor:

1. Select the object.

2. Choose the Format➪AutoShape command. The AutoShape dialog box appears.

3. Select the Position tab.

4. Choose the Lock anchor option.

5. Choose OK.

To display and move anchors:

1. Choose Tools➪Options.

2. Select the View tab.

3. Choose the Object anchors option in the Show group, and click OK.

4. Select an object to display its anchor.

5. Drag the anchor to another paragraph to move the anchor.

Aligning objects using the Snap to Grid dialog box

Word contains a built-in invisible grid that aligns drawing objects to the nearest 1/10 inch and lets you line up objects. You can change the horizontal or vertical spacing of the grid or turn the grid off altogether by choosing Draw➪Grid, which opens the Snap to Grid dialog box (see Figure 13-25). In this dialog box, you can determine the grid's beginning point so that you can specify no grid on part of your screen.

The Grid dialog box also includes a Snap to shapes check box that lets you choose to automatically align objects with gridlines that go through the vertical and horizontal edges of AutoShapes.

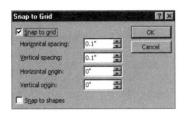

Figure 13-25: The Snap to Grid dialog box.

The grid constrains the movement of your crosshair as you draw. As a result, you can use the drawing grid to help you draw straight lines and draw the sides of objects in certain increments. For example, if you want to draw squares that have 1/2-inch sides, set your drawing grid to .5".

By default, the grid starts at the top-left corner of the page. You can change this origin, however. For example, you may want the grid to originate at the top left of a column.

To change the size and placement of the drawing grid:

1. Choose Draw⇨Grid from the Drawing toolbar to display the Snap to Grid dialog box.

2. Choose the Snap to grid check box. To turn the grid off, clear the Snap to grid check box.

3. Choose Horizontal spacing, and type the side-to-side spacing increment you desire. You can also click the arrows, or use the arrow keys to increase or decrease the increment.

4. Choose Vertical spacing and type the top-to-bottom spacing increment you desire; click the arrows; or use the arrow keys to increase or decrease the increment.

5. To set the origin of the grid, do one of the following:

   • Choose Horizontal origin, and type the distance from the left edge of the page where you want the grid to begin. You can also click the arrows or use the arrow keys to increase or decrease the increment.

   • Choose Vertical origin, and type the distance from the top edge of the page where you want the grid to begin. You can also click the arrows or use the arrow keys to increase or decrease the increment.

6. Choose OK.

Tip If the grid is off, you can turn it on temporarily by holding down the Alt key as you drag. Alternatively, if the grid is on, you can turn it off temporarily by holding down Alt as you drag.

Aligning objects using the Align dialog box

You can align objects to each other or to the page. When you align objects to each other, they line up either on the side you specify (left, right, top, or bottom) or at their centers. Similarly, when you align objects to the page, they align with the left, right, top, bottom, or center of the page. You can also distribute objects horizontally or vertically. Figure 13-26 shows three objects centered on the page.

To align objects to each other, you must select more than one object; however, you can align a single object to the page. After an object is aligned, you can drag it to move it to another location.

To align objects:

1. Select the objects you want to align to each other or the object you want to align to the page.

2. Choose Draw⇨Align or Distribute from the Drawing toolbar. You can select the align or distribute option from the callout menu or click and drag on the bar at the top of the menu to show the Align or Distribute floating toolbar.

3. Choose Align Left, Center, or Right to align horizontally. Choose Align Top, Middle or Bottom to align vertically. Choose Distribute Horizontally or Vertically to align your images evenly in either direction.

4. Choose Relative to Page if you selected one or more objects and want to align them relative to the edges of the page.

Layering drawing objects

The Word program provides three layers in which you can work:

✦ The text layer, the layer you're accustomed to working in when you use a word processing program

✦ The drawing layer, the layer above the text

✦ The layer behind the text

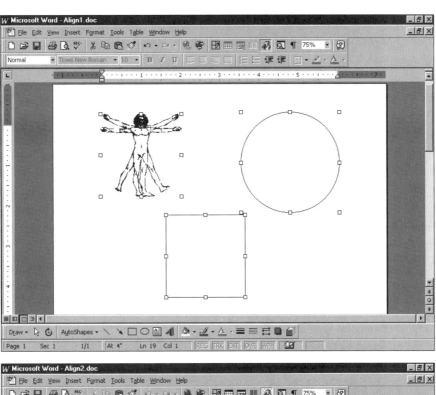

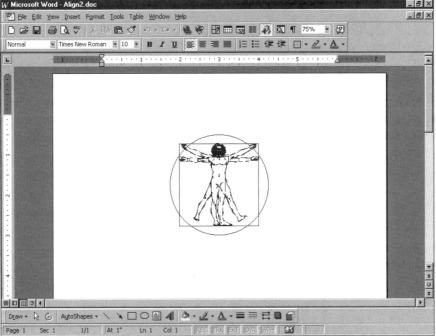

Figure 13-26: Three objects centered on a page.

The Draw⇨Order command on the Drawing toolbar lets you move any object (or even your entire picture) between the layers above and below the text. If you move an image to the layer below the text, you can see the drawing through your text. Use this technique to create backgrounds for your text. For example, by layering an object behind text, you can create a watermark or add a graphic border around your text. A *watermark* is a graphic that appears behind the text. Chapter 10 explained one method of creating a watermark. You can add a border around your page by choosing the Format⇨Borders and Shading, and then clicking the Page Border tab. Another technique for adding a graphic border around the edge of your page is to insert a drawing or a WordArt object in a header or footer and then choose Draw⇨Order⇨Send Behind Text.

Selecting objects that are behind the text layer works the same as selecting objects that are in the drawing layer. (Remember, when you first draw objects, they appear in the drawing layer on top of the text.) If an object is hidden behind another object, select the topmost object and move it behind the hidden object.

Figure 13-27 shows an example of Word's layering. Objects or pictures in the drawing layer obscure text. Objects in the text layer force the text to wrap. This feature is apparent when you choose Page Layout view or Print Preview. Objects behind the text show through the text. The Drawing toolbar has four separate tools for rearranging layers: two for moving objects in front of and behind other objects in the drawing layer and two for moving objects behind or in front of the text layer.

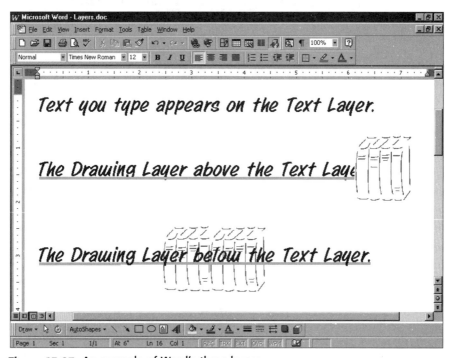

Figure 13-27: An example of Word's three layers.

Objects you draw appear on top of other objects in the drawing layer. You can select any object and move it to the top of or bottom. How you layer objects determines how much of an object is visible. For example, you can layer multiple objects by selecting the top object and moving it to the back, selecting the next object and moving it to the back, and so on until only the portions of the objects you want to show are displayed. Figure 13-28 shows an object layered behind text.

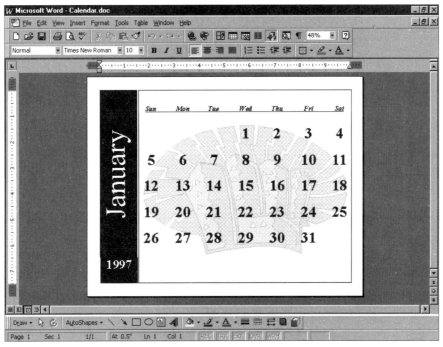

Figure 13-28: You can see through the text to an object layered behind the text.

To layer drawing objects and text:

1. Select the object(s) you want to move.

2. Choose Draw➪Order, or right-click to display the shortcut menu and choose Order. Then, do one of the following:

   • Choose the Send Behind Text option to move the object(s) behind the text layer.

   • Choose the Bring in Front of Text option to move the object(s) in front of the text layer.

   • Choose the Bring to Front option to move the object(s) to the front of all the other objects in the drawing layer.

   • Choose the Send to Back option to move the object(s) behind all the other objects in the drawing layer.

Adding callouts

A *callout* is a type of text box that also includes a line for pointing to any location on the document. A callout is helpful when you need to identify and explain parts of a picture (see Figure 13-29). You can include text and insert pictures in a callout. As with text boxes, you can define a fill color, line style, and color. If you want a callout to appear as text only, select None as your fill and choose your line colors. You can change, move, and layer callouts.

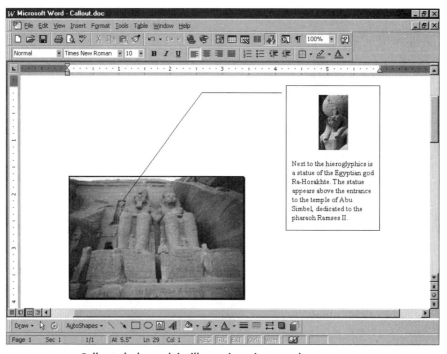

Figure 13-29: Callouts help explain illustrations in your document.

When you insert a callout, you draw a line from where you want the callout to point to where you want the callout text to be inserted. To insert a callout:

1. Choose the AutoShapes⇨Callouts command on the Drawing toolbar and select the style of callout you want to use. Choose the Callout button.

2. Move the crosshair to where you want the callout to point.

3. Click and hold the mouse button, and drag to where you want to place the callout text.

4. Release the mouse button.

5. Type the callout text.

Formatting callouts

You apply colors and line styles to a callout just as you do for any object you draw. To change the format of a callout, select the callout and choose Format⇨AutoShape, and then click the Text Box tab. Click Format Callout to display a dialog box for changing the callout's formatting. Using this dialog box, you can determine the style and angle of the callout line, how the callout line is attached to the callout text, and whether a border will appear around the callout text.

The Format Callout dialog box appears as shown in Figure 13-30. You can choose one of four callout styles for the pointer and text box by using the Type box. The selections you make in the Format Callout dialog box apply to the current callout and the next callouts you create.

Figure 13-30: The Format Callout dialog box.

To format a callout:

1. Select the callout you want to format.

2. Choose Format⇨AutoShape, and then click the Text Box tab. Click the Format Callout button to display a dialog box for changing the callout's formatting.

3. In the Type group, select one of the four callout types shown. Types One and Two create straight lines; type Three creates a two-part line; and type Four creates a three-part line.

4. Choose from among the options in Table 13-4 (not all options are available for all callout types).

5. Choose OK.

Table 13-4
Format Callout Dialog Box Options

Option	Description
Gap	The distance between the callout line and the callout text.
Angle	The angle of the line from the item you're calling out.
Drop	The space between the top of the callout text and the beginning of the first part of the callout line. The position where you want the callout line attached to the callout text, attached at an exact distance from the top or attached at the Top, Center, or Bottom.
Length	The length of the callout line: Best Fit or a measurement that you specify.
Text border	Places a border around the callout text.
Auto attach	Places the callout line at the bottom of the callout text when text is to the left of the callout line. This action ensures that the callout line doesn't overlap the callout text.
Add accent bar	Places a vertical line next to the callout text.

Adding Special Effects with WordArt

WordArt lets you turn ordinary words into graphics objects. You can sculpt text into a variety of shapes, flip or stretch letters, rotate or angle words, or add shading, colors, borders, or shadows to text, and more. By mixing WordArt effects, you can create hundreds of interesting designs. Figure 13-31 shows some samples of WordArt images.

You treat a WordArt image just like any other graphic in Word: after you create a WordArt image, you can edit and manipulate it like you do any graphic. In fact, using Word's standard graphics editing tools, you can move, copy, resize, crop, or add a caption to a WordArt image. You can apply the editing techniques explained earlier in this chapter to WordArt images.

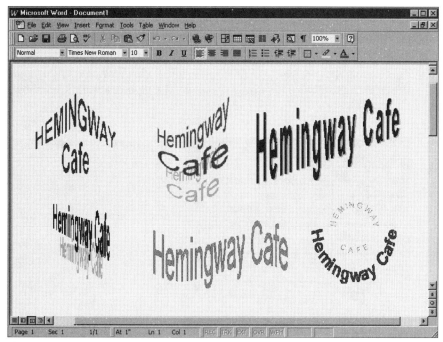

Figure 13-31: Samples of WordArt generated images.

You insert a WordArt image by using the Insert⇨Picture⇨WordArt command. Alternatively, you can click the Insert WordArt button on the Drawing toolbar. After starting WordArt, creating a WordArt image involves choosing a style and then typing the text to be included in the image and adding whatever special effects you want. At any time, you can change the text or the special effects. You never leave your document when you work with WordArt: you create your WordArt image directly on your document's page by using WordArt commands and buttons from the floating toolbar that appears after you include WordArt.

WordArt lets you experiment with different effects because when you change special effects, the WordArt image changes immediately, and you instantly see the result of each effect. All special effects apply to the text rather than to the border or background of your text, and all special effects apply to all the text in the Edit WordArt Text dialog box. You cannot apply an effect to just a few letters.

To start WordArt:

1. Position the insertion point where you want the WordArt object to appear in your document.

2. Choose Insert⭢Picture⭢WordArt or click the Insert WordArt button on the Drawing toolbar. The WordArt Gallery dialog box appears, as shown in Figure 13-32.

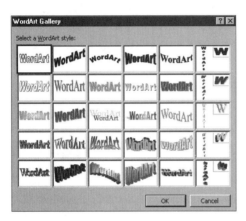

Figure 13-32: The WordArt Gallery dialog box.

3. Select the WordArt effect you like, and then click OK or double-click the effect you want to use. The Edit WordArt Text dialog box appears as shown in Figure 13-33.

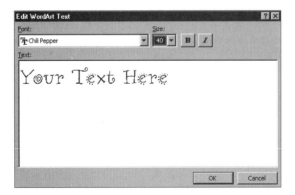

Figure 13-33: The Edit WordArt Text dialog box.

4. Type the text you want to appear in WordArt.

5. Choose OK.

Editing WordArt graphics

You can redisplay the WordArt screen or display a WordArt dialog box at any time to edit an existing WordArt image. All the techniques for editing a WordArt image share one rule: Select, and then do. In other words, you must select your WordArt image before you change it. Here are ways you can activate WordArt to edit an image:

✦ Double-click your WordArt image. The Edit Text dialog box appears.

✦ Select your WordArt image, and choose Edit Text from the WordArt toolbar.

To change the formatting of your WordArt, click your WordArt image and choose Format⇨WordArt, or right-click with the mouse pointer on the WordArt image and choose the Format WordArt option from the shortcut menu. The Format WordArt dialog box appears, as shown in Figure 13-34.

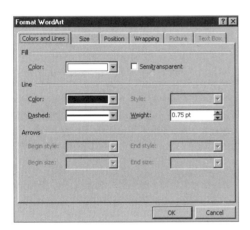

Figure 13-34: The Format WordArt dialog box.

A WordArt image selected with the mouse appears with square selection handles on all sides and corners, and a WordArt image selected with the keyboard appears reversed. A selected WordArt image has selection handles on the sides and corners: these handles let you resize the image.

Entering text

The text in the Edit WordArt Text dialog box is selected when you start WordArt. You can type as much text as will fit on your page. In other words, the size of the WordArt image is limited by the size of your page. By default, a new WordArt image is two inches wide and as tall as the text you type. The shaded box marks the spot where your finished WordArt image appears in your document.

Changing font or font size

You can change the *font* (the letters' style) or font size of your WordArt image by selecting the font and font size from the <u>F</u>ont and <u>S</u>ize drop-down lists in the Edit WordArt Text dialog box. You can use the same TrueType fonts in WordArt that you use in Word. If you select a different font size, the size of the WordArt frame changes to fit your text.

Applying bold, italics, and other formats

WordArt lets you apply bold and italics to characters in an image, as well as make all the letters in your text the same height, regardless of case. You can toggle each effect (bold, italic, and even caps) via the buttons on the WordArt toolbar. For example, to apply even caps, click the WordArt Same Letter Heights; to remove them, click the button a second time. To apply (or remove) bold, italics, or the same letter heights to text in the Edit WordArt Text dialog box, select the text you want to affect, and click the appropriate button.

Shaping text

The Shape button on the WordArt toolbar displays a grid of different shapes (see Figure 13-35). When you select one of the shape options, the text in the Edit WordArt Text dialog box changes into that shape. Some shapes produce different results depending on how many lines of text you're shaping. For example, the circle shape turns a single line of text into a circle, but multiple lines of text are changed into a vertical half-circles. Experiment to get the result you want.

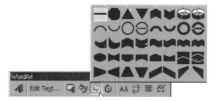

Figure 13-35: WordArt Shape list options.

To shape text:

1. Start WordArt, and type text in the Edit WordArt Text dialog box.

2. Choose the Shapes button to display the available shape options.

3. Select the shape you want. The text in the shade box changes to the selected shape.

4. Repeat Steps 2 and 3 to select any different shapes.

Flipping vertical and stretching

The WordArt Vertical text button lets you flip your text so it appears vertically on the page. "Stretching" letters stretches them to fit the WordArt frame. Although you can change the size of letters in a WordArt image by changing the size of the WordArt frame, stretching text is the only way to lengthen text vertically. To stretch letters, first enter the text in the Edit WordArt Text dialog box. Then, start WordArt and click the Stretch button. Figure 13-36 shows vertical and horizontal text, and text before and after stretching.

Figure 13-36: Samples of text before and after it is flipped and stretched.

Skewing and rotating WordArt text

You can rotate your WordArt image, using the Free Rotate button. Figure 13-37 shows some of the effects you can achieve with the Free Rotate button. When you select a WordArt image in your document, a yellow diamond appears dead-center. To skew your text, drag the yellow diamond in the opposite direction that you want your text to slant. To quickly return to your original, unskewed text, double-click the yellow diamond.

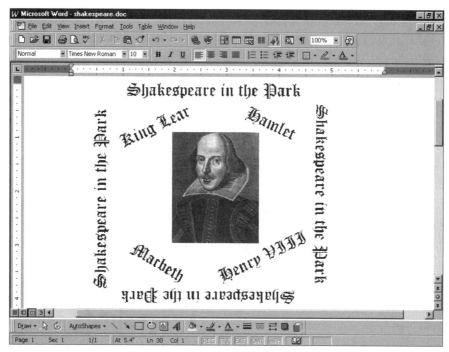

Figure 13-37: Samples of rotating WordArt text.

Aligning WordArt text

WordArt text is centered by default; you can align WordArt text flush left or right. You also can *stretch justify* text to stretch the letters to fit the WordArt frame, *letter justify* text to space the letters out to fit the frame, or *word justify* text to space the words to fit the frame.

To change alignment, with your text entered in the Edit WordArt Text dialog box, click the WordArt Alignment button on the WordArt toolbar. A list of alignment options appears (shown in Figure 13-38). Select the alignment style you want.

Figure 13-38: The Alignment options list.

Kerning adjusting spacing between characters

WordArt lets you control the spacing between letter pairs or all the letters in an image. You can turn on *kerning*, the adjustment of spacing between character pairs, to improve your document's look. In general, kerning tightens the spacing between letter pairs such as To or Wa. If your type is larger than normal reading size, kerning can make your text more readable. *Tracking*, meanwhile, is the adjustment of spacing between all letters. In WordArt, you can loosen or tighten tracking. You can even set tracking to an exact percent of normal spacing. To adjust the spacing between letters and words:

1. Select the WordArt image in your document.

2. Click the WordArt Character Spacing button on the WordArt toolbar. The WordArt Character Spacing menu appears.

3. Do one of the following:

   • Choose a tracking option: Very Tight (60% of normal), Tight (80%), Normal (100%), Loose (120%), or Very Loose (150%). You can also choose Custom and select a percent of normal.

   • Choose the Kern Character Pairs option if you want WordArt to automatically kern character pairs. Clearing the check box turns off kerning.

Adding color outlines and shadows to your WordArt

Applying color, shading, or a pattern fills all the characters in a WordArt image. For both shades and patterns, you can choose a foreground and background color. To change the color of text, choose a different foreground color in the solid foreground pattern. To add color or shading to a WordArt image:

1. Select your WordArt image in your document.

2. Click the Format WordArt button. The Format WordArt dialog box appears. Then do one of the following:

   • **To change the color**. Choose the Color from the fill options and select the color you want from the palette. If you want to fill the letters with a gradient, texture or a pattern, choose More Colors from the Color drop-down list box. You can also choose the Semitransparent check box to make the selected solid-color fill partially transparent. Clear this check box to make the selected fill completely opaque.

   • **To change the border of the letters**. In the Line group, choose a color from the Color drop-down list box. To make the outline thinner or wider, enter the point size of the border you want to surround your letters in the Weight text box. If you want, you can use a dashed line border by using a line style from the Dashed Line list box.

3. Choose OK to see the effects of your choices on your text.

To add a border around a WordArt image, use a shape from one of the AutoShape menus and drag the mouse around your WordArt image. The image will cover the WordArt. Choose the Draw➪Order➪Send to Back option. Your WordArt now appears with a surrounding border.

Like any image inserted in your document, you can apply different types of shadows and 3-D effects to your WordArt image. To add a shadow or 3-D effect, select your WordArt image and use the Shadow button or the 3-D button on the Drawing toolbar. Figure 13-39 shows some sample shadow and 3-D effects added to a WordArt image.

Figure 13-39: Shadow effects applied to WordArt images.

Summary

Word lets you bridge the chasm of diverse graphic formats to let you work with almost any graphical application. In addition, Word gives you a tremendous amount of options for creating and adding drawings and adding special effects from within Word. Using this chapter as a guide, you can now:

✦ Import graphics from other applications into your documents.

✦ Position a graphic anywhere on the page.

✦ Resize and crop pictures.

✦ Add graphics as objects.

✦ Include links to images so that you can minimize the size of a document.

✦ Layer text and graphics using text boxes.

✦ Convert images to Word Picture format so that you can work with Word's drawing tools on the picture.

✦ Use Word's drawing tools to create lines, shapes, and callouts to your document.

✦ Use WordArt to add text as a graphic that you can position in any angle or insert in a predefined shape.

Where to go next...

✦ For a more in-depth explanation of working with frames, see Chapter 14.

✦ For more information on creating links to other applications, see Chapter 15.

✦ For more information on captioning figures and illustrations in a document, see Chapter 23.

✦ To find step-by-step instructions for creating a watermark, turn to Chapter 9.

✦ To gain greater control of Word, check out Chapter 25 for ways to customize how Word displays text and graphics.

✦　　✦　　✦

Positioning Text and Graphics with Text Boxes

A text box is a fantastic formatting feature in Word that lets you move objects, including text, anywhere you want on the page. You can insert a text box around any amount of text in your document. You can also insert an empty text box as a placeholder and add the object or text later. In either case, after you insert the text box, you can resize it and move it anywhere on the page. This chapter explains how to insert, position, and apply formats to text boxes. It also shows some desktop publishing layout techniques for working with text boxes.

Understanding Text Boxes and Frames

Text boxes are new Word 97 drawing objects that replace the frames you used in earlier versions of Word. Text boxes give you more flexibility in manipulating your text and graphics. A text box is actually a container into which you can place any amount of text and graphics and treat the collection as a single object. You can move it around in the document, anchor it to a particular paragraph. You can wrap text around a text box and add some sophisticated formatting with the Drawing toolbar such as 3-D effects, shadows, colors, and background fills and textures.

Frames are still used for a limited number of purposes such as positioning text or graphics that contain comment or note reference marks. You must also use frames to position text that contains certain fields, including those dealing with tables of contents, indexes, document references, and tables of authorities.

When you open a document created in Word 95 that contains frames, Word 97 keeps the frames. If you open the F̲ormat menu, you will see Fra̲me in place of Text Bo̲x. The process of converting frames to Word 97 text boxes is discussed later in this chapter.

Inserting a Text Box

You can insert a text box around selected text in your document, or you can insert an empty text box to act as a placeholder into which you can paste text or a graphic object. If you are inserting an empty text box, you can draw the box to fit the space in your document or simply click in the document and size it later. When you insert a text box around selected text, the text box appears in the default size, approximately 1 $^3/_4$ inches wide and 2 inches high. The selected text is config-ured to fit in the new box and the remaining text wraps around it. If you click in the document to insert an empty text box, a small box appears, approximately 1 inch square.

Another way to insert a text box is to use the Text Box button (see Figure 14-1), which is on the Drawing toolbar. You can always add the Text Box button to the Standard or Formatting toolbars by using the V̲iew⇨T̲oolbars⇨C̲ustomize command. See Chapter 25 for information on customizing your toolbars.

Figure 14-1: The Text Box button on the Drawing toolbar.

When a text box is inserted into the document, you can change the format of the text box using the F̲ormat⇨Text Bo̲x command and the buttons on the Drawing toolbar. You see more about changing the text box appearance later in this chapter.

Inserting a text box around selected text

Word inserts an empty text box when nothing is selected in the document, but selecting text first creates a text box around the selected text. Figure 14-2 shows the result of selecting the first paragraph of text and choosing I̲nsert⇨Te̲xt Box. To restore the paragraph to the page width, use the handles to resize the text box.

After inserting a text box, it is automatically selected so that you can work with it immediately. You can tell when a text box is selected by the cross-hatch border and the eight square handles around the text box. Figure 14-3 shows the resized text box around a paragraph.

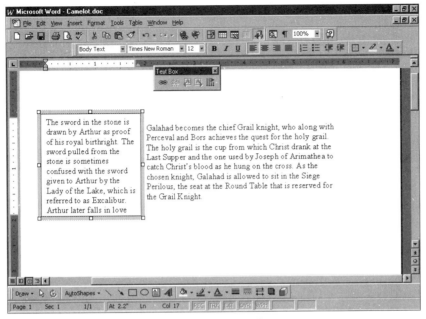

Figure 14-2: A text box inserted around selected text.

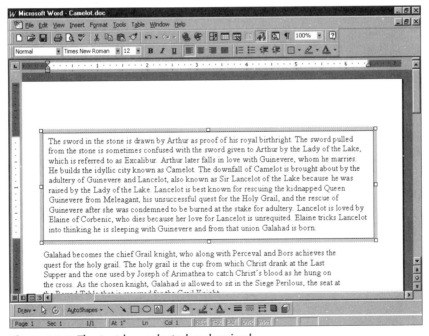

Figure 14-3: The text box selected and resized.

Caution you want to place an existing graphic object in a text box, insert an empty text box first. Then paste the graphic in it. If you try to draw a text box around the graphic object, the text box will not contain the object and they will not move together.

If you insert a text box around a selection while in Normal view, Word automatically switches to Page Layout view. To insert a text box around selected text:

1. Select the text you want to include in the text box.

2. Choose Insert⇨Text Box. Alternatively, click the Text Box button on the Drawing toolbar. Word displays the text box with a cross-hatch border and eight handles so that you can immediately work with the text box.

Tip When you insert a text box around a paragraph, the paragraph keeps its formatting. If the indents in the paragraph are too large in relation to the text box, however, the text box may appear empty. To correct this, either widen the text box or decrease or remove the paragraph indentation.

Inserting an empty text box

Inserting an empty text box in a document leaves space for an object that you intend to insert later. For example, if the document is a newsletter and you want to add a graphic, inserting an empty text box reserves the correct space for the graphic and enables you to edit the document with an accurate view of its layout.

Another benefit of inserting an empty text box is that you can draw the text box to your specifications, unlike inserting a text box around an existing object. When not selected, an empty text box appears in your document as a box with a single-line border. To insert an empty text box:

1. Make sure that nothing is selected. (Otherwise, Word inserts a text box around the selected text.) Choose Insert⇨Text Box, or click the Text Box button. The pointer changes to a crosshair.

2. Position the crosshair where you want to place the upper-left corner of the text box.

3. Click once to insert a small square text box or drag the crosshair to create a custom text box outline. To control how the text box is drawn, do one of the following:

   • To create the text box from the center out, press Ctrl as you drag the crosshair.

   • To create a square text box, hold down Shift while you drag the crosshair.

- To create a square text box using the starting point as the center of the square, press Ctrl+Shift while you drag the crosshair.

4. Release the mouse button to create the text box.

Adding text and drawing objects

To enter text in the new text box, simply place the insertion point in the box and begin typing. The text automatically wraps in the box; however, if you type more text than is visible on-screen, the box does not automatically expand to show the text (the way frames used to). The text is there, though. You must resize the text box to show all the text.

When you insert or paste a picture or other drawing object in a text box, the picture resizes to fit the box. If the aspect ratio was locked when the picture was saved, the picture retains its width-to-height proportion. You may have to do some small adjusting of the text box after all, but mostly it shows the whole picture.

To add a picture or other drawing object to your text box, you can choose an option from the Insert menu or use the Cut/Copy and Paste editing tools on the Standard toolbar or the shortcut menu. Figure 14-4 shows a text box with both text and a picture in it.

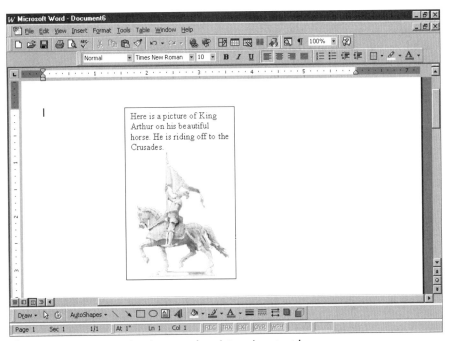

Figure 14-4: An example of text and a picture in a text box.

Selecting a Text Box

Selecting a text box that contains text is a little different than selecting other items in Word because you can select the text in the text box without selecting the text box itself. To see this, start by inserting a text box around selected text. Then select something outside the text box so that neither the box nor the text inside the box is selected. The framed paragraph will have a single-line border around it. Slowly drag the mouse pointer (which should be the familiar I-beam shape) over the border to the text. As you drag the pointer, notice that the pointer briefly changes to an outline arrow pointing to the upper-right, and then changes to a four-headed arrow as you cross the border. The four-headed arrow is known as the *positioning pointer*. After you pass over the border and move the pointer into the text, the pointer changes back to the I-beam shape.

If you click when the pointer becomes the positioning pointer, you select the text box itself and the crosshatch border appears with the handles. If you click inside the border when the pointer has returned to the I-beam shape, you position the insertion point in the text and the border now appears with single diagonal lined border — but still has the handles.

Selecting a text box containing a graphic object is a little more complicated. When you drag the mouse pointer over the border, the pointer becomes the positioning pointer and stays that way as you move over the graphic itself. If you click the mouse button as the positioning pointer passes over the border, you select the text box. If you click on the graphic, you select the graphic instead.

Tip   You have two shortcut menus at your disposal when working with text boxes. Right-click the text box border to open the full shortcut menu that contains options for editing, grouping, ordering, linking, and formatting text boxes. Press Shift+F10 when the text box is selected to display a brief shortcut menu with the Cut/Copy and Paste editing options and a choice that opens the Borders and Shadings dialog box.

Positioning and Formatting a Text Box

The most precise method of working with text boxes is to use the Format Text Box dialog box (see Figure 14-5). This dialog box contains six tabs, each containing groups of related object formatting options:

✦ Specifying color and style for fill, lines, and arrows

✦ Setting the style and spacing for wrapping text around the text box

✦ Positioning the text box horizontally and vertically on the page

✦ Specifying sizing options for the text box

✦ Setting the internal margins for text within the text box

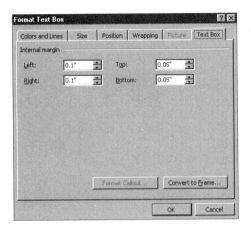

Figure 14-5: The Format Text Box dialog box.

You must first select a text box before you can open the Format Text Box dialog box; otherwise, the Text Box option is not available from the Format menu. The Picture tab of the Format Text Box dialog box is not available for text boxes. The options in each of the available tabs are described in the following sections.

Tip   You can also choose Format Text Box from the text box shortcut menu.

A shortcut to display the Format Text Box dialog box when working with a text box containing text is to select the text box and double-click a text box border.

Positioning a text box on the page

When you first insert a text box, Word uses default position settings and anchors the text box to the nearest paragraph. If that paragraph moves, the text box also moves with it. Because the defaults cover most situations, you may never have to worry about the precise positioning of a text box. Even if you do have to move one, the easiest method is to use the mouse to drag the text box to the new location.

If you want the text box at a particular position on the page, such as centered horizontally, you can use the Drawing toolbar. To position a text box with the Drawing toolbar:

1. Select the text box you want to place.

2. Click D<u>r</u>aw on the Drawing toolbar and point to <u>A</u>lign or Distribute. The menu (Figure 14-6) shows six options for placement. The first three options refer to horizontal alignment; the next three refer to vertical alignment. The option at the bottom of the menu specifies that the position be related to the whole page.

Figure 14-6: The Align or Distribute options.

3. Do one of the following:

   • If the alignment is to refer to the whole page, select Relative t<u>o</u> Page. Then repeat Step 2 and select the desired alignment.

   • If the alignment refers to an alignment relative to the current position of the text box, make sure the Relative t<u>o</u> Page option is cleared and choose the desired alignment.

Sometimes, however, greater precision is necessary. In a newsletter, for example, you may need to position a text box relative to a specific column or paragraph on a page. In a business document, you may need to text box a graphic such as a logo and anchor it to specific text so that, even if the text moves to another page, the text box stays with it.

Before you can specify an exact horizontal or vertical position for the text box on the page, you must choose the reference from which to measure the position. The horizontal position determines where the left edge of the text box will appear. You have a choice of measuring with respect to the page, the left margin, or a column. The vertical position determines where the top edge of the text box will appear. You can choose to measure with respect to the page, the top margin, or the nearest paragraph. Using the page or margin references, you can place text boxes in any of the page margins.

Figure 14-7 shows the Position tab of the Format Text Box dialog box. Table 14-1 describes each of the Position options.

Figure 14-7: The Position tab of the Format Text Box dialog box.

Table 14-1
Format Text Box Position Options

Option	Effect
Horizontal	Specifies the horizontal position of the left edge of the text box. Enter a numeric value in the box or use the spin box to select a value.
From	Specifies the reference for measuring the horizontal distance: Page, Margin, or Column (if you are working with multiple columns). For example, if you select Margin in the From box, the value you entered in the Horizontal box is relative to the margin.
Vertical	Specifies the vertical position of the text box. Enter a numeric value in the Vertical box or use the spin box to select a value.
From	Specifies the reference for measuring the vertical position of the text box: Page, Margin, or Paragraph.
Move object with text	Determines whether the text box moves with the paragraph to which it is anchored. This setting has no bearing on the horizontal positioning options selected, but it does set the Vertical From setting to Paragraph.
Lock anchor	Makes sure that the text box always appears on the same page as the paragraph to which it is anchored.

If you want the text box to appear in the left margin, enter a negative number in the Horizontal box and choose Margin in the From box. To place the text box in the right margin, enter a number that equals or exceeds the value on the Ruler that marks the right margin, for example, 6.5". Entering a negative number in the Vertical box and choosing Margin places the text box in the top margin of the page. Figure 14-8 illustrates text boxes positioned horizontally and vertically in various positions.

The text box will not fit entirely in the margin unless the margin is wider than the text box. If the text box is wider than the margin, the text box either extends into the text or falls off the page. To position a text box:

1. Select the text box.

2. Choose Format⇨Text Box to display the Format Text Box dialog box.

3. Click the From arrow next to Horizontal and choose the reference from which you want to position the left edge of the text box: Page, Margin, or Column.

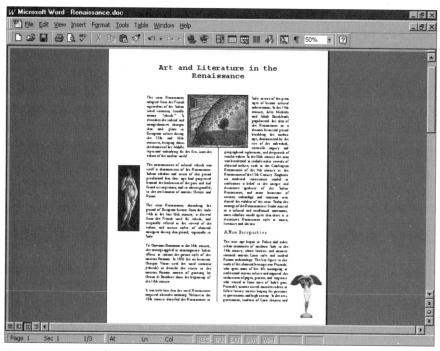

Figure 14-8: Some horizontal and vertical positioning options.

4. Enter the measurement in the Horizontal box. A positive number positions the left edge of the text box that distance to the right of the selected reference; a negative number, to the left of the reference; and zero places the left edge at the reference.

5. Click the From arrow next to Vertical and choose the reference for positioning the text box vertically on the page: Paragraph, Page, or Margin.

6. Enter the measurement in the Vertical box. A positive number positions the top edge of the text box that distance below the selected reference; a negative number positions the top edge of the text box that distance above the reference; and zero positions the top edge at the reference.

7. Click OK.

Tip
If you create a text box for a margin note and the note appears at the end of the page, format both the paragraph to the right of the text box and the text in the text box using the Keep with next option (choose Format⇨Paragraph, and click the Line and Page Breaks tab). This ensures that the text box and the paragraph text are not separated.

Anchoring a text box

Word anchors every text box to a paragraph, using the closest paragraph by default when the text box is first inserted. Word also enables the Move with text option in the Position tab of the Format Text Box dialog box by default. So, if you move the paragraph to which the text box is anchored, the text box moves with the paragraph. If, on the other hand, you drag the text box to a different location on the page, Word breaks the connection and anchors it to the nearest paragraph when you drop it.

In addition to dragging the text box away from its anchoring paragraph, you can drag the anchor to a different paragraph instead of moving the text box. This happens because Word disables the Move with text option when you drag the anchor. Thus, you can have a text box anchored to a paragraph that is not the closest paragraph to the text box.

You can see the anchor if you select the Show/Hide button on the Standard toolbar to display paragraph marks and other nonprinting symbols. Then select the text box, and you will see the anchor symbol in the closest paragraph. You can anchor a text box to a different paragraph by dragging the anchor symbol. (Figure 14-9 shows a text box anchored to a paragraph above the current one.)

You can lock the anchor to a specific paragraph so that the text box stays on the same page as that paragraph no matter how the text box is otherwise positioned. If that paragraph moves to a different page because of editing, the text box also moves to the new page. For example, if the text box was formatted to be positioned at the bottom of the page, that is where it will also appear on the new page. When you lock the anchor, a small padlock icon appears with the anchor.

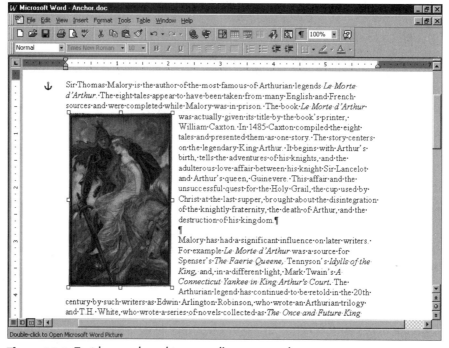

Figure 14-9: Text box anchored to preceding paragraph.

To lock an anchor to a paragraph:

1. Select the text box.

2. Click the Show/Hide button on the Standard toolbar to show nonprinting characters. The anchor will now be visible.

3. Drag the anchor to the desired paragraph.

4. Choose Format⇨Text Box to display the Format Text Box dialog box, and then click the Position tab.

5. Check the Lock anchor box to lock the anchor to the selected paragraph.

6. Choose OK. A small lock appears next to the anchor icon.

Note You can keep a text box on a specific page by clearing both the Lock anchor and Move with text check boxes.

Aligning a group of text boxes

You can align a group of text boxes on a page just as you can other types of drawing objects. Hold down Shift while you select all the text boxes you want to line up; then choose Draw from the Drawing toolbar and point to the Align or

Distribute option. The pop-up menu includes the same options as before: align the group by their left or right edges or vertical centers, their top or bottom edges or horizontal middle, or distribute them horizontally or vertically. When you choose to align the text boxes at the left, all the boxes in the group move left to align with the left-most edge. As before, if you select the Relative to Page option, the alignment related to the whole page rather than to the current positions of the group.

Once you have selected a group of text boxes, you can use the mouse to drag them as a group to a new position on the page.

Resizing a text box

The easiest way to resize a text box is to select the text box so that its handles show, and then click and drag one of the sizing handles. To change the size of a text box from the center out, hold down Ctrl while you drag the handle. You also can resize a text box by specifying measurements in the Format Text Box dialog box.

If you want to change the size of a text box proportionally, select the text box and position the pointer on one of the corner handles. The pointer changes to a two-headed diagonal arrow. Hold down Shift while you drag the pointer in the direction you want to size the text box.

To set the dimensions of a text box more precisely, use the Size tab of the Format Text Box dialog box (Figure 14-10). The Size options set the actual measurements of the text box while the Scale options set the dimensions as a percentage of the original size. You can change the height and width independently. You can enter measurements in centimeters (cm), inches (in or "), points (pt), or picas (pi). Word converts your entries, however, to the current default measurement type as set in the General tab of the Options dialog box.

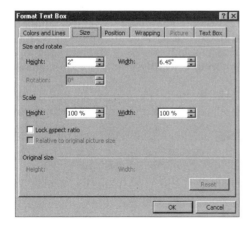

Figure 14-10: The Size tab of the Format Text Box dialog box.

The Lock aspect ratio option forces the height and width to stay in their original proportion. If you have checked this option and change the height or width of the text box, the other setting will change in relation to the original aspect ratio.

Note The dimmed options relate to pictures and are not available to text boxes.

Wrapping text around text boxes

You have several options for wrapping text around text boxes, both in style and arrangement. You can also specify how much space to leave around the text box. Figure 14-11 shows the Wrapping tab of the Format Text Box dialog box.

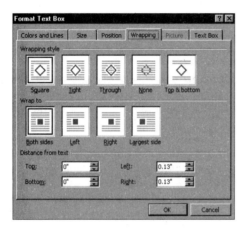

Figure 14-11: The Wrapping tab of the Format Text Box dialog box.

The wrapping style determines how the accompanying text is arranged around the text box. You have five styles to choose from. The Wrap to options tell Word where you want the text with respect to the text box. The Distance from text options specify the amount of space between the text box and the surrounding wrapped text. Distance from text options are not available if you have chosen None as the wrapping style. Table 14-2 describes the options available in the Wrapping tab.

The first three styles wrap text around the text box the same way because text boxes are rectangular. They have more effect on pictures and odd-shaped graphic objects.

To set the text wrap option:

1. In Page Layout view, choose Format⇨Text Box to display the Format Text Box dialog box.

2. Choose the Wrapping tab and select a wrapping style, such as Square.

3. Move to the Distance from text and set the desired space around the sides of the text box. The available options depend on the selected style.

4. Click OK.

Table 14-2
Text Wrapping Options

Option	Effect
Square	Wraps text around all sides of the square bounding the text box.
Tight	Follows contours of drawing object instead of wrapping to bounding rectangle.
Through	Same as Tight, but wraps inside any part of the object that is empty.
None	Removes text wrapping and text box appears in front or behind text, depending on which layer the text box is stacked in. (More about layers later in the "Layering Text Boxes and Other Objects" section.)
Top & bottom	Wraps text at the top and bottom of the text box but not at the sides.
Both sides	Places text on both sides of the text box if there is room.
Left	Wraps text only on the left side of text box, if there is room. If not enough room, wraps at top and bottom.
Right	Wraps text only on the right side of text box, if there is room. If not enough room, wraps at top and bottom.
Largest side	Wraps text on the left or right side, whichever is wider.
Top	Sets space between text and the top of the text box. Unavailable if Tight or Through style is chosen.
Bottom	Sets space between text and the bottom of the text box. Unavailable if Tight or Through style is chosen.
Right (distance from text)	Sets space between text and the right border of the text box. Unavailable if Top & bottom style is chosen.
Left (distance from text)	Sets space between text and the left border of the text box. Unavailable if Top & bottom style is chosen.

Figure 14-12 shows a text box containing a picture with the wrapping style set to Square and .2-inch space on all four sides of the text box. Figure 14-13 shows the text box moved slightly to the right and with the Largest side wrapping style selected. A .2-inch space is set for the right and left sides.

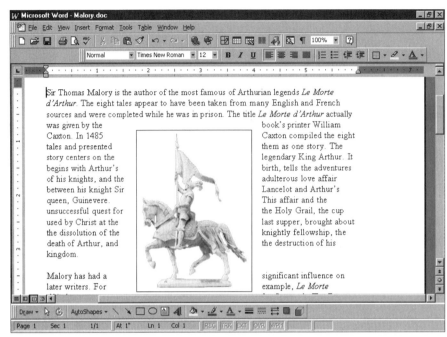

Figure 14-12: An example of a text box with text wrapping set to Square.

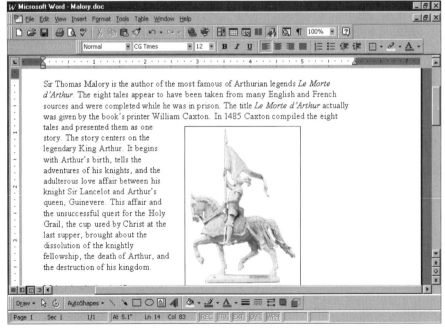

Figure 14-13: An example of a text box with text wrapping set to Largest side.

Setting internal margins

The internal margins in a text box are the property of the text box and determine the space within the text box border that is free of text. You can set the indent and line spacing with the usual paragraph formatting options, but you need the Format Text Box dialog box to set the internal margins. Refer to Figure 14-5 to see the Text Box tab. You can enter measurements in the Left, Right, Top, and Bottom boxes or you can use the spin boxes. The measurements are in the default unit of measure as set in the General tab of the Options dialog box. If you enter measures in inches (in), centimeters (cm), points (pt), or picas (pi), Word converts them to the default.

Copying and moving a text box

To copy a text box and its contents, right-click the text box border and choose Copy from the shortcut menu. This creates a Clipboard copy of the current text box that you can paste to another location. To paste the text box, right-click in the document and choose Paste from the shortcut menu. The copy is slightly offset from the original, and you can click and drag the copy to the desired position.

To move a text box and its contents from its present position to a new location, select the text box and move the pointer on the border. When the pointer changes to the positioning pointer, you can drag the text box to a new location. Alternatively, you can choose Cut from the shortcut menu, and then choose Paste, as above.

If you copy or move a text box to a part of the page that has text, the text box either obscures or displaces the existing text, depending on your wrapping setting. You can choose in the Wrapping tab of the Format Text Box dialog box whether you want the text to wrap around the text box or stop above the text box and resume below it.

Adding colors and lines

When you insert a text box around text or create an empty text box, Word adds a single-line border around the text box. The text box also has a plain white background. You can use the Colors and Lines tab of the Format Text Box to add some more interest to your text boxes (Figure 14-14). The Fill Color arrow displays a palette of colors as well as a Fill Effects option. The fill effects include special gradients, textures, patterns, and pictures that you can apply to a text box. The Semi-transparent option fills the text box only partially with the selected color. This option is not available if you have chosen one of the Fill Effects.

The Line options refer to the border of the text box. You can change the color (solid or dash style) and weight, or choose to show no line at all. The Arrows options are available only for picture objects. See Chapter 13 for more information on selecting color, fill, and line options.

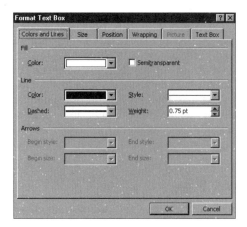

Figure 14-14: The Colors and Lines tab of the Format Text Box dialog box.

The Drawing toolbar includes buttons for formatting the lines and color of the text box. It also includes some dramatic 3-D and shadow effects.

The options you select using Borders and Shading from the Format menu apply to the text within the text box, not the box itself. For example, if you choose to add a border style, it would appear inside the text box border.

If you want to remove the text box and its contents, just select the text box in Page Layout view, and press Delete or Backspace. If you want to take the text or graphic out of the text box and remove only the text box, you must first use Copy or Cut to take the contents out of the text box. Paste the contents to another position in your document and then select the text box and press Delete or Backspace.

Formatting Text in a Text Box

Formatting text in a text box is the same as formatting uncontained text with one added feature: you can change the text direction so that it reads vertically. As mentioned earlier, when you type in a text box, the text wraps in the text box. If you type more text than the box will hold, the additional text is accepted but hidden from view until you resize the text box. The text box does not expand vertically to accommodate the new text.

If you want to format the contents of the text box quickly, select the text, and apply the formatting. If you use styles, apply the style before you draw the text box around the text. If you apply the style after enclosing the text, the style may change the text box appearance or its position on the page. Adding text box formatting to a style lets you quickly format and position text in your document. For example, if you commonly position a side head in the left margin for a certain type of document, you can create a style that includes both the text and text box formatting. When you apply the style, the text has the correct position as well as the correct formatting.

You can use paragraph formatting in a text box for even more precise alignment. Text boxes treat the contained text as a block that you can drag to different locations on the page. With paragraph formatting, you can align text in the text box, but it has no bearing on the position of the text box. For example, centering text in a text box is different than centering the text box itself. If you drag a text box with centered text to a different location on the page, the text remains centered in the text box. This is also true of indentation applied to text in a text box.

A new feature in Word 97 is the ability to orient the text in a text box either horizontally or vertically. You can choose Format⇨Text Direction to open the Text Direction - Text Box dialog box (Figure 14-15). The dialog box shows three text direction options: horizontal, vertical reading up, and vertical reading down. The Preview pane shows what the text will look like in the selected orientation. The Text Box toolbar also has a button, Change Text Direction, that cycles through the three orientations when you click it.

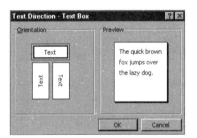

Figure 14-15: The Text Direction - Text Box dialog box.

After you have set the text orientation, you can use the alignment buttons on the Formatting toolbar to further align the text. If you have selected the horizontal orientation, you have a choice of aligning left, right, center, or justify. If the text is oriented vertically, the toolbar buttons change to Align Top, Align Center, Align Bottom, and Justify.

Layering Text Boxes and Other Objects

One thing you could not do with frames is layer. *Layering* means placing an object on top of text or another object. If you want to layer text, you can use a text box that does not force text on a page to flow around it. The major benefit of using a text box is that Word sees the text box as a drawing object; therefore, you can place text or a graphic behind or in front of the main text in a Word document. And you can use the mouse to pick up the box and drag it to any location on the page. A text box also doesn't automatically resize when you add text or graphics so the proportions are preserved in your document. A graphic added to a text box resizes itself to fit the text box, and if you type more text than a text box will hold, you must resize the box to make the text visible.

Figure 14-16 shows an example of a graphic in a text box layered over the document's main text. Figure 14-17 shows an example of the same graphic layered behind the text. Both of these examples have no text wrapping specified. The text box in back of the text resembles a watermark because the thin border line has been removed. To use a text box as a watermark, you must insert it in the header of footer of the document. See Chapter 9 for more information on adding headers and footers.

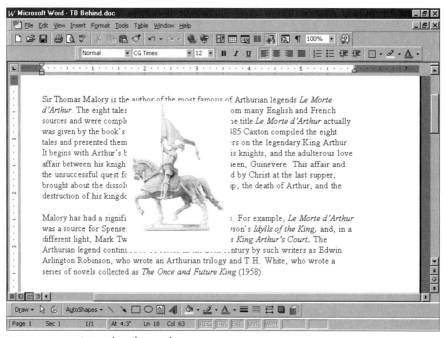

Figure 14-16: A text box layered over text.

To layer a text box in a document:

1. With a document containing text open, choose <u>V</u>iew⇨<u>T</u>oolbars, and select Drawing to display the Drawing toolbar, if not already visible.

2. Select the Text Box button. The pointer changes to a crosshair.

3. Drag to create a text box within the existing text. The insertion point is positioned inside the text box.

4. Choose Insert⇨Picture to insert a graphic. Or, if you copied a graphic previously, paste it into the box. Size the text box, if necessary. The text box covers some of the text.

5. Select the text box, choose Draw on the Drawing toolbar, and point to Order. The Order pop-up menu contains six options that move the selected drawing object forward and backward in the stack.

6. Choose Send Behind Text. The contents of the text box appear behind the text.

7. To bring the text box in front of the text again, repeat Step 5 and choose Bring in Front of Text.

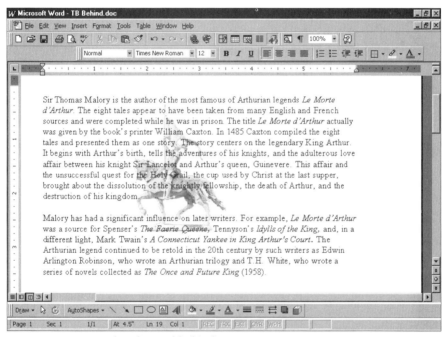

Figure 14-17: A text box layered behind text.

Text boxes and Publishing Techniques

You can use text boxes to lay out and add special effects in your documents. For example, you can use text boxes to create side headings instead of the usual headings positioned above a paragraph. A common layout for newsletters and reports is to add a centered graphic to break up the page. Another nice effect is to display a graphic in the header or margin of every page of your document. The margin display of graphics can include text formatted in WordArt, which is treated as a graphic. The following sections explain each of these layout techniques.

Creating a side heading with a text box

A *side heading* is a heading placed to the left of text rather than above it. Figure 14-18 illustrates a side heading. Side headings are commonly used in text books and manuals. They provide a nice visual emphasis for any type of document. The key to using side headings is to create a margin large enough for the heading. The example in Figure 14-18 has a 2.25" margin. Assuming that the margin is wide enough, you can create the heading, text box it, and drag it into position.

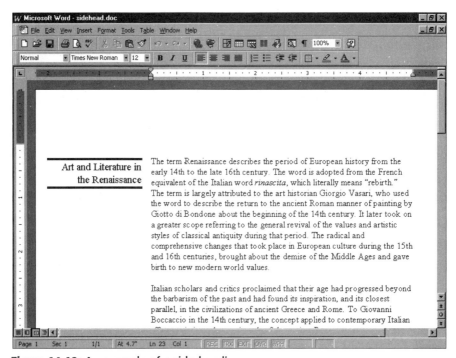

Figure 14-18: An example of a side heading.

If you use side headings, be sure to set the width of the text box to an exact figure so that the heading wraps around rather than extends into the text. The width of the text box must be less than the margin. If the text box initially is so wide that it extends into the text, use the mouse to resize the width. You should also lock the anchor to the paragraph next to the heading and enable the <u>M</u>ove with text setting so that the heading stays with its text regardless of future editing. You can also use paragraph formatting to further define the side heading. The side heading in Figure 14-18, for example, is right-justified.

Centering a text box between columns

A common task for those who produce newsletters is to center a graphic using a two-column layout. (A two-column layout refers to *snaking* columns, or newspaper-style, not two columns in a table.) The following steps explain how to center a text box as shown in Figure 14-19. Although you can use these steps as a guideline for this type of task, you may need to adjust some settings for your layout. (You can drag the text box to the position you want, but using the Drawing toolbar is more precise.)

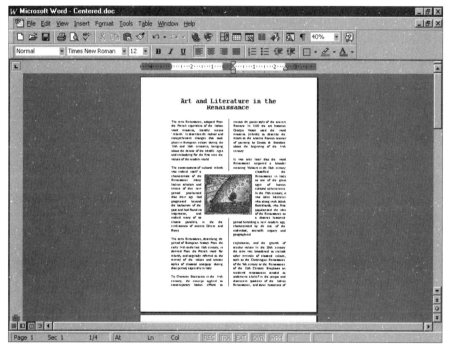

Figure 14-19: A centered text box.

To center a text box over a two-column layout:

1. Switch to Page Layout view if you are in a different view.

2. Select the text box in the document.

3. Choose Draw on the Drawing toolbar and then point to Align or Distribute.

4. Select Relative to Page, if not already selected, and repeat Step 3.

5. Select Align Center. The text box is aligned horizontally.

6. Repeat Step 3 and select Align Middle. The text box is now aligned in the center of the page both horizontally and vertically.

7. Right-click the text box border and choose Format Text Box from the shortcut menu. Choose the Wrapping tab.

8. Choose the Square wrapping style and enter .15" in all the Distance from text boxes. This is the measurement used in Figure 14-19. If you want more space between the text box and the text, increase the value. For less space, decrease the value.

9. Click OK.

Repeating text and graphics with text boxes

One of the more intriguing things that you can do with text boxes is to repeat them on every page. For example, you can have a logo or text formatted in WordArt appear on every page in the left margin. You can use this technique to create striking visual images. As with side headings (described in the preceding section), the key is to have a margin wide enough to accommodate the object. To repeat a graphic on every page:

1. Choose File⇨Page Setup to specify a top margin wide enough to accommodate the text box.

2. Choose View⇨Header and Footer. This action switches you to Header/Footer view and automatically displays the Header and Footer toolbar (see Figure 14-20). See Chapter 9 for information about creating headers and footers.

3. Type the text you want for the header, if any. If you do type text, press Enter after it to create a separate paragraph for your graphic insertion.

4. Draw an empty text box in the header and size to the desired dimensions.

5. Insert the graphic or picture. You can do this by pasting (if you copied the graphic previously), or by choosing Insert⇨Picture.

6. Crop and size the graphic as necessary.

7. Select the text box, and drag the graphic to the position you want. Alternatively, you can use the Drawing toolbar Align or Distribute options.

8. If you don't want the graphic to appear on the first page of the document; or, if you want to specify odd or even pages, click the Page Setup button on the Header and Footer toolbar to open the Page Setup dialog box (see Figure 14-21). Select the Layout tab, and make your selections under the Headers and Footers section. Then choose OK.

9. Click Close on the Header and Footer toolbar to return to your document. You can see the new header in Page Layout view and in Print Preview. Figure 14-22 shows pages with a header graphic repeated on every page.

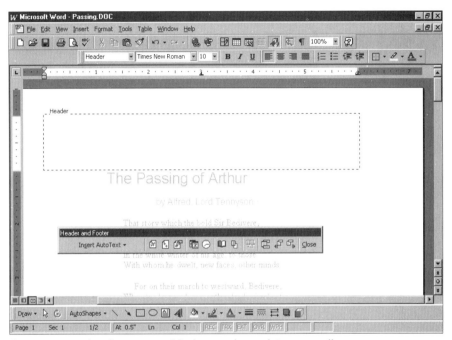

Figure 14-20: The document with the Header and Footer toolbar.

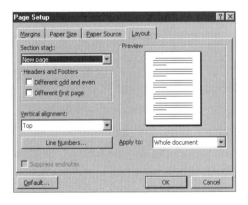

Figure 14-21: The Page Setup dialog box.

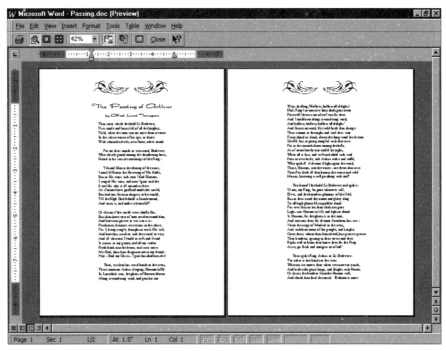

Figure 14-22: Pages with a graphic header repeated on every page.

Changing Between Text Boxes and Frames

In those cases in which you must use a frame instead of a text box, you can insert a text box and then convert it to a frame. For example, if you need to place text that contains comments and comments marks in a container, you cannot use a text box.

To convert a text box to a frame:

1. Double-click the text box frame to open the Format Text Box dialog box.

2. Choose the Text Box tab.

3. Choose Convert to Frame, and then choose OK. Word displays a warning message that some formatting may be lost.

4. Choose OK. The text box is now a frame with a single diagonal line border instead of the typical text box crosshatched border.

When you are updating the documents you created with earlier versions of Word, you may want to replace the frames with text boxes. Unfortunately, you can not convert them directly; you must first insert a new text box of the same size, and then cut and paste the objects from the frame object to the text box.

Linking Text Boxes into a Story

New One of the great new tools in Word 97 enables you to link text boxes together so the text flows from one part of your document to another to create a story. A *story* is a chain of text contained in linked text boxes each of which can be placed in different locations within the document. For example, a rather long article in a newsletter may begin on page one and be continued on page four. When you edit the text in either segment, the text in the linked box accommodates the changes seamlessly.

When you are laying out the newsletter, you insert empty text boxes in the size and position where you want the continuing story to appear. They may appear on different pages. You can enter text in the first text box before linking the boxes, but the others must be empty. Figure 14-23 shows three linked text boxes. As text was entered into the first text box, it overflowed into the second and then the third.

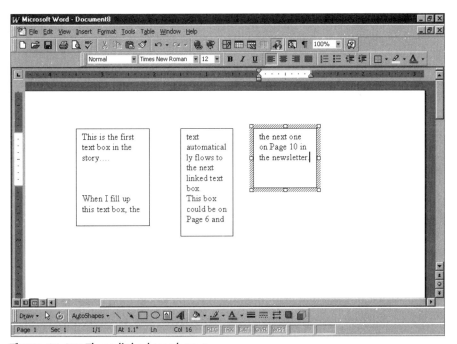

Figure 14-23: Three linked text boxes.

To create text box links:

1. Draw the text boxes in the locations where they will appear in the document and resize them as necessary.

2. Right-click the first text box and choose Create Text Box Link from the shortcut menu. If the Text Box toolbar is visible, click the Create Text Box Link button. A pitcher icon appears in place of the mouse pointer.

3. Move the pitcher icon to the second text box. As it moves over the second box, the pitcher turns into a pouring pitcher.

4. Click in the text box you want the text to flow into.

5. Repeat Step 2 in the second text box and move to the third box to click the pouring pitcher. The three boxes are now linked.

You can enter text only in the first of the linked text boxes. As the first text box fills up, the text continues in the next box in the story.

Tip   If you get stuck with the pitcher icon, press Esc to remove it and return to the normal document window.

Each text box has only one forward link and one backward link. You can break the link between any two text boxes in the chain and create two stories. All the other links remain intact, but the text boxes after the break will be empty, ready for the new story. To break a link, select the text box you want to stop text flowing into and choose Break Forward Link from the shortcut menu or the Text Box toolbar.

Summary

This chapter gave you some powerful ways for using text boxes to lay out your pages. It included several tips for formatting text and graphics in a text box. As you can see, text boxes can save you a lot of time when positioning text and graphics on a page. Using this chapter as a guide, you can:

✦ Insert and position a text box, and use it as a placeholder for laying out complex documents, such as a newsletter.

✦ Copy or move a text box anywhere in a document.

✦ Determine whether and how text wraps around a text box.

✦ Apply colors and lines formatting to a text box.

✦ Create a side heading with a text box in the margin.

✦ Add a text box to a heading to print on every page of your document.

✦ Link text boxes to create a continuing story in a document.

Where to go next...

✦ For more information on working with graphics, turn back to Chapter 13.

✦ For more information on adding borders and shading, see Chapter 8.

✦ For more information on laying out pages with columns and sections with different formatting, see Chapter 9.

✦ For more information on working with text and graphics in tables, see Chapter 12.

✦ For more information on creating attractive headers and footers, refer to Chapter 9.

✦   ✦   ✦

Linking Information from Other Applications

L inking information across different Windows applications lets you include sophisticated charts and data in your Word documents. The most important tool for exchanging information among Windows applications is OLE (Object Linking and Embedding). OLE provides a way to create compound documents. To the user, a compound document appears to be a single set of information; however, it contains elements created by two or more different applications. For example, you might combine a spreadsheet created using Microsoft Excel with a text document created using Microsoft Word. Compound documents could be created either by linking two separate documents together or by completely embedding one document in another. The idea behind OLE is to give users a document-centric view of computing instead of an application-centric view.

Component Object Model (COM) provided the foundation for OLE 2. COM defined a common format for interaction among all sorts of software. The term *OLE* was used for anything built around COM technology. COM defines the standard approach by which one chunk of software supplies its services to another. COM is transforming the way software is constructed. It is the underlying force behind the dramatic changes in Word 97.

In early 1996, Microsoft introduced ActiveX, which is associated with Internet technologies but now has been integrated into Office 97 applications, including Word 97. Both OLE and ActiveX are built on the Component Object Model, but OLE now represents only the technology used to create compound documents. The diverse group of COM technologies, once grouped under the OLE banner, are now labeled ActiveX.

As a result of ActiveX technology, Word 97 (and Office 97) offers an impressive collection of improvements and new features for linking information. Chief among these linking information additions is the integration of Internet applications into Word 97. For example, you can create hyperlinks in Word 97 documents and activate them simply by clicking them. These hyperlinks can be connected to a site on the Internet or another Office 97 document. You can also use Internet Explorer (3.0 or higher) to seamlessly browse Office 97 documents. Working with Word 97's Web-linking features is explained in Part IV.

This chapter explains sharing information based on OLE for creating compound documents. It also discusses creating compound documents made of Word and Excel components and working with Office 97's Binder application. The Binder lets you group files from Word, Excel, PowerPoint, or any Office-compatible application into a document that can be edited, stored, printed, and distributed as a single file that is independent of the applications used to create it.

Zen and the Art of OLE, Linking, and Embedding

OLE uses object technology. *Object* is the term used to define the information that is exchanged among applications. Objects can include text, documents, images, charts, tables, voice annotations, and video clips. Thus, when you copy an Excel chart and embed it in your Word document, that chart becomes an object.

Although linking and embedding are similar, there are some substantial differences. One method may be more practical than the other, depending on the type of task you need to accomplish.

Linking refers to establishing a connection between files. For example, you decide that you need to include information from an Excel spreadsheet in your Word document. You copy the information you need to the Clipboard, paste it into your Word document, and link the copied information so that, if you later make a change to the original Excel file, the change occurs automatically in the Word document. What actually happens is that Word stores the link in the form of a field code that keeps information about the source application and file. The field code acts as a pointer to the original application. Word also stores a visual representation of the field code so that you can see and print either the code or the linked object.

Note Word 97 includes a new Insert➪Hyperlink command and Insert Hyperlink button on the Standard toolbar that lets you create hyperlinks in your documents in the form of Web URLs or file paths to other documents. You can also use the Edit➪Paste as Hyperlink command to copy and paste hyperlinks from other sources, such as the Internet Explorer. Working with hyperlinks is explained in Chapter 17 .

Embedding means using another application to create the object but storing it entirely in Word. All the information necessary to edit the object is contained in the embedded field code in Word. No file is created in the original application. If you want to modify the embedded information later, you just need to double-click the embedded object. Windows automatically opens the application that created the embedded object so that you can make the necessary changes. When you close the application, the changes are updated in the Word document.

The subtle difference between linking and embedding has a number of ramifications. For one, embedding makes your Word document substantially larger than linking does because embedding stores the entire object and all the information about the originating application in the Word document. Linking, on the other hand, requires fewer system resources than embedding because Word stores only the linked code and a picture of the linked object.

What all this means is that OLE provides several ways for you to exchange information with other applications. However, it also means that you need to decide which approach is better for your particular situation. Table 15-1 offers some guidelines for making this decision.

<table>
<tr><td colspan="2" align="center">Table 15-1
Linking Versus Embedding</td></tr>
<tr><td>*Task*</td><td>*Approach and Comments*</td></tr>
<tr><td>Include information in your Word document that becomes part of the document and is always available, even if the original source file is not.</td><td>Use embedding. The problem with this approach occurs when you open the Word file on a computer that doesn't have the original application. If this is the case, you cannot use the original application to update the embedded object.</td></tr>
<tr><td>Include information maintained in a separate file, such as an Excel spreadsheet. Changes made to original file are reflected in the Word document.</td><td>Use linking. This approach is especially advantageous when you copy the source data (for instance, the Excel spreadsheet) to a number of different files (such as Word documents or PowerPoint graphs).</td></tr>
<tr><td>Include a very large object, such as a sound or video clip.</td><td>Use linking to keep the size of your Word file manageable. Embedding such a large object makes the Word file extremely large.</td></tr>
</table>

Embedding Objects in Word Documents

When you embed information from another application (or another Word document), you create an object. That object resides entirely in your Word document and not in the originating application. All the information Word needs to edit the object is stored with the object. However, to edit an embedded object created in another application, you must have the other application installed on your computer or have an application that can read objects of that type.

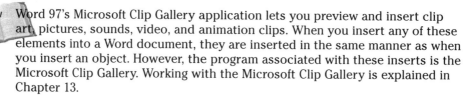

New Word 97's Microsoft Clip Gallery application lets you preview and insert clip art, pictures, sounds, video, and animation clips. When you insert any of these elements into a Word document, they are inserted in the same manner as when you insert an object. However, the program associated with these inserts is the Microsoft Clip Gallery. Working with the Microsoft Clip Gallery is explained in Chapter 13.

Embedding objects in Word

While you are working in Word, you can create an object in a different application and embed it in your Word document, or you can embed an existing file. If you embed an existing file, Word stores an independent copy of that file as the object. Updates to the object do not affect the original file, nor do changes to the original file affect the object. To create an embedded object:

1. Position the cursor where you want to embed the object.

2. Choose Insert⇨Object to display the Object dialog box.

3. Click the Create New tab, if necessary. Figure 15-1 shows the Object dialog box and the Create New tab. The items displayed in the Object type list depend on which Windows applications are installed on your computer.

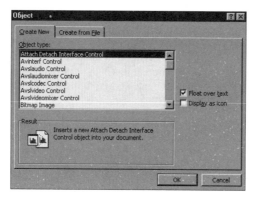

Figure 15-1: The Create New tab in the Object dialog box.

4. To display the embedded object as an icon, choose the Display as icon option. This causes the Change Icon button to appear (see Figure 15-2). Click this button to open the Change Icon dialog box (see Figure 15-3), and choose an icon different from the suggested one. The selection of available icons depends on the application you choose. To see more icons, use the Browse button to choose a different file.

The Float over text setting places the object in the drawing layer, where you can position it in front of or behind text and other objects using commands on the Draw menu. Clear this check box to place the object inline, in the current paragraph, where it behaves like regular text.

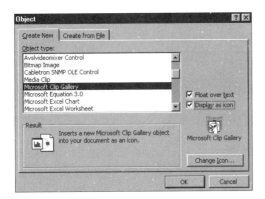

Figure 15-2: The Change Icon button appears when you choose the Display as Icon option.

Figure 15-3: The Change Icon dialog box.

5. Select the application you want to use to create the object, and click OK. The application window appears.

6. Create the object in the application.

7. After you create the object, return to Word by clicking anywhere outside the application window, click the Close button, or you can choose File⇨Exit in the application window.

Note When you install any Windows application that supports OLE, Windows automatically makes that application available to other applications for OLE tasks. This means that any application that supports OLE appears automatically in the Object dialog box. If you install an application and it doesn't appear in the Object dialog box, it doesn't support OLE.

To embed an existing file:

1. Position the cursor where you want to embed the file. If you want to embed only part of an existing file, follow the instructions in the next section.

2. Choose Insert⇨Object to display the Object dialog box.

3. Click the Create from File tab (see Figure 15-4).

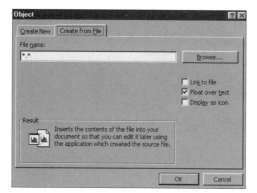

Figure 15-4: The Object dialog box, Create from File tab.

4. Enter the path name for your file in the File name text box, or click the Browse button and choose the drive and directory of the file you want to embed. If you aren't sure where the file is stored, click the Find File button to search for the file (see Chapter 6 for information about using the Find File feature).

5. To link the object rather than embed it, enable the Link to file option.

6. To display the embedded object as an icon, enable the Display as icon option. Doing so causes the Change Icon button to appear. Click this button to open the Change Icon dialog box and choose a different icon. Your selection of available icons depends on the application you choose.

7. After you make your selections, click OK to embed the file.

Note Most of the time, you will probably want to display an embedded object as the actual object. If you embed an Excel chart, you want Word to display the actual chart, not an icon representing the chart. However, icons are useful for representing embedded sound and video clips. When you embed a sound or video object, double-clicking the icon representing the object causes the object to play. To edit such an object, you must first select it and use Edit⇨Object.

Embedding objects in Word from another application

You can embed an object in a Word document while you work in a different application. For this approach, you use the Edit⇨Copy and Edit⇨Paste Special commands. To embed while working in the source application:

1. Select the information you want to embed.

2. Choose Edit⇨Copy. Doing so places a copy of the selection on the Clipboard.

3. Switch to Word.

4. Open the file in which you want to embed the object, and position the cursor where you want the object to be embedded.

5. Choose Edit⇨Paste Special to display the Paste Special dialog box (see Figure 15-5). The options in the Paste Special dialog box depend on the type of information you selected in Step 1. Table 15-2 describes the various options in the Paste Special dialog box.

6. When you have chosen the options you want, click OK to embed the object. (Note that you can use this dialog box to link as well as to paste.)

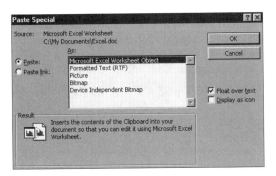

Figure 15-5: The Paste Special dialog box.

Tip   You can quickly insert an Excel spreadsheet as a table into your Word document by clicking the Insert Microsoft Excel Spreadsheet button on the Standard toolbar.

When you embed an object, Word inserts an embed field {EMBED...} into the document. If you see the field rather than the object when you embed an object, select the object and press Shift+F9. This keystroke toggles the view between showing the code and showing the object. Figure 15-6 shows an example of an embedded field code.

By default, the field codes are turned off. In most cases, you'll want them turned off because they can quickly clutter up a screen. However, if you want to display field codes choose Tools➪Options, click the View tab, and click Field codes. For more information on working with field codes, see Chapter 26.

`{EMBED·Excel.Sheet.8··}`   **Figure 15-6:** Embed field code.

Table 15-2 Paste Special Options	
Option	**Action**
Source object	Displays the name of the source file and its location. If you copied the object from an application that did not provide the source data, the display shows Unknown. If Unknown is displayed, you cannot use the originating application to edit the embedded object.
Paste	Inserts the contents of the Clipboard into the document. The option you choose in the As list box determines the type of object that is pasted. This option does not create a link to the original application. If you choose this option and choose an object in the As list box, the selection is pasted with no connection to the original application.
Paste link	Inserts the contents of the Clipboard into the document and creates a link to the contents of the Clipboard's source application. If the source application does not support linking, this option is not available. If you choose this option, you can have Word update the object automatically if you make changes to the original data, or you can specify manual updating.

Option	Action
As	Lets you specify the type of object to paste.
Worksheet Object	This is one choice for embedding in the As list box. This selection pastes a graphical representation of the contents of the Clipboard and all the data needed to edit the object. The name of the object in the list depends on the application used to create the object.
Formatted Text (RTF)	Pastes the selection with text formatting. For example, an Excel table is pasted as a Word table.
Picture	Pastes the selection as a graphical representation, such as a Windows metafile.
Bitmap	Pastes the selection as a graphical representation used by other applications, such as Paintbrush.
Device Independent Bitmap	Inserts the contents of the Clipboard as a bitmap picture that is an exact representation of what you see on the screen. Be aware that this format demands a lot of memory and disk space.
Float over text	Places the object in the drawing layer, where you can position it in front of or behind text and other objects using commands on the Draw menu. Clear this check box to place the object inline, in the current paragraph, where it behaves like regular text.
Display as icon	Displays the selection as an icon. This option is available only if you choose to link or embed the selection.
Result	Describes the result of your selections.
Change Icon	Enables you to choose a different icon to represent the linked or embedded object. This button is not available unless you enable the Display as Icon option. (Refer back to Figure 15-2 to see this button.)

Editing embedded objects

One of the major reasons for using OLE is the simplicity of editing objects. You can edit an embedded object directly or by using the Edit⇨Object command. You must use Edit⇨Object to edit embedded video and sound clips because double-clicking these objects causes them to play. Also, you may prefer to use Edit⇨Object, even if in-place editing is available because, when you switch to the original application, you can use the entire screen.

Note   The Edit⇨Object command changes to the name of the object your editing. For example, if you inserted a chart from Excel into your document, the Edit⇨Object command appears as Edit⇨Chart Object.

To edit an embedded object directly:

1. Double-click the embedded object. The application window opens with the object's contents displayed.

2. Edit the object as desired.

3. After you edit the object, return to Word by clicking anywhere outside the object in the Word document.

Tip   Right-clicking anywhere on the object displays the shortcut menu, from which you can access the editing tools for that object. The contents of this menu change depending on the object.

To edit an embedded object by using the Edit⇨Object command:

1. Select the embedded object.

2. Choose Edit⇨Object. The name of the application appears on the menu. If both Open and Edit appear on the menu, choosing Open enables you to edit the object in the original application, whereas selecting Edit enables you to edit the object in the Word document.

3. After you edit the object, return to Word by clicking anywhere outside the object in the Word document.

Converting embedded objects to different file formats

When you embed an object, the entire object is stored in the Word document, including information about the application that created the object. When you want to edit the object, double-click it to use the original application for editing. Sometimes, though, the original application isn't available, such as when you copy the Word file to a computer that doesn't have the original application installed. What you can do in this case is convert the object to a different file format. You can permanently or temporarily convert the object.

Note   If you create an object with an application (such as Excel 95) and then upgrade that application (to Excel 97), before you can edit the object, you must convert it to the upgraded version of the application by opening the file in the upgraded application.

To convert an embedded object to a different file format:

1. Select the object you want to convert.

2. Choose Edit➪Object. Doing so opens a pop-up menu.

3. Choose Convert to open the Convert dialog box (see Figure 15-7).

4. Choose the Convert to option to see a list of applications in the Object type list box. Use this option for a permanent conversion.

   Or choose the Activate as option if you want to convert the object temporarily to a different type of object for editing purposes. When you save the object, it is saved in its original file format. The list of options in the Object type list box may change, and the option to display the object as an icon is not available. The Activate as setting may not be available if there aren't any translators for the selected object. This is confusing because the Convert to option may still be available even though there aren't any options to choose in the Convert dialog box.

5. To display the embedded object as an icon, enable the Display as icon option. This causes the Change Icon button to appear. Click this button to open the Change Icon dialog box (refer to Figure 15-3), and choose an icon different from the suggested one. The selection of available icons depends on the application you choose.

6. In the Object type list box, select the application to which you want to convert the object, and click OK.

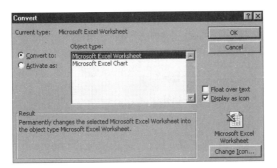

Figure 15-7: The Convert dialog box.

Converting embedded objects to graphics

When you convert an embedded object to a graphic, you can no longer edit it in its original application. If you double-click the graphic after converting it from an object, Word opens a separate window and displays the Drawing toolbar so that you can edit the graphic as a Word Picture. The significant advantage of converting an embedded object to a graphic is that you reduce the file size of the Word document.

To convert the object to a graphic, select it, and press Ctrl+Shift+F9. You cannot convert the graphic back to an embedded object, but you can undo the conversion with the Edit⇨Undo command (Ctrl+Z) if you change your mind.

Linking Objects in Word

Linking differs from embedding in that Word doesn't store the entire linked object. Instead, Word stores a field code that indicates the source of the object and a visual representation of the linked object. (Figure 15-8 shows an example of a link field code.) You are actually linking to another file where the information is stored. After you establish a link, many options are available in Word for using the link. For example, you can specify that Word update the original file automatically, or you can manually update changes.

{Link·Excel.Sheet.8"C:\\MSOffice97\\Excel\\royalties.xls"·""\a\p}   **Figure 15-8:** Sample link field code.

Creating links

As with embedding, you can create a link either while working in Word or while working in another application. If you want to link to a selection within a file, you must first switch to the other application to select the item you want to link. To create a link while working in Word:

1. Position the cursor where you want the link.

2. Choose Insert⇨Object to display the Object dialog box.

3. Choose the Create from File tab (refer to Figure 15-4).

4. Enter the file path name or choose the Browse button to navigate to the file you want.

5. To display the linked file as an icon, enable the Display as icon option. Doing so causes the Change Icon button to appear (refer to Figure 15-2). Click this button to open the Change Icon dialog box (refer to Figure 15-3), and choose a different icon.

6. Choose the Link to file option, and click OK.

To create a link from another application:

1. Save the file in the other application before linking.

2. Select the information you want to link.

3. Choose Edit⇨Copy to place the information on the Clipboard.

4. Switch to the Word document, and place the cursor where you want the linked object.

5. Choose Edit⇨Paste Special to display the Paste Special dialog box (refer to Figure 15-5). The options in the Paste Special dialog box depend on the type of information you selected in Step 2. Review Table 15-2 for the various options in the Paste Special dialog box.

6. To link the selection, click the Paste Link option.

7. In the As list box, choose the format you want and click OK.

Updating links

Word can update links in two ways: automatically and manually. With automatic links, Word updates the links each time you open the file containing the links, as well as any time the source information changes while the Word document is open. With manual links, Word updates the links only when you decide. Word's default is to update all links automatically when the information in the source file changes, but you can specify either updating method for any link.

If you change any of the linked information in the Word document, Word over-writes the changes the next time it updates the link. However, any formatting you apply to the linked object is not affected.

Controlling link updates

You can use the procedure outlined in the following steps not only to specify automatic or manual updating for your links but also to break and lock links and to change the source file. To specify how links are updated:

1. Choose Edit⇨Links to display the Links dialog box (see Figure 15-9). (Table 15-3 describes the options in the Links dialog box.) The Links command is not available unless you have at least one link in the document.

2. The Links dialog box lists all links in the active Word document. Select one or more links. To select multiple links, click once on the first link, press Ctrl, and click once on each of the other links that you want to edit. If you have several links and want to select them all, click once on the top link, press Shift, and click once on the last link in the list. All the links are then selected.

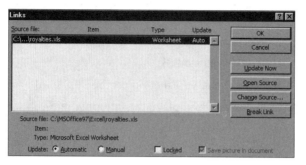

Figure 15-9: The Links dialog box.

3. Choose Automatic for automatic links, or choose Manual for manual links. You can specify different options for different links.

4. Click OK.

Table 15-3
Links Dialog Box Options

Option	Action
Source file	Displays the name and location of the source file.
Item	Defines the range of data within the file if the object doesn't contain the whole file. If the linked object is a file, this option is blank.
Type	Displays the application that created the linked object.
Update	Determines how to update the links. You specify how you want to update the selected links.
Automatic	Updates the link each time the source data changes.
Manual	Doesn't automatically update the link. You must take an action to update the link.
Update Now	Updates all selected links in the Links list box. This is one of the ways to update manual links.
Open Source	Opens the selected file in the source application so that you can edit it.
Change Source	Enables you to specify a different source file for a selected link. When you click this button, the Change Source dialog box opens. It looks and works the same as the File Open dialog box.

Option	Action
Break Link	Breaks the link for selected links.
Locked	Locks the selected link so that it doesn't update until you unlock the link. If you lock a link, the Update Now option is unavailable for that link.
Save picture in document	Saves a graphical representation of the linked object in the Word document. This option is available only if you select a link to a graphics file. If you don't choose this option, Word stores only the link in the document; the file size does not increase appreciably. If the source file is available, Word displays a picture of the graphics object but not the actual object. If the source file is unavailable, Word displays a placeholder.

Note   If you break the link for an object that displayed an icon, the icon remains in your Word document but becomes a Word picture. There is no longer any connection between the icon and the original file. If you break the link for text, the text remains in your Word document but is no longer linked with the original.

Updating links manually

There are two methods for manually updating links. The simplest one is to position the cursor somewhere in the linked object and press F9. The other way is to use Edit⇨Links. Using Edit⇨Links may be quicker if you have several links in your document because you can see a list of all the links. To update links manually:

1. Choose Edit⇨Links to display the Links dialog box (refer to Figure 15-9 and also Table 15-3, which lists the options in the Links dialog box). The Links command is not available unless you have at least one link in the document.

2. The Links dialog box lists all links in the active Word document. Select one or more links. To select multiple links, click once on the first link, press Ctrl, and click once on each of the other links that you want to edit. If you have a number of links and want to select them all, click once on the top link, press Shift, and click once on the last link in the list. All the links are then selected.

3. Click the Update Now button. Word updates the selected links.

Updating links each time you print the document

Another option you have is to update all the links in your Word document when you print the document. If you choose this option, all links are updated. You cannot update selected links when this option is enabled. To update links each time you print the document:

1. Choose Tools⇨Options. Click the Print tab to display the print options (see Figure 15-10).

2. Enable the Update links option.

3. Click OK.

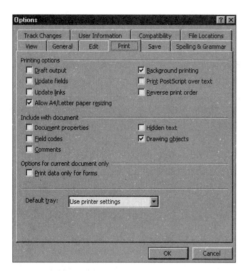

Figure 15-10: The Options dialog box, Print tab.

Editing links

You should edit linked information in the source file. If you edit it directly in your Word document, any update of the link in the future will overwrite your changes. You cannot double-click a linked object to edit the link. If you are in Word, choose Edit⇨Object (the menu displays the type of link object). This option is usually at the bottom of the Edit menu, unless you've changed your Edit menu. Choose Edit from the pop-up menu, and the original application opens with the linked file. When you have made the changes you want, save the file and close the application. If the linked object updates automatically, the changes are reflected immediately; otherwise, select the linked object, and press F9.

One of the benefits of linking information is that you can open the source application anytime and change whatever information you want. If the information you change is linked, the linked data changes as well.

Breaking links

Breaking a link means the linked information remains in your Word document, but you cannot update it from the source application. Displaying an icon to represent the linked data causes the data not to appear when you break the link. Instead, the icon becomes a Word picture.

The simplest method of breaking a link is to select the linked object and press Ctrl+Shift+F9. After you break the link, you cannot restore it, but you can undo it (Ctrl+Z).

Locking and unlocking links

Locking a link prevents it from being updated. The difference between locking a link and breaking it is that you can later unlock the link. After you break a link, you cannot restore it. To lock and unlock a link:

1. Choose Edit⇨Links to display the Links dialog box (refer to Figure 15-9). (Table 15-3 describes the options in the Links dialog box.) The Links command is not available unless you have at least one link in the document.

2. The Links dialog box lists all links in the active Word document. Select one or more links. To select multiple links, click once on the first link, press Ctrl, and click once on each of the other links that you want to edit. If you have several links and want to select them all, click once on the top link, press Shift, and click once on the last link in the list. Word then selects all the links.

3. Enable the Locked option to lock the selected links. If the link you selected is locked, you can unlock it by clearing the Locked option.

4. Click OK.

Instead of using the menu commands as described previously, you can lock a link by selecting it and pressing Ctrl+F11. To unlock, select the link, and press Ctrl+Shift+F11.

Shading links

Word lets you shade fields, including linked and embedded objects. The advantage to doing so is that you can see at a glance which parts of your document are linked. You don't waste time, therefore, editing the documents when the next update overwrites any edits. To shade a link, choose Tools⇨Options, and click the View tab. Under Show, choose Always in the Field shading box. All fields, including linked and embedded objects, are shaded. Graphics objects, however, do not show shading. The shading does not print.

You may also want to shade information that serves as a source for links to another file because any change you make to such information results in a change to the linked data. You can do this by choosing Tools➪Options and clicking the View tab. Under Show, enable the Bookmarks option. All bookmarks and link sources are displayed in large gray brackets. The brackets do not print.

Embedding an Excel Worksheet

Embedding an Excel worksheet in Word enables you to use Excel's powerful spreadsheet tools to create complex tables and store them in your Word document. The advantage to embedding them in a Word document is that you can copy the Word document to a different computer and the embedded objects remain a part of the Word file. If the other computer has Excel installed, you need only double-click the embedded Excel worksheet to edit the object.

To create and embed a worksheet, place the cursor where you want the worksheet to appear. Choose Insert➪Object, and click the Create New tab. Choose Microsoft Excel in the Object type list box, and click OK. Doing so opens the Excel window (Figure 15-11). You can now build your worksheet.

When you finish, choose File➪Exit. Click Yes to the message asking you whether you want to update the worksheet in your document. Doing so embeds the worksheet in your Word document. You can edit it anytime by double-clicking it.

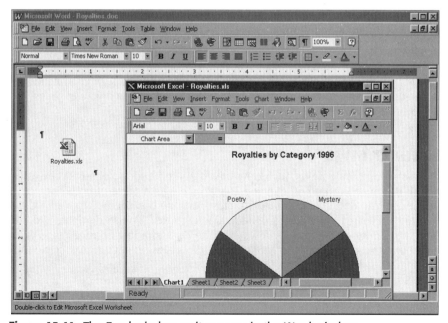

Figure 15-11: The Excel window as it appears in the Word window.

Linking an Excel Worksheet

When you embed a worksheet, it is stored in the Word document, and you simply use Excel to edit the worksheet data. When you link a worksheet, however, you save the worksheet as an Excel file. Then, if you edit the data in the original Excel worksheet, the edits are reflected in the linked data in your Word document. The advantage here is that you can copy and link the same data in any number of Word (and other) files. You don't have to worry about updating each Word file. Linking takes care of updating for you.

Although you can create a link while working in Word, it is best to open Excel and work in the file you want to use. If the worksheet already exists, open it; otherwise, create a new worksheet. Then, select the data you want to add to your Word document, and choose Edit⇨Copy to place the data on the Clipboard. Switch to the Word file, and place the cursor where you want to paste the linked data. Choose Edit⇨Paste Special, and choose Paste Link. In the As list box, choose the type of format you want to use. The Result box explains each option. Click OK to link the worksheet.

The best way to become familiar with all the options is to try them. Create a test worksheet and copy it to the Clipboard. Use Paste Link to paste the linked data into your Word document several times, selecting different formats each time.

Working with the Office 97 Binder

Office 97 brings new options for creating compound documents from many applications by using the Microsoft Binder. The Binder lets you group files from Word, Excel, PowerPoint, any Office-compatible application, and Web documents into a compound document that can be edited, stored, printed, and distributed as a single file that is independent of the applications used to create it.

You can create binders that act as master copies for sets of documents. You can create your own binder templates or use the four binder templates that come with Office 97, which include Client Billing, Meeting Organizer, Proposal and Marketing Plan, and Report.

Use the original application to edit documents that you assemble in a binder. The collection of editing tools available in the Binder are limited.

Starting Binder

When you start Binder, a new blank binder appears in the Binder window, as shown in Figure 15-12. The left pane will display the file icons and the right pane will display the file's contents with the application window that generated the file.

The button at the far left of the menu bar hides or displays the left pane. Each document you add to the Binder is called a section.

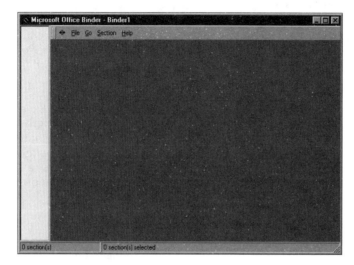

Figure 15-12: The Binder window.

To create a binder:

1. Choose Start⇨Programs⇨Microsoft Binder. The Binder window appears with a blank binder based on the default blank binder template.

2. Do one of the following:

   • Drag a file icon to the left pane of the Binder window. The file icon appears in the left pane, and the application window with the file appears in the right pane. For example, drag a Word document file, and the Word 97 application appears with the document file in the Binder window, as shown in Figure 15-13.

   • Choose Section⇨Add from File. The Add from File dialog box appears. Choose the file you want to add, and then click Add. The file icon appears in the left pane, and the application window with the file appears in the right pane. The Binder's File and Section menus are added to the menu bar of the application.

3. Repeat Step 2 to add additional files to your binder.

4. Choose File⇨Save Binder to save your binder. The file is saved as a binder file.

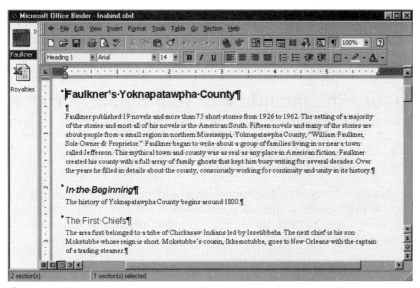

Figure 15-13: The Binder window with a Word 97 document added.

Performing common Binder tasks

After you add all the documents you want into a binder, you can navigate among them in the Binder window by clicking the file icon in the left pane. The following items explain basic tasks you can perform on your binder documents:

✦ To rearrange the order of the documents in your binder, choose Section⇨Rearrange. The Rearrange dialog box appears Select the document that you want to move, and then click the Move Up or Move Down button. After you rearrange your documents, click OK.

✦ To delete a document in your binder, click the document you want to delete in the left pane of the Binder window. Click the right mouse button on the icon to display a shortcut menu, and then choose delete. You can also choose Section⇨Delete.

✦ To print a binder, choose File⇨Print Binder.

✦ To open an existing binder, choose File⇨Open Binder.

✦ To open a new binder, choose File⇨New Binder to display the New Binder dialog box . The General tab includes the default Blank Binder template. Click the Binder tab to display the four premade binder templates that come with Office 97. You can view the layout of each template by clicking it and viewing it in the Preview area of the New Binder dialog box. Choose the binder template you want, and then click OK.

✦ To print all sections with the same header and footer, choose File⇨Binder Page Set<u>u</u>p, and then click the Header/Footer tab. Under Apply header/footer, click All supported sections. You can also choose Only sections selected below to print several sections with the same header and footer.

Integrating the Internet into your Binder documents

The Binder in included with the Microsoft Office 97 supports integrating resources from the Internet directly into your Binder documents. This handy features lets you bring in Web pages directly into your binder documents or create hyperlinks to resources anywhere on the Internet.

You can also open binders on the Web or anywhere on the Internet from the Open dialog box in any Office 97 application, including Word 97. For this feature to work, you must have access to the Internet. The <u>G</u>o menu includes all the commands for integrating Internet resources into your binders.

The following explain the common commands in the <u>G</u>o menu:

✦ To search the Web, choose <u>G</u>o⇨Search the <u>W</u>eb.

✦ To start your Web exploration from the start document used in your Web browser choose <u>G</u>o⇨<u>S</u>tart Page.

✦ To display the Web toolbar, choose <u>G</u>o⇨Sh<u>o</u>w Web Toolbar.

✦ To add a Web document link to a binder, choose <u>G</u>o⇨<u>O</u>pen. The Open Internet Address dialog box appears (see Figure 15-14). Enter the URL in the Address field, such as **http://www.microsoft.com**, and then click OK.

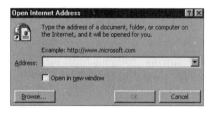

Figure 15-14: The Open Internet Address dialog box.

Summary

Linking information across different Windows applications lets you produce sophisticated documents and incorporate features that go beyond what Word offers. In this chapter, you learned about linking and embedding information in Word documents, including how to:

✦ Differentiate between linking and embedding. Linking information creates a link to a separate file, such as an Excel spreadsheet. Changes made to the file are reflected in the link in your Word document. Embedding a file as an object keeps the file with your Word document without links to the original file. This lets you share the document with other users, even if they don't have Excel on their systems.

✦ Create an embedded object by choosing Insert⇨Object. In the Object dialog box, choose the Create New tab, select the application you want to use in the Object Type list, click Display as Icon, and click OK.

✦ Embed an existing file by displaying the Object dialog box (Insert⇨Object). In the Object dialog box, choose the Create from File tab and enter the path name for the file in the File Name text box. Click the Display as icon option, and choose OK.

✦ Edit an embedded object by double-clicking the object in your Word document. Edit the object in its native application, and click anywhere outside the object to return to Word.

✦ Create a link to an existing file by displaying the Object dialog box (Insert⇨Object) and choosing the Create from File tab. Enter the path name for the file, or choose the Browse button to navigate to the file, choose the Link to File option, and click OK.

Where to go next...

✦ To learn more about working with graphics objects, see Chapter 13.

✦ To learn more on positioning objects in your document, check out Chapter 14.

✦   ✦   ✦

Working with Microsoft Graph 97 Chart and Microsoft Equation 3.0

This chapter covers working with two programs included with Word 97: Microsoft Graph 97 Chart and Microsoft Equation 3.0. Microsoft Graph 97 Chart (referred to as Graph in this chapter) is a charting application that lets you create quick and easy charts to include in your Word document. Using Graph, you can display numeric data in graphic form, making it clearer, more interesting, and easier to read than just a table. Microsoft Equation 3.0 is an equation editor that lets you incorporate mathematical symbols to create mathematical equations in your Word document.

About Graph

The Graph program lets you create charts for your Word documents. A chart you create using Graph is inserted as an embedded object into Word's document. As with other embedded objects, you can copy, delete, or resize the chart using the main application's commands. To edit the chart's data or format any part of the chart, you activate the chart by double-clicking it and then you work in Graph.

When you begin creating a new chart, the default chart and Datasheet window appear in your current Word document (see Figure 16-1). The default chart appears as an image in your document with a border around it. The chart displays data in 3-D columns with a legend displayed and with some other standard formatting. The Datasheet window appears as a spreadsheet with default entries in the columns and rows. The data in the Datasheet window appears automatically in the chart. You can enter your own data to replace the sample data or import data from another document. In either case, the chart is updated to display the new data. Once you enter or import your data in the Datasheet window, you can choose different types of charts to represent your data. For example, you can change the default 3-D bar chart to a pie chart. Graph has 14 basic chart types you can choose from, and you can customize these charts.

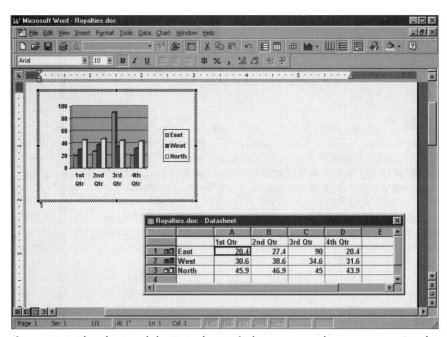

Figure 16-1: The chart and the Datasheet window appear when you open Graph.

Starting and Quitting Graph

You can start Graph anytime while working in Word. By default, the Graph program is available only from the menu, but you can add the Chart button to your toolbar. If you plan to use Graph routinely, you may want to do this. Just choose Tools⇨Customize to display the Customize dialog box. Choose the

Commands tab, and select the Insert option in the Categories list. The available toolbar buttons (and menu items) for Insert menu commands appears in the Commands list, (see Figure 16-2). Drag the Chart button from the Customize dialog box to the location on the toolbar you want. Click Close to close the Customize dialog box.

Tip

You can do a quick load of the Graph program by choosing Insert⇨Picture⇨Chart.

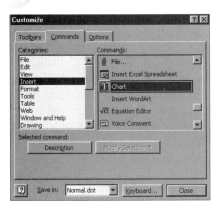

Figure 16-2: The Commands tab in the Customize dialog box.

To start and quit Graph:

1. Place the insertion point at the location in your document where you want to create a chart.

2. Choose Insert⇨Object to display the Object dialog box (see Figure 16-3). Choose Microsoft Graph 97 Chart from the Object type list in the Create New tab and click OK, or click the Graph button on the toolbar. The default chart and Datasheet window appear in the Word window (refer back to Figure 16-1).

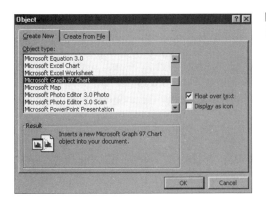

Figure 16-3: The Object dialog box's Create New tab.

3. Make any changes to your data in the Datasheet window or changes to your chart.

4. Point anywhere outside the chart or the Datasheet window, and click. The Datasheet window disappears as well as the Graph program menus and toolbars. The Word program window reappears with your chart embedded in the document.

5. To open the Graph program with a chart in your Word document, double-click the chart.

Choosing the Display as icon in the Object dialog box's Create New tab embeds the Graph program as an icon in your Word document, as shown in Figure 16-4. When you double-click the icon, the Graph program appears in its own window. You work with the Graph program in the same way except that your chart closes to an icon instead of appearing as a picture in your document. To exit the Graph window and return to Word, choose File⇨Exit & Return in the Graph window, or click the Minimize or Close button. If the Graph program is minimized, the Graph icon in your Word document appears shaded.

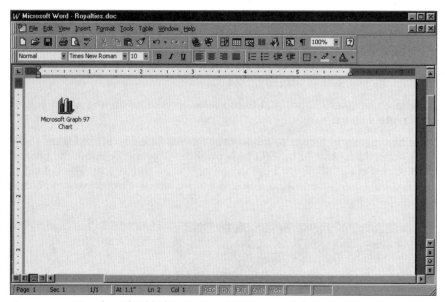

Figure 16-4: Graph embedded as an icon in your Word document.

You can also start Graph by choosing an existing file from the Create From File tab (as shown in Figure 16-5) in the Object dialog box (Insert⇨Object). You can enter the name of the file in the File name field, or choose the Browse button to navigate to the file you want. If you want to display the object as an icon, choose the Display as icon check box. To maintain a link to the original file, select the Link to file check box.

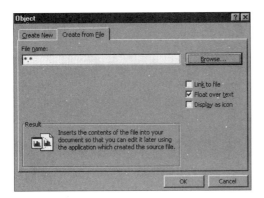

Figure 16-5: The Create from File tab in the Object dialog box.

Note You can't use the Object command to insert many graphic file formats. Instead, use the Insert⇨Picture command. Working with this command is explained in Chapter 13.

In most cases, you'll work with a chart as a graphic in your document. This chapter focuses on working with a chart appearing as a graphic in your document, but the techniques are fundamentally the same regardless of the way you work with Graph.

A Quick Orientation of Graph

When you open Graph, the Microsoft Graph window appears with its own menus and toolbars along with the chart and Datasheet window (see Figure 16-6). Graph includes two toolbars. Like toolbars in Word, you can drag these toolbars to place them where you want, and you can move your pointer on the button to display the button's label.

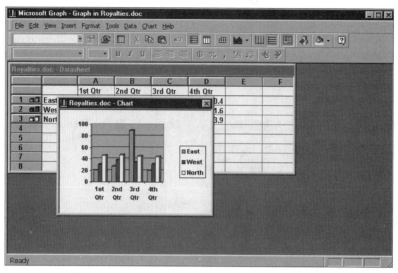

Figure 16-6: The Microsoft Graph window.

Working in the Datasheet Window

The Datasheet window is similar to a typical spreadsheet used in a Windows spreadsheet program, such as Microsoft Excel. The top row of the datasheet contains the names of the classes of things being reported on: in this case, the 1st, 2nd, 3rd, and 4th quarters. The leftmost column, meanwhile, contains the names of the things within the classes (East, West, and North regions). In Graph talk, the top row represents the names of the *categories,* and the left column lists the names of the elements in each *series.* A data series is one row or column of values (data points) that is displayed as a set of data markers on the chart. What you type in the first row and column of cells and which orientation you choose (series in rows or series in columns) determines how the data is plotted on the chart.

Although initially the Datasheet window shows only a few columns and rows, you can expand the display of the window by moving the pointer to any window edge and dragging outward to expand it or inward to reduce its size. The scroll bars at the right and bottom let you navigate around a datasheet. Figure 16-7 shows the Datasheet window.

Figure 16-7: The Datasheet window.

		A	B	C	D	E
		1st Qtr	2nd Qtr	3rd Qtr	4th Qtr	
1	East	20.4	27.4	90	20.4	
2	West	30.6	38.6	34.6	31.6	
3	North	45.9	46.9	45	43.9	
4						

Entering data in a datasheet

Graph automatically opens a sample chart and datasheet when you open it. You can enter new data over the existing data or select the text in the Datasheet window and delete it, as explained later. If you need to enter more data than the number of rows that appear in the Datasheet by default, you can scroll to display new columns and rows. When you enter data in the cell, a new row or column is automatically created, and the chart automatically reflects the additions. You can expand the Datasheet window by pointing to a corner or side and dragging outward to expand the window size.

A cell in the Datasheet window can display up to eight characters. If your data takes up more than eight characters, the data in the cell is noted with a series of number signs (#) across the width of the cell. The data you entered in the cell is there, but it's too big to display in the default eight-character width of the column. However, you can enlarge the width of any column by pointing to the vertical line to the right of the column heading (the column headings are the A, B, C, and so on at the top of the Datasheet window). When the pointer changes to a vertical bar with arrows on each side, drag to the right to widen the column. When you reach the width of your data in the column, the actual data replaces the number signs.

To enter data in the Datasheet window:

1. Click a cell in the datasheet. A border appears around the cell.

2. Enter your data in the cell. If you enter data in a new column or row, make sure you label it at the top or right side of the spreadsheet.

3. Press a direction key to move to the next cell.

4. Enter your data in the cell.

5. After you're finished entering your data, click anywhere outside the Datasheet or Chart windows to return to Word.

Entering data in an existing datasheet

When you exit Graph, the Datasheet window disappears. To display the Datasheet window again to make any changes, simply double-click the chart. The Graph program menus and toolbars appear but not the Datasheet window. To display the Datasheet window, click the View Datasheet button on the Standard toolbar (third button from the left). The Datasheet window appears. Now you can edit your datasheet. To edit information in a datasheet, select the appropriate cell, click it, and enter your information.

Selecting data and moving within the datasheet

The easiest way to move about in a datasheet is to click where you want to go with the mouse. As you select cells with the mouse, remember the following:

✦ One cell — the active cell — is always selected. To make another cell active, click it.

✦ If you want to select several cells, drag the mouse over them.

✦ If you want to select an entire row or column, click the shaded area (header) to the left (for a row) or above (column).

✦ To select several rows or columns, drag the mouse over their headers.

✦ To select the entire datasheet, click the area where the row and column headers meet or press Ctrl+A.

Sometimes, you may want to use the keyboard to navigate a datasheet and then select a cell. Tables 16-1 and 16-2 list important key combinations.

Table 16-1
Navigating a Datasheet Using the Keyboard

Press This	To Move Here
Arrow keys	One cell in the direction of the arrow
Home	First cell in row
End	Last cell in row
Ctrl+Home	Top left cell
Ctrl+End	Lower right cell
Page Up (Page Down)	One screen up (down)
Ctrl+Page Up (Ctrl+Page Down)	One screen left (right)

Moving and copying information in the datasheet

To move or copy cells in a Graph datasheet, use the Cut, Copy, and Paste buttons on the Standard toolbar, or use the Edit⇨Cut, Copy, and Paste commands. Select the cells you want to copy or move. Then choose either the Cut or Copy button or the command to place the cells on the Clipboard. Position the cursor where you want the information to move, and choose the Paste button or command to move or copy the data to its new location. If you want to replace existing cells with the new information, select the cells to be replaced before pasting the copies.

Table 16-2 Selecting Cells Using the Keyboard	
Press This	**To Select This**
Arrow key	One cell in the direction of the arrow
Shift+arrow key (you also can use the extend selection function key, F8)	Series of cells
Shift+spacebar	A row
Ctrl+spacebar	A column
Ctrl+Shift+spacebar	Entire datasheet

Deleting and inserting information in the datasheet

To delete a row or column, select a cell in the column or row, and choose Edit⇨Delete. The Delete dialog box appears, as shown in Figure 16-8. Choose the Entire row or Entire column option, and choose OK. To delete a cell or selection of cells, click the cell or select the group of cells. Choose the Shift cells left to delete the cells and shift the remaining cells to the left, or choose Shift cells up to delete the cells and shift the remaining cells up.

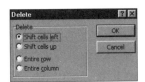

Figure 16-8: The Delete dialog box.

If you want to delete the contents of a cell, row, or column without any confirmation, just select the cell or cells you want to delete, and press the Delete key. The contents of the selected cells are deleted.

To insert a row or celi, select the cell in the row or column you want to insert above in the case of a row or before in the case of a column. Choose Insert⇨Cells to display the Insert dialog box. The Insert dialog box appears, as shown in Figure 16-9. Choose the Entire row or Entire column option, and click OK. To insert a cell or selection of cells, click the cell, or select the group of cells. Choose the Shift cells right to insert the cells and shift the remaining cells to the right, or choose Shift cells down to delete the cells and shift the remaining cells up.

You can also use the Edit⇨Clear commands to remove information in cells.

Figure 16-9: The Insert dialog box.

Formatting data in the datasheet

You can format data in your datasheet quickly by using the Formatting toolbar. It includes the standard Word formatting features, which you can apply to the entire data sheet. You can change the font and font size used for data entries, and you can boldface, italicize, or underline data entries.

Unique to the Graph toolbar are its last five buttons. These buttons let you format your data entries. You can apply a currency, percent, or comma style to data or increase or decrease the decimal point value. For example, if you want all the values in your datasheet to represent dollars, select the entire datasheet by pressing Ctrl+A and then click the dollar sign ($) button.

Working with Charts

Data entered in your datasheet automatically appears in the default bar chart. The Graph program provides a variety of chart styles to choose from as well as tools for customizing how your chart looks. The parts of a chart typically include such items as a chart title, axis values, data labels, gridlines, data series, a chart area, a plot area, and a legend. The following items explain the key elements of charts:

✦ A data series is one row or column of values, called data points, that are displayed as a set of data markers on the chart, such as bars, lines, or pie slices. What you enter in the first row and column of cells and which orientation you choose (series in rows or series in columns) determines how the data is plotted on the chart. The default chart is plotted with series in rows.

✦ A data marker is a bar, area, dot, slice, or other symbol in a chart that represents a single data point or value originating from a datasheet cell. Related data markers in a chart comprise a data series.

✦ Tick marks are the small lines that intersect an axis like divisions on a ruler. Tick marks are part of and can be formatted with the axis. Tick-mark labels identify the categories, values, and series in a chart. They come from and are automatically linked to cells in your worksheet selection.

✦ Data points are individual values plotted in a chart that originate from single cells in the datasheet. Data points are represented by bars, columns, lines, pie slices, and other shapes in charts. These shapes are called data markers.

✦ An axis consists of the lines bordering the plot area that provide the frame of reference for measurement or comparison on a chart. A 2-D chart has two axes, and a 3-D chart has two or three axes. For most charts, data values are plotted along the value (y) axis, which is usually vertical, and categories are plotted along the category (x) axis, which is usually horizontal. Pie and doughnut charts don't have axes.

✦ Gridlines are lines you can add to your chart that extend from the tick marks on an axis across the plot area. Gridlines come in various forms to make it easier to view and evaluate data.

✦ A category is groupings of data usually plotted along the category (x) axis on a chart. If you define data series in rows on the datasheet, then the categories are the columns; if you define the data series in columns, then the categories are in rows.

✦ A legend is a box containing entries and keys that help identify the data series or categories in a chart. The legend keys, to the left of each entry, show the patterns and colors assigned to the data series or categories in the chart.

✦ After you create a chart, you can position it in your document by using standard Word paragraph formatting and positioning commands. You can enlarge a chart by clicking it to display its sizing handles and dragging a sizing handle.

Changing chart types

With your data entered in a datasheet, you can view the data using other chart types. Table 16-3 lists the available chart styles available in Graph. To display the data in your datasheet in different chart styles, click the down arrow on the Chart Type button, and choose the chart type you want. Graph automatically converts the data into the specified chart. You can also choose a chart by using the Chart⇨Chart Type, which displays the Chart Type dialog box (see Figure 16-10). Select a chart type from the Chart type list. The available charts within the selected category appear in the Chart sub-type area of the dialog box. Double-click the one you want.

Figure 16-10: The Chart Type dialog box.

	Table 16-3 **Chart Types Available in Graph**
Chart Type	**Use**
Area	Shows how values change in proportion to a total. An area chart does not handle multiple series very well, though, and large values tend to swallow the representation of smaller ones.
Bar	Compares items or shows individual figures at a specific time. A bar chart can handle multiple series well.
Bubble	Displays data with x-axis and y-axis as bubbles.
Column	Shows variations over time. Two options (stacked and 100%) show relationships to a whole.
Cone	Shows data as clustered cone columns.
Cylinder	Shows data as clustered cylinder columns.
Doughnut	Shows parts to a whole like a pie chart, but it can show more than one data series, unlike the pie chart.
Line	Shows trends in data or changes in a group of values over time.
Pie	Portrays one series as a relationship to a whole.
Pyramid	Displays data as clustered pyramid columns.
Radar	Shows changes or frequencies of data series relative to a center point and to one another.
Stock	Displays stock High-Low-Close data.
Surface	Shows relationships between large amounts of data. Appears as if a rubber sheet were stretched over a 3-D column chart.
XY (Scatter)	Shows the relationship between two sets of numbers. You can use XY charts to discover patterns.

Excluding data in a chart

At times, you may not want Word to include some rows or columns of data in a chart. For example, you may input data for several different charts in one data-sheet. As a result, you may want to display only some of the information in a certain chart. Inserting and removing rows and columns lets you see changes in the chart by adding or removing data. It does not actually remove the data in rows and columns but suspends the selected information from appearing in the chart.

Position the cursor where you want to exclude a row or column, and choose the Data⇨Exclude Row/Col to exclude the data from the chart. The adjustment to the chart occurs automatically. To restore the excluded data to the chart, choose Data⇨Include Row/Col. You can also include or exclude rows and columns by double-clicking the column or row header in the datasheet.

Customizing and Refining Charts

Once you've created a chart, you can make a variety of changes to a chart using the Chart Options dialog box (see Figure 16-11). Choose Chart➪Chart Options to display the Chart Options dialog box. The following paragraphs describe the functions of the six tabs (Titles, Axes, Gridlines, Legend, Data Labels, and Data Table) in the dialog box:

✦ The Titles tab (see Figure 16-11) lets you add titles for your chart and the X and Y axes. An *axis* consists of the lines bordering the plot area of a chart that provide a frame of reference for comparison of data. A 2-D chart usually has two axes, and a 3-D chart has two or three axes. For most charts, data values are plotted along the value (y) axis, which is usually vertical, and categories are plotted on the (x) axis, which is usually horizontal. Pie and doughnut charts don't have axes.

✦ The Axes tab lets you turn on or off the display of axis values. By default, the chart appears with axis labels and values.

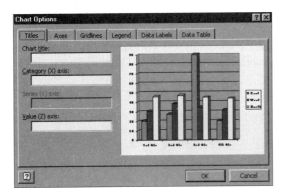

Figure 16-11: The Chart Options dialog box.

✦ The Gridlines tab lets you add vertical and horizontal gridlines. When you create a chart, by default it has some gridlines to make reading data values and categories easier. You can change the kind of gridlines displayed. Major gridlines delineate larger ranges of values or categories along the axis. Minor gridlines break down the ranges further. Choose the Gridlines tab in the Chart Options dialog box.

✦ The Legend tab lets you display or not display the Legend, and it lets you decide where you want to position it. When you create a chart, by default it has a legend to identify the different data series displayed. A chart *legend* details the name of each series and indicates how each series is represented (color or shading, for example). If you deleted the legend from an existing chart, you can add it by clicking the Legend button on the Standard toolbar.

✦ The Data Labels tab lets you add data labels to a data series, to an individual data point or marker, or to all data points on the chart. The chart type assigned to your selected data points determines the kinds of labels you can add. A data marker is a bar, area, dot, slice, or other symbol in a chart that represents a single data point or value originating from a datasheet cell. Related data markers in a chart comprise a data series.

✦ The Data Table tab lets you turn on or off the display of the chart's corresponding data table.

Formatting Charts

When the Graph program is activated, you can format different parts of a chart by double-clicking the particular part in the chart display. For example, double-clicking a chart legend displays a Format Legend dialog box, which lets you format and fine-tune the chart's legend. Depending on the chart type you choose, different dialog boxes may appear or different options may appear in the dialog boxes. The following items explain the formatting dialog boxes that appear when you double-click particular sections of a 3-D bar chart after activating the Graph program:

✦ Double-clicking a chart's gridlines displays the Format Gridlines dialog box (see Figure 16-12). The Patterns tab lets you specify the style, color, and weight of the gridlines. The Scale tab lets you specify the scale used for your gridlines.

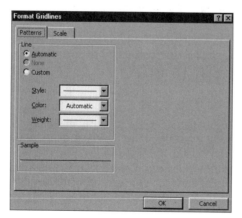

Figure 16-12: The Format Gridlines dialog box.

✦ Double-clicking a chart's data series displays the Format Data Series dialog box (see Figure 16-13). The tabs in this dialog box change, depending on the type of chart you're using.

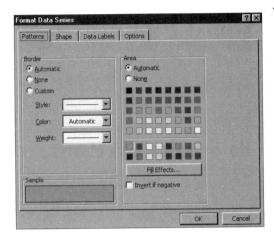

Figure 16-13: The Format Data Series dialog box.

✦ Double-clicking a chart's data axis displays the Format Axis dialog box (see Figure 16-14).

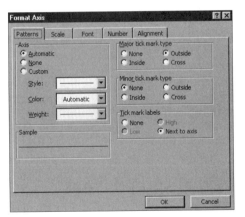

Figure 16-14: The Format Axis dialog box.

✦ Double-clicking the chart's legend displays the Format Legend dialog box.

✦ Double-clicking in the white space of the chart area displays the Format Chart Area dialog box. This dialog box includes the Patterns and Font tabs.

✦ Double-clicking the wall of a chart displays the Format Walls dialog box.

✦ Double-clicking anywhere in the Plot Area (the white space at the intersection of the X axis and the Y axis) displays the Format Plot Area dialog box.

Getting Data and Charts from Other Sources

In many cases, you already have the data you want to chart in a table or in a spreadsheet file. You can import into Graph's datasheet any information that you have developed in another application, or tables in Word documents. The following sections explain how to bring in data from a Word table or an Excel spreadsheet.

Getting data from Word tables into charts

Graph lets you easily copy information in a Word table into the datasheet. After the data is in the datasheet, you can create the type of chart you want in the same way you do when you enter the information in the datasheet. This handy feature saves you the tedious task of reentering in a datasheet the data that's already in a table. Converting data from a table to a chart lets you show data in the table and in the chart. To convert tables into charts:

1. Enter the data and text in a table. (Choose the Table button on the toolbar to insert a table. Refer to Chapter 12 for information on tables.)

2. Select the table.

3. Choose Insert⇨Picture⇨Chart or choose the Insert⇨Object⇨Create New tab and select Microsoft Graph 97 Chart. The standard Datasheet window and graph windows appear.

You can also select the data in the table by using the Copy button or the Edit⇨Copy command in Word. You then activate Graph, display the Datasheet window, select the data you want to replace or click the cell from which you want the table data to start, and then choose Edit⇨Paste (or press Ctrl+V). The data from the table appears in the Datasheet window.

Getting data from an Excel spreadsheet

If you use Excel, you may want to use information that you already used in a spreadsheet and bring it into the Datasheet window. You can import spreadsheet data directly into Graph's datasheets from Excel spreadsheets.

You can also link or embed a spreadsheet from Excel by using Word's linking and embedding features, which are explained in Chapter 15. Linking a spreadsheet from Excel to Word lets you use Excel's full features. To import spreadsheet data into Graph's datasheet:

1. Place the insertion point where you want the chart, and open Graph by clicking the Chart button or choosing the Insert⇨Object⇨Create New tab⇨Microsoft Graph 97 Chart.

2. To erase all the sample data from the datasheet, click the datasheet. Press Ctrl+A to select all the data, or click the area where the row and column headers meet. Press the Delete key to delete the data.

3. Position the cursor in the top left row of the now-blank datasheet, and click it to make the cell active.

4. Click the Import Data button or choose Edit⇨Import File to open the Import File dialog box, shown in Figure 16-15.

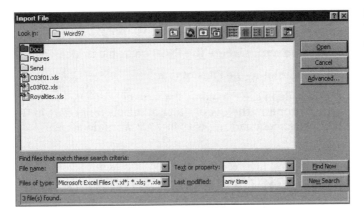

Figure 16-15: The Import File dialog box.

5. Choose the worksheet file you want to import and click Open. The Import Data Options dialog box appears (see Figure 16-16). Do one of the following:

   • To import the entire worksheet, choose the Entire sheet radio button in the Import group.

   • To tell Word what range of cells to import from the Excel spreadsheet, choose the Range radio button.

Figure 16-16: The Import Data Options dialog box.

6. Choose OK. The data is automatically entered in the Datasheet window.

Importing charts from Excel

The Graph program lets you import a chart generated in Excel. Once you import the chart, you can work with it by using the Graph program. To import a chart from Excel:

1. Position the cursor where you want the chart to appear in your Word document.

2. Open the Graph program.

3. Click the Import Chart button on the Graph Standard toolbar, or choose Edit➪Import File. The Import File dialog box appears.

4. Navigate to the directory where the Excel chart file is located.

5. Choose the file format in the Files of type list.

6. Select the chart file in the File name list, and choose OK. A message box prompts you to confirm the overwriting of the current chart in Graph. Choose OK. The Excel chart appears in your Word document.

Working with Microsoft Equation 3.0

You can use Microsoft Equation 3.0 to add fractions, exponents, integrals, and so on to Word documents. You start building an equation by opening Equation, shown in Figure 16-17. The Greek-looking items in the top row of the toolbar are symbols, such as operators or letters, that you may want to insert into an equation. The items on the bottom row are called *templates:* essentially, they are the fences that hold the mathematical symbols.

You build an equation by assembling templates and associated symbols in the *slot* (a box bounded by dotted lines), which appears in the work area. As you build the formula, the slot changes in position and size. In fact, more than one slot may be associated with a formula.

Microsoft Equation 3.0 is not installed automatically when you install Office 97. If you want to use Equation, you need to install it from the original Microsoft distribution media (CD-ROM):

1. Run the Office 97 Setup.

2. Click the Add/Remove button.

3. Select Office Tools and then click the Change Option button.

4. Click the Equation Editor check box and then click OK.

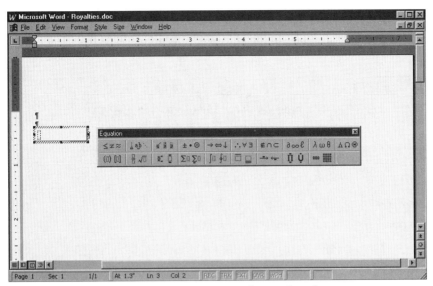

Figure 16-17: The Microsoft Equation 3.0 window and toolbar.

To open Equation:

1. Position the insertion point where you want to place the equation.

2. Choose Insert⇨Object.

3. Choose the Create New tab.

4. Under Object type, select Microsoft Equation 3.0. Choose OK. The Equation Editor opens.

You can start Equation Editor anytime while working in Word. By default, the Equation Editor is available only from the menu, but you can add the Equation Editor button to your toolbar. If you plan to use the Equation Editor routinely, you may want to add the button to your toolbar.

To add the Equation button to the toolbar, choose Tools⇨Customize to display the Customize dialog box. Choose the Toolbars tab, and select the Insert option in the Categories list. The available toolbar buttons for the Insert menu commands appear in the Buttons area. Drag the Equation Editor button (the button with the square root sign on it) from the Toolbars dialog box to your toolbar. Click OK to close the Customize dialog box.

Positioning the insertion point

To move within a formula, use the keystrokes listed in Table 16-4.

Table 16-4 Keystrokes for Moving the Cursor	
Press	*The Cursor Moves*
Tab	To the end of the slot or to the next logical slot
Shift+Tab	To the end of the preceding slot
Right-arrow key	Right one unit in the current slot
Left-arrow key	Left one unit in the current slot
Up-arrow key	Up one line
Down-arrow key	Down one line
Home	To the beginning of the current slot
End	To the end of the current slot

Building a sample equation

You never can tell when you may feel that indescribable need to write to your mother about frictionless incompressible fluids and Torricelli's Equation. (Torricelli's Equation states that velocity equals two times the square root of the acceleration due to gravity times the distance between the liquid surface and the center of the nozzle.) Luckily, Equation Editor can ease your discomfort. To build Torricelli's Equation:

1. Position the insertion point where you want to place the equation.

2. Choose Insert➪Object.

3. Choose the Create New tab.

4. Under Object type, select Microsoft Equation 3.0, and then choose OK. The Equation Editor opens.

5. Type **V=**.

6. Click the Fractions and Radicals button, and select the square root symbol.

7. Type **2gH** in the slot under the square root.

Adjusting spacing and alignment

You should have little need to adjust an equation's formatting because Equation Editor automatically handles subscripts and superscripts, as well as most other formatting. Nonetheless, you can manually adjust the spacing and alignment of equations in three ways.

First, you can use the Spaces and Ellipses button on the Equation toolbar. This button allows you to include spaces that act just like characters, taking up room from zero length to the equivalent of a quad space.

Second, when Equation Editor is open, you can choose Format➪Spacing, which displays the Spacing dialog box (see Figure 16-18). You can use this dialog box to adjust line, matrix, subscript, and superscript spacing.

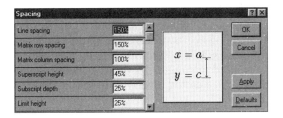

Figure 16-18: The Spacing dialog box.

The final method, called *nudging,* is more precise. Select the item you want to adjust, hold down the Ctrl key, and click the arrow pointing in the direction you want the element to move. The selected element moves one pixel per click. (Pixel is short for picture element, which represents the smallest element of a video display.) Your computer screen is broken up into thousands of pixels (dots).

Summary

You now have the fundamentals for working with Microsoft Graph 97 Chart and Microsoft Equation 3.0, which come with Word. In this chapter, you learned how to:

✦ Start the Graph program by choosing Insert⇨Object to display the Object dialog box, choosing Microsoft Graph 97 Chart from the Create New tab, and clicking OK. You also learned how to place the Graph button on a toolbar by choosing Tools⇨Customize to display the Customize dialog box and dragging the Graph icon to the toolbar.

✦ Format data in a data sheet as currency or percentage, add commas, and increase or decrease the decimal point placement by using the last five buttons on the Formatting toolbar.

✦ Change the chart type by clicking the down arrow on the Chart Type button or choosing Format⇨Chart Type.

✦ Display the Format Gridlines dialog box by double-clicking a chart's gridlines; display the Format Data Series dialog box by double-clicking a chart's data series; display the Format Axis dialog box by double-clicking a chart's data axis; display the Format Legend dialog box by double-clicking a chart's legend; display the Format Chart Area dialog box by double-clicking a chart's chart area; and display the Format Plot Area dialog box by double-clicking a chart's plot area.

✦ Get data from a Word table by selecting the table, then opening the Graph program from the Object dialog box, and clicking OK.

✦ Import data from an Excel spreadsheet by choosing Edit⇨Import Data or clicking the Import Data button on the Standard toolbar.

✦ Open the Equation Editor by choosing Insert⇨Object to display the Object dialog box and selecting Microsoft Equation 3.0. The Equation Editor toolbar appears, so you can add mathematical symbols by choosing the appropriate symbol from buttons on the Equation Editor toolbar.

Where to go next...

✦ To learn more about linking other Windows 95 applications to your Word documents, see Chapter 15.

✦ To learn more about the laying out charts and equations in a Word document, see Chapter 14.

✦   ✦   ✦

Spreading the Word: Publishing Web Documents and Working with Workgroups

Creating Basic HTML Documents with Word 97

CHAPTER

17

Word 97 includes a new, built-in Web authoring environment for creating your own Web pages. Word's Web authoring tools are based on many of the same commands you use to create Word documents making it easy to create a Web document. Word simplifies authoring Web pages by providing WYSIWYG (What You See Is What You Get) support for authoring Web pages. You can build Web documents and forms quickly by using wizards, templates, and dragging and dropping Web page elements. You can also choose predefined visual elements for these pages including background colors, bullets, horizontal lines, and many other elements. For your text documents, you can tap into Word's powerful proofing tools to check spelling and grammar. This chapter takes you through creating Web pages using Word's Web authoring tools. Because many of these tools are the same as the ones used in Word, you can reference the appropriate chapters for more details on a topic.

Note   ᵔ Web authoring tools in Word 97 allow you to create ⸺ressive multimedia Web pages. However, they don't ⸺ide the more powerful features needed to create image ⸺ps, scripts, server includes, timestamps, and other capabilities that are linked to a Web server. For these capabilities, you'll need a more advanced Web authoring program, such as Microsoft FrontPage 97 or, for more advanced users, Microsoft Internet Studio.

Creating a Web Page

Word gives you two ways to create Web pages. The first method is using a Wizard or template. The second way is to convert an existing Word document to HTML. Converting an existing Word document into HTML formats is explained later in this chapter.

The easiest way to get started creating a Web page is using the Web Page Wizard. This Wizard provides a collection of different layouts, color themes, and text organizations to work from. You can easily customize these templates to make them yours. If you want to create your Web page from scratch, you can choose a Blank Web Page template.

To create a Web page using the Web Page Wizard:

1. Choose File⇨New to display the New dialog box.

2. Click the Web Pages tab. Figure 17-1 shows the Web Pages tab.

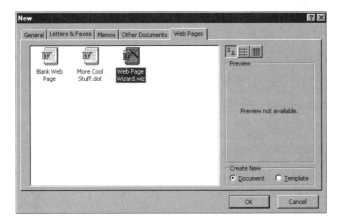

Figure 17-1: The Web Pages tab in the New dialog box.

3. Double-click the Web Page Wizard icon. A new Web document appears with the Web Page Wizard dialog box displayed. You can select the type of Web page style you want to preview. For example, selecting 2-Column Layout shows how the Web page appears in the document window behind the Web Page Wizard dialog box (see Figure 17-2). You can preview any Web page type in the list by simply clicking it.

4. Select the Web page type you want to use, and then click Next. The next Web Page Wizard page displays a list of visual style options. Like the layout styles, selecting a visual style displays it in the document window. For example, clicking the Outdoors visual style displays an outdoor motif, as shown in Figure 17-3.

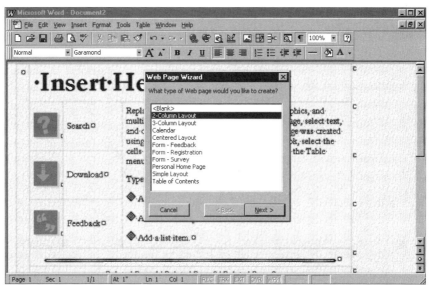

Figure 17-2: The 2-Column Layout displayed in the document window.

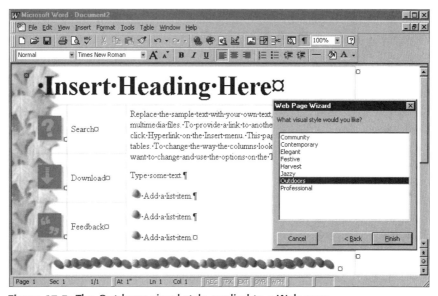

Figure 17-3: The Outdoors visual style applied to a Web page.

5. Select the visual style you want, and then click Finish. The Web page appears as a document in Word's Web authoring environment.

6. Choose File➪Save to save the document. The document is saved as an HTML document with an .html filename extension.

Once you have created a Web page using the Wizard, the page appears as any document would in Word. However, you're in Word's Web authoring environment. The menus and available toolbars reflect the subset of Word features you can use in creating and editing your Web pages.

You can also create Web pages using the Blank Web Page template. Choose File⇨New to display the New dialog box, and then click the Web Pages tab. Double-click the Blank Web Page template. You can then build your Web document using Word's tools just as you would if you used the Wizard.

The More Cool Stuff icon in the Web Pages tab (in the New dialog box) displays the document shown in Figure 17-4. Clicking the Microsoft Word Web Site connects you to the site so you can download stuff if you have Internet access setup in Windows 95.

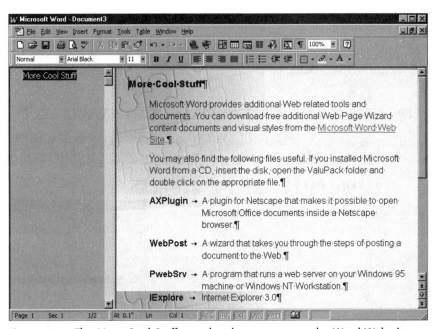

Figure 17-4: The More Cool Stuff template lets you access the Word Web site.

Using Styles to Insert HTML Markup

Word provides three methods for inserting HTML tags. The first way is using styles to add the most common HTML tags. With a Web document in Word, the Style box on the Formatting toolbar contains a collection of common HTML formats along with some basic Word document styles that work within the Web authoring environment. The second method is entering the HTML tags that you want, selecting it, and then choosing the HTML Markup style from the Style box. The final option is to enter HTML tags directly when you are viewing the source code of the Web page.

Adding HTML tags as styles

To add any HTML style, enter the text of object you want in the Web page, and then select it. Choose the HTML style option from the Style box on the Formatting toolbar.

Tip To see the complete list of styles in the Style box on the Formatting toolbar, first click somewhere in the document to deselect the Style box. Then press the Shift key and click the down arrow on the Style box. All the style names appear in the list.

The HTML Markup style is the generic style for defining any HTML tag in your Web page. You enter the tag and text or object, and then select it. Choose the HTML Markup style from the Style box on the Formatting toolbar. Applying the HTML Markup style will format the text as hidden if the Show/Hide button is not active. Clicking the button displays the HTML source code as hidden text.

Like working with styles in Word documents, you can add styles to the Style box. If you want to see all the HTML styles that come with Word and their definitions, choose Format➪Style to display the Style dialog box (see Figure 17-5). Choose All styles under List at the bottom-left corner of the dialog box to show all the styles that come with Word, including HTML styles.

Note For more information on working with styles, see Chapter 11.

Figure 17-5: The Style dialog box.

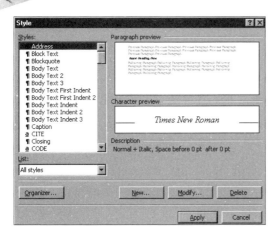

Entering HTML tags in the HTML Source view

By default Word hides the HTML tags, which are collectively referred to as source code. However, you can easily view HTML source code and work with HTML source code directly using the HTML Source view. With a previously saved Web page opened, choose View⇨HTML Source. The HTML source code appears in the document window, as shown in Figure 17-6. You can enter and edit HTML tags in the document using the same tools you use to work with text in a Word document. To exit the HTML Source view, choose the Exit HTML Source button on the Standard toolbar, or choose View⇨Exit HTML Source.

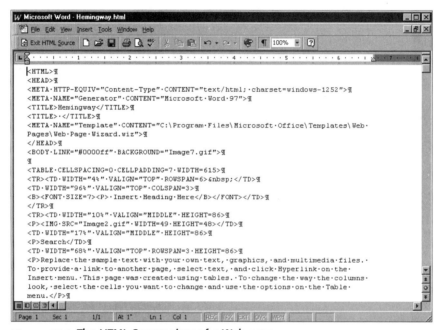

Figure 17-6: The HTML Source view of a Web page.

Inserting Hyperlinks

Hyperlinks are what make the connections to information possible via the World Wide Web. A hyperlink can jump to a location in the current document or Web page, to a different document, or to a file. You can also use hyperlinks to jump to multimedia files, such as sound files or video clips. To insert a hyperlink, do the following:

1. In a previously saved Web page, position the insertion pointer where you want the hyperlink, or select the text or object you want to become a hyperlink.

2. Choose Insert⇨Hyperlink, press Ctrl+K, or click the Insert Hyperlink button. The Insert Hyperlink dialog box appears. (see Figure 17-7).

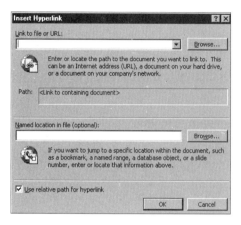

Figure 17-7: The Insert Hyperlink dialog box.

3. Enter the file or URL you want to link to in the Link to file or URL box. If you want to add a hyperlink to a part of a file by using a named location (book-mark, a named range, or a database object) enter the path in the Named location in file box or locate the information source using the Browse button.

4. Click the Use relative path for hyperlink check box to base the hyperlink on the location of the current file relative to the Web page with the hyperlink. This setting lets you create hyperlinks to files you may want to move later. Clear this check box if you want to use the absolute path for the hyperlink.

5. Click OK. The selected object in your Web page appears as a hyperlink. For a text hyperlink, the text appears as underlined blue text.

When you move the pointer over any hyperlink in your Web page, a ScreenTip appears to show the path and file of the linked object.

Drag and drop hyperlinks

You can create a hyperlink by dragging selected text or graphics from a Word document or PowerPoint slide, a selected range in Excel, or a selected database object in Microsoft Access to your Web page. When you drag text and graphics from an Office 97 program to a Web page, Word recognizes the location of the information:

1. Display both files on the screen.

2. In the destination document, select the text, graphic, or other item you want to jump to.

3. Use the right mouse button to drag the selection to your Web page.

4. Click Create Hyperlink Here.

You can also copy and paste text as a hyperlink to achieve the same effect using the Edit⇨Paste as Hyperlink command.

Turning filenames into hyperlinks using automatic formatting

By using the automatic formatting features in Word, you can create a hyperlink just by typing the address of the file you want to jump to. Network paths and Internet addresses can automatically become hyperlink display text (hot spots) that the reader clicks to jump to the hyperlink destination.

1. Choose Tools⇨AutoCorrect.

2. Click the AutoFormat As You Type tab.

3. Under the Replace as you type setting, click the Internet and network paths with hyperlinks check box.

4. Click OK.

When you type the address of the file located on a network or on the Internet, Word changes the address to a hyperlink. The address of the file becomes the display text the reader clicks.

Managing Files and Links on Web Pages

When authoring Web pages, you need to manage the related files and plan the hyperlinks so the related files will be activated correctly when the pages are placed on a Web server. When files are connected with your Web pages, such as images or video clips, you need to use the relative links. When you apply links to any files in your Web pages, Word automatically saves these items as separate files in the same location as your Web page. You'll need to move these files along with your Web pages so your links will work.

Previewing Your Web Page

While your Web page in Word's authoring environment looks a lot like the finished Web page as a user would view it — it's not. You need to choose File⇨Web Page Preview or click the Web Page Preview button on the Standard toolbar to display your Web document in the Internet Explorer Web browser (see Figure 17-8). If you have made any changes that you didn't save before choosing Web Page Preview, Word prompts you to save your changes before executing the preview. Click OK. Word automatically saves your changes and displays your Web document in the Internet Explorer. From the Web browser, you can return to the Word Web authoring mode by clicking the Edit button on the Internet Explorer's toolbar.

Figure 17-8: A Web document displayed in Internet Explorer.

Adding Basic Visual Elements to Your Web Pages

Web pages are a visual medium that requires the use of visual elements to enhance the presentation of your material and to provide structure to your documents. These basic visual elements include background colors, horizontal lines, colored text, bullets, and numbering.

Backgrounds

One of the first things you may want to add to your Web document is a different background color. By default, when you use the Blank Web Page template, the background color is white. You can choose a different color or add a textured background. To add a different background to your Web page:

1. Open the Web page on which you want to change the background color.

2. Choose Format⇨Background or the Background button on the Formatting toolbar. A pop-up menu of fill options appears.

3. If you want to add a solid color background, click the color you want; or choose More Colors to display more color options in the Colors dialog box (see Figure 17-9). This dialog box lets you choose from an expanded color palette or create your own custom colors.

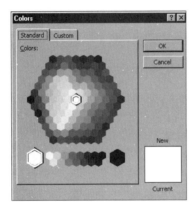

Figure 17-9: The Colors dialog box.

4. If you want to add a texture, choose Fill Effects. The Fill Effects dialog box appears (see Figure 17-10). You can select from the pre-made textures, or you can click the Other Textures button to access other graphic files to use as a background texture.

5. Click OK.

If you're using Office 97, navigating to Backgrounds folder via the Fill Effects dialog box (Program Files/Microsoft Office/Clip Art/Backgrounds) displays a list of several other background textures in GIF format. The Word 97 ValuPack also includes a Texture folder that includes a collection of texture files in JPEG format. You can display these textures using the Other Textures button in the Fill Effects dialog box.

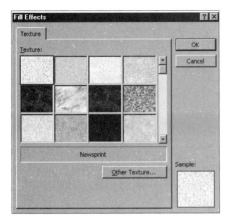

Figure 17-10: The Fill Effects dialog box.

Text colors

You can change the color of text in your Web documents on an as-needed basis or by defining what colors are used for different types of text. Choosing Format⇨Text Colors displays the Text Colors dialog box (see Figure 17-11). In this dialog box, you can specify text colors for your body text, hyperlink text, and the text following a hyperlink. You can also select any text in your Web page, and then click the Font Color button on the Formatting toolbar. You can specify the color for the Font Color button by clicking the down arrow to the right of the button, which displays a color palette.

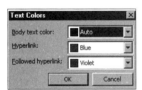

Figure 17-11: The Text Colors dialog box.

Horizontal lines

Horizontal lines are commonly used on Web pages to separate logical sections. Word provides a number of line styles you can use. To add a horizontal line:

1. Click where you want to insert the line in your Web document.

2. Choose Insert⇨Horizontal Line. The Horizontal Line dialog box appears (see Figure 17-12).

Figure 17-12: The Horizontal Line dialog box.

3. Click the line style you want; or choose the <u>M</u>ore button to display the Insert Picture dialog box with additional line styles, as shown in Figure 17-13.

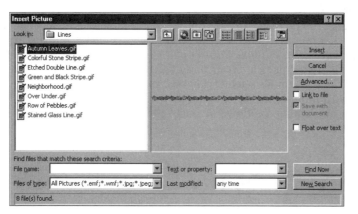

Figure 17-13: The Insert Picture dialog box with more line styles.

4. After selecting a line style, click OK. The line is inserted into your Web page.

Bullets and numbering

You can create bulleted and numbered lists when authoring Web pages similarly to how you create bulleted lists in Word documents. Choosing F<u>o</u>rmat⇨Bullets and <u>N</u>umbering displays the Bullets and Numbering dialog box (see Figure 17-14). You can choose graphic bullets for your Web documents. Clicking the <u>M</u>ore button displays more bullet graphic options in the Insert Picture dialog box (see Figure 17-15). Selecting the bullet item previews the button in the Preview area of the dialog box. Clicking the Numbered tab in the Bullets and Numbering dialog box lets you format your numbered lists.

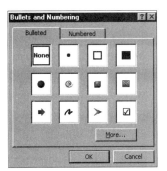

Figure 17-14: The Bullets and Numbering dialog box.

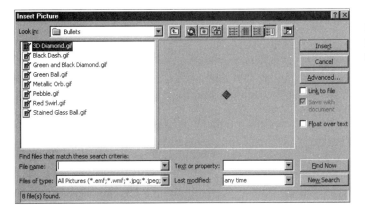

Figure 17-15: The Insert Picture dialog box with more bullet graphic options.

Adding Multimedia Elements to Your Web Pages

Images, sounds, and video clips make your Web pages come alive. Word's Web authoring environment provides tools for adding images, audio, and video clips. Keep in mind that sound and video files can be large files that can be a problem for Web users accessing the Web using slower speed modems (9.6Kbps and 14.4Kbps).

Note If you're creating Web pages for the Internet, make sure you use file formats that are de facto standards for the Internet. These file formats include GIF and JPEG for images, AU for audio, and MOV (Movie) for videos.

Images

Pictures are big part of Web documents, and Word makes it easy to add them to a Web document. Once the picture is inserted in your Web document, you can work with it as you would a picture in Word. If you insert an image that is not either a GIF or JPEG format file, the image will automatically be converted to GIF. Word saves the images as Image.gif, Image1.gif, Image2.gif, and so on. If you insert a JPEG image, the JPEG format and filename extension (.jpg) are retained. To add any picture to your Web document

1. Click where you want to insert the picture, and then choose Insert⟶Picture⟶ From File or click the Insert Picture button on the Standard toolbar. The Insert Picture dialog box appears (refer to Figure 17-15).

2. Navigate to the folder containing the image you want to use and select the file.

3. Click Insert. The picture is inserted into your Web page.

The Clipart folder on the Office 97 CD-ROM includes a number of images in GIF and JPEG formats. Check out the Photo folder for a large collection of images. Another way to add images to your Web pages is choosing Insert⟶Picture⟶Clip Art, which displays the Microsoft Clip Gallery 3.0 dialog box (see Figure 17-16). Click the Pictures tab to display images. All the images in the Pictures tab are JPEG files.

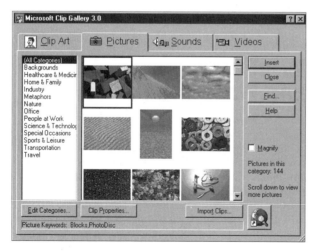

Figure 17-16: The Microsoft Clip Gallery 3.0 dialog box.

You can use the pictures in the Clip Art tab. These pictures are in the Windows Metafiles format, which is not a standard file format on the World Wide Web. However, when you insert the file, Word automatically converts it to a GIF format. You can always check the file type by clicking the Clip Properties button in Microsoft Clip Gallery 3.0 dialog box.

Note   You can use Microsoft Photo Editor, which comes with Microsoft Office, to create GIF images with transparent areas for Web pages. When an image contains a transparent area, the background color or texture of the page shows through the image.

Animated images

Animated images are GIF files that display movements. For example, using an animated GIF file of a pair of scissors shows them cutting. Another animated GIF image might show a bouncing ball. You can use these to create activity for your bullets or buttons. You insert an animated GIF file as you would any graphic file, as explained earlier. Because they are GIF files, they are supported by most Web browsers.

Drawing objects

Drawing objects, such as AutoShapes, text boxes, and WordArt effects, can be inserted into Web pages as GIF files. You can insert drawing objects into Web pages by first creating a Microsoft Word Picture object, and then using the options on the Drawing toolbar. When you save your Web page, Word converts these objects to GIF images. Once you close your file, you will not be able to edit the image in Word again. If you need to update a drawing, save a copy of your file as a Word document (*.doc).

Sounds

Word's Web authoring environment provides several tools for integrating sounds into your Web documents. For Web users to hear background sounds, they must have a sound system installed, and their Web browser must support the sound format of the file you inserted. You can insert sound files in WAV, MID, AU, AIF, RMI, SND, and MP2 (MPEG audio) formats. The most common sound file formats on the Internet are AU.

You can add a sound file to a Web document using the Sounds tab in the Microsoft Clip Gallery. Once the file is inserted in your Web page, it appears with a speaker icon. Double-clicking the icon plays the sound. You can also insert a hyperlink that the user can click to download the sound file instead of playing it. See the "Inserting Hyperlinks" section in this chapter.

Word also lets you add a background sound to a Web page. A background sound activates a sound anytime a user opens or returns to the Web page. To insert a background sound:

1. Choose Insert⇨Background Sound⇨Properties. The Background Sound dialog box appears (see Figure 17-17).

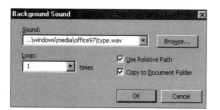

Figure 17-17: The Background Sound dialog box.

2. In the Background Sound dialog box, enter the path or URL of the sound file, or click Browse to locate the file.

3. In the Loop box, click the number of times you want the sound to repeat.

4. To copy the sound to the same folder as your Web page, select the Copy to Document Folder check box. To use a relative path, a path that is relative to your current page, select the Use Relative Path check box.

5. Click OK.

To review the sound while you're authoring the Web page, choose Insert⇨Background Sound⇨Play.

Caution The background sound is played automatically every time your page is opened or returned to. For frequently opened pages, such as home pages, this repetition can become annoying. Also avoid using the Infinite option in the Loop setting, because the sound will play continually.

Videos

You can add an inline video to your Web page, which means the video is downloaded when the user opens the page. You can determine whether the video will play when the page is opened, or when the user points to the video. You can also insert a hyperlink to a video, which means the user can click the hyperlink to download the video and play it.

Note Microsoft videos are in the AVI format, which is not the standard format for video clips on the Internet. Instead use the QuickTime .MOV format for your video files.

To insert a video into a Web document:

1. Make sure you save your Web document before you add a video clip.

2. Choose Insert⇨Video. The Video Clip dialog box appears (see Figure 17-18).

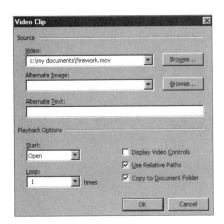

Figure 17-18: The Video Clip dialog box.

3. Enter the address or URL of the video file you want in the Video box, or click Browse to search for the file.

4. Enter the address or URL of the graphics file in the Alternate Image box that you want to designate as a substitute when the user's browser doesn't support video.

5. Type the text you want to appear in place of the video or alternative image in the Alternate Text box when the user's browser doesn't support videos, or when the server where the video or image is located is not available.

6. In the Start list, choose an option to specify how the video will play. The Open option causes the video to play when the users downloads the Web page. The Mouse-ver option causes the video to play when the pointer moves over the video. The Both option causes the video to play in both ways.

7. Enter the number of times you want the video to repeat playing in the Loop box. You can choose 1 through 5 times or Infinite.

8. If you want to display video controls while you're authoring Web pages, click the Display Video Controls check box. To copy the video to the same folder as your Web page, use the Copy to Document Folder setting. To use a relative path to the current Web page, use the Use Relative Paths.

9. Click OK. Word displays a information message telling you some browsers don't support inline videos. Choose Continue, and the video clip is added to your Web page.

Caution Video clips are typically large files; use them sparingly.

Text marquee

Word 97's scrolling text feature lets you operate a text marquee that displays text moving across a Web page. After you create your scrolling text, the scrolling text box appears as a box in your Web document. You can adjust the size of the scrolling text box by dragging the handles. To create scrolling text:

1. Choose Insert⇨Scrolling Text. The Scrolling Text dialog box appears (see Figure 17-19).

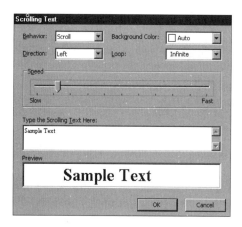

Figure 17-19: The Scrolling Text dialog box.

2. Type the text you want to appear as scrolling text in the Type the Scrolling Text Here text box.

3. In the Loop box, click the number of times you want the text to scroll. The default Infinite makes the text continuously scroll. You can also choose 1, 2, 3, 4, or 5.

4. To adjust the speed the text scrolls, move the slider control in the Speed setting.

5. To define the behavior of the scrolling text, choose an option in the Behavior list. The settings are Scroll, Slide, Alternate. The default setting is Scroll. The Slide setting makes the text slide from side to side, and the Alternate setting alternates between the Scroll and Slide settings.

6. To specify the direction the text scrolls, choose the Left or Right option in the Direction setting.

7. To specify a background color for the scrolling text, choose the color you want from Background Color list.

8. Click OK.

Adding Tables

Working with tables in Web pages is similar to working with tables in Word documents. You can use the Table➪Draw Table to create and modify the structure of your tables. You can insert a table grid by using the Table➪Insert Table command or the Insert Table button on the Standard toolbar.

You can add borders to tables on Web pages using the Table➪Borders command, which displays the Table Borders dialog box (see Figure 17-20). Borders that you apply to tables on Web pages have a 3-D appearance in Web browsers, as shown in Figure 17-21.

Figure 17-20: The Table Borders dialog box.

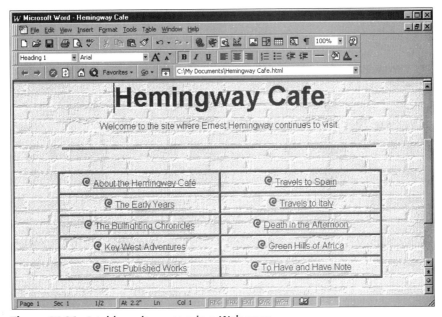

Figure 17-21: A table as it appears in a Web page.

You can change the background color or shading of tables by using the Table⇨ Table Properties command. The Table Properties dialog box appears (see Figure 17-22). You can change the way that text wraps around the table, the distance between the table and surrounding text, and the spacing between columns.

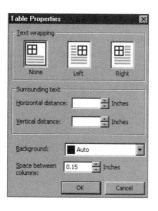

Figure 17-22: The Table Properties dialog box.

The Table⇨Cell Properties command displays the Cell Properties dialog box (see Figure 17-23). This command lets you align the contents of a table cell in a table. You can change the height of selected rows and the width of selected columns. You can also change of background of selected cells.

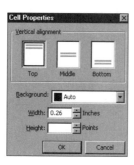

Figure 17-23: The Cell Properties dialog box.

Note   For more information on working with Tables, see Chapter 12.

Saving Word Documents in HTML

You can also create a Web page by saving an existing Word document in HTML. However, some aspects of your document may not be available in HTML and, therefore, may not appear correctly. When you save a Word document as a Web page, Word closes the document and then reopens it in HTML format. Formatting and other items that aren't supported by HTML are removed from the file. Table 17-1 describes the elements that Word changes or removes upon conversion.

To save an existing Word document into HTML format, choose <u>F</u>ile⇨Save as <u>H</u>TML. The Save As HTML dialog box appears. Enter the filename, if you want to change the name, and then choose <u>S</u>ave. The file is saved with an .html filename extension.

Table 17-1
Word Elements that Change or Are Removed Upon Conversion to an HTML Document

Element	Description of Changes
Comments	Comments you insert with the Insert⇨Comments command are removed. After saving the document in HTML format, you can enter comments and apply the Comments style. The comments will not appear when the Web page is displayed in a Web browser.
Font sizes	Fonts are mapped to the closest HTML size available, which ranges from size 1 to 7. These numbers are not point sizes but are used as instructions for font sizes by Web browsers. Word displays the fonts in sizes ranging from 9 to 36.
Emboss, shadow, engrave, small caps, double all caps, strikethrough, and outline text effects	All these character formats are lost in conversion, but the text remains.
Bold, strikethrough, italic, and underline	All these effects are converted. However, some special underline effects such as dotted underlines are converted to a single underline, and some underline effects aren't converted.
Animated text	Animations are lost, but the text remains. For an animated effect, insert scrolling text into your page using Word's Scrolling text feature.

(continued)

Table 17-1 *(continued)*

Element	Description of Changes
Graphics	Graphics are converted to .gif format, unless the graphics are in .jpg (JPEG) format. Drawing objects, such as text boxes and shapes, are not converted. Lines are converted to horizontal lines.
Tabs	Tabs are converted to the HTML tab character, represented in HTML source as &#9. Tabs may appear as spaces in some Web browsers, so you may want to use indents or a table instead.
Fields	Field codes are removed and field results are converted to text. For example, if you insert a DATE field, the text of the date converts, but the date will not be automatically updated.
Table of contents, table of authorities, and indexes	The information is converted, but indexes and tables of contents, figures, and authorities can't be updated automatically after conversion because they are based on field codes. The table of contents displays asterisks in place of page numbers; these asterisks are hyperlinks that the reader can click to navigate through the Web page. You can replace the asterisks with text that you want to have displayed for the hyperlinks.
Drop caps	Drop caps are removed. In the Web page authoring environment, you can increase the size of one letter by selecting it and then clicking the Increase Font Size button. If you have a graphic image of a letter, you can insert it in front of the text to create a drop cap effect.
Drawing objects (Auto, Shapes, text effects text boxes, and shadows)	Drawing objects are removed. You can use drawing tools in the Web page authoring environment by inserting Word Picture Objects. The object is converted to GIF format.
Equations, charts and other OLE objects	These items are converted to GIF images. The appearance is retained, but you won't be able to update these items.
Tables	Tables are converted, although settings that aren't supported in the Web page authoring environment are lost. Colored and variable width borders are lost. By default, tables are converted with a fixed width.
Highlighting	Highlighting is lost.

Element	Description of Changes
Revision marks	Changes entered with the track changes feature are retained, but the revision marks are removed.
Page numbering	Because an HTML document is considered a single Web page, regardless of its length, page numbering is removed.
Margins	Margins are removed. To control the layout of your page, you can use a table.
Borders around paragraphs and words	Borders around paragraphs and words are removed. You can place borders around a table, and you can use horizontal lines to help emphasize or separate parts of your Web page.
Page borders	There isn't an HTML equivalent for a page border. You can place borders around a table, and you can use horizontal lines to help emphasize or separate parts of your Web page.
Headers, footers, footnotes, and endnotes	There are no equivalents in HTML for any of these elements.
Newspaper columns	No conversion. For a multicolumn effect, use tables.
Styles	User-defined styles are converted to direct formatting, provided the formatting is supported in HTML.

Summary

Word 97's Web authoring tools let you carry over many of the techniques you use in creating Word documents to creating Web documents. This chapter explained working with Word's Web authoring features, including how to:

✦ Create Web pages using the Web Page Wizard. Choosing File➪New displays the New dialog box. Clicking the Web Pages tab displays the Web Page Wizard. You can also use the Blank Web Page template to create a new Web page without any formatting.

✦ Apply HTML tags as styles by choosing the style from the Style box on the Formatting toolbar. You can also manage the 80 HTML styles using the Style dialog box (Format➪Style).

✦ Insert hyperlinks by choosing Insert➪Hyperlink, pressing Ctrl+K, or clicking the Insert Hyperlink button. In the Insert Hyperlink dialog box, you can specify a path or URL to the object you want.

✦ Apply basic visual elements to your Web pages including; adding background colors or textures (Format➪Background), changing text colors (Format➪Text Colors), adding horizontal lines (Insert➪Horizontal Line), and creating bulleted and numbered lists (Format➪Bullets and Numbering).

✦ Insert Images into your Web pages by clicking the Insert Picture button on the Standard toolbar or choosing Insert➪Picture➪From File.

✦ Insert video clips by choosing Insert➪Video, which displays the Video Clip dialog box to specify the video file and how it is going to be played on the Web page.

✦ Create a text marquee in your Web pages by choosing Insert➪Scrolling Text.

✦ Add tables to your Web pages by choosing Table➪Insert Table.

✦ Save a Word document as an HTML document by choosing File➪Save as HTML.

Where to go next...

✦ If you want to know how to create more sophisticated Web documents, see Chapter 18.

✦   ✦   ✦

Advanced HTML Publishing with Word

◆ ◆ ◆ ◆

In This Chapter

Creating clickable images

Making the background of an image transparent

Creating HTML forms

Using a CGI script to process forms

Publishing your Web page

◆ ◆ ◆ ◆

The World Wide Web lets you do more than just publish a static HTML document. To really get the most out of the Web, you should create pages that allow you to interact with your reader. This chapter explains how to add a clickable image using a client-side image map and how to create and process a form. Creating a Web page and testing it by loading the page in your browser is great, but you most likely will want to publish your page so anyone on the Web can view it. This chapter also explains the process of publishing your Web page.

Working with Graphics

The previous chapter explained how to add an image or animated GIF to your page. Images with a solid background appear as square blocks on your page. With just a little work, you can make the background of an image transparent so the objects in the image appear to float on the page. You also may want to create images with hot spots, sometimes called clickable images, so when the reader clicks an area in the image, the browser opens a new document or moves to another location. There are two types of clickable image mapping techniques: server-side image maps and client-side image maps. Server-side image maps have been used for quite some time, but are being replaced by client-side image maps. Client side image maps are easier to create and don't require that you have a Web server running in order to work. The following sections explain how to create an image with a transparent background and create a clickable image so you can add them to your Web document using Word 97.

Creating a transparent background

In order to make an object appear to float on a page, you need to set the background color in a GIF or PNG image to be transparent. When you specify a background color as transparent, the background color disappears, so the image appears to float on the page. If you are using a white background on your page and are using a white background in your image, the objects may already appear to float, but specifying a transparent background color ensures that the objects float on a page no matter what color background or background tiled image you use.

Figure 18-1 shows an image without a transparent background displayed next to the image saved with a transparent background color. To specify a transparent color you will need an image editor, such as the Microsoft Photo Editor that comes with Word 97. The following steps explain how to specify a transparent background color for an existing image using Microsoft Photo Editor.

If Microsoft Photo Editor isn't installed, run the Setup program again and install it. For more information on installing Word 97 components, see Appendix B.

Caution When you specify a transparent color, all instances of the color will become transparent. So if you have a white background and the image is a picture of a face, the whites of the person's eyes and teeth may also become transparent. To avoid this, you may want to fill the background with a unique solid color before specifying the transparent color.

Figure 18-1: An image with a transparent background floats on the page.

The following steps explain how to use the Microsoft Photo Editor that comes with Office 97 to create a transparent background.

1. Start Microsoft Photo Editor and load the GIF image that you want to have a transparent background.

2. Click the Set Transparent Color button in the toolbar.

3. Click the color you want to make transparent. The Change Color to Transparent dialog box appears. The preview window shows the color that will change to transparent, as shown in Figure 18-2. You can also indicate a range of colors that you want become transparent or change the degree of transparency.

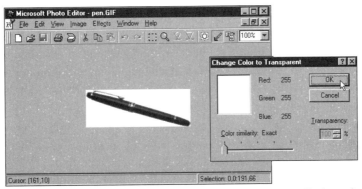

Figure 18-2: The Set Transparent Color tool lets you specify the color you want to be transparent.

4. Choose OK and repeat step three for each color you want to be transparent.

5. Choose File⇨Save to save your image. Start Word and use the Insert Picture button to add the image with a transparent background to your Web page.

Creating a clickable image

Most browsers support client-side image mapping, including Netscape Navigator 3.0 and higher and Microsoft Internet Explorer 3.0 and higher. A clickable image is an image that has areas designated as hot spots, so when a person clicks an area, the browser loads a new URL to display a different site or page or begins downloading a file. In order to create a clickable image, you have to designate the image's hot spot areas. While it's possible to manually define the coordinates of an image using an image editor, using an image mapping program is an easier and faster way to map an image's hot spot coordinates. One of the best image mapping programs is Todd Wilson's Map This, which is free and can be downloaded off the Web.

Defining image map coordinates

A client-side image map (CSIM) exists in the same HTML document and consists of HTML tags that specify the coordinates for the hot spots in a clickable image. Unfortunately, Word doesn't have a toolbar button for inserting image map tags, so you'll have to choose the View⇨HTML Source to add the image map information to your HTML document.

To map the hot spots in your image, you'll need to download an image mapping program like Map This. The home page for the Map This program is http:// galadriel.ecaetc.ohio-state.edu/tc/mt/. You can also download the program from the FTP site at ftp://faramir.ecaetc.ohio-state.edu/pub/tcfiles/ mapthis/. The latest version of Map This (version 1.3) is distributed as an executable file (.exe). Once you have downloaded the program, simply double-click the mpths13.exe file to install the Map This program. The following steps explain how to use Map This to create a map of clickable coordinates for the image.

1. Choose Map This from the Windows Start menu.

2. Choose File⇨New. The Make New Image Map dialog box appears, as shown in Figure 18-3.

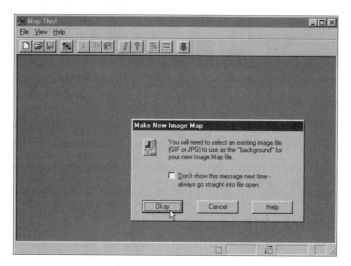

Figure 18-3:
The Make New Image Map dialog box.

3. Choose the Okay button. The Open existing Image (GIF/JPEG) file dialog box appears, as shown in Figure 18-4.

Figure 18-4: The Open existing Image (GIF/JPG) file dialog box.

4. Locate and select the GIF or JPEG image file you want to map and choose the Open button. The image appears in the Map This window for you to begin editing. Figure 18-5 shows the Map This window with a GIF image.

Figure 18-5: A GIF image displayed in Map This.

5. Click the Mapping toolbar item or choose the Mapping menu item that specifies the shape you want to use to define a hot spot. If the image is small, you may need to maximize the image so you can see and use the Mapping toolbar. The Mapping toolbar buttons include the Rectangle, Circle, and Polygon. The following explains how to define different regions using the Mapping toolbar. If two defined areas overlap, the first matching shape in the map file determines the URL that will be returned.

- **Rectangle:** Click the left mouse button in one corner of a rectangular region of interest in the image. Now move the mouse pointer to the opposite corner, dragging the rectangle marquee. The rectangle appears with cross-hatch lines indicating the hot spot you just defined.

- **Circle:** Position the mouse pointer in the upper-right portion of the circle. Click the left mouse button, and you can then move the mouse pointer to any point on the edge of the desired circle. The circle appears with cross-hatch lines indicating the hot spot you just defined.

- **Polygon:** Click the left mouse button on the edge of the area you want to begin map-ping. Move the mouse pointer to outline the edge. Note that a line follows you from the point of the initial click. Click again at second point that continues to outline the area you want to map. Continue click-ing to create points until you have outlined all but the final connection back to the first point. Click the mouse button on the original point to finish defining the shape. The shape appears with cross-hatch lines indicating the hot spot you just defined.

6. Click the Select existing area button (the arrow button), and then click the Show/hide area list button. The Show/hide area list appears, as shown in Figure 18-6.

Figure 18-6: The Show/hide area list.

7. Select the first area from the list and click the Edit button, shown as a pencil in the area list. Alternatively, you can double-click inside of the first area. The Area #1 Settings dialog box appears, as shown in Figure 18-7. Enter the URL you want to link to. You can also add any comments in the Internal comment about this area text box. Choose OK when you're finished.

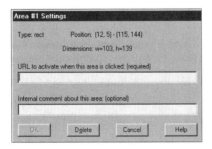

Figure 18-7: The Area #1 Settings dialog box.

8. Repeat step 7 for each hot spot you want to define. For this example, we used other HTML documents such as news.html for the microphone, web-tour.html for the suitcase, index.html for the statue, and contact.html for the phone. This example uses a simple HTML file reference, but you can point to any URL.

9. Choose the File➪Save command. The Settings for this Mapfile dialog box appears, as shown in Figure 18-8.

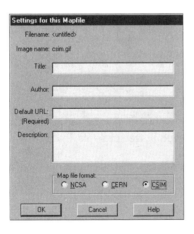

Figure 18-8: The Settings for this Mapfile dialog box.

10. Enter a name for your map information in the Title text box. For this example, we titled the map "navigate."

11. Enter the document or URL you want to use if the person clicks outside one of hot spot areas in the default URL text box. For example, you may want to point to an HTML document that displays a message informing the reader that he needs to click an image. In this example, we used default.htm.

12. If you want, you can enter your name in the Author text box and a description of the hot spot in the Description text box. Both of these text boxes are optional. The text you enter here will appear as comments in your HTML document.

13. Click the CSIM radio button (CSIM stands for Client Side Image Map) and click the OK button. The Save the Image Map file dialog box appears.

14. Enter the name of a temporary HTML file you want to create in the File name text box. You can name the file with an htm or html extension. Figure 18-9 shows the mapped image loaded in Netscape Navigator. The HTML file you created with Map This contains the map coordinates. Pay attention to the folder you're saving the temporary HTML document to because you'll need to retrieve the file later.

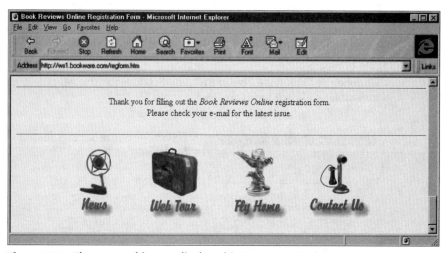

Figure 18-9: The mapped image displayed in Netscape Navigator.

15. Click the Save button to save your map coordinates to a file.

16. Choose File⇨Exit to close Map This.

Adding the image map coordinates using Word 97

To use an image map you need to add the USEMAP attribute to the IMG tag, assign the map name, and add the MAP tag and image map coordinates. The USEMAP attribute setting instructs the browser where to look for the MAP tag that contains the client-side image mapping information in the document. Unfortunately, Word 97 doesn't have menu items or toolbar buttons for inserting the USEMAP and MAP tags, so you'll have to choose the View⇨HTML Source to add the image map information to your HTML document in Word. The following steps explain how to add the image map information you generated using Map This to your HTML document using Word 97.

1. Start Word 97 and open the HTML document to which you want to add the clickable image. Choose the Insert Picture button to add the image to your HTML document if it isn't already in your page.

2. Choose View⇨HTML Source and choose Yes when you are prompted to save your file. You can now add the USEMAP attribute to your IMG tag. The map name is the same name you entered as the title in step 10 in the previous section. You can also specify that the image map doesn't appear with a border and assign alternate text for non-text browsers using the ALT tag. For this example, we entered

   ```
   <IMG SRC="csim.gif" BORDER="0" ALT="Navigation bar"
        USEMAP="#navigate">
   ```

3. Choose File⇨Open to open the HTML file you created with Map This. Nothing will appear on your screen at this time.

4. Choose View⇨HTML Source. The HTML source code containing your map coordinates appear.

5. Select and copy (Ctrl+C) the section starting with the <MAP> tag and ending with the </MAP> tag. The closing </MAP> tag is before the closing </BODY> tag in your HTML file.

6. Choose File⇨Close to return to the document to which you are adding the clickable image.

7. Paste (Ctrl+V) the section after the IMG tag. The following shows all the code for a client side image map:

   ```
   <HTML>
   <HEAD>
   <TITLE>A Client Side Image Map Example</TITLE>
   </HEAD>
   <BODY>
   <H1 ALIGN="CENTER">A Client Side Image Map Example</H1>
   ```

(continued)

```
<IMG SRC="csim.gif" BORDER="0" ALT="Navigation bar"
      USEMAP="#navigate">
<MAP NAME="navigate">
<!-- #$-:Image Map file created by Map THIS! -->
<!-- #$-:Map THIS! free image map editor by Todd C.
      Wilson -->
<!-- #$-:Please do not edit lines starting with "#$" -->
<!-- #$VERSION:1.30 -->
<!-- #$DATE:Sun Nov 10 10:05:46 1996 -->
<!-- #$PATH:I:\ -->
<!-- #$GIF:csimap.GIF -->
<AREA SHAPE=RECT COORDS="11,6,110,143" HREF="news.html">
<AREA SHAPE=RECT COORDS="159,5,269,144" HREF="webtour.html">
<AREA SHAPE=RECT COORDS="316,6,428,144" HREF="index.html">
<AREA SHAPE=RECT COORDS="459,5,590,144" HREF="contact.html">
<AREA SHAPE=default HREF="default.htm">
</MAP>
</BODY>
</HTML>
```

8. Choose Exit HTML <u>S</u>ource button, and Word displays a dialog box asking if you'd like to save your changes. Choose <u>Y</u>es to save your changes.

9. Choose <u>F</u>ile⇨<u>W</u>eb Page Preview or click the Web Page Preview toolbar button to load your page, and move the mouse on the hot spots. Notice that when you move the mouse pointer over a hot spot the status bar lists the location. Click the hot spot and the page loads or you are transported to the new location.

Creating Forms

Forms let you interact with your readers and provide dynamic data. For example, you might want to add a form that lets readers provide feedback about your site, conduct a survey, or add an order form. The Control Toolbox lets you add form elements and set the properties for the form elements.

Information entered in a form is stored as name value pairs; for example, if a form had a text box to let the reader enter his or her first name, you might specify that the name you want to use for the name value pair would be called *fname*. The text that the person enters in the text box would be the value of the name value pairs. If a person entered the name **Hermann**, the name value pair would be stored as the following name value pair:

```
fname=Hermann
```

When all the contents of the form are submitted, the data is sent in a special format known as *URL encoded data*. URL encoded data joins each name value pair entered in the form with an ampersand (&). Spaces are converted to plus signs and some characters, such as quotes, appear as numbers preceded by a percent sign. The following shows an example of three name value pairs (fname, lname, and book) sent as URL encoded data.

```
fname=Hermann&lname=Melville&book=Moby+Dick
```

The following sections explain how to create a simple form and have the URL encoded results sent to you via e-mail. In order to decode the URL encoded data so it appears on separate lines, you need to set the ACTION of a form to use a CGI script that decodes the information. This means you have to create a script using a language like VBScript or Perl or at least download a prewritten program that decodes form data. Perl is the safest language to use because it can be used on just about any platform: Windows, UNIX, or Macintosh. Portability is especially important because most service providers are currently running UNIX. One of the best Perl library programs that includes a special function for processing form data is a Perl program named cgi-lib.pl. So we don't leave you hanging, this chapter includes the information you need to process a form. Keep in mind that this is only a cursory introduction; to really master working with forms, you need to get a book that covers working with CGI.

Caution Although Word 97 Help states that you can submit forms using the mailto: protocol followed by the Internet e-mail address that you want to send the URL encoded data to, Internet Explorer 3.0 *does NOT* support using mailto: to process forms. Netscape Navigator does support using mailto; if you have Netscape Navigator, you can test your form to make sure that it works. Keep in mind that the person submitting the form must be using a browser that can work with the mailto: protocol in order to process the form.

Creating forms using the Web Page Wizard

Sample forms, such as feedback and survey forms, are available from the Web Page Wizard. You can use the Wizard to create a basic form and then modify it to fit your needs. The following explains creating a form using the Web Page Wizard:

1. Choose File⇨New and then select the Web Pages tab.

2. Double-click the Web Page Wizard icon. The Web Wizard dialog box appears for you to choose from several HTML page templates including a feedback, registration, and survey form. You can see the basic format of a form template by clicking the form you want to view.

3. Choose the form you want to create, and add or change any text or formatting you want. Then choose Next. The Web Wizard displays a variety of styles to choose from.

4. Select a style and choose <u>F</u>inish.

5. Right-click a toolbar and choose Control Toolbox. The Control Toolbox toolbar appears, as shown in Figure 18-10.

Figure 18-10: The Control Toolbox toolbar.

6. Click the Design Mode button to enter the Design mode.

7. Double-click the element you want define as a name value pair. Use the information on form elements in the following sections to specify the name value pairs for the form element.

8. Repeat step 7 for each element in your form.

9. Choose the Exit Design Mode button, and then choose <u>F</u>ile⇨<u>S</u>ave to save your HTML document.

> **Note** If you don't see the Web Pages tab or files, the Web page authoring component may not be installed. Run Setup again, and then select the Web page authoring components.

Adding form elements without the Web Wizard

If you are creating a form without using the Wizard, use the Blank Web Page template.

1. Choose <u>F</u>ile⇨<u>N</u>ew, select the Web Pages tab, and then double-click the Blank Web Page icon. A blank page appears for you to begin creating your form.

2. Right-click a toolbar and choose Control Toolbox. The Control Toolbox toolbar appears, as shown in Figure 18-10.

3. Click the form element you want to add. Alternatively, you can choose Insert⇨<u>F</u>orms, and select the form element you want to add. Word automatically changes to Design mode.

4. Double-click the form element. The Properties dialog box appears for the Text Area form element appears. Figure 18-11 shows the Properties dialog box for the Text Area form element.

Figure 18-11: The Properties dialog box for the Text Area form element.

5. Enter the properties for the form element. For help with form elements and properties, see the following section.

6. Repeat steps 2 through 5 until you've added all the form controls you want. Make sure that the last form control you add is a Submit or an Image Submit control element so the reader can submit the form.

7. Add or modify any content that you want to introduce your form elements.

8. Click the Exit Design Mode button when you are finished editing your form and choose File⇨Save to save your HTML document.

Understanding form elements and properties

The form elements in Word 97 are not standard HTML tags but are ActiveX controls that are based on standard form elements used on the World Wide Web. When you insert a form element, a Top of Form boundary and a Bottom of Form boundary is inserted. You insert other form elements you want in the form between those boundaries. It is possible to have more than one form on the same Web page. The boundaries appear only in Design mode and will not appear when the page is viewed in a Web browser.

To modify the properties of a form element you've already inserted, choose View⇨Form Design Mode, and then double-click the control to display the properties.

As mentioned earlier, form data is stored as name value pairs. If you look at the properties for a form, you will see the HTMLName property. This setting is the name portion of the name value pair. You can assign any name you want to the form element. The Value property is the value portion of the name value pair. Typically, any text you enter in the Value setting appears as the default value. The following sections explain how to add form elements to a form. Figure 18-12 shows a sample form created using Word 97.

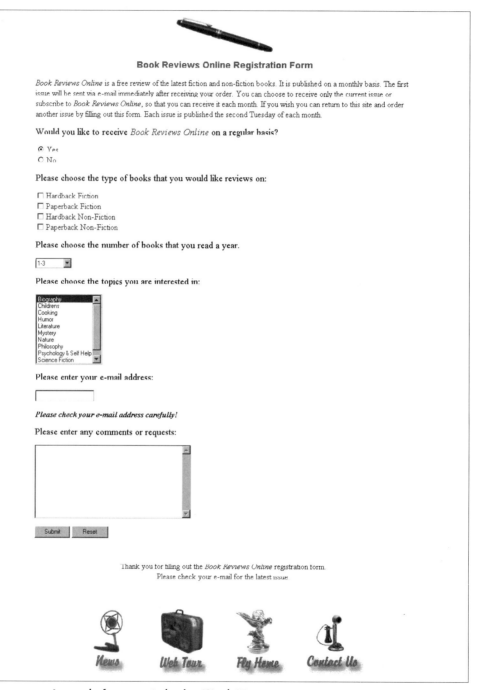

Figure 18-12: A sample form created using Word 97.

Including option buttons

Option buttons, sometimes called radio buttons, are for a group of items that are mutually exclusive. The reader can only select one option button from a group of option buttons. A option button is either on or off, so that when you receive the name value pair only one option button from a group of option buttons will be set to on. As with check boxes, you can enter checked to select the option button by default. Because only one option button can be set on, you can use the same HTMLName for each option button element in the same group. The Value setting is the value to return if the button is selected. Multiple groups are permitted within the same form.

Adding check boxes

Check boxes let a reader select one or more items. If you want the check box to be selected by default enter Checked. In the example shown in Figure 18-12, the HTMLName is set for each of the check boxes to hardfict, paperfict, hardnon, and papernon. Set the Value to the name you want to use to identify the check box. Check boxes that aren't checked are ignored when a form is submitted. When you receive the name value pair, the setting for the check box will be set on for all the check boxes that are checked.

Adding a drop-down box

The Dropdown Box inserts a list box that displays available choices in a drop-down list format. If the list exceeds the box size, the user can scroll through the list to view additional choices. You enter the items you want to appear in the list in the DisplayValues property box. Each list item needs to be separated by a semicolon in the DisplayValues property box. Don't type spaces between the items. In the example shown in Figure 18-12, we have asked that the person select from the drop-down box the number of books read each year. The DisplayValues properties is set to the following:

```
1-3;4-6;6-10;10+
```

The HTMLName is the name you assign to the name value pair. The Value property is the value returned for each item in the list. The names of the values can differ from the display values, but the number of values must be equal to or greater than the number of display values. Values are also separated with a semicolon; don't type spaces between them.

The Selected property determines whether the first item appears in the box and is selected by default. You can let a person select more than one item from a list by setting the MultiSelect property to True. MultiSelect defaults to False. If you change MultiSelect to True, the control becomes a list box. If you change MultiSelect settings, the settings for Selected are cleared. The Size property refers to the size of the font. The default font size for a drop-down list is 1.

Adding a list box

A list box displays the values of a list of items. If the number of items is larger than the displayed list box, a scroll bar appears. To add items to a list box, select the DisplayValues and enter the items for the list, separated by a semicolon. You don't need to type spaces between them. The HTMLName is the name portion of the name value pair that is assigned to the form element. The Value property is the value returned for each item in the list.

The names of the values can differ from the display values, but the number of values must be equal to or greater than the number of display values. Values are also separated with a semicolon; as with the values in the drop-down list, don't type spaces between them.

You can determine whether the reader can select more than one item from a list box by using the MultiSelect. By default, MultiSelect is set to True. If you change MultiSelect settings, the settings for Selected are cleared. The Selected property determines whether the first item appears selected by default. By default, the size of the list box is set to display three items. You can change the size by entering the number of list items in the Size property box.

Adding a text box

Clicking the Text Box button in the Control Toolbox inserts a text box that lets the reader enter a single line of text. In the example shown in Figure 18-12, we added a text box for the reader to enter his or her e-mail address. The HTMLName is set to e-mail. Because we don't want to have default address appear, we have left the text box properties value blank. You can specify the maximum numbers of characters that a person can enter by filling in the MaxLength property. The default is 0, which doesn't restrict the length.

Creating a text area

One of the simplest and most functional form elements is the Text Area box. You can easily create a feedback form that consists of a text area box and a Submit and Reset button. Text Area inserts a control in which the user can enter multiple lines of text. When you create a text area box, you can specify the number of columns and rows to display. In Design mode, when you double-click the text area box the properties box is displayed. Click Columns to change the width of the text area in number of columns or click Rows to change the height of the text area. You can have default text appear in the Text Area box by entering text in the Value field.

Because the text area lets the reader type in whatever he or she wants, you will most likely want to control how text is handled in your text area. The WordWrap options let you specify how words are handled in the text area. The three settings you can choose from are Virtual, Physical, or Off. Words automatically wraps in the box if WordWrap is set to Virtual or Physical. If the setting is set to Off, and words will not wrap as a line fills up with text. Not all Web browsers support WordWrap.

Adding a password

Don't be fooled by the Password element. It isn't a safe method of protecting a form. The password is similar to the text field, but instead of displaying the characters that the person types, asterisks appear in the text box. The HTMLName is the name portion of the name value pair. Although you can add a default value to the password field, doing so would defeat its purpose. You can restrict the number of characters that can be entered in a Password text box by changing the MaxLength property. MaxLength defaults to 0, which doesn't restrict the length.

Including a hidden field

The hidden field hides information from the reader. This field can be used to pass information to the server, such as information about the browser's environment. When the person submits the form. The Hidden field is not visible unless you are in the form's Design mode or when hidden text is showing in your document. The HTMLName is the name portion of the name value pair. The Value property is the default text that is sent to the server.

Adding the Submit button or Image Submit button

To process the contents of a form, you must add a Submit button. The Submit button displays the properties that are used to submit the data that the user fills in the form. Inserting a Submit button adds a button to the page. You can change the text that appears on a Submit button by entering a new button name in the Caption properties box. By default the Caption is set to submit. The Caption property is the equivalent of the VALUE attribute in HTML for the HTML <INPUT TYPE=SUBMIT> tag.

Tip   There are two methods used for submitting the form data: POST or GET. GET is the default. GET adds the URL encoded data to the end of the URL. The POST Method is used to store the data as standard input. Unless a program instructs you to use GET, you should change the method from GET to POST for submitting the form data.

Another way to present a Submit button to the reader is to use the Image Submit button. This lets you choose an image to use as a button. When you click the Image Submit button control, the Picture dialog box appears for you to select the image you want to use as the button. When you copy the Web page to the server, be sure to copy the button image, also. Other than the Source property, which is the name of the image source file, the Image Submit properties are the same as the Submit button.

Note If you are familiar with HTML FORM tags, you may find how Word adds attributes to the FORM tag a little confusing. In HTML you use the ACTION attribute to specify the location of the file that is run when the user clicks the Submit button. Unlike HTML where you assign a CGI program to the FORM's ACTION attribute, Word 97 adds the CGI program file name using the Action property of the Submit button. If you look at the source after setting the Action property, you will notice that the Action property is added as the URL of the FORM's ACTION attribute.

Including a Reset button

The Reset button lets a reader quickly remove his or her form entry data, so the form only displays the forms default settings. The value setting specifies the text that appears on the button. The default setting is Reset. The Caption is equivalent to the HTML VALUE attribute for the HTML <INPUT TYPE=RESET> tag.

Processing the form

Unless you can get the results back from a form, adding a form to your Web page won't do you much good. To process a form, you need to use a special program that conforms to the Common Gateway Interface (CGI). You can use any language to write a CGI script, but because most Internet Service Providers (ISPs) run UNIX, you will most likely need to create a CGI script, using a programming language such as Perl, that uses the UNIX sendmail program to have the form data sent to your e-mail address. The name of the CGI script file is added to the URL following your Web site's domain name or IP address as the Submit action property setting.

A few kind sites let you use an existing CGI form mail script that runs on another server, but you cannot always be sure that the service will be available. If you want to test your script using Windows 95 or NT, we suggest you use a form mail program that is already written, such as the Windows port of Matt Wright's FormMail program. The following sections explain the essentials of setting up a CGI script to process a form for a service provider running UNIX, and using the FormMail program to process a script using Windows 95.

Processing a form using a UNIX-based ISP

Because writing Perl scripts is really beyond the scope of this book, we will simply give you the steps and an example script that you can use to process your form from a UNIX server. Numerous books exist on CGI and Perl. An excellent introduction to CGI and Perl is Robert Farrell's *60 Minute Guide to CGI Programming with Perl 5*, which is published by IDG Books Worldwide. Most Internet service providers already have Perl installed. The following gives you the steps you will need to follow to process a form using an ISP running UNIX.

Tip   The following example uses the command-line FTP program that comes with Windows 95, but some excellent graphical Windows-based FTP tools exist. The Windows FTP tools are a lot easier than using FTP from the command line. WS_FTP and CuteFTP are two of the better FTP graphical-based shareware programs. You can download WS_FTP at `ftp://ftp1.ipswitch.com/pub/win32`. You can download Cute FTP from `ftp://ftp.cuteftp.com/pub/cuteftp/`.

1. Start Word and enter the following Perl script replacing yourname\ @domain.com with your e-mail address and the names references (name1, name2, and name3) with the HTML names you assigned your form elements. Be sure to leave the backslash before the @ sign. Save the file as ASCII text only and name the file form.cgi.

```perl
#!usr/local/bin/perl

require ('cgi-lib.pl');

&ReadParse;

print "Content-type: text/html\n\n";
open(MAIL, "| /usr/lib/sendmail yourname\@domain.com");
print<<_END_
The form was sent with following entries\n
The first entry was $in{'name1'}\n
The second entry was $in{'name2'}\n
The third entry was $in{'name3'}\n
_END_
;
```

2. Using Word 97, open your HTML file that contains your form. Click the Design Mode button and double-click the Submit button. The properties dialog box appears. Assign the Submit property setting to your Web site's URL and add **/cgi/form.cgi**. For example, it might be `http://www.authors .com/cgi/form.cgi`. Save your HTML document and close Word.

3. Download cgi-lib.pl Perl library program from `http://software.ora.com/ techsupport/software/PL_CGI-LIB.ZIP`.

4. Unzip the CGI-lib program in the same folder that you stored your form.cgi program.

5. Open an MS-DOS window and change directories to the directory where you stored your CGI script form.cgi and the cgi-lib.pl file. Steps 1- 15 will all be performed from the DOS window.

6. Enter **ftp** followed by your service provider's domain name or the domain name that your ISP specifies to use to transfer your HTML files.

7. Enter your login name and password at the prompts. An ftp> prompt appears.

8. Enter **ascii**. The message Type set to A appears.

9. Change to the directory that your service provider has created for your HTML documents, for example, enter **cd public_html** if public_html is the directory used to store your HTML files. The message CWD command successful appears.

10. Enter **put form.html** to copy your HTML document to your Web site. A message appears telling you that the Port command was successful and the transfer was complete.

11. Enter **mkdir cgi** to create a directory for your CGI script. The message MKD command successful appears.

12. Enter **cd cgi**. The message CWD command successful appears.

13. Enter **put cgi-li.pl** to copy the cgi-lib.pl file and press Enter to copy the cgi-lib.pl file to your cgi directory.

14. Enter **put form.cgi** and press Enter to copy the form.cgi script to your cgi directory.

15. Enter **quit**. The MS DOS prompt appears.

16. At the DOS prompt, enter **telnet**. The Telnet window opens.

17. Choose Connect⇨Remote System. A dialog box appears for you to enter your Host name, Port, and Term type. Enter your service provider's domain name in the Host Name field. This is the domain name of the server that you specified in step 6 to transfer files your site.

18. Choose the Connect button and enter your login name and password at the prompts.

19. Change directories to the directory where your HTML files are located. For example you might enter cd public_html if your HTML files are stored in the public_html directory.

20. Enter **chmod 755 cgi** to change the permissions for the directory. In some rare cases your service provider may require you to set the last number to 0. Check with your service provider if your script doesn't run to make sure that you have the permission set correctly.

21. Enter **cd cgi**.

22. Enter **chmod 644 cgi-lib.pl** to change the permissions for the CGI library program. In some rare cases your service provider may require you to set the last number to 0. Check with your service provider if your script doesn't run to make sure that you have the permission set correctly.

23. Enter **chmod 755 form.cgi** to change the permissions for the CGI/Perl script. In some rare cases, your service provider may require you to set the last

number to 0. Check with your service provider if your script doesn't run to make sure that you have the permission set correctly.

24. Choose Connect⇨Exit to end the Telnet session.

Setting up a script to process your forms using FormMail

If you want to test your forms on your own PC using the prewritten FormMail Perl program, there are a few programs you need to set up. First you need to have a Windows 95 or Windows NT Web server running. You can download an evaluation version of the WebSite server from O'Reilly and Associates free at the URL http://website.ora.com.

You can also get a version of NetManage's Web server for free from Microsoft at http://www.microsoft.com/ie/download/ieadd.htm, but we highly recommend using WebSite server.

Although you can use any programming language to run a CGI script, most people who create and process forms use Perl. The FormMail program is written in Perl, so you need to set up Perl on your PC. You can download a version of Perl for Windows 95 from http://www.perl.hip.com.

The FormMail program is a Windows 32-bit port of Matt Wright's FormMail script. You can download the FormMail script for Windows 95 from http://www2. webbernet.net/~dgorski/formmail/formmail.zip.

In order to use this program you must also have a copy of BLAT. BLAT is a Simple Mail Transfer Protocol utility written for Windows NT that can also be used with Windows 95. You can download a copy of BLAT from http://gepasi.dbs.aber. ac.uk/softw/Blat.html.

Before you install the program, you need to install Perl and associate the extension .pl with the perl program (perl.exe). The formhandler.cgi script needs to be renamed to formhandler.pl, so that Windows and WebSite know to use the Perl program to run the script.

If you set up the FormMail script, keep in mind that the e-mail addresses *should NOT* contain the characters <,>,or |. This is due to the fact that BLAT needs From:, To:, and CC: addresses on the command line, and COMMAND.COM/CMD. EXE will attempt to perform a redirection operation if these characters are found. This means that you *do NOT* want to use the e-mail convention Brent Heslop <bheslop@bookware.com>, instead simply use your e-mail address (for example, bheslop@bookware.com).

Another thing to keep in mind is that Perl and your Web server expect paths to folders to be in the UNIX format, so file and folder paths should use forward slashes (/) rather than back slashes (\) (for example, C:/Website/FormHandler.txt).

Publishing your Web documents

Once you have created your HTML documents with Word, you will want to find a service provider that allows you to make your pages available to the world. You could easily download a Web server program and publish your Web pages from your site, but it is a lot less expensive to use a service provider than to pay for a dedicated connection to the Internet. If you want to use your own company name as a part of your URL, make sure to ask if the service provider supports virtual domain names. If you publish your pages with an ISP that doesn't support virtual domains, you and others will likely have to use the service provider's address followed by a tilde and your name in order to view your Web pages.

Tip   If you are connecting to the World Wide Web using an online service provider, such as America Online, CompuServe, or Prodigy, and want to switch to an ISP that will give you a virtual domain name and let you run CGI scripts, check out the URL `http://thelist.com`. This is one of the most comprehensive ISP lists you're likely to find.

To publish your pages using an ISP, you need to transfer the HTML documents and image files to your HTML document directory at your ISP. The Microsoft Office 97 ValuPack includes the Web Publishing Wizard that will transfer your Web pages to your service provider. You can also download the Web Publishing Wizard from Microsoft at `http://www.microsoft.com/msdownload/`. To install the Web Publishing Wizard, create a temporary folder on your hard disk. Download or copy the `web-post.exe` file in temporary folder. In that folder, double-click the webpost.exe icon.

In order to publish your pages, you must have an access to the Internet through a proxy server at your company or through an ISP. If you are publishing from your company, check with your system administrator to make sure you have write access to your company's Web server's directories. To use the Web publishing Wizard, the Web server must be set up to work with the Web Publishing Wizard.

Note   If your ISP or corporate Web Server isn't set up to work with Microsoft's Web Publishing Wizard, you can ask to have your ISP or system administrator get the simple instructions for setting up the server for Microsoft's Web Publishing Wizard from `http://www.microsoft.com/windows/software/webpost/wp2.htm`.

If you have multiple files, such as images that you want to include on your page or pages, first copy all the files you want to publish to a directory and then do the following to use the Web Publishing Wizard to publish your HTML documents:

1. Click the Start menu; then choose Programs⇨Accessories⇨Internet Tools⇨Web Publishing Wizard. The Web Publishing Wizard starts and

displays a dialog box informing you that the Web Publishing Wizard will copy your HTML documents and images to a Web server (see Figure 18-13).

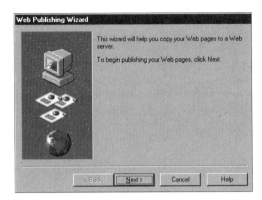

Figure 18-13: The Web Publishing Wizard lets you copy your HTML documents and related files to a Web server.

2. Choose <u>N</u>ext. A dialog box appears, prompting you to select the files or folder you want to publish. You can choose not to include subfolders by clearing the check mark from the <u>I</u>nclude subfolders check box. Do one of the following:

   • Choose Br<u>o</u>wse Folders to select all the files you want to publish.

   • Choose B<u>r</u>owse Files if you want to only publish a single file.

3. Choose <u>N</u>ext. A dialog box prompts you to either choose or create a new entry for your Web site. If you're using CompuServe's Our World or SPRYNET SPRY Society, you can choose the one you're using from the drop-down list. Otherwise, choose N<u>e</u>w.

4. Enter the name you want to use to identify your Web site in Type a name to describe your Web server. The default is My Web site. Make sure <Other Internet Provider> is selected in the <u>S</u>elect your service provider from a list drop-down list box.

5. Choose <u>N</u>ext and enter your URL in the <u>U</u>RL or Internet Address text box (see Figure 18-14). If you don't know your URL, enter the domain name of your ISP; the Wizard will try to detect it for you. If you're are not using a virtual domain name, your address will typically be your service provider's URL followed by a forward slash, a tilde, and your login name.

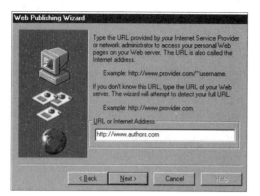

Figure 18-14: The Web Publishing Wizard prompts you for your URL or Internet address.

6. Choose Next. A dialog box appears asking you to choose the type of connection you are using to connect to the Internet. Choose Local Area Network (Intranet) if you are using an network connection or choose Dial up networking to access the Internet if you are using a modem.

7. Choose Next. A dialog box appears informing you that the Web Publishing Wizard will verify your information when you click Next.

8. Choose Next. The Web Publishing Wizard verifies the FTP connection, the LAN server or dial-up connection, and the Web server Internet address. If you're trying to connect to your ISP, the Wizard will display dialog boxes one at a time for you to manually enter the information for your Web server, which includes the protocol you're using, your user name and password, your FTP server name, the subfolder that contains your Web pages on the server, and your URL. The user name and password will default to your Window settings, so most likely these will have to be changed to have the Web Publishing Wizard transfer your files. Figure 18-15 shows the dialog box for entering your user name and password.

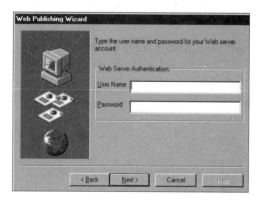

Figure 18-15: A dialog box appears for you to enter your login name and password.

9. Choose the Finish button. Your files are transferred and a dialog box appears informing you that your files were transferred successfully.

10. Choose OK to close the dialog box.

If your ISP doesn't allow you to use the Web Publishing Wizard, you can always use Windows 95 FTP tool. To use Windows 95's FTP tool, start an MS-DOS window and enter **ftp** followed by your service provider's domain name, and then enter your login and password. You can use the **cd** command to change directories. To move the files enter put followed by the name of the file you want to copy. You can use asterisk wildcards to copy all the files in the directory. To end your FTP session, enter **exit** at the DOS prompt. Check the second Tip in the forms section of this chapter ("Processing a form using a UNIX-based ISP"), which includes URLs to two graphical-based FTP shareware tools.

Summary

This chapter has covered using Word 97 in conjunction with other programs to let you create impressive Web pages. In this chapter you have learned:

✦ How to specify that a background color is set to transparent.

✦ How to create a client side image map.

✦ How to add form elements to your pages.

✦ How to process a form.

✦ What you need to do to publish your Web pages.

Where to go next...

✦ The Web is a great way to share documents. In the next chapter you can learn about sharing documents and working with Workgroups to create and revise documents.

✦   ✦   ✦

Sharing Documents and Working with Workgroups Using Word 97

CHAPTER 19

In This Chapter

Sharing Word 97 documents with others

E-mailing and faxing documents

Routing documents

Adding text and voice comments

Revising documents

Protecting shared documents

In most office environments, documents are shared with others to disseminate information or to solicit comments and track revisions. Word 97 includes several new collaboration features that allow you to work with others to share, review, and revise documents in a workgroup environment. For example, you can let more than one person simultaneously edit the same document, you can store different versions of the same document in the same file, or you can track revisions made by others reviewing your documents. If you are on a network that uses Office 97's new Outlook, Windows 95's Microsoft Exchange, or a compatible e-mail system, you can send or route documents to others on the network. If you have set up Microsoft Fax, you can fax your document directly from within Word. This chapter explains how to share documents with others whether they are across the room or around the world.

Sharing Word Document Files

In order to share Word document files, you need to take into account the delivery options available to the person you want to receive the document. You also will need to make sure that the person can read the Word document. As previously mentioned, you have several options available to share Word 97 documents. If you want to share a document with someone at a remote location, you may want to e-mail or fax the document from Word. To share a document with another person on a network, copy the shared document to a network location or shared folder where other users can gain access to it. The following sections explain the options available for sharing Word document files with others.

Sharing different versions of Word documents

Microsoft Word 97 has a different file format from earlier versions of Word. If you are sharing documents with someone who is using Word 95, Word 6.x, Word for Windows NT, or Word for the Macintosh, you can share documents and templates among these versions. In order to share a Word 97 document, all the recipients must also have Word 97 or a previous version of Word and a Word converter or a Word viewer installed on their systems to read the document. You can open files created in Word 95 or Word 6.x directly in Word 97. Formatting created in Word 95 or Word 6.x is fully supported by Word 97. However, if you need to share Word 97 documents with someone using an earlier version of Word, you will need to either save the document in Word 6.0/95 (*.doc) format or have the person receiving your document install the Word 97 converter. Once the converter is installed, the person can directly open Word 97 documents. Be aware that you will lose any Word 97-specific formatting features.

If you need to share a document with a person who is using a previous version of Word, the person will need to have a copy of the Word 97 converter (Wrd97cnv.exe). The Wrd97cnv.exe file is included on the Word and Office 97 CD-ROM. To install the converter, simply double-click the Wrd97cnv.exe file in Explorer. Depending on the version of Word the person is using, Word installs either the Mswrd832.cnv file (the 32-bit version for people running Word 95) or the Msword8.cnv file (the 16-bit version for people running Word 6.x). The Wrd97cnv.exe program also updates the necessary registry settings. Anyone can obtain the Word 97 file format converter and other converters that are not included with Word. To obtain the Word 97 file format converter or other Word converters free of charge, download the file from Microsoft Support on the World Wide Web at http://www.microsoft.com/support or from the MS Software Library on MSN, or call the Microsoft Order Desk at (800) 360-7561.

Tip You can customize the way a file converter works. If you don't have the template Convert8.dot on your system, run the Microsoft Word 97 Setup program to install the template. After you select the Wizards, templates, and letters check box, select the Macro templates check box. For information on customizing macros, see Chapter 27.

Sharing Word documents with non-Word users

Windows 95 ships with the Quick Viewer program for viewing Word document files. A more robust tool is Microsoft's Word Viewer that lets anyone running Windows 95 open, view, and print Word for Windows and Word for the Macintosh (versions 4.0 and greater) document files. The Word Viewer doesn't allow you to edit a Word document, although it does support dragging and dropping text and copying and pasting text. The Word Viewer is freeware that is included on the Office 97 CD-ROM as a part of the ValuPack. It is also available for downloading from Microsoft's Web site at `http://www.microsoft.com/word/Internet/Viewer/default.htm`. Microsoft encourages you to distribute the Word Viewer along with your Word documents to anyone who isn't using Microsoft Word for Windows. Figure 19-1 shows a document open in the Word Viewer window.

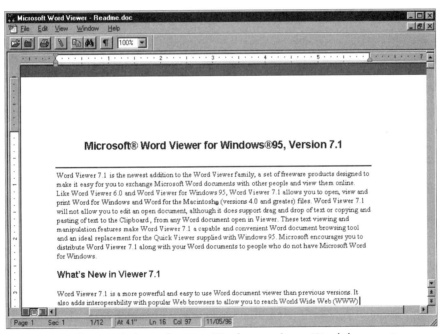

Figure 19-1: The Word Viewer lets non-Word users view a Word document.

Sharing documents via e-mail

To send e-mail using Word and Office 97, you must have Microsoft Exchange or Outlook set up, and you must add an information service for e-mail. If you're using Word with Office 97, you most likely will want to set up mail using Outlook 97. Outlook 97 is an information manager program that replaces the Microsoft Exchange Inbox and Schedule+. Outlook 97 works in conjunction with Word, enabling you to use a common address book and use Word as your e-mail editor. You don't have to use Outlook 97 to use Word to share documents via e-mail. If you're working on a network that is using Microsoft Exchange, you can easily use Exchange to send documents via e-mail. The following sections explain how to install an e-mail service using Outlook and use Word to send and route documents via e-mail.

Installing an e-mail service

If you try to send e-mail from Word and Exchange or Outlook 97 and see a subject line informing you that the message was undeliverable, it is likely that you need to add an e-mail service to your Microsoft Exchange or Outlook 97 profile. Using Exchange, you can double-click the Inbox icon on the Windows 95 desktop to start the Inbox Wizard.

Unless a Microsoft mail workgroup post office has been set up, the Exchange client can only be partially configured. Creating and administering an Microsoft Exchange post office is typically a task reserved for your network's system administrator. If the workgroup post office is already set up, the post office location automatically appears in the post office location box when using the Inbox setup Wizard.

To add an information service for e-mail using Outlook, do the following:

1. Double-click the Microsoft Outlook icon or open the Start menu and choose Microsoft Outlook from the Programs menu. The Outlook window appears, as shown in Figure 19-2.

   • If you're opening Microsoft Outlook for the first time, a message appears asking if you want to turn on Word as your e-mail editor. Click Yes.

   • If the Office Assistant displays a Welcome message and starting options, choose OK to close the Office Assistant dialog box so you can begin installing an e-mail service.

2. Click the Inbox icon in the Outlook bar.

3. Choose Tools⇨Services. The Services dialog box appears with the Services tab selected, as shown in Figure 19-3.

4. Click Add. The Add Service to Profile dialog box appears, as shown in Figure 19-4.

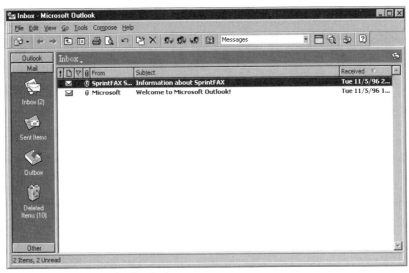

Figure 19-2: The Outlook window.

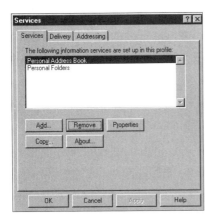

Figure 19-3: The Services dialog box.

Figure 19-4: The Add Service to Profile dialog box.

5. Choose Internet Mail if you are using an Internet Service Provider, MSN, or CompuServe to retrieve your e-mail. Choose Microsoft Mail if you are going to retrieve your mail from a local area network. A dialog box appears for the type of e-mail service you want to add.

6. Fill in the fields in the dialog box with the information provided by your ISP or your system administrator and click OK to close each of the open dialog boxes when you are finished.

Using WordMail as your e-mail editor

Using Microsoft Exchange or Outlook, you can use Word as your e-mail editor. When you first start Outlook, the Office Assistant appears asking if you want to use WordMail as your default e-mail editor. WordMail lets you use Word's editing and formatting features when you compose e-mail messages. WordMail includes a special e-mail toolbar and Compose menu (Alt+M) commands to create, send, read, reply to, and forward messages.

To use Word as your e-mail editor if you didn't specify it when you opened Outlook for the first time, open Microsoft Outlook and choose Tools⇨Options and then click the E-mail tab (see Figure 19-5). Click the Use Microsoft Word as the e-mail editor check box.

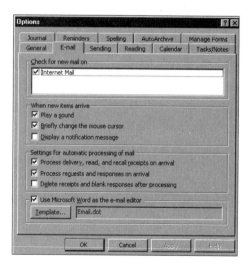

Figure 19-5: The E-mail tab in Outlook's Options dialog box lets you choose Word as your default e-mail editor.

Using WordMail templates and AutoSignature

Word includes several e-mail templates that you can choose from when you use WordMail as your editor. To select a template, choose Compose⇨Choose Template in the Outlook window and choose the template you want to use. If you want to change the default WordMail template, open Microsoft Outlook and choose Tools⇨Options, click the E-mail tab, and then click the Template button. The WordMail Template dialog box appears (see Figure 19-6). Double-click the template you want to use as your default.

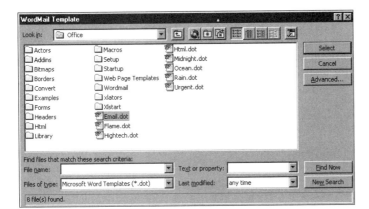

Figure 19-6: The WordMail Template dialog box

If you're using Microsoft Exchange, choose Compose⇨New Message. The Message dialog box appears. Choose Compose⇨Choose Template. The WordMail Template dialog box appears. Click the template you want to use.

In addition to using WordMail's templates to speed up composing e-mail messages, you can also create an automatic signature for e-mail messages and add the signature with the click of a button. First open a message that contains your signature information, such as your name, title, company name, e-mail address, and so on. Select the text you want to use as an automatic signature in e-mail messages, and then choose Tools⇨AutoSignature. A dialog box appears, asking you to confirm that you want to use the selection as your AutoSignature (see Figure 19-7). Click Yes. The signature will be automatically added to the bottom of every message. You can quickly remove an AutoSignature from a single message by selecting the AutoSignature and pressing the Delete key.

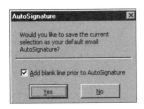

Figure 19-7: Word confirms that you want to use the selected text as an AutoSignature.

E-mailing a document from Word

To send a Word document file using e-mail, you can send it as an attachment to any recipient not using WordMail. If the recipient is using Outlook with WordMail, the Word document can also be added into the message. If the document you want to send as an attachment to a mail message is open in Word, choose File➪Send To➪Mail Recipient option to send the current file. The Choose Profile dialog box appears. Choose OK to accept the default profile. The Message window appears for you to enter the e-mail address, carbon copy address, subject line, and any text you want to appear in the e-mail message accompanying your Word attachment (see Figure 19-8). Outlook and most e-mail programs support three Content-Transfer-Encoding formats: 7-bit, Quoted-printable, and Base 64.

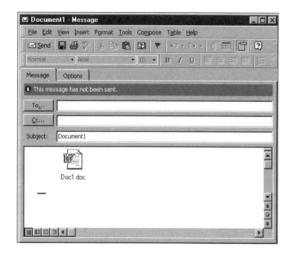

Figure 19-8: The Message window.

In Windows Explorer, right-click the document file icon for the file you want to send and choose the Send To➪Mail Recipient Using Microsoft Outlook. The Send To option in the shortcut menu is also available when you choose File➪Open in Word. In the Open dialog box, right-click the name of the file you want to send, select Send To from the shortcut menu, and enter the required message information in the mail system.

Viewing a Word Document in Netscape Mail

When you receive a Word document attachment in Netscape mail, you will see base64 at the bottom of the message window, as shown in Figure 19-9. In order to read the Word document in Netscape, you need to set up Word or Word Viewer as a helper application. To do this, start Navigator and choose Options➪General and click the Helpers tab. Click the MSWord application and choose the Launch application radio button. Enter the path to Word; for example, enter C:\Program Files\Microsoft Office\Winword.exe. The next time you click a Word document sent as an attachment, Word will start and load the attached document.

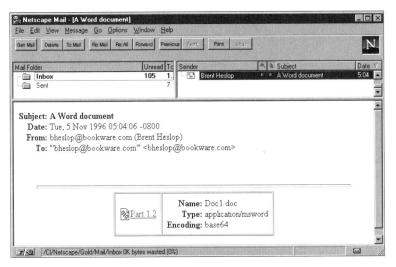

Figure 19-9:
A Word document attachment in Netscape Mail.

Note You can route documents online by using any 32-bit e-mail program that is compatible with the Messaging Application Programming Interface (MAPI) or by using any 16-bit e-mail program that is compatible with Vendor Independent Messaging (VIM). The Mail Recipient and Routing Recipient options appear when you select Send To on the File menu.

Using WordMail instead of Netscape Navigator

If you would prefer to use Word to edit your e-mail messages and use Outlook to send and receive your e-mail rather than Netscape's e-mail client, do the following:

1. Start Netscape Navigator.

2. Choose Options⇨Mail and News Preferences and click the Appearance tab.

3. Click the Use Exchange Client for Mail and News and choose OK.

Routing a document

If you want to share a document, simply e-mail a copy to all the recipients. If you want the others to see it in a particular sequence and also get feedback on the annotations and revisions, route the document instead. When you route a document, you can either send it as an attachment in an e-mail message to the recipients one at a time so that each person can see the changes made by the previous recipients, or you can send it to everyone at once. You will automatically be informed as each recipient forwards the document to the next. You can also remind the recipient to forward the document to the next person. After all the recipients have completed their review of the document, it automatically returns to you.

When you review the document later, you can see the changes by turning on the revision marks. The revision marks will show where text or graphics have been changed in any way. Before you can route a document, you must prepare a routing slip for it with the names and addresses of all recipients, presented in the desired order. To create a routing slip:

1. Open the document you want to route and click File⇨Send To⇨Routing Recipient. (This command will not appear if you do not have a mail system installed.)

2. Click Address to select the recipients and other routing options. The Address Book dialog box appears.

3. In the Type Name or Select from List box, type a recipient's name or select the name from the list box, and then click To. Once you've entered the last recipient name in the To box, click OK.

4. Click Route.

If you don't want to route the document just yet, click Add Slip to save the routing. Then when you're ready to route the document, choose File⇨Send to⇨Next Routing Recipient.

Note If the document has a routing slip associated with it but you don't want to send it to all the recipients on the list, or maybe you want it routed in a different sequence, you can send the document without using the routing slip.

When you want the recipients to review the document only and not make any permanent changes, you can add password protection. To prevent others from changing a routed document:

1. Open the document, and then choose Tools⇨Protect Document. The Protect Document dialog box opens (see Figure 19-10).

Figure 19-10: The Protect Document dialog box.

2. Click Tracked changes to let recipients change the document but add revision marks at all changes.

3. Click Comments to let recipients insert comments but not change any of the content.

4. Type a password in the Password text box, and click OK.

Using Microsoft Fax with Word

Microsoft Fax enables you to send fax messages directly from Word. You can fax messages from Word in three ways: by choosing File⇨New, clicking the Letters Faxes tab, and then double-clicking the Fax Wizard; Choosing the File⇨Send to⇨ Fax Recipient; or Choosing the Fax printer driver and printing the file.

You need to install and configure both Outlook and Microsoft Fax, and you must have a fax modem installed in order to send and receive fax messages using Word. If you don't see the Outlook icon on your desktop, it's likely that Outlook is not installed. If you try to send a fax and Office 97 displays an error message informing you that `awfext32.dll` is not installed, you need to install Microsoft Fax.

Installing and setting up Microsoft Fax

To install Microsoft Fax, open the Control Panel, and double-click the Add/Remove Programs icon. This displays the Add/Remove Programs Properties dialog box. Click the Windows Setup tab, and click in the check box for Microsoft Fax. Click OK to close the dialog box. If you originally installed Windows 95 using a CD-ROM or floppy disks, you may be prompted to insert the Windows installation disks in your PC. After you have added the Microsoft Fax program, you need to configure Microsoft Fax and add the Microsoft Fax service to your profile.

The following explains how to add the Microsoft Fax service to your default profile using Outlook.

1. Double-click the Microsoft Outlook icon or open the Start menu and choose Microsoft Outlook from the Programs menu. The Outlook window appears. If the Office Assistant displays a Welcome message and starting options, choose OK to close the Office Assistant dialog box, so you can begin installing Microsoft Fax.

2. Click the Inbox icon in the Outlook bar.

3. Choose Tools⇨Services. The Services dialog box appears with the Services tab selected.

4. Click Add. The Add Service to Profile dialog box appears.

5. Select Microsoft Fax and choose OK. A message box appears informing you that you will need to add your name, fax number, and the fax modem you will use when sending faxes.

6. Choose Yes. The Microsoft Fax Properties window appears. Enter your user information. The information you enter in the User properties tab will automatically appear on the cover page of a fax you send from Word. You must enter a return fax number. If you don't have a fax number, enter your voice phone number.

7. Click the Modem tab and select your fax modem from the A̲vailable fax modems list.

8. Click the Set as Active F̲ax Modem button and click OK. A message appears informing you that you must choose Exit and L̲og off and restart Outlook or Exchange for your changes to take effect.

9. Click OK to close the message box and the Services dialog box, and then choose F̲ile⇨Exit and L̲og off.

Sending a fax from Word

When you send a fax, the cover sheet includes information about you that it gets from Outlook. This includes your name, your fax number, and your business and home phone numbers. If you want to edit your fax cover sheet information, double-click the Microsoft Outlook icon. The Outlook window appears. Choose T̲ools⇨Microsoft Fa̲x Tools⇨O̲ptions. The Microsoft Fax Properties dialog box appears. Click the User tab so you can enter or edit Y̲our full name, F̲ax Number, H̲ome Telephone number, and Office T̲elephone Number fields in your fax cover sheet. The follow-ing steps explain how to send a fax from Word using Outlook:

1. Turn on your modem.

2. Start Word, and open the document you want to fax.

3. Choose F̲ile⇨Sen̲d To⇨F̲ax Recipient. The Fax Wizard window appears, as shown in Figure 19-11.

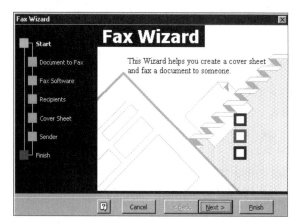

Figure 19-11: The Fax Wizard.

4. Choose N̲ext. Choose to fax the opened document with a cover sheet. You also have the option to send the document without a cover sheet or just send a cover sheet with a note.

5. Choose Next. Choose to send your fax with Microsoft Fax. Alternatively, you can choose to use a different fax program or print the document so you can send it from a separate fax machine.

6. Choose Next. The Recipients window appears. Enter the name of the person you want to receive the fax. If you have entered names and phone numbers in your Address book, click the Address Book button and select the person to receive the fax.

7. Choose Next. The cover sheet window appears so you can choose from three types of cover sheets: Professional, Contemporary, or Elegant. Choose the style you want to use.

8. Choose Next. The Sender window appears with information you entered when you set up Microsoft Fax. Fill in any missing information you want added to your fax cover sheet.

9. Click the Finish button to send the fax. The Send Fax Now button appears.

10. Click Send Fax Now to send your fax.

To send a fax from Word using the Print command:

1. Turn on your modem.

2. Start Word, and open the document you want to send.

3. Choose File⇨Print (Ctrl+P). The Print dialog box appears.

4. Choose the Microsoft Fax printer driver from the Name drop-down list.

5. Click the OK button. The Compose New Fax dialog box appears, as shown in Figure 19-12.

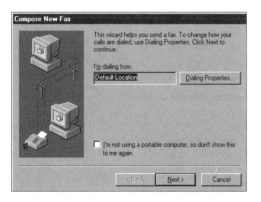

Figure 19-12: The Compose New Fax dialog box.

6. Click the Next button to accept the default location. The dialog box changes to let you enter the recipient information, as shown in Figure 19-13.

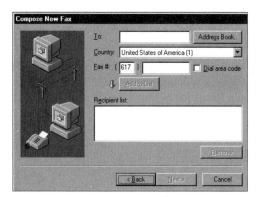

Figure 19-13: The Compose New Fax dialog box changes to let you enter recipient information.

7. Enter the recipient's name in the To text box and the person's fax number in the Fax # text box. If you want to use the Address Book, click the Address Book button. The Address dialog box appears. Select the name of the person to whom you want to send the fax. If the person isn't already in your address book, click the New button. If you choose New, the New Entry dialog box appears. Choose Fax, and choose OK. Enter the recipient's name in the Name to show on the cover page text box, and then enter the fax number in the Area code and fax number field. You must fill in these two fields. The other fields in the different tabs are optional. The Company (Business tab) and the Business phone (Phone Numbers tab) fields also show in the To portion of the fax cover sheet. Click the To button, and choose OK. The name appears in the Recipient list.

8. Click the Next button. The Compose New Fax dialog box displays options for adding a cover sheet, as shown in Figure 19-14.

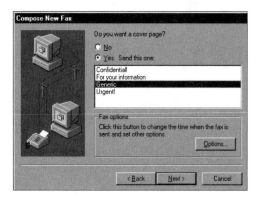

Figure 19-14: The Compose New Fax dialog box changes to display options for adding a fax cover sheet.

9. Click the cover sheet that you want to use from the list, or click the No option button to send the fax without a cover sheet. Click the Next> button. The Compose New Fax dialog box displays options for adding a subject line and an additional note.

10. Enter the topic for your fax in the Subject text box. If you want, enter comments in the Note text box. Click the Next button.

11. Click the Finish button to send the fax. The Microsoft Fax Status dialog box appears showing the progress of your fax. Don't click the Hang Up button; the program will automatically hang up after it finishes sending the fax.

Reviewing and Revising Documents

You can use the Highlight or the Track Changes feature to keep track of changes made to a document, no matter how many different people work on it. Instead of each person actually changing the original document as that person edits it, changes are marked as revisions that can later be accepted and incorporated into the document or rejected and discarded. The new Word 97 Reviewing toolbar has all the tools you need for tracking and processing changes to your documents.

Reviewing a document

Use comments to leave notes to yourself or others—they're much neater than "yellow stickies." Comments are great for reviewers' comments and reminders to yourself about things that you need to check or add later. Comments don't affect a document's formatting, nor do they print with the document (unless you specifically tell them to), so you can insert comments anywhere without worrying that they may end up in your final print-out by mistake.

Note   Word's Reviewing feature allows reviewers to make changes directly in the document. For more information about this feature, see the section "Adding revision marks" later in this chapter.

You can insert a comment using the Insert menu, but working with comments and revisions of your document is easier with the new Reviewing toolbar. To display the toolbar, choose Toolbars from the View menu, and then select Reviewing from the list. You can also right-click another toolbar in an empty area between buttons and select Reviewing from the shortcut menu. See Figure 19-15 for a description of the Reviewing tools.

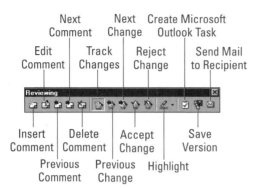

Next Comment

Next Change

Create Microsoft Outlook Task

Edit Comment

Track Changes

Reject Change

Send Mail to Recipient

Insert Comment

Delete Comment

Accept Change

Save Version

Previous Comment

Previous Change

Highlight

Figure 19-15: The Reviewing toolbar tools.

Inserting comments

When you create a comment, Word opens a comment pane, in which you enter the text for the comment. The Comment pane is just like any other pane: you can switch between it and your document editing area by clicking in either area or by pressing F6. You can adjust the size of the Comment pane (or any other pane) by dragging the split bar that separates the two panes. To close the Comment pane, choose Close, click the Edit Comment button on the Reviewing toolbar, double-click a comment mark in the Comment pane, or double-click anywhere on the split bar.

To reopen the Comment pane, double-click a comment mark in the document or choose Edit Comment on the Reviewing toolbar. If you will be inserting or editing multiple comments, you can leave the Comment pane open while you work on your document.

When you insert a comment, Word automatically highlights the word in the document immediately preceding the insertion point. Conversely, when you select a comment in the Comment pane, the corresponding document text is highlighted. If you want the comment to refer to more than one word in the document, select the text before inserting the comment.

To insert a comment:

1. Position your insertion point where you want the comment mark to appear. Or, if you want the comment to refer to a specific section, select the text before you proceed.

2. Click the Insert Comment button on the Reviewing toolbar.

   Word places your initials (from the User Information tab of the Options dialog box) inside a comment mark in your document and opens the Comments pane, as shown in Figure 19-16. Each comment is also numbered, VFA1, VFA2, and so on.

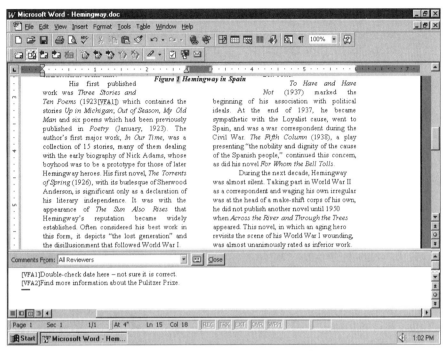

Figure 19-16: The Comments pane in the document window.

3. Type the text for your comment in the Comments pane. You can use any of Word's character and paragraph formatting options.

4. When you are finished, close the Comment pane by choosing <u>C</u>lose or using one of the methods mentioned above.

When you rest the mouse pointer on a highlighted comment marker in the text, the author's name and the comment text are displayed in a ScreenTip.

How Word identifies the reviewer

How does Word identify the reviewer? When you create a comment, Word assigns reviewer initials based on the information in the User Information tab in the Options dialog box (<u>T</u>ools⇨<u>O</u>ptions) dialog box. The ScreenTip displayed in the document includes the author's full name. If you want to be identified differently, edit the User Information tab. If more than one reviewer uses the same system, be sure to change the User Information.

Using sound and pen comments

If your computer has sound capabilities, you can use voice comments to add some personality to your comments. You can combine text and voice comments for the same reference area. Just create a standard text comment by using the techniques described in the preceding section. Then, with your insertion point directly after the comment mark in the document window, add the voice comment. To insert a voice comment:

1. Position your insertion point where you want the voice comment to appear. Or, if you want the comment to refer to a specific section, select the text before you proceed.

2. Choose the Insert Comment button on the Reviewing toolbar to open the Comment pane.

3. Choose the Insert Sound Object button (the button that looks like an audio cassette) on the Comment pane. The Sound Object dialog box appears (see Figure 19-17), and a loud speaker icon appears in the comment text. (If your computer does not have sound capabilities, nothing will happen when you click this button.)

4. Record or insert your comment.

5. If Word prompts you to update the object, do so.

Figure 19-17: Use the Sound Object dialog box to add a voice comment.

6. Close the Comments pane.

Caution   Before you create sound comments, make sure that you know whether the people who will be looking at the document also have sound capabilities on their computers. If they don't, they won't be able to listen to your comments and will miss them.

To listen to a sound comment, double-click the loud speaker icon in the Comment pane. You can also right-click the icon and point to Wave Sound Object in the shortcut menu, and then choose Play.

If your computer system is pen-equipped, you can add hand-written pen comments. Pen comments are treated like drawing objects.

Changing and manipulating the comments

Working in the Comment pane, you can edit and format comments just like any other text. Use any of the techniques in the next section to find the comment that you want to edit or format and fire away. You can include any Word elements in a comment: graphics, frames, and tables are all fair game. The TC (table of contents entry) and XE (index entry) fields cannot be inserted in comments. Other than these elements, anything that you can do in a document can be done in a comment.

You can move, copy, or delete comments just like any other element. The only thing to keep in mind is that you must first select the comment mark before you can move, copy, or delete it. When you move, copy, or delete comments, Word automatically renumbers the comment marks in the document window and in the Comment pane.

To move or copy a selected comment to different locations in the same document or even to different documents use any standard cut, copy, or paste technique, including dragging and dropping with the mouse. When you move a comment mark to a new location, the ScreenTip shows "Inserted" instead of the original comment text.

If you decide you want to remove a comment you inserted, you can delete it. Deleting comment text in the Comment pane does not delete the comment itself. You must delete the comment mark in the document window to delete a comment. To delete a comment, place the insertion point on the comment marker in the document and then click the Delete Comment button on the Reviewing toolbar. You can also simply press Delete or Backspace. The Next Comment and Previous Com-ment buttons will locate other comment markers in the document. You should keep your comment marks visible during editing because if you don't, you may delete a comment unintentionally. If you delete text surrounding a comment mark, the comment is also deleted with no warning.

The Replace feature can globally delete all comments in your document. Just choose Edit⇨Replace, select Comment Mark from the Special pop-up list (or type ^a in the Find what text box). Leave the Replace with text box blank, and choose the Replace All button. (You may need to click the More button in the Replace dialog box to see the Special button.)

If you will be passing the document back to the original reviewer (or to someone else for further edits), you can *answer* a comment inserted by someone else. After you view a particular comment in the ScreenTip and you want to respond to it, place the insertion point to the right of the mark, and then click the Insert Comment button on the Reviewing toolbar. Word inserts a new comment directly following the current one and moves the insertion point to the Comment pane where you enter your comment. The new comment with your initials will appear right after the original reviewer's comment and the comments will be renumbered accordingly. Figure 19-18 shows a new comment inserted in response to an existing comment. Notice the different initials and the renumbering of the other comments. Comments by different reviewers are displayed in different colors in the document and the Comment pane.

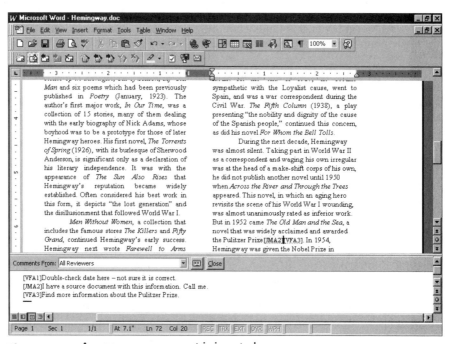

Figure 19-18: An response comment is inserted.

Reviewing comments

When the Comment pane is open, you can view all comments attached to the document by scrolling through the pane, just as you scroll through any other text. By default, all comments are visible when the Comment pane is open. If you want to see only the comments made by a specific reviewer, make a selection from the From list in the Comment pane's toolbar.

Without the Comment pane open, you can still see the text of the comments while viewing the document in the document pane. You don't need to see the comment marks to find where comments are inserted in your document. If you have Screen-Tips activated, the text the comment refers to is highlighted in light yellow. When you move the insertion point over the highlighted text, the color brightens. If you have chosen to display the comment marks, both the text and the marks are highlighted.

Note Comment marks are formatted as hidden text, so the comment marks display only if the display of hidden text is activated. You control the display of hidden text by choosing Tools⇨Options and selecting or clearing the Hidden text check box in the Nonprinting characters section of the View tab. Hidden text is also displayed when All is selected in the Nonprinting characters section of the View tab.

Whether or not the comment marks are visible, you can view the comment online in a ScreenTip, a small pop-up box that appears when you rest the pointer on the highlighted text (see Figure 19-19). The comment ScreenTips appear only if Screen-Tips are selected in the View tab of the Options dialog box.

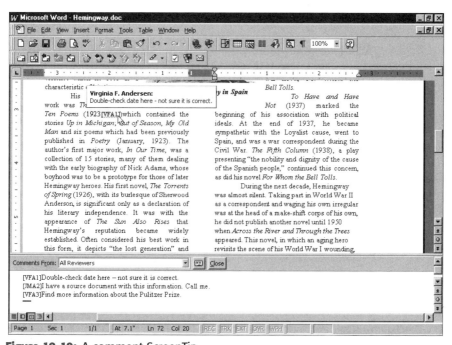

Figure 19-19: A comment ScreenTip.

If you want to review comments sequentially, you can use the Next Comment and Previous Comment buttons on the Reviewing toolbar. The vertical scroll bars in both the document and comment panes also contain Next Comment and Previous Comment buttons below the scroll arrows. The button between the Next and Previous is the Select Browse Object button, which you use to specify the type of object you want to review. To move through comments, click the Select Browse Object button and select Browse by Comment from the displayed palette (see Figure 19-20).

Figure 19-20: The Select
Browse Object palette.

If you want to search for a specific comment or comments from specific reviewers,
use the Go To feature (Edit⇨Go To). Word numbers comments sequentially for all
reviewers throughout a document, but the comments for individual reviewers are
not numbered separately. As more comments are inserted or some deleted, the
existing comments are renumbered accordingly. To search for a specific comment:

1. Choose Edit⇨Go To (or press F5).

2. Select Comment in the Go to what list. Figure 19-21 shows the Go To dialog
   box with Comment selected.

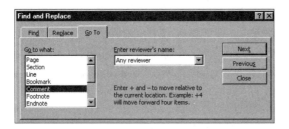

Figure 19-21: The Go To dialog
box with Comment selected.

3. Do one of the following:

   • To find a specific reviewer's comment, select the reviewer's name from the
     Enter reviewer's name drop-down list. The names of all the reviewers who
     have added comments to the document will appear on the list.

   • To find a specific comment, enter the number of the comment (without the
     reviewer's initials) that you want to find in the Enter reviewer's name text
     box. Notice that when you enter a number, the Next button in the Go To
     dialog box is replaced by a Go To button.

   • To find a comment that is positioned relative to your current location,
     enter a number preceded by a plus or minus sign. For example, if you want
     to find the third comment following your current position, enter **+3** in the
     text box.

4. If you specified a comment number or a relative position, choose the Go To
   button. If you specified a reviewer, choose the Next or Previous button to
   jump to the next or preceding comment for that reviewer.

The insertion point will jump to the specified comment mark in your document window. You can then view, edit, or delete the comment.

Note You can also use Word's Find feature to search for comment marks if you don't want to specify a particular comment or reviewer. Just choose Edit⇨Find to open the Find and Replace dialog box. Then choose the Special button, and select Comment Mark from the pop-up list. (You may need to choose More to expand the dialog box to include the Special button.) When you use this feature to find a comment, Word opens the Comment pane and moves the insertion point to the next or preceding comment inside the Comment pane, depending on your Search rule.

Including comments in your document

In many cases, you will want to include text from a comment in your document, and Word's drag-and-drop techniques allow you to do so with ease. With the Comment pane open, just select the text that you want to move or copy into your document and use any of Word's standard cut, copy, and paste techniques.

Protecting documents for comments

If you want to prevent reviewers from making changes to a document, you can protect the document for comments. When you do this, the only elements that anyone can add to the document are comments. As with any other kind of protection, many menu options are dimmed. To protect a document for comments:

1. Choose Tools⇨Protect Document. The Protect Document dialog box appears, as shown in Figure 19-22.

Figure 19-22: The Protect Document dialog box gives you choices for protecting your document.

2. Select Comments.

3. Enter a password in the Password text box if you don't want anyone else to be able to unprotect the document.

   Note that passwords *are* case-sensitive. If you enter the password in all capital letters, that is how you will have to type the password when you access or unprotect the document.

4. Choose OK.

If you entered a password, Word asks you to reenter the password as confirmation.

To unprotect the document, choose Tools⇨Unprotect Document. If you specified a password, you will be prompted to enter the password before you can unprotect the document.

Printing comments

You can print comments, either by themselves or on a separate page at the end of the document. To print comments by themselves:

1. Choose File⇨Print (or press Ctrl+P).

2. Select Comments from the Print what drop-down list.

3. Choose OK.

To print comments at the end of the document:

1. Choose File⇨Print (or press Ctrl+P).

2. Choose Options.

3. Select Comments from the Include with document group in the Print tab, and choose OK.

   Note that selecting Comments also selects the Hidden text box. Because comments are formatted as hidden text, you cannot print comments along with your document without also printing any other hidden text. You can, however, print hidden text without printing comments.

4. Print your document or selected portions of it as desired.

   The comments will print at the end of the document, and each comment will include a reference to the page number on which the referenced text appears, along with the reviewer's initials.

Revising a document

Besides annotating a document with comments, you can highlight portions of text and add revision marks to mark where you have added or deleted text and made formatting changes. Using revision marks, you can later choose whether to accept or reject the revisions. Word also includes options for customizing the marks used to identify revisions. Additionally, Word lets you compare a revised document with the original document to see the changes that were made. The following sections explain how to highlight text, add revision marks, and track revisions using Word.

Highlighting text

The Highlight button on the Reviewing or the Formatting toolbar is a tool for online document revision. The Highlight ScreenTip indicates the current color selection. When you click the Highlight down-arrow key, you see a drop-down palette of colors that you can apply to selected text (see Figure 19-23). When you return to the text and the mouse pointer changes shape to a paintbrush drawing short yellow lines, select the text you want to highlight. If it is just a single word, double-click the word.

Figure 19-23: The Highlight Pen drop-down color palette.

To discontinue highlighting, click the Highlight button again, or select None from the drop-down palette. The highlight gives the effect of having marked the text with a colored felt pen. Figure 19-24 shows some text highlighted with various colors.

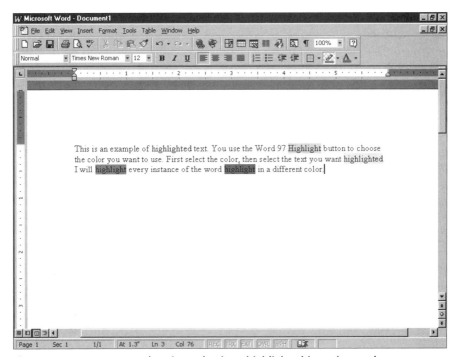

Figure 19-24: Some text showing selections highlighted in various colors.

Caution If you plan to print the document on a monochrome printer, be sure to use a light color so that the text will show through the highlight.

After you have added highlighted comments or revisions, you can use Edit⇨Find to locate each occurrence. First select Highlight in the Format list, and then choose Find Next. To remove the highlight, choose None from the Highlight palette, and then select each highlighted text you want to clear.

To change the highlight color already in your document, select the text and then click the Highlight down arrow and select a new color. If you want to change the color of all the highlighted text in the document, you can use the Replace option on the Edit menu. To replace the highlighted color:

1. Click the Highlight arrow and select a new color from the palette.

2. Choose Edit⇨Replace then select More to expand the Find and Replace dialog box, if necessary.

3. Delete any text and formatting from the Find what and Replace with boxes.

4. Place the insertion point in the Find what box, choose Format and select Highlight from the pop-up list.

5. Repeat Step 4 with the insertion point in the Replace with box.

6. Then do one of the following:

   • Choose Replace to replace the color with the currently selected color on the palette. If you replace the current highlight color, Word automatically moves to the next highlighted text.

   • Choose Find Next to skip this highlight.

   • Choose Replace All to change them all at once.

7. When finished, choose Close.

The View tab of the Options dialog box includes the options for showing or hiding the highlight both on the screen and when printing.

Adding revision marks

In order to have Word automatically mark additions, deletions, and format changes, turn on change tracking. After you turn on change tracking, any changes you make will be marked. If you move text, the text in the original location doesn't disappear; it remains but is marked for deletion. The text in the new location is marked for insertion. If you delete text that you've added while editing, that text is actually deleted. Word 97 now offers change tracking for changes in formatting as well as text.

If you want Word to keep track of revisions to all of your documents automatically, open `Normal.dot`, turn on change tracking, and choose File⇨Save. This command saves the change to the default template that Word uses for your documents. Note that if you use any other template, you will have to activate change tracking manually unless you also modify that template to track changes.

Before you begin marking a document, save a copy of the document with a different name. That way, you can always go back to the original if any problems arise or if you need to double-check something. To turn on change tracking:

1. Choose Tools, point to Track Changes and choose Highlight Changes.

   The Highlight Changes dialog box appears, as shown in Figure 19-25.

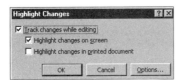

Figure 19-25: The Highlight Changes dialog box.

2. Select Track changes while editing.

3. If you don't want the revision marks to be displayed while you work, clear the Highlight changes on screen check box. As long as Track changes while editing is selected, Word keeps track of your revisions, even when they're not visible on-screen.

4. If you don't want the revision marks to appear in the printed document, clear the Highlight changes in printed document check box.

5. If you want to change the display of revision marks, choose Options to open the Track Changes tab of the Options dialog box and make the desired changes. Changing revision mark options is covered later in this section.

6. Choose OK.

   As you edit the document, all additions, deletions, and reformatting will be marked by either the default markings or those that you select in the Track Changes tab. Figure 19-26 shows a sample document using the default revision markings. Notice that there's a vertical line in the margin next to any line where text has been added or deleted. Each author is automatically assigned a different display color (up to eight). Both new and deleted text is assigned the display color according to the author. Deleted text has a line through it, and new text is underlined. Format changes are hidden by default, but you can have them displayed if you want.

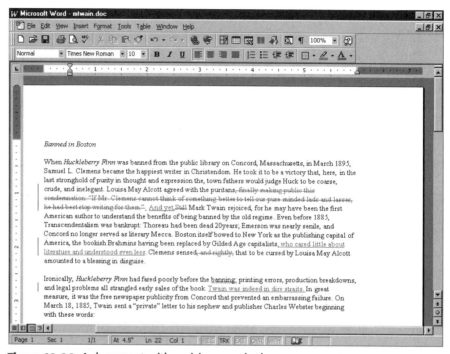

Figure 19-26: A document with revisions marked.

Once you have set the change tracking options, you can use the Reviewing toolbar to review, accept, and reject the marked changes.

You can click the Track Changes button on the Reviewing toolbar to turn the feature on and off. You can also turn off change tracking at any time by clearing the <u>T</u>rack changes while editing check box in the Highlight Changes dialog box. If the revisions marks are visible on the screen, when you rest the insertion point on a revision mark, a ScreenTip displays the name of the reviewer, the date and time the change was marked, and the type of change.

Note You can tell whether change tracking is turned on by looking at the status bar. The letters "TRK" are bolded when revision marking is active. Double-clicking TRK on the status bar is a shortcut for turning off change tracking. If you right-click TRK, the shortcut menu (see Figure 19-27) contains some of the same options as the <u>T</u>rack Changes menu, plus you can open the Track Changes tab of the Options dialog box.

Figure 19-27: The TRK shortcut menu.

Reviewing, accepting, or rejecting changes

After you have marked a revised document, you can go over it and decide which changes you want to keep. When you accept a change, the revision marking for that item is removed. Text marked for deletion is cut from the document; text marked as inserted text is incorporated into the document; and text marked for reformatting is changed.

You can incorporate all the revisions at once by choosing Accept All from the Accept or Reject Changes dialog box. Answer Yes when you are asked whether you want to accept all revisions for the document. Before you decide on such a drastic measure, you can take a look at how the document would look after accepting all the changes by choosing Changes without highlighting in the View area of the Accept or Reject Changes dialog box. This option simply hides the revision marks. To review the original document, choose Original.

You may want to return the document to its original state before any edits were made. You can do so by choosing Reject All from the Accept or Reject Changes dialog box and answering Yes when you are asked whether you want to reject all revisions.

Caution   Undo will not back you out of a global acceptance or rejection of revisions. Pay careful attention before you answer the confirmation prompt. Better yet (and in addition to being careful), make sure that you have a backup copy of the original document, as suggested earlier.

You can also review revisions one at a time, accepting or rejecting as you go:

1. Choose Tools and point to Track Changes; then choose Accept or Reject Changes. The Accept or Reject Changes dialog box appears, as shown in Figure 19-28. For each revision, Word tells you who marked the change and when it was done.

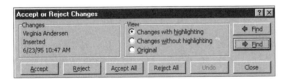

Figure 19-28: The Accept or Reject Changes dialog box.

2. To review a change, do one of the following:

   • To move to the preceding revision mark, choose the Find button with the left arrow.

- To skip this revision mark and move to the next revision mark, choose the Find button with the right arrow.

- Click a revision mark in the document area.

3. With a revision mark selected, do one of the following:

  - Choose Accept to incorporate added text, remove text marked for deletion, or make the format change. Word automatically moves to the next revision mark every time you accept or reject a revision.

  - Choose Reject to reject the revision. When you reject inserted text, the revision mark is removed, and the text is deleted. When you reject deleted text, the revision mark is removed, and the text remains in your document. When you reject a format change, the mark is removed and the appearance of the text is unchanged.

  - To reverse the action after you've accepted or rejected a change, choose Undo.

4. Repeat Steps 2 and 3 until you have completed your review of the document. Then choose Close.

New The new Reviewing toolbar offers you a quick and easy way to review and accept or reject each change the reviewers have marked in your document. Click the Track Changes button to toggle change marking on and off. The Next Change and Previous Change buttons take you to other marks. Click Accept Change or Reject Change to resolve the recommendation. The revision marks need not be visible on the screen for the Reviewing toolbar buttons to work. You will not, however, see an explanation of the revision mark if the marks are hidden.

Customizing the revision marks

Unless you specify otherwise, Word uses the following defaults for revision marks:

✦ Inserted text is marked with an underline.

✦ Deleted text is marked with strikethrough (a line through the characters).

✦ Reformatted text is not marked.

✦ For both inserted and deleted text, a unique color is assigned for up to eight reviewers. If there are more than eight reviewers, Word begins recycling colors.

✦ A vertical line is displayed in the margin next to any line that contains inserted or deleted text. The line color is set to Auto.

You can change the options that control revision mark appearance when you activate revision marking or at any other time. The following instructions in this section take you through the Track Changes dialog box. If you want to change revision marking options outside of the Track Changes dialog box, just choose Tools⇨Options, select the Track Changes tab, and make any changes that you want. The changes that you make affect only the current document unless you save the changes to `Normal.dot` or another template. To change the appearance of revision marks:

1. Choose <u>T</u>ools, point to <u>T</u>rack Changes and choose <u>H</u>ighlight Changes. You can also open this dialog box by right-clicking TRK in the status bar and choosing <u>H</u>ighlight Changes from the shortcut menu. TRK need not be bolded at the time.

2. Choose <u>O</u>ptions to open the Track Changes tab of the Options dialog box, shown in Figure 19-29.

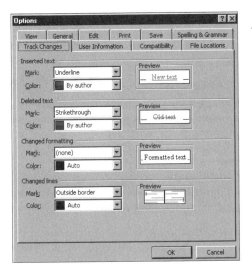

Figure 19-29: The Track Changes tab of the Options dialog box.

3. Change marking options by using the following guidelines:

• To change how inserted text is marked, make a selection from the <u>M</u>ark drop-down list in the Inserted text area. The choices are (none), Bold, Italic, Underline (the default), and Double Underline.

• To change how deleted text is marked, make a selection from the M<u>a</u>rk drop-down list in the Deleted text area. The choices are Hidden, Strikethrough (the default), a caret symbol (^), or a pound sign (#).

• To change how reformatted text is marked, make a selection from the Ma<u>r</u>k drop-down list in the Changed formatting area. The choices are the default (none), Bold, Italic, Underline, and Double Underline.

• To change the placement of the vertical mark that identifies lines containing revised text, make a selection from the Mar<u>k</u> drop-down list in the Changed lines area. The choices are (none), Left Border, Right Border, or Outside Border (the default, which places the mark in the left or right margin on alternating pages).

- To specify a color for any of the marking options, open the Color drop-down list in the desired area and make a selection. Because the default color option (By Author) assigns unique colors to only eight reviewers, you may want to specify custom colors if you have more than eight reviewers.

4. Choose OK twice.

Note   If you don't see revision marks in a document that you have reason to believe was marked or if you see a revision mark in the margin but no text is marked as inserted or deleted, check the settings in the Track Changes tab in the Options dialog box. Deletions can be marked as hidden and not be visible on screen even if hidden text is displayed. To see deletions, reset the change mark to one of the other options. Also keep in mind that the revisions can be inside comments and field codes.

Comparing two versions of a document

You can add revision marks to a revised version of a document that was edited with the change tracking feature turned off. When you use this feature, the original document is not changed. The revised document is marked for your review. Text that appears in the original document but not in the revised version is marked for deletion; text that appears for the first time in the revised document is marked for insertion. In order to compare two versions of a document, you must have two documents with different filenames (or the files must be in different directories). To compare two versions of a document:

1. Open the revised version of the document.

2. Choose <u>T</u>ools, point to <u>T</u>rack Changes and choose <u>C</u>ompare Documents. You select the original filename from the Select File to Compare With Current Document dialog box, shown in Figure 19-30.

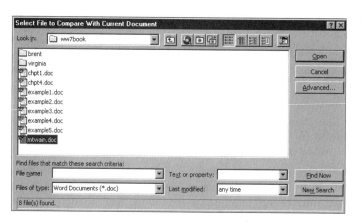

Figure 19-30: The Select File to Compare With Current Document dialog box.

3. Select the original filename from the file list or type the name in the File name text box.

   Note that the Select File to Compare With Current Document dialog box contains all of the same options for searching through drives and folders as the Open dialog box.

4. Choose Open. Word goes through the document and marks the revised document with the differences, highlighting in a different color. Depending on the size of the document, this process could take a little while. After you have marked a document using this technique, you can follow the procedures described earlier for accepting or rejecting the changes. Rest the mouse pointer on each revision mark to see a description of the revision.

Protecting documents for revision

If you want to prevent reviewers from making changes to a document other than those reflected in revision markings, you can protect the document for tracked changes. When you protect a document for tracked changes, the only elements that anyone can add to the document are text and format changes. When tracked change protection is activated, revision marking can't be turned off, nor can a reviewer accept or reject any revisions. Tracked change protection also prevents others from making any nontext changes other than formatting. As with any other kind of protection, many menu options are dimmed. To protect a document for tracked changes:

1. Choose Tools⇨Protect Document.

2. Select Tracked changes in the Protect Document dialog box.

3. Enter a password in the Password text box if you don't want anyone else to be able to unprotect the document. Passwords *are* case-sensitive. If you enter the password in all capital letters, you will have to type the password in that manner when you access the document.

4. Choose OK. If you entered a password, Word asks you to reenter the password as confirmation.

To unprotect the document, choose Tools⇨Unprotect Document. If you specified a password, you will be prompted to enter the password before the document can be unprotected.

Merging comments and revisions from multiple reviewers

In many cases, a document will make its way through several reviewers during the editing process, with each reviewer adding properly identified comments and/or tracked changes to a separate copy of the document. To combine all the comments and proposed changes into one document, all you need is the original document and each revised version.

To merge comments and tracked changes:

1. Make sure that all the revised documents that you want to merge have been marked for revisions. If changes weren't tracked for any of the documents, compare the revised document to the original and add revision marks.

2. Open a copy of the original document that you want to merge the changes to.

3. Choose Tools⇨Merge Documents. The Select File to Merge Into Current Document dialog box opens, as shown in Figure 19-31.

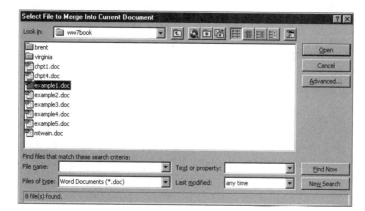

Figure 19-31: The Select File to Merge Into Current Document dialog box.

4. Select one of the shared documents that has changes you want to merge with the original file.

   The Select File to Merge Into Current Document dialog box contains all the same options for searching through drives and folders as the Open dialog box. You can select the name of the file from the displayed name list or type the name in the File name text box.

5. Choose Open.

6. Repeat Steps 3 through 5 for each revised version of the original document.

   Any comments or revisions that were already in the original document remain, and Word uses different colors to distinguish the merged comments and revisions for each of up to eight reviewers.

After merging all the reviewed copies of the document, you can examine all the comments and proposed changes and accept or reject them as before.

Summary

This chapter has covered many of the Word tools that let you share documents with others and add comments and revisions during the document preparation process. In this chapter you have learned how to:

✦ Send a document via e-mail or fax.

✦ Route a document across the network.

✦ Review documents and highlight specific text and relate comments to co-authors.

✦ Revise a document with one or more reviewers.

✦ Merge several versions into one document.

Where to go next...

✦ In many cases, when you work with long documents you will need to share them with others for review and revisions, and you will need to apply the review and revision tools you worked with in this chapter. For information on working with long documents, see Chapter 23.

✦   ✦   ✦

The Great Plays: Mail Merge, Forms, Outlines, and Long Documents

P A R T

V

Creating Form Letters, Envelopes, Labels, and Catalogs

✦ ✦ ✦ ✦

In This Chapter

Creating and printing form letters

Producing envelopes, mailing labels, and lists

Using documents from other applications

Screening records before printing

Changing the order of printing

Exploring some advanced concepts

✦ ✦ ✦ ✦

In this chapter, you learn about the fundamentals for creating and printing various kinds of merged documents, as well as some of the more advanced techniques such as selecting certain letters or labels to print, sorting the documents before printing, and varying the text of the letter based on field value.

Merging Letter and Address Files

Word's capability to insert information from one file into another is the key to some very useful and powerful work that you can accomplish. With the process called *merging*, you can do any of the following:

✦ Print personalized letters addressed to any number of recipients.

✦ Print envelopes for the letters.

✦ Print mailing labels.

✦ Print lists and catalogs.

Briefly, merging involves creating a main document that contains text with some placemarkers embedded within the text. Separately, you create a data source document that lists sets of text that will replace the placemarkers in the main document. Then, when Word merges the two files, the result is a set of documents, one document for each set of text in the data source document. Each of these resulting documents contains the text of the original main document with the text from the data source document inserted in place of the markers.

The best known use for merging is creating form letters, such as those announcing that you, personally, have won millions of dollars in the sweepstakes. A typical main document for a form letter consists of the text of the letter with markers indicating positions for an addressee's name, street address, city, state, and ZIP code. The data source document contains a list of the actual addressees' names and addresses. Word merges the two documents together to print personalized letters.

In addition to creating form letters, you can use Word to merge data for printing envelopes and mailing labels. Word can also merge data between a main document and a data source document to produce formatted lists, such as catalogs and directories.

That is just the beginning of what merging can do. A main document can include fields that define conditions. A condition in the main document might define the conditions under which data in the data source document will be used. You can print letters, envelopes, or labels for people who live in a certain city, for example, or whose addresses are within a certain range of ZIP codes. Or you can print letters to remind them to renew their soon-to-expire magazine subscriptions. The possibilities arc limitless.

Like many of Word's features, you can use merging in a straightforward way to satisfy many of your needs. You can also explore its advanced capabilities. Suppose that you work in a billing department and want to automate the process of sending reminder letters to customers who are more than 30 days delinquent in paying their bills. You create a suitable letter and save it as the main document. You also create a data source document that contains customers' names and addresses, together with the date on which they were originally billed. Then you can ask Word to merge the two documents, selecting only those customers who were billed more than 30 days before the current date. You can even increase the severity of the reminder as the account becomes more delinquent.

The first part of this chapter deals with straightforward merging to print form letters, envelopes, mailing labels, and lists. Later sections of the chapter cover some of the more sophisticated ways in which you can use Word's versatile merge feature.

Just What Is Merging?

The beginning of this chapter introduced you to the concept of two documents used by Word in the merge process: a main document and a data source document. Now is the time to look at these documents in more detail before getting down to the specific task of creating typical merged documents. For the present, think only about using Mail Merge to create personalized form letters. Later in this chapter, you'll see how the same concepts and techniques apply to addressing envelopes, printing labels, and creating lists and catalogs.

Take a few minutes now to get a general understanding of the main and data source documents. After that, you'll learn how to create these documents.

The main document

The *main document* for a form letter contains the text, and perhaps graphics, that should be in every letter. It also contains markers, called *field codes*, where the personalizing text should go. Figure 20-1 shows a typical main document.

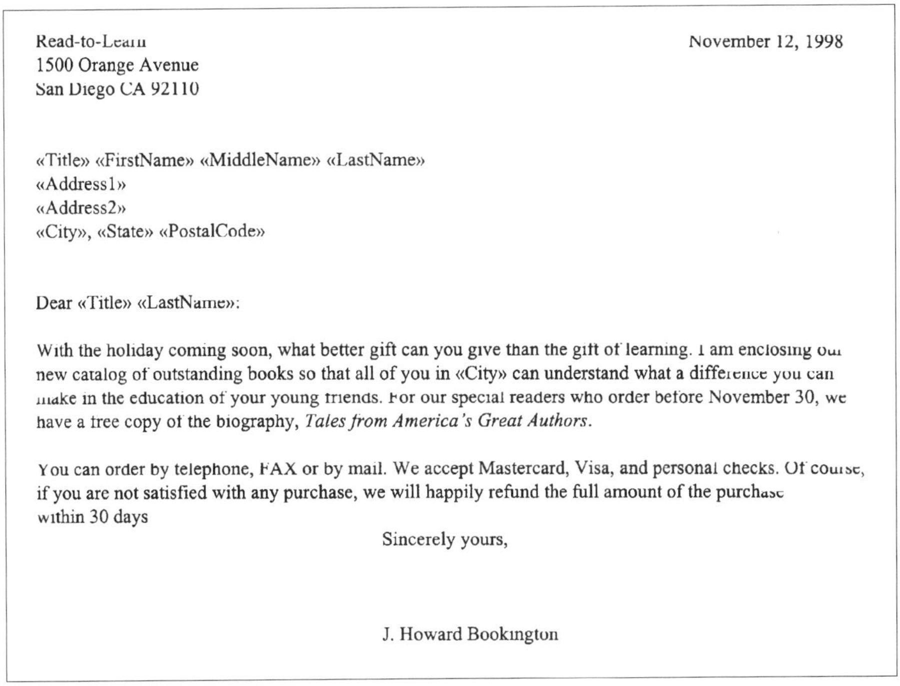

Read-to-Learn   November 12, 1998
1500 Orange Avenue
San Diego CA 92110

«Title» «FirstName» «MiddleName» «LastName»
«Address1»
«Address2»
«City», «State» «PostalCode»

Dear «Title» «LastName»:

With the holiday coming soon, what better gift can you give than the gift of learning. I am enclosing our new catalog of outstanding books so that all of you in «City» can understand what a difference you can make in the education of your young friends. For our special readers who order before November 30, we have a free copy of the biography, *Tales from America's Great Authors*.

You can order by telephone, FAX or by mail. We accept Mastercard, Visa, and personal checks. Of course, if you are not satisfied with any purchase, we will happily refund the full amount of the purchase within 30 days

Sincerely yours,

J. Howard Bookington

Figure 20-1: A typical main document.

The words enclosed in chevrons (« and ») in the main document are the field codes that identify data to be inserted from the data source document. Other text in the main document (text not enclosed in chevrons) will appear in every letter.

Note   You don't type the chevrons and the field codes they enclose. As you'll learn later in this chapter, you use convenient Word tools to place the field codes in your document.

The data source document

The *data source document* contains the information that replaces field codes in the main document. Figure 20-2 shows a typical data source document.

Title	FirstName	MiddleName	LastName	Address1	Address2	City	State	PostalCode
Mr.	Alexander		Parsons	6701 Willow Way		El Cajon	CA	92020
Ms.	Patricia	B.	Burnham	1702 Morningside Ave.		Louisville	KY	40243
Dr.	Marilyn	L.	Fletcher	Snow Village	P.O. Box 49	Londonderry	VT	05148
Mr.	Philipe	V.	Renoir	1709 W. Ranchera St.		Beaumont	KS	67012
Mrs.	Ruth	K.	Farwell	5 Normal St.		Cambridge	MA	02146
Mr.	Jacob	L.	Jones	Rt. 3 Box 2209		Gloucester	VA	23061
Mrs.	Francine	H.	Kellogg	6612 Orange Ave.		Pasadena	CA	91105
Ms.	Susanne	A.	Waterside	702 Jasmine Circle		Coronado	CA	92118

Figure 20-2: The beginning of a typical data source document.

The data source document is actually just a table. The row at the top of the table contains the field names. The same names are used in the main document to mark where text from the data source document is to be placed. After the first row, each row of the table contains information about one person.

Although you can create a data source document just as you create a table for any other document, as described in Chapter 12, Word provides an easier way to create the data source document, as you will see a little later.

Putting the two together

After you create a main document and a data source document, you need only tell Word to merge them. The result is a set of customized letters, such as the one shown in Figure 20-3.

Here are some important facts about merging:

✦ Each letter contains data from the data source document in its proper place.

✦ Some of the fields (Title, LastName, and City) are used more than once.

✦ Most of the customized letters do not use one of the fields (Address2) in the data source document. In these cases, Word does not leave a blank line in its place.

✦ The customized letters are created in the same order as the names are listed in the data source document. You can easily change this order.

✦ The fields in the data source document need not be in any special order.

Writing Form Letters

Word guides you smoothly through the process of creating a form letter. You simply follow the instructions in a sequence of dialog boxes.

Read-to-Learn   November 12, 1998
1500 Orange Avenue
San Diego CA 92110

Mr. Alexander Parsons
6701 Willow Way
El Cajon, CA 92020

Dear Mr. Parsons:

With the holiday coming soon, what better gift can you give than the gift of learning. I am enclosing our
new catalog of outstanding books so that all of you in El Cajon can understand what a difference you can
make in the education of your young friends. For our special readers who order before November 30, we
have a free copy of the biography, *Tales from America's Great Authors*.

You can order by telephone, FAX or by mail. We accept Mastercard, Visa, and personal checks. Of course
if you are not satisfied with any purchase, we will happily refund the full amount of the purchase
within 30 days
                              Sincerely yours,

                              J. Howard Bookington

Figure 20-3: A typical customized letter.

If you follow the steps in the following section, you create several files. Before you
start, however, use the Windows Explorer or DOS to create a folder for these files
so that you can save them all together in the folder. These steps assume you have
created a folder named My Mail Merge within your own or the main Word
directory.

Building a new merge structure

The process described here assumes that you are not basing your form letters on
an existing letter and that you do not have a list of people to whom you want to
address the letters. Later in this chapter, you learn how to adapt an existing letter
and how to use an existing list of names and addresses. To begin creating a set of
form letters:

1. With an empty document open, choose Tools⇨Mail Merge to open the Mail
   Merge Helper dialog box, as shown in Figure 20-4. The information box at the
   top tells you what to do next.

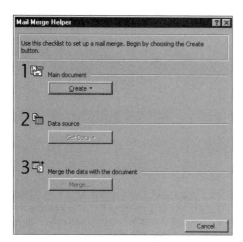

Figure 20-4: The initial Mail Merge Helper dialog box.

2. Choose the <u>C</u>reate button to open a list of the types of documents you can create, as shown in Figure 20-5.

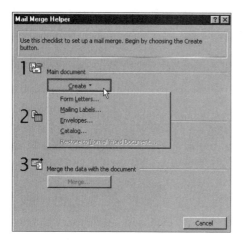

Figure 20-5: The list of document types you can create.

3. Choose Form <u>L</u>etters to open a dialog box that asks you whether you want to use the current <u>A</u>ctive Window as the basis of your form letter or create a <u>N</u>ew Main Document.

4. Choose <u>N</u>ew Main Document to return to the Mail Merge Helper dialog box, which again tells you that the next step is to specify a data source by choosing the <u>G</u>et Data button.

Creating the data source document

The data source document is a table in which the first row, known as the *header row,* contains field names. The remaining rows of the table contain data for each person. In the following steps, you choose the field names that go into the header row. To define the source data:

1. As suggested in the message at the top of the Mail Merge Helper dialog box, choose the Get Data button to display a list box, as shown in Figure 20-6.

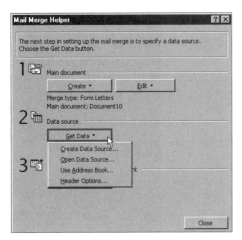

Figure 20-6: The choice of creating a data source or using an existing data source.

2. Because you don't already have a source of data, choose Create Data Source to display the Create Data Source dialog box, as shown in Figure 20-7.

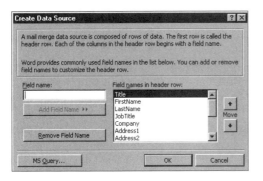

Figure 20-7: The Create Data Source dialog box.

The Create Data Source dialog box offers you a list of commonly used field names. You can use this list as it is, change or delete some of the field names, or add other field names.

Field names can consist of up to 40 characters. Each field name must be unique in the same data source document. Field names must start with a letter; subsequent characters can be letters, numbers, or the underscore character. Field names cannot contain spaces.

Tip As you work through the next few steps, you remove some of the field names provided and add a field name of your own.

You have a good reason for using separate fields for a person's first and last names. By doing so, you can sort names in the list alphabetically by order of last name.

Selecting just the right field names

The form letter you are creating is a personal one, so you don't need the JobTitle and Company fields, nor do you need the country field and the two telephone number fields. To remove field names:

1. In the Field names in header row list box, select the JobTitle field name.

2. Choose Remove Field Name to remove JobTitle from the list. Word removes that field name and automatically selects the next name in the list, Company in this case.

3. Choose Remove Field Name again to remove Company from the list.

4. Scroll down the list, and select Country. Choose Remove Field Name to remove that name.

5. Choose Remove Field Name twice more to remove HomePhone and WorkPhone.

Tip Immediately after you remove a field name from the list, that name appears in the Field Name text box. If you remove a name by mistake, choose Add Field Name to put that name back into the list.

Adding a field name

The list suggested by Word provides FirstName and LastName fields, but it doesn't provide a field for a person's middle name or initial. This omission can be a problem if you want to send a letter to Mr. A. John Brown or anyone else who uses a middle name. For this reason, you might want to insert a field for a person's middle name into the list. To insert a name into the list:

1. If necessary, select the Field name text box.

2. Type a name for the field you want to insert. Remember that the name must start with a letter, must not contain spaces, and can have up to 40 characters. In this case, type **MiddleName**.

3. Choose Add Field Name to append the new name to the end of the list.

Changing the order of the field names

After you place data into the data source document, the order of field names doesn't matter because Word merges the data into the main document on the basis of field names, not on the basis of their order in the data source document. When you are entering data into the data source document, however, having the fields in some logical order is convenient. For this reason, you should move the new MiddleName field so that it is between FirstName and LastName. To move a field name in the list:

1. Select the field name you want to move. In this case, select MiddleName.

2. Point to the up arrow at the right side of the Create Data Source dialog box, just above the word Move.

3. Click the mouse button several times to move the MiddleName up until it is between FirstName and LastName. You have now completed naming the fields in your data source document.

You can, of course, use the down arrow to move a field name down the list.

Naming and saving the empty data source document

At this stage, you have created just the skeleton of a data source document. Word, however, expects you to name the document and save it:

1. Choose OK at the bottom of the Create Data Source dialog box to display the Save As dialog box.

2. Open the My Mail Merge (or other) folder you created for your Mail Merge files.

3. In the File name text box, type a name, such as **NAMELIST**, and choose Save. Word saves the file and displays the dialog box shown in Figure 20-8. You can choose Edit Data Source if you want to enter information about the people to whom your letter is addressed, or you can choose Edit Main Document if you want to work on the letter itself.

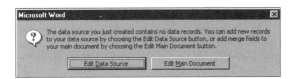

Figure 20-8: Choosing what you want to do next.

4. Choose Edit Data Source in this case to display the Data Form dialog box, as shown in Figure 20-9.

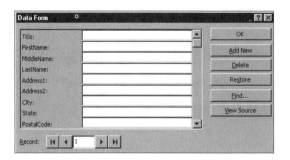

Figure 20-9: The Data Form dialog box.

Note   You are free to decide whether you want to place data in the data source document before you complete the main document or work on the main document first and then place data in the data source document.

Putting names and addresses in the data source document

In the Data Form dialog box, you provide the specific text that replaces field codes for each person when you merge the two files. The dialog box lists the field names at the left with text boxes at the right in which you can type text for each field. You are not limited to the width of the text box on the screen. If you type more characters than will fit, your typed characters automatically scroll to the left to provide more space. You can enter as much text as you need into each field. Do not include the Tab character.

When you first open the Data Form dialog box, a flashing insertion point appears at the beginning of the first field. The Record box at the bottom of the dialog box contains the number 1 to indicate that the information you are about to type goes into the first record in the data source document.

Suppose that the first person on your list is Mr. Alexander Parsons. To place the data for the first person into the data source document:

1. Type **Mr.** for the Title field. Include the period if you want it to appear in your form letter. If you make a typing mistake, press the backspace key to delete what you typed, and type the correct characters.

2. Press Enter or Tab to move to the FirstName field.

3. Type **Alexander**. Then press Enter or Tab to move to the MiddleName field.

4. Press Enter or Tab to leave this field empty and move to the LastName field.

5. Type **Parsons**. Then press Enter or Tab.

6. Continue in this way, using your imagination or copying the data shown earlier in Figure 20-2 to place data in the remaining fields. Leave the Address2 field blank unless the person's address requires two lines.

7. After you have placed information in all the fields, choose <u>A</u>dd New (or press Enter if the insertion point is in the last field) to accept all the information for the record. Word then displays blank fields ready for you to type data for the next record and the record number shows **2**.

Note In Step 1 of the "To place the data for the first person into the data source document" task, you typed the person's title (Mr) followed by a period. You should include the period here rather than in the main document because you may want to spell out the title in full for some people, in which case you don't want the period to appear in the merged letter.

To have a data source document that you can work with in the remainder of this chapter, you need to enter records for several more people. Repeat the steps in the preceding procedure nine more times so that you have 10 records. You can use imaginary information as is done here, or you can copy information from your personal address book. So that you can follow the examples later in this chapter, make sure that at least one record contains an address in Vermont (use the abbreviation VT in the State field) and another record contains an address in California (use CA in the State field).

At any time while you are entering the data, you can move from record to record by choosing the buttons at the bottom of the Data Form dialog box, to the right of the word <u>R</u>ecord. Table 20-1 summarizes the purpose of these buttons. The number in the box enclosed by these buttons indicates which record is currently displayed.

Table 20-1
Data Form Dialog Box Buttons

Button	Action
⏮	Go to first record.
◀	Go to previous record.
▶	Go to next record.
⏭	Go to last record.

With any record selected, you can use normal editing methods to change the content of any field in that record.

After you have entered data for eight or ten records, save that data to disk as explained in the next section.

Saving the filled-in data source document

When you saved the data source document previously, you saved only the header row with the field names. Now you need to save it again with the data you have just entered. To save the data source document with its data:

1. Choose the View Source button in the Data Form dialog box to display the data source document as a table, as shown in Figure 20-10. Don't be concerned about the way data wraps within the narrow columns. The wrapping has no effect on the way the data is formatted in your form letters. (Refer to Chapter 12 for information about tables.) Notice that the Mail Merge toolbar is temporarily replaced by the Standard toolbar.

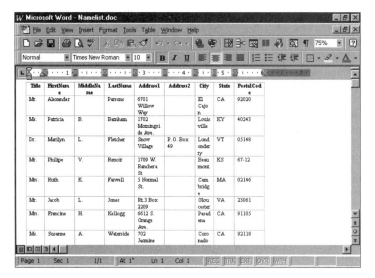

Figure 20-10: The data source document displayed as a table.

2. Choose File⇨Save to save the data source document with the new data. Then close the file and the Mail Merge toolbar returns.

3. Choose the Mail Merge Helper button in the Mail Merge toolbar to reopen the Mail Merge Helper dialog box where you can work on the form letter's main document.

Now that you've completed the data source document, you're ready to work on the main document.

Using an Address Book

If you have created a mailing list and saved it in your Personal Address Book, in the Microsoft Schedule+ Contact list, or with the new Office 97 Outlook information manager, you can use it as your data source. When you choose Get

Data Source in the Mail Merge Helper dialog box, choose Use <u>A</u>ddress Book from the list. The Use Address Book dialog box opens (see Figure 20-11) where you can choose the source of the addresses.

Figure 20-11: The Use Address Book dialog box.

After you select the address source to use as the data source document, Word opens the Choose Profile dialog box where you choose the information services to use with Windows Messaging. The list depends on how you installed Windows.

Cruising the Mail Merge toolbar

As soon as you begin Mail Merge, the Mail Merge toolbar appears behind the dialog box. While you are working with Mail Merge, you frequently use buttons in the Mail Merge toolbar. When you start creating the main document you have a clear view of the toolbar and all the buttons. Table 20-2 defines the functions of the buttons in the Mail Merge toolbar.

Table 20-2
Functions of the Mail Merge Toolbar Buttons

Button	Name	Function
Insert Merge Field ▾	Insert Merge Field	Insert a merge field into the main document.
Insert Word Field ▾	Insert Word Field	Insert a Word field into the main document.
«»ABC	View Merged Data	Toggle between viewing merge fields and merged data.
▮◀	First Record	Go to the first record in a data source document.
◀	Previous Record	Go to the previous record in a data source document.
1	Go to Record	Go to a specific record in the data source document.
▶	Next Record	Go to the next record in a data source document.

(continued)

		Table 20-2 *(continued)*	
Button	**Name**	**Function**
	Last Record	Go to the last record in a data source document.
	Mail Merge Helper	Display the Mail Merge Helper dialog box.
	Check for Errors	Check for errors in merged documents.
	Merge to New Document	Display merged documents on-screen.
	Merge to Printer	Print merged documents.
	Mail Merge	Display Merge dialog box.
	Find Record	Find a record in the data source document.
	Edit Data Source	Edit the data source document.

Creating the form letter

When you first see the main document, it is empty. You have to place two types of data in it:

✦ Text that appears in every letter

✦ Field codes to mark the positions where text from the data source document will be inserted

For this example, create a conventional letter that starts with the return address on the left and the date on the right. Follow the heading with the recipient's name and address, a salutation, the body of the letter, and the sender's signature.

Starting with the return address

Because the return address is text that appears in every copy of the letter, type it as you normally do so that it appears at the top of the document. Leave two blank lines, and then type the date on which you plan to mail the letters. If you like, copy the text in Figure 20-12 for the return address.

Refer to Chapter 26 for information about using a date field instead of typing the date. If you use a date field, Word prints the actual date on which the letter is printed.

At this stage, the beginning of the main document should look like the one shown in Figure 20-12. Press Enter three times to move to the next line and add two blank lines.

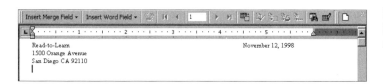

Figure 20-12: The beginning of the main document.

Inserting merge field

Now you are ready to place fields for the recipient's name and address. This is information that will be merged from the data source document. To place the recipient's name and address:

1. Choose the Insert Merge Field button at the left end of the Mail Merge toolbar to display a list of fields in the data source document, as shown in Figure 20-13.

Figure 20-13: The list of fields in the data source document.

2. Select Title from the list. The Title field name, enclosed in chevrons, appears at the insertion point in your document.

3. Press the spacebar to leave a space, and choose the Insert Merge Field button in the toolbar again. If you forget the space, you can always add it later by placing the insertion point between the fields and pressing the spacebar.

4. Select FirstName to place that field name in the document.

5. Press the spacebar again, and choose the Insert Merge Field button to insert MiddleName in the document.

6. Press the spacebar one more time, and choose the Insert Merge Field button to insert LastName in the document. Your document should now look like the one shown in Figure 20-14.

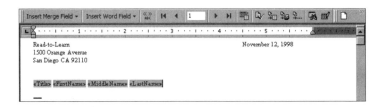

Figure 20-14: The four recipient-name fields in the main document.

> **Note**   You must use the Insert Merge Field button to place field names in the main document. You cannot type these names, nor can you use Insert➪Symbol to insert the chevrons.

After you place fields for the first line of the recipient's address, continue in a similar manner to place the fields for the remaining recipient-address:

1. Press Enter to start a new line.

2. Use the Insert Merge Field button to insert the Address1 field. Press Enter.

3. Insert the Address2 field. Press Enter.

4. Insert the City field, type a comma, press the spacebar, insert the State field, press the spacebar and insert the PostalCode field. At this stage, the main document should look like the one shown in Figure 20-15.

Figure 20-15: The completed recipient-address section of the main document.

> **Note**   You might wonder what happens when Word merges an empty field from the data source document with the main document. Normally, Word ignores empty fields and closes up the text. Therefore, if the MiddleName field is empty for a particular record, Word omits that field in the merged document. Similarly, if the Address2 field is empty, Word omits that field and does not leave a blank line where that field would have been.

Completing the main document

Now you are ready to place the salutation at the beginning of the form letter. To enter the salutation:

1. Leave a blank line. Then type **Dear**, followed by a space.

2. Use the Insert Merge Field button to insert the Title field.

3. Leave a space, and insert the LastName field followed by a colon.

Now type the body of the letter. Include a reference to the recipient's city by using the City field code. Conclude the letter with a space for your signature, and type your name. Figure 20-16 shows most of the letter. The field codes are set to be shaded only when selected.

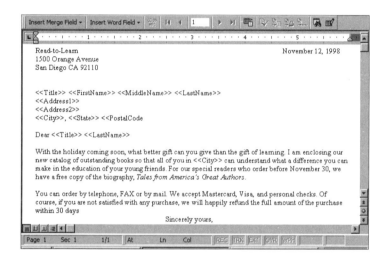

Figure 20-16: The form letter showing inserted codes.

If you want to save time, scan your signature, and insert it as a graphic at the end of the main document. That way, you don't have to sign each letter by hand. See Chapter 13 for information about graphics.

Naming and saving the main document

After you complete the main document, you must save it. You save the same way you save any other document: by choosing File⇨Save and entering a name.

You now have the main document and the data source document complete. The next step is to merge the two documents.

Merging the main and data source documents

At this stage, you can immediately merge and print the letters. If your data source document contains more than two or three names, however, you should check that everything is working correctly before you print all the letters. If you have hundreds of names in your list, you don't want to print all the letters and then find out you've made a minor mistake.

Word provides several ways you can check your documents before you print the letters.

Letting Word check your documents for errors

After you choose, or create, a data source document and a main document, you are ready to check for errors, an important step before you start printing. To check your main and data source documents for errors, choose Check Errors in the Merge dialog box or choose the Check for Errors button in the Mail Merge toolbar. In the resulting dialog box, you can choose to do the following:

✦ Simulate the merge, and report errors in a new document.

✦ Complete the merge, pausing to report each error as it occurs.

✦ Complete the merge without pausing. Report errors in a new document.

You can choose any of these error-reporting modes to check your documents. Word initially proposes the second mode and, generally, it is the most useful. To check for errors:

1. Choose Merge in the Mail Merge Helper dialog box to display the Merge dialog box, as shown in Figure 20-17.

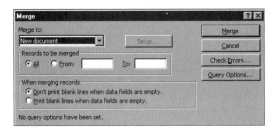

Figure 20-17: The Merge dialog box.

2. Choose Check Errors to display the Checking and Reporting Errors dialog box, as shown in Figure 20-18.

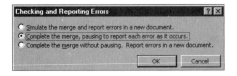

Figure 20-18: The Checking and Reporting Errors dialog box.

3. Choose Complete the merge, pausing to report each error as it occurs (the default option), or one of the other options if you prefer, and then choose OK. If Word detects no errors, the Merge dialog box reappears.

If Word finds an error, it displays a message box to tell you the nature of that error. Then you must correct the main document or the data source document and check for errors again before proceeding.

If you've followed the steps in this chapter, Word should not find any errors. In this case, Word creates a single document containing all the letters, each one separated from the next by a Section Break (Next Page) marker, as shown in Figure 20-19. (We've scrolled down the screen so that you can see the section break.) Examine all the letters in this document to make sure that they are what you intended, and print this document to create your letters.

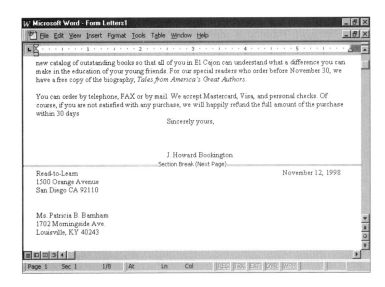

Figure 20-19: The beginning of a document that contains all your form letters.

You can choose File➪Print Preview to see on-screen how the letters will look when they are printed. Or you can choose File➪Print, and print any or all of the form letters. Make any necessary changes to the Print dialog box, as described in Chapter 5, and choose OK to print the letters.

Merging the files to a new document

If you used the error-checking procedure described in the preceding section, you have already merged your files to a new document. As an alternative, you can choose the Merge to New Document button in the Mail Merge toolbar to create a new document that contains all your merged documents as a single document. Merge to a new document if you want to do the following:

✦ Edit individual letters.

✦ Create a file copy of your letters that you can print from another computer.

If you choose this method, you can use normal editing procedures to edit the individual letters in the document. When you are satisfied with your letters, choose the Merge to Printer button in the Mail Merge toolbar to display the Print dialog box as before.

Creating Envelopes, Mailing Labels, and Lists

In addition to creating form letters, you can use Word's Mail Merge to print envelopes or labels for those letters. You can also print a list of names and addresses, using the data source document you already have.

Using Mail Merge to print envelopes

The steps you follow to print envelopes, using an already-existing data source document, are similar to those you use to create form letters except that the envelope is the main document.

Word helps you create the envelope layout as a main document. To do so, Word needs to know what type of printer you plan to use to print the envelopes. Before you begin these steps, select that printer so that Word configures the envelopes correctly. Selecting the correct printer (the printer you will use to print envelopes) before proceeding is very important.

Word uses the text in the Mailing Address section of the User Information tab of the Options dialog box as the default return address on envelopes. Make sure this information is correct before you prepare to print envelopes. Refer to Chapter 5 for information about setting this address.

Designating a printer

For detailed information about selecting a printer that Word uses to print a document, refer to Chapter 5. To select the desired printer:

1. With an empty document on the screen, choose File⇨Print to display the Print dialog box.

2. Click the Name down arrow, and select the printer you plan to use to print your envelopes from the list of installed printers.

3. Choose OK to close the Print dialog box with the printer selected. Word passes a blank page through the printer.

After you select the correct printer, you are ready to prepare for printing envelopes.

Getting ready to print envelopes

Preparing to print envelopes is a matter of identifying the data source document, or creating one if it doesn't already exist, and selecting the envelope size and layout. To identify the data source document:

1. Choose Tools⇨Mail Merge to display the Mail Merge dialog box.

2. Choose Create, choose Envelopes, and choose New Main Document.

3. In the Mail Merge Helper dialog box, choose Get Data.

4. To use the existing data source document, select Open Data Source. Word displays the Open Data Source dialog box.

5. Open the folder (My Mail Merge) that contains the existing data source document. Select the data source document and choose Open. Word tells you that the next step is to set up the main document.

The steps in identifying the data source document assume that you already have a data source document. If you do not have one, in Step 4, choose Create Data Source, and use the Create Data Source dialog box to create a new data source document, as described previously in the section about creating form letters.

Now, you are ready to select an envelope size and layout:

1. Choose Set Up Main Document to display the Envelope Options tab of the Envelope Options dialog box, as shown in Figure 20-20.

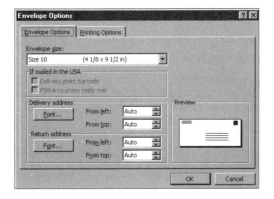

Figure 20-20: The Envelope Options tab of the Envelope Options dialog box.

2. In the Envelope size list box, select the type of envelope you are using. If you select anything other than Custom, Word displays the envelope size. If you select Custom, Word displays a dialog box in which you can set the envelope size.

    The Preview section at the bottom right of the dialog box displays a miniature view of the selected envelope, together with the placement of the recipient and return addresses. For most purposes, you can accept the envelope layout Word proposes. However, you can modify the position and font for the addresses.

3. Select the Printing Options tab of the Envelope Options dialog box. The name of the current default printer appears at the top of the dialog box. If it is not the printer you intend to use, you must cancel this complete sequence of steps, select the correct default printer as previously described, and start this sequence of steps again from the beginning. Figure 20-21 shows a typical Printing Options tab.

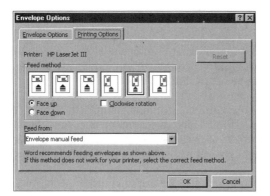

Figure 20-21: The Printing Options tab of the Envelope Options dialog box.

4. If necessary, in the Feed from list box, select the feeder you will use to feed envelopes into your printer.

5. Word shows you several ways to feed the envelope into the printer. In Figure 20-21, for example, you see that the envelope should be face up, centered in the feeder, and with the stamp edge leading. In most instances, you do not change these settings, so just choose OK to display the Envelope address dialog box.

6. The Envelope address dialog box contains a blank box that represents the recipient-address area on an envelope. Choose Insert Merge Field to display a list of field names in the data source document, as shown in Figure 20-22.

Figure 20-22: The Envelope address dialog box listing available fields.

7. Select the first field you want in the address. In this case, select Title to display that field name at the top left of the address space.

8. Proceed as you did when creating a form letter to place the remaining fields in the address space with spaces and punctuation marks. The completed address should look similar to the one shown in Figure 20-23.

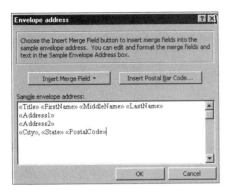

Figure 20-23: The Envelope address dialog box showing field codes.

9. If you want Word to print the postal bar code on each envelope, choose Insert Postal Bar Code to display the Insert Postal Bar Code dialog box, as shown in Figure 20-24. In this dialog box, use the Merge Field with ZIP Code list box to choose the field that contains the ZIP code in your data source document. In this case, select PostalCode. You can also choose to include the FIM-A courtesy reply mail code with the bar code. Then choose OK to return to the Envelope address dialog box, which now indicates where the bar code will appear on the envelope.

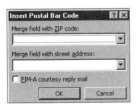

Figure 20-24: The Insert Postal Bar Code dialog box.

10. Choose OK to return to the Mail Merge Helper dialog box, which now indicates that the next step is to complete the merge.

Checking for errors

As before, check for errors before you start printing the envelopes. You check for errors in the envelopes the same as for the main document or the data source document. If any are found, you must correct them before proceeding.

Printing the envelopes

Before you start to print a large number of envelopes, see how one or two look on your screen, and then, if you are satisfied, print one or two samples to make sure the envelope stock feeds properly. To display sample envelopes on-screen:

1. In the Merge dialog box, select New Document in the Merge To list box.

2. Enter 1 in the From text box and 2 in the To text box.

3. Choose Merge to display the first two envelopes as a new document on-screen.

4. Close the new document without saving it.

If you are satisfied with the appearance of the envelopes, you can print one or two sample envelopes:

1. Choose the Mail Merge Helper button in the Mail Merge toolbar to display the Mail Merge Helper dialog box.

2. Choose Merge to display the Merge dialog box again.

3. Check the Options in effect notes at the bottom of the Merge dialog box. If it tells you Query Options have been set, the merge may not occur as you intended. See the sections about selecting records to be merged and sorting records later in this chapter for information.

4. In the Merge to list box, select Printer.

5. If you want to print the same number of envelopes that you previously displayed, you don't need to change the Records to be merged section of the Merge dialog box. However, you can change the range of envelopes to be printed.

6. Choose Merge to display the Print dialog box.

7. Choose OK to print the envelopes.

Note   Step 6 assumes that your printer's feeder contains blank envelopes. If your envelope feeder holds a stack of envelopes, printing should start soon after you choose OK. If you are using a manual feeder that holds only one envelope, however, you must insert an envelope into the feeder and press a button on the printer to print each envelope. The printer button is labeled *Continue* on many printers but may have a different name on your printer. Some printers automatically print the next envelope when they sense it in the feeder.

If you are satisfied with the sample envelopes, you can print all the envelopes now. Then be sure to save the new main document with the envelope layout. Choose File⇨Save, and name the file. To print all the envelopes:

1. Choose the Merge to Printer button in the Mail Merge toolbar to display the Print dialog box.

2. If you need to make any changes to the settings in this box, make them now.

3. Choose OK to print the envelopes.

You can also use one of the new Word 97 wizards to create and print your envelopes. Choose File⇨New and choose the Envelope Wizard from the New dialog box. When you choose OK, the Wizard asks if you want to print a single envelope or envelopes for your entire mailing list. If you choose to print only one, the Wizard opens the Envelopes and Labels dialog box with no addresses entered. See Chapter 5 for information on creating envelopes with this dialog box.

If you chose to print envelopes for your mailing list, the Wizard opens the Mail Merge Helper dialog box with Envelopes selected as the merge type. Proceed as described previously to create and print the envelopes.

Letting Mail Merge print your labels

Using Mail Merge to print mailing labels is not much different than using it to print envelopes. Using the small changes described in the following sections, you can just follow the steps described for envelopes.

Getting ready to print mailing labels

You start the process of preparing and printing mailing labels the same way as for envelopes, by choosing Tools➪Mail Merge in the main menu. Then choose Create in the Mail Merger Helper dialog box, and select Mailing Labels rather than Envelopes from the list box. Continue the same steps to create a new main document, and select a data source document. When you choose Open to select the data source document, Word prompts you to set up your main document. Choose Set Up Main Document to display the Label Options dialog box, as shown in Figure 20-25. Use this dialog box to specify the type of labels you plan to print.

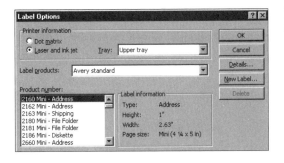

Figure 20-25: The Label Options dialog box.

Use only labels that are manufactured for use with your specific printer. If you use unsuitable labels, you can damage your printer.

To specify the labels:

1. In the Printer Information box at the top of the Label Options dialog box, choose Dot matrix if you plan to print labels on a dot-matrix printer with pin feed, or choose Laser and ink jet if you plan to print labels on a laser, ink jet, or similar sheet feed printer.

2. If you chose Laser and ink jet in Step 1, select the paper tray in the Tray list box that contains the sheets of labels (normally the default tray). This choice is not available if you chose Dot matrix in Step 1.

3. In the Label products list box, select the general type of labels, which, in most cases, is the name of the label manufacturer.

4. In the Product number list box, select the specific product number of the label you plan to use. (The product number is printed on the label package.) The Label information box displays the label type and dimensions.

5. To display information about the label size and the layout of labels on the sheet, you can choose Details to display an information dialog box which contains all the margin and spacing dimensions for the selected label type.

6. Choose OK to return to the Label Options dialog box.

7. Choose OK to accept your choice of labels and to display the Create Labels dialog box which is very similar to the Create Envelope dialog box.

If you want to use labels that are not defined within Word, you can choose a type of label with similar dimensions, and, in Step 5 of specifying the labels, change the dimensions to suit your needs or design a new label from scratch. See Chapter 5 for more details about creating custom label designs.

Caution Use the Create Labels dialog box to place merge fields from the data source document into the label, in the way previously described for envelopes.

You can also use the Mailing Label Wizard to create and print labels. The Wizard asks if you want to print a single sheet of labels or labels for your entire mailing list. The Mailing Label Wizard works much like the Envelope Wizard.

Printing labels

To print your labels, follow the same process of merging, checking, and printing labels as you did for envelopes.

Letting Mail Merge compile your mailing list catalog

You can use Mail Merge to create a list based on the data in a data source document. For example, you can create a list of the names and addresses in the data source document that you created when you were preparing form letters.

The procedure for creating a list (which Word calls a *catalog*) is similar to printing envelopes or mailing labels. As you did with envelopes, start by choosing Tools⇨Mail Merge in the main menu to display the Mail Merge Helper dialog box. Then choose Create, and, in the list box, select Catalog. Now continue the same steps you used when printing envelopes to create a new main document and select a data source document. When you choose OK to open the selected data source document, Word prompts you to edit your main document. Choose Edit Main Document to display the empty main document.

Use the Insert Merge Field button in the Mail Merge toolbar to place fields from the data source document in the main document. Figure 20-26 shows an example of a typical main document of this type. Be sure to press Enter after inserting the PostalCode field or the next name in the list will be on the same line.

Figure 20-26: A typical main document for a catalog.

Save the main document in the folder you created for Mail Merge documents.

To display the list in a new document, click the Merge to New Document button on the Mail Merge toolbar. Figure 20-27 shows a typical mailing list. Notice that the records in the data source document are repeated one under the other in the new document rather than as separate sections.

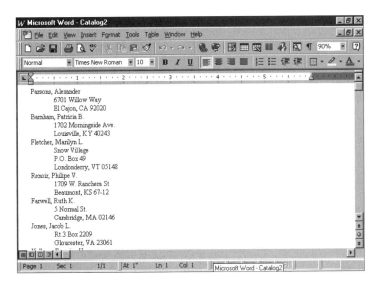

Figure 20-27: A typical list created from a data source document.

The document you produce in this way is a normal Word file that you can edit, save, and print in the usual manner.

Using an Existing Main Document

Earlier in this chapter, you created a main document as part of the process of using Mail Merge. You also can create a main document independently, use an already-existing Word document, or use a document that was created in another application.

Using a Word document

Instead of creating a main document as part of the Mail Merge process, as described previously in the section about creating form letters, you can start by creating a form letter just as you create any other Word document. Don't try to place the field codes at this stage; just mark the places where you want to place the field codes, for example, by using three or four asterisks. It doesn't matter what you use because you delete these markers later.

After you finish the main document, keep the document open. Choose Tools⇨Mail Merge, choose Create, and select Form Letters. Next, select Active Window to use the open document as the main document. After you select a data source, Word indicates that the next step is to edit your main document. Choose Edit Main Document to display the document. Then replace your temporary field markers with actual field codes, using the Insert Merge Field button in the Mail Merge toolbar.

After you place all the field codes, continue as before to check and print your letters. You can, of course, open an existing Word document and use it as a main document by adding merge fields to it.

Using non-Word documents

You can use documents created in other applications as Mail Merge main documents. Table 20-3 lists various source applications you can use to create main documents.

Table 20-3 Sources of Main Documents	
Source	**Notes**
Word for Windows version 6.x	Can be used directly.
Word for Windows version 2.x	Can be used directly.
Word for Windows version 1.x	Must contain a DATA field that identifies the data source document.

Source	Notes
Word MS-DOS	Must contain a DATA instruction that identifies the data source document.
Word for Macintosh	Must contain a DATA instruction that identifies the data source document.
WordPerfect	Word converts each WordPerfect merge field to a Word merge field with the same name.

If you have the necessary filters installed in Word, you can open documents created in several other word processors and text editors and use them as the basis of main documents.

Making an ordinary document look like a main document

You can edit and format text and graphics in a main document the same way as in any other Word document.

You cannot edit merge fields in the main document without displaying them as field codes, as explained in the next section. However, you can delete merge fields, and you can apply formats to them. You also can use the Clipboard to copy or move complete fields.

If you have placed a field in the wrong position in a main document or if you have placed the wrong merge field, delete that field, and then insert the correct merge field in the proper position. To delete a merge field:

1. Click and drag the insertion point over the whole field including the chevrons. When the field code is selected, the characters in the field appear in reverse video, white on dark gray.

2. With the entire field and the chevrons that enclose it highlighted, press Delete to completely remove the field.

3. To delete all the merge fields in one line, select them all by dragging the insertion point over them or by triple-clicking in one field. Press Delete.

Note You may notice that you can edit the characters within a field name. Although you can see these changes on-screen, Word ignores them. You cannot change from one merge field to another by editing its name in this way. See the section about editing field codes for information about replacing fields. Chapter 26 describes more fully working with field codes.

After you delete an incorrect field, you can insert the correct field by choosing the Insert Merge Field button in the Mail Merge toolbar and choosing from the list of available fields.

When Word merges the data from the data source document into the main document, that data is displayed in the font and font size of the merge field and is formatted according to the format of the field. The font, font size, and formatting of the data in the data source document do not affect the appearance of text in merged documents. If you want the text that replaces merge fields to appear in a specific font and font size or to have specific formatting, format the field in the main document accordingly.

Editing field codes

So far you've seen fields in main documents indicated by a field name enclosed within chevrons, which is Word's default way of showing fields. This method is usually convenient. However, Word can display fields as full field codes. For example, <<LastName>> would appear as { MERGEFIELD LastName }.

Knowing about this alternative format is important because you may have Word set to display these codes. Also you can use this format to change field names. For example, if you have incorrectly placed the FirstName field where there should be a LastName field, you can correct the mistake by editing the field name.

You can switch between displaying fields as field names and displaying them as full field codes in two ways. The easier method is to press Alt+F9. The other method is to choose Tools⇨Options to display the Options dialog box, choose the View tab, and check the Field codes option box. Use either of the methods again to switch back to normally displayed merge fields. If you want to display only one or two fields as field codes, click in the field and press Shift+F9. Repeat to remove the field code.

Figure 20-28 shows field names in a main document displayed as full field codes. Compare this with the way Mail Merge normally displays fields, which was shown earlier.

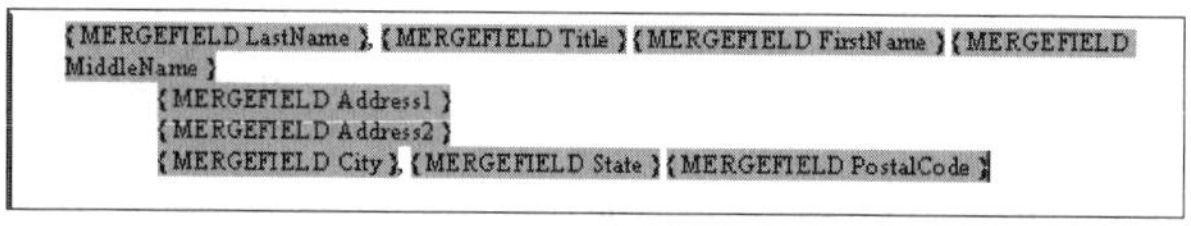

{ MERGEFIELD LastName }, { MERGEFIELD Title } { MERGEFIELD FirstName } { MERGEFIELD MiddleName }
{ MERGEFIELD Address1 }
{ MERGEFIELD Address2 }
{ MERGEFIELD City }, { MERGEFIELD State } { MERGEFIELD PostalCode }

Figure 20-28: Field names displayed as full field codes.

With full field codes displayed, you can (with caution) edit field names to replace one field with another. To replace a field name, carefully backspace over just the characters, leaving the spaces just inside the curly brackets. Type the new name exactly as it appears in the header row of the data source document. You may find it easier to delete the wrong field and replace it by using the buttons on the Mail Merge toolbar.

In the View tab of the Options dialog box, you also have a choice of when you want the merge fields and field codes shaded: Never, Always, or When selected.

Using an Existing Data Source Document

Earlier in this chapter, you created a data source document as part of the process of using Mail Merge. You can also create a data source document independently, use an already-existing Word document, or use a document that was created in another application.

Using a Word Document

Instead of creating a data source document as part of the process of creating Mail Merge documents, you can use Word independently to create the document. You can create the data source document:

✦ **As a table.** See Chapter 12 for information about tables.

✦ **As text.** Each record must be separated from the next by a specific character called the *record delimiter*. Within every record, each field must be separated from the next by a specific character called the *field delimiter*.

Whether you use a table or text, the first record must consist of the field names.

To use text as the data source, choose a character to use as a record delimiter and another character as a field delimiter. These characters, of course, must not occur in the text of the source data. The Enter (paragraph) character is often used as the record delimiter and the Tab character as the field delimiter.

Using Enter as the record delimiter and Tab as the field delimiter, type the source data as shown in the example in Figure 20-29. Notice that if there is no value in a field such as the middle name field, you must press Tab again to preserve the uniformity. Save the data as a named file, and then close the file.

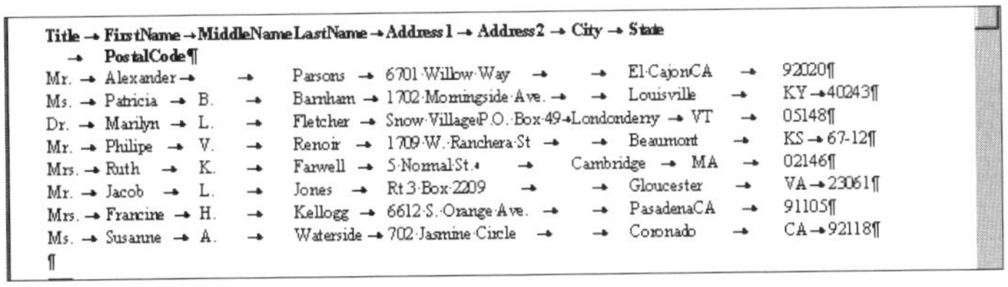

Figure 20-29: An example of text as a data source.

Note For the sake of displaying this example clearly, the Tab and Paragraph markers are showing in Figure 20-29. To show the markers, click the Show/Hide button on the Standard toolbar or use the Options dialog box. You do not need to turn on the display, however, to use Tab and Enter as delimiters.

After you save the text, start Mail Merge as usual and, as you proceed, select the new file as your data source document.

If you already have a suitable document in Word or in any other application that creates files Word can open, you can use it—perhaps after editing to make field and record delimiters consistent—as a Mail Merge data source document.

Using documents from other applications

When creating a list of names and addresses to use as a mail merge data source, you should give some thought to the best application for the job. For example, if your list is short or medium in length, use Word. Word can also create an automatically numbered list, if desired. If your list is long and you expect to make a lot of changes to it or you want special sorting and searching capabilities, you are better off using a spreadsheet such as Excel or a database application such as Access.

The Word Mail Merge Helper can also get data from one of the address books you created for use with the Microsoft Exchange Server, Outlook or Schedule+ 7.0. In fact, you can use any address list created with a Message Application Programming Interface (MAPI)-compatible messaging system.

If you have installed the proper converters with Word, you can use the following file formats in Word mail merge:

✦ ASCII

✦ Microsoft Word for Macintosh versions 3.0-6.x

✦ Microsoft Word versions 3.0-6.0 for MS-DOS

✦ Microsoft Excel versions 2.0-8.x

✦ WordPerfect version 6.x for MS-DOS

✦ WordPerfect version 6.x for Windows

✦ Lotus 1-2-3 versions 2.x-4.x

Word can also use Borland Paradox and dBASE files via the open database connectivity (ODBC) driver or text files and rich-text-format (RTF) files that you can create in many other applications.

Using a separate header file

Earlier in this chapter, you read that the first record in a data source document is a header record in which field names are defined. This is not necessarily so. You can omit this record, but if you do, you must have a separate header file.

Having a separate header source file can be convenient if you have several data source documents, all with the same fields. By using a separate header file, you avoid the necessity of placing the same header record in every document. You might also prefer to have a separate header file when you are using a data source document created in another application and that document does not already have a header record.

A separate header file is, in effect, a one-record data source document. Create it as a table or as delimited text as already described. Alternatively, you can create the separate header file as you do in the Mail Merge process described next.

If you are using a separate header file, proceed as normal with Mail Merge until you open the Get Data list box. At this point, select Header Options to display the Header Options dialog box, in which you can choose to create a new header file or open an existing one.

If you choose Open in this dialog box, Word opens the Open Header Source dialog box in which you can choose an existing header file. If you choose Create, Word opens the Create Header Source dialog box in which you can choose field names from a list or type your own, as described earlier in the section about creating form letters. After you choose field names, Word prompts you to type a name for the header source and save it.

To Print or Not to Print Blank Lines

As already mentioned, by default Word omits any line in a merged document that contains only an empty field. In the example near the beginning of this chapter, the Address2 field was empty for most records in the data source document. Even though this field was present in the recipient-address part of the main document, the form letters based on records for which the Address2 field was empty omitted this line. If you are using the data source to fill out a preprinted form, it may be necessary to retain the blank line.

In fact, you can control whether Word omits blank lines by making a choice in the Merge dialog box (refer to Figure 20-17). In the When merging records section near the bottom of the dialog box, you can choose whether to print blank lines. Choose the appropriate button according to your needs.

Merging Specific Records

The simple situation you've been working with in this chapter produces one letter, envelope, or label, or one item in a list, for every record in the data source document. Often, you want to be selective. If your data source document contains a record for each of your customers but you want to send letters only to those customers who live in a particular state, what do you do? The answer is simple: you use a query.

A *query* enables you to specify conditions under which a record in the data source document is included when you merge. A query can be quite simple, such as asking for records for people in one state, or more complex, such as asking for all the Smiths west of the Rocky Mountains.

Selecting records for one state

The following example shows how you can select records for people who live in Vermont: records in which the State field contains VT. The steps assume that you have the main document for a letter in a file named Form Letter and a data source document containing people's names and addresses in a file named Name List. The steps also assume that at least one record in the list has the State field as VT.

The Query Options dialog box is where you specify the records you want to merge. The Filter Records tab contains three principal columns. In the column labeled Field, you choose a field in the data source document. In the column labeled Comparison, you select how you want to compare the content of the field. In the column labeled Compare to, you enter the value with which you want to compare the contents of the field. To prepare to specify a query:

1. Open the main document, Form Letter.

2. Choose Tools⇨Mail Merge to open the Mail Merge Helper dialog box.

3. Choose Create, and select Form Letters.

4. If you have already merged Form Letter with Name List, the message at the top of the dialog box tells you that the main document and data source are ready to merge. Otherwise, you need to define a data source document at this stage.

5. Choose Query Options to display the Query Options dialog box with the Filter Records tab selected, where you can construct your query.

To specify the state for which you want to merge records:

1. In the first row of the Query Options dialog box, select the name of the field you want to use from the list box. In this case, select State.

2. The phrase "Equal to" appears in the Comparison box to the right. You want to look for the content of the State field to be equal to something, so make no change here.

3. In the Compare to box, type **VT** (or the abbreviation for a different state in your list) to indicate that you want to select records from that state. At this time, the dialog box looks like the one shown in Figure 20-30. Word automatically prepares for an additional query condition by adding And to the second line. You can ignore this for now.

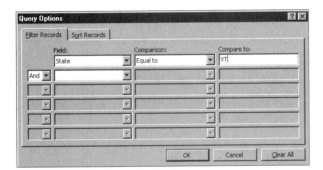

Figure 20-30: The Query Options dialog box with a query specified.

Now you're ready to complete the merge:

1. At the bottom of the Query Options dialog box, choose OK to return to the Mail Merge Helper dialog box.

2. Choose Merge to display the Merge dialog box.

3. In the Merge dialog box, select New Document in the Merge to list box and the All button in the Records to be merged section, and choose Merge.

After a short delay, Word displays a new document containing form letters addressed to those people in your list who live in Vermont.

Note   After you complete Step 2, the note at the bottom of the Merge dialog box tells you that query options have been set. It's important to check this message before you continue the merge.

Using other comparison operators

By default, Word offers "Equal to" as the type of comparison between the content of a field and what you place in the Compare to box. If you open the Comparison list box, however, you have a choice of other methods of comparison, as listed in Table 20-4. One of the comparisons, "is blank," is handy for finding records lacking data in a critical field, such as the ZIP code field.

	Table 20-4 **Comparison Types**	
Comparison	**Explanation**	
Equal to	Contents of the field exactly match the comparison text.	
Not equal to	Contents of the field do not match the comparison text.	
Less than	Contents of the field are less than the comparison text.	
Greater than	Contents of the field are greater than the comparison text.	
Less than or equal	Contents of the field are less than or equal to the comparison text.	
Greater than or equal	Contents of the field are greater than or equal to the comparison text.	
is blank	The field is empty (the Compare to box is empty).	
is not blank	The field is not empty (the Compare to box is empty).	

If the field contains a number and the comparison text is a number, the meanings of the comparisons are clear. If the field contains text and the comparison is text, as in the preceding example, the comparison is based on the ANSI value of characters but without regard to whether characters are uppercase or lowercase. If the field or the comparison text contains anything other than alphabetic characters, the comparison is also based on the ANSI value of characters.

Selecting with two rules

Each comparison is called a *rule*. In the preceding example, the content of the State field is compared with some text, using a single rule. Word enables you to specify up to six rules. When you have two rules, you can specify that a record is selected only if both rules are satisfied or that a record is selected if either or both rules are satisfied. Suppose that you want to select records of people if the State field contains VT or if the field contains CA.

Now, if you merge, you get all records in which the State field contains VT and all records in which the State field contains CA.

Note   If you leave And in the box at the left end of the second row, you are asking for two comparisons that cannot be true at the same time. No State field can satisfy both of these conditions. If you try this comparison and try to merge, Word displays a message saying that no data records match your query.

To define two rules:

1. Define the first rule to compare the content of the State field with VT. By default, Word places And in the small box at the left end of the second row.

2. Click the down arrow just to the right of And to open a small list box and select Or from the list.

3. Select State for the field in this row.

4. Type **CA** as the comparison text.

5. Choose OK to accept these rules.

You don't need to have the same field in both rules. You can have one rule that selects records in which the state is CA, for example, and another that selects records in which the FirstName field is George. If the second rule starts with Or, merging gives you records for all residents of California together with all people whose first name is George, whatever state they live in. On the other hand, if the second rule starts with And, merging gives you only records for anyone who lives in California and whose first name is George.

Selecting by using more than two rules

When you define more than two rules in the Query Options dialog box, three possibilities exist:

✦ Each rule is related to the previous one by Or. In this case, a record is included in the merge if one or more rules are satisfied.

✦ Each rule is related to the previous one by And. In this case, a record is included in the merge only if all rules are satisfied.

✦ Some rules are related to the previous one by Or and others by And. This possibility requires further explanation.

You must understand two principles about how Word selects records when Or and And both occur in rules:

✦ Or or And define the relationship between a rule and the rule that immediately precedes it.

✦ And takes precedence over Or.

To understand these principles, look at the four rules shown in Figure 20-31.

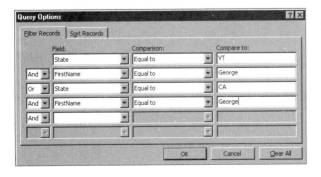

Figure 20-31: Four rules that use And and Or.

Note After you finish creating each rule, Word automatically starts the next rule by placing And at the beginning of the next row. Word ignores the And in the last (empty) row when it runs the query.

Because the And rules have precedence, think about them first. The second rule starts with And. Therefore, for the record to be used in the merge, the first and second rules both must be satisfied. The fourth rule also starts with And, so the third and fourth rules both must be satisfied. The third rule starts with Or. The result is that the record is used if the first and second rules are satisfied or if the third and fourth rules are satisfied. The record is also used if both pairs of rules are satisfied. To summarize, this set of rules will select records for people whose first name is George if they live in either California or Vermont.

Adding ranges to rules

With some of the comparison conditions, you can specify a range of values for which merge uses a record. In that case, you can use one rule as the lower limit of the range and another as the upper limit. For example, if you want to print letters for people who live in states for which the ZIP code is in the range 40000 to 49999, you use two rules. To ask for records in that range, you select the PostalCode field (or whichever other field contains ZIP codes) for Field in the Query Options dialog box. The first rule should contain a Greater than or equal comparison of 40000, the lower limit. The second rule, starting with And, should contain a Less than or equal comparison of 49999, the upper limit.

Sometimes you need to use only one rule to specify a range. For example, suppose that you want to print letters for only those people who live in the western states. To do so, ask for records in which the ZIP code is in the range 90000 to 99999. Select the appropriate field, and then select Greater than or equal for the Comparison and 90000 for the Compare To text. No five-character ZIP codes are larger than 99999, so you don't have to be concerned about an upper limit.

Removing rules

After you set rules, those rules apply to all merges until you either cancel them or terminate your Word session. To clear rules without terminating your Word session, choose the Clear All button in the Query Options dialog box, and choose OK.

Setting the Record Order

By default, Word prints merge documents in the same order as records occur in the data source document. You can change this order based on the values in any field. You might want to print records (and envelopes or labels) in ZIP code order, for example, or you might want to print a catalog in alphabetical order of last names.

To sort records in ZIP code order, display the Query Options dialog box as described in previous sections. Then display the Sort Records tab, as shown in Figure 20-32.

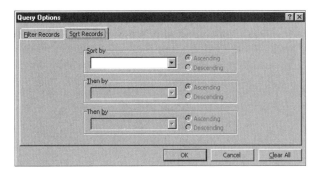

Figure 20-32: The Sort Records tab of the Query Options dialog box.

To sort records by ZIP code:

1. In the Sort by list box, select the field that contains ZIP codes.

2. Choose the Ascending or Descending option according to your preference.

3. Choose OK to return to the Merge dialog box.

Note After you complete Step 3 of sorting records by ZIP code, the note at the bottom of the Merge dialog box tells you that query options have been set. It's important to check this message before you continue the merge.

When you proceed to merge, the form letters are arranged in ZIP code order. However, you are not limited to sorting in one field. You might want to sort primarily in order of last names, for example; and, if two or more people have the same last name, to sort them in first name order. If two or more people have the same first and last names, you can sort them in middle name order. Just select the first sort field in the Sort by box, the second sort field in the first Then by box, and the third sort field in the second Then by box.

As in the case of comparisons, sort specifications remain in effect until you clear them or terminate your Word session. To clear sort specifications, choose Clear All at the bottom of the Query Options dialog box.

Adding Special Word Fields to a Main Document

You have already seen how you can place merge fields in a main document. These fields are replaced with text from the data source document when you merge the two documents. In addition to merge fields, you can place Word fields in a main document. Word fields are instructions that tell Word to perform an action when the merge occurs.

As an example, the main document used earlier in this chapter offered a certain book to people. Suppose that you want to offer that book to most people on your list but want to offer a different book to readers who live in California. By using a Word field in the main document, Merge can do just that, as illustrated in the first example that follows.

Another time you might find Word fields useful is when you want to add a personal message to some of the letters you are sending. You may, for example, be preparing a holiday greeting letter to send to your clients. In many cases, you end the letter with a traditional greeting, but in some cases you might want to replace that greeting with a more personal message. The second example shows how to fill in special text.

Specifying text to appear in merged documents

This example creates merged letters that contain the book name *Tales from America's Great Authors* for records in which the State field is not CA and prints the book name *Tales from California's Great Authors* for records in which the State field is CA.

To start, create the main document shown in Figure 20-33. You use this document if you want to send exactly the same letter to everyone.

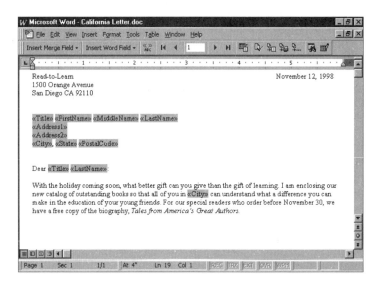

Figure 20-33:
The main document you use to start.

To insert a Word field:

1. Delete *Tales from America's Great Authors* from the main document, being careful not to delete the space before the phrase or the period after the phrase.

2. Place the insertion point where you want to insert the Word field. In this case, place the insertion point just before the period at the end of the paragraph.

3. Choose the Insert Word Field button (the second from the left) in the Mail Merge toolbar to display a list of available Word fields, as shown in Figure 20-34.

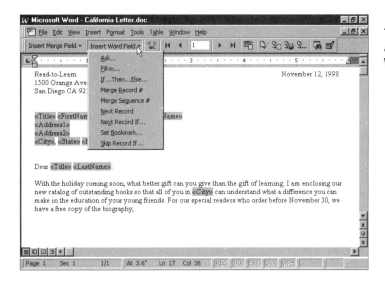

Figure 20-34: The list of available Word fields.

4. Choose If...Then...Else... to display the Insert Word Field: IF dialog box, in which you specify the text to include when the State field is CA and the alternate text to include when it is not.

5. In the Field name list box, select the field you want to use as a basis for the decision. In this case, you want to base the decision on the content of the State field, so select that field.

6. In the Comparison list box, select the basis for the decision, in this case, Equal to.

7. In the Compare to text box, type the comparison text. In this case, type **CA**.

8. Place the insertion point in the Insert this text box, and type what should appear in a letter if the comparison is satisfied. In this case, type **Tales from California's Great Authors**.

9. Place the insertion point in the Otherwise Insert this text box, and then type what should appear in the letter if the comparison is not satisfied. In this case, type **Tales from America's Great Authors**. The completed dialog box should look similar to the one shown in Figure 20-35.

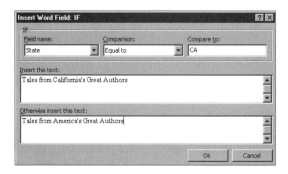

Figure 20-35: The completed dialog box.

10. Choose OK to return to the main document.

When you return to the main document, all you see of the Word field is the text that appears if the condition is satisfied. Select the text in the field and format it as you would any other text, italic in this case. If you want to see the field in more detail, press Alt+F9 to reveal field codes. After you press this key combination, all field codes in the main document are shown, as explained earlier in this chapter. The Word field, shown in Figure 20-36, shows the instruction in detail.

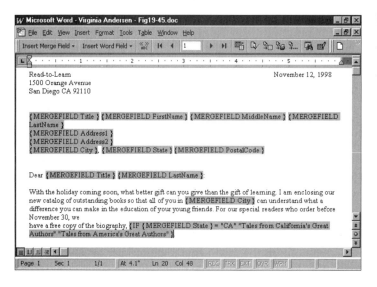

Figure 20-36: The main document with the Word field inserted and with field codes revealed.

To return to the normal display in which field codes are not shown, press Alt+F9 again.

To verify that the Word field acts as you intended, you can display some form letters on your screen as follows:

1. Choose the Merge to New Document button in the Mail Merge toolbar to display the merged letters as a new document on your screen.

2. Scroll through the merged letters to confirm that those addressed to California and those addressed to other states have the correct text.

3. Close the new merged document without saving it.

Using a Fill-In field in a merged document

Suppose that you have written a holiday greeting letter as a main document. You are content to end most letters with a traditional phrase, such as "Wishing you and your staff a happy holiday and a prosperous New Year." For some clients, though, you want to replace that message with a more personal greeting. You can use the Fill-in Word field for this purpose as follows:

1. At the end of your letter, go to a new paragraph.

2. Choose the Insert Word Field button in the Mail Merge toolbar.

3. Choose Fill-in to display the Insert Word Field: Fill-in dialog box as shown in Figure 20-37.

Figure 20-37: The Insert Word Field: Fill-in dialog box.

4. In the Prompt box, type the words you want Word to use to request a greeting, such as **Type greeting here**.

5. In the Default fill-in text box, type the standard greeting with which you close most letters.

6. Choose OK to return to the letter with the standard greeting displayed.

7. Choose the Merge to New Document button in the Mail Merge dialog box. During the merge, Word displays a dialog box as each letter is merged.

8. Either choose OK to accept the standard greeting; or, to insert a special greeting in a letter, type that greeting, and choose OK.

Summary

You now have the basics for creating and printing several types of merged documents with Word. You learned how to

✦ Print form letters that are personalized for each recipient.

✦ Print envelopes by using the letters' files of names and addresses.

✦ Use Word's merge feature to print mailing labels for larger packages.

✦ Print a list of your addresses by creating what Word calls a catalog.

✦ Print only selected merge documents.

✦ Change the order of printed merge documents.

✦ Vary the text of a letter, based on a field value.

Where to go next...

✦ For information about using the Word 97 Wizards to create letters, envelopes and mailing labels, turn to Chapter 10.

✦ To learn more about creating innovative forms that you can add to your mailings, go to Chapter 21.

✦ To find more information about using field codes to automate some chores, go to Chapter 26.

✦   ✦   ✦

Creating Forms

◆ ◆ ◆ ◆

In This Chapter

Creating a new form

Adding text and form fields

Using the Forms toolbar

Protecting your forms

Changing form field properties

Adding Help messages

Using and printing the form

◆ ◆ ◆ ◆

From the local library or supermarket to the Internal Revenue Service, forms have become a way of life. A form is a way to collect all of the essential pieces of information (and no more) about a subject, whether it is a job application or a list of itemized deductions. In Chapter 12, you learned how to create online and fill-in forms by using tables. In this chapter, you will create new data entry forms with text and form fields.

Understanding Word Forms

The application you use to create your form depends on the purpose of the form and the type of data you intend to collect with it. Word, Access, and Excel all provide form creation capabilities. If your form contains complex text and data formatting, pictures, check boxes, drop-down lists, or linked objects, use Word or Access to design your form. If you are collecting a large amount of information, or need relational database capabilities, use Access. If you are planning to collect information for use in calculations, statistical analyses, or financial reports, use Excel.

In Word, a form is a special kind of template, and each time you use the form to collect data, you are actually creating a new document based on the form template. To keep the user from changing the form in any way, you protect the form before you save it. In this way, the user can only move from one data entry field to another and enter the desired information.

Word provides several predesigned document templates that you can use to create common types of forms, such as invoices, purchase orders, FAX cover sheets, and weekly time sheets. You can use these templates as they are, or customize one of them to suit your needs. You can create a form for almost any use, such as filling out contracts, invoices, job applications, or any other repetitive data-gathering purpose.

Creating a New Form in Word

If you already have a printed form that you want to duplicate in Word, you can go right ahead and create a new form template using the printed form as a pattern. Otherwise, you should sketch the form design, and make sure that you have spaces for all the desired information and sufficient explanatory text for the user. You should also decide what kind of data will be entered in each field and how you want it to look. After careful review of the design, you are ready to create the form.

Creating a new form is a four-step process. First, you start a new template. Then you enter the desired text, interspersed with (properly identified) form fields where the data will be entered. Next, you protect the form template with a password so that the user has access only to the data entry fields. Finally, you save the form in the template folder. Figure 21-1 shows a typical Word form, which can be used to gather information about new customers of an educational book mail-order business. The shaded areas represent the data entry fields. The rest of the form is inaccessible to the user.

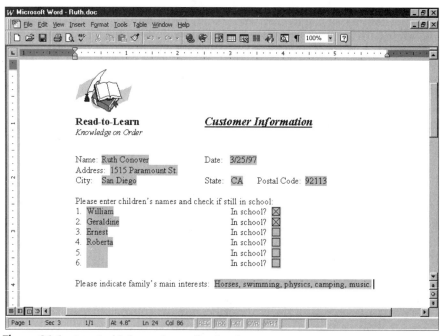

Figure 21-1: A typical information collection form.

To start a new form, open a new template and treat it just like any other document by setting the page layout, font style, size, and other document properties.

Creating a new form

The first step in creating a new form is to start a new template by using an existing template as a pattern. To open a new form:

1. Choose New from the File menu. The New dialog box opens.

2. Select the Template radio button (see Figure 21-2).

3. Select an existing template to use as a guide, or choose Blank Document.

4. Click OK.

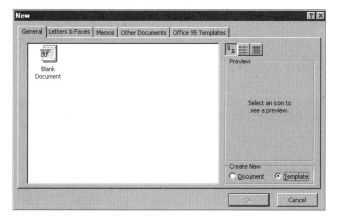

Figure 21-2: Opening a new template.

Saving your new template right away under a different name is often helpful. That way, you won't chance inadvertently making changes to the template you chose. To save the new form:

1. Choose Save As from the File menu.

2. Enter the template name in the File name box (see Figure 21-3).

3. Select Save.

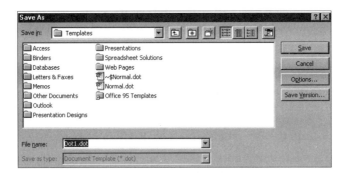

Figure 21-3: Naming a new template.

Note   By default, Word saves templates in the Program Files\Microsoft Office\Templates folder. You can specify a different folder if you want, by changing the Save in entry. To change the default location for template files, use the File Locations tab of the Options dialog box.

Developing the form's structure

At this point, adjust the margins, and put the basic information in place. Treat your form template exactly the same way as you would treat any document. A form has access to all the document character formatting options.

Form fields will be inserted in the document where you want to place fill-in information. See the next section to learn how to insert form fields.

Adding Text and Inserting Form Fields

After you type the form title and introductory text, you move to the beginning of the data entry area where you insert one or more form fields. You have a choice of three types of form fields: text, check box, and drop-down list. The type you insert depends on what kind of information you expect from the user, how it is entered, and how you want it displayed.

You insert a form field by using the Forms toolbar. (The Form Field option is no longer part of the Insert menu.) The Forms toolbar is specifically designed for working with forms. To display the Forms toolbar, select Toolbars from the View menu, and then click the Forms check box in the list of available toolbars.

The floating Forms toolbar (see Figure 21-4) includes buttons for inserting each type of form field, a table, or a text box. Table 21-1 describes the Forms toolbar buttons. You can also click the Form Field Options button to open the Options dialog box for the selected field. Other buttons toggle the field shading and form protection on and off. Emphasizing the data entry fields with shading is a handy way to find the fields quickly, especially in a large, complicated form.

Figure 21-4: The Forms toolbar.

Table 21-1 Forms Toolbar Buttons	
Button	*Description*
abl	Insert Text form field
☑	Insert Check Box form field
🔲	Insert Drop-Down form field
🔳	Open form field options box
✏	Draw table
▦	Insert table
▥	Insert frame
ⓐ	Toggle form field shading
🔒	Protect form

An easy way to open Word's activity-specific toolbars is to right-click anywhere in a currently displayed toolbar. Doing so opens a drop-down list of toolbars, from which you can select the one that you want to see. Like other Word toolbars, you can drag the toolbar to any position on the screen, dock it at a margin, and change its dimensions by dragging its borders with the mouse. To insert a form field:

1. Position the cursor where you want to place the field.

2. Click one of the form field tools in the Forms toolbar. A form field appears as a shaded rectangle in your document.

3. Click the field shading button in the Forms toolbar. The field shading is removed. Figure 21-5 shows the Customer Information form with field shading turned off.

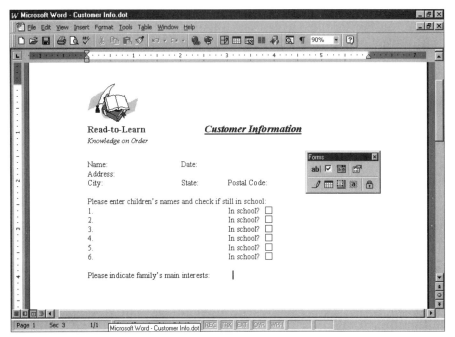

Figure 21-5: The Customer Information form without field shading.

After inserting a form field, you can move it by clicking and dragging to a new position. You can also add or delete spaces or text before it in the template. To delete a field, select the field and press Delete.

To remove the Forms toolbar from the screen, click the Close button in the toolbar. You can also choose <u>T</u>oolbars from the <u>V</u>iew menu, uncheck Forms, and choose OK.

Protecting the Form

After the form's structure is created and the fields are inserted, you need to protect the form. Protecting the form will lock all of your work into place and prevent anything from being changed other than the information contained in the form fields. Protecting the form accomplishes several things:

✦ A user cannot edit a protected form. Neither can a user make changes to the body of the form. Only information to be included in form fields can be changed.

✦ Most menu commands are not available. Any command that will change the way that the form prints, including almost all of the commands in the Insert, Format, Tools, and Table menus, is disabled.

✦ Fields that contain formulas display the results of the formula, and the underlying formulas cannot be viewed or changed.

The Protect Document dialog box prompts you to enter a password for your form template. This feature can be quite useful, but it also carries some risk. To password protect your document, simply enter a password into the Protect Document dialog box. You then must re-enter the password to confirm it. To protect a form:

1. Select Protect Document from the Tools menu to open the Protect Document dialog box shown in Figure 21-6.

Figure 21-6: The Protect Document dialog box.

2. Select the Forms radio button.

3. Enter your password, if desired.

4. Choose OK, and repeat the password entry.

5. Choose OK.

Once protected, a template cannot be edited without unlocking it with the password, which keeps busy fingers away from your work. Dare we mention that you shouldn't forget your password!

To unprotect the form, select Unprotect Document from the Tools menu, or click the Protect Form button in the Forms toolbar again. You are then asked to enter your password, if you provided one when you protected the form.

Note   You can also protect your form by clicking the Protect Document button in the Forms toolbar. Word automatically protects the document without asking for a password. Then, to unprotect the form, click the Protect Document button again, or choose Unprotect Document from the Tools menu. You will not be asked for a password because none was specified. Protecting your form this way is handy during the design because you can switch back and forth to see how the form design is coming without having to enter a password every time.

You do not necessarily have to protect all of the document. If, while constructing the body of the form, you divide it into parts by using section breaks (see Chapter 9 for information on sections), you can protect any combination of sections that you want.

To protect certain sections, click Sections in the Protect Document dialog box. This button is only available if the document contains section breaks. Selecting this button opens a Section Protection dialog box listing all the sections in the document (see Figure 21-7). Check the sections that you want protected, and continue in the normal manner.

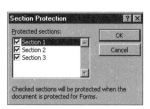

Figure 21-7: The Section Protection dialog box.

Understanding Form Fields

As mentioned earlier, form fields come in three basic types: Text, Check Box, and Drop-Down. You can customize each of these form field types in turn by changing their options. Each type has its own set of custom features that you can change through its Options dialog box. Once you have inserted a field in the form, Word gives you three ways to open the Options dialog box for that field. First, select the field, and do one of the following:

✦ Double-click the form field.

✦ Right-click the form field, and choose Properties from the shortcut menu.

✦ Click the Form Field Options button on the Forms toolbar.

Note To edit a form field after it has been placed in a document, you must first unprotect the document.

Changing Text form field options

You can change the data type and display format, limit the number of characters that can be entered into a field, and specify a default value for all Text type form fields except the current date and time, which get their values from your computer. You can also add a custom bookmark to name the field so that you can use the value in this field (perhaps the result of a formula or other expression) elsewhere in the form. (See Chapter 23 for more information about bookmarks.) You can even add some Help text that can be displayed in the status bar when a field is highlighted or in a dialog box when the user presses F1.

To modify Text form fields, begin by selecting the field and then opening the Text Form Field Options dialog box (see Figure 21-8), using one of the methods listed previously.

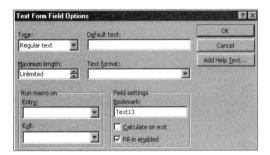

Figure 21-8: The Text Form Field Options dialog box.

Clicking the Type down arrow in the Text Form Field Options dialog box opens a drop-down list containing six different types of text entries: Regular text, Number, Date, Current date, Current time, and Calculation. The following paragraphs describe each of these text field types and their formatting options.

You can set the maximum allowable length of any of the Text form field types by filling in the Maximum length box. This box is particularly helpful if you need to limit the length of an answer to fit into an existing database field. The default is Unlimited, but you can enter any other number.

Regular text

You insert a Regular Text form field when you want the user to enter text, numbers, symbols or spaces. An example is a field following the question "In what city do you live?" that will hold the user's response.

When you specify a regular text field, you have the option of entering a value in the Default text box. You can enter, for example, **Indianapolis**, if your form will be primarily distributed there. The field then displays *Indianapolis*, so that users do not have to type an entry unless they want to change the answer.

You can set the format by selecting options from the Text format drop-down list. Leave the Text format box blank if you want to leave the user's entry as is with no special formatting. Table 21-2 shows examples using these options.

Table 21-2 Text Format Options	
Option	*Result*
Uppercase	EVERYTHING IS IN CAPITAL LETTERS.
Lowercase	everything is in lowercase letters.
First capital	The first letter of the first word is capitalized.
Title case	The First Letter Of Each Word Is Capitalized.

Number

When your form requires a numeric entry, change the text field to a Number type. The user's response may be used in a calculation, or it may be an answer to a question such as "How old are you?" Unlike a text field, which can accept text as well as numbers, number fields will only accept numeric entries. If someone answered the preceding question by typing **eighteen**, an error message will appear, and the insertion point will remain in the field until the user changes the answer to **18** or some other number.

The Number format list displays pictures of the number formats that can be applied to a number form field. Table 21-3 describes these formats. You can also specify a default numeric value in the Default Number box.

Table 21-3 Number Formats	
Option	*Result*
0	123
0.00	123.45
#,##0	1,234
#,##0.00	1,234.56
$#,##0.00;($#,##0.00)	$1,234.56 or ($1,234.56) if a negative number
0%	1%
0.00%	1.00%

Chapter 26 describes all of the possible number placeholders and formatting codes. You can choose from the list or construct a custom number format for any display that you desire. The following sections briefly explain what the symbols mean.

0 (zero) placeholder

A zero in a number format indicates that you want a digit to appear in that place, no matter what. If a digit is in the place occupied by a zero placeholder, the digit is displayed. If not, a zero appears in its place. For example, if you are formatting dollars and cents and you want every entry to include two decimal places, you end the numeric picture with .00; 4 will appear as $4.00, and 4.1 as $4.10. Additionally, if a result is longer than the number of digits specified by the instruction, it will be rounded off to conform to the specified number format.

(number sign) placeholder

A number sign in the number format indicates that you want a digit to appear if one exists. If the result does not have a digit to display, a space (instead of a zero) is inserted in its place.

; (semicolon)

The semicolon acts as a formatting separator in several types of format specifications. When you want different formats to apply to positive and negative numbers, you can specify two number formats separated by a semicolon. For example, a form field with the predefined number format $#,##0.00;($#,##0.00) will display positive numbers as usual, but negative numbers will be enclosed in parentheses.

Date

Use a Date form field if the form requires a date entry. Date fields won't accept entries other than date entries. If someone types an invalid date, an error message will appear and the insertion point will remain in the field until the user makes a proper response.

The Date format list includes pictures of the date formats that can be applied to a Date form field. Table 21-4 describes these formats.

Table 21-4 Date Formats	
Option	**Result**
M/d/yy	1/15/98
dddd, MMMM dd, yyyy	Saturday, January 15, 1998
MMMM d,yyyy	January 15, 1998

(continued)

Table 21-4 *(continued)*	
Option	*Result*
M/d/yyyy	1/15/1998
yyyy-MM-dd	1998-Jan-15
d-MMM-yy	15-Jan-98
M.d.yy	1.15.98
MMM. d,yy	Jan. 15,98
d MMMM, yyyy	15 January, 1998
MMMM, yy	January, 98
MMM-yy	Jan-98
M/d/yy h:mm am/pm	1/15/98 6:25 pm
M/d/yy h:mm:ss am/pm	1/15/98 6:25:15 pm
h:mm am/pm	6:25 pm
h:mm:ss am/pm	6:25:15 pm
HH:mm	18:25
HH:mm:ss	18:25:15

Chapter 26 describes all of the available time and date placeholders. (You are not limited to the predefined formats found in the drop-down lists, and you can construct a custom date or time picture in any format that you desire.)

Current date and current time

These fields are used to insert the current date and time as shown by the computer's clock. You can use all of the date and time placeholders described in the previous section and in Chapter 26 in any combination that you desire.

Note   Because the current date and time are taken directly from your computer system, you can't specify a default.

You can have Word update the Current Date or Current Time form field when the document is printed by selecting the Update fields check box in the Printing options area of the Print tab. The Print tab is found under Options in the Tools menu.

Calculation

Use a Calculation form field whenever you want to insert an *expression* that derives a value from other fields in the form. An expression is constructed with a leading

= sign and then a formula. An example would be =Amount*Percent, which multiplies the value found in the field named Amount by the value in the field named Percent. You can enter an expression to do almost anything that you want.

The operators listed in Table 21-5 are supported in expressions.

Table 21-5 Operators Supported in Expressions	
Operator	*Description*
+	Addition
-	Subtraction
*	Multiplication
/	Division
%	Percent
^	Powers and roots
=	Equal to
<	Less than
<=	Less than or equal to
>	Greater than
>=	Greater than or equal to
<>	Not equal to

Expressions are not confined to the usual numerical operators listed previously. Because Word will recognize the cell-naming conventions of most spreadsheets and apply these conventions to tables, you can construct some pretty sophisticated equations.

For example, if you want to sum all of the information in a column on an invoice, you can enter a Calculation field that looks like =SUM(D4:D9). SUM() is a Word function that adds the values specified in the argument (enclosed in the parentheses). If you wanted to figure the amount of sales tax due on the total sales, you could insert an expression that looks like =PRODUCT(totsale,.05), where totsale is the bookmark assigned to the field Total Sale. For more information on expressions and functions, refer to Chapter 26.

The Calculation field can use the same formatting specifications as discussed in the Number field mentioned earlier.

You can set the maximum allowable length of the Calculation field by filling in the Maximum length box. This feature is particularly helpful if you make a calculation that returns a value like pi.

Inserting and modifying Check Box form fields

Check Box form fields do not lend themselves to much modification other than size. By their nature, they are either on or off: selected or not selected, whichever is the default setting. However, like Text form fields, the results of the field can be named as a bookmark, and Help text can be included. You can also record a macro to be played either when the cursor enters or leaves the check box.

You modify check box fields by opening the Check Box Form Field Options dialog box, shown in Figure 21-9.

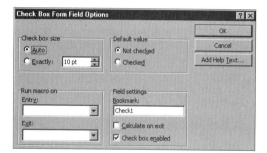

Figure 21-9: The Check Box Form Field Options dialog box.

Check box size

You can set the size of the check box within the form automatically by selecting Auto (the default setting). This sets the size of the check box to conform to the size of the surrounding text font. You can increase or decrease the size of the check box by selecting the Exactly radio button, and entering a value (in points) in the spin box.

You can change the check box size to a specific font size (points) and set the default setting to checked or not checked. To insert and modify a Check Box form field:

1. Position the insertion point where you want to place the new check box field.

2. Click the Check Box Form Field tool on the Forms toolbar.

3. Right-click the new field, and choose Properties from the shortcut menu.

4. Change the size or default setting as necessary, and then select OK.

Default value

Because a check box must be either checked or not, you can select the value that will be used as a default. If you want the box to be checked when you open the form, choose Checked. If you don't want the box to be checked, choose Not checked (the default setting).

Adding Drop-Down form fields

To make sure that no invalid values are entered into a form, such as an incorrect state abbreviation or unacceptable method of payment, you can add a Drop-Down form field to your template. Then the user must choose one from a limited list of valid values. No other values will be accepted. After inserting the drop-down field, you enter the items you want to appear in the list for user selection. To enter the items, open the Drop-Down Form Field Options dialog box, as shown in Figure 21-10.

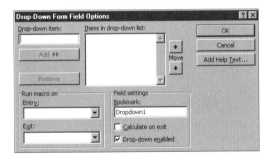

Figure 21-10: The Drop-Down Form Field Options dialog box.

Drop-down fields give the user a choice of valid field values from which to choose. To add a drop-down form field:

1. Position the insertion point where you want to place the new Drop-Down form field.

2. Click the Drop-Down Form Field tool on the Forms toolbar.

3. Double-click the new field to open the Drop-Down Form Field Options dialog box.

4. One by one, enter the items that you want to include in the drop-down list in the Drop-down item box, and choose Add or press Enter.

5. When you have added all the items you want on the list, choose OK.

Figure 21-11 shows an example of a field used to answer a question about book preferences. The drop-down arrow does not appear with the field until you have protected the form. The first item in the list appears as the default value in the form field.

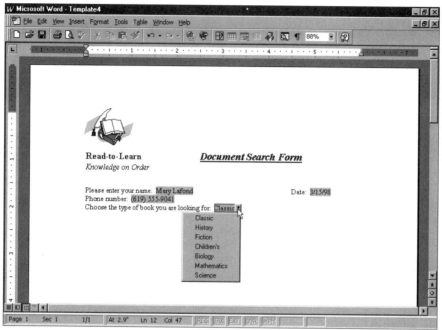

Figure 21-11: A sample Drop-Down field list.

After the items have been added to the list, you can remove them or rearrange their order in the Items in drop-down list box. You may want to move the most likely response to the top of the list because the first entry will display as default text:

- ✦ To move an entry, select it and press the up or down arrow to the right of the list. Each click moves the entry up or down one position in the list.

- ✦ To remove an entry, select it and choose Remove.

- ✦ To add a new entry, go back to the Drop-down item box.

Attaching a macro to a field

Use the options in the Run macro on area to name a macro that you want to run when entering or leaving the field. You may want to build a macro that will update the fields and perform calculations while the form is being filled. You can also have macros run when a user enters data in a particular field within the form, for example, to get additional information about the data just entered. (See Chapter 27 for a complete discussion of macros.)

Changing field settings

Word automatically assigns a bookmark to every form field. You can change the name of this default bookmark to something more meaningful than "Dropdown1" by entering a new name in the Bookmark box. Bookmarks are used in calculations and in macros to represent the results of the field, as in the following example: =SUM(Sales96,Sales97).

The Calculate on exit field setting updates any calculations that involve the field when the user moves to another field. By default, this is not checked because if your form contains a lot of calculations, it can slow down data entry. You can always update the fields after you have finished entering data.

The Fill-in enabled option setting for Text form fields toggles the read-only status of the field. When the option is cleared, the user may not enter data in the field. The Drop-down enabled option setting for Drop-Down fields allows the user to select a value from the drop-down list. When the option is cleared, the list does not appear and the first item in the list is the uneditable default value. If the Check box enabled option for a Check Box form field is cleared, the user cannot change the preset default value.

Adding Help text

Each type of form field allows you to include helpful text to guide the users of your form. This Help message can be displayed in the status bar, in a Help dialog box, or both.

Selecting Add Help Text from any of the form field options dialog boxes opens the Form Field Help Text dialog box, shown in Figure 21-12.

Figure 21-12: The Form Field Help Text dialog box.

The Form Field Help Text dialog box contains two identical tabs. Use the Status Bar tab to specify the help text you want displayed on the status bar when the insertion point is in the field. Use the Help Key (F1) tab to specify the help text to display in a dialog box that will open if F1 is pressed while the cursor is in the associated form field. Table 21-6 lists the options available in both tabs of the Form Field Help Text dialog box. The AutoText entry option gives you a list of available AutoText entries to use as Help text. The list includes predefined entries as well as items from the User Information tab of the Options dialog box and any AutoText entries you have defined.

Note Word limits the amount of Help text that you can display. If you want the Help text displayed in a dialog box, you can enter up to 255 characters. In the status bar, you are limited to 138 characters because it must all be displayed on one line across the bottom of the screen.

Table 21-6
Options in the Form Field Help Text Dialog Box

Selection	Action
None	Displays no help text for the form field.
AutoText entry	Allows you to retrieve text that you have previously defined as AutoText, and place that text either on the status bar or in a Help Text dialog box.
Type your own	Allows you to type in the information that you want the user to see on the status bar or in a Help Text dialog box.

Note Status bar Help messages display whenever a user enters a field. You can display a simple Help message on the status bar to act as a reminder to the user; you can store a more complete Help message in the Help Key (F1) tab. Figure 21-13 shows a Help message displayed in the status bar and in a dialog box opened by pressing F1.

Drawing and inserting tables

The Draw Table and Insert Table buttons on the Forms toolbar work the same way as the same buttons on the Standard toolbar. With Draw Table, you first draw the outside boundaries of the table, and then draw the lines to configure the rows and columns. When you use Insert Table, you drag the mouse pointer over the table grid to define the number of rows and columns you want in the table. See Chapter 12 for information on working with tables.

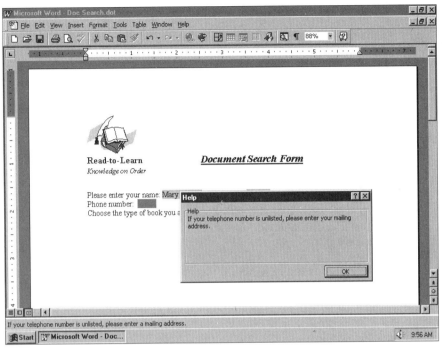

Figure 21-13: Help text in a form.

Adding text boxes

Text boxes add emphasis and visual appeal to forms just as they do to documents. You can add a text box to hold special text or to enclose one or more form fields. In order to view the text box when you insert it, you must be in the Page Layout view. Add a text box to your form design by clicking the Text Box button on the Forms toolbar. After the text box is in your form, you can resize it and change the format of the borders and shading the same as in any other document. See Chapter 14 for more information on text boxes. If you want a form field to appear in a text box, insert the text box first and then add the form field. Text boxes have taken the place of frames in Word 97. If you have documents created with earlier versions, Word 97 usually supports them.

Filling Out a Form

After your new form template is completed, protected, and saved in the template folder, anyone can use it to enter the information. You use the form just like you use any other template in creating a new document.

As you fill in the information in the fields, you are actually creating a new document using the form as a template. The new document will contain all the text in the form as well as the field values entered by the user. To create a new document with a form template:

1. Choose New from the File menu. The New dialog box opens for you to select a template.

2. Select the form template you just created, and choose OK. The form appears on the screen with the first form field highlighted.

3. Enter the requested information, select from the drop-down list or check the check box, and then press Tab to move the cursor to the next form field.

4. Repeat Step 3 as often as needed to complete the form. You can return to a field to change the entry using standard Word editing methods.

5. Name and save the new document, or simply print the document and close without saving.

To check a check box, either press Tab to move to the field and press the space-bar or simply click in the check box. To delete an entry from the form, select the field and press Delete.

Printing a Form

Printing a form is not much different from printing any other document. You can click the Print button on the Standard toolbar or open the Print dialog box to select print options. If your form contains many graphic objects and explanatory text, which can slow down your printing, you may want to print only the data that has been entered into the form. To limit the printing, choose Options in the Print dialog box to open the Print tab of the Options dialog box. In the Options for current document only, choose Print data only for forms, then choose OK twice to print your form data. The text is printed in exactly the positions in which it appears in the form.

Summary

In this chapter, you learned the basics of creating forms for use as templates for data collection. You saw that Word provides the tools to build any kind of form you may need. Armed with these versatile Word tools, you can create a form for any purpose. Here are two fundamentals well worth remembering:

✦ Forms are composed of text and data entry fields.

✦ The form can control the values entered and offer help to the user.

Where to go next...

✦ To make a form more user-interactive by attaching macros that run when you enter or leave a field, see Chapter 27.

✦ To learn about all the switches and formatting options that are available to change the appearance of the data in your form fields, go to Chapter 26.

✦   ✦   ✦

Getting Organized with Outlines and Master Documents

In this chapter, you learn how to use outlines to organize your thoughts and give focus to your ideas. In addition, the Master Document feature, which builds on Word's outlin-ing techniques, makes it easy to apply consistent formatting to long documents by combining small documents into a large framework.

Understanding How Outlines Work

Word's outline feature is intertwined with its heading styles. When you create an outline, Word automatically assigns the appropriate heading style to each outline level. For example, a level one heading uses the Heading 1 style. If you change the heading to level two, it automatically takes on the Heading 2 style. Conversely, assigning a standard heading style to text in Normal or Page Layout view automatically prepares the document for an outline. Therefore, if you use the standard heading styles as you create a document, you can make an outline of the document simply by switching to Outline view.

Note You can format heading styles as you do any style in Word. Chapter 11 explains working with styles.

This marriage of outlines and styles gives you considerable flexibility in approaching the outlining process. You can create an outline from scratch by turning on Outline view and assigning levels to your headings and body text as you type. Or you can write your document in Normal or Page Layout view and switch to Outline view to make it easier to arrange sections and assign or reassign heading levels. Because Outline view enables you to control the amount of text visible on the screen, you can move large chunks of text with minimal effort.

You can use outlines as a brainstorming aid: just type your thoughts without worrying where they fit in the overall picture. After you put a basic outline in place, you can change heading levels and rearrange entire sections of data. Creating an outline has other benefits. For example, you can use an outline to create a table of contents, number headings, or build a master document.

Understanding Outline View

Whether you want to create an outline from scratch or work with an existing document in outline format, you must first turn on Outline view. To do so, choose View⇨Outline, or choose the Outline View button from the horizontal scroll bar. Figure 22-1 shows a document in Normal view. Figure 22-2 shows the same document in Outline view.

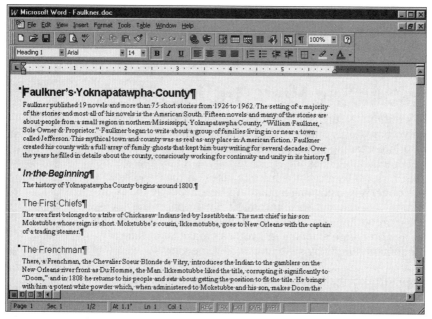

Figure 22-1: A document in Normal view. All headings are formatted by using Word's built-in heading styles.

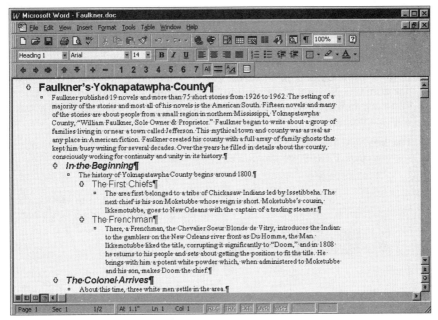

Figure 22-2: The same document in Outline view.

When you activate Outline view, the Outlining toolbar replaces the ruler. In addition, each heading or text paragraph is indented to its respective level and is preceded by a plus sign, minus sign, or box. Table 22-1 describes the heading icons.

Table 22-1
Outline Icons

Icon	Meaning
✛	Body text, headings, or both are below the heading.
▭	Body text or headings are not below the heading.
▫	Indicates a body text paragraph.

As you work with an outline, you can switch to Normal, Online Layout, or Page Layout view at any time. Outline view affects only the on-screen appearance of the document, not the document itself.

Note Online Layout view optimizes the layout of a document to make online reading easier. Text appears larger and wraps to fit the window, rather than the way it prints.

There are four ways to switch among Normal, Outline Layout, Page Layout, and Outline views:

✦ **The <u>V</u>iew menu.** Choose <u>N</u>ormal, Onlin<u>e</u> Layout, <u>P</u>age Layout, or <u>O</u>utline.

✦ **Buttons on the horizontal scroll bar.** The left edge of the horizontal scroll bar contains Normal View, Online Layout View, Page Layout View, and Outline View buttons. Figure 22-3 shows the horizontal scroll bar with the view buttons labeled.

✦ **The keyboard.** Press Alt+Ctrl+N for Normal view, Alt+Ctrl+O for Outline view, and Alt+Ctrl+P for Page Layout view.

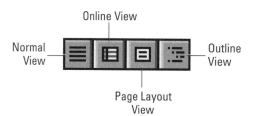

Figure 22-3: The View buttons on the horizontal scroll bar.

Note   Although headings and text appear indented in Outline view, the outline display doesn't have anything to do with the document's formatting. Don't be deceived by Outline view: make sure that you do document formatting in Normal or Page Layout view. (Word's paragraph formatting features are not even accessible from Outline view.)

Creating Outlines

To create an outline from scratch or to outline an existing document, switch to Outline view and assign outline levels to your headings and paragraphs. To create a new outline:

1. Switch to Outline view by choosing <u>V</u>iew⇨<u>O</u>utline, or by choosing the Outline View button from the horizontal scroll bar. Figure 22-4 shows the Outlining toolbar and identifies its buttons, and Table 22-2 describes the buttons on the Outlining toolbar.

   Word assigns the Heading 1 style to the paragraph. If you don't want the entry to be at the first level, promote or demote the heading by using the techniques in Step 4 before proceeding to Step 2.

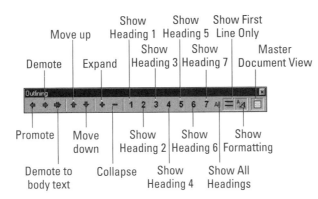

Figure 22-4: The Outlining toolbar with its buttons identified.

2. Type your first heading.

3. Press Enter when you're finished with the first heading.

   Each time you press Enter, Word begins a new paragraph at the same level as the previous heading.

4. To promote or demote a heading, do one of the following:

   • To change to a lower level (demote a heading), choose the Demote button on the Outlining toolbar, or press Alt+Shift+right arrow until the heading is at the level you want.

   • To change to a higher level (promote a heading), choose the Promote button on the Outlining toolbar, or press Alt+Shift+left arrow as many times as necessary.

5. To change to body text, choose the Demote to Body Text button on the Outlining toolbar, or press Ctrl+Shift+N.

6. Continue entering text, promoting and demoting levels as desired.

Table 22-2
Outlining Toolbar

Button Name	Action
Promote	Promotes a heading to the next higher level, or promotes body text to the level of the preceding heading.
Demote	Demotes a heading to the next lower level, or changes body text to a heading at a level below the level of the preceding heading.
Demote to Body Text	Demotes a heading to body text.

(continued)

	Table 22-2 *(continued)*
Button Name	**Action**
Move Up	Moves a heading or body text above the previous heading or body text paragraph. Note that only visible paragraphs are taken into account, and moved headings and body text retain their current levels.
Move Down	Moves a heading or body text below the next outline item. Only visible items are taken into account, and the moved headings and body text retain their current levels.
Expand	Expands the heading in which the insertion point is placed to show the next level of headings.
Collapse	Collapses all headings and body text subordinate to the selected heading.
Show Heading #	Shows all headings and body text through the selected level.
Show All	Shows all headings and body text if any text is currently collapsed. If all headings and text are currently expanded, collapsed body text will continue to display all heading levels.
Show First Line Only	Toggles between displaying the full text of each body text paragraph or only the first line of each paragraph.
Show Formatting	Toggles between displaying and hiding character formatting.
Master Document view	Switches to Master Document view and displays the Master Document toolbar.

Note Don't worry if you find dealing with styles easier than outline levels. Assigning heading levels from the style box has the same effect as promoting or demoting a heading level by using any of the outline techniques.

To create an outline from existing text:

1. With your document on-screen, switch to Outline view.

   Unless you have applied standard heading styles to your text, each paragraph is initially designated as body text. The document in Outline view in Figure 22-5 was not created by using heading styles.

2. With your insertion point anywhere in the heading or body text paragraph, promote and demote levels as desired, using the techniques in Step 4 of the preceding task.

   Assigning outline levels automatically adds standard heading styles to your text.

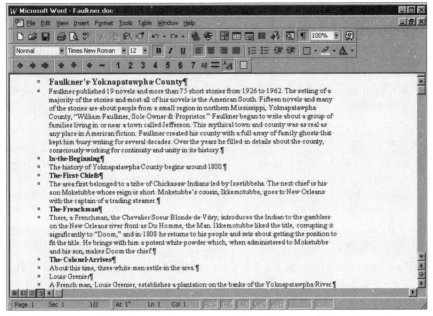

Figure 22-5: This document was not created by using Word's heading styles. In Outline view, each paragraph initially appears as body text.

As you promote and demote headings, you can see the level by looking at the Style box on the Formatting toolbar. In addition, if you want to view all your styles at once, you can display the style area. Choose Tools⇨Options, select the View tab, and enter a measurement in the Style area width box. When the style area is displayed, you can adjust its width by dragging the vertical line that divides the style area from your document text. Or, you can close the style area display by dragging the vertical line to the left until it disappears.

Rearranging Your Outline

As you create an outline, you don't need to worry about getting the arrangement and levels exactly the way you want them. The beauty of working with outlines is that you can enter thoughts as they occur and rearrange the text in a flash by changing the level or moving whole sections.

Selecting in Outline view

Before you start rearranging an outline, you need to understand how selection works in Outline view. The following list describes selection techniques that apply specifically to outlines:

✦ When you click a plus icon, the heading and all of its subordinate levels are selected.

✦ When you click the box symbol for a body text paragraph, you select only that paragraph of body text.

✦ When you click in the selection bar to the left of a paragraph, only that paragraph is selected. Therefore, if you click in the selection bar next to a heading with a plus sign, you select only that heading, not any of its subordinate levels.

✦ You can select multiple headings or paragraphs by dragging through the selection bar.

✦ You can use any standard Word technique for selecting text in an outline paragraph, but as soon as a selection crosses to a new paragraph, both paragraphs are selected in their entirety. In other words, you cannot select only a portion of more than one paragraph in Outline view.

Note If your text moves when you try to select it, you may have accidentally dragged a plus or minus symbol instead of just clicking it. Just choose Edit⇨Undo, and try again.

Promoting and demoting outline levels

To promote or demote a heading, place your insertion point anywhere in the heading, and use one of the following three methods:

✦ Use the buttons on the Outlining toolbar. Choose the Promote or Demote button to change the heading level. Choose the Demote to Body Text button to change any heading to body text.

✦ Use keystroke shortcuts. Press Alt+Shift+left arrow to promote a heading to the next level or Alt+Shift+right arrow to demote a heading one level. For the first three heading levels, you can also press Alt+Ctrl+#, with # standing for the outline level to which you want the text assigned. For example, to change a heading to level two, press Alt+Ctrl+2.

✦ Use the mouse to drag heading icons. Drag the plus symbol to the left or right. When you place the mouse pointer over an outline icon, the pointer changes to a four-headed arrow. As you drag, a vertical line appears at each heading level. Release the mouse button when you reach the desired level.

You can promote or demote multiple headings or body text paragraphs by selecting them before you use one of the preceding methods.

Tip   Here's a great trick for globally promoting or demoting outline headings. Suppose that you want to change all level two headings to level three. Simply use Word's Find and Replace feature. Choose Edit➪Replace. With your insertion point in the Find what text box, choose More➪Format➪Style, and select the Heading 2 style from the Find what style list box. In the Replace with text box, select the Heading 3 style from the Replace With Style list box. Choose Replace All.

What happens when you promote or demote text?

When you use the Outlining toolbar buttons to promote or demote a heading, only the actual paragraph in which your insertion point is positioned is moved. Unless you select an entire section by clicking the plus icon or using any other selection method, subordinate levels are not affected, with the following exceptions:

✦ Body text is always promoted or demoted along with its heading.

✦ Any outline elements that are collapsed under the heading are always moved along with the heading.

If a heading is collapsed, any structural changes you make to that heading affect subordinate headings or body text paragraphs. This makes it easy to move sections of a document. Simply collapse your outline to its highest level, and promote, demote, and move the headings.

Using keyboard shortcuts when working with outlines

Because working with outlines primarily involves text manipulation, using the keyboard as much as possible can speed things, particularly when you're entering text. When your fingers are already on the keyboard, pressing a keystroke combination is often easier than lifting your fingers off the keyboard to use the mouse. For example, if you are all set to type a body text entry, consider pressing Ctrl+ Shift+N rather than choosing the Demote to Body Text button. There's no right or wrong: Think about which method makes the most sense in a particular situation. In general, keyboard shortcuts make more sense during text entry, and mouse techniques can save you time when you're rearranging large chunks of text. Table 22-3 lists some of the most useful keystroke shortcuts when you are working with an outline.

Tip   Tab and Shift+Tab are two handy keystroke shortcuts in Outline view. Pressing the Tab key with your insertion point in a heading demotes the heading to the next level. Pressing Shift+Tab promotes a heading to the next level or promotes body text to a heading. These keystrokes have this effect only in Outline view. To promote or demote a heading in Normal view, you must use the Alt+Shift+arrow key combinations.

Caution   Pressing the Tab key in Outline view can produce unpredictable results if you're not aware of what's happening. As noted in the preceding tip, pressing Tab demotes a heading and pressing Shift+Tab promotes a heading. To insert an actual tab character in Outline view, you must press Ctrl+Tab.

Table 22-3
Keystroke Shortcuts in Outlines

To Do This	Use These Keys
Switch to Outline view	Alt+Ctrl+O
Switch to Normal view	Alt+Ctrl+N
Promote a heading or body text to the next level	Alt+Shift+left arrow (or press Tab)
Demote a heading to the next level	Alt+Shift+right arrow (or press Shift+Tab)
Promote or demote a heading to a specific level.	Alt+Ctrl+1 through Alt+Ctrl+3. Note that keystrokes are assigned for only the first three levels. If desired, you can assign keystroke shortcuts for any additional levels.
Demote a heading to body text	Ctrl+Shift+N
Move a paragraph up	Alt+Shift+up arrow
Move a paragraph down	Alt+Shift+down arrow
Show headings up to a specified level	Alt+Shift+1 through Alt+Shift+9 on the numeric keypad
Show all headings and body text or show all headings without body text	Alt+Shift+A
Show only the first line of body text or show all body text	Alt+Shift+L
Show or hide character formatting	/ on the numeric keypad
Expand selected headings	Alt+Shift++ on the numeric keypad
Collapse selected headings	Alt+Shift+- on the numeric keypad

Moving outline headings

Before you move headings, decide whether you want to move only a particular heading or all subheadings and body text associated with the heading. If a heading is collapsed when you move it, any subordinate text moves with the heading. If the heading is expanded to show its subordinate levels, some movement techniques move only the specified heading. You can take advantage of this to move whole sections without going through the process of selecting text. Figure 22-6 shows the sample outline collapsed to level one and two headings. With the outline collapsed, dragging any plus icon will move all its associated text.

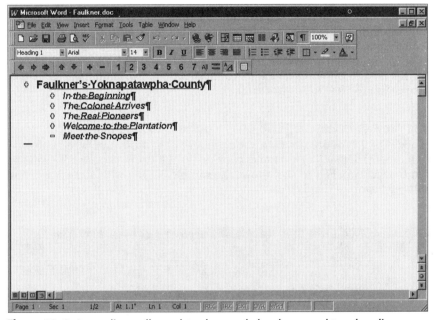

Figure 22-6: An outline collapsed to show only level one and two headings.

To move a heading without moving any of its associated subheadings or body text, you must use the Move Up or Move Down button on the Outlining toolbar, or press the Alt+Shift keys in combination with an up- or down-arrow key. Whenever you drag a plus icon, all text associated with the heading is moved.

When you place your mouse pointer on a plus icon, the pointer changes to a four-headed arrow. As you drag up or down, a horizontal line with a right arrow is displayed. Release the mouse button when the line is positioned where you want the text moved.

To move multiple headings, select the headings you want to move. Then hold down the Shift key while you drag the last heading icon in your selection. Make sure that you don't drag any heading except the last one. As soon as you click any heading in a selection other than the last one, the selection is cleared and only the heading at your mouse pointer position is selected.

Tip   Outline view is a handy way to rearrange table rows. When you're working in a
       table, switching to Outline view enables you to move a row or selected rows to a
       new location by dragging them.

Expanding and collapsing headings

You can expand or collapse any portion of an outline to show only the headings
you want. Collapsing an outline to show only the main headings gives you a quick
overview of your document and simplifies the task of rearranging sections. You
can also expand or collapse any individual heading section by double-clicking the
plus icon. You have the best of both worlds: you can work with most of your outline collapsed to get an overview of your document, but instantly expand a particular section to view it or work on it.

Expanding or collapsing the entire outline to a specific level

To specify which outline level to show, choose one of the numbered buttons on
the Outlining toolbar. For example, clicking the 2 button displays all headings
down to level two. Figure 22-7 shows the sample outline with all level one, two,
and three headings displayed.

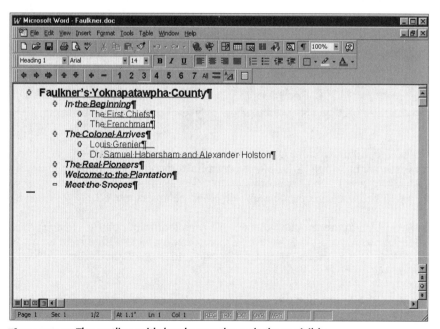

Figure 22-7: The outline with levels one through three visible.

To display your entire outline, choose the All button. The first time you choose All, all heading levels and body text are displayed. If you choose All again, the outline collapses to display all headings without any body text.

Expanding or collapsing a particular level

You can expand or collapse any heading by double-clicking its plus icon. If the heading is expanded, double-clicking the plus icon collapses any subheadings and body text subordinate to the heading. If the heading is collapsed, double-clicking the plus icon displays any subordinate levels. Figure 22-8 shows the sample outline collapsed to level three headings, with one section expanded.

You can also use the Expand and Collapse buttons on the Outlining toolbar to expand or collapse a heading or selected headings. In addition, you can press Alt+Shift+-(hyphen) to collapse a heading, or Alt+Shift++ (plus) to expand a heading.

When a heading is collapsed, a gray line appears under a portion of the heading text.

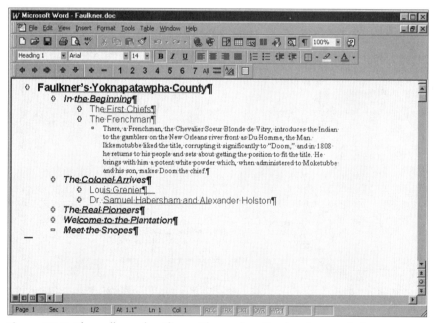

Figure 22-8: The collapsed outline with one heading level expanded.

Seeing more of your outline

The Outlining toolbar contains two buttons that enable you to see more of your outline, even when it's expanded:

✦ The Show First Line Only button displays only the first line of each body text paragraph. This feature enables you to see an overview of your document by displaying headings along with a small portion of text under each heading. Figure 22-9 shows the outline with Show First Line Only selected.

✦ The Show Formatting button toggles character formatting on and off. If you're using the outline mainly to organize your thoughts or prepare a table of contents, consider turning the display of character formatting off. Fonts and attributes can unnecessarily add to the size of the text displayed on the screen, reducing the amount of text a screen can display. Note that this option affects only the display: choosing it does not delete any character formatting you have applied. As soon as you switch to Normal or Page Layout view, you will see all your formatting. Figure 22-10 shows the sample outline with formatting hidden.

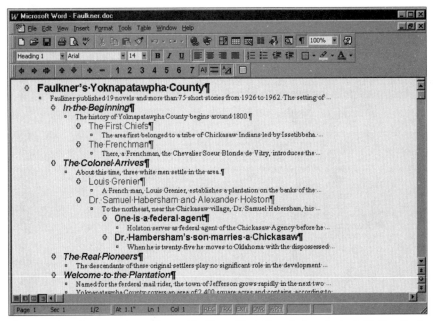

Figure 22-9: The sample outline with Show First Line Only selected. Notice that only the first line of each body text paragraph is visible.

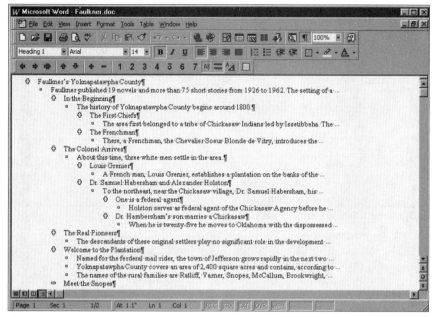

Figure 22-10: The sample outline with Show Formatting turned off.

Both of these buttons are toggles. If the feature is active, choosing the button turns it off; if the feature is inactive, choosing the button turns it on.

Displaying your document in Outline and Normal view at once

One way to work effectively with outlines is to split the document screen into two panes. You can display your document in Outline view in one pane and in Normal view in the other. This enables you to take advantage of Outline view to rearrange your text while viewing the result of your actions in the full document.

To split your document into two equal panes, double-click the split bar (at the top of the vertical scroll bar), or choose Window⇨Split. Or you can just drag the split bar to tailor the panes' size. (Of course, if you first split the screen into equal panes, you later can drag the split bar to resize the panes.) To restore the split window to its original condition, double-click the split bar, or choose Window⇨ Remove Split. Figure 22-11 shows the outline in split view.

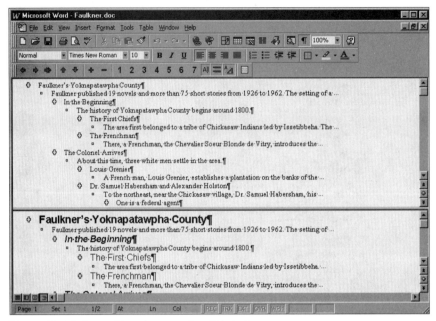

Figure 22-11: An outline document split into two panes.

Numbering headings in Outline view

Although you can add automatic numbering to any text where you have assigned a heading style, this technique is especially relevant to outlines. When you assign a numbering style, all heading numbers automatically adjust when you move a heading or change its level. For more information about numbering, see Chapter 9. To add numbers to an outline:

1. From any view, choose Format⇨Bullets and Numbering, or choose Format⇨Bullets and Numbering from the shortcut menu.

2. From the Bullets and Numbering dialog box, choose the Outline Numbered tab.

3. Choose one of the sample heading styles. If you want to modify the option, click Customize to assign a custom numbering changes.

4. Click OK when you have made all of your selections.

Figure 22-12 shows the sample document with heading numbering applied. If you want to remove numbering from your headings, just choose <u>R</u>emove from the Heading Numbering dialog box.

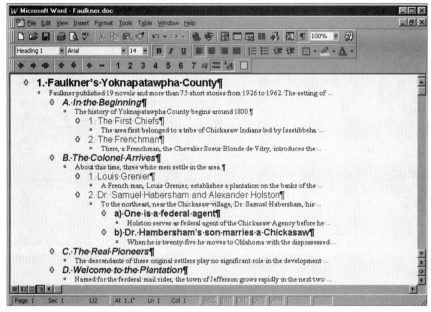

Figure 22-12: The sample outline with automatic numbering added.

Browsing Outlines

You can use Word 97's Document Map and Select Browse Object features to easily navigate a long outline.

Choosing <u>V</u>iew⇨<u>D</u>ocument Map while in any document view displays a vertical pane along the left edge of the document window that outlines the documents structure. Figure 22-13 shows the Document Map as it appears in the Normal view. Notice the headings listed in the left pane. You can use Document Map to quickly browse a long or online document and to keep track of your location in it.

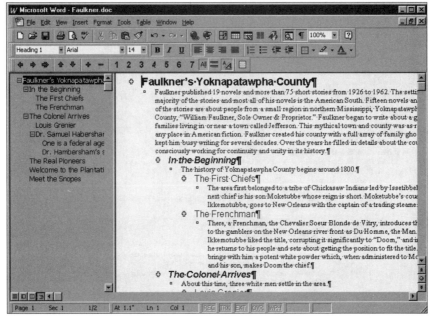

Figure 22-13: The Document Map lets you easily move around a document using its headers.

Click the Select Browse Object button (located at the bottom of the vertical scroll bar), which displays the menu of browse options (Figure 22-14). Click the Browse by Heading option. To move up one heading at a time, click the Next button; to move down one heading at a time, click the Previous button.

Browse by Heading

Figure 22-14: The Select Browse Object's menu of browsing choices.

Formatting an Outline

Remember that the formatting you see in Outline view is not necessarily the document formatting. The headings are indented only in Outline view unless you specifically modify the heading styles.

Each built-in heading style has its own format. If you want a heading style formatted differently, you can modify it. To modify a style, choose Format⇨Style, select the heading you want to change, and choose Modify. When you modify a style, the changes affect every instance of that style in the document. For more information about working with styles, see Chapter 11.

Note You can use AutoFormat to apply the standard heading styles to a document before you switch to Outline view. Just type each heading on a separate line as you create your document, and choose Format⇨AutoFormat. For more information about using AutoFormat, see Chapter 11.

Printing an Outline

When you print from Outline view, only the visible portion of your document is printed. For example, if your outline is collapsed to level one, only the level one headings are printed.

Note Outline symbols don't appear on a document printout.

Before you print from Outline view, expand or collapse your outline to display what you want printed. If you want to print your document as it will appear in its final form, switch to Normal view or Page Layout view before you print.

Understanding Master Documents

The most obvious way to create a large document is to add all your data to one colossal document. If you've already created several documents, you can use the Insert⇨File command to retrieve the documents into one location. There are a few problems with this approach, however. One problem is that Word begins to function less efficiently when a document is larger than 20 to 30 pages. Certain tasks such as scrolling and searching can take longer to accomplish, and the possibility of system errors increases.

Another problem is that only one person can work on any given file at one time. Therefore, if everything is crammed into the same file, you lose the ability to have different people working on the project.

Word's master document feature enables you to consolidate several documents into a large framework, providing the consistency and other advantages inherent in working with one large document, while retaining the convenience of working with individual subdocuments.

In addition to these advantages, the master document feature enables you to:

✦ Cross-reference items among several documents

✦ Use the Outline view tools to rearrange items spread among several documents

✦ Create indexes, tables of contents, and lists that span several documents

✦ Easily assign consistent page numbering, headers, and other formatting across multiple documents

✦ Print multiple documents with one command

A book is ideally suited to the master document feature. Each chapter can be a subdocument, and elements common to the entire book can be contained in the master document itself.

The Master Document View

The key to working with master documents is Master Document view, which is an extension of Outline view. You have all the features of Outline view (such as the capability to promote, demote, expand, or collapse headings) with several added attractions.

Whether you want to create a master document from scratch or combine existing documents into a master document, you must first turn on Master Document view by choosing View➪Master Document. If the Outlining toolbar is displayed, you can switch to Master Document view also by choosing the Master Document View button from the Outlining toolbar. Figure 22-15 shows the Master Document toolbar and identifies its buttons. Figure 22-16 shows the initial Master Document view of a document.

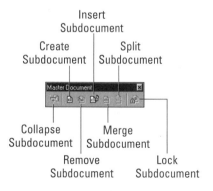

Insert
Subdocument

Create
Subdocument

Split
Subdocument

Collapse
Subdocument

Merge
Subdocument

Remove
Subdocument

Lock
Subdocument

Figure 22-15: The Master Document toolbar.

The Master Document toolbar is an extension of the Outlining toolbar, which was detailed in Table 22-2. Table 22-4 covers the buttons on the Master Document toolbar that are not included on the Outlining toolbar.

Table 22-4 **Master Document Toolbar**	
Button Name	**Action**
Collapse Subdocument	Expands or collapses subdocuments.
Create Subdocument	Turns selected headings and associated text into subdocuments.
Remove Subdocument	Turns selected subdocuments back into part of the master document. Note that this button does not delete the subdocument text.
Insert Subdocument	Inserts an existing file as a subdocument.
Merge Subdocument	Combines multiple subdocuments into one subdocument.
Split Subdocument	Divides one subdocument into two subdocuments.
Lock Document	Toggles the entire document or selected subdocuments to a locked or unlocked state. Note that this provides only cursory protection: any user can unlock the subdocument simply by choosing the Lock Document button again. For more protection, use one of Word's file sharing options.

Note After you have used Master Document view in a Word session, the Outline View button on the horizontal scroll bar turns into a Master Document View button, enabling you to switch among the Master Document view and other views.

Building a Master Document

There are three main methods of building a master document:

✦ Begin a new document in Master Document view. Create an outline for your master document, and use the headings to break the outline into separate subdocuments.

✦ Break an existing document into subdocuments.

✦ Combine existing documents into a master document by inserting them as subdocuments. Any existing Word document can be treated as a subdocument.

Master documents, like outlines, use Word's built-in heading styles (Heading 1 through Heading 9).

Note You can create a table of contents or an index from an outline or master document. See Chapter 24 for details. Chapter 23 tells you how to use master documents to create cross-references that span several documents.

To build a master document from scratch in Master Document view:

1. Open a new document window.

2. Switch to Master Document view by choosing View⇨Master Document.

3. Create an outline for your master document, using any of the techniques covered previously in this chapter. Before you create the outline, however, decide which heading level you want to use to begin each subdocument.

4. When you are ready to break portions of the document into subdocuments, select all the headings and text that you want to convert. (You can expedite this process by collapsing the outline to the heading level at which you want to begin your subdocuments before you select.)

   Word uses the level of the first heading in your selection to determine where each subdocument will begin. For example, if your selection begins with a level two heading, Word will begin a new subdocument at each level two heading in your selected text area.

5. Click the Create Subdocument button.

   Each subdocument is enclosed in a box, and a subdocument icon is displayed in the upper-left corner of each box, as shown in Figure 22-16.

6. Save the master document.

   When you save a master document, Word assigns a unique filename to each subdocument based on the first eight characters (not including spaces) in the heading at the beginning of the subdocument. When you open a sub-document, its filename appears in the title bar.

   Notice that Word adds a body text paragraph between each subdocument. This makes it easy to add additional text or subdocuments outside existing subdocument boundaries.

Because Word automatically assigns subdocument filenames, you can end up with strange results if your headings have similar names or if the filenames assigned by Word would conflict with files already in the destination directory.

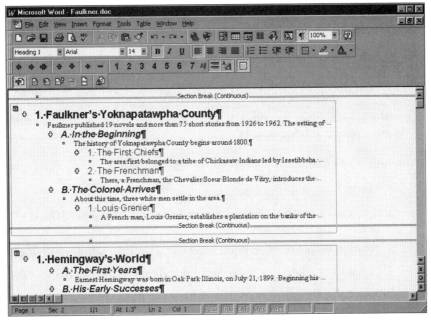

Figure 22-16: A master document divided into subdocuments.

As a simple demonstration, suppose that your directory contains a document called Chapter1.doc. You create a subdocument in which the first heading is titled Chapter 1. When you save the master document, Word assigns the name Chapter2.doc to your subdocument because Chapter1.doc is already taken. When a naming conflict occurs, Word uses numbers to differentiate filenames. Therefore, your neatly numbered headings may not correspond to their sub-document filenames. For this reason, you should check and, if necessary, rename subdocument filenames before you close the master document. See the "Renam-ing or moving a subdocument" section later in this chapter for instructions. To convert an existing document to a master document:

1. Open the document you want to convert.

2. Switch to Master Document view.

3. If the document is not already organized in outline format, promote and demote headings as desired.

4. Select the section you want to split into subdocuments, making sure that the first selected heading is the level at which you want each subdocument to start.

5. Click the Create Subdocument button.

6. Save the master document.

If you want to insert a document into a master document without turning the document into a subdocument, use the Insert⇨File command. The text of the inserted document becomes part of the master document, but there is no link to the original document. You can use this technique to insert a subdocument into an existing master document, or to create a master document from scratch by inserting previously created subdocuments.

To convert an existing document to a subdocument:

1. Switch to Master Document view.

2. If you want to use an existing master document, open it. Otherwise, open a new document window.

3. Position your insertion point where you want to add the subdocument.

4. Choose the Insert Subdocument button on the Master Document toolbar.

5. Select the file you want to insert from the Insert Subdocument dialog box.

   The document retains its original filename. In addition, when you open a subdocument from within its master document, the template and formatting assigned to the master document take precedence over any formatting originally assigned to the subdocument. If you open the subdocument separately, it reverts to its original formatting.

Working with Master Documents

After you build a master document, you have several options for working with it. In Outline view, you can treat the entire document as one large outline: expand, collapse, promote, and demote sections at will. In Normal view, you can work with the document as you would any other document: cut and paste text or graphics between sections, add formatting, or perform any other document tasks. You also can open an individual subdocument and work on it separately by double-clicking the subdocument icon.

Note   Master Document has been enhanced to make opening master documents faster by collapsing all subdocuments and using hyperlinks to navigate through the document.

Be aware that Word inserts section breaks for each subdocument. This action may affect your formatting decisions. You can apply different formatting (including headers, footers, margins, paper size, page orientation, and page numbering) for different sections. You can view the section breaks in Normal view or Master Document view by choosing the Show/Hide button on the Standard toolbar.

The maximum size of a master document is 32MB, not including any graphics, and you can't have more than 80 subdocuments in any master document. You probably won't have to worry about this. In most cases, you will reach the limits of your computer's capacity to deal with a master document before you reach Word's limits.

Note Working with a master document in Normal view or Page Layout view is just like working with any other document. You can apply formatting to the entire document or any part of it. Because each subdocument is a section, you can apply or modify any section-level formatting, such as page numbering or margins. In addition, you can insert new sections within subdocuments for formatting purposes.

If you follow the next two rules, you won't have a problem with formatting master documents:

✦ If you want the formatting (for example, page numbering) to apply to the entire document, make sure that you apply the formatting in the master document rather than in a subdocument.

✦ If you want the formatting to apply to only one subdocument, place your insertion point inside the subdocument to which you want to apply the formatting (or open the subdocument) before you proceed.

Also, keep in mind that if you insert an existing document as a subdocument, the document retains its original section formatting except where that formatting would be overridden by the master document's template or styles. If you want one header or footer to continue throughout the entire master document, make sure that your individual subdocuments don't contain their own headers or footers. If you want to create different headers or footers for each subdocument, set them up in the individual subdocuments.

Working with the entire master document in Normal view or Page Layout view makes it easy to move text and graphics among subdocuments using Word's standard cut and paste techniques, including drag-and-drop. You can also navigate through a large document and use Word's Find and Replace feature to make global changes across several documents.

Working with Subdocuments

From Master Document view, you can open any subdocument to work on it separately. This option is especially useful if several people are working on a project. Different people can open and edit several subdocuments simultaneously. You also can change the order of the subdocuments, combine subdocuments, nest subdocuments within other subdocuments, or break a portion of a subdocument into a new subdocument.

Opening a subdocument

You can open an individual subdocument from within a master document by double-clicking its subdocument icon in Master Document view. If you make changes to the subdocument, be sure that you save both the edited subdocument and the master document before closing the master document. If someone else may need to work on another part of the master document while you're editing the subdocument, be sure that you close the master document as soon as you open the subdocument where you want to work. As long as your subdocument has been previously saved with the master document, the subdocument retains its link to the master document even after you close the master document file.

You can also open a subdocument using Word's File⇨Open command, but certain changes may not be properly updated in the master document. To ensure that a subdocument's links are accurately updated in the master document, opening subdocuments from the master document is best.

If you opened the subdocument from the master document, closing the subdocument returns you to the master document. If you opened the subdocument as a normal document, or, if you opened it from the master document but closed the master document with the subdocument still open, closing the subdocument is the same as closing any regular document.

Renaming or moving a subdocument

If you want to rename a subdocument, or move it to a different directory or drive, make sure that you open the subdocument from the master document and use the File⇨Save As command. Then resave the master document. If you move or rename a subdocument through the Windows Explorer, or use any method other than the one just described, the master document loses its link with the subdocument.

Removing subdocuments

To merge a subdocument into a master document, click the subdocument icon to select the subdocument, and choose the Remove Subdocument button. When you do this, the text remains in the master document, but it is no longer attached to the subdocument.

If you want to remove the subdocument text from the master document entirely, click the subdocument icon and press Delete. The subdocument text is deleted from the master document.

Neither of these actions deletes the subdocument file from disk: They only break the subdocument's attachment to the master document. If you want to delete the file from the disk, you must do so from Windows File Manager or use another standard file deletion method.

Caution Don't delete a subdocument from disk without first deleting it from the master document. If you delete the subdocument file first, you will get an error message the next time you open the master document.

Rearranging the order of subdocuments

Master Document view makes reorganizing your subdocuments a snap. You can accomplish the same end by selecting and moving text in Normal view, but in Master Document view, reorganizing subdocuments is a simple matter of dragging the subdocument icon. To rearrange subdocuments:

1. Open the master document and switch to Master Document view.

2. Click the subdocument icon you want to move. This selects the entire subdocument.

3. Drag the subdocument to its new position.

You can also move a subdocument by positioning your insertion point anywhere in the subdocument and holding down the Alt+Shift keys while you press an up- or down-arrow key.

If you move a subdocument inside the boundaries of another subdocument, the subdocument you move becomes part of the destination subdocument. If you want a subdocument to retain its integrity as a separate subdocument when you move it, be sure to move it to a location outside any subdocument boundaries.

Splitting subdocuments

A subdocument may become too large for you to work with effectively, or you may want more than one person to work on different portions of the subdocument at the same time. You can split a subdocument into two separate subdocuments:

1. Open the master document and switch to Master Document view.

2. Select the entire heading or body text paragraph that will begin the new subdocument.

3. Click the Split Subdocument button on the Master Document toolbar. The subdocument splits just above the selected paragraph.

Merging subdocuments

You can combine several small files into one subdocument. You may want to do some editing afterwards. To merge multiple subdocuments into one:

1. Open the master document that contains the subdocuments you want to merge, and switch to Master Document view.

2. Make sure that the subdocuments you want to merge are adjacent.

3. Select the subdocuments you want to merge.

4. Click the Merge Subdocument button on the Master Document toolbar.

When you save the master document, Word assigns the filename of the first document in your selection to the merged subdocument.

Sharing subdocuments

Word uses the Author information in Summary Info to determine the owner of each subdocument. If you are the owner, you have full rights to open and edit the document. If you did not originally create the document, a small padlock icon appears just under the subdocument icon. Figure 22-17 shows a master document in Master Document view with one subdocument locked.

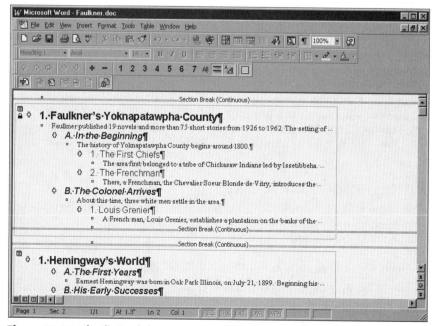

Figure 22-17: The first subdocument on this screen has been locked by using the Lock Document button. Notice the padlock under the subdocument icon.

To lock or unlock a subdocument:

1. Select the subdocument you want to lock or unlock.

2. Choose the Lock Document button on the Master Document toolbar.

Keep in mind that the master document's Lock Document option does not provide real protection. Anyone can unlock the document simply by clicking the Lock Document button. If you need a higher level of protection, use one of Word's file sharing options to add a Protection Password or a Write Reservation Password. These options can be accessed by choosing Tools⇨Options, and selecting the Save tab. For more information about passwords, see Chapter 6.

Summary

Word's outline feature allows you to organize your thoughts into headers and rearrange them as needed. The Master Document feature lets you create large documents by creating subdocuments, which gives you more efficiency in Word. In this chapter, you learned how to:

✦ Create and work with outlines by using the Outlining toolbar, which appears when you choose View⇨Outline or the Outline View button on the horizontal scroll bar. Word's outline feature is essential for helping you organize your thoughts in a document by using headings.

✦ Create and work with Master Documents by choosing View⇨Master Documents, or by clicking the Master Document View button on the Outlining toolbar. Word's Master Document feature lets you work efficiently with large documents by organizing them into subdocuments.

Where to go next...

✦ To format your outline heading styles differently than Word's default settings, see Chapters 7 and 8 for basic character and paragraph formatting. See Chapter 11 for creating and modifying styles.

✦ To learn other Word features for working with long documents beyond Master Document, see Chapters 23 and 24. Chapter 23 explains the collection of Word features for working with long documents. Chapter 24 explains how to create tables of contents and indexes.

✦　　✦　　✦

Working with Long Documents

♦   ♦   ♦   ♦

In This Chapter

Inserting bookmarks

Writing captions

Creating cross-references

Creating footnotes and endnotes

♦   ♦   ♦   ♦

Word provides tools to help you create a formal, business-like document complete with figure captions, footnotes, endnotes, and accurate cross-references. This chapter introduces you to these tools and shows you how to use them to produce a complete and professional document.

Can This Chapter Help You?

The Word features introduced in this chapter were originally intended for long documents. Most of these features interact with one another to form a web of continuity throughout the document. For example, you can create a cross-reference to a caption or a footnote. And when you create a cross-reference (unless it's to a reference that's already a bookmark), Word inserts a bookmark at the reference location. As you modify the document, Word automatically revises the cross-references and bookmarks accordingly.

Although this chapter is titled "Working with Long Documents," many of the features discussed can also work well in shorter documents. You may, for example, want to add a footnote in even a one-page document.

Introducing Fields

Several of the features discussed in this chapter use fields. Chapter 26 covers fields in detail, but the following pointers will help you as you work through this chapter:

♦ By default, fields look just like any other document text unless they are selected, so you may have trouble telling what's a field and what's not. If you want, Word identifies your document fields by shading them. Choose Tools⇨ Options, and select the View tab. Then select Always from the Field Shading drop-down list. Now all of your fields will be shaded, making them easy to spot.

✦ Fields are displayed as either codes or results. For example, a date field's result is the actual date, but the field code looks something like: { DATE \@ "M/d/yy" }. The code is a set of instructions that tells Word what to do.

✦ To toggle between displaying field codes and field results for a particular field, place your insertion point in the field and press Shift+F9. You can also click the right mouse button when your insertion point is in a field, and choose the Toggle Field Codes option from the shortcut menu.

✦ To toggle field codes for the entire document, press Alt+F9, or choose Tools⇨Options and select Field codes from the Show area on the View tab.

✦ You can activate the Office Assistant and display a list of relevant Help topics by pressing F1 with your insertion point anywhere in the field code.

✦ To update a field, place your insertion point in the field, and press F9. You can also choose Update Field from the shortcut menu.

✦ To update all fields in a document, select the entire document (the fastest way to select the entire document is to press Ctrl+A), and press F9.

✦ To move your insertion point to the next field, press F11. Or press Shift+F11 to move to the preceding field.

✦ To edit a field's results, move your insertion point inside the field. If Field Shading is activated, the field results are a lighter shade of gray than when the entire field is selected. Select the text that you want to edit and change, or format the text by using any of Word's character formatting options.

✦ To delete a field, select the entire field (the text appears in reverse video), including the opening and closing brackets, and press Delete. Deleting fields is easier when the field codes are displayed.

Working with Bookmarks

Forget about those ratty old pieces of paper you use (and lose) to mark your place in printed books. Word's electronic bookmarks give the term *bookmark* a whole new meaning. You can have a virtually unlimited number of bookmarks in any document. And don't let the name deceive you: Word's bookmarks do much more than mark your place. They can mark any item or selection in a Word document, including text, graphics, tables, or any combination. If you select items before you create a bookmark, moving to that bookmark selects the entire section. The bookmark feature thus enables you to mark items for cross-referencing, indexing, moving, or copying.

Bookmarked items can also be used in fields and macros. You can even use bookmarks in calculations, which is similar to using a range name in a spreadsheet.

Later in this chapter, you will learn how to use bookmarks when creating cross-references, and in the next chapter, you'll see how you can use bookmarks to mark page ranges for indexes.

Inserting bookmarks

Creating a bookmark involves two steps: you choose the location that you want to mark, and you assign a name for the bookmark so that you can identify it later. To create a bookmark:

1. Position your insertion point at the location that you want to mark. Or, if you want the bookmark to mark a section, select the text and/or objects before you proceed.

2. Choose Insert⇨Bookmark (or press Ctrl+Shift+F5). The Bookmark dialog box appears, as shown in Figure 23-1.

Figure 23-1: The Bookmark dialog box shows a list of existing bookmarks in the current document.

3. Enter a name for the bookmark in the Bookmark name text box.

   A bookmark name can contain up to 40 characters, and you can use both letters and numbers (but the first character must be a letter). A bookmark name cannot include spaces, nor can you use any symbol except the underscore character to separate words.

4. Choose Add. The dialog box automatically closes.

Caution If the Add button is dimmed after you enter your bookmark name, the name may be invalid. Word dims the Add button if the name includes any characters that are not allowed. The name cannot include any characters other than letters, numbers, or underscore characters. You can use numbers in a bookmark name, but the first character must be a letter.

Viewing bookmarks

Word allows you to control the display of bookmark markers in your document. Choose Tools⇨Options, and select or clear the Bookmarks check box on the View tab. When this check box is selected, bookmarks are displayed, as shown in Figure 23-2. If you selected a block of text before creating the bookmark, the selected text is surrounded by square brackets. If no text was selected before you created the bookmark, an I-beam symbol is displayed at your insertion point location. The I-beam looks like the mouse pointer that Word uses inside a text entry area. You can see the bookmarks in both Normal and Page Layout views if they are checked on the View tab.

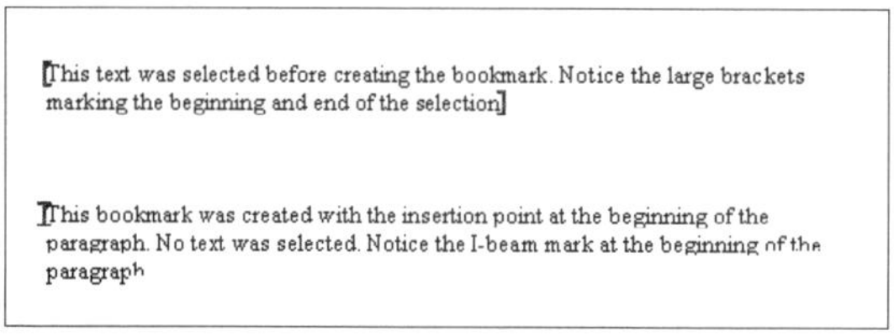

[This text was selected before creating the bookmark. Notice the large brackets marking the beginning and end of the selection]

[This bookmark was created with the insertion point at the beginning of the paragraph. No text was selected. Notice the I-beam mark at the beginning of the paragraph

Figure 23-2: The first bookmark on this screen was created with text selected. The second was created without any text selected.

Moving to bookmarks

You can use either the Bookmark dialog box (Insert⇨Bookmark) or the Go To tab of the Find and Replace dialog box (Edit⇨Go To) to jump to a specified bookmark. Both methods will be covered in this section, but the Bookmark dialog box is the most direct route. As you will see, using the Go To dialog box involves at least one extra step or keystroke. If, however, you know the exact name of the bookmark, the fastest way to jump to it is to press F5 to open the Go To tab, type the bookmark name, and press Enter.

If several bookmarks are in a particular area, you may have difficulty telling where one bookmark ends and the next one begins. You can quickly identify the bookmark that you want by using one of the methods described in the following two exercises. Either method will select the entire bookmarked area. To find a bookmark by using the Bookmark dialog box:

1. Choose Insert⇨Bookmark.

2. Select the bookmark that you want to go to from the Bookmark name list (refer to Figure 23-1).

3. Choose Go To (or press Enter).

   Notice that Go To is the default button: all you have to do is select a bookmark and press Enter. You can also move to a bookmark directly after opening the Bookmark dialog box just by double-clicking the bookmark's name. You may need to drag the dialog box aside to see the insertion point at the bookmark.

Note The Bookmark dialog box allows you to sort your bookmarks either alphabetically or by their location in the document. Sorting by location allows you to easily identify bookmarks based on their relative positions in a document. By default, however, bookmarks are sorted by name. To sort them by location, select the Location radio button near the bottom of the Bookmark dialog box.

To find a bookmark by using the Go To dialog box:

1. Choose Edit⇨Go To.

2. Choose Bookmarks from the Go to what list.

3. Select the bookmark that you want to go to from the Enter bookmark name drop-down list, or type the bookmark name in the text box (see Figure 23-3). Notice the bookmarks are in alphabetic order by name.

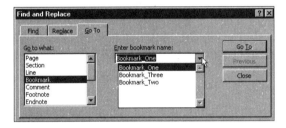

Figure 23-3: The bookmark list in the Go To tab.

4. Choose Go To (or press Enter).

Manipulating bookmarks

Table 23-1 describes what happens when you move, copy, or delete bookmarked items.

Table 23-1
Moving, Copying, and Deleting Bookmarked Items

Action	Result
Add text with your insertion point inside bookmark brackets.	The text is included in the bookmark.
Move text that contains a bookmark to another location in the current document.	The bookmark moves with the text.
Move text that contains a bookmark to another document.	The bookmark moves with the text unless the recipient document already contains a bookmark with the same name.

(continued)

Table 23-1 *(continued)*

Action	Result
Copy text that contains a bookmark to another location in the same document.	The bookmark stays in the original location. The copied text does not contain a bookmark.
Copy text that contains a bookmark to another document.	Both documents contain the same text and bookmarks. If, however, the other document already contains a bookmark with the same name, the bookmark is not copied.
Delete all the text or objects between two bookmark brackets.	The bookmark is deleted.
Delete a portion of the text or objects in a bookmark selection.	The remaining items retain the bookmark.

The following exercise tells you how to delete a bookmark from the list without deleting any of the items that it references.

Caution You should work with your bookmark markers displayed; otherwise, you may inadvertently delete a bookmark. You may also end up with a bookmark that references a larger section than you intend. If your insertion point is immediately after text that's bookmarked, everything that you type will be included in the bookmark, unless your insertion point is outside the bookmark closing marker when you begin typing. To delete a bookmark without deleting the bookmarked items:

1. Open the Bookmark dialog box (Insert⇨Bookmark).

2. Select the bookmark that you want to delete.

3. Choose Delete.

4. Close the Bookmark dialog box.

Placing the contents of a bookmark in your document

You can insert the contents of a bookmark field anywhere in a document. Just press Ctrl+F9 to insert the opening and closing field characters, and type the name of the bookmark between the brackets. If your bookmark name is the same as one of Word's built-in field names, type **REF** in front of the bookmark name inside the field. For example, to insert the contents of a bookmark called MY_BOOKMARK, enter **MY_BOOKMARK** in the field. But, if you have a bookmark called AUTHOR, which is also the name of a Word field, enter **REF AUTHOR** in the field.

You can use the techniques in the preceding paragraph to insert bookmark contents anywhere in a current document or in documents linked in a master document. To insert the contents of a bookmark in a different document, use the INCLUDEPICTURE or INCLUDETEXT fields. To replace the field with the contents of the bookmark, right-click and choose Update Fields from the shortcut menu. For more information about using fields to refer to other documents, see Chapter 26.

When you insert the contents of a bookmark field, the object or text that is marked by the bookmark is actually inserted in your document. The inserted items take on the paragraph formatting in effect at the insertion point location, unless you included a paragraph mark in the selected area when you created the bookmark. In that case, the bookmark's formatting takes precedence.

Calculating with bookmarks

You can use bookmarks to identify values you want to use in calculations. You can then insert the bookmarked items in formulas anywhere in a document. If the numbers change, you can recalculate the results by updating your fields. To create a bookmark for use in calculations, select the number and create the bookmark by using the techniques covered earlier in this section.

To insert a formula to calculate numbers in bookmark fields, position your insertion point where you want the result of the formula to appear, and choose Insert⇨ Field. Select Equations and Formulas from the Categories list and =(Formula) from the Field names list, as shown in Figure 23-4. Create a formula using the bookmark names in place of numbers. Depending on whether you are displaying field codes or results, you will see either the formula or the result. For information about creating formulas and other expressions, see Chapter 26.

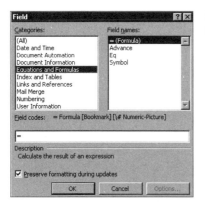

Figure 23-4: The Field dialog box with the Formula field selected.

Word has two special bookmarks to help you address envelopes. If you have more than one address in a document, select the address that you want to use for the delivery address, and create a bookmark called EnvelopeAddress. Select the address that you want to use for the return address, and create a bookmark called EnvelopeReturn. When you select Tools⇨Envelopes and Labels, the text included in these bookmarks is placed in the delivery and return address windows, respectively.

Captions

Have you noticed the captions that accompany each figure in this book? Word has a special feature that allows you to add captions to figures, tables, selected text, or other items. The caption numbers increase automatically as you add additional cap-tions. And, if you move or delete a caption, the surrounding caption numbers adjust automatically. In addition, you can use the Cross-reference command to refer to specific captions in your document text or in other document areas.

You can either type captions manually or let Word create the caption for you. If you want to add captions automatically to all items of a particular type (for example, charts or equations), Word's AutoCaption feature does most of the work for you.

Entering captions directly

You can use Word's caption feature to manually add captions to specific items. If you've already inserted objects that require captions into your document, use this feature. To add captions manually:

1. Select the object that you want to caption.

2. Choose Insert⇨Caption. Figure 23-5 shows the Caption dialog box.

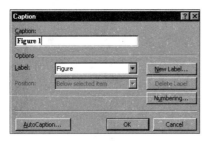

Figure 23-5: The Caption dialog box shows an example of a figure caption using default numbering.

The Caption text box initially contains a default label name and an item number. The label identifies the object and appears in front of your caption text. Captions for each label name are numbered sequentially.

3. To add text after the label, type it in the Caption text box.

Note that Word will not allow you to delete the label text in the Caption text box. To change the label, follow the instructions in Step 4.

Look at Figure 23-6 for an example of a caption with a label and additional text. The label identifies the object as the first figure in this section, and the text describes the particular figure.

Figure 23-6:
A figure caption appears below the picture.

4. To edit or change the label, do one of the following:

   • To choose an existing label, make a selection from the Label drop-down list.

   • To add a custom label name, choose New Label, type a name in the Label text box, and choose OK. After you create a new label, its name appears on the Label drop-down list and can be selected like any other label.

5. To change the numbering options, choose Numbering, modify the selections in the Caption Numbering dialog box, and choose OK. (Caption numbering options are covered a little later in this section.)

6. To change the caption's position relative to the object, select Below selected item or Above selected item from the Position drop-down list.

7. Choose OK to insert the caption. Word inserts the caption and ensures that the caption remains on the same page as its object.

Because captions use the Caption style, make sure that no other text is included in the same paragraph as your caption. Any text in the same paragraph will be formatted with the Caption style.

Caution If you move a figure or other object that has a caption, the caption won't automatically move with the object. To be sure that your captions stay with their associated objects, add a text box to the document as a container for each caption with its object. To do so, create the text box by choosing Insert⇨Text Box. Then insert the object and its caption into the text box. Framing objects and captions together makes it easy to move both items in a single action: just drag the container. For more information about text boxes and framing, see Chapter 14.

Adding captions with AutoCaption

Use AutoCaption if you want to automatically add captions to all items of a particular type. After you turn on AutoCaption for an object type, each object that matches the criteria will be automatically captioned, using the label and any other options that you specify.

Word uses caption labels to determine the numbering sequence. All captions with the same label are numbered sequentially. If you want a particular set of captions to be numbered separately, make sure that you use a unique label name.

It's a good idea to plan ahead if you want to use automatic captioning. If you decide to use AutoCaption for all of your figures after you've inserted several figures in your document, only the figures you insert *after* you turn on automatic captioning will be captioned. To add captions automatically:

1. Choose Insert⇨Caption.

2. Choose AutoCaption. The AutoCaption dialog box, shown in Figure 23-7 appears.

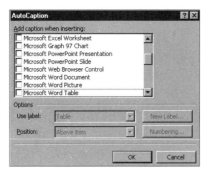

Figure 23-7: The AutoCaption dialog box.

3. Select the type of object that you want to caption from the list labeled Add caption when inserting. If you want several object types to use the same label and numbering scheme, just select as many objects as you want. Each type of object will be numbered sequentially within its own group.

4. Choose Use label, and select a label from the drop-down list; or choose New Label, and type a new label name.

5. Choose Position, and select Above item or Below item.

6. Choose Numbering if you want to change any of the numbering options.

7. Click OK.

You can add descriptive text to an automatic caption by placing your insertion point directly after the caption number in your document and typing additional information.

Updating your captions

Captions are inserted as fields, which means that they can be displayed, edited, updated, and used in macros just like any other field. (For more information about fields and field codes, see Chapter 26.) You may see a caption that looks like this:

```
{SEQ Figure \* ARABIC}
```

In this case, the field codes for the caption are being displayed rather than the caption text. You can switch between displaying field codes or results by pressing Alt+F9.

In most cases, Word takes care of updating and renumbering your captions. You can move, copy, add, or delete captions to your heart's content without worrying about the numbers. The only time that you have to do something about caption numbering is when you move or delete an object that a caption references. Because captions are fields, all you have to do is update the field—select the caption and press F9. Or you can update all fields in your document at one time (including any captions) by selecting the entire document and pressing F9.

Editing caption labels

Word comes with three built-in caption labels: Equation, Figure, and Table. When you create a caption, you can either choose one of these labels or create a new one. After you have created captions, you can easily change the label for all captions of the same type.

Note   Because captions of a particular type are linked for numbering purposes, you can't just change a label name for an individual caption. If you want only one caption to be relabeled, select the caption and press Backspace or Delete to delete it. Then create a new caption by using the techniques covered earlier in this chapter. To change caption labels:

1. Select a caption that uses the label you want to change.

2. Choose Insert⇨Caption.

3. Do one of the following:

   - Select a label name from the Label drop-down list.

   - Choose New Label, and type a new label name.

4. Choose OK.

   All the captions of the same type will be relabeled. For example, if the label of your selected caption was *Figure* and you changed it to *Drawing,* all of the captions that used the label *Figure* will now be labeled *Drawing.*

Deleting labels and captions

You can't delete any of the built-in label names (Equation, Figure, or Table), but you can delete any labels that you create. To do so, just open the Caption dialog box (Insert➪Caption), select the label that you want to delete, and choose Delete Label.

Because captions are inserted as fields, you delete a caption as you delete any other field. Select the entire field, and press Delete or Backspace. It's easier to select a field for a deletion when you have the field codes displayed. To display the field codes, press Alt+F9 or choose Field codes in the View tab of the Options dialog box.

Changing caption style

Word assigns a built-in style called Caption to all captions. This style is basically the Normal style with bold added and a line space above and below the paragraph. You can modify this style as you do any other style. See Chapter 11 for more information on working with styles. If you make changes to the Caption style, all of the captions in your document will reflect the changes.

If you want to change the formatting for a particular caption, just select that caption and use any standard Word formatting technique to make changes. You can edit a caption's text just as you edit any other document's text.

Changing caption numbering style

By default, Figure and Table captions are numbered by using Arabic numerals (1,2,3), and Equation captions use lowercase letters (a,b,c). You can change the style to uppercase or lowercase letters or Roman numerals. To change the appearance of caption numbers, follow the steps outlined in the following exercise:

1. Select an item that uses the label type you want to renumber.

   For example, if you select an item that uses the Figure label, all figure captions in your document will reflect any changes that you make.

2. Choose Insert➪Caption.

3. Choose Numbering. Figure 23-8 shows the Caption Numbering dialog box.

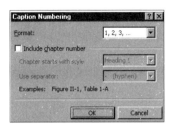

Figure 23-8: The Caption Numbering dialog box gives you several options for formatting captions.

4. Select a numbering style from the Format drop-down list.

5. Choose OK twice.

Using chapter numbers in a caption

If your document consists of chapters, you can instruct Word to include chapter numbers in your captions. Take a look at the figures in this book. Each figure caption begins with the word Figure followed by the chapter number and a hyphen. After that, the figures are numbered sequentially within each chapter. If you use one of Word's built-in heading styles for your chapter titles, you can include the chapter number in your captions. Note that this technique can be used for any headings that use the standard heading styles — it's not limited to chapter titles.

Make sure that your chapter headings use one of the nine built-in heading styles, such as Heading 1, and that each chapter heading uses the same style. Also, be certain that the heading style you use for chapter titles is not used anywhere else in the document. To choose a style for your chapter titles:

1. Choose Format➪Bullets and Numbering to display the Bullets and Numbering dialog box, and then click the Outline Numbered tab (see Figure 23-9).

2. Select a numbering style, and choose OK.

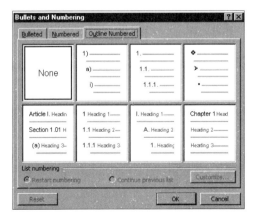

Figure 23-9: The Outline Numbered tab shows several numbering styles.

After you have selected a style for the titles, you can specify that style as the source for the chapter numbers to add to the captions. To include chapter numbers in captions:

1. Select an item that uses the label type in which you want to include chapter numbers.

2. Choose Insert⇨Caption.

3. Choose Numbering.

4. Select Include chapter number.

5. Select Chapter starts with style, and select the heading style that you used for your chapter titles (usually Heading 1).

6. Select Use separator, and select the character you want to use to separate the chapter number from the item number.

7. Choose OK to return to the Caption dialog box, and choose OK again.

Working with Cross-References

Cross-references tell readers where to look for more information. For example, placed throughout this chapter are several references that direct you to other chapters for details. To direct you to the chapter that discusses sections, you can just type **See Chapter 10**. But what if a chapter gets added or deleted, and the chapter on fields is no longer 10? Going back and changing every reference to that chapter (and any other chapter) could be a major headache.

Cross-referencing comes to the rescue. If, instead of typing **See Chapter 10**, you type **See** and then insert a cross-reference code that links to the heading of the chapter that we want to reference, Word can automatically update the reference number no matter how many times it changes. You can cross-reference the following items:

✦ Headings that use one of Word's built-in heading styles

✦ Footnotes and endnotes

✦ Captions

✦ Bookmarked items

Cross-references are inserted as fields, so all the field information discussed at the beginning of this chapter applies.

Creating in-document cross-references

Creating a cross-reference is a simple matter of typing some fixed text and inserting a reference to the item.

A cross-reference can include multiple references. You could say, for example, "See Chapter 10 on page 263." In this example, you would type **See** and insert a reference to the chapter number. You would then type **on page** and insert a reference to the page number on which the chapter heading appears. Notice that the fixed text includes any spaces or punctuation that you want to include.

You can also use cross-referencing to insert a chapter name or number inside your header or footer. Just open the header or footer area, place your insertion point where you want to insert the reference, and use the steps listed in the following exercise to create a cross-reference:

1. Place your insertion point where you want the cross-reference, and type any introductory text (for example, **For more information, see**); make sure that your insertion point ends up at the exact spot where you want the cross-reference inserted.

2. Choose Insert➪Cross-reference. The Cross-reference dialog box appears, as shown in Figure 23-10.

Figure 23-10: The Cross-reference dialog box lists several types of references.

3. Make a selection from the Reference type drop-down list to select the general reference category.

   Depending on the reference type that you select, the Insert reference to and For which lists will contain different options, and the name of the For which list changes. (For example, if your reference type is Heading, you get a For which heading list that includes all the headings in your document.)

4. Select an option from the Insert reference to drop-down list to specify the information from the reference category that should be inserted in the cross-reference. Note that each reference category contains a Page number option, which enables you to refer to the page on which the referenced item occurs.

5. Specify the exact reference that you want by making a selection from the For which list. For example, if you choose Bookmark as the reference type, the For which bookmark list contains a list of all bookmarks in the document.

6. Choose Insert. The Cross-reference dialog box remains open so that you can add information to your reference or add additional references.

7. When you are finished, close the Cross-reference dialog box.

Another option in the Cross-reference dialog box, Insert as hyperlink, allows you to jump quickly to the referenced item in the same document. The Include Above/below option adds the word "above" or "below" to refer to the location of the referenced item with respect to the cross-reference. For example, "See Table 4 above."

Note If you want to create cross-references across document boundaries, all the involved documents must be part of a master document. See Chapter 22 for more information about working with master documents.

Keeping cross-references up to date

Cross-references are inserted as fields. They are automatically updated whenever you print your document, and you can use standard field updating techniques to update them at any time. Press F9 with your insertion point in a cross-reference field to update that field, or select the entire document, and press F9 to update all fields in the document.

The introductory text for a cross-reference can be revised just like any other text. If your fields are shaded, as suggested at the beginning of this chapter, you can easily tell where the introductory text ends and the cross-reference field begins.

You can change the reference information for a particular reference by selecting the reference, choosing Insert➪Cross-reference and making any changes that you want in the Cross-reference dialog box.

Note Whenever you insert a cross-reference, Word creates a bookmark at the reference location. See the section on bookmarks earlier in this chapter for more information about working with bookmarks.

Working with Footnotes and Endnotes

If you do any kind of academic or business writing, you will probably deal with footnotes or endnotes at one time or another. Word can't help you compose your text, but it will streamline every other aspect of the process.

Every footnote or endnote includes a reference in the document text and the note itself. The reference is usually a number, but it can also be a letter or any other symbol. The only difference between footnotes and endnotes is that footnotes appear on the same page as the material they reference while endnotes appear at the end of a section or document.

Creating a footnote or endnote

Creating a footnote or endnote involves two steps: inserting the reference in your document text and writing the note itself. There are many footnote and endnote options that you can change (positioning, formatting, numbering style, and so on), but the basic technique for inserting a note is always the same. To create a footnote or endnote:

1. Position your insertion point immediately after the text you want to reference. If no text is selected, the reference mark will be placed at your insertion point location. Or, select a section of text that you want to reference. If text is selected, the reference mark is placed at the beginning of the selection.

2. Choose Insert⇨Footnote.

   Note that you make the same menu selection even if you are planning to create an endnote. The resulting Footnote and Endnote dialog box, as shown in Figure 23-11, allows you to specify whether you want a footnote or endnote.

Figure 23-11: The Footnote and Endnote dialog box helps define the note and set the numbering style.

3. Select Footnote or Endnote.

4. In the Numbering section, do one of the following:

   • Select AutoNumber (the default setting) if you want Word to automatically number your footnotes or endnotes.

   • Select Custom mark if you want to use symbols or other custom options for your numbering. See the section about customizing footnote and endnote options later in this chapter for information on this topic.

5. Choose OK.

   If you are in Normal view, Word opens the note pane, in which you type the text for your note. Figure 23-12 shows a footnote being entered in Normal view. The text pane is in the top part of the screen, and the note pane is in the lower part of the screen.

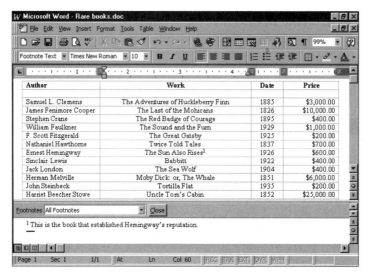

Figure 23-12: The note pane at the bottom of the screen is where you enter footnote or endnote text in Normal view.

If you are in Page Layout view, Word moves the insertion point to the footnote area at the bottom of the page or the endnote area at the end of the document. Figure 23-13 shows a footnote being entered in Page Layout view.

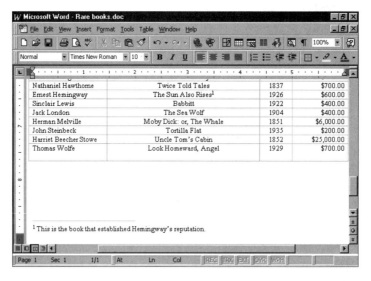

Figure 23-13: In Page Layout view, you enter footnote or endnote text directly on the page.

6. Type the text for your note.

7. Close the note pane.

When you rest the mouse pointer on a footnote or endnote mark, a ScreenTip displays the text of the note.

Tip   You can quickly insert a footnote or endnote without going through the Footnote and Endnote dialog box by pressing Alt+Ctrl+F for a footnote or Alt+Ctrl+E for an endnote. Either of these keystroke shortcuts will insert a reference mark at your insertion point location and take you directly to the note pane where you can type your note text.

Referring to the same footnote or endnote

There may be times when you want several areas in a document to refer to the same footnote or endnote. You can accomplish this feat with a Cross-reference command and the NOTEREF field. To insert multiple references to the same footnote or endnote:

1. Create one footnote or endnote for the reference using the techniques covered in the preceding exercise.

2. Position your insertion point at the location where you want to insert an additional reference.

3. Choose Insert⇨Cross-reference.

4. Select Footnote or Endnote from the Reference type drop-down list.

5. Select Footnote number or Endnote number from the Insert reference to drop-down list.

6. Select the footnote or endnote that you want to refer to in the For which footnote or For which endnote list box.

7. Choose Insert; then choose Close (or press Enter).

8. Select the reference mark that you just inserted.

9. Choose Format⇨Style to open the Style dialog box.

10. Choose Footnote Reference or Endnote Reference from the Styles list, and then choose Apply to apply the appropriate style to the reference mark.

11. To insert additional references to the same note or additional notes, repeat Steps 2 through 10.

Instead of opening the Style dialog box, you can simply click the drop-down arrow next to the Style button on the Standard toolbar and select Footnote Reference or Endnote Reference from the list.

Keeping footnotes and endnotes

One way to work with footnotes or endnotes is to keep the note pane open (View⇨Footnotes) as you work on your document. The note pane will scroll with your document so that you can always see any notes that are referenced in the visible portion of your document. You can switch back and forth between your document and the note pane by clicking in either pane or by pressing F6.

When the note pane is open, you can specify whether you want to view footnotes, endnotes, or both by choosing your option from the drop-down list in the note pane menu bar.

If the note pane isn't open, you can use one of the following methods to view your notes:

✦ Rest the insertion point on the reference mark in the document pane and the note text displays in a ScreenTip above the mark.

✦ Double-click any footnote or endnote reference mark to open the pane and view the note. Double-clicking any note reference in the note pane closes the pane and returns your insertion point to the location of the reference mark for that note in your document.

✦ Hold down the Shift key while you drag the split box on the vertical scroll bar. This action opens the note pane so that you can view or edit your notes. Close the note pane by double-clicking the split box or by dragging the split bar up until the pane disappears.

✦ Choose <u>V</u>iew↣<u>F</u>ootnotes.

If your document includes both footnotes and endnotes, you can switch between displaying footnotes and endnotes in the note pane by selecting All Footnotes or All Endnotes from the notes drop-down list in the note pane menu bar.

Moving to footnotes and endnotes

With or without the note pane open, you can scroll through all of your footnotes and/or endnotes by using the object scroll buttons at the bottom of the vertical scroll bars. Click the Browse by Object button and select Browse by Footnote (or Endnote) from the pop-up palette (see Figure 23-14). Then click the Next or Previous buttons to scroll through the notes sequentially. If the insertion point is in the document pane, it moves to the next (or previous) note mark. If it is in the note pane, it moves to the next (or previous) note itself.

Figure 23-14: The Browse by Object pop-up palette with Browse by Footnote selected.

What if you want to locate a particular note? Or what if you want to return to a particular reference location in your document? The following exercise answers the first question. As for the second question, if you double-click any note reference, either in the note pane or in the note area in Page Layout view, Word returns you to the reference mark for that note in your document. To find footnotes or endnotes using Go To:

1. Choose Edit⇨Go To.

2. Select Footnote or Endnote in the Go to what list.

3. Do one of the following:

   - To jump to the next or preceding footnote or endnote, choose Next or Previous.

   - To move to a specific footnote or endnote, type a number in the Enter footnote number text box.

4. Choose Close or Go To.

You can also use the Edit⇨Find command to locate footnotes or endnotes. In the Find dialog box, just select Footnote Mark or Endnote Mark from the Special pop-up list. (You may need to click More to see the Special button.) You cannot use this method to find a specific footnote number, but you can keep choosing Find Next to cycle through all of the footnotes or endnotes in your document until you find the one you want.

Modifying footnotes and endnotes

Unless you specify otherwise, all footnote and endnote text is formatted in a 10-point font. Footnotes use a built-in style called Footnote Text, and endnotes use a style called Endnote Text. The default font size for reference marks is also 10 points, and the style names are Footnote Reference and Endnote Reference. To modify any of these styles, choose Format⇨Style, select the style that you want to change, choose the Modify button, and then the Format button. Make your desired changes, and choose OK. Choose the Apply button in the Style dialog box to apply your changes to the style. For more information about working with styles, see Chapter 11.

Modifying a footnote or endnote style affects all of the footnotes or endnotes for a particular document, but you can also edit the text or change the formatting for specific footnotes or endnotes just as you can for any other Word text. With your insertion point in the note pane, scroll to the note that you want to work with and change it, using the toolbars, the Ruler, or any of Word's menus or keystrokes.

If you're working in Normal view, the only thing you need to do before you edit footnote or endnote text is to open the note pane using any of the techniques described earlier. If you're working in Page Layout view, you can simply scroll to the area containing the footnote or endnote text.

Manipulating footnotes and endnotes

Deleting a footnote or endnote is as simple as selecting the reference mark in the document and pressing Delete or Backspace. Moving or copying a selected reference mark also moves or copies the associated footnote or endnote text. You can use any of Word's cut, copy, and paste commands. When you move, copy, or delete footnotes or endnotes, Word automatically renumbers the notes to reflect any changes.

You can delete all of the footnotes or endnotes in a document by using the Replace feature. Choose Edit⇨Replace, select Endnote Mark (^e) or Footnote Mark (^f) from the Special pop-up list, leave the Replace with text box blank, and choose Replace All.

Converting footnotes to endnotes and vice versa

You can be sure that with any electronic document, everything is subject to change. All of your carefully positioned footnotes may look great, but what happens when the powers-that-be decide that the footnotes should all appear at the end of the document as endnotes. Word's way ahead of you here: the conversion process is virtually automatic. To convert all footnotes to endnotes (or vice versa):

1. Choose Insert⇨Footnote.

2. Choose Options.

3. Choose Convert.

4. Select the option that you want from the Convert Notes dialog box, shown in Figure 23-15.

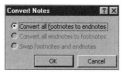 **Figure 23-15:** The Convert Notes dialog box.

5. Choose OK.

Now that you know all about mass conversion, what about converting notes one at a time? To convert individual footnotes or endnotes:

1. Make sure that the note text is visible, either through the note pane in Normal view or on the page in Page Layout view.

2. With your insertion point anywhere in the note that you want to convert, click the right mouse button to open the Footnotes shortcut menu, shown in Figure 23-16.

Figure 23-16: Choose from the Footnotes shortcut menu to convert a footnote to an endnote.

3. Choose Convert to Footnote or Convert to Endnote, as applicable.

Setting custom footnote and endnote options

If you create a footnote or endnote without specifying any options, Word uses the following default settings:

✦ Footnotes use Arabic numerals (1,2,3) as reference symbols, and endnotes use lowercase Roman numerals (i,ii,iii).

✦ Footnotes appear at the bottom of the page that contains the reference mark, and endnotes appear at the end of the document.

✦ Note numbering is consecutive throughout a document.

✦ A two-inch horizontal line separates footnotes and endnotes from document text. If a footnote or endnote must wrap to the following page, Word uses a line that extends from the left to the right margin (a *continuation separator*) to indicate the continuation of a note.

Of course, Word makes it easy for you to customize any of these settings with the Note Options dialog box. To open the Note Options dialog box:

1. Choose Insert⇨Footnote.

2. Choose Options.

3. Select the All Footnotes or All Endnotes tab, depending on which type of note you want to reformat.

Altering the appearance of reference marks

The following exercise tells you how to change the numbering style for automatically numbered footnotes or endnotes:

1. In the Note Options dialog box, select a numbering style from the Number format drop-down list, shown in Figure 23-17.

Figure 23-17: The Number format drop-down list in the Note Options dialog box.

2. Choose OK and then Close.

You can also create custom marks that don't renumber along with your other footnotes or endnotes. Choose Custom mark from the Footnote and Endnote dialog box. Your custom mark can consist of up to ten characters, and you can use any keyboard character. For additional choices, choose Symbol from the Footnote and Endnote dialog box. This selection opens the Symbol dialog box, shown in Figure 23-18. Double-click any symbol to close the Symbol dialog box, and insert that symbol in the Custom Mark text box. If you want to insert more symbols, just choose Symbol again and repeat the process.

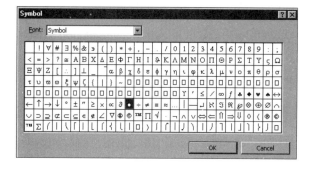

Figure 23-18: The Symbol dialog box contains over 200 symbols that you can use in custom marks.

The simplest way to change the numbering style is to do so when you create the footnote or endnote. If you've already created the footnote or endnote, though, you can easily change its style by selecting the reference mark in your document and following the procedures in this section.

Note Word does not update custom reference marks. For example, if you change a footnote reference mark to an asterisk, that footnote mark remains an asterisk no matter how many footnotes are added or deleted. In addition, the custom setting applies only to the individual footnote to which you assign it. If you want to assign a custom mark to additional footnotes or endnotes, you must do so on an individual basis.

Moving footnotes and endnotes

You can make two changes to footnote and endnote placement: you can tell Word that you want your footnotes to follow right after the last text on the page instead of appearing at the bottom of the page, and you can direct endnotes to appear at the end of each section instead of all together at the end of the document. To change the placement of footnotes and endnotes:

1. From the Place at drop-down list in the Note Options dialog box, select Beneath text to place footnotes immediately following text instead of at the bottom of the page, or select End of section to place endnotes at the end of each section instead of at the end of the document.

2. Choose OK and then Close.

Controlling footnote and endnote numbering

You can direct Word to restart footnote or endnote numbering on each page, or you can stipulate a specific starting number. To restart footnote or endnote numbering on each page:

1. In the Note Options dialog box, select the Continuous, Restart each page, or Restart each section radio button.

2. Choose OK and then Close.

To specify a starting number for footnotes or endnotes:

1. Type or select the starting number in the Start at text box. Notice that Word automatically selects the Continuous radio button as soon as you begin entering text in the Start at text box.

2. Select the Numbering option that you want.

3. Choose OK and then Close.

Note When you use the master document feature, Word automatically numbers footnotes and endnotes consecutively across subdocuments.

Changing footnote and endnote separators

Word allows you to change the appearance of separator and continuation separator lines—you can even get rid of them altogether. Note that these changes must be made from Normal view: you cannot edit separator lines in Page Layout view. To change footnote and endnote separators:

1. Switch to Normal view.

2. Choose <u>V</u>iew➪<u>F</u>ootnotes to open the notes pane.

3. Choose All Footnotes or All Endnotes from the notes drop-down list to view your footnotes or endnotes, as applicable.

4. Choose one of the following from the notes drop-down list:

   • Footnote Separator or Endnote Separator to edit the separator line.

   • Footnote Continuation Separator or Endnote Continuation Separator to edit the continuation separator line.

5. Do one of the following:

   • Edit the separator by making any changes you want.

   • Delete the separator by selecting it and pressing Delete or Backspace.

6. Close the notes pane when finished.

Note   You can return to the default separators at any time by choosing <u>R</u>eset from the notes pane menu bar.

By default, there is no text to indicate to readers that a footnote or endnote continues to a new page. You can direct Word to add some identifying text whenever a footnote or endnote continues to another page. This feature is called a *continuation notice.* You can, for example, insert something like **Continued on next page** as a continuation notice. To add a continuation notice:

1. Switch to Normal view.

2. Choose <u>V</u>iew➪<u>F</u>ootnotes.

3. Select All Footnotes or All Endnotes, as applicable.

4. Select Footnote Continuation Notice or Endnote Continuation Notice from the notes drop-down list.

5. Type the text that you want for your continuation notice.

6. Choose <u>C</u>lose.

After making the desired changes to the footnote and endnote formatting and text, you can view them on the page in the Page Layout view or continue to edit the notes in the note pane of the Normal view document window.

Summary

This chapter has covered many of the Word tools that operate in the background of the document preparation process. You have learned

✦ How to add and reference bookmarks, captions, and cross-references in the document.

✦ How to include and customize footnotes and endnotes.

Where to go next...

✦ To learn how to enter comments and deal with revisions made by one or more reviewers, see Chapter 19.

✦ For information about creating tables of contents and indexes for long documents, see Chapter 24.

✦ To delve deeper into the realm of fields and field codes and learn more about what is behind all the codes and marks you met in this chapter, see Chapter 26.

✦   ✦   ✦

Creating Tables of Contents and Indexes

C H A P T E R

24

Indexes and tables of contents are both valuable additions to long documents. Readers can thumb through the table of contents to determine which sections may be of interest, and a well-planned index can enable readers to zero in on a specific topic. You can also create tables to list your figures, charts, equations, or any other document items. Word's indexing and tables features make it easy to add these important finishing touches to your long documents.

Index and table of contents entries, the indexes themselves, tables of contents, and figures are all fields. The techniques covered in this chapter will help you automate the process of creating and updating fields, and you can apply everything you know about fields to indexes and tables of contents. For example, you can add any of the general field switches to INDEX, TOC, or TOA fields.

Feel free to use the Insert⇨Field command to create any of the fields discussed in this chapter without going through the feature-specific dialog boxes. You can also create fields from scratch by first pressing Ctrl+F9 to insert the opening and closing field characters in your document and typing the field name along with any additional text and switches. Chapter 26 contains a detailed discussion of fields and their codes and switches. See Chapter 23 for a brief overview of fields that will provide just enough information to work with the fields covered in this chapter.

✦ ✦ ✦ ✦

In This Chapter

Creating indexes for your documents

Creating tables of contents for your documents

Creating tables of figures, tables of authorities, and other tables

✦ ✦ ✦ ✦

Adding Indexes to Your Documents

In global terms, the process of creating an index includes two steps: you first mark all the items in your document that you want included in the index, and then you instruct Word to assemble the index from the marked entries. Index entries are contained in the XE field, and the information for the index itself is contained in the INDEX field.

Note If you are creating your index from a master document, doing your index work in the master document itself works better than in the individual documents, as working in the master document will help to ensure that items are marked consistently and that page number references in the index are accurate.

Creating, formatting, and modifying index entries

Before Word can assemble your index, you must first specify the items you want referenced in the index. The easiest way to mark index entries in your document is with a *concordance file,* which is a standard two-column Word table that contains all the words or phrases that you want to include in your index. You type all the words or phrases, tell Word how you want those items listed in the index, and let Word use the concordance file to search through your document and mark all occurrences of the items you've listed.

But no matter how thorough you are in the creation of your concordance file, you can't get around the tedious task of combing through your document and individually marking those items that you may have missed. For example, even if you include "banned in Boston" and "Banned in Boston" in your concordance file, an instance may occur in your document where you refer to the event without using one of the precise phrases. You may have used the word "banned" in a paragraph, with the word "Boston" somewhere later in the paragraph. Because the phrase "banned in Boston" (in any permutation) is not used, no reference to this paragraph will appear in your index unless you mark it separately.

In addition, because the concordance file marks *every* occurrence of the listed items, you may end up with some items marked that really shouldn't be. There may be places where you used a word or phrase without relating it to the topic that you want to index.

So the best indexing technique is to start by creating a concordance file that's as inclusive as possible and adding manual index entries as necessary, while deleting any unneeded entries.

Note Plan your index carefully. Indexing is an art: no automated indexing feature, regardless of its power, can take the place of careful planning and design. You must go through your document and determine which index layout will best serve your readers. Ask yourself some of the following questions: How detailed does the index need to be? Should you include cross-references to refer readers to other topics? Would multilevel categories make it easier for readers to find information? After settling these issues, make a list of all of your index topics and decide how you want each item to appear in the index. This chapter will tell you how to accomplish your goals by using Word's indexing tools, but the clearer your goals are at the outset, the more useful your index will be.

Marking index entries automatically

Two steps are involved in the process of using a concordance file: creating the file and using it to mark entries. Don't worry about alphabetizing the items as you create your concordance file: Word will take care of that job when it creates the index. To create a concordance file:

1. Open a new document window by choosing File➪New and choosing Blank Document in the New dialog box, or clicking the New button on the Standard toolbar.

2. Create a two-column table by choosing Table➪Insert Table and choosing OK. You don't have to make any changes in the Insert Table dialog box because a two-column table is the default.

3. In the first column, type the word or phrase that you want indexed and press Tab to move to the second column.

   The word or phrase in the first column must be the exact word or phrase that you want Word to search for, capitalized and punctuated exactly as it appears in your document. For example, if "Up in Michigan" and "up in Michigan" are both used in your document and you want them indexed, you must include them as two separate entries in your concordance file.

4. In the second column, type the index entry exactly as you want it to appear in the index, and press Tab to create a new row.

   The main index entry may not be the same as the item in the first column. Proper names are one area where your document text (the first column entry) will probably differ from the resulting index entry (the second column entry). In an index, proper names are usually listed with the last name first. So you can list "Ernest Hemingway" in the first column and "Hemingway, Ernest" in the second column.

   Another instance where the document text may differ from the index entry is in the case of subentries. For example, you may want "Kansas City Star" to appear in your index as a subentry under "Hemingway, Ernest." To do this, type **Hemingway, Ernest:Kansas City Star** in the second column. The colon tells Word to insert the second item as a subentry. You can have up to nine levels of subentries, and you separate each level with a colon.

5. Repeat Steps 3 and 4 for each index reference and entry.

When you've completed your entries, you should spell check and proofread the file before you use it to mark your document.

6. Save the file as a standard Word document. Figure 24-1 shows a sample concordance file.

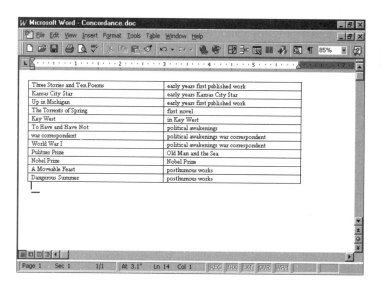

Figure 24-1: A sample concordance file.

Three Stories and Ten Poems	early years first published work
Kansas City Star	early years Kansas City Star
Up in Michigan	early years first published work
The Torrents of Spring	first novel
Key West	in Key West
To Have and Have Not	political awakenings
war correspondent	political awakenings war correspondent
World War I	political awakenings war correspondent
Pulitzer Prize	Old Man and the Sea
Nobel Prize	Nobel Prize
A Moveable Feast	posthumous works
Dangerous Summer	posthumous works

Note You can streamline the process of creating a concordance file by copying and pasting text from the document that you want to index instead of typing the text directly in the concordance table. Copying text can also reduce the potential for errors. Any time you type new text, you open yourself to the possibility of typographical errors. With a concordance file, even something as seemingly insignificant as a lowercase letter that should really be uppercase can prevent Word from finding and marking the text for your index entry.

If you plan to copy text from an existing document into your concordance file, the easiest way to set yourself up is to open both files and choose Window⇨Arrange All. This command causes both document windows to be visible, and you can copy text from one document to the other.

After you've created a concordance file, you can use it to mark index entries in a document automatically:

1. Open the document that you want to mark.

2. Choose Insert⇨Index and Tables and select the Index tab. The Index and Tables dialog box should appear, as shown in Figure 24-2.

3. Choose AutoMark. The Open Index AutoMark File dialog box appears, as shown in Figure 24-3.

4. Select the name of the concordance file that you want to use.

5. Choose OK.

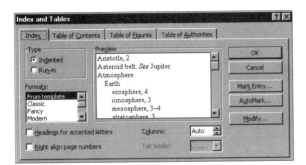

Figure 24-2: The Index tab in the Index and Tables dialog box.

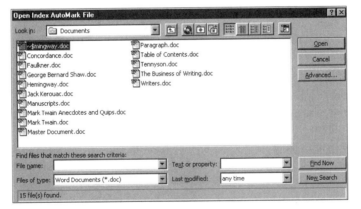

Figure 24-3: The Open Index AutoMark File dialog box.

Marking index entries manually

After you create your concordance file and use it to mark your document, go through the document to find any items that you missed. If the entry that you want to mark is exactly the way you want it to appear in the index, you can select the text before you create the entry. Or you can simply place your insertion point at the location of the text and type the entry directly in the Mark Index Entry text box. To mark an index entry manually:

1. Select the text that you want to mark, or position your insertion point where you want to insert the index entry.

2. Press Alt+Shift+X to open the Mark Index Entry dialog box shown in Figure 24-4. You can also open the Mark Index Entry dialog box by choosing Insert⇨Index and Tables and choosing Mark Entry from the Index tab in the Index and Tables dialog box.

Figure 24-4: The Mark Index Entry dialog box.

3. If you selected text before accessing the Mark Entry dialog box, Word places that text in the Main entry text box. As necessary, type new text or edit the existing text in the Main entry text box. You can add character formatting to any portion of the entry by selecting the text that you want to format and pressing Ctrl+B for bold, Ctrl+I for italic, or Ctrl+U for underline.

4. If you want to create a subentry, type it in the Subentry text box. Later in this chapter, you will discover how to work with subentries and sub-subentries.

5. By default, the index entry refers only to the current page. Select one of the other choices in the Options area if desired:

   • Select Cross-reference to create a cross-reference for the entry. See the section "Cross-referencing index entries" later in this chapter for instructions on creating index cross-references.

   • Select Page range and select a bookmark name (or type a new bookmark name) if you want the entry to refer to a range of pages. See the section "Using page ranges in index entries" later in this chapter for instructions on referencing page ranges.

6. Select Bold or Italic from the Page number format area if you want to print the page number for the index entry in bold or italic.

7. Do one of the following:

   • Choose Mark to mark the entry.

- Choose Mark <u>A</u>ll to have Word mark every place it finds an occurrence of the text (but it won't mark more than one occurrence of an item in each paragraph, so you don't have to worry about a bunch of extra entry codes). If you choose this option, the status bar tells you how many entries were marked. Note that this option is case-sensitive: Word will mark only entries that exactly match your entry. If, for example, you specify the index entry as "book sales," choosing Mark <u>A</u>ll will not mark any instances where the phrase appears as "Book Sales."

8. Mark additional entries by repeating Steps 1-7. You can move between the Mark Index Entry dialog box and the document editing area by clicking in either area.

9. When you have completed marking index entries, close the Mark Index Entry dialog box.

Note If the text you select for an index entry contains a colon, Word adds a backslash in front of the colon in the Main <u>e</u>ntry box. Because Word uses a colon to indicate an index subentry, the backslash lets Word know that the colon should be inserted in the index as regular text. If you type the entry from scratch, be sure that you type a backslash in front of any colons that you want to include. In addition, if your index entry includes quotation marks, Word adds backslashes in front of each mark in the entry field (but the backslash doesn't appear in the Main <u>e</u>ntry box). Field text is enclosed in quotation marks, so the backslash is necessary to direct Word to insert the quotation marks as text.

When you choose Mark <u>A</u>ll, Word displays all hidden text and any other nonprinting characters in your document, and it doesn't close the dialog box when it's finished marking. This quirk isn't a real problem, but it could throw you if you don't know what's happening. To stop displaying hidden text and nonprinting characters after choosing Mark <u>A</u>ll, just click the Show/Hide button on the Standard toolbar.

In some cases, you may want to include an individual symbol in the document index. To mark a symbol, select it and press Alt+Shift+X to open the Mark Index Entry dialog box as before. In the Main <u>e</u>ntry box, type **;#** (semicolon followed by a number sign) immediately following the symbol. Then choose <u>M</u>ark and OK. Word places symbols first in the index before any alphabetic entries.

Using page ranges in index entries

In many cases, you may want an index entry to reference a range of pages (for example, "Hemingway in Spain, 33-38"). Before you can have such an entry, you must create a bookmark that refers to the specified pages. See Chapter 23 for more information on creating bookmarks. To use a range of pages in an index entry (Steps 1-3 lead you through the process of creating a bookmark for your page range. If you have already created a bookmark, skip to Step 4.):

1. Select the pages that contain the text that you want to refer to in the index entry.

2. Choose Insert⇨Bookmark.

3. Type a name for the bookmark in the Bookmark name box in the Bookmark dialog box, and choose Add.

4. Select the text that you want to mark as an index entry. Or position your insertion point where you want to insert the index entry.

5. Press Alt+Shift+X to open the Mark Index Entry dialog box. Or choose Insert⇨Index and Tables, and choose Mark Entry from the Index tab in the Index and Tables dialog box.

6. If necessary, type new text or edit the existing text in the Main Entry text box.

7. If you want to create a subentry, type it in the Subentry text box.

8. Choose Page range and type the name of the bookmark in the Bookmark text box, or select the bookmark's name from the drop-down list.

9. Choose Mark and then Close if you are through marking index entries. The text now shows the XE field code followed by the text you entered, an \r switch, and the name of your bookmark. You'll read more about switches later. Click the Show/Hide button on the Standard toolbar to remove the field code from the display.

Cross-referencing index entries

Use the following steps if you want to insert text that will direct readers to another location in the index. When you use a cross-reference, the cross-reference text replaces the page number that normally appears in the index. To create a cross-reference for an index entry:

1. Follow Steps 1-4 in the earlier task marking an index entry.

2. In the Mark Index Entry dialog box, select Cross-reference.

3. Type the text for the cross-reference in the Cross-reference text box. Word automatically inserts the word "See" in italics. In most cases you will want the reference to begin with "See" (for example, "*See* Hemingway's early years"). You can add your text after "See" or delete "See" and start from scratch.

4. Choose Mark to mark an individual entry or Mark All to mark all occurrences of the entry text.

Creating multilevel indexes

In many cases, breaking an index entry into levels can make it easier for your readers to locate specific topics. Take a look at the following entry that lists all of the references to Ernest Hemingway:

Hemingway 5, 33, 59, 160

The references don't give the reader any information other than that there's *something* about Hemingway on the referenced pages. Now look at this entry:

Hemingway

early years 5

in Key West 33

as war correspondent 59

Nobel Prize 160

The second example uses multiple levels to more clearly delineate the topics. Creating multilevel entries is not difficult. As with the entire indexing process, however, it requires some planning. You must decide exactly how you want your entries to appear: what the main headings should be and how detailed the sub-headings should be. You must also be consistent as you mark the headings or create your concordance file.

To create a multilevel entry when you are marking an index entry manually, you must insert text in both the Main entry and Subentry text boxes in the Mark Index Entry dialog box. To create the index entry for Hemingway's early years, type **Hemingway** in the Main entry text box and **early years** in the Subentry text box.

You can have up to nine levels of subentries. You add additional subentries in the Subentry text box by separating each entry with a colon. For example, to add a sub-subentry of "first published work" under "early years," type **early years:first published work** in the Subentry text box.

You can create multilevel entries in a concordance file by placing colons between the main entry and each level of subentries. To insert the entry in the preceding paragraph into a concordance file, type **Hemingway:early years:first published work** in the second column next to the first-column item containing the document text that you want indexed.

Formatting index entries

As you create an entry, you can select text in the Main entry or Subentry text boxes in the Mark Index Entry dialog box and apply character formatting to the text. You can also apply formatting directly to the text within an existing XE (index entry) field. If you format the text within the Mark Index Entry dialog box, you are limited to the Ctrl+B (bold), Ctrl+I (italic), and Ctrl+U (underline) shortcut keys because you cannot access menus or toolbars from within a dialog box.

If you want to make character formatting changes that go beyond the addition of bold, italic, or underline, you must select the text in the XE field and select the formatting options that you want. If your index entries are not visible, display hidden text by clicking the Show/Hide button on the Standard toolbar or by choosing Hidden text in the Nonprinting characters area of the View tab of the Options dialog box.

When you edit the text in the index entry field, you have access to all of Word's standard character formatting options accessible through the Formatting toolbar or accessible when choosing Format⇨Font. Any character formatting that you add to an individual index entry is retained when you update the index or change its style.

Modifying index entry fields

An XE field contains all of the information for an index entry as it will appear in the index. Table 24-1 lists the switches that you can use to modify the field to customize your entries. Many of these switches are inserted automatically when you mark an index entry. This table will help you recognize switches that may already be present in your index entry fields. It also provides options for modifying the switches. You cannot use general switches that modify the format of or prevent changes to the field results in XE fields.

Table 24-1
Switches for the XE Field

Switch	What It Does
\b	Applies bold formatting to the page number for the index entry.
\f	Defines an entry type. This switch works in conjunction with the \f switch for the INDEX field. You can add a letter enclosed in quotation marks after this switch in an XE field and add the same letter following a \f switch in an INDEX field to compile an index consisting of only those XE fields that contain the same entry type.
\i	Applies italic formatting to the page number for the index entry.

Switch	What It Does
\r	This switch is always followed by a bookmark name and directs Word to include the range of pages marked by the specified bookmark in the index entry. This is the switch that Word inserts when you select Page range and specify a bookmark name in the Mark Index Entry dialog box.
\t	This switch is always followed by text and directs Word to use the specified text instead of a page number for the index entry. The text following the switch must be enclosed in quotation marks. This is the switch that Word inserts when you add a cross-reference in the Mark Index Entry dialog box.

You modify switches or insert new ones within a field just as you add or edit any other text. To add switches or modify any of the existing switches in an index entry field, place your insertion point anywhere in the field. Word inserts index entry fields as hidden text. If you don't see any XE fields, you can enable the display of hidden text by clicking the Show/Hide button on the Standard toolbar or by choosing Tools⇨Options and selecting Hidden Text on the View tab. Then you can move your insertion point inside the field and add or delete text and switches as desired.

Formatting and compiling an index

After you have marked your index entries manually or with the help of a concordance, you are ready to format and compile the index itself. To format and compile an index:

1. Position your insertion point where you want the index to appear. If you are indexing a master document, switch to Master Document view and make sure that your insertion point is not inside a subdocument. If you want the index to begin on a new page, insert a page break in front of your insertion point location.

2. Choose Insert⇨Index and Tables, and select the Index tab.

3. Make one of the following selections in the Type area:

   • Indented to indent subentries under main entries.

   • Run-in to place subentries on the same line as the main entry (entries will wrap to a second line as required).

4. Select a format from the Formats list. The Preview box displays a sample of the selected format so that you can see how your index will appear in that format.

5. Make selections in the following areas as desired:

- Select <u>H</u>eadings for accented letters to sort words that begin with an accented letter under a separate heading. For example, É and E are listed separately.

- Select <u>R</u>ight align page numbers if you want the page numbers aligned at the right edge of each column (or at the right margin if the index is not formatted in columns).

- Type a number in the C<u>o</u>lumns text box if you want the index formatted in more than the default two-column layout (enter **1** if you don't want the index formatted in multiple columns).

- Select Ta<u>b</u> leader if you want a line between the text and the page number. You can choose a dashed, dotted, or solid line. This option is dimmed unless <u>R</u>ight align page numbers is selected.

6. Choose OK. Word repaginates the document and creates the index at your insertion point location. The index is formatted as a separate section, which means that you can use any of Word's section formatting options to work with the index. Figure 24-5 shows a sample index with the section markers displayed.

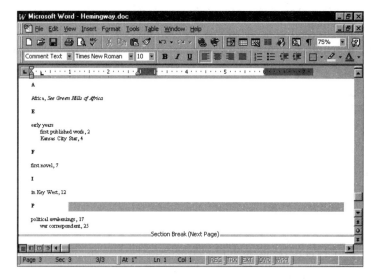

Figure 24-5:
A sample index.

Note   The entire index is actually a field (INDEX). If you press Shift+F9 with your insertion point anywhere inside the index, you can view the field code as shown in Figure 24-6. The INDEX field switches are described later in this chapter.

Figure 24-6:
The field code for
the sample index.

Customizing your index style

If you want to design your own index format, just choose Insert⟶Index and
Tables⟶Index. Choose Custom style from the Formats list in the Index tab, and
modify the styles for Index 1 through Index 9. Each index level uses a built-in Word
style, Index 1-Index 9. To create your own index format, modify these styles as you
do any other style:

1. Choose Insert⟶Index and Tables, and select the Index tab.

2. Select From template from the Formats list.

3. Choose the Modify button. The Style dialog box appears with a list of the
   nine index styles for each entry or subentry level, as shown in Figure 24-7.

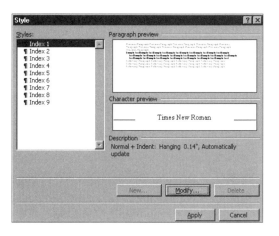

Figure 24-7: The Style dialog
box with the nine built-in index
styles listed.

4. Select the index style that you want to modify from the Styles list and choose
   Modify.

5. Edit the style to meet your needs and then choose Apply. See Chapter 11 if
   you need help working with styles.

6. Choose OK or Close until all the dialog boxes are closed. If you are modifying the style for an index that you have already created, answer Yes when Word asks you if you want to replace the selected index.

Note A built-in style called Index Heading does not appear in the Styles list when you choose the Modify button from the Index and Tables dialog box, but Word uses it to format the area that separates your alphabetical groups of entries. To modify this style, choose Format➪Style, select Index Heading from the Styles list, choose Modify, and make changes as you do to any other style. If the Index Heading style doesn't appear on the Styles list, select All styles from the List drop-down list in the Style dialog box to make sure that all of Word's built-in styles are listed.

Updating an index

Because the index is actually a field, you can update your index at anytime by updating the field. You should update the index when you add new index entries, when you make any editing or formatting changes to XE fields, or any time you make changes to your document that may affect pagination.

Any formatting changes that you make in the index itself will be lost when you update. For this reason, the best way to change the index's appearance is by editing the field code rather than the field result (the index text). If, however, you are certain that the document's pagination will not change and that there will be no further entries added to the index, you can convert an index field to text by placing your insertion point anywhere in the index and pressing Ctrl+Shift+F9. (It doesn't matter whether the field code or the index is displayed when you issue this command.) After you convert a field to text, it can no longer be updated or revised as a field. To update an index:

1. If the index is displayed, place your insertion point anywhere inside it (because the index is a field, placing your insertion point inside the index selects the entire field). If the index field is currently displayed, select the field.

2. Press F9, or choose Update Field from the shortcut menu.

Editing the INDEX field

All the information Word uses to build your index is contained in the INDEX field. Table 24-2 lists the switches that you can use to modify the field and customize your index in various ways. Many of these switches are inserted automatically when you make selections in the Index and Tables dialog box. This table will help you recognize switches that may already be present in your field code, and it will give you some options for modifying these switches.

You modify switches or insert new ones within a field just as you add or edit any other text. To add switches or modify any of the existing switches in your index field, place your insertion point anywhere in the index. If the field code is not currently displayed, press Shift+F9. Then move your insertion point to the location that you want to edit and add or delete text as desired.

Note When adding separator characters, be sure to put spaces before and after them within the quotation marks if you don't want them to run in with the entry and the page number.

	Table 24-2 **Switches for the INDEX Field**	
Switch	**What It Does**	**Example**
\b	Instructs Word to index only the portion of the document marked by the specified bookmark. You can use this switch to create separate indexes for different parts of a document.	{ INDEX \b hemingway } builds an index using the index entries in the range designated by the bookmark named "hemingway."
\c	Instructs Word to divide the index into a specified number of columns.	{ INDEX \c \3 } builds a three-column index. By default, an index contains two columns, and it can contain a maximum of four columns.
\d	Designates the separator characters used between a character and a page number. This switch is used with the \s switch. The separator can contain up to five characters, and you must enclose the characters in quotation marks.	{ INDEX \s chapter \d ":" } gives you an index in which the entries look like sequence Twain, 3:5. In this example, 3 is the chapter number, and 5 is the page number within the chapter. The default separator is a hyphen.
\e	Designates the separator characters used between index entries and page numbers. The separator can contain up to five characters, and you must enclose the characters in quotation marks.	{ INDEX \e " –> " } gives you an index in which the entries look like this: Twain–>5. The default separators are a comma followed by a space.
\f	Creates an index that uses only the entry type that you specify.	Corresponds to an entry type with the XE field. If you designated an entry type for your XE fields, you can refer to that entry type in the INDEX field to compile an index comprising only those XE fields that contain the same entry type.

(continued)

	Table 24-2 *(continued)*	
Switch	*What It Does*	*Example*
\g	Used to designate the separator characters between the limits of the page range. You can have up to five separator characters; you must enclose the separator characters in quotation marks.	{ INDEX \g " to " } gives you an index in which the entries for page ranges look like this: Twain, 25 to 32.
\h	Inserts headings between index groups.	{ INDEX \h "*** A ***" } separates each alphabetical group with a line that looks like this: *** A ***. The "A" in the field is actually a code that tells Word to move to the next letter of the alphabet for each group, so that your second group's heading would be *** B ***, and so on.
\l	Used to designate the separator characters between page numbers for entries that refer to more than one page (but not a page range). You can have up to five separator characters; you must enclose the separator characters in quotation marks.	{ INDEX \l " and " } gives you an index in which multiple page references are separated as follows: Twain, 25 and 32 and 51. The default is a comma followed by a space, as in this example: Twain, 25, 32, 51.
\p	Creates an index from entries for only the specified characters or that includes special characters. You can use an exclamation point with this switch to include special characters.	{ INDEX \p a-c} compiles an index for entries beginning with the letters a, b, or c. { INDEX \p ! } includes entries that begin with non-alphabetic characters. { INDEX \p !-f }compiles an index for entries beginning with letters *a* through *f* as well as any special characters.
\r	This switch is added automatically when you choose Run-in in the Index tab of the Index and Tables dialog box to have your subentries follow right after the main entries on the same line. Adding this switch to the field yourself has the same effect as selecting Run-in.	{ INDEX \r } Hemingway: early years 5; in Key West 33; as war correspondent 59.

Switch	What It Does	Example
\s	Use this switch in conjunction with the SEQ field to include chapter or other numbers along with the page numbers in your index (for example, 5-1, 5-2, and so on). You first format each segment in a separate section and instruct Word to restart the page numbering at 1 for that section. Then, insert a SEQ field at the beginning of the section.	Assume you insert a { SEQ chapter } field at the beginning of each chapter to assign the name "chapter" to the SEQ field: { INDEX \s chapter } includes the chapter-page number sequence in your index. Use the \d switch to specify a separator character other than the default hyphen.

Tip   By default, the From template index format does not insert any separators between groups of letters: your index ends up as one long, unbroken list unless you use the \h switch to add a heading between groups. The basic separator is a blank line between each alphabetical group (all of the entries starting with a same letter). To insert a basic heading separator into your index field, add the \h switch to your index field code and follow the switch with a space enclosed in quotation marks, as shown below:

{ INDEX \h " " }

This example shows only the heading switch. Your field code may contain several other switches in addition to this one.

Deleting an index

You can delete an index just like any other field. Simply select the entire field and press Delete. The quickest way to select the field is with the field code displayed: triple-clicking anywhere in the field selects it. If the index itself is displayed, click in the left margin on one of the section breaks at the beginning or end of the index. You must be in Normal view to see the section breaks.

Adding Tables of Contents to Your Documents

As with creating an index, creating a table of contents is a two-step process. First, mark the items in your document that you want to appear in the table of contents, and then instruct Word to assemble the table of contents from the marked entries. The TC field contains table of contents entries, and the TOC field contains the assembled and formatted information for the table of contents.

Preparing your document for adding a table of contents

You can prepare a document for a table of contents in several ways:

✦ Use Word's built-in heading styles (Heading 1 through Heading 9) as you create your document. Word automatically recognizes these styles when it compiles a table of contents, so applying the styles to your headings is all the preparation you need.

✦ You can, of course, apply the heading styles to each heading as you type your document. Or you can type your document without worrying about styles and let AutoFormat do the work for you. See Chapter 11 for more information about applying styles manually and using the AutoFormat feature to apply them automatically.

✦ Another option is to build your document in Outline view. As you promote and demote outline levels, Word automatically applies the appropriate heading style. See Chapter 22 for more information about working with outlines.

✦ Using the built-in styles is definitely the easiest way to go, and you can change the formatting of these styles to meet your needs. Simply modify the styles Heading 1 through Heading 9 as you do any other style. See the section about assembling a table of contents from built-in heading styles, later in this chapter to learn how to compile a basic table of contents.

✦ Use your own custom styles. If Word's built-in heading styles can't meet your needs, you can create any styles you choose and assign them to headings or any other text that you want included in your table of contents. See Chapter 11 for more information about working with styles. And later in this chapter, you will find how to get Word to recognize your custom styles when it compiles the table of contents.

✦ Mark items for the table of contents with the TC entry field. You can mark any document text for inclusion in a table of contents by inserting a field code. The following steps teach you how to mark text as a table of contents entry, and the section "Assembling a table of contents by using TC entry fields," later in this chapter, shows you how to use the field entries to build your table of contents.

To use a TC field to mark a table of contents entry:

1. Select the text that you want to include in the table of contents. Or place your insertion point at the location of the text that you want marked for inclusion.

2. Press Alt+Shift+O to open the Mark Table of Contents Entry dialog box shown in Figure 24-8.

3. If you selected text before pressing Alt+Shift+O, that text appears in the Entry text box. If necessary, edit the text as you want it to appear in the table of contents. If you did not select text, type your table of contents entry in the Entry text box.

   The text will be displayed in your table of contents exactly as it appears in the Entry text box, including any capitalization and character formatting. If you choose, you can add character formatting to the text in the Entry box by selecting the portion of text that you want to format and pressing Ctrl+B (Bold), Ctrl+I (Italic), or Ctrl+U (Underline).

4. Make a selection from the Table identifier list.

   The Table identifier tells Word in which table the entry belongs. By default, a table of contents entry uses the *C* identifier; a table of figures entry uses *F.*

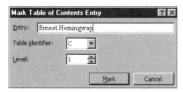

Figure 24-8: The Mark Table of Contents Entry dialog box.

5. Type or select a heading level in the Level box.

   The Level designation tells Word how to treat the entry when it compiles your table of contents (level one, level two, and so on). When you use the built-in heading styles, Word takes care of this setting for you, but when you create a table of contents entry with the TC field, you need to give Word some help.

6. Choose Mark.

   Word places a TC entry field at your insertion point location (or at the end of your selected text). Figure 24-9 shows a sample TC entry field.

Figure 24-9: A sample TC entry field.

Note   You can also build a TC entry field from scratch, using any of the field techniques covered in Chapter 26. The Mark Table of Contents Entry dialog box is just a tool that assists you in creating a TC field. The end result is the same whether you use the dialog box or create the field with the Insert⇨Field command.

Modifying a TC entry field

A TC field contains all the information for a table of contents entry. Table 24-3 lists the switches that you can use to modify the field to customize your entries. Many of these switches are inserted automatically when you mark a table of contents entry. This table will help you recognize switches that may already be present in your table of contents entry fields. It also provides options for modifying the switches.

<table>
<tr><th colspan="2">Table 24-3
Switches for the TC Field</th></tr>
<tr><td>**Switch**</td><td>**What It Does**</td></tr>
<tr><td>\f</td><td>Defines an entry type such as illustrations. This switch works in conjunction with the \f switch for the TOC field. You can add a letter enclosed in quotation marks after this switch in a TC field and then add the same letter following a \f switch in a TOC field to compile a table of contents comprising only those TC fields that contain the same entry type.</td></tr>
<tr><td>\l</td><td>Designates the heading level. Level 1 is assumed if none is specified.</td></tr>
<tr><td>\n</td><td>Use this switch to keep the page number for a table of contents entry from displaying.</td></tr>
</table>

Compiling a table of contents

The techniques for compiling a table of contents vary somewhat depending on the method you used to prepare your document. The following sections take you through all three methods.

Assembling a table of contents from Word's heading styles

Before you begin to build the table of contents, make sure that you have applied one of Word's built-in heading styles (Heading 1 through Heading 9) to all the headings that you want included in the table of contents. Remember to turn off the display of hidden text and field codes, as both of these text elements can affect pagination. To assemble a table of contents from built-in heading styles:

1. Position your insertion point where you want the table of contents to start. If you are using a master document to create your table of contents, switch to Master Document view and make sure that your insertion point is not in a subdocument.

2. Choose Insert⇨Index and Tables and select the Table of Contents tab (see Figure 24-10).

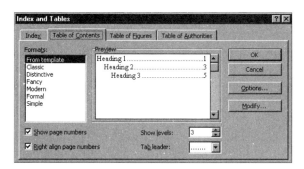

Figure 24-10: The Table of Contents tab of the Index and Tables dialog box.

3. Select a format from the Formats list. As you select different formats, a sample is displayed in the Preview box.

   If you select From template, you can choose Modify, which opens the Style dialog box with a list of the TOC styles (1-9) displayed. Each style refers to the heading level of the same number. You can change the appearance of any heading level in your table of contents by modifying the applicable style. (For example, to modify all your first level headings, modify the TOC 1 style.)

4. Make selections in the following areas as desired. The default settings for some of these options vary, depending on which table of contents format is selected:

   • By default, all the table of contents formats display page numbers. Clear the Show page numbers check box if you want a table without page numbers.

   • Select Right align page numbers if you want the page numbers aligned at the right margin.

   • By default, all the table of contents formats build a table using only the first three heading levels. Enter a number in the Show levels text box if you want your table of contents to display a different number of levels.

   • Select Tab leader if you want a line between the headings and the page numbers. You can choose a dashed, dotted, or solid line. Different formats show different or no tab leaders. This option is dimmed unless Right align page numbers is selected.

5. Choose OK. Word repaginates the document and creates the table of contents at your insertion point location. The table of contents is formatted as a separate section, which means that you can use any of Word's section formatting options to work with the table of contents. Figure 24-11 shows a sample table of contents displayed. The entire table of contents is actually a field. If you press Shift+F9 with your insertion point anywhere inside the table of contents, you can view the field code as shown in Figure 24-12.

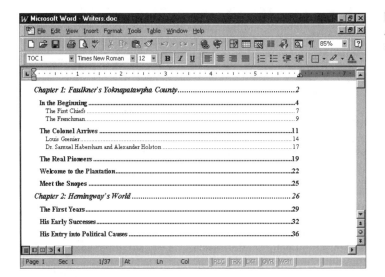

Figure 24-11: A sample table of contents.

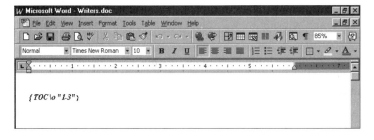

Figure 24-12: The field code for the sample table of contents.

Tip   After you compile a table of contents or a table of figures (using any method), you can use the table to navigate through your document quickly. Just double-click any page number in the table to move your insertion point to the referenced location.

Assembling a table of contents by using custom styles

If you used styles other than Heading 1 through Heading 9, you can still create a table of contents. Before you begin, make sure that you have applied styles to all the headings that you want included in your table of contents and that the styles are applied in a consistent fashion. If, for example, you created a style for level one headings called "Chapter Title," *each* level one heading must be formatted with this style or it won't be correctly included in the table of contents. Don't forget to turn off the display of hidden text and field codes, because both of these elements can affect pagination.

To assemble a table of contents from custom styles:

1. Position your insertion point where you want the table of contents to start.

   If you are using a master document to create your table of contents, switch to Master Document view and make sure that your insertion point is not in a subdocument.

2. Choose Insert⇨Index and Tables and select the Table of Contents tab.

3. Select a format from the Formats list and select other options as before. As you select different formats, a sample is displayed in the Preview box.

4. Choose Options. The Table of Contents Options dialog box, as shown in Figure 24-13, lists all your available styles, including any captions, comments, footnotes an other styles in the current document. There is a check mark to the left of each heading style used in your current document.

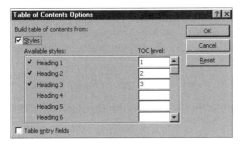

Figure 24-13: The Table of Contents Options dialog box.

5. To instruct Word to include all headings marked with a specified style in the table of contents, type a number from 1-9 (to assign a heading level to the style) in the TOC level text box next to the style.

6. Repeat the process for each style that you want to include.

   Make sure that the TOC level text box is blank for any styles you don't want included. If at any time you want to return to the default settings, just choose the Reset button.

7. Unless you have added some TC fields that you want to include in your table along with your custom styles, make sure that the Table entry fields check box is cleared.

8. Choose OK. Notice that the Preview box in the Table of Contents tab now displays your custom styles.

9. Choose OK to compile the table of contents.

Note   You can also use the Table of Contents Options dialog box to trick Word into formatting the built-in heading styles for a different level than the one for which they were designed. Suppose, for example, that you want all the headings to which you applied the Heading 4 style to be formatted as level two in your table of contents. Just type **2** in the TOC level box next to Heading 4. This technique changes the heading format only for your table of contents: it doesn't affect the formatting in your document text.

Assembling a table of contents by using TC entry fields

After you have created TC fields at each location that you want included in your table of contents, the procedure for compiling the table is much the same as for compiling a table that uses styles. To assemble a table of contents by using TC entry fields:

1. Position your insertion point where you want the table of contents to start. If you are using a master document to create your table of contents, switch to Master Document view and make sure that your insertion point is not in a subdocument.

2. Choose Insert⇨Index and Tables and select the Table of Contents tab.

3. Select a format from the Formats list and change settings as necessary.

4. Choose Options.

5. Check the Table entry fields check box.

6. Unless you want headings to which you have applied specific styles included in your table of contents, make sure that the Styles check box is cleared.

   If you do want Word to use some of your custom styles as it compiles the table of contents, follow the instructions in the preceding task and make sure that both the Styles and Table entry fields check boxes are selected.

7. Choose OK to return to the Table of Contents tab.

8. Choose OK to compile the table of contents.

Updating a table of contents

Because the table of contents is actually a field, you can update your table of contents at any time by updating the field. You should update the table of contents any time you make changes to your document that may affect pagination. You should also update the table of contents when you add new table of contents entries (either by marking entries with TC fields or by adding new headings to which you applied built-in or custom styles).

Any formatting changes you make to the table of contents itself will be lost when you update. For this reason, the best way to change the table's appearance is by editing the field code rather than the field text. If, however, you are certain that the document's pagination will not change and that you will not be adding any entries to your table of contents, you can convert the TOC field to text by placing your insertion point anywhere in the index and pressing Ctrl+Shift+F9. (It doesn't matter whether the field code or the index is displayed when you issue this command.) After you convert a field to text, you can no longer update or revise the text as a field. To update a table of contents:

1. Place your insertion point anywhere inside the table (because the table of contents is a field, placing your insertion point inside the table selects the entire field). If the TOC field is currently displayed, select the field.

2. Press F9 or choose Update Field from the shortcut menu. Word displays the Update Table of Contents dialog box shown in Figure 24-14.

Figure 24-14: The Update Table of Contents dialog box.

3. Do one of the following:

   • Choose Update page numbers only if you want to update the page numbers in your table without updating any entries. Your formatting is preserved.

   • Choose Update entire table if you want to update the names of the entries and any other options in addition to the page numbers. With this option, any formatting that is applied directly to the table (rather than in a field code) will be lost.

4. Choose OK.

Creating Tables of Figures and Other Tables

In addition to a table of contents, you may want to include tables that list figures, equations, charts, or other elements. For the purpose of this section, all such tables will be referred to as tables of figures. Keep in mind that a table of figures can include many different document elements, and you can have many different tables in one document.

You can prepare figures (or other document items) for inclusion in a table of figures by using three different methods:

✦ You can add captions to the items using Word's Insert⇨Caption command. Adding captions to items automates the process of creating a table of figures in the same way that using Word's built-in heading styles automates the process of creating a table of contents. Word automatically recognizes captions created with the Caption command when it compiles a table of figures.

✦ You can apply styles to the items that you want to include in a table. You can use any style that you want as long as you apply the same style to all the items that you want included in a particular table. If, for example, you want to create a table that lists all the drawings in your document, you can create a style called "drawing" and apply that style to every drawing. See Chapter 11 for more information about working with styles. Later in this chapter, you'll find how to get Word to recognize your custom styles when it compiles the table of figures.

✦ You can mark items for the table of figures with the TC entry field. This field code is the same one that is used to mark text for a table of contents: marking text or an object for inclusion in a table of figures is just a matter of changing a few options. The following steps teach you how to mark an item as a table of figures entry, and the section "Assembling a table of figures from styles or TC fields" later in this chapter shows you how to use the field entries to build your table of figures.

Marking table entries

To use a TC field to mark a table of figures entry:

1. Select the figure or other item that you want to include in the table of figures.

2. Press Alt+Shift+O to open the Mark Table of Contents Entry dialog box, shown in Figure 24-15.

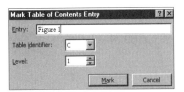

Figure 24-15: The Mark Table of Contents Entry dialog box.

3. If you selected a caption before pressing Alt+Shift+O, that caption text appears in the Entry text box. If necessary, edit the text as you want it to appear in the table of figures. If you did not select text, type your table of figures entry in the Entry text box.

   The text will be displayed in your table of figures exactly as it appears in the Entry text box, including any capitalization and character formatting. If you choose, you can add character formatting to the text in the Entry text box by selecting the portion of text that you want to format and pressing Ctrl+B (Bold), Ctrl+I (Italic), or Ctrl+U (Underline).

4. Make a selection from the Table identifier list. The Table identifier tells Word in which table the entry belongs. By default, a table of contents entry uses the *C* identifier, and a table of figures entry uses *F*. The actual letters don't really matter: the main thing is to make sure that you use the same identifier for all the items in a specific table.

   All entries in a table of figures are at the same level, so you don't have to make a selection in the Level box.

5. Choose Mark. Word places a TC entry field at your insertion point location (or at the end of your selected text). Figure 24-16 shows the field code for the marked caption.

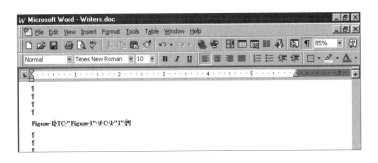

Figure 24-16: The field code for the sample figure entry.

Compiling a table of figures

Once you mark your entries or apply styles to your figure captions, you're ready to compile them. The following sections explain how to assemble a table of figures from captions, styles or TC fields.

Assembling a table of figures from captions

Before you proceed, make sure that you have used the Insert⇨Caption command to add captions to all the items that you want to include in the table of figures. To assemble a table of figures from captions:

1. Position your insertion point where you want the table to begin.

2. Choose Insert⇨Index and Tables, and select the Table of Figures tab. Figure 24-17 shows the Table of Figures tab.

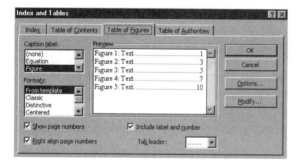

Figure 24-17: The Table of Figures tab in the Index and Tables dialog box.

3. Select the label type that you want to compile from the Caption label list. The label type is the same one that you selected (or created) when you first added the captions.

4. Select one of the built-in formats from the Formats list. Or select From template and choose the Modify button to define your own format.

5. Make selections in the following areas as desired. The default settings for some of these options vary depending on which format is selected:

   • By default, all the table of figures formats display page numbers. Clear the Show page numbers check box if you want a table without page numbers.

   • Check the Right align page numbers check box if you want the page numbers aligned at the right margin.

   • Check the Include label and number check box if you want the caption label included in the table.

- Select Ta<u>b</u> leader if you want a line between the entries and the page numbers. You can choose a dashed, dotted, solid line, or no line at all. This option is dimmed unless <u>R</u>ight align page numbers is selected.

6. Choose OK.

Assembling a table of figures from styles or TC fields

To assemble a table of figures from styles or TC fields:

1. Position the insertion point where you want the table to begin.

2. Choose <u>I</u>nsert⇨In<u>d</u>ex and Tables.

3. Select one of the built-in formats from the Forma<u>t</u>s list, or define your own format and then choose page number and tab leader options as before.

4. Choose the <u>O</u>ptions button to open the Table of Figures Options dialog box, shown in Figure 24-18.

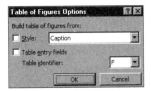

Figure 24-18: The Table of Figures Options dialog box.

5. Do one or both of the following:

- To build the table of figures from styles, check the <u>S</u>tyle check box, and then select the style that you applied to your list items from the Styles drop-down list.

- To build the table of figures from TC entry fields, check the Table <u>e</u>ntry fields check box and select the table identifier you used in the TC fields from the Table <u>i</u>dentifier drop-down list.

6. Click OK twice.

Creating Tables of Authorities

Unless you work in the legal profession or otherwise have reason to work with legal documents, chances are that you can safely skip this section. A table of authorities is a highly specialized tool that most lawyers can't live without and that other mere mortals can survive quite nicely without ever encountering.

Before Word, compiling citations in a table of authorities was a tedious, time-consuming, and error-prone proposition. But with Word, marking a citation is as easy as marking text for inclusion in any table. Compiling the table of authorities is very much like compiling a table of contents or a table of figures. You just tell Word where you want the table to go and choose from several style formats or create your own custom style.

Marking citation entries

The first step in creating a table of authorities is to mark your citations. There are two types of citation entries:

✦ A long citation is always used the first time the citation appears in your document. The long citation contains the full reference to the case, statute, or rule: for example, Twain v. Alcott, 352 Win 2d 901 (4th Cir. 1952).

✦ A short citation is used for each subsequent appearance of the citation. The short citation for the above example may simply be Twain, or, if there is more than one case involving Twain in your document, Twain v. Alcott.

To mark citations for a table of authorities:

1. Select the citation that you want to mark.

2. Press Alt+Shift+I to open the Mark Citation dialog box, shown in Figure 24-19. Notice that your selected text is displayed in both the Selected text and the Short citation boxes.

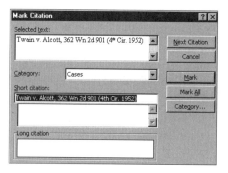

Figure 24-19: The Mark Citation dialog box.

3. Edit and format the text in the Selected text box as necessary. You can use the following shortcut keys to add character formatting to the citation: Ctrl+B (Bold), Ctrl+I (Italic), or Ctrl+U (Underline).

4. Select a category from the Category drop-down list. The list includes most common citation categories. To modify these categories or create your own, see "Creating and editing citation categories" later in this chapter.

5. Edit the text in the Short citation box as you want it to appear in the table of authorities.

6. Do one of the following:

   - Choose the Mark button to mark the individual entry.

   - Choose the Mark All button if you want Word to search through your document and mark all occurrences of the citation. Word will mark only those occurrences that are precise matches for the long and short citation entries in the Mark Citation dialog box.

7. Choose the Next Citation button. Word tries to find the next citation in your document by searching for words like "in re" or "v" that are typically found in citations. Next Citation is not foolproof: some of your cites may not include the buzzwords that Word scans. Be sure that you check for unmarked citations before finalizing the table of authorities.

8. Repeat Steps 1-7 for each citation.

9. Choose the Close button when you finish marking citations.

Compiling a table of authorities

After you mark the citations, all that remains is to format and compile the table of authorities. Compiling a table of authorities is similar to compiling an index or a table of contents. You tell Word how you want the table of authorities to look and where you want it inserted. To assemble a table of authorities:

1. Position your insertion point where you want the table of authorities to start. If you are using a master document to create your table of authorities, switch to Master Document view and make sure that your insertion point is not in a subdocument.

2. Choose Insert➪Index and Tables and select the Table of Authorities tab (shown in Figure 24-20).

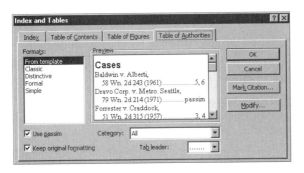

Figure 24-20: The Table of Authorities tab in the Index and Tables dialog box.

3. Select a format from the Formats list. As you select different formats, a sample is displayed in the Preview box.

   If you select From template, you can choose Modify, which opens the Style dialog box with the Table of Authorities and TOA Heading styles listed. Choose the Modify button from the Style dialog box to change either of these styles and then choose Apply to make the change take effect.

4. Select the category of citations that you want to compile from the Category drop-down list. The default selection is All, so you don't need to do anything if you want to include all citation categories in your table of authorities.

   When Word compiles the table of authorities, it creates a separate section for each category with the citations arranged alphabetically within their sections.

5. Make selections in the following areas as desired:

   • Check the Use passim check box if you want Word to use the term passim in place of page numbers for each citation that is referred to on more than five different pages.

   • Check the Keep original formatting check box if you want to retain any character formatting that you applied to the citation in the document.

   • Select Tab leader to change the default setting for the line between citation entries and page numbers. You can choose to have a dashed, dotted, or solid line, or no line at all. The default setting varies depending on which format you choose.

6. Choose OK. Word repaginates the document and creates the table of authorities at your insertion point location.

Updating a table of authorities

You should update your table of authorities whenever you make changes to your document that may affect pagination. You should also update your table of authorities when you make changes to any of your citations that should be reflected in this table. To update a table of authorities:

1. Choose Insert⇨Index and Tables and select the Table of Authorities tab.

2. Choose OK. Word selects the existing table of authorities and displays a dialog box that asks whether you want to replace the selected category.

3. Choose Yes to update the table of authorities. If you choose No, Word keeps your old table of authorities and adds a new one, so you can use this technique to add new categories or sections to your table.

Note You can also update a table of authorities by placing your insertion point in the TOA field (or anywhere in the table of authorities if the field result is displayed) and pressing F9.

Creating and editing citation categories

Word includes most commonly used citation categories, but you can add your own categories or edit the existing ones. You can have a maximum of 16 categories in a table of authorities. To create and edit citation categories:

1. Press Alt+Shift+I to open the Mark Citation dialog box.

2. Choose Category to display the Edit Category dialog box shown in Figure 24-21.

Figure 24-21: The Edit Category dialog box.

3. Make a selection from the Category list as follows:

   - Select the name of one of the seven existing categories that you want to replace, or

   - Select a number from 8 to 16 to create a new category.

4. Type the name of the new or modified category in the Replace with text box.

5. Choose the Replace button.

6. Choose OK, and then close the Mark Citation dialog box.

Note You can easily include chapter numbers along with page numbers in an index or table. You need only use the Insert⇨Page Numbers command, check the Include chapter number check box in the Page Number Format dialog box, and select the style that you applied to your chapter numbers.

Summary

This chapter covered working with Word's tools for creating an index and tables of contents. Both of these features are essential for creating long documents, such as a manuscript or term paper. Word lets you create a table of contents, a table of figures, or a table of citations. You can also choose from several formats to create impressive-looking indexes and tables of contents. In this chapter, you learned how to

✦ Create index entries by using two methods. The first method is creating a concordance file, which is a table of index entries and then telling Word to search a document for all the entries in the table of index entries. The other method is manually marking each index entry in a document by selecting the text and pressing Alt+Shift+X.

✦ Create and format an index by using the Insert➪Index and Tables command.

✦ Create a table of contents from heading styles in a document by choosing Insert➪Index and Tables, choosing the Table of Contents tab, and specifying the formatting of your table of contents.

✦ Create a table of figures based on figure caption styles in a document by choosing Insert➪Index and Tables and choosing the Table of Figures tab.

✦ Create a table of citations document by choosing Insert➪Index and Tables and choosing the Table of Authorities tab.

Where to go next...

✦ To learn more about other Word features for working with long documents, check out Chapter 23.

✦ Word uses fields to create indexes and tables of contents. To learn more about working with field codes and their switches, go to Chapter 26.

✦   ✦   ✦

The Perfect Word: Customizing Word

Customizing Menus, Options, Toolbars, and Keys

The preceding chapters of this book dealt, for the most part, with Word as it appears before you make changes to it.

In this chapter, you'll find information about customizing Word to better suit your needs. Bear in mind, though, that no description of customizing Word can be complete because Word, though a word processor, is in fact a versatile programming language (as you'll discover by the time you read about macros in Chapter 27).

Customizing Word 97

When you use Word after installation, it has certain default settings for its commands and options. Some of these settings include

- ✦ The menu bar with nine named menus; the Standard and Formatting toolbars, each with certain buttons; the status bar at the bottom of the window; and the horizontal and vertical scroll bars — which all appear on your screen.

- ✦ When you type nonprinting characters, such as a space or a tab, you see only white space on-screen.

✦ The keystrokes you use to edit a document cause Word to respond in a default way.

✦ Word looks for certain types of information, such as templates and documents, in specific directories.

✦ Shortcut keys are assigned to some commands.

These are just a few of the Word defaults you can accept and use. Alternatively, you can change most aspects of Word to suit your own needs. You probably have already used many of these options as you've worked with many of Word's features.

Working with the Options Dialog Box

Options control the way you interact with Word. Certain options, for example, affect what you see on-screen; others affect what Word does when you press certain keys. To change optional Word settings, display the Options dialog box, and choose the options you want. All the options you choose remain in effect throughout the current Word session. When you terminate your Word session, all the options in effect are saved so that the next time you open Word, the same options apply. The following sections describe all the options available in the ten tabs of the Options dialog box. In the option tables, the following conventions are used:

✦ The Option column contains option names.

✦ The Default column shows the default state of the option.

✦ The View column indicates in which view the option operates.

✦ The Effect column contains a brief description of the effect of the option when you choose it.

✦ All the options are listed alphabetically and with groups, as defined in the tab.

Note Clicking the Question Mark button on the right side of the dialog box title bar calls up Word's Help system, which describes an option in any of the Options dialog box's tabs. When you click the Question Mark button, the pointer includes a question mark. Click the option for which you want more information, and a pop-up text description appears.

Changing an option

To become familiar with the general procedure for changing an option, try this example. Suppose that you don't want to display the status bar, but you do want to show your style names. The procedure outlined in the following task assumes that the default view options are currently in effect. To change view options:

1. Choose Tools⇨Options to display the Options dialog box, shown in Figure 25-1.

2. If the View tab of the Options dialog box is not displayed, click that tab so that you see the View options.

3. In the Window group at the bottom-left corner of the dialog box, choose the Status bar option box to remove the X and turn off that option.

4. Choose OK to accept the changes and remove the dialog box from the screen. The Word window reappears with the status bar removed.

Figure 25-1: The Options dialog box with the View tab displayed and default options selected.

After making changes to options such as these, those options remain in effect throughout your current Word session. If you terminate Word normally, the changed options are in effect the next time you open Word. However, if Word terminates abnormally, perhaps due to a power failure, the changed options are not saved.

If you make changes to anything in the Options dialog box, and then decide you don't want these changes, you can choose Cancel in the dialog box. This procedure removes the dialog box from your screen without making any of the changes.

View tab

Choices in the View tab modify the appearance of the application and document windows and the appearance of documents. Table 25-1 lists the options available in the View Tab (refer to Figure 25-1). Some view options are available in Normal view, Outline view, and Page Layout view. Other options are available only in certain views. Switch to the Normal view or Outline view before opening the Options dialog box to choose options that apply to these views. Switch to the Page Layout view before opening the Options dialog box to choose options that apply to this view.

Table 25-1
Options in the View Tab*

Show Group Option	Default	View	Effect
Animated text	Checked	All	Displays text animation on the screen. Clear the Animated text check box to see how text will look when printed.
Bookmarks	Not checked	All	Displays bookmarks and links.
Draft font	Not checked	Normal	Displays most character formatting as underlined and bold, and displays graphics as empty boxes. Select the Draft font check box to speed up screen display in documents with extensive formatting.
Field codes	Not checked	All	Displays field codes instead of field values.
Field shading	When selected	All	Identifies field results when selected, always, or never.
Highlight	Checked	All	Displays and prints highlighted text in a document.
Picture placeholders	Not checked	All	Displays graphics as empty boxes.

Show Group Option	Default	View	Effect
ScreenTips	Checked	All	Displays reviewers' comments in yellow pop-up boxes on the screen when you hover with the mouse above the comment reference mark.

Nonprinting Characters Group Option	Default	View	Effect
All	Not checked	All	Displays all nonprinting characters.
Hidden text	Not checked	All	Displays hidden text.
Optional hyphens	Not checked	All	Displays optional hyphens.
Paragraph marks	Not checked	All	Displays paragraph marks.
Spaces	Not checked	All	Displays spaces as dots.
Tab characters	Not checked	All	Displays tab characters.

Window Group Option	Default	View	Effect
Horizontal scroll bar	Checked	All	Displays horizontal scroll bar.
Status bar	Checked	All	Displays status bar.
Style area width	0"	Normal, Outline	Provides space at left of document window for style name.
Vertical scroll bar	Checked	All	Displays horizontal scroll bar.
Wrap to window	Not checked	All	Wraps the text to the document window, which makes it easier to read on the screen. To wrap the text as it will appear when printed, clear the Wrap to window check box.

*You can switch between displaying and hiding all nonprinting characters by choosing the Show/Hide button on the Standard toolbar.

General tab

Choices in the General tab modify various Word settings that don't fit in any of the other Options dialog box tabs. Table 25-2 lists the options available in the Options dialog box General tab, shown in Figure 25-2.

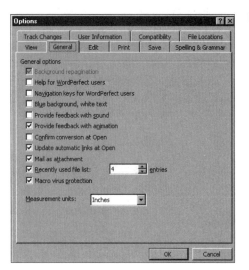

Figure 25-2: The General tab in the Options dialog box.

Table 25-2
Options in the General Tab

Option	Default	Effect
Background repagination	Checked	Repagination occurs while you work.
Blue background, white text	Not checked	Displays white text on blue background.
Confirm conversion at Open	Not checked	Selects the converter that Word will use to open a file created in another application.
Help for WordPerfect users	Not checked	Shows Word equivalent when you press a WordPerfect for MS-DOS key combination. When this check box is selected, WPH appears in the status bar.
Macro virus protection	Checked	Turns on a warning message that appears whenever you open a document that might contain macro viruses.

Option	Default	Effect
Mail as attachment	Checked	Attaches the current document to an electronic mail message when you choose File⇨Send To Mail Recipient. Clear this check box if you want Word to insert the contents of the current document into a mail message instead of attaching it. This check box is available only if an e-mail application is installed on your computer.
Measurement units	Inches	Sets the measurement units to inches, centimeters, points, or picas for measurements in dialog boxes and on the horizontal ruler.
Navigation keys for WordPerfect users	Not checked	Changes functions of PgUp, PgDn, Home, End, and Esc keys to their equivalent WordPerfect actions.
Provide feedback with animation	Checked	Animates the movement of your mouse in Word, and uses special animated cursors in place of standard static cursors for a variety of Word actions.
Provide feedback with sound	Checked	Beep occurs when you make certain actions. To change the sound that is associated with an event, open the Sounds folder in the Windows Control Panel.
Recently used file list	4	Determines number of filenames displayed at the bottom of the File menu. You can choose up to nine entries in the entries box.
Update automatic links at Open	Checked	Updates information linked to other files at Open when you open documents.

Edit tab

Choices in the Edit tab modify certain editing actions performed by Word. For more information on working with Word's editing features, see Chapter 2. Table 25-3 lists the options available in the Options dialog box Edit tab, shown in Figure 25-3.

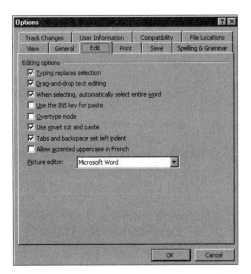

Figure 25-3: The Edit tab in the Options dialog box.

Table 25-3
Options in the Edit Tab

Option	Default	Effect
Allow accented uppercase in French	Not checked	For text formatted as French, allows accents over uppercase letters.
Drag-and-drop text editing	Checked	Moves or copies selected text without need for cut and paste.
Overtype mode	Not checked	Replaces existing text as you type.
Picture editor	Microsoft Word	Selects the application to use for editing pictures.
Tabs and backspace set left indent	Checked	Sets left indents by pressing the Tab and to set Left Indent Backspace keys.
Typing replaces selection	Checked	Deletes selected text as soon as you start typing.
Use smart cut and paste	Checked	Removes unneeded spaces when you cut; adds necessary spaces when you paste.
Use the INS key for paste	Not checked	Pastes Clipboard contents when you press Insert.
When selecting, automatically select entire word	Checked	Selects the entire word when part of the word is selected.

Print tab

Choices in the Print tab modify the way documents are printed and control what is printed. For more information on printing documents in Word, check out Chapter 6. Table 25-4 lists the options available in the Options dialog box Print tab, shown in Figure 25-4.

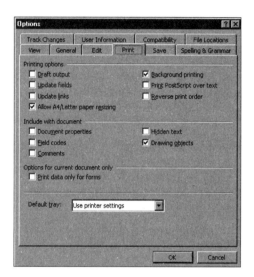

Figure 25-4: The Print tab in the Options dialog box.

Table 25-4
Options in the Print Tab

Printing Options/Group Option	Default	Effect
Allow A4/Letter paper resizing	Checked	For some countries, the standard paper size is Letter, for others, the standard size is A4. Select this check box if you want Word to automatically adjust documents formatted for another country's standard paper size so they can print correctly on your country's standard paper size.
Background printing	Checked	Allows you to work while a document is being printed.
Draft output	Not checked	Prints a document with minimum formatting (the effect depends on the printer in use).

(continued)

Table 25-4 *(continued)*		
Printing Options/Group Option	***Default***	***Effect***
Print PostScript over text	Not checked	Prints PostScript code in a converted Word for the Macintosh document on top of the document text instead of underneath it.
Reverse print order	Not checked	Prints pages starting with the last page.
Update fields	Not checked	Updates all fields in a document before printing.
Update links	Not checked	Updates all linked information in a document before printing.
Include with Document Group Option	***Default***	***Effect***
Comments	Not checked	Prints comments on separate page at end of the document.
Document properties	Not checked	Prints summary information on separate page at end of document.
Drawing objects	Checked	Prints Drawing objects.
Field codes	Not checked	Prints field codes instead of field results.
Hidden text	Not checked	Prints all hidden text.
Other Option	***Default***	***Effect***
Print data only for forms	Not checked	Prints form input only.
Default tray	From Control Panel	Chooses the paper tray in the printer

Track Changes tab

Choices in the Track Changes tab modify the way Word displays changes to a document. Chapter 19 explains how to work with Word's revision features. Table 25-5 lists the options available in the Options dialog box Revisions tab, shown in Figure 25-5. Preview boxes in this tab show the effects of your choices.

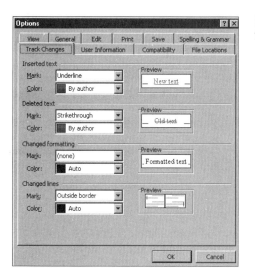

Figure 25-5: The Track Changes tab in the Options dialog box.

Table 25-5
Options in the Track Changes Tab

Inserted Text Option	Default	Effect
Mark	Underline	Chooses among none, bold, italic, underline, or double underline to mark inserted text.
Color	By Author	Chooses color for inserted text.
Mark	Strikethrough	Chooses among strikethrough or hidden text to mark deleted text.
Color	By Author	Chooses color for deleted text.
Changed Formatting Option	**Default**	**Effect**
Mark	None	Chooses the options you want for marking text with formatting changes in your document.
Color	Auto	Chooses color for revision bars.

(continued)

	Table 25-5 *(continued)*	
Changed Lines Option	**Default**	**Effect**
Mark	Outside Border	Chooses None to clear revision bars; chooses Left Border to place revision bars in left margin; chooses Right Border to place revision bars in right margin; or chooses Outside Border to place revision bars in the outside margins of facing pages.
Color	Auto	Chooses color for revision bars.

Note   The default Color selection for Inserted text and Deleted text is By author. This selection causes Word to use unique colors for the first eight authors who revise the text. Alternatively, you can choose Auto (Word uses the default text color set in the Windows Control Panel) or a specific color.

User Information tab

Choices in the User Information tab enable you to specify the name, initials, and address of the primary user; information that Word uses in certain kinds of documents. Word initially places information about the registered user in this tab. You can change this information. Table 25-6 lists the options available in the Options dialog box User Information tab, shown in Figure 25-6.

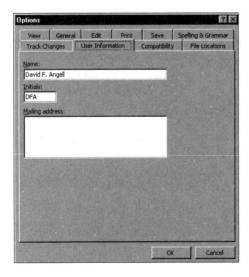

Figure 25-6: The User Information tab in the Options dialog box.

	Table 25-6 Options in the User Information Tab	
Option	**Default**	**Effect**
Name	Name of registered user	Word uses the text here as the author's name in document summary information.
Initials	Initials of registered user	Word uses your initials when you use annotations to identify your comments.
Mailing address	Address of registered user	Word uses the text here as the return address on envelopes.

Compatibility tab

Choices in the Compatibility tab control how Word displays documents created in older versions of Word and in other word processors. Table 25-7 lists the options available in the Options dialog box Compatibility tab, shown in Figure 25-7. You can use these options to display a document created in older versions of Word or in other word processors so that it more closely matches the original. The options you choose here affect only the way Word displays the document; they do not affect the actual document.

Figure 25-7: The Compatibility tab in the Options dialog box.

Note Word can automatically choose appropriate options for displaying and printing a document created in certain other applications. To choose these options, select the appropriate application in the Recommended Options For list box. When you do this, Word automatically checks the appropriate options. If a suitable combination of options is not available, you can manually choose the options that you want.

Table 25-7	
Options in the Compatibility Tab	
Option	**Effect**
Font substitution	Selects fonts available on your system to substitute for those unavailable in the current document.
Recommended options for	Selects the word-processing application that you want to set options for, including Microsoft Word 6.0-7.0, Word for Windows 1.0, Word for Windows 2.0, Word for the Macintosh 5.x, Word for MS-DOS, WordPerfect 5.x, WordPerfect 6.x for Windows, WordPerfect 6.0 for DOS, and Custom.
Options	Lists options that affect the way a document from a non-Word 97 source displays in Word. Selected options affect how the document is displayed only while you're working with it in Word.

After you have chosen the appropriate options, you can choose the Default button to save those options in the active template. If you open a document, open the Options dialog box, and then choose the Compatibility tab, you can choose the Font Substitution button to determine whether fonts in the document are available on your computer. If all required fonts are available, Word displays an information box to tell you that all fonts are available. If one or more fonts are not available, Word displays a Font Substitution dialog box in which you can specify the fonts that you wish to substitute for those that are missing.

File Locations tab

Choices in the File Locations tab enable you to specify where Word should look for certain kinds of files. This tab lists the directories in which Word looks for certain kinds of files. If you wish, you can move specific types of files to different directories, but if you do this, you must define the new location of these files by making changes in the File Locations tab. Table 25-8 lists the options available in the Options dialog box File Locations tab, shown in Figure 25-8. The specific default locations of files may vary according to whether you're using a stand-alone version of Word 97 or Office 97.

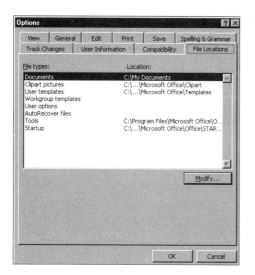

Figure 25-8: The File Locations tab in the Options dialog box.

Table 25-8
Options in the File Locations Tab

File Type	Default Location
Documents	C:\My Documents
Clip art pictures	D:\Clipart (CD-ROM) or E:\Clipart (CD-ROM)
User Templates	C:\...\Microsoft Office\Templates
Workgroup templates	See note below*
User options	No entry
AutoRecover files	See note below†
Tools	C:\Program Files\Microsoft Office\Office
Startup	C:\.Program Files\Microsoft Office\Office\STARTUP

*If you install Word on a network, you can share templates among the workgroup, and individual users can have their own templates. In this case, the Workgroup Templates row in the dialog box indicates the location of the shared templates.

†By default, the AutoRecover files row does not indicate a file location. However, AutoRecover files are saved in the C:\WINDOWS\Desktop directory.

To modify any location, select that location, and then choose the Modify button to display the Modify Location dialog box shown in Figure 25-9. Navigate to the new directory, and choose OK. To create a new directory, choose the Create New Folder button, and choose OK.

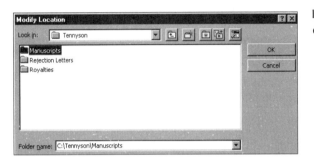

Figure 25-9: The Modify Location dialog box.

Save tab

Choices in the Save tab modify the way in which Word saves documents. For more information on saving your documents in Word, see Chapters 1 and 6. Table 25-9 lists the options available in the Options dialog box Save tab, shown in Figure 25-10.

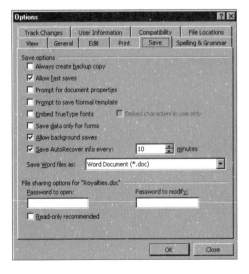

Figure 25-10: The Save tab in the Options dialog box.

Table 25-9
Options in the Save Tab

Save Options Group Option	Default	Effect
Allow background saves	Checked	Saves documents in the background, so you can continue working in Word while you save a document. A pulsing disk icon appears in the status bar when Word is saving in the background.
Allow fast saves	Checked	Speeds up saving your work by recording only changes to document.
Always create backup copy	Not checked	When you save a document, creates a backup copy with .bak extension in the same folder as the original. When you select Always create backup copy, Word clears the Allow fast saves check box because can create backup copies only when it performs a full save.
Embed TrueType fonts*	Not checked	When you save document, also saves TrueType fonts used (see note following). The Embed characters in use only check box becomes active when you activate the Embed TrueType fonts. This lets you specify saving only the specific characters of a font instead of the entire character set, if you used 32 or fewer characters.
Prompt for document properties	Not checked	Displays Summary Information dialog box when you save new document.
Save Options Group Option	**Default**	**Effect**
Prompt to save Normal template	Not checked	When you close Word, displays a message asking whether you want to save changes to Normal.dot.
Save AutoRecover info every	10 minutes	Automatically saves document at defined time interval.
Save data only for forms	Not checked	Saves the data entered in an online form as a single, tab-delimited record so you can use the record in a database. Word saves the file in a text-only format.

(continued)

Table 25-9 (continued)		
Save Options Group Option	**Default**	**Effect**
Save Word files as	Word Document	Selects the file format you want Word to use by default each time you save a (*.doc) document.
File Sharing Options for Option	**Default**	**Effect**
Password to open	None	Password (up to 15 characters) required before anyone can open document. Password is applied to the current active document.
File Sharing Options for Option	**Default**	**Effect**
Password to modify	None	Password (up to 15 characters) required before anyone can save changes to document. Password is added to the current active document.
Read-only recommended	Not checked	When anyone requests to open document, Word displays message recommending that the document be opened as read-only.

*When you check the Embed TrueType fonts option, the document's fonts become part of the saved file — as long as the fonts in question allow this kind of save. This option is advantageous because it enables you to open, view, and print a file using the original fonts even when you're working on a computer where the required fonts are not installed.

Spelling & Grammar tab

Choices in the Spelling tab control how Word checks spelling and let you create custom dictionaries. Refer to Chapter 4 for detailed information about spell checking. Table 25-10 lists the options available in the Options dialog box Spelling tab, shown in Figure 25-11.

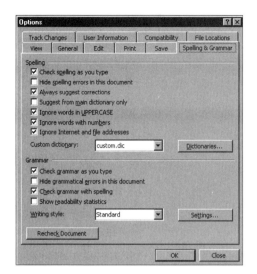

Figure 25-11: The Spelling & Grammar tab in the Options dialog box.

Table 25-10
Options in the Spelling & Grammar Tab

Spell Group Option	Default	Effect
Check spelling as you type	Not checked	Checks spelling automatically and marks errors as you type. When unchecked, the Hide spelling errors in this document check box is not available.
Hide spelling errors in this document	Not active	Hides the wavy red lines that denote possible spelling errors.
Always suggest corrections	Checked	Always suggests spellings for misspelled words.
Suggest from main dictionary only	Checked	Suggests spelling from the main dictionary, but not from custom dictionaries.
Ignore words in UPPERCASE	Checked	Ignores words in all uppercase letters.

(continued)

Table 25-10 (continued)

Spell Group Option	Default	Effect
Ignore words with numbers	Checked	Ignores words that contain numbers.
Ignore Internet and file addresses	Checked	Ignores Internet addresses, file names, and e-mail addresses.
Custom dictionary	CUSTOM.DIC	Lists the active custom user dictionaries. When you click Add during a spelling check, Word adds the entry into the currently selected dictionary in the Custom dictionary list.
Dictionaries	Active	Displays the Custom Dictionaries dialog box for creating, editing, and deleting custom dictionaries.

Grammar Group Option	Default	Effect
Check grammar as you type	Not checked	Checks grammar automatically and marks errors as you type.
Hide grammatical errors in this document	Not Active	Hides the wavy green line under possible grammatical errors in your document.
Check grammar with spelling	Not checked	Checks grammar at the same time spell checking is done.
Show readability statistics	Not active	Displays readability statistics at end of grammar check.
Writing style	Standard	Selects the writing style you want Word to use to check grammar in this document. You can choose from Standard, Formal, Technical, and Custom.

Grammar Group Option	Default	Effect
Settings	Active	Displays the Grammar Settings dialog box for customizing the writing style and grammar rules that Word uses for the selected style in the Writing style list.
Check Document/Recheck Document	Active	This button name is Check Document if you haven't yet run the spelling and grammar checker during the current Word session. After you change spelling or grammar options or open a custom dictionary, the Check Document button changes to Recheck Document so you can recheck your document.

Working with Toolbars

The more you work with Word, the more you may come to rely on the buttons in toolbars for quick access to what you want to do. Although Word comes with two toolbars—the Standard and Formatting toolbars that contain buttons you use frequently—and other toolbars such as the Drawing and Tables and Borders toolbars that contain special-purpose buttons you use occasionally, you probably want more. You would like to have buttons to suit your personal needs. That's why Word lets you customize toolbars.

You can customize toolbars in several ways:

✦ Add buttons to existing toolbars.

✦ Delete buttons from existing toolbars.

✦ Move buttons between toolbars.

✦ Change the icons in existing buttons.

✦ Modify the action of existing buttons.

✦ Create new toolbars that contain existing or new buttons.

Before continuing with this subject, you should understand how Word saves the changes that you make to toolbars and to the buttons in toolbars. All changes you make are saved in a template, either in the template on which your current document is based, or in the Normal template. If you save toolbar changes in any template other than Normal, those changes are available only when you are working with documents based on that template. However, if you save toolbar changes in the Normal template, those changes apply to all documents. Normally, the toolbar changes you want to make are useful only in certain kinds of documents, so you should save these changes in the templates on which those documents are based.

Note   You can move toolbars from templates or documents into other templates or documents using the Organizer dialog box (Format➪Style➪Organizer). Moving toolbars is done in the same way you move styles, which is explained in Chapter 11.

How toolbars appear in Word

Before you begin to work with toolbars, you need to understand how Word displays toolbars on your screen. Open any document based on the Normal template and look carefully at the default Standard and Formatting toolbars, shown in Figure 25-12.

Figure 25-12: The default Standard and Formatting toolbars.

The individual, small rectangular buttons in each toolbar are enclosed within a large rectangle. For buttons to be part of a toolbar, they must be within the large rectangle. As you learn later in this chapter, you can move tools out of large rectangle. When you do this, those tools are no longer part of the toolbar, even if they are in line with the other tools. In fact, they now are in another toolbar.

The size of toolbar buttons depends on your monitor's resolution. The icon in each button is a bitmap image, 24 pixels wide × 23 pixels high. If you have a monitor that displays 640 × 480 pixels, the icons are much larger than those displayed on a higher-definition monitor that displays 800 × 600 or 1,024 × 768 pixels. If you are using a monitor that displays only 640 × 480 pixels, the Standard toolbar occupies the full width of the screen, so you have no room to add buttons. The higher-definition monitor used to capture the screens printed in this book displays smaller buttons, so there is room to add buttons.

Adding a button to a toolbar

A toolbar button represents a Word action. Before you add a button to a toolbar, therefore, the action represented by that button must be defined. Word comes with many predefined buttons, some of which are already in toolbars. Other buttons, however, are defined but not initially available in toolbars. You can add any predefined button into any toolbar; you can even add a button that appears in one toolbar to another toolbar.

Note As you'll discover in Chapter 27, you also can define your own buttons and add them to toolbars. In this chapter, we work only with buttons already defined in Word.

To access buttons defined in Word, Choose Tools⇨Customize to display the Customize dialog box shown in Figure 25-13. You can also display the Customize dialog box by choosing View⇨Toolbars and, in the Toolbars dialog box, choosing Customize. Yet another way to display the Customize dialog box is to point to a toolbar, click the right mouse button to display a shortcut menu, and choose Customize.

Figure 25-13: The Customize dialog box.

The Toolbars tab (refer to Figure 25-13) lists all the toolbar options you can customize. The Categories list box in the Commands tab (see Figure 25-14) displays categories of commands, organized by menu name or by type. If you scroll down the list, you see various categories of tools. Click a category to change the list of commands in the Commands box. For example, choose File in the Categories list. The list of available commands and buttons appear in the Commands list. To see what any button is defined to do, just choose the entry in the Commands list, then click the Description button. Likewise to view the buttons available for the Drawing toolbar, select Drawing in the Categories list. The Modify Selection button displays the shortcut menu for edit buttons and menus.

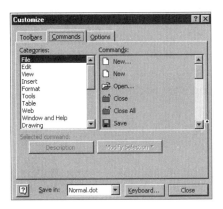

Figure 25-14: The Commands tab in the Customize dialog box.

The Options tab (see Figure 25-15) in the Customize dialog box lets you display larger icons, show or not show ScreenTips, and display shortcut keys in the ScreenTips. ScreenTips are the labels that appear whenever you move the pointer over a button on a toolbar.

Figure 25-15: The Options tab in the Customize dialog box.

Adding buttons to a toolbar

You can add buttons to any of Word's toolbars listed in the Toolbars list in the Toolbars tab (refer to Figure 25-13). Any toolbar or menu bar already displayed is checked. For example, the Standard and Formatting toolbars are checked because they are displayed. The following procedure shows you how to add buttons to any toolbar:

1. Open a new document based on the template you want to use.

2. Choose Tools⇨Customize to open the Customize dialog box. If necessary, choose the Toolbars tab in the dialog box.

3. Click the check box for the toolbar you want to add the button to. The toolbar appears on your screen.

4. Choose the Commands tab.

5. Drop down the Save in list box at the bottom of the dialog box, and choose the template or document in which you want to save toolbar changes.

6. Choose an option in the Categories list box.

7. Choose the button from the Commands list. Clicking the Description button displays a description of the button.

8. Drag the button to a position on the toolbar. You can place the button anywhere you like within a toolbar. If you place the new button outside the rectangle that encloses the buttons on a toolbar, the new button exists in a new toolbar.

9. Choose Close to close the dialog box. The toolbar you selected remains displayed. Click the Close button.

The new button on your toolbar behaves like the standard buttons. Notice that when you point to the new button, a ToolTip appears identifying the button. To use the button, choose it just as you choose any other button.

Tip   The Reset button in the Toolbars tab removes any changes you made to the selected toolbar and restores the original settings. For more information on resetting a toolbar, see "Restoring a toolbar to its original state" in this chapter.

Moving and copying toolbar buttons

When you added buttons to the Standard and Formatting toolbars, you were probably not entirely satisfied with their positions. You can adjust the spacing between buttons and move a button from one place to another in a toolbar, or even from one toolbar to another. You also can copy a button in one toolbar to another toolbar.

Buttons in Word's toolbars are grouped by function. For example, the first four buttons in the Standard toolbar relate to file operations. When you add a button to an existing toolbar, you can place it with a group of related buttons, as explained earlier in this chapter. If you want to move buttons or adjust their spacing, you can do so by *dragging* the buttons, as outlined in the following task:

1. Open a new document based on the template you want.

2. Choose Tools➪Customize to open the Customize dialog box and, if necessary, choose the Toolbars tab.

3. Check the toolbars you want to move or copy buttons between. The toolbars appear on your screen.

4. To move a button, point to the button you want to move, and drag it to the new location you want.

5. To copy a button, point to the button you want to copy, press and hold down the Ctrl key while you drag the button from one toolbar to the other.

Deleting toolbar buttons

You may never use some buttons that are on toolbars, or your needs may change when your working on different projects. In many cases, you'll want to delete buttons to simplify your toolbars. You can delete any toolbar button simply by dragging it out of the toolbar and into the document area:

1. Open any document based on the template that contains the toolbar with the button that you want to delete.

2. Choose Tools➪Customize to open the Customize dialog box and, if necessary, choose the Toolbars tab.

3. Check the toolbar(s) you want to delete buttons from. The toolbar(s) appears on your screen.

4. Point to the button you want to delete, click and drag the button into the document area, and release the mouse button.

After you delete a predefined or default button, you can choose it in the Customize dialog box to add it back into a toolbar. However, if you delete a button you created from a macro, you cannot retrieve that button.

Restoring a toolbar to its original state

You can restore any of the toolbars supplied with Word to their original state. For example, you can restore the Standard toolbar (you added two new buttons to it) to its original state:

1. Open a document based on the template you want.

2. Choose Tools⇨Customize to open the Customize dialog box, and choose the Toolbars tab, if necessary.

3. Highlight the toolbar you want to reset from the Toolbars list.

4. Choose Reset to display the Reset Toolbar dialog box (see Figure 25-16).

Figure 25-16: The Reset Toolbar dialog box.

5. In the list box, choose the document or template.

6. Click OK. The toolbar changes to its original configuration and Word returns to the Customize dialog box.

7. Click Close to exit the Customize dialog box.

Note   You cannot restore changes that you have made to custom toolbars.

Changing a button's image

You can change any of the icons Word uses in toolbar buttons by choosing from a collection of ready-made icons or you can create your own icons. To change a button icon to another ready-made one, do the following:

1. Open any document based on the template that contains the toolbar with the button that you want to delete.

2. Choose Tools⇨Customize to open the Customize dialog box and, if necessary, choose the Toolbars tab.

3. Check the toolbar(s) on which you want to change button images.

4. Point to the button you want to change, click right to display a shortcut menu (see Figure 25-17).

Figure 25-17: The shortcut menu with ready-made button images.

5. Select the Change Button Image command to display a collection of icon images (refer to Figure 25-17).

6. Click the button image you want. The button changes to the selected image.

If you want to get more involved in the look of your icon, you can use Button Editor. To edit a button using the Button Editor, do the following:

1. Open a document based on a template that includes the Standard toolbar.

2. Open the Customize dialog box, choose the Toolbars tab, if necessary.

3. Point to a button in the toolbar and right-click to display a shortcut menu.

4. In the shortcut menu, choose Edit Button Image to display the Button Editor dialog box shown in Figure 25-18. The Edit Button Image dialog box shows an enlarged picture of the toolbar button you selected.

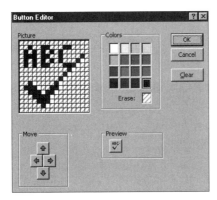

Figure 25-18: The Button Editor dialog box.

Note You must use the mouse to edit toolbar buttons. Word provides no keyboard commands for this action.

You can edit this image by clicking individual pixels. To change the color of a pixel, click the color you want to use in the Colors box, and click the pixel in the enlarged image. If you want to change a pixel to the background color, click erase in the Colors box, and click the pixel. To clear all pixels to the background color so that you can design your own icon, choose the Clear button. Instead of picking a color from the Colors box, you can point to a pixel that has the color you want to use in the enlarged button image, and click the right mouse button.

To move all image pixels one pixel to the left, right, up, or down, click the appropriate arrow in the Move box. While you are editing a button, you can see the effect on the button as it appears in the toolbar in the Preview box.

When you've finished editing, choose OK to close the dialog box, and replace the old version of the button in the toolbar with the edited version. Alternatively, if you want to abandon your changes, choose the Cancel button.

Working with custom toolbars

You have already seen how you can modify existing toolbars by adding, deleting, moving, and changing buttons. You also can create custom toolbars. For example, you may want to consolidate frequently used commands from several toolbars into a single toolbar name Handy Tools.

Creating a custom toolbar

You can create a custom toolbar that contains any of the buttons available in the Customize dialog box and also any buttons you define as macros. To create a custom toolbar:

1. Open a document based on the template in which you want to save the new toolbar.

2. Choose Tools⇨Customize to open the Customize dialog box, and choose the Toolbars tab, if necessary.

3. Choose New to display the New Toolbar dialog box (see Figure 25-19).

Figure 25-19: The New Toolbar dialog box.

4. In the Make toolbar available to list box, choose the template name.

5. In the Toolbar name box, type a name (such as **Handy Tools**) for the new template.

6. Choose OK to close the New Toolbar dialog box. Word automatically opens a new toolbar and the toolbar appears in the Toolbars list. The new toolbar initially appears with room for only one button.

7. After you have finished adding buttons, choose Close to close the Customize dialog box, leaving the new toolbar displayed, as shown in Figure 25-20.

Figure 25-20: The new custom toolbar with buttons.

As described earlier in this chapter, you can add buttons into the new toolbar by dragging them one at a time from the Customize dialog box. Be sure to choose the template in which you want to save these new buttons before you drag buttons into the toolbar. If you add more than one button, the new toolbar automatically widens.

To move the new toolbar into an area above the horizontal ruler, double-click an unoccupied area within the toolbar. You can now work with this toolbar, just as you can work with the toolbars originally available in Word. Remember, though, to save the template so that the new toolbar is available whenever you open a document based on that template. The next time you choose Tools⇨Customize to open the Customize dialog box, you will see the name of the new toolbar in the Toolbars list in the Toolbars tab. You can choose whether to display the new toolbar by checking the option box adjacent to its name in the list.

Renaming a custom toolbar

You can change the name of any custom toolbar quite easily. To rename a custom toolbar:

1. Open a document based on the template that contains the custom toolbar you want to rename.

2. Choose Tools⇨Customize to open the Customize dialog box.

3. Click the Toolbars tab, if necessary.

4. Choose the name of the toolbar you want to rename in the Toolbars list.

5. Click the Rename button to open the Rename Toolbar dialog box (see Figure 25-21).

6. Type a new name for the toolbar, and then choose OK.

Figure 25-21: The Rename Toolbar dialog box.

Deleting a custom toolbar

You can delete a custom toolbar, but you can't delete any of Word's built-in toolbars. To delete a custom toolbar:

1. Open a document based on the template that contains the custom toolbar you want to delete.

2. Choose Tools⇨Customize to open the Customize dialog box.

3. Click the Toolbars tab, if necessary.

4. Select the toolbar you want to delete in the Toolbars list.

5. Click the Delete button. Word prompts you to confirm that you want to delete the toolbar.

6. Click OK. The toolbar is deleted.

Customizing Menus

Word enables you to customize menus and shortcut menus (the menus you see when you right-click the mouse). You also can add your own menus.

There are several reasons for customizing menus:

✦ To provide extra facilities by adding commands to menus

✦ To simplify the Word interface by deleting commands from menus

✦ To address certain tasks by adding menus

Just as it does when saving changes to toolbars, Word saves changes to menus in templates or documents.

Word offers two types of menus: the menus accessible from the menu bar and shortcut menus. Menus are the lists of commands you see when you choose a command in the menu bar or from a shortcut menu. Shortcut menus appear when you right-click the mouse. You can add or delete commands to or from any of these menu types in the same way.

Adding a command to a menu

Word makes adding commands to menu as easy as using drag-and-drop. To add a command to a menu on the menu bar or a shortcut menu, do the following:

1. Open a document based on the template in which you want to save the menu with the added command.

2. Choose Tools⇨Customize to open the Customize dialog box.

3. Choose the Toolbars tab, if necessary.

4. If you want to add a command to a shortcut menu, click the check box labeled Shortcut Menus in the Toolbars list. The Shortcut Menus toolbar appears (see Figure 25-22). Click the Text, Table, or Draw buttons to access the appropriate menu of available shortcut menus. Open the shortcut menu that you want to change.

Figure 25-22: The Shortcut Menus toolbar.

5. If you want to add a command to a menu on the menu bar, open the menu on the menu toolbar.

6. Click the Commands tab in the Customize dialog box.

7. Choose the category of commands you want to add from in the Categories list. The commands for the selected category appears in the Commands list.

8. Drag and drop the commands you want to add from the Commands list to the location in the menu where you want the command to appear.

Changing shortcut keys and command names

As you know, every command in the menus has a shortcut key underlined in the command name. For most commands, the shortcut key is the first character in the command name. Each command in a menu, however, must have a different shortcut key. If two or more commands in a menu have the same first character, characters other than the first are used as shortcut keys. For example, the File menu contains Save and Save As.

Word automatically assigns the shortcut keys for any existing commands you add to a menu. However, you can assign a different shortcut key. Before you start the process of adding a command to a menu, you should make a note of the shortcut keys used by commands already in that menu so that you can pick a new short-cut key.

Right-click the command for which you want to change the shortcut key. A shortcut menu appears. In the Name text field the name of the command appears with an ampersand character (&) immediately in front of the assigned shortcut key for the current command. For example, the two Save commands in the File menu are written as &Save and Save &As, which means the commands appear with the underlined shortcut keys as Save and Save As.

To change a shortcut key for the selected command, reposition the ampersand character (&) to immediately in front of the desired shortcut key. You must, of course, designate a shortcut key not already used by any other command in the menu.

When you add a new command to a menu, Word automatically uses the existing name of the command. You can accept the default name, or you can choose a different name if you prefer. You should make a note of the names of commands already in the menu so that your command name isn't the same as an existing name.

Changing a command name is done in the Name text field. Simply right-click the command you want to rename to display a shortcut menu, then enter your new name in the Name text field and press Enter or click anywhere outside the short-cut menu.

Organizing commands into groups

In addition to the names of commands, Word menus contain separators that divide commands into related groups:

1. Open a document based on the template that contains the menu with the command you want to remove.

2. Choose Tools⇨Customize to open the Customize dialog box.

3. Open the menu to which you want to add a separator.

4. Right-click the a command in a menu that you want to be first in the new command group. A shortcut menu appears.

5. Choose Begin a Group. The separator appears above the selected command and a check mark appears at the left of the Begin a Group command.

Removing a command or separator from a menu

You can remove commands or separators already existing in a menu or those you have added to a menu. To delete a command from a menu:

1. Open a document based on the template that contains the menu with the command you want to remove.

2. Open the Customize dialog box.

3. Open the menu you want to delete a command or separator from.

4. Right-click a command in a menu that you want to delete or the command that is directly under the separator you want to delete. A shortcut menu appears.

5. To delete a command, choose Delete.

6. To delete a separator, choose the Begin a Group command to deactivate it.

There's a quicker way to remove commands from a menu. Press Alt+Ctrl+- to change the mouse pointer to a bold minus sign. Open the menu that contains the command you want to remove, and choose that command. As soon as you do so, the menu closes and the mouse pointer changes to its normal shape. The next time you open the menu, the command you chose is no longer there. This shortcut does not work with separators.

You can also drag and drop a command from a menu to anywhere in the document to delete a command. The Customize dialog box must be displayed to delete a command using drag-and-drop.

Customizing Shortcut Keys

If you use Word for anything more than writing simple letters, you probably spend a great deal of time opening menus, choosing commands, and choosing options in dialog boxes. Wouldn't you be more productive if you could use simple key combinations instead? That's what shortcut keys do.

Shortcut keys are key combinations that give you fast access to commands, fonts, symbols, AutoText entries, styles, and macros. Many shortcut keys are built into Word. You can change the meaning of the built-in shortcut keys, and you can define other shortcut keys. For a complete list of Word's built-in shortcut keys, choose Help⇨Contents and Index. Click the Index tab, and type **shortcut keys**. You can choose various categories of shortcut keys in this way. You can see the format of shortcut keys in Table 25-11. This table lists just a few examples of Word's built-in shortcut keys.

The shortcut keys listed in the Help menu are only the ones built into Word. By looking in the Help menu, you cannot tell whether you, or someone else, has already assigned a shortcut key to a particular command.

Table 25-11
Examples of Word's Built-In Shortcut Keys

Shortcut Key	Action
Ctrl+]	Increases the font size by one point
Ctrl+[	Decreases the font size by one point
Ctrl+B	Makes text bold
Ctrl+I	Makes text italic
Ctrl+Shift+*	Displays nonprinting characters
Ctrl+E	Centers a paragraph
Ctrl+L	Left-aligns a paragraph
Ctrl+K	Starts AutoFormat
Alt+Ctrl+1	Applies the Heading 1 style
Alt+Ctrl+2	Applies the Heading 2 style
Ctrl+F3	Cuts to the Spike
F1	Accesses Help
F2	Moves text or graphics
Alt+Shift+D	Inserts a Date field
Shift+F9	Switches between field code and result
Alt+F9	Switches between all field codes and results

As you can see from Table 25-11, some built-in shortcut keys consist of a single function key. Most, though, entail pressing Shift, Ctrl, or Alt (or a combination of these keys) while pressing another character. The custom shortcut keys you create consist of similar key combinations. As you see later in this chapter, you also can create two-part shortcut keys that contain a key combination followed by another key. Like changes to toolbars and menus, the custom keyboard shortcuts you create are saved in the active template.

Creating a shortcut key for a style

You can create shortcut key combinations to make your life with Word more enjoyable and productive. Suppose, for example, that you frequently use certain styles in your work. Instead of dropping down the Style list box in the Formatting toolbar and scrolling up or down to find the style you want, you can create short-cut key combinations that give you fast access to specific styles.

As an example, suppose that you frequently use the Normal, Heading 1, Heading 2, Heading 3, and Heading 4 styles. You can work faster if shortcut keys give you instant access to these styles.

Before going ahead to create shortcut keys for these styles, you should determine whether they already exist in Word. The easiest way to do so is to look in the Help menu, as previously explained. If you do so, you find that

✦ Ctrl+Shift+N applies the Normal style.

✦ Alt+Ctrl+1 applies the Heading 1 style.

✦ Alt+Ctrl+2 applies the Heading 2 style.

✦ Alt+Ctrl+3 applies the Heading 3 style.

Word does not have a shortcut key to apply the Heading 4 style. The following steps explain how to assign a shortcut key to the Heading 4 style:

1. Open a document based on the template in which you want to save the new shortcut key.

2. Apply the appropriate style (in this case, the Heading 4 style) to some text in the document using the Format⇨Style command.

3. Choose Tools⇨Customize to open the Customize dialog box.

4. Choose the Keyboard button. The Customize Keyboard dialog box appears, as shown in Figure 25-23.

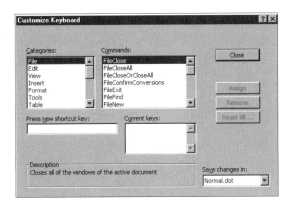

Figure 25-23: The Customize Keyboard dialog box.

5. In the Categories list choose Styles.

6. Choose Heading 4 in the Styles list. Notice that the Description box at the bottom of the dialog box contains a description of the style that you choose. Also, if someone has already assigned a shortcut key to the Heading 4 style, that shortcut key appears in the Current keys list box.

7. Place the insertion point in the Press new shortcut key text box, and press Alt+Ctrl+4 (the shortcut key you want to assign to the Heading 4 style). Notice that [unassigned] appears under Currently assigned to, indicating that the shortcut key you have chosen is not currently assigned.

8. Choose Assign to assign the keyboard shortcut to the style. Word confirms the assignment by displaying the shortcut in the Current keys list box.

9. Click Close to close the dialog box.

If a shortcut key has previously been assigned to the Heading 4 style, that shortcut is displayed in the Current keys list box in Step 6.

In the preceding steps, you assigned a one-part shortcut key (Alt+Ctrl+4) to perform a specific task. Word also enables you to assign two-part shortcut keys. You can, for example, assign

✦ Alt+Ctrl+H,1 to the Heading 1 style

✦ Alt+Ctrl+H,2 to the Heading 2 style

✦ Alt+Ctrl+H,3 to the Heading 3 style

✦ Alt+Ctrl+H,4 to the Heading 4 style

To assign Alt+Ctrl+H,4 to the Heading 4 style, proceed as before in Step 7, press Alt+Ctrl+H, and press 4. Word automatically places a comma between Alt+Ctrl+H and 4. After you have assigned a two-part shortcut key, use it by pressing the first part, Alt+Ctrl+H in this case, and pressing the second part, 4 in this case. Don't type the comma.

Assigning shortcut keys for other purposes

Using shortcut keys to provide quick access to styles is only one of many productive ways to use shortcut keys. The Categories list box in the Keyboard tab of the Customize dialog box, shown in Figure 25-23, contains many categories for which you can assign shortcut keys. These are

✦ All Commands (those in the menus as well as others)

✦ Macros

✦ Fonts

✦ AutoText entries

✦ Styles

✦ Common symbols

Before you get too enthusiastic about styles, a word of caution is appropriate. Shortcut keys are easy to create, but difficult to remember. You can create many shortcut keys and have different shortcut keys in separate templates. Unless you have a supercomputer for a brain, you won't be able to remember all of them. You can easily become counterproductive by creating too many shortcut keys. Avoid a situation where you spend more time trying to find the right shortcut key than you would spend selecting what you need from a menu or dialog box.

Be systematic. Decide which shortcut keys you need on a regular basis, and assign only those. As much as possible, save your shortcut keys in the Normal template so that the same shortcuts are available in all your documents. If you are a member of a workgroup, make it a high priority that every member of the group uses the same shortcut keys. You can follow this procedure by making one person responsible for updating the template.

Restoring shortcut key assignments

Just a few steps can restore all original shortcut key assignments in a template:

1. Open a document based on the template for which you want to restore shortcut keys.

2. Choose Tools⇨Customize to open the Customize dialog box., and then click the Keyboard button.

3. Choose Reset All to open a dialog box in which Word asks you to confirm that you want to restore shortcut key assignments.

4. Choose Yes to restore these assignments and return to the Customize dialog box.

5. Choose Close to close the dialog box.

6. Choose File⇨Save All to save changes to the template.

Summary

To the naked eye, Word appears as a word-processing program. But it's actually one giant collection of customizing options. You can tap into Word's power by mastering its customizing features, including changing its default settings, changing toolbars and menus, as well as defining shortcut keys. In this chapter, you learned how to:

✦ Work with the 12 tabs in the Options dialog box (Tools⇨Options), which include View, General, Edit, Print, Track Changes, User Information, Compatibility, File Locations, Save, and Spelling & Grammar.

✦ Create your own custom toolbars using the Customize dialog box (Tools⇨Customize).

✦ Add and delete buttons on existing toolbars using the Customize dialog box (Tools⇨Customize).

✦ Customize menus by adding your own menu items or deleting existing menu items using the Menus tab in the Customize dialog box (Tools⇨Customize).

✦ Customize shortcut keys by using the Keyboard button in the Customize dialog box (Tools⇨Customize).

Where to go next...

✦ For more in-depth coverage of Word's customizing capabilities at the macro level, check out Chapter 27. This chapter tells you how to create your own Word commands.

✦ To automate Word tasks, flip to Chapter 26. This chapter covers working with field codes, which is a collection of instructions that you create for Word to automatically follow.

✦   ✦   ✦

Using Field Codes

You worked with fields in earlier chapters when you inserted names and addresses in form letters and mailing labels. Fields were also important for creating fill-in forms, other forms, and for marking topics for a document index. How does Word know exactly what you want when you insert a field? By the instructions contained in the field code.

Just What Are Field Codes?

Field codes are flexible and powerful behind-the-scenes tools that help you automate many repetitive chores associated with word processing. They can keep boilerplate text updated without having to retype it whenever a value changes. At the simplest, a field code is a set of instructions that tells Word what information to insert in the document and how it should look. A field code may tell Word to insert the date in the header or the author's name in the footer. On the other hand, it may tell Word to do something complex, such as "take whatever it was that you put in over here, copy it to over there, add it together with this other stuff, and place the result in this table, formatted bold and italic." A field code is still just a set of instructions, no matter how complicated.

The most comforting thing about field codes is that they are extremely logical, consistent, and not that difficult to master. You don't have to remember the names of all the field codes. Word gives you the tools to select and then modify them for just the result you want.

Working with Field Codes

You seldom see field codes looking at you from the screen: they lurk in the background. What you see is the result of the field code's actions. If, for example, you insert an author's name in a document (Insert⇨Field⇨Document Information⇨Author), you will see something on the order of "Ernest Hemingway." Word sees this command as { AUTHOR * MERGEFORMAT }, which loosely translates as "Go to the User Information Tab in the Options menu, pull out the information stored in the Name field, and plop it in here. Oh, and by the way, keep the same character format as the rest of the paragraph." (The * MERGEFORMAT part of the field code will be discussed later in this chapter.)

Finding fields

Normally as you work on a document, you see the results of all the field codes you have inserted instead of the codes themselves. These may be difficult to distinguish from normal text, so Word has added a feature called *shading* that helps you locate field results. When the feature is turned on, the information that represents the results of a field code will assume a gray shading.

To change the shading setting, choose Options from the Tools menu, and click the View tab (see Figure 26-1). The setting applies to both the field results and the field codes themselves.

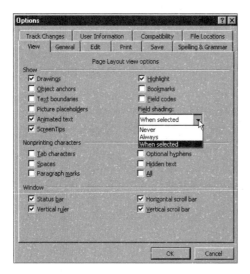

Figure 26-1: The Field Shading options in the View tab of the Options dialog box.

The Field shading drop-down list gives you three different options: Never, which turns off the shading feature altogether; Always, which displays all field codes as shaded all the time (see Figure 26-2); and When selected, which displays field codes, or their results, as shaded whenever the cursor is placed on them.

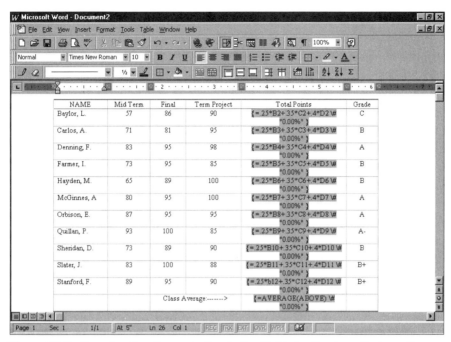

Figure 26-2: Choosing the Always option in the Field shading box displays all formula field codes as shaded.

Note Field shading primarily lets you know where fields are located within a document. The shading does not show in Print Preview, and it does not print with the document.

As you work on your document, you may want to skip from one field to the next to verify that you have inserted the ones you want. You can use shortcut key combinations to move to the next or previous field code. Press F11 to move to the next inserted field code or Shift+F11 to move back to the previous field.

The new Word 97 Select Browse Object button on the vertical scroll bar gives you another way to move quickly from field to field in your document. Click the button and choose Browse by Field from the palette (see Figure 26-3). Then just click the navigation buttons by the Select Browse Object button to move to the previous or next field.

Figure 26-3: Use the Select Browse Object button to move among fields.

Displaying field codes

The shading feature is handy if you just want to see where field codes are located within a document. However, because only the field results are usually displayed, shading is not always useful for examining the actual instructions given by Word to the document.

If you want to see the directions given by a particular field, use the Shift+F9 key combination or choose from the field shortcut menu. To view field codes with keyboard commands:

1. Insert a field code into a document by pressing the Alt+Shift+T keyboard shortcut to insert the time.

2. Position the cursor in the time field. If When selected is chosen from the Field shading drop-down list in the View tab of the Options dialog box, the time will become grayed when it is selected. If you chose Always, all the fields are automatically shaded.

3. Be sure the insertion point is in the field, and then press Shift+F9. You will see a field code that looks like Figure 26-4.

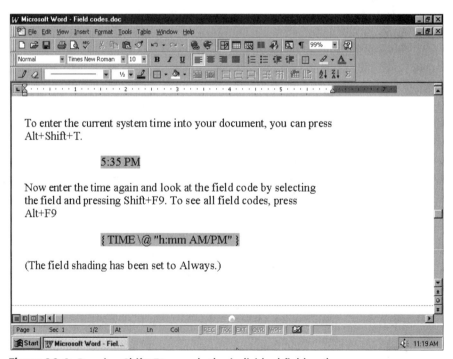

Figure 26-4: Pressing Shift+F9 reveals the individual field code.

4. Right-click in the field code and select T̲oggle Field Codes from the shortcut menu (see Figure 26-5) to return to the results view.

Figure 26-5: The shortcut menu also toggles between field results and codes.

If you want to view all the field codes in a document, press the Alt+F9 key combination. This command toggles all of the fields between displaying the codes or the results. The insertion point need not be in any field to use Alt+F9.

Note   Another option exists that allows you to view all the field codes as the default. Select O̲ptions from the T̲ools menu, select the View tab, and check the F̲ield codes box in the Show area. Use this option with caution because it changes the default setting for all your documents, not just the current document. Be aware that the field codes and their results are of differing lengths; therefore, formatting and page length may not display correctly. Your best bet is to leave this option off and use the Shift+F9 or Alt+F9 key combinations or the shortcut menu to toggle between viewing field codes and viewing their results.

Updating fields

After you have added a new field or changed an existing field, you need to update the field results. Word doesn't know you have given it instructions until you call attention to the new field code. Press F9 to update a selected field. You can also choose U̲pdate Field from the shortcut menu to update the results of the selected field.

To update all the fields in the document at once, choose E̲dit⇨Select A̲ll and then press F9. If you want to make sure the field results are all up-to-date when you print your document, you can set a print option by choosing F̲ile⇨Print⇨O̲ptions⇨U̲pdate fields (see Figure 26-6).

If you want to print the field codes in your document instead of the results, check the F̲ield codes option in the same Print dialog box. Word automatically changes all fields to field codes before printing.

Figure 26-6: Using a print option to update fields before printing.

Inserting Field Codes

You already know several ways to enter fields into your document. Mail merge does it, as does just about every command under the Insert menu. This section discusses three ways of inserting field codes: using shortcut key combinations, selecting them from the Insert⇨Field menu, and manually adding them from the keyboard.

Using the shortcut keys

Three fields are inserted in document headers and footers so often that Word has provided you with shortcut key combinations to do the job:

- ✦ To insert the current system date, press Alt+Shift+D.
- ✦ To insert the current system time, press Alt+Shift+T.
- ✦ To insert the page number, press Alt+Shift+P.

Using the Insert Field menu

Inserting a field by using the dialog boxes available from the Insert⇨Field menu is the easiest and most straightforward way to place a field code in a document. You also have quick access to all of Word's more than 70 field types. To make things even easier, the field types are grouped into categories such as Date and Time, Index and Tables, and User Information. To insert a field containing the name of the current file:

1. Place the cursor where you want to enter the field.

2. Select Field from the Insert menu. This selection will open the Field dialog box, shown in Figure 26-7. With the Preserve formatting during updates option checked, Word automatically includes the MERGEFORMAT switch with the field code. More about MERGEFORMAT and other switches later in this chapter.

Figure 26-7: The Field dialog box.

3. Click Document Information in the Categories list. You can also select (All), but this shows all the field codes in the Field names list, which makes finding a specific field a little harder than necessary.

4. Select FileName from the Field names list.

5. If you want to change the formatting for the way the name appears or if you want to add the file system path to the name, select the Options button. Then choose the formatting or the switch that you want. You learn more about formatting and switches a little later in this chapter.

6. Click OK.

The field entered in the preceding exercise returns a name, probably Document1 unless you have a document open. To see the actual code, place the cursor in the field and press Shift+F9 to toggle the code on. It looks something like { FILENAME * MERGEFORMAT }. Each part of this field will be discussed later in this chapter. It is important to notice that there are always spaces just inside the bracket characters separating them from the field code.

Note Field codes contain special characters that look a lot like braces { }. Unfortunately, these characters are *not* braces, and, if you try to insert them from the keyboard in the usual manner, your field codes will not work. If you want to insert just the special characters, do so by pressing Ctrl+F9. Then you can create the field manually.

Inserting field codes directly

If you are an advanced user and know just what you want or if you are using a code that you have customized in some manner, you may want to enter the codes directly from the keyboard instead of using the Field dialog box.

Manually entering field codes is not an exercise for the faint-at-heart. You will not see friendly dialog boxes that guide your fingers to the successful completion of the task, and you can make some simple, but highly frustrating, errors. To add a field manually:

1. Position the cursor where you want to place the field.

2. Press Ctrl+F9. This command places a set of braces { } in the document and inserts the cursor between them. These braces are special characters that tell Word where a field begins and ends, and you cannot enter them by using the keys next to the "P" on your keyboard.

3. Enter the field name followed by a space and then any field instructions or switches that you want. For this task, use the AUTHOR field by itself. See the upcoming section, "Looking at Fields," for a discussion of the various parts of a field code.

4. Update the field code by pressing F9. You should see your name in the field result.

Caution   It's easy to make two errors when inserting fields from the keyboard:

✦ If you put in the first character of the field code name and receive only beeps, Overtype has probably been turned on. To fix this problem, press the Insert key on the keyboard until the letters OVR disappear from Word's status line.

✦ If everything seems to disappear after you enter the field code, you probably forgot to update the field. To solve this problem, press Alt+F9 to toggle all the fields in the document and show the field codes. Next position the cursor anywhere within the offending field, and press F9 to update it. You can then toggle the field codes off again by using the Alt+F9 key combination.

Looking at Fields

Different fields act in different ways in Word. Some fields insert information, some tell Word to take some action, and others simply provide location markers. This section discusses each kind of field.

Fields that insert information are called result fields. Examples of result fields are the { DATE } field, most of the fields used in a mail merge, the { FILLIN } field, and any other field that directs Word to retrieve some information and put it in the document.

Fields that do something to the document, but don't insert text, are called *action fields*. An example of an action field is the { GOTOBUTTON }. Clicking { GOTOBUTTON } in a Word document will transport you to another location within the document. This function is useful in documentation and instructional works.

Marker fields are location markers. They don't take any action, and they don't insert any text, but they do act as sign posts and guides. The fields marking table of contents entries { TC } and index entries { XE } are two examples of marker fields.

One of the marker fields, the bookmark, is particularly useful when you are constructing long documents and find that you are skipping about and copying and pasting stuff from one place to another. Before you go hopping forward or backward in the document, press Ctrl+Shift+F5 to open the Bookmark dialog box, and type the word **here** to place a bookmark called here. You can then go looking throughout your document for whatever you want, confident that you can always get back to where you were by pressing F5, typing **here**, and pressing Enter.

Taking a field apart

Fields, like Gaul, are divided into three parts: field characters, field type, and field instructions.

The following field inserts the current time into the document in the format 12:34 AM:

```
{ TIME \@ "hh:mm AM/PM" }
```

The two characters that look like braces (but aren't) are field characters: TIME is the field type, and \@ "hh:mm AM/PM" is the field instruction.

Field characters

Field characters that resemble braces ({}) define the beginning and end of a field. You can create field characters in two ways: by choosing <u>F</u>ield from the <u>I</u>nsert menu and selecting a field from the Field dialog box or by pressing the Ctrl+F9 key combination. For more information on putting fields in a document, see the "Inserting Field Codes" section earlier in this chapter.

Field types

The field type defines what the field is supposed to do, and it immediately follows the space after the first field character ({).

Field types are not case-sensitive, meaning that { fillin } and { FILLIN } will both work.

Field instructions

Field instructions provide a great deal of flexibility to the field. They define and refine the actions to be performed, and you can modify them to do some pretty amazing stuff. If your word processing demands are rather simple and you choose most of your field codes directly from a menu, you probably know enough about the anatomy of a field code at this point to go ahead and skip to the "Changing the Appearance of Field Results" section. If you have a burning desire to master field codes, however, continue on with the next section.

Dissecting field instructions

If you really want to get into the nitty gritty of field codes, you need to delve into the world of field instructions. Like field codes, field instructions can consist of several different parts.

The following is a list of all the possible parts of a field instruction:

✦ Arguments

✦ Bookmarks

✦ Expressions

✦ Identifiers

✦ Text

✦ Switches

Arguments

Arguments are information placed in a field instruction to help a field decide what to do. For example, the field { AUTHOR } all by itself would insert the name of the author as shown in the document's summary field. If you include the argument Fred Farkle in the field—changing the field to { AUTHOR "Fred Farkle" }—the code will first change the name of the author in the document summary to Fred Farkle and then insert that text into the document.

Text arguments that include spaces must be enclosed in quotation marks (usually). In other words, Fred Farkle, if used as an argument in the preceding example, will not work, but "Fred Farkle" will. Exceptions to this rule are shown in the Description area of the Field dialog box. If one of your field codes returns only the first word of an argument, you probably forgot the quotation marks.

You can also use arguments to give directions to users. Using the Field code FILLIN along with the argument "Please enter your name here" { FILLIN "Please enter the customer's name" }, will open a dialog box prompting for the user's name (as shown in Figure 26-8). You may remember inserting FILLIN fields with prompt arguments when you created fill-in forms in Chapter 12.

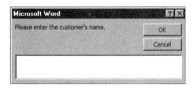

Figure 26-8: The field code and argument { FILLIN "Please enter the customer's name" } will open this dialog box.

Bookmarks

The second part of a field instruction is called a *bookmark*. At first glance, this description may be confusing because bookmarks are also used in the text of a document. However, suppose that you have a chart, table, or several paragraphs of text that you want to refer to several times. Using a field code with a bookmark will insert the text or graphic represented by the bookmark anywhere in the text. To set and use a bookmark in a field:

1. Type some text and select it, or select text that you have already written.

2. Create a normal bookmark by pressing Ctrl+Shift+F5, and give it a name. The name **George** will do nicely.

3. Move to another place in your document, and choose Field from the Insert menu to open the Field dialog box, shown earlier in Figure 26-7.

4. Choose Links and References in the Categories box, and choose Ref in the Field names list.

5. Choose Options, and click the Bookmarks tab of the Field Options dialog box. The Bookmarks tab shows all the bookmarks you have added to the current document. (See Figure 26-9.)

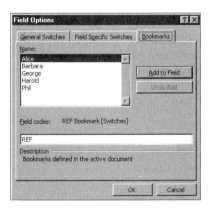

Figure 26-9: The Bookmarks tab of the Field Options dialog box displays a list of existing bookmarks.

6. Select the bookmark that you created in Step 2, choose Add to Field, and then click OK.

7. Click OK to return to the document. Depending on whether field codes are being displayed, you will see { REF George * MERGEFORMAT } in the document.

8. Place the insertion point in the field code, and press Shift+F9 to toggle to the field results and the text that you named George appears.

Instead of selecting the bookmark from the Options dialog box, you can type the name of the bookmark that you created in Step 2 directly into the Field codes box after the field name. Or you can skip choosing Ref and type the whole field code **REF George** (no quotes) directly in the Field codes box. Figure 26-10 shows the Field dialog box set up to insert the bookmark George.

Figure 26-10: The Field dialog box set up to insert the bookmark called George.

Note Inserting stuff that is already placed in the document may seem unnecessary. Why not just copy and paste? However, consider the case when the bookmark represents a chart depicting the corporate share of the market by region. If this chart is inserted in several places in the document by pasting from one original, updating every copy of the chart will be quite a nuisance. It will be much easier to update the chart once and then press F9 to update all other instances of it in the document.

Expressions

If you are familiar with a spreadsheet, you will be at home dealing with expressions. You can include expressions (formulas) right in a field instruction. Insert { =24-10 } in a field instruction, and you will see the display 14.

Far from an exciting event, for sure, but couple this feature with some other information that you already know, and you can make numbers into bookmarks and then add, subtract, multiply, divide, raise to powers, average, and compare those bookmarks. Consider the use of the IF field in the following example (be sure to put spaces around the > operator):

```
{ IF midwest > northeast, "Great job midwest region!" "Let's
    show a better effort next quarter!" }
```

Translated, this field code says "If the value of the midwest bookmark is greater than that of the northeast bookmark, return the result 'Great job midwest region!' If, however, the value of the midwest bookmark is less than that of the northeast bookmark, return the result 'Let's show a better effort next quarter!'" I am sure you can think of lots of other uses. Expressions can include one or more of the operators listed in Table 26-1.

Table 26-1
Operators Used in Expressions

Operator	Description
+	Addition
-	Subtraction
*	Multiplication
/	Division
%	Percent
^	Powers and roots
=	Equal to
<	Less than
<=	Less than or equal to
>	Greater than
>=	Greater than or equal to
<>	Not equal to

Expressions are not confined to the usual numerical operators listed in Table 26-1. If the results referred to by the expression are found in a table, you can use many mathematical formulas. Word recognizes the cell-naming conventions of most spreadsheets, and Word applies these conventions to tables.

When working with tables, rows are numbered and columns are lettered; therefore, the cell in the second column and the third row has the unique name of B3. Ranges of cells are indicated by naming the first cell, inserting a colon, and then naming the last cell. So, you name the block of cells between the very first cell in the upper-left corner and the cell in the eighth row and eighth column as A1:H8.

Cell naming can be a little confusing, but, if you make the effort to learn the proper methods, you can use any of the Word functions in formulas, but only a few accept cell references as arguments. Table 26-2 lists functions that you can use with cell references.

Table 26-2 **Functions and Their Descriptions**	
Function	*Description*
SUM (B2:C3)	Add the contents of all the cells between B2 and C3.
PRODUCT (B2:C3)	Multiply the contents of all the cells between B2 and C3.
MAX (B2:C3)	Show the largest value in the cells between B2 and C3.
MIN (B2:C3)	Show the smallest value in the cells between B2 and C3.
AVERAGE (B2:C3)	What is the average of the values in the cells between B2 and C3?
COUNT (B2:C3)	How many cells are in the range between B2 and C3?

The mathematically inclined can easily use the information in Table 26-2 to put together the formula for a standard deviation or whatever else you need for calculating meaningful field results.

Identifiers

You use *identifiers* to distinguish between different parts of a document or to name a series of items to number, such as figures or tables. Perhaps the best example of an identifier is the sequence field. If you are writing a book about college football, you may want to start each game description with a title like this: Game Plays from Game { SEQ Game }. Word keeps track of the number of times that the { SEQ Game } field is in the document. When you assemble the book, the first game description will read Game Plays from Game 1; the second will read Game Plays from Game 2, and so on.

If you are keeping track of Charts, the SEQ field can be { SEQ Chart }; if tables are the object, the SEQ field can be { SEQ Table }; or if you are tracking the Golden Oldies of the '60s, you can construct the SEQ field as { SEQ Oldies }, or some such identifier. An identifier can contain up to 40 characters including letters, numbers, and the underline character, but no spaces.

Note   The Caption command in the Insert menu is another way to construct sequence identifiers. Selecting this command will open the dialog box shown in Figure 26-11. You can select New Label to use labels such as Oldies or Yogurt. For more information on inserting fields, see "Inserting Field Codes" earlier in this chapter.

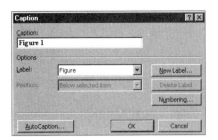

Figure 26-11: The Caption dialog box.

Text

Text is just what you would expect: words that you want to appear in the document or on the screen. The ASK and FILLIN fields are good examples of asking for text to be used in a field. If you are constructing an order form and want to find out who sold the product, you can include the { ASK salesperson "Who received this order?" } field, bookmark, and text field instruction combination to get a text response. The text response is assigned to the salesperson bookmark and inserted wherever that bookmark appears in the document.

Switches

Switches come in two broad categories: general and field specific. *General switches* are optional instructions that either change the way field results look or lock fields to prevent change. The *field specific* switches are also optional and vary depending on the type of field you insert.

All Word field code switches start with a backslash, and the switches appear after all other instructions. You can add more than one switch to a field code. An example of a switch in use is { ASK salesperson "Who received this order?" * Caps }, where the * is the formatting switch and the *Caps* option tells Word to capitalize the first letter of every word in the result as is appropriate for a person's name.

The four general switches can be used with most fields. Table 26-3 describes the general switches and how they can be used. These four general switches work with most fields, but you cannot use them with the following field types:

AUTONUM	FORMDROPDOWN
AUTONUMLGL	GOTOBUTTON
	LISTNUM
AUTONUMOUT	MACROBUTTON
EMBED	RD (Referenced Document)
EQ (EQUATION)	TA (Table Of Authorities)

FORMTEXT   TC (Table Of Contents Entry)

FORMCHECKBOX   XE (Index Entry)

Table 26-3
General Switches and Their Uses

Switch	Usage
*	(character format). Use this switch to specify the character and number format of the field result, or to specify Arabic or roman numerals. You can also use this switch to prevent changes to the existing format of the field results.
\#	(number format). Use this switch to specify how numbers will appear. With this switch, you can specify the number of decimal places, whether to use commas, any leading character such as $, and you can change numbers to their text equivalents.
\@	(date and time formatting). Use this general switch to format date and time field results. It indicates the form of date or time to be reported, such as 10/2/98 or Thursday, 1:42 p.m..
\!	(lock field). Use this switch to prevent updating of the results of BOOKMARK, INCLUDETEXT and REF fields.

You can reach the field-specific switch by choosing the Options button in the Field dialog box. Figure 26-12 shows the field-specific switches for the XE (Index Entry) field. The XE field marks topics to be included in the document index. Select the switch you want, and choose Add to Field. As you add switches, you can see the field code building in the Field codes box. Some field types, such as the REF field, have more than one tab that contain groups of field switches in the Field Options dialog box, as shown in Figure 26-13. If your document has no bookmarks, the Bookmarks tab does not appear.

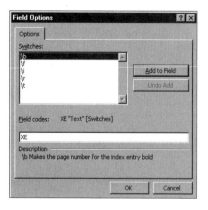

Figure 26-12: Field-specific switches for the XE (Index Entry) field.

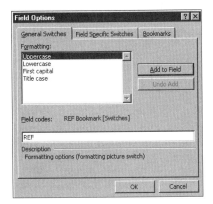

Figure 26-13: The Field Options dialog box for the REF field has three tabs.

Changing the Appearance of Field Results

With the exception of the lock field switch (\!), each of the general switches discussed earlier (*, \# and \@) has a host of options that will tell Word exactly how you want the results to look.

You may, for example, have the identical field in several places. In one location, you want the results to be bold and underlined and in a format that looks like **1,560**. Elsewhere, you want the sum spelled out with initial caps, such as One Thousand Five Hundred Sixty.

You can accomplish basic character formatting (bold, italic, underline, font, and so on) in two ways: you can simply select the field code result and apply the formatting that you want, or you can include a switch within the field. The latter method is preferred simply because it won't change as fields are updated. The appearance of the results formatted by using the first method may change as you update fields, and so they may have to be renewed.

Using the text field switch (*)

The text field switch has three categories of format names: character formatting, case conversion, and number conversion. Some types of fields adopt the same format as the source of the results. The two character formatting options offer a way to control the result in an independent field. We'll discuss the two powerful character formatting options first, and then move on to the other text field switches.

Character formatting

The first character formatting switch applies the format of the previous result to the new result. The second character formatting switch lets you specify the format of all the characters in the result by doctoring the first character of the field name. The following sections describe these two very useful switches.

* MERGEFORMAT

Word automatically includes this switch if the Preserve formatting during updates option is checked in the Field dialog box. It is included when you choose Field from the Insert menu, or insert the field directly from the keyboard. Use this option when you want to format a field result and keep it the same, even with new field results. For example, a field result, say a bookmark named freddie, is formatted to look like the following:

The flock of fowl Fred found _finally_ finished fishing.

Whenever that bookmark is called by the field code { REF freddie * MERGEFORMAT }, the formatting will apply on a word-for-word basis: the seventh word will always be italicized and underlined.

Note   Word takes this option literally; when the switch says that the seventh word will be italicized and underlined, it means it. So, if you change the words in the previous bookmark to read, "The flock of fowl finally found Fred flying," the seventh word, Fred, will be italicized and underlined.

* CHARFORMAT

While the MERGEFORMAT switch takes the formatting characteristics from the source of the field results, the * CHARFORMAT option takes its instructions from the appearance of the first character in the field type (the first character after the opening bracket).

Referring back to the freddie bookmark we used in the preceding section, if you change the REF field code to { REF freddie * CHARFORMAT }, where the "R" in REF has been formatted to be bold, underlined, and a small cap, the freddie bookmark will be inserted in your text as "THE FLOCK OF FOWL FRED FOUND FINALLY FINISHED FISHING."

Note   When using CHARFORMAT, you need to understand two points. First, it is an all or nothing deal. All of your field results will take on the formatting of the first letter of the field type, no matter how long it is. Second, formatting applied by using CHARFORMAT takes precedence over all other formatting that may have been applied to the result.

Case conversion

You can use the text-formatting switch (*) to convert the first or all letters in the field results to uppercase or lowercase.

* Caps

This option changes the first letter of every word in the field results to uppercase.

* FirstCap

This option changes only the first letter of the first word in the field results to uppercase. Any initial caps in the bookmark text, such as in the name Fred, are preserved.

* Lower

This option changes all of the letters in the field results to all lowercase. It has no effect if the field is already formatted as small caps.

* Upper

This option changes all of the letters in the field results to uppercase.

Number conversion

You can use the text formatting switch * to change the way numbers are displayed in the field results. Use the following options to see the described results. In the switches that convert numbers to their text equivalents, you can add a second switch to control the capitalization as described in the previous paragraph.

* alphabetic

This option instructs Word to convert numbers to their letter equivalents: 1 becomes a, 2 becomes b, 3 becomes c, and so on. Type the option as * ALPHABETIC to display the field results in uppercase: A, B, C, and so on.

* Arabic

This option instructs Word to convert the field results to Arabic cardinal numbers. For example, { NumPages * Arabic } may display the result as 156.

* CardText

This option instructs Word to convert the field results to cardinal text numbers, such as one hundred fifty-six. Lowercase is the default, but you can add another switch (* Caps) to change the capitalization to show One Hundred Fifty-Six.

* DollarText

This option instructs Word to convert the field results to cardinal text numbers, but it also includes the wording "and 00/100 dollars." For example, one hundred three and 59/100. Adding the switch * Upper results in ONE HUNDRED THREE AND 59/100.

* Hex

This option instructs Word to convert the field results to hexadecimal numbers, such as A, B, and C, to represent 10, 11, and 12.

* Ordinal

This option instructs Word to convert the field results to ordinal numbers, such as 1st, 2nd, and 3rd.

* OrdText

This option instructs Word to convert the field results to ordinal text numbers, such as first, second, and third. You can add another switch to change the capitalization.

* roman

This option instructs Word to convert the field results to roman numerals, such as i, ii, and iii. Type the option as ***ROMAN** to get I, II, and III.

Using the number field switch (#)

The number field switch is used to draw a picture of how you want numeric results to be printed or displayed in field results. If, for example, you want results listed in dollars and cents, you draw a picture that looks like $#,###,###.00 and place it in a field code by using the number switch. The switch with the picture looks like this: \# $#,###,###.00.

The number switch is almost always used in expression fields, for example { =bookmarka*bookmarkb \# $#,###,##0.00. } or { =22/7 \# #.####### }.

The number switch comprises three types of picture items called *placeholders* (0, #, and x), and several instructions are described next. Use them to build a picture that will represent numbers just the way that you want them to look. If the field results are not numeric, this switch is ignored.

0 (zero) placeholder

A zero in a numeric picture indicates that you want some kind of digit to appear in that place, no matter what. If some digit is in the place occupied by a zero placeholder, it is displayed; if not, a zero is displayed. For example, if you are formatting dollars and cents and you want every entry to include cent values, you would end the numeric picture with .00.

If a field result ends as a number with no decimals, two zeros will be added; 4 is displayed as 4.00, and 4.1 is displayed as 4.10. Additionally, if a result is longer than the number of digits specified by the instruction, it will be rounded off to conform to the number picture. { =4.666+3.21 \# #.00 } shows the result 7.88.

(number sign) placeholder

A number sign in the numeric picture indicates that you want a digit to appear here only if the field result includes one. If the result does not include a digit, a space is inserted in its place.

{ =4.666+3.21 \# #,###,###.## } will still display the result 7.88; spaces are substituted for the first six number signs. Like the 0 placeholder, extra digits are rounded off to conform to the number picture.

x (truncate) placeholder

When this placeholder is on the left of the decimal character, it drops any digits to its left. When the truncate placeholder is on the right of the decimal, it rounds the value to that place and drops any subsequent digits.

{ =966.466 \# x.x } displays 6.5. The 9 and the 6 are truncated (dropped) from the front of the number; the 4 is rounded up to a 5 and the two 6s are dropped from the end.

decimal point instruction (period or comma)

The character used as a decimal point is set in the Regional Settings Properties dialog box in the Windows Control Panel. In the United States, it is a period, but a comma is used in many other countries.

Inserting the decimal point character in the number picture inserts it in the field result. For example, { =5x3 \# ###.00 } displays 15.00.

digit grouping symbol (comma or period)

The digit grouping symbol is used to separate groups of three digits in large numbers and, like the decimal point, varies between a comma and a period — depending on where you live. Select the proper option for you in the Regional Settings Properties dialog box in the Windows Control Panel.

Inserting the digit grouping symbol in the number picture inserts it in the field result. For example, { =GrossSales \# $#,###,### } may display $5,426,705.

- (minus sign)

This instruction adds a minus sign if the result is negative. If the field result is a positive number, a space is inserted. For example, { = 6-9 \# -## } displays the result -3 and { =9-6 \# ## } displays (space)3.

+ (plus sign)

This instruction is a little more demanding than the simple minus sign. It adds a plus sign if the result is positive, a minus sign if the result is negative, or a space if the result is zero. For example, { = 6-9 \# +## } displays the result -3; { = 6+9 \# +## } displays the result +15; and { = 6-6 \# +## } displays a space.

; (semicolon)

The semicolon separates number formatting sections. If you want one format to apply to positive numbers, another to apply to negative numbers, and still a third to apply zero sum results, use the semicolon to separate the arguments, and enclose all in quotation marks.

The third argument, formatting zero sum results, is optional.

For example, the field { =taxesdue \# "$#,##0.00;-$#,##0.00;'None, congratulations!'" } will return a normally formatted number if the value of the bookmark taxesdue is a positive number, a bold and italic number with a leading minus sign if the value is negative, and the words None, congratulations! if the value of taxesdue is zero.

' (single quotation marks) literal text

Single quotation marks are used to include text in a field result. The text to be included must be surrounded by single quotation marks.

A field switch that contains any spaces should be enclosed in double quotation marks.

For example, { =3-1 \# "# 'is the value of this field.'" } returns the following phrase: 2 is the value of this field.

` (accent grave) sequence value

This instruction includes the value of a sequence, such as the current value of the { SEQ Game } field or the current caption number. Use the value of a sequence by enclosing the sequence name in accent graves. The result is displayed in Arabic format. For an example, examine the following field: { =bookmarka+bookmarkb \# "### 'is the total number of first downs in game' `Game`"}. This may display **12 is the total number of first downs in game 4**.

character

Simply typing a desired character will include it in the field result. If you want to include the Yen sign, the Pound sign, or any other character in a result, just include it where you want it to be, as the following two samples illustrate:

{ =17+39 \# ¥## } displays ¥56

{ =2500/100 \# ##% } displays 25%

Using the date and time field switch \@

Using the date and time field switch is similar to using the number field switch. You include characters to paint a picture of how you want the results to appear. For example, the field { DATE \@ "MMMM d, yyyy', at 'h:mm AM/PM" } displays the field results in the following form: January 6, 1998, at 12:50 PM.

M (month) placeholder

The M placeholder is used to control the appearance of the month. The M must be in uppercase, to distinguish it from m, the placeholder for minutes. The month can display in one of four possible formats, depending on how many Ms you include in the placeholder:

M   Displays the month number without a leading zero. December is displayed as 12 and January as 1.

MM   Displays the month number with a leading zero. December is displayed as 12 and January as 01.

MMM   Displays the month as a three-letter abbreviation. December is displayed as Dec and January as Jan.

MMMM   Displays the full name of the month, December or January.

d (day) placeholder

The d placeholder is used to display the day of the month. The day can display in one of four possible formats, depending on how many Ds you include:

d   Displays the day number without a leading zero. The sixth day of the month is displayed as a 6.

dd   Displays the day number with a leading zero. The sixth day of the month is displayed as a 06.

ddd   Displays the day as a three letter abbreviation. Monday is displayed as Mon and Tuesday as Tue.

dddd   Displays the full name of the day: Monday or Tuesday.

y (year) placeholder

The y placeholder is used to control the appearance of the year. The year can display as two or four digits, depending on how many Ys you include in the placeholder:

yy	Displays the year as a two digit number with a leading zero as necessary. 1997 is displayed as 98, and 2002 is displayed as 02.
yyyy	Displays the full number of the year: 1998 or 2002.

h (hour) placeholder

The h placeholder is used to control the appearance of the hour. The hour can display in one of four possible formats, depending on and the number of Hs and their case:

h	Displays the hour on a 12-hour clock without a leading zero. 9 PM is displayed as 9.
hh	Displays the hour on a 12-hour clock with a leading zero. 9 PM is displayed as 09.
H	Displays the hour on a 24-hour clock without a leading zero. 9 PM is displayed as 21, and 9 AM is displayed as 9.
HH	Displays the hour on a 24-hour clock with a leading zero. 9 PM is displayed as 21, and 9 AM is displayed as 09.

m (minutes) placeholder

The m placeholder—lowercase m to distinguish it from the month placeholder—is used to display minutes in one of two possible formats, depending on how many ms you include in the placeholder:

m	Displays the minutes without a leading zero. Five minutes after the hour displays as 5.
mm	Displays the minutes with a leading zero. Five minutes after the hour displays as 05.

am/pm placeholder

This placeholder displays a.m. or p.m. in one of four formats:

AM/PM	Displays the morning or afternoon indicator in uppercase. 9 in the evening is displayed as 9 PM.
am/pm	Displays the morning or afternoon indicator in lowercase. 9 in the evening is displayed as 9 pm.

A/P   Displays the morning or afternoon indicator in uppercase as an abbreviation. 9 in the evening is displayed as 9 P.

a/p   Displays the morning or afternoon indicator in lowercase as an abbreviation. 9 in the evening is displayed as 9 p.

' (single quotation marks) literal text

The single quotation marks are used to include text in a date/time field result the same as for a number field. You must enclose the text to be included in single quotation marks.

You should surround a field switch that contains spaces with quotation marks. Here's an example: { DATE \@ " ' Date Read: 'dddd, MMMM dd, yyyy" } displays as Date Read: Sunday, January 26, 1998.

Again, if your text includes any spaces, the whole expression must be contained in double quotations marks.

` (accent grave) sequence value

This instruction includes the value of a sequence, such as the current value of the { SEQ Game } field, or the current number reported by any of the caption fields included in your document using the Caption command in the Insert menu. Use this instruction the same as with number fields by enclosing the sequence name in accent grave marks. The result displays in Arabic format. The following example illustrates how to use the accent grave:

{ CREATEDATE \@ "M/d/yy 'is the day I wrote about game' `Game` "} displays as: 3/4/98 is the day I wrote about game 6.

character

Simply typing a desired character will include it in the field result. To add a colon or a hyphen to a date, include it where you want it to be, the same as for a number field (be sure to enclose the field switch in quotation marks), as shown in the following example:

{ DATE \@ "HH:mm MMM-d" } displays 21:09 Apr-2.

Editing Field Codes

When you want to change the format or content of any of the field results, you can edit its field code. For example, you can change the formula field { =bonus/4 } to calculate one-third of the bonus rather than one-fourth. Click in the field to select it. Be careful not to include either of the field characters ({ or }) in the selection. If you see the field results, press Shift+F9 to toggle to the field code. Change the 4 to a 3, and press F9 to update the field. When you press Shift+F9 again, you'll see the new field results.

Protecting Fields

Sometimes, you just don't want anybody meddling with your fields. You can disassociate your fields from the source information to retain the current values. This requires the process of locking, unlocking, and unlinking fields. Locking a field prevents it from being updated whenever its BOOKMARK, INCLUDETEXT, or REF field is updated. When a field is linked to a document, every time there is a change in the referenced text, the field result is subject to change.

Locking and unlocking fields

Locking a field can keep it from updating without your direct control. You can lock fields temporarily in one of two ways: you can use the \! switch in the field, or you can lock fields on-the-fly from the keyboard.

To lock a field result with a field switch, add \! as the last switch in the field code. For example, { INCLUDETEXT C:\Sales\gross sales.doc \# $#,###,### \! } displays the value found in the gross sales document at the time the field was first evaluated. Subsequent changes in the document will not affect the field results.

To lock a field on-the-fly:

1. Position the cursor in the field that you want to lock. (If you want to lock several fields, select them all.)

2. Press Ctrl+F11.

After a field is locked, if you try to update it, a rewarding beep will greet you, and not much else will happen. Unlocking a field so that you can update it is just about as hard as locking it:

1. Position the cursor in the field that you want to unlock. (If you want to unlock several fields, select them all.)

2. Press Ctrl+Shift+F11.

Unlinking fields

Sometimes, you will want to disassociate the current field results from the source information so that they will never be updated. Perhaps you have finalized a project or a report, or you are sending something off to the printer. Word gives you the option to unlink your fields, but use it with caution because the unlink is permanent and the only way to restore the link is to reinsert the field. To unlink a field:

1. Place the insertion point in the field that you unlink.

2. Press Ctrl+Shift+F9.

Summary

In this chapter, you saw how to build field codes that instruct Word to insert fields and display them just the way you want. You learned how to:

✦ Display field codes and field results.

✦ Insert field codes in a document.

✦ Add formatting switches.

Where to go next...

✦ To compare the Word fields in this chapter with form fields, see Chapter 21.

✦ To review the use of bookmarks in your document, turn to Chapter 23.

✦ Make life a lot easier by automating codes with macros. See Chapter 27 for information on how to let Word do the job for you.

✦   ✦   ✦

Working with Macros

Word consists of a galaxy of pre-made commands created by using Visual Basic, the programming language behind Word and many other applications. All Word menu selections and dialog box options are carried out by built-in macros containing Visual Basic commands. You can create your own custom commands using Word's macro features to record keystrokes and mouse actions. Word also lets you construct more complex macros from scratch by using the Visual Basic Editor. This chapter explains creating, editing, managing, and using macros in Word, as well as an introduction to Visual Basic.

Understanding Macros

With macros, you can automate a set of procedures and run them with a single command. They can be simple recordings of keystrokes, commands, and mouse button clicks or sophisticated programs that you create. Using macros can significantly improve your efficiency; so, if you find that there are particular tasks you are performing repeatedly, create a macro to do the job. Even simple recorded macros can noticeably improve your work efficiency. Some of the simple tasks and procedures that you can automate with a macro include the following:

- ◆ Opening and arranging a group of files that are used together
- ◆ Speeding up routine text formatting and editing
- ◆ Opening a document and immediately moving to the last location edited
- ◆ Simplifying dialog box selections
- ◆ Automating a series of related tasks
- ◆ Switching automatically to Outline view

The easiest way to create a macro is to record your keystrokes and command selections with Word's macro recorder. The recording process is much like using a VCR to record a television program. When you turn on the macro recorder, Word stores all your keystrokes and command choices as Visual Basic macro commands until you turn it off.

Visual Basic, the programming language included with Word, is the language used to develop all commands in Word. When you create a macro, you are creating your own custom Word command in the Visual Basic programming language. You can assign your macros to buttons on toolbars or to shortcut keys. After you record a macro, you can play it back at any time by clicking a button or pressing shortcut keys, or using the Macro dialog box. You can also modify a recorded macro or write a macro from scratch using Visual Basic. Visual Basic enables you to develop sophisticated macros that present choices, display dialog boxes, get data from the user, and perform virtually any Word task. A Word macro can consist of only a few lines or up to several hundred lines of code.

Storing Global and Template Macros

You can store a macro in a single document template or in a global template. By default, Word stores macros in the Normal template (Normal.dot), so you can use them with any document. When you store a macro in a document template, it is available only to documents based on that template. If you change your mind later about the location of the stored macro, you can use the Organizer to copy macros from one template to another, as explained later in this chapter. Save macros as global macros only when many documents need to share them. Macros designed for a specific type of document or specialized purpose should be saved with the template associated with that document type.

Recording and Saving Macros

Before you record a macro, you need to understand what Word records while the macro recorder is on. This information will help you to set up Word prior to starting the macro recorder, and it will also prevent you from recording unwanted steps. You can always remove them later, but it is easier to record only the steps you want in the macro.

With the macro recorder on, Word records mouse clicks that select menu commands or dialog box options but not mouse movements in the document window. You must use the keyboard if you want to record selecting, copying, or clicking and dragging document text. If you are unfamiliar with using the keyboard to select or move text and graphics, see Chapter 3. You can pause recording any time and then resume where you left off.

Selections made in dialog boxes are recorded within macros only if you choose OK to close the box. This action records the current settings for all options in the dialog box. In the case of dialog boxes that contain tabs, such as Tools⇨Options, you only can record the settings of one tab at a time by choosing OK in that tab. If, for example, you want to record Save, View, and Edit options, you must choose the Tools⇨Options for each set of options, select the tab, select the options, and choose OK rather than switching to another tab. If you are in a dialog box, choosing Cancel or pressing Esc prevents the dialog box from being recorded. If you backspace over text that you have just typed, the deleted text will not be recorded.

Some items (such as the Ruler) toggle between conditions, in which case, the macro recorder records a single statement, DisplayRulers. If the Ruler is already on, DisplayRulers turns the Ruler off. If the Ruler is off, DisplayRulers turns the Ruler on. As a result, running a recorded macro could actually turn off the Ruler when you want it to stay on.

If you intend to use the new macro in another document, make sure none of its commands depend on the contents of the original document.

Recording macros

Before you create a macro, you need to decide whether the macro affects a specific portion of the document, a selected portion of the document, or the entire document. If the macro always affects a specific part of a document, insert bookmarks in the document that name the specific text or graphic so that the macro can move to these locations. See Chapter 23 for more information on working with bookmarks. If you want a macro to work on whatever you have selected when you run the macro, make your selection before you begin recording the macro. To record a macro that affects the whole document, make sure nothing is selected when you begin recording.

Open the template in which you want your macro stored, and prepare the document so it is in the same condition that, in the future, will warrant running the macro. If you want the macro available to all documents, you should base the document on the Normal template. If you want to use the macro only with documents from a specific template, open a document based on that template. You can see which template a document is based on by choosing the File⇨Properties command and reading the template name in the General tab. To record a macro:

1. Open a document based on the template to which you want to apply the macro. If you plan to make the macro global, you can open any document based on any template, and then select the Normal.dot option from the Record Macro dialog box.

2. Do one of the following to open the Record Macro dialog box (see Figure 27-1):

- Choose Tools➪Macro➪Record New Macro.

- Double-click the REC indicator in the status bar.

Figure 27-1: The Record Macro dialog box.

3. Type a name for the macro in the Macro name text box. Macro names must begin with a letter, but you can include numbers after the first letter. Macro names can be up to 80 characters long, and they cannot contain spaces or symbols. Use a combination of uppercase and lowercase letters to identify the macro more easily.

4. If you want the macro stored as a global macro, make sure that you choose the All Documents (Normal.dot) from the Store macro in list. This list includes the global Normal.dot template and templates for all documents that are currently open.

5. Enter a description in the Description text box to help you remember what the macro does. This description displays in the status bar of the Macros dialog box when the macro name is selected. The current date and author are automatically entered as the description, but you may find it useful to have a more informative description when working with and managing your macros.

6. Choose OK. The REC indicator in the status bar changes to bold, and the Stop Recording toolbar (see Figure 27-2) displays in the document window. The toolbar contains only two buttons: Stop Recording and Pause Recording. The mouse pointer changes to show an icon of a cassette tape.

Figure 27-2: The Macro Recording toolbar.

7. Perform the actions that you want to record. If you want to pause the macro, click the Pause Recording button on the Stop Recording toolbar. Click this button (now called Resume Recording) a second time to restart macro recording.

8. When you are finished entering the macro actions, do one of the following:

- Choose the Stop Recording button on the Stop Recording toolbar to stop the recording. The REC indicator in the status bar dims when the recording stops and the toolbar and cassette-tape icon disappear.

- Choose the Tools➪Macro➪Stop Recording to turn off the macro recorder.

Be careful not to name your new macro with the same name as an existing Word macro. The new macro commands will replace the existing ones and Word may not work the way it should. To make sure you don't use a Word macro name, choose Tools➪Macro➪Macros and choose Word Commands from the Macros in list. Scroll down the names in the alphabetic list of the built-in Word macros to see if the name is already in use. If you do use the same name as a built-in macro, the new macro actions will replace the old.

Tip   You must use one of the procedures in Step 8 to stop recording. Closing the Stop Recording toolbar doesn't stop recording. If you notice that your mouse and keyboard are running much slower than usual, you may have left the macro recorder on.

Assigning a macro to a toolbar

To make a macro even easier to use, you can create a button on any toolbar, and then you can click the button to run the macro. If you prefer to use shortcut keys, you can assign the macro to a specific key combination. You can assign the same macro to both methods for flexibility.

To assign a new macro to a toolbar:

1. Choose Tools➪Macro➪Record New Macro to open the Record Macro dialog box. Enter the macro name and description, and select the storage template.

2. Choose Toolbars in the Assign macro to area of the Record Macro dialog box. The Customize dialog box opens (see Figure 27-3).

Figure 27-3: The Commands tab of the Customize dialog box.

3. Choose the <u>C</u>ommands tab, if not already showing, and then do one of the following:

- If the toolbar you want to add the macro button to is visible in the document window, click the macro in the Comman<u>d</u>s box and drag it from the dialog box to a position on the toolbar. Then release the mouse button. The new button appears on the toolbar.

- If the toolbar you want is not visible, click the Tool<u>b</u>ars tab and check the desired toolbar. The toolbar is displayed immediately. Return to the <u>C</u>ommands tab and click and drag the macro command to the toolbar.

4. To change the macro button options, choose the <u>O</u>ptions tab (see Figure 27-4). Table 27-1 describes the toolbar button options.

Figure 27-4: The Options tab of the Customize dialog box.

5. Choose Close to begin recording the macro.

Table 27-1
Toolbar Button Options

Option	Description
Large icons	Increases the button size.
Show Screen<u>T</u>ips on toolbars	Displays the macro description in a ScreenTip when the mouse pointer rests on the button.
Show <u>s</u>hortcut keys in ScreenTips	Displays the keyboard shortcut key combination in the ScreenTip with the description.
<u>M</u>enu animations	Specifies the way to display menus when a command is clicked. Choices are (none), Random, Unfold, and Slide.

Many people prefer to use the keyboard for most actions rather than the mouse. To assign a macro to a key combination:

1. In the Record Macro dialog box, choose Keyboard from the Assign macro to area after entering the other information and before beginning to record the macro. The Customize Keyboard dialog box opens (see Figure 27-5).

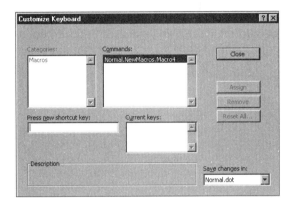

Figure 27-5: The Customize Keyboard dialog box.

2. With the insertion point in the Press new shortcut key text box, press the keys you want to assign the macro to. If the key combination is already assigned to something else, Word lists the current assignments below the Press new shortcut key box. For example, if you enter **Alt+F9** as the shortcut key, Word tells you that that combination is currently assigned to the Word macro ViewFieldCodes (see Figure 27-6).

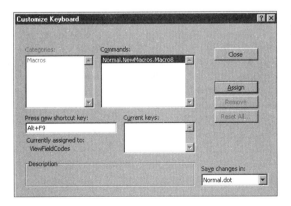

Figure 27-6: Entering a shortcut that is already assigned.

3. Change the key combination to one which is not already assigned then choose Assign.

4. Choose Close to close the dialog box and begin recording the macro.

If you assign a new macro to a key combination already in use, you will replace the existing assignment. For example, Alt+F9 will no longer display field codes in your document.

If you want to assign an existing macro to a toolbar or shortcut key—one you have already recorded or one provided by Word—you can use the Customize dialog box available through the Tools menu. In the Commands tab of the Customize dialog box, scroll down the list of categories and select Macros. A list of macros available in the current template is displayed (see Figure 27-7). Click and drag the macro command to the toolbar as before, or use the Keyboard button to open the Customize Keyboard dialog box where you can select the macro you want and assign a shortcut key combination. For more information about customizing toolbars and shortcut keys, see Chapter 25.

Figure 27-7: The Commands tab of the Customize dialog box showing available macros.

Saving macros

A new macro is only stored in memory, not automatically saved to disk. You must save template macros before you close the template to which they are attached. Global macros must be saved before you exit Word. When you save a document whose template you have changed by adding a macro, Word will ask if you want to save the changes to the template. If you attempt to exit Word and have not saved the macros you added to the Normal template, Word will ask whether you want to save those changes.

Running Macros

How you run a macro depends on how you assigned it. If you assigned your macro to a shortcut key or a toolbar, you run the macro by pressing the shortcut key combination or by clicking the button on the toolbar. If you did not assign the macro to one of these, you run the macro using the Macros dialog box. You can run a global macro at any time because the Normal template is always available. If you want to run a macro that you have stored in a specific template, you must either open the template itself, or open a document that is based on that template. If the macro is designed to work with selected items, select those items first. Press the macro shortcut key or choose the button from the toolbar to run your macro.

To run a macro using the Macros dialog box:

1. Open a document on which the macro is designed to work. Before running the macro, select your text if the macro is designed to work with selected text.

2. Choose the Tools⇨Macro⇨Macros command. The Macros dialog box appears (see Figure 27-8).

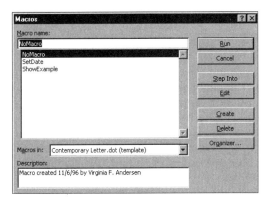

Figure 27-8: The Macros dialog box showing available macros in the Contemporary Letter template.

3. Select or type the macro name in the Macro name list box.

4. Choose the Run button.

If the macro you want does not appear in the Macros dialog box's Macro name list, make sure that you have opened a document based on the template that contains your macro. If you want the macro to be available at all times, use the Organizer to transfer a copy of the macro out of its current template and into the Normal template, as explained later in the "Managing macros" section of this chapter.

Because Word commands themselves are really macros, you can display them and execute them directly from the Macro dialog box. Choosing the Word Commands option in the Macros in list displays a list of nearly 1000 macros that correspond to Word's built-in commands (see Figure 27-9). You'll find many commands listed that don't appear in Word's menu. FileCloseAll, for example, is a file-related command that doesn't appear on the File menu, but you can run it from the Macros dialog box as though it were a menu selection. The Description box shows a short explanation of the selected macro. Notice the Edit, Create, and Delete buttons are dimmed, indicating that you can't change the Word command list or any of the command macros.

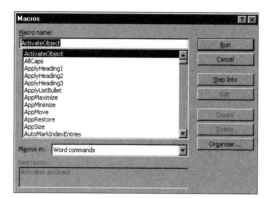

Figure 27-9: Word 97 includes nearly 1,000 built-in macros.

Checking for viruses

When you choose to run a macro from another source, such as another system or from e-mail, Word displays a warning box about macro viruses (see Figure 27-10). A macro virus can be activated by opening a document or template that contains a macro infected with the virus. It then invades your system where it infects every document you save. The virus can also be transmitted to others who open these infected documents. If you are sure of the source of the macro, you can go ahead and enable the macros. If there is a chance of a virus, you can open the document or template with the macros disabled or not open it at all. There is also the option of displaying the Word 97 Help topic that deals with checking documents for macros that may contain certain viruses.

Figure 27-10: Word 97 displays a warning against macro viruses.

Running WordBasic macros

Word 97 automatically converts macros created in earlier versions of Word the first time you open the template that contains the macros, create a new document based on the template, or attach the template to a document with the Templates and Add-Ins command of the Tools menu. The WordBasic commands are converted to Visual Basic for use in Word 97. The status bar displays a message during conversion. After the conversion is complete, you must save the template in order to save the conversion. Otherwise, Word will have to convert the macros again the next time you want to use the template.

Caution Always save the converted template to a new name. If you save the template over the original template, you will lose the WordBasic macros, and previous versions of Word will not be able to run them.

If you have any macros created in Word 2.x, Word 97 cannot directly convert them. You must first convert them to Word 6.x or Word 95 WordBasic macros, and then use Word 97 to convert them to Visual Basic macros.

Running automatic macros

Word lets you create automatic macros (auto macros) that run when you open or close a document or start or exit Word. While creating a macro that will run automatically, you have to name it using one of the five unique macro names listed in Table 27-2. The name that you choose depends on when you want the macro to run. You can, for example, create a macro that does any of the following:

✦ Automatically opens the last document on which you were working

✦ Prompts users for information when they create a new document with a particular template

✦ Reverts your settings upon quitting Word to the way they were when you first started Word, eliminating any special settings that you temporarily added during a session

✦ Performs operations that format a document when it opens

Table 27-2
Word's Auto Macros

Macro name	Function
AutoExec	Runs when you start Word
AutoExit	Runs when you quit Word
AutoNew	Runs when you create a new document based on a template containing the macro
AutoOpen	Runs when you open an existing document based on a template containing the macro
AutoClose	Runs when you close a document based on a template containing the macro

You can create only one macro using the AutoExec and AutoExit macro names because they are global macros. You can create AutoNew, AutoOpen, and Auto-Close macros for different templates or as global macros. All these macros are contained in the Word macro library.

Note   The AutoNew macro combined with the UpdateFields macro is useful for updating all fields in a given document when you open a template for that document. These macros are especially useful for form or document templates containing date and time fields and { FILLIN } field codes. When a new document opens from a template having these macros, each field code is updated. All the { FILLIN } input boxes, for example, are displayed in turn.

Auto macros can be stored in the Normal template or another template or in a document. The exception is the AutoExec macro, which must be stored in the Normal template or another global template in the Startup folder in order to run automatically when you start Word.

Preventing automatic macros from running

To prevent an automatic macro from running, hold down the Shift key while you perform the action that starts the macro. For example, to prevent AutoOpen from running when you open a document, hold down the Shift key while you choose the Open button from the Open dialog box.

Running macros from a field code

If you want to get really fancy, you can insert a Word field into a document that will run a macro. The field, { MACROBUTTON }, can be displayed as text or a graphic in your document. When you double-click the field, Word runs the macro assigned to it. See Chapter 26 for more information on using field codes. You will see an example of using macro field codes later in this chapter.

Editing Macros

The macro recorder records and stores each action that you perform as one or more Visual Basic statement in a macro document. Issuing a Visual Basic statement is the same as choosing the corresponding command. Visual Basic, a version of the popular BASIC programming language, is used in all Microsoft Office applications. You can use it to edit macro statements much like text in a normal document.

With the Visual Basic Editor, you can correct typos, delete unwanted commands, copy parts of a macro from one document or template to another, and reorganize macros by cutting and pasting. You edit macro text in the same way that you edit document text.

To edit a macro:

1. Open the template containing the macro you want to edit, or open a document based on that template.

2. Choose the Tools⇨Macro⇨Macros command.

3. Select the name of the macro from the Macro name list box in the Macros dialog box.

4. Choose the Edit button. The Visual Basic Editor opens with the text of the macro in the editing window. Figure 27-11 shows most of a recorded macro named CodeStyle that sets the font appearance for selected text to 12-point Courier with small caps.

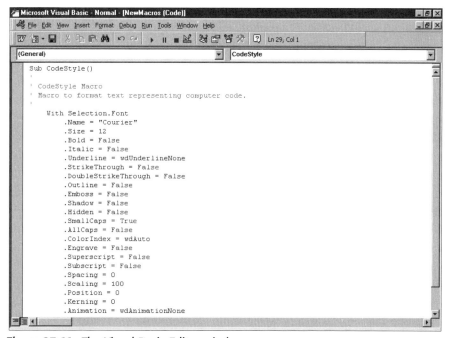

Figure 27-11: The Visual Basic Editor window.

5. Make the desired changes just as you would in a normal document. For example, change the statement .Size = 12 to .Size = 10 to change the font size to 10 points.

6. When all the changes have been made, choose File⇨Close and Return to Microsoft Word. The macro is saved to memory, but you still have to save it with the document to save it to your disk.

Dissecting a macro

Before moving on, let's take a look at the Visual Basic code that was generated by recording the macro shown in Figure 27-11.

```
Sub CodeStyle()
'
'CodeStyle Macro
'Macro to format text representing computer code.
'
    With Selection.Font
        .Name = "Courier"
        .Size = 12
        .Bold = False
        .Italic = False
        .Underline = False
        .StrikeThrough = False
        .DoubleStrikeThrough = False
        .Outline = False
        .Emboss = False
        .Shadow = False
        .Hidden = False
        .SmallCaps = True
        .AllCaps = False
        .ColorIndex = wdAuto
        .Engrave = False
        .SuperScript = False
        .Spacing = 0
        .Scaling = 100
        .Position = 0
        .Kerning = 0
        .Animation = wdAnimationNone
    End With
End Sub
```

The first few lines of the macro show the macro name and some comments. Any line that begins with an apostrophe is ignored by Word and can contain any amount of descriptive information that will help you remember what the macro is supposed to do.

With and End With enclose the macro instructions that refer to the same object. In this case, the selected text. The line, With Selection.Font indicates that text is selected and the Font dialog box is opened.

Most of the remaining statements in the CodeStyle macro represent choices made in the Font dialog box during the recording of the macro. Each setting is called a *property*. Any text selection such as the font name, Courier, is contained in quotation marks. Numeric settings appear as regular numbers (.Size = 12). False means that the option was not selected, and True means that it was. All the Font dialog box options are represented in the macro. The last two lines close the macro and return control to Word.

Deleting unnecessary commands

As you can see in the CodeStyle macro above, most of the Font dialog box selections were left in the default setting. Only the font name, size, and SmallCaps properties were changed. You can delete all the Visual Basic statements relating to the unchanged properties without disturbing the macro's performance. You delete commands from a macro the same way as any other text: select the line and press Delete.

The condensed macro will run faster than the original because it sets only three properties instead of all 21.

Adding remarks and comments to a macro

Remarks and comments are helpful for reminding you what is going on in a macro. In Visual Basic, you have two ways of adding information to a macro that Word will ignore. The REM statement is a hold-over from early BASIC and was used to identify the line as a remark. The apostrophe is now generally used to indicate remarks and comments that you want to see in the macro but you want Word to ignore. Tabs can be used to indent text, which helps understand the hierarchical structure of the macro. Using tabs, remarks, and comments makes your macros easier to decipher. The following is an example of using comments and tabs to explain the beep command in a macro:

```
Sub BeepMacro()
'
'      The Beep Command
'
'The Beep statement emits a beeping sound.
'
Beep

End Sub
```

Managing Macros

You will eventually accumulate macros that have outlived their usefulness. Keeping your macros up-to-date and well-organized is a good idea. Word lets you manage your macros in many ways. You can rename and delete macros, as well as copy macros between templates. Using the Organizer dialog box (see Figure 27-12), you can manage your macros by copying them into different templates or renaming them. By default, Word stores macros in the Normal template so that they are available for use with every Word document. If, however, you create macros for a specific document, save those macros to a template for that document. This technique helps you keep your Normal template less cluttered.

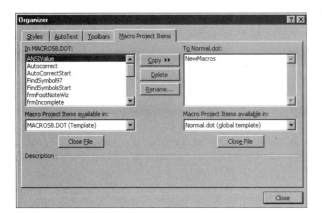

Figure 27-12: The Macro Project Items tab in the Organizer dialog box.

The Word Organizer is a flexible tool for managing macro project items as well as toolbars, styles, and AutoText entries. The Macro Project Items tab is divided into two major areas, right and left, that contain lists of macros in selected templates. When you select a macro name from either list, that template becomes the focus of the operation, and, if you want to copy a macro, it is the source of the macro. The headings above the lists alternate between In and To, depending on which list contains the selected macro. The Copy arrows also change direction accordingly.

If you have recorded a number of new macros in the current template or document, they will be lumped together in a macro project named NewMacros rather than listed separately.

Note If a template is protected, you must unprotect it before you can delete or rename a macro. To unprotect a template, choose the Tools⇨Unprotect Document command. You may be prompted to enter the password if one was assigned when the document was protected.

Copying or moving macros between templates

At times, you will want to copy or move a macro from one template to another. Word lets you copy or move macros between open templates:

1. Choose the Tools⇨Macro⇨Macros command.

2. Choose the Organizer button from the Macros dialog box. The Macro Project Items tab of the Organizer dialog box appears.

3. In the Macro Project Items available in box (on the left side, by default), select the template that contains the macro that you want to copy or move.

   If you want to copy a macro stored in a template that is not open, choose the left Close File button to close the open template (the button changes to Open File), and then choose the Open File button to find and open the template that you want. The Open dialog box appears, as shown in Figure 27-13. (Your file names will be different.) Select the template and choose Open.

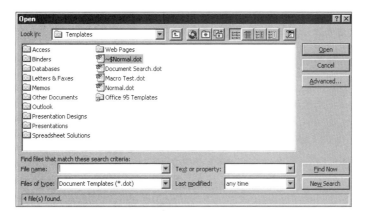

Figure 27-13: The Open dialog box.

4. Select the template into which you want to copy or move macros from the Macro Project Items available in list box (right side). If you want to move or copy a macro to a template that is not open, choose the right Close File button, and then choose the right Open File button. Select the desired template and choose OK to open that template.

5. Select the macros in the In list that you want to move or copy. To select a series of macros, hold down the Shift key and click the first and last items in the series. To select multiple macros individually, hold down Ctrl and click each item.

6. Do one of the following:

   • To copy the macros, choose the Copy button.

   • To move the macros, first choose the Copy button to copy the selected macros. Next, you need to delete the macros from the original template, as described in the next section.

7. If you want to copy or move additional macros from other templates, repeat Steps 3 through 6.

8. Choose the Close button. Make sure that you choose the Yes button to save your template and macros when you close the documents (or templates) or exit Word.

Deleting and renaming macros

If a macro is stored either globally or in the active template, you can delete it with the Delete button in the Macros dialog box. To delete a macro stored in an unopened template, use the Organizer dialog box. You can also rename a macro using the Organizer dialog box.

Renaming a macro comes in handy when you want to base a new macro on one that comes with Word. Because you are not permitted to edit a Word-supplied macro, you can first copy the macro and then rename it so you can edit the new version.

To delete or rename macros using the Organizer dialog box:

1. Choose the Tools⇨Macro⇨Macros command. The Macros dialog box appears.

2. Choose the Organizer button from the Macros dialog box. The Organizer dialog box appears.

3. In the Macro Project Items available in box (left side), select the template that contains the macro that you want to delete or rename.

   If you want to delete or rename a macro stored in a template that is not open, close this template and open the one you want, as described in the previous section.

4. Do one of the following:

   • To delete a macro, select the macro that you want to delete. To select a series of macros, hold down the Shift key and click the first and last items in the series. To select multiple macros individually, hold down Ctrl and click each item. Choose the Delete button. A confirmation box appears asking you to confirm the deletion (see Figure 27-14). Choose Yes to delete a single macro or multiple macros one at a time. Choose Yes to All to delete multiple macros without a confirmation before each deletion. If you change your mind about deleting one of the macros, choose No.

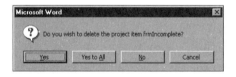

Figure 27-14: The deletion confirmation dialog box.

   • To rename a macro, select the macro. (You can only rename one macro at a time.) Choose the Rename button. The Rename dialog box appears (see Figure 27-15). Type the new name, and choose OK.

Figure 27-15: The Rename dialog box.

5. Choose the Close button to close the Organizer dialog box. All your changes are stored in memory until you save them to disk.

Note You cannot delete a macro that is open in the Visual Basic Editor window. If you delete a macro currently assigned to a toolbar, Word unassigns the macro when it is deleted.

Using Word's Sample Macros

In addition to the macros that comprise the extensive list of Word commands, Word 97 has a set of sample macros that you can examine and run. The sample macros were created by the Microsoft Product Support Services and are stored in the Macros subfolder of the Office folder. The macro files are not installed with the Typical installation, but you can run the Office 97 Setup again and include that option. After they are installed, you can use the Organizer to copy or move some or all of the macro files to the Normal or another document template.

To install the sample macros:

1. Run Office 97 Setup again and choose Add/Remove.

2. Select Microsoft Word and choose Change Option.

3. Select Wizards and Templates, and choose Change Option to open the Wizards and Templates options dialog box (see Figure 27-16).

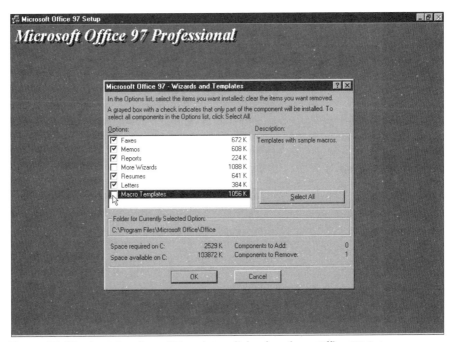

Figure 27-16: The Wizards and Templates dialog box from Office 97 Setup.

4. Choose Macro Templates then choose OK twice and complete the installation with no further changes. The Macros subfolder is installed in the Program Files\Microsoft Office\Office folder.

You can now open the Macros8 template and look at the sample macros. The Support8 template contains two macros relating to changing Windows registry settings and advanced print flags. Table 27-3 lists the macros that are available in the Macros8 and Support8 templates.

Table 27-3 Word 97 Sample Macros	
Macros8.dot	**Function**
ANSIValue	Displays the ANSI value of the selected character(s).
AutoCorrectUtility	Creates a backup copy of the AutoCorrect entries in the current document. You can use the AutoCorrect Backup.doc to copy entries to another computer.
FindSymbol	Allows the searching and replacing of symbol characters.
InsertFootnote	Displays a Wizard that assists in inserting a footnote in the selected publication style.
TableCellHelper	Displays the row and column number of the currently selected table cell.
SuperDocStatistics	Displays information about the formatting and styles used in the document and its sections, such as fonts, styles, sections, hyperlinks, and bookmarks.
NormalViewHeaderFooter	Displays the header and footer panes in Normal view.
CopySpike	Similar to the Spike command, which places multiple items on the Clipboard. CopySpike copies rather than cuts the items to the Clipboard.
Support8.dot	**Function**
RegOptions	Used to change Word settings stored in the Windows registration database.
PrintFlags	Provides modifications for advanced printing functions.

To run the ANSIValue macro in the Macros8 template:

1. Open the Macros8 template, responding <u>E</u>nable Macros when Word displays the Warning box. Figure 27-17 shows the open template with a Sample Macros toolbar.

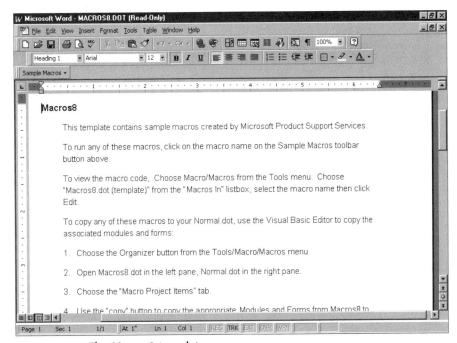

Figure 27-17: The Macros8 template.

2. Select the first word in the template, "This," and then click the Sample Macros toolbar to see the list of sample macros that you can run (see Figure 27-18).

3. Choose the ANSIValue macro. Word runs the macro and returns the ANSI value of the word "This," as shown in Figure 27-19.

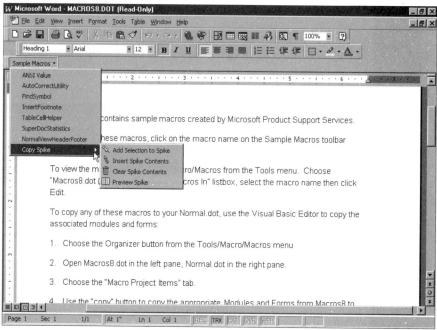

Figure 27-18: The Sample Macros toolbar.

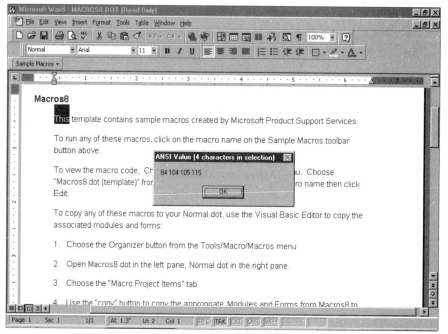

Figure 27-19: The result of running the ANSIValue macro.

To see the commands in the ANSIValue macro:

1. Choose the <u>T</u>ools⮕<u>M</u>acro⮕<u>M</u>acros command. The Macros dialog box appears.

2. Change the M<u>a</u>cros in selection to Macros8.dot and select ANSIValue in the <u>M</u>acro name list.

3. Choose <u>E</u>dit. Figure 27-20 shows the macro commands in the Visual Basic Editor window.

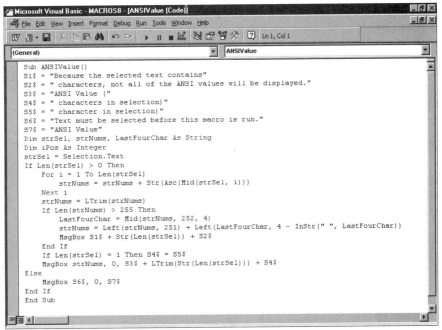

Figure 27-20: The ANSIValue macro in the Visual Basic Editor window.

Note In the next section, you will be introduced to Visual Basic program construction, using this macro as an example.

The two macros in the Support8 template are assigned to field codes in the template. As you can see from Figure 27-21, you are instructed to double-click the macro name to run the macro. Double-clicking the RegOptions macro button displays the Set Registry Options dialog box shown in Figure 27-22. Double-clicking the PrintFlags macro button displays the Set Print Flags dialog box shown in Figure 27-23.

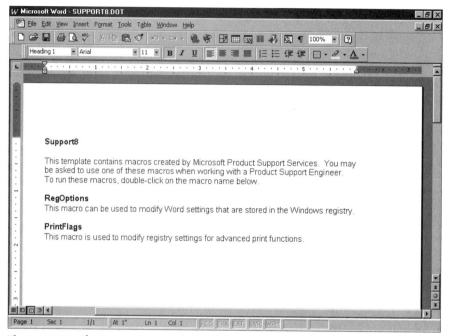

Figure 27-21: The Support8 template.

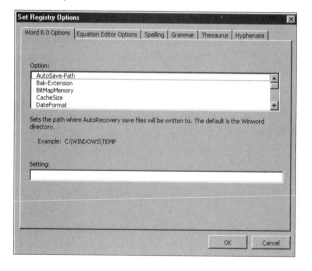

Figure 27-22: The Set Registry Options dialog box displayed by the RegOptions macro.

Figure 27-23: The Set Print Flags dialog box displayed by the PrintFlags macro.

If you toggle the field codes (Alt+F9) in the Support8 template, you can see the MACROBUTTON fields in place of the macro titles (see Figure 27-24).

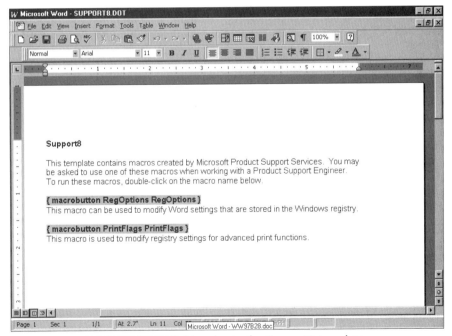

Figure 27-24: MACROBUTTON field codes in the Support8 template.

Introducing Visual Basic

Visual Basic is a sophisticated descendent of the original **B**eginner's **A**ll-Purpose **S**ymbolic **I**nstructional **C**ode (BASIC) that was developed at Dartmouth College in the 1960s and is still taught in schools today. Word 97 uses Visual Basic as the underlying programming language to create commands and macros. Word 6.x and Word 95 used the earlier version, WordBasic.

The main difference between WordBasic and Visual Basic is a matter of dimension. The WordBasic language is built around a two-dimensional flat list of commands while Visual Basic consists of a three-dimensional hierarchy of objects. Each object in turn has access to a specific set of methods (actions) and properties similar to the statements and functions found in WordBasic.

For example, if you want to apply italic formatting to selected text, the WordBasic statement would be

```
Italic 1
```

while the more definitive Visual Basic statement would be

```
Selection.Font.Italic = True
```

The object is the selected text (Selection). Font is a property of the Selection, and Italic is a property of Font. The equal sign sets the property to the value True (on).

Notice that the object, Selection, may have many other properties such as borders, columns, footnotes, comments, and dozens more. Each of these properties in turn has another set of related properties.

Method are actions that can be applied to an object. The Selection object is exposed to nearly 100 methods such as copy, cut, delete, insert, move, paste, and sort.

Using Visual Basic code for common Word tasks

You've already seen an example of using Visual Basic to apply formatting to selected text in the CodeStyle macro. You can also apply formatting to a range object such as the first four paragraphs of the active document. Visual Basic can also change page margins and the line spacing before or after a paragraph.

Other typical uses for Visual Basic macros include:

✦ Finding and replacing text or formatting

✦ Editing and inserting text

✦ Changing the view of the active window

✦ Placing text in headers and footers

✦ Customizing menus and toolbars

✦ Creating tables, inserting text and applying formatting

✦ Creating new documents, opening, saving, and closing documents

✦ Displaying custom dialog boxes for user input

Examining the ANSIValue macro

As described in the previous section, the ANSIValue macro examines the selected characters, converts them to their corresponding ANSI values, and displays the results in a message box. The macro is repeated here for reference:

```
Sub ANSIValue()
S1$ = "Because the selected text contains"
S2$ = " characters, not all of the ANSI values will be
    displayed."
S3$ = "ANSI Value ("
S4$ = " characters in selection)"
S5$ = " character in selection)"
S6$ = "Text must be selected before this macro is run."
S7$ = "ANSI Value"
Dim strSel, strNums, LastFourChar As String
Dim iPos As Integer
strSel = Selection.Text
If Len(strSel) > 0 Then
    For i = 1 To Len(strSel)
        strNums = strNums + Str(Asc(Mid(strSel, i)))
    Next i
    strNums = LTrim(strNums)
    If Len(strNums) > 255 Then
        LastFourChar = Mid(strNums, 252, 4)
        strNums = Left(strNums, 251) + Left(LastFourChar, 4 -
    InStr(" ", LastFourChar))
        MsgBox S1$ + Str(Len(strSel)) + S2$
    End If
    If Len(strSel) = 1 Then S4$ = S5$
    MsgBox strNums, 0, S3$ + LTrim(Str(Len(strSel))) + S4$
Else
    MsgBox S6$, 0, S7$
End If
End Sub
```

The first seven lines (after the title line) specify the text to be displayed in the message box as a set of string variables. Variables are named objects that contain information to be used in the macro. The two lines beginning with Dim declare three variables as string (character) type variables and one as an integer type.

The command `strSel = Selection.Text` sets the value of the strSel variable to the characters in the text you have selected.

The remainder of the macro is an `If...Then...Else` structure that first tests the length of the string to see of any characters at all were selected. If the length of the string is 0 (no characters were selected) the macro branches to the Else alternative, which includes the statement

```
MsgBox S6$, 0, S7$
```

which displays a message box with the text contained in the variables S6$ and S7$ ("ANSI Value" (Text must be selected before this macro is run)") in the title bar. Actually, if you run the macro with no character selected, the macro returns the ANSI value of the character to the right of the insertion point instead of this message.

Next, the macro processes a loop that steps through the selected characters, one by one, converting each to its equivalent ANSI value as it goes. Each number is concatenated to the previous group with the statement

```
strNums = strNums + Str(Asc(Mid(strSel, i)))
```

The next If statement checks to see if the concatenated string of ANSI numbers exceeds the capacity of the message box (255 characters). If so, it constructs a message using the text in variables, S1$ and S2$ to explain that not all of the ANSI values will be displayed.

The last If statement substitutes the singular text of S5$ for the plural text of S4$ if only one character was selected. Finally, the message box is displayed with "ANSI Values (*number of characters selected* characters in selection)" in the title bar and the resulting ANSI values in the box.

Getting Help with Visual Basic

A complete set of online Help topics is available in Word if you have selected the Online Help for Visual Basic option during Setup. To access Visual Basic Help, open the Contents tab of the Word Help dialog box and scroll down to Microsoft Word Visual Basic Reference. Double-click the book icon and select Visual Basic Reference, and then choose <u>D</u>isplay. Figure 27-25 shows the Contents tab of the Visual Basic Help topics dialog box.

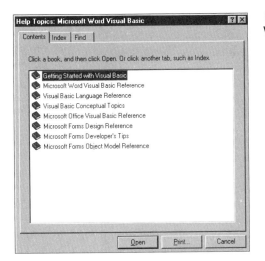

Figure 27-25: The Contents of the Visual Basic Help topics.

Starting a new macro with Visual Basic

You will probably start most of your new macros with a few recorded keystrokes or with an existing macro. However, if you really want to start from scratch:

1. Choose Tools⇨Macro⇨Macros command.

2. Enter the macro name and description.

3. Choose the template or document you want to store the macro in. Then choose Create. The Visual Basic Editor window opens with the beginnings of the new macro (see Figure 27-26), including the name and description you entered.

Once you have completed entering your macro commands, you can use the Editor to help you debug it. You can also print the macro from the Editor window.

Note   The Visual Basic Editor toolbar contains many handy tools for working with macros and troubleshooting problems with macros. Visual Basic is far too complex to delve very far into it in this book. If you are interested in the programming language itself and its uses in application development, the Microsoft Office 97/Visual Basic Programmer's Guide is available in most computer book stores. You can also order a copy directly from Microsoft by calling 1-800-677-7377 or via CompuServe GO MSP.

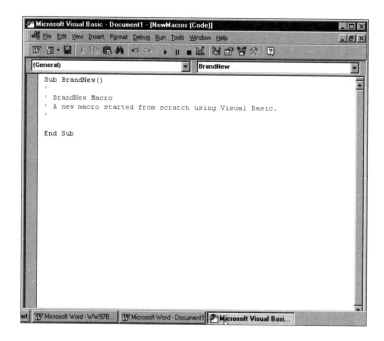

Figure 27-26: Starting a new macro with Visual Basic.

Summary

In this chapter, you learned to master macros for getting more of what you need from Word. You were also introduced to the powerful Visual Basic programming language that is the basis for all Word commands. You learned how to:

✦ Record a macro by choosing Tools⇨Macro⇨Record New Macro, or by double-clicking REC in the Status bar.

✦ Run a macro by using the Run button in the Macros dialog box.

✦ Copy and move macros among templates by using the Organizer dialog box.

✦ Use the sample macros that come with Word, which can be installed in the Macros subfolder in the Microsoft Office\Office folder.

Where to go next...

✦ If you want to continue your exploration of Word's powerful customizing features, check out Chapter 25.

✦ To find out more about using field codes in your document, see Chapter 26.

✦ To learn more about what you can do with templates, see Chapter 10.

✦   ✦   ✦

Appendixes

What's New in Word 97

Whereas Word 95 Introduced a "document-centered" approach to the program, Word 97 strives to provide more interconnectivity—between you and the world by linking Word documents to the World Wide Web, and between you and other office-mates by allowing many people to edit the same document without confusion. In the world of Word 97, your "office-mates" could be in the next cubicle or the next continent. There are lots of online features here, such as the ability for several people in different parts of the world to have access to the same document and post their changes, merging everybody's various versions into one seamless document.

When working with the Office 97 version of Word 97, it's hard to tell where Word leaves off and other applications begin. You are encouraged to use tools such as the new Microsoft Outlook, which incorporates e-mail, intra-office messaging, scheduling, and task management on one clever screen (see Figure A-1).You cannot help but share the same clip art collection with other Microsoft products such as Microsoft Publisher, if they reside on your computer. And the same Office Assistant pops up on any Office 97 application, ready to provide intelligent responses to questions such as, "What do I do next?"

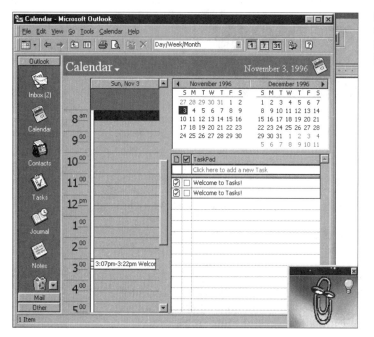

Figure A-1: The Microsoft Outlook screen, available from the desktop after installing Office 97.

You'll find that Word 97 is more than willing to tell you what to do next. The Wizards, templates, and Help system are more complete and thorough than earlier versions. You'll find yourself getting acquainted with Word 97's newer features in the few minutes it takes to click on and search for a topic.

Word 97 is installed in a new place. Although the default directory for many Word 97 files is `C:\Program Files\Microsoft Office`, there is no single tidy location that holds everything about Word. Some files will be stored in `C:\Program Files\Shared Applications`, and your documents will be stored by default in `C:\My Documents`. Word 97 files involving the World Wide Web, Microsoft Mail, and e-mail will be stored in the same directory as all other Microsoft Web-related programs.

Because Office 97 and Word 97 are geared towards integration with the Internet and the World Wide Web, Word's links to sites for upgrading your Internet software are very important. Improved Web tools and browser upgrades appear regularly; Microsoft does not intend for you to wait until a full new version of Word appears for you to get those improvements. Word 97's Help menu contains links to many important Web sites.

How to explore the new Word 97 features

You can get a good look at Word 97's new features at any time by typing **What's new in Word 97?** in the Office Assistant dialog box, as shown in Figure A-2. This way, you won't be shown an exhaustive laundry list of everything on the Office 97 CD, but you can limit your exploration to Word features alone.

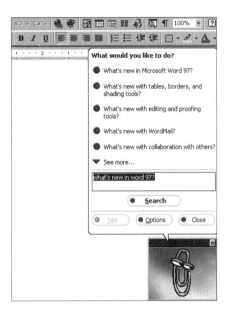

Figure A-2: Typing an inquiry about new Word 97 features in the Office Assistant dialog box brings helpful results.

If you have more time to spare, put the Office 97 CD in your CD-ROM drive and click the ValuPack Folder. Happily, you don't have to open each subfolder and read all the ReadMe files to find out what's worthwhile here. Figure A-3 shows two icons that provide a helpful tour of the new features. Double-click the `Valupkh8.hlp` icon to see the screen shown in Figure A-3, and scroll through to find the new features that interest you. There are many, *many* templates, patches, free demos, and tools of all sorts that are available in this ValuPack folder. Also, pains were taken to provide good instructions and explanations as well. (A full version of Microsoft Publisher is included on the CD. You can try it for 60 days.)

Viewing the ValuPack Demo

`Overview.PPS`, the other icon shown in Figure A-3, starts a PowerPoint Demo that guides you through a more pictorial explanation of the ValuPack features. Pictured in Figure A-4 is the opening screen of the Demo. Figure A-5 shows that at the end of each description is either an icon to set up the feature, or a reference to its location on the ValuPack CD.

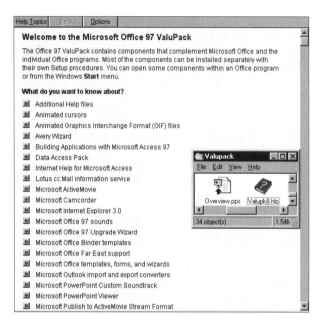

Figure A-3: Clicking the *Valupkh8.hlp* icon opens this branching Help file.

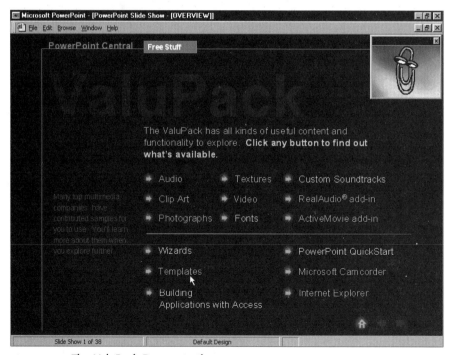

Figure A-4: The ValuPack Demo starting screen.

Figure A-5: At the end of each description, a reference to its location on the CD appears.

Installing new features from the ValuPack

As you explore the ValuPack description files, instructions are given as to how to install each feature. If you explore the ValuPack subfolders on your own, you'll notice each feature has a Setup icon that begins a painless installation.

One ValuPack directory that is certainly worth a visit is the Software Patch folder. It includes patches to solve incompatibility issues with older software and provide "fix-its" that might improve Word 97's performance on your computer. One issue of special importance to Microsoft Plus users is that the JPEG scheme used by Microsoft Plus's Theme Pack is not compatible with Word 97. The ValuPack's Software Patch folder contains a fix for that problem.

New features of Word 97

This section provides a quick overview of Word 97's newest features. These are all covered generously throughout the book as the subject arises.

The Office Assistant

The Office Assistant replaces Office 95's Answer Wizard and uses an advanced technology that recognizes natural language patterns, not just keyword location. Go ahead and type in a question phrased similarly to your normal speech pattern. You'll be amazed at the specific answers you get. By default, the Office Assistant is on your screen at all times. It is your gateway to all Word 97 Help resources. Although you can customize Office Assistance appearances and animations, each Office Assistant answers questions the same way. Figure A-6 shows a typical pattern of interactivity with the Office Assistant. After opening the Tables and Borders dialog box, I made a simple rectangle, and Office Assistant appeared with a light bulb over its head. (Get used to it.) Clicking the light bulb revealed a comment that I could turn the rectangle into a fully formatted table with a couple of mouse clicks.

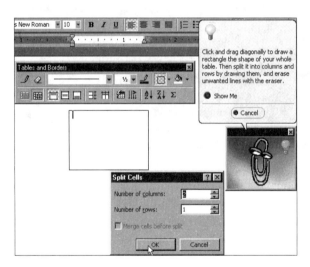

Figure A-6: Opening the Tables and Borders dialog box and creating a rectangle prompts a suggestion from Office Assistant.

Internet, intranet, and WWW features

Just as Word 95 tried to get you to think in terms of working with a document rather than a program, Word 97 again tries to get us to think differently about our computers. You'll find references to Web sites built into many of Word 97's features. When you compose your document on Word 97, think of having all the resources of the World Wide Web at your disposal, rather than just those found on your computer. Help files, access to new features as soon as they become available, and the ability to build hyperlinks right into your document are just some of the new features Word 97 offers.

Web Page Wizards

Word 97 provides Web Page Wizards that provide ready-made Web pages that you can simply type your own content into. These include areas for you to type hyperlinks and graphics already set aside as image maps for buttons, watermarks, sounds, and other visuals. Web Page Wizards of several styles are provided, such as for home pages or soliciting business.

Web page authoring tools

Even without the Wizards, Word 97 provides plenty of Web page authoring tools. These employ "What-You-See-Is-What-You-Get" technology, so that you can place sound icons, videos, text, and pictures on your screen, while Word 97 handles the HTML coding in the background. Over 80 HTML tags are supported.

Automatic hyperlink formatting

If you type **http://www.winsock.com/**, for example, in your Word 97 document, it will automatically create a hyperlink to that location (providing it exists!) through Microsoft Outlook and Exchange.

Automatic hyperlink creation

You can create a link that instantly takes you to any place in your current document, any Office 97 document on your computer, or any online hyperlink location. This feature nicely supplements the new Document Mapping tool, which provides an instant heading-based outline for instant scanning of your document structure and switching between locations.

Document collaboration

With Word 97, many people can edit your document, and you can keep track of who did what and when. You can easily restore your document to an earlier version without having to maintain multiple copies of this document each time someone makes a change. While reviewing a document online, multiple reviewers can post "sticky-notes" on your work without their comments becoming part of the original text. Each reviewer can be assigned a different color to help you identify his comments.

Microsoft Outlook

The introduction of Microsoft Outlook virtually combines Schedule Plus, Word Mail, and Microsoft Exchange into one seamless application. The Inbox, Outbox, e-mail composition and delivery, and address lists are now found in Outlook, which initially installs itself as an icon on your desktop. A two-month calendar, task list, and day-by-day scheduler are all in view as you deal with your e-mail and all communication-related tasks on your computer. Chapter 15 covers linking information with other applications, and Chapter 19 covers working with workgroups.

Office 97 online update access

Office 97 provides tools to obtain new templates, clip art, patches, add-ons, and Web authoring tools through online locations available on the Word 97 Help menu. The Active Web feature, available from the ValuPack CD, enriches your online access by providing the latest browsing tools and online documents. World Wide Web and HTML concepts are covered thoroughly in chapters 17 and 18.

Online Document View

Located right next to the familiar Outline View and Normal View icons on your Word 97 document, you'll see an Online Document View icon, which changes your view of your document to how it would look if it were viewed as a Web page. Editing and navigating documents are covered in Chapter 2 of this book.

Office 97 drawing tools

Office 97 provides a rich collection of 3-D shape creation tools, AutoShapes, shadow effects, textures, and semi-transparent fills. Word 97 includes a toolbar just for drawing tools. Word 97 includes a Send Behind Text option that provides unique layering possibilities for your documents. You'll learn about Word 97 and graphics in Chapters 13 and 14.

Office Art

Office Art provides powerful artistic tools to all Office 97 programs. Any Auto-Shapes you create or edit, or clip art you create and save will be available to all Office 97 applications.

Linked text boxes

Ideal for creating newsletters and brochures, you can now create text boxes of any width or height that flow from page to page, much like a Desktop Publishing program. These include text overflow features that automatically send extra text to the next linked box. Chapter 9 covers text boxes and discusses sections, columns, and page formatting.

Text wrapping around irregular objects

Rather than wrapping text around the rectangular shape surrounding a picture, you can now wrap your text so very little room is left between the text and the picture. The effect is less boxy and more interesting to look at. See Chapter 14 for more on this topic.

Table and border tools

Microsoft has conveniently placed table and border tools onto one toolbar. Having this toolbar handy allows quick access to creating custom border and tables at any point in your document.

Table creation tools

The new Tables and Borders toolbar lets you create custom tables simply by dragging them onto the page as you would any drawing tool. Adjusting the width and height of a cell is done with a single mouse click. You can now merge cells simply by deleting the partition between them, rather than hunting for a Merged Cells command. Tables are covered in Chapter 12.

Border tools

You have access to over 150 border styles to apply to any document. It's now easy to put a border on a single side of each page, or around single words or paragraphs. There are new tools for text shading and creating graduated blends across portions of your page. Callout boxes are easier than ever to create. See Chapter 14 for more on this.

Editing and proofing tools

Word 97 checks grammar as you type. It provides tips to improve your writing skills, tighten up grammar and sentence structure, verb agreement, and so on. Word 97 also has improved spelling and Find capabilities. It recognizes many proper nouns, figures of American speech, and company names. It also knows to ignore Internet URLs and file addresses like C:\DOS. The Find and Replace feature will now change multiple forms of the word you're searching for. If you want to replace "talk" with "speak" throughout your document, Word 97 will also replace "talking" with "speaking." Chapter 4 covers proofing documents.

Automating tasks

See Chapter 11 for a complete discussion on styles and AutoFormat, Chapter 4 for proofing documents, and Chapter 3 for finding and replacing text and formatting.

AutoComplete

If you type **thur** and press Enter, Word 97 automatically finishes the word Thursday. Similarly, typing the first couple letters in your name prompts Word 97 to finish it. This feature extends to months, the current date, and your own AutoText entries.

AutoSummarize

Word 97 automatically summarizes the main points of your document based on complex linguistic analysis. It doesn't merely regurgitate the first sentence of each paragraph. The AutoSummarize feature can create a single paragraph or multipage summary, depending on what you specify.

Advanced Letter Wizard

Combined with the Office Assistant, Word 97's Letter Wizard removes most of the mundane aspects of letter writing. Addressing, return addressing, headings, and letter formatting are all automated. Chapter 10 covers Wizards and templates.

Other new Office 97 tools worth noting

Some new Office 97 features resist categorization. You'll find them on your Office 97 CD, and they fully compliment Word 97. Here is a handful of highlights.

Microsoft Word 97 converter

This tool allows you to open Word 97 documents in many other versions of Word, including Macintosh and Windows NT. Like many "extra" features, it is found on the ValuPack CD. Learn more about working with workgroups and Word 97 in Chapter 19.

Microsoft Word Viewer

This is a great tool! You can send your Word document to anyone that has a Windows 95 computer and he can read and print your document, even if he doesn't have Word. Distribute the Microsoft Word Viewer to anyone with Windows 95 on his computer, and he can open your Word documents.

Avery Wizard

Avery, "the label company," has provided this add-in to make it easier to work with all Avery's products. Mail merging goes smoother, and text on the labels always ends up in the right place, rather than half the sheet looking off-centered. Avery Wizard is found on the ValuPack CD. Printing your documents is covered in Chapter 5. Creating labels and envelopes is covered in Chapter 20.

ClipArt Editing Features

Word 97 has provided new tools for locating, recoloring and reshaping clip art. With a little editing, you can add a piece of clip art to your document that looks more like an original work.

Microsoft Publisher trial version

Included on the ValuPack CD is a full version of Microsoft's excellent Desktop Publishing program, Publisher. The '97 version of Publisher has been revamped as thoroughly as Word has, and the program is definitely worth a look. The trial lasts for two months after you install it. At that point, it will refuse to turn on unless you register it.

✦   ✦   ✦

Installing Word 97

How you install Word for Windows 97 varies according to whether you bought it separately or as part of Microsoft Office for Windows 97. This appendix explains how to install Word 97 in the context of installing Microsoft Office 97. In this appendix, you learn what hardware is required to run Word and how to install the program with different features and settings. These instructions center on installing Office 97 from a CD-ROM, but you can use the instructions for floppy disk installations. The only difference is the drive, switching of floppy disks, and the number of extras and add-ons. This appendix also explains how to install and remove Word 97 components after you have installed the program. Finally, you learn how to remove and reinstall Word 97.

Requirements for Office 97

Word and Office 97 run only with Windows 95 or Windows NT 3.51 or higher. The following are requirements for running Word 97 For Windows optimally:

- ✦ A PC running Windows 95, preferably using a Pentium system.

- ✦ At least 8MB of memory.

- ✦ A Super VGA or higher graphics card compatible with Windows 95. High-resolution monitors can take better advantage of Word's features.

- ✦ Minimum disk space for installation is discussed later in this appendix. To run Word 97 well, you need at the very least twice as much free disk space as required for installation.

✦ A double- or quad-speed CD-ROM drive or higher.

✦ A mouse or other pointing device.

✦ A printer supported by Windows 95, preferably a laser printer.

Note

You cannot run Office 97 on Windows 3.1 or Windows for Workgroups.

Installing Word 97 for Windows

Before you begin setting up Word, decide where you want to install it. The default folder is C:\Program Files\Microsoft Office. There really isn't a single folder where you can find all files related to Word 97. Your documents will be stored in a folder called My Documents (unless you designate otherwise), and most of the files required to run Office 97 are stored in common folders with other Word 97 components.

During the installation process, you can use the mouse to make selections. If you use the keyboard, press Tab to move to options or buttons. After moving to a check box or button with the Tab key, press the spacebar to make the selection. Pressing Enter is the same as clicking OK, and pressing Esc is the same as clicking Cancel.

Depending on your configuration options, the complete installation of Office 97 takes between 60MB and 191MB.

The following steps explain how to install Microsoft Office 97 for Windows and specifically Word 97:

1. Make sure that no applications are running on your system.

2. Insert the Microsoft Office 97 CD-ROM in your CD-ROM drive.

3. The Microsoft Office 97 opening screen appears. (See Figure B-1.)

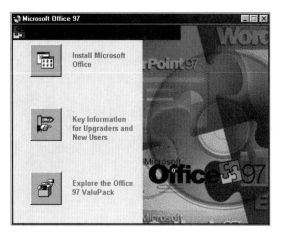

Figure B-1: The Microsoft Office 97 opening screen.

4. Click the Install Microsoft Office icon to proceed immediately, or select one of the other two icons to gain more information before installing. You'll learn about the other two icons later. Clicking the Install Microsoft Office icon causes the Microsoft Office 97 Setup dialog box to appear.

5. If you have disabled AutoRun on your computer, steps for installing are as follows:

   • Insert the Microsoft Office 97 CD in your CD-ROM drive.

   • Double-click the My Computer icon.

   • Double-click the CD drive icon.

   • Double-click the Setup.exe icon. The Microsoft Office 97 Setup dialog box appears.

6. Click the Continue button to continue with the installation. The Name and Organization Information dialog box appears, as shown in Figure B-2.

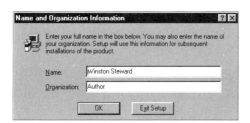

Figure B-2: The Name and Organization Information dialog box.

7. Enter your name and any organization name you want, and then click OK. Setup prompts you for a confirmation. If your entries are correct, click OK. If you want to make a change, select the text you want to replace and type over it. After making your changes, choose OK.

Caution If an older version of Office is detected on your computer, Setup will ask permission to remove some of the older files. Do not say yes to this if you plan to use any older Office programs.

8. You will be asked to provide your 10-digit CD Key. This code number can be found on a sticker on your CD jewel case. If it is lost, you'll have a hard time getting a replacement.

9. A dialog box appears with your Product ID (see Figure B-3), which you use for your product registration and technical support identification. After installation, if you ever want to view this number, use the Help⇨About Microsoft Word command. Click OK.

10. The program then searches your computer for older Microsoft Office components, and checks for necessary disk space. This could take a few minutes. Avoid the temptation to reset your computer. It is not likely that anything has gone wrong; be patient.

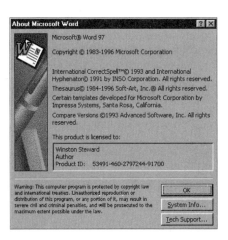

Figure B-3: The Product ID. This number is needed for registration and technical assistance.

11. After a few moments, the Microsoft Office 97 Setup dialog box shown in Figure B-4 appears. It specifies the destination folder for your Office 97 files. The default folder is C:\Program Files\Microsoft Office.

Figure B-4: The Microsoft Office 97 Setup dialog box.

12. If you want to change the folder, choose Change Folder. The Change Folder dialog box appears, as shown in Figure B-5. Choose your folder and choose OK to return to the Setup dialog box. Choose OK to continue. Here are three points regarding changing directories:

   • If you have more than one hard drive on your computer, install Office 97 on the drive that is fastest and has the most free space. For Office 97 to run comfortably, your computer ought to have three times as much free space as is required by installation alone.

- Just because you choose to install Office 97 on some other drive besides C:\, many Microsoft "Shared Components" are going to end up installed inside your Windows folder anyway. So if your Windows 95 files are installed on your C:\ drive, you can expect as much as 50MB of new data to be installed on C:\, no matter which drive you decide to install Office 97 on.

- If you choose to install Office 97 in a new folder, You will be prompted with: "This folder does not exist. Do you want us to create it?" If you select No, Office files are installed in your root folder, so be sure to select Yes.

Figure B-5: The Change Folder dialog box.

13. Setup may again search your system for installed components, and, after a few moments, the installation type dialog box for Setup appears, as shown in Figure B-6.

Figure B-6: The installation type dialog box.

How do I know what to install?

The Setup dialog box offers three types of installations for Office 97:

✦ Typical, which installs all the Office applications and most of their components

✦ Custom, which displays lists of applications and components from which to choose

✦ Run from CD-ROM, which runs Office from your CD and copies only the shared components to your hard disk.

The choice you make depends on (1) how you plan to use Office and Word and (2) the amount of free disk space. You can always run the setup program later and add or remove components.

Choosing Custom installation rather than Typical requires careful thought. Here are some issues to consider:

1. You can choose Typical installation and find that some components you require were not installed. (Figure B-7 shows which Word components will be installed with Typical installation.) Happily, Office 97 makes it quite painless to go back and reinstall new components. If, however, you choose Custom installation now, you might find yourself having to choose amongst lists of dozens of options, and not having much information to base your decision on. To learn a bit about Word 97 and Office 97 components *before* you install them, you can click either of the bottom two icons on the Microsoft Office 97 AutoRun screen (refer to Figure B-1). that appears when you first put the CD in your computer:

   • Selecting Key Information for Upgraders and New Users brings up the Help menu pictured in Figure B-8. Exploring this menu helps you make an informed decision about what Office 97 features you want available to you. If AutoRun is disabled, open the Office 97 CD and click ofnew8.hlp.

   • Selecting Explore the Office 97 ValuPack (see Figure B-9) gives you a detailed explanation of a feature before you install it. If AutoRun is disabled, open the ValuPack folder and click the valupk8.hlp icon.

2. Once you click the Custom button from the Microsoft Office 97 Setup screen (refer to Figure B-6), you are asked to choose which Office 97 programs to install, for example Word or Excel, and then choose which features of those programs you want on your computer.

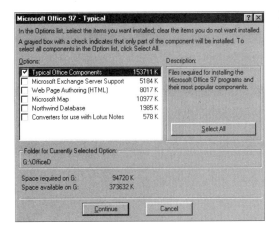

Figure B-7: Components installed with Typical installation selected.

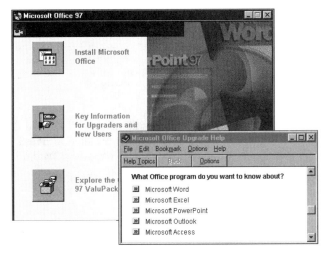

Figure B-8: The Microsoft Office Upgrade Help menu.

3. Having selected Custom installation, choose Microsoft Word in the Options list, and click the Change Option button. The Microsoft Word 97 Installation dialog box appears, as shown in Figure B-10. The default options, which are for the typical installation option, appear checked in the Options list. Options without a check mark aren't installed. If an item listed in the Options list has suboptions, the Change Option button becomes active when you click the item. If no suboptions exist, the button is dimmed.

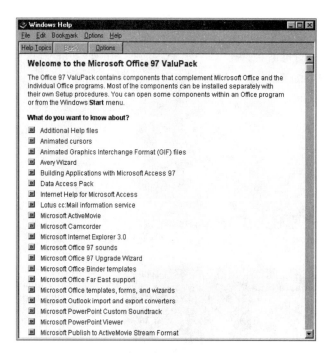

Figure B-9:
The ValuPack
exploration menu.

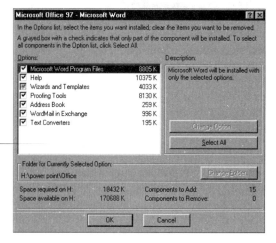

Figure B-10: The Options
available for Word 97 after
choosing Custom installation.

Do one of the following:

• To select all the options for Word 97, choose the Select All button. Setup
  returns you to the Custom dialog box.

- To select specific Word 97 options beyond the default Options, click the item and choose the Change Option button. For example, click the Wizards and Templates item, and choose the Change Option button. The Wizards and Templates dialog box appears, as shown in Figure B-11. Click the check boxes for the item or items you want, and then choose OK twice.

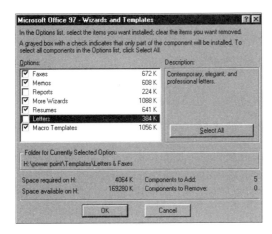

Figure B-11: The Wizards and Templates dialog box from the Word 97 suboptions menu.

4. Setup returns you to the Custom dialog box. Select Office Tools from the Options list dialog box in the Custom dialog box, and then choose the Change Option button.

5. Select the Equation Editor and Clip Gallery items in the Options list. A check mark appears in the appropriate check box. Click OK.

6. Click Continue. Setup installs Office 97 on your system. After Office 97 is installed, Setup displays a message box stating it is done. Click OK.

You may be asked if you want to delete components of earlier versions of Office or Word. If you have no more use for them, choose Yes to remove them all. You will use less disk space by removing unnecessary versions.

Aborting Office 97 installation after you've started

Installing Office 97 on some computers will be worth a good couple of trips to the coffee machine before the process is truly finished. If you find you must press the Cancel button to abort installation, your files will be restored as they were originally. But canceling installation takes a long time. Windows must restore files saved in a backup area to their original locations. You may find that canceling installation takes longer than allowing installation to progress.

Adding and Removing Word Components

After you install Word 97, you can run the Office Setup program again at any time to add or remove components of the Word 97 itself or any other Office 97 program.

Note You can use the Office Shortcut Bar or Add/Remove Programs in the Control Panel to affect the entire Office 97 suite. To make changes for Word 97 specifically, you must use the Office 97 Setup icon in your Microsoft Office folder.

To install or remove Word components:

1. Click the box in the upper-left corner of the Office 97 Shortcut bar, the Control Menu icon, and choose Add/Remove Office Programs.

2. If the Office Shortcut bar is not visible, choose Settings from the Start menu and then choose Control Panel.

3. Double-click the Add/Remove Programs icon and then select Microsoft Office 97 from the options list in the Install/Uninstall tab of the Add/Remove Programs Properties dialog box. Click Add/Remove. You will be asked to insert the Office 97 CD into your drive.

4. Choose OK. The Microsoft Office 97 Setup dialog box appears with a choice of four changes in the installation, as shown in Figure B-12.

Figure B-12: The Microsoft Office 97 Setup dialog box.

5. Choose Add/Remove. The Microsoft Office 97 Maintenance dialog box appears with a list of all the Office 97 options.

6. Select the Word item in the Options list, and then click the Change Option button. The Microsoft Word dialog box appears.

7. Select the check boxes for additional components that you want to install. If you want to remove a component, click to clear the check box. If you don't want to remove an entire group that is already installed, leave its check box selected. Setup will not reinstall selected groups of items.

8. To add or remove specific items of an option group, select the component in the Options list and click the Change Option button. Repeat Step 7 for the specific components you want to add or remove, and click the OK button twice.

9. Click the Continue button in the Maintenance dialog box. Setup displays a confirmation dialog box informing you of the number of selected components to remove.

10. Click Yes to add or remove the selected components. Setup installs the selected components or removes the cleared components (check boxes without an X). A dialog box appears informing you that the Setup program was successful.

11. Click the OK button to close the Setup dialog box. Then choose OK to return to the desktop.

Note   If you are going to share your Word documents with other Word users, they must be using Word 97 as well. If they don't have Word 97, make sure you save your Word documents in a file format the other users can read.

Removing and Reinstalling Word 97

The Setup program also includes options to remove the entire Word 97 program. If you have installed Word and find that it's not running correctly, you can run the Setup program to remove Word and then run Setup again to reinstall it. Reinstalling Word 97 without uninstalling it first will probably not fix the problem you've been having. Generally speaking, in order to have a successful reinstall, the older files must be removed first. The Remove All button in the Setup dialog box (refer to Figure B-12) removes the entire Office 97 program. To specifically remove Word 97, do the following steps:

1. Click the box in the upper-left corner of the Office 97 Shortcut bar, the Control Menu icon, and choose Add/Remove Office Programs.

2. If the Office Shortcut bar is not visible, choose Settings from the Start menu and then choose Control Panel.

3. Double-click the Add/Remove Programs icon and then select Microsoft Office 97 from the options list in the Install/Uninstall tab of the Add/Remove Programs Properties dialog box. Click Add/Remove. You will be asked to insert the Office 97 CD into your drive.

4. Choose OK. The Microsoft Office 97 Setup dialog box appears with a choice of four changes in the installation, as shown in Figure B-12.

5. Choose Add/Remove. The Microsoft Office 97 Maintenance dialog box appears with a list of all the Office 97 options.

6. Choose the Word 97 item in the Options list to remove the check mark from the check box.

7. Click continue. A message appears asking you to confirm the removal of the Office 97 components.

8. Click Yes. Setup removes Word 97. A dialog box appears telling you the operation was completed. Click OK twice.

Your Word documents are not affected by removing the Word 97 program.

To reinstall Word 97, open the Maintenance dialog box as before and follow these steps:

1. Choose the Word 97 item in the Options list to add the check mark from the check box. The settings for the last installation of Word 97 are used. If you want to change any of the settings, do so before choosing Continue.

2. Click Continue. The Word 97 program is installed. A dialog box appears telling you the operation was completed; click OK twice.

Summary

Congratulations! You've installed Office 97 and Word 97. You've learned how to add and remove components at will by using the Office 97 Setup program.

Where to go next...

✦ To get started with Word 97, go to Chapter 1.

✦ To learn more about what's new in Word 97, check out Appendix A.

✦   ✦   ✦

A Word 97 HTML Reference

The following is a reference to common HTML tags that Word 97 supports. You can insert any of the HTML tags manually to create or edit a Web page. We have pointed out the Microsoft Internet Explorer extensions so that you can omit these tags if you want to create a page for other browsers. If you add tags that are Microsoft Internet Explorer extensions, only people using Internet Explorer will be able to see the effect. If a browser doesn't support the tag, it will disregard the tag and only display the text that follows the tag.

This reference lists HTML tags in the order they appear as options on the formatting toolbar and Word menus. You can find additional information about Web publishing and HTML tags at Microsoft's Web site http://www.microsoft.com/ or at http://www.authors.com.

Word Formatting and HTML tags

When you create and save a Word document as an HTML document, the next time you load the document, Word displays the options available for editing an HTML document. Word displays the Web page similar to the way it will appear in a Web browser. An HTML document is pure ASCII text. Word saves a document in the HTML format; any Word formatting that doesn't have equivalent HTML tags are removed from the file. This reference identifies the elements that Word inserts or changes and removes when saving an HTML document or converting a document from Word to HTML.

Understanding HTML tags

HTML tags consist of a tag name and can include tag attributes. Tags appear within open and closing angle brackets (<>). Most tags have beginning and closing tags. The end tag is the same as the opening tag, except that it includes a forward slash before the tag name. Not all tags have opening and closing tags. Tags for inserting horizontal lines and images for example don't have closing tags. To format text in bold, the text to format in boldface is surrounded by an opening <B> tag and a closing </B> tag, as shown in the following example:

```
<B>This text will appear in boldface</B>
```

If you are adding an attribute to a tag, it is added to the opening tag. For example, to center a paragraph, you can add the ALIGN=CENTER attribute to the <P> tag. The paragraph with the align attribute would appear as follows:

```
<P ALIGN="CENTER'>This is a centered paragraph</P>
```

HTML tags are not case sensitive, so you can use either uppercase or lowercase letters or both. To help you easily identify the tags and attributes, this reference shows all HTML tags and attributes in uppercase. The attribute settings that you can replace with your own values appear in lowercase.

When more than one type of attribute setting is available, we have included the settings separated by a | character. For example, the ALIGN="LEFT | CENTER | RIGHT" attribute entry for the paragraph tag, <P>, indicates that you can use either "LEFT," "CENTER" or "RIGHT" to set the alignment of a paragraph.

Basic HTML tags added by Word

When you create a Web page with the Blank Web Page template or the Web Page Wizard, Word automatically adds the basic tags used to create an HTML document. An HTML document is broken into two sections: head and body, as shown in the listing that follows. The sections that follow the listing explain each of the tags Word adds to create an HTML document.

```
<HTML>
<HEAD>
<META HTTP-EQUIV="Content-Type" CONTENT="text/html;
      charset=windows-1252">
<META NAME="Generator" CONTENT="Microsoft Word 97">
<TITLE>Test</TITLE>
<META NAME="Version" CONTENT="8.0.3410">
<META NAME="Date" CONTENT="10/11/96">
<META NAME="Template" CONTENT="D:\Microsoft Office
      97\Office\HTML.DOT">
</HEAD>
<BODY TEXT="#000000" BGCOLOR="#ffffff">
```

```
<P> </P></BODY>
</HTML>

<HTML> . . . </HTML>
```

HTML documents always begin with the <HTML> tag and end with a closing </HTML> tag. Notice that the closing tag has a forward slash after the left angle bracket.

<!DOCTYPE>

The !DOCTYPE tag indicates the version of HTML used. The latest version of HTML is 3.2.

<HEAD>

The <HEAD> . . . </HEAD> tags mark the heading portion of a document to help keep document data separate from the BODY elements.

<TITLE>

The <TITLE> . . . </TITLE> tags identify the purpose of the page. The title appears in the window bar used to identify the contents of the window. You can change the title by choosing File⇨Properties and entering the title in the Title text box in the Document Properties dialog box.

<META>

The <META> tags supply meta information about the document as name/value pairs. By default Word includes information about the version of Word, the date, and the template used to create the page.

The <META> tag attributes are as follows:

```
HTTP-EQUIV="string"
```

This attribute specifies the HTTP (Hypertext transfer protocol) equivalent name for the meta information and causes the Web server, also known as an HTTP server, to include the name and type content in the HTTP header for the document when the document is sent to the browser. For example, Word informs the browser that the document is an HTML document and that it uses the Windows character set.

```
CONTENT="string"
```

This attribute specifies the value for meta-information about a document.

```
NAME="string"
```

You use this attribute to specify the name of the meta-information.

\<BODY\>

\<BODY\> tag attributes are as follows:

```
BGCOLOR="color | #rrggbb"
```

This attribute specifies the background color of the document. The color is added as the hexadecimal equivalent (for example, "#C0FFC0") of the color you chose from the palette (Format⇨Background). It is possible to edit the color with one of the following standard 16 colors supported with the Windows VGA palette: aqua, black, blue, fuchsia, gray, green, lime, maroon, navy, olive, purple, red, silver, teal, white, and yellow.

```
BACKGROUND="URL | file"
```

This BACKGROUND attribute sets the URL or image file used to create a tile background. You can specify the file to which the BACKGROUND attribute is set by choosing the Format⇨Background⇨Fill Effects⇨Other Texture.

There isn't an HTML equivalent for a page border. If you want, you can place borders around a table and use horizontal lines to help emphasize or separate parts of your Web page.

```
TEXT="color | #rrggbb"
```

specifies the color of the text in the document. The color is added as the hexa-decimal equivalent ("#C0FFC0", for example) of the color you chose from the palette (Format/⇨Font). It is possible to edit the color with the name of one of the standard 16 colors supported with the Windows VGA palette: aqua, black, blue, fuchsia, gray, green, lime, maroon, navy, olive, purple, red, silver, teal, white, and yellow.

```
ALINK="color | #rrggbb"
```

This attribute sets the color of the active link.

```
LINK="color | #rrggbb"
```

This attribute sets the color of the links. For more information on the LINK attribute, see the Hyperlink entry in the "Styles" section of this Appendix.

```
VLINK="color | #rrggbb"
```

The VLINK attribute sets the color of visited links. For more information on the VLINK attribute, see the Hyperlink entry in the "Styles" section of this Appendix.

Paragraphs and line breaks

To designate paragraphs in HTML, you use the paragraph tags:

```
<P> . . . </P>
```

Word automatically adds paragraph tags containing a non-breaking space
<P> </P>. Word replaces the non-breaking space ( ) when you begin
entering text. Pressing Enter adds opening and closing paragraph tags. Paragraph
alignment attributes are covered later in this Appendix.

To designate a line break, you use the line break tag:

```
<BR>
```

You can insert a line break tag by pressing Ctrl+Enter.

Styles

Just as you apply styles in Word using the Styles list box, you can format text to
be converted to HTML tags using the Styles list box. If you modify a Word built-
in style, such as Heading 1, the formatting associated with the style will be
exported to a corresponding HTML tag—provided that the formatting is
supported in HTML.

User-defined styles are also converted to direct formatting, provided that the
formatting is supported in HTML. For example, if you convert a style that includes
bold and shadow formatting, the bold formatting is retained as a direct formatting,
but the shadow formatting is lost.

Logical and physical formatting

There are two types of HTML formatting: *logical tags* and *physical tags*. Logical tags are more desirable for use than physical tags. If you specify a physical tag, the formatting option must be available for the format to be applied. Logical formatting, however, lets the person use other formatting to identify the formatted text. For example if the person is using a text-based browser that doesn't include bold or italics, the person can specify that the text be formatted to appear emphasized using inverse video. Using the logical tag <EM> for emphasis instead of the physical italics tag <I> enables the person to see the text in reverse video.

Headings (Heading 1)

Word includes headings styles that you should not confuse with HTML headings. To create headings that use true HTML heading tags, instead use the H1 through H6 styles. When you use a Heading 1 style, you may think that Word is going to use H1 tags, but Word uses BOLD and FONT tags instead, as the following examples show.

Heading 1

```
<B><FONT FACE="Arial" SIZE=4><P>Heading One</P></B></FONT>
```

Heading 2

```
<B><I><FONT FACE="Arial"><P>Heading Two</P></B></I></FONT>
```

Heading 3

```
<FONT FACE="Arial"><P>Heading Three</P></FONT>
```

Normal

The Normal style sets the paragraph to the settings specified by the normal text formatting style.

Address

To present address information, such as a street address or an e-mail address, use the address tag pair:

```
<ADDRESS> . . . </ADDRESS>
```

Blockquote

To format a block of quoted text, you use the blockquote tags:

```
<BLOCKQUOTE> . . . </BLOCKQUOTE>
```

Citation

To display the text as a citation, use the cite tags:

```
<CITE> . . . </CITE>
```

Code

The code tag pair displays text as a programming code sample. Code text typically displays in the browser in a monospaced font, such as Courier:

```
<CODE> . . . </CODE>
```

To add a comment to your HTML source, you use the comment tag pair:

```
<!-- Comment text -->
```

Comment text displays as hidden text in Word. Comments do not appear on the Web page but can be viewed using a Web browser's View⇨Source command. You can enter comments and apply the Comments style.

Definition

To display text as a definition, surround the text with the definition tag pair:

```
<DFN>definition</DFN>
```

Definition List

This tag pair displays text using definition term <DT> (see the following section) and definition data <DD> tags. Definition lists include a descriptive term and definition description. Definition lists are sometimes referred to as a glossary list.

```
<DL>            ·
<DD>Defined data</DD>
</DL>
```

<DL> tag attributes include this one:

```
COMPACT
```

This attribute generates a definition list requiring less space.

Definition term

To format the term to be defined, you use the definition term tags:

```
<DT>Definition term</DT>
```

The following example shows how this tag pair can be used with a definition list:

```
<DL>
<DT>First term to be defined
<DD>Definition of first term
<DT>Next term to be defined
<DD>Next definition
</DL>
```

Headings (H1)

The headings H1 to H6 refer to HTML headings. Headings one through six display headings in differing font sizes from large to small. Headings are used to organize your page similar to outline headings.

H1
```
<H1> . . . </H1>
```

H2
```
<H2> . . . </H2>
```

H3
```
<H3> . . . </H3>
```

H4
```
<H4> . . . </H4>
```

H5
```
<H5> . . . </H5>
```

H6
```
<H6> . . . </H6>
```

HTML Markup

When you choose the HTML Markup style, you can insert any HTML tags directly into the source without having to choose the Edit⇨HTML Source command:

```
< > . . . </ >
```

The tags appear as hidden text in a red font in Word:

Keyboard
```
<KBD> . . . </KBD>
```

This tag pair displays text that should be entered from the keyboard.

Preformatted text

The preformatted text tags display text as it appears, so that you don't lose the formatting:

```
<PRE> . . . </PRE>
```

Preformatted text may include embedded tags, but not all tag types are permitted. The <PRE> tag displays text in a mono-spaced font such as Courier and can be used to include a small table of data in a document.

Sample

```
<SAMP> . . . </SAMP>
```

This tag pair displays text that is being used as sample text.

Typewriter

```
<TT> . . . </TT>
```

This tag pair displays text in a typewriter font.

Variable

```
<VAR> . . . </VAR>
```

This tag pair displays a name of a variable:

Default Paragraph Font

This style returns the paragraph's font to the default paragraph's font settings.

Emphasis

```
<EM> . . . </EM>
```

This tag pair displays text in italics or in a format to show emphasis. Emphasis is the logical equivalent of italics.

Followed Hyperlink

```
VLINK="color | #rrggbb"
```

This tag pair determines the color of a link that has been visited. VLINK is an attribute of the BODY tag.

Hyperlink

```
LINK="color | #rrggbb"
```

This tag determines the color of all links in a document. LINK is an attribute of the BODY tag.

Strong

```
<STRONG> . . . </STRONG>
```

This tag pair displays text in bold or in a format to show importance. Strong is the logical equivalent of bold.

Fonts

An HTML tag is available that you can use to designate fonts:

```
<FONT>
```

When you choose a different font from the font list box or specify a font size, Word surrounds the text with <FONT></FONT> tags with the appropriate attribute. Keep in mind that others viewing your Web pages may not have the same fonts on their systems.

When you increase the size of text by selecting it and then clicking Increase Font Size, Word adds or changes the SIZE attribute. Drop caps created with Word are removed; if you have a graphic image of a letter, you can insert it in front of the text.

<FONT> tag attributes are as follows:

```
SIZE="value"
```

Font sizes are not measured in point sizes but are mapped to the closest HTML size available, which ranges from size 1 to 7. Word displays the fonts in sizes ranging from 9 points to 36 points.

When you click the Increase Font Size button, the font changes to the next available size and the HTML source for the Font tag. Use Decrease Font Size to quickly switch to the next available font size. You can also change the type of font, but keep in mind that others viewing your Web pages may not have the same fonts on their systems. Also, some Web browsers display text in a default font only.

```
COLOR="color | #rrggbb"
```

When you change the color of selected text by clicking the Font Color button that appears at the end of the Formatting toolbar or choose the Format⇨Font command and choose the Color option in the Fonts tab, Word adds the COLOR attribute to the <FONT> tag.

Formatting

Common Word formatting, such as bold, strikethrough, italic, and underlines, are converted to HTML tags. Some special underline effects, such as dotted underlines, are converted to a single underline; however, other underline effects aren't converted. Highlighting is lost.

Several Word formatting features (Format⇨Font) are not available. Animated text and font formatting such as emboss, shadow, engrave, all caps, small caps, double strikethrough, and outline text effects are lost, but the text is retained.

You can manually add scrolling text into your page for readers viewing your page in Microsoft Internet Explorer by adding the MARQUEE tag, which is explained later.

The following tags are the equivalent tags that appear when you apply formatting by using the font and paragraph buttons that appear on the Formatting toolbar. These formats can also be applied by choosing the Format⇨Font or Format⇨ Paragraph commands.

This tag

```
<B> . . . </B>
```

displays text in boldface.

To display text in italics, you use these tags:

```
<I> . . . </I>
```

To display text with an underline, use this tag pair:

```
<U> . . . </U>
```

To align paragraphs, use the paragraph alignment tag

```
<P>
```

The default paragraph is left aligned.

Paragraph <P> tag attributes are as follows:

```
ALIGN="LEFT | CENTER | RIGHT"
```

Numbered and bulleted lists

An ordered list (numbered list) automatically numbers each item in the list:

```
<OL>
<LI>The first item</LI>
<LI>The second item</LI>
<LI>The third item</LI></OL>
</OL>
```

Unordered list (bulleted list) adds a bullet before each list item:

```
<UL>
<LI>The first item</LI>
<LI>The second item</LI>
<LI>The third item</LI>
</UL>
```

Indents

Word applies indents using the DIR tag. The DIR tag was designed to create indented directory lists:

```
<DIR><P>Paragraph indent</P></DIR>
```

Horizontal lines

To place a horizontal rule or separator between sections of text, you use the horizontal rule tag:

```
<HR>
```

By default, Word places the HR tag within centered paragraphs, so that choosing a horizontal line appears similar to the following:

```
<P ALIGN="CENTER"><HR></P>
```

The horizontal rule tag attributes are as follows:

```
ALIGN="LEFT | CENTER | RIGHT"
```

The ALIGN attribute specifies the alignment of the horizontal rule.

```
WIDTH="value"
```

The WIDTH attribute determines the width of the horizontal rule. For example, you can resize the line like a Word drawing object. You can also specify the width as number of pixels or a percentage. To specify a percentage, add the percent sign to the value, such as shown here:

```
<P ALIGN="CENTER"><HR ALIGN="LEFT" WIDTH="50%"></P>
```

Hyperlinks or anchors

When you click on the Insert Hyperlink button or choose Insert⇨Hyperlink, Word displays the Insert Hyperlink dialog box. The filename or URL you enter in the Link to file or URL text box appears in an anchor tag. The following example shows a link to a URL:

<A HREF="URL">hyperlink text</A>

If you type a named location to create a hyperlink to a specific part of a file—such as a bookmark in Word, a named cell in Microsoft Excel, or a named object in

Microsoft Access—in the Named location in file text box, the anchor appears similar to the following:

```
<A HREF="#ANCHOR_NAME"> . . . </A>
```

When you create a bookmark to define a target location in a document, the link appears similar to the following:

```
<A NAME="ANCHOR_NAME">hyperlink text</A>
```

The following shows a link to a target location in another document:

<A HREF="URL#anchor_name">hyperlink text</A>

Images

When you choose the Insert Picture button or select Insert⇨Picture, Word inserts the IMG tag in your document:

```
<IMG SRC="image.gif">
```

Graphics, such as pictures and clip art, are converted to GIF (.gif) format, unless the graphics are already in JPEG (.jpg) format. Drawing objects, such as text boxes and shapes, are not converted. Lines are converted to horizontal lines.

Drawing objects, such as AutoShapes, text effects, text boxes, and shadows, are not retained. You can use drawing tools in the Web page authoring environment by inserting Word Picture Objects. The object is converted to GIF format.

Equations, charts, and other OLE objects are converted to GIF images. The appearance is retained, but you won't be able to update these items.

Image <IMG> tag attributes are as follows:

```
SRC="URL | file"
```

The SRC attribute specifies the location of the image file.

```
ALT="Alternate Text"
```

The ALT attribute displays a text string in place of the image for browsers that cannot display images. This text also appears in graphics-capable browsers while the image is loading.

```
ALIGN="TOP | MIDDLE | BOTTOM"
```

The ALIGN attribute specifies the alignment in relation to surrounding text.

```
ISMAP
```

ISMAP is used to specify a server-side image map. If ISMAP is present, the image tag is within an anchor, and a corresponding map file exists, the image will become a "clickable" image. The pixel coordinates of the cursor will be appended to the URL specified in the anchor if the user clicks within the mapped image. Server-side image maps have been superceded by client-side image maps. Chapter 18 covers how to create clickable image maps.

```
USEMAP="map_name"
```

USEMAP is used to specify a client-side image map. USEMAP works in conjunction with the <MAP></MAP> tags. The coordinates of the mapped image appear within <MAP> </MAP> tags. If USEMAP is present, the image tag is within an anchor, and the MAP tags include the image map coordinates, the image will become a clickable image.

Special characters (entities)

Tabs are converted to the HTML tab character, represented in HTML source code as &#9. Tabs may appear as spaces in some Web browsers, so you may want to use indents or a table instead.

```
&keyword;
```

This character set displays a particular character identified by a special keyword.

```
&amp;
```

This set specifies the ampersand (&).

```
&lt;
```

This set specifies the less than (<) character.

```
&gt;
```

This set specifies the greater than (>) character.

The semicolon following the keyword is required. You can check a keyword list at the following URL:

```
http://www.w3.org/pub/WWW/MarkUp/html-spec/html-
      spec_9.html#SEC9.7
```

If you insert a character that doesn't include a special keyword, Word instructs the browser to display a character literally by inserting code similar to the following:

```
&#ascii_equivalent;
```

Tables

When you create a table, Word converts the table settings to HTML settings. Settings that aren't supported in the Web page authoring environment are lost. For example, colored and variable width borders are not retained. You can place borders around a table, however, and you can use horizontal lines to help emphasize or separate parts of your Web page.

Tables are converted with a fixed width. If you are an experienced Windows 95 user and are familiar with the Windows Registry, you can choose to convert a table with percentage width (so that the table is sized relative to the browser window) by setting the option PercentageTableWidth=1 in the following Windows 95 Registry location: HKEY_LOCAL_MACHINE\Software\Microsoft\Shared Tools\Text Converters\Export\HTML\Options.

Choosing the Insert Table button and selecting the number of cells automatically adds the tags for a table:

```
<TABLE> . . . </TABLE>
```

<TABLE> tag attributes are as follows:

```
BORDER="value"
```

The BORDER attribute defines the width of the table's border in pixels.

```
WIDTH="percent%" | WIDTH="value"
```

The WIDTH attribute defines the width of the table in percentage or in pixels.

```
CELLSPACING="value"
```

The CELLSPACING attribute defines in pixels the spacing between cells.

```
CELLPADDING="value"
```

The CELLPADDING attribute defines in pixels the distance between the data and the edge of the cell.

Table row

Once you have the basic table tag, you need to add tags for table elements, such as the table row tag:

```
<TR>
```

Table row <TR> attributes are as follows:

```
ALIGN="LEFT | CENTER | RIGHT"
```

The ALIGN attribute aligns the cell contents according to the type of alignment specified.

```
VALIGN="TOP | CENTER | BASELINE | BOTTOM"
```

The VALIGN attribute vertically aligns the contents of the cell in the row according to the type of alignment specified.

```
BACKGROUND="image"
```

This attribute should be familiar; it specifies an image to be tiled in the background of a cell.

```
BGCOLOR="color | #rrggbb"
```

This attribute defines the background color for the current row.

Table header

To add a header to your table, you use the following table header tag:

```
<TH>
```

Table header <TH> attributes are as follows:

```
ALIGN="LEFT | CENTER | RIGHT"
```

This attribute aligns the table header cell's contents according to the type of alignment specified.

```
BACKGROUND="URL | file"
```

This attribute specifies an image file to be tiled in the background of the table header cell.

```
BGCOLOR="color | #rrggbb"
```

This attribute defines the background color for the table header cell.

```
COLSPAN="value"
```

This attribute determines the number of adjoining columns for the table header cell to span.

```
ROWSPAN="value"
```

The ROWSPAN attribute determines the number of adjoining rows for the table header cell to span.

```
WIDTH="value"
```

This attribute sets the width of the table header cell to the number of pixels or a percentage.

```
NOWRAP
```

The NOWRAP attribute instructs the browser not to automatically wrap text to fit the width of the cell.

Table data

To define a table data cell, you need the table data tag:

```
<TD>
```

Table data <TD> attributes are as follows:

```
ROWSPAN="value"
```

This attribute specifies how many rows the cell spans.

```
COLSPAN="value"
```

This attribute specifies how many columns the cell spans.

```
VALIGN="TOP | CENTER | RIGHT"
```

This attribute aligns the data vertically.

```
ALIGN="TOP | CENTER | RIGHT"
```

The ALIGN attribute aligns the data horizontally according to the type of alignment specified.

```
NOWRAP
```

The NOWRAP attribute instructs the browser not to automatically wrap text to fit the width of the cell.

Caption

Suppose that you want to add a caption for your table. To do so, you need the table caption tag:

```
<CAPTION>Caption for the table</CAPTION>
```

<CAPTION> tag attributes are as follows:

```
ALIGN="TOP | BOTTOM"
```

This attribute aligns the caption at either the top or the bottom of the table. Captions always appear centered in relation to the table.

Forms

HTML forms let you define HTML documents containing text boxes, check boxes, and other form fields that readers can fill in when visiting your Web pages. When a person fills out the form and clicks on a Submit button, the information in the form is sent to a Web server and passed to a program for processing the form data. You need to add a program to get the information supplied by the user and return it to the browser for display or send the results to yourself via e-mail. Chapter 18 explains how to add form elements and process data input in an HTML form.

The basic form tags are as follows:

```
<FORM> . . . </FORM>
```

This tag pair defines a form area within an HTML document. A document may contain multiple <FORM> elements, but <FORM> elements may not be nested. You can use formatting and other non-form related tags inside a form.

<FORM> tag attributes are as follows:

```
ACTION="URL"
```

The ACTION attribute points to the location of the CGI program that will be used process the form.

```
METHOD=POST
```

The METHOD=POST attribute determines the method of exchanging data between the client and the program used to process the form. GET is the default; however, POST is the preferred method. The following example shows how the ACTION and METHOD attributes might appear:

```
<FORM ACTION="http://www.authors.com/cgi/process.cgi"
      METHOD=POST>
```

Check box

When you select Insert⇨Forms⇨Check Box or choose Check Box from the Control Toolbox, Word adds a check box to your page with this tag:

```
<INPUT TYPE=CHECKBOX>
```

CHECKBOX attributes are as follows:

```
CHECKED
```

This attribute adds a check mark to make the check box selected by default.

```
NAME="string"
```

This attribute specifies the name that is passed to the form processing script.

```
VALUE="string"
```

This attribute sets the value that the name is set to when processing the form.

Option button

When you select Insert⇨Forms⇨Option Button or choose the Option Button from the Control Toolbox, Word inserts this tag to display an option button (also known here as a *radio button*) that allows for selection of only one from of a group of option buttons:

```
<INPUT TYPE="RADIO">
```

The RADIO attributes are as follows:

```
NAME="string"
```

The NAME attribute specifies the name that is passed to the form processing script.

```
VALUE="string"
```

This attribute designates the value to which the name is set when processing the form.

Drop-down box and list box

Creating these elements in a form is not quite as straightforward as some of the others discussed here. The following tag pair defines a drop-down box or a list box that displays a set of list items from which the reader can select one or more items:

```
<SELECT> . . . </SELECT>
```

Each item in the selection lists appears with an <OPTION> tag. SELECT attributes are as follows:

```
NAME="string"
```

The NAME attribute, in this case, sets the name of the option values that, when selected, are passed to the script used to process the form.

```
SIZE="value"
```

This attribute determines the number of items displayed in the list.

```
MULTIPLE
```

The MULTIPLE attribute enables the reader to select more than one option from the list of items.

```
<OPTION>
```

This attribute defines a select field option. The <OPTION> tags are used to define the values for the select field. In the following example, all three options may be chosen, but Item two is selected by default (which is indicated by the SELECTED attribute):

```
<SELECT MULTIPLE>
<OPTION>Item one
<OPTION SELECTED>Item two
<OPTION>Item three
</SELECT>
```

Text box

When you select Insert⇨Forms⇨Text Box or click on the Text Box button in the Control Toolbox, Word inserts this tag to display a text box that accepts character data:

```
<INPUT TYPE=TEXT>
```

The TEXT attributes are as follows:

```
SIZE="value"
```

The SIZE attribute here determines the number of characters displayed for the text box.

```
MAXLENGTH="value"
```

This attribute defines the maximum number of characters allowed in the text box.

```
NAME="string"
```

This attribute specifies the name that is passed to the form processing script.

Text area

The TEXTAREA tag pair defines a text area where the user may enter text. If *default text* is present between the opening and closing tags, it will be displayed when the field appears.

<TEXTAREA>default text</TEXTAREA>

TEXTAREA attributes are as follows:

```
NAME="string"
```

This attribute specifies the name for the text-area value that is passed to the form processing script.

```
ROWS="value"
```

The ROWS attribute determines the height, by number of characters, of the text area box.

```
COLS="value"
```

The COLS attribute determines the number of characters wide the text area box will be.

Submit Button

When you select Insert⇨Forms⇨Submit Button, Word displays a Submit button that sends the completed form to the server to be processed by the program set using the FORM tags ACTION attribute. The tag for the Submit button is as follows:

```
<INPUT TYPE="SUBMIT">
```

SUBMIT attributes are as follows:

```
VALUE="string"
```

The VALUE attribute specifies a label to be displayed on the Submit button.

```
NAME="string"
```

This attribute specifies the name that is passed to the form processing script.

Reset button

When you select Insert⇨Forms⇨Reset Button, Word displays a button that resets the form variables to their default values, using this tag:

```
<INPUT TYPE="RESET">
```

RESET attributes are as follows:

```
VALUE="string"
```

The VALUE attribute specifies a label to be displayed on the Reset button.

```
NAME="string"
```

This attribute specifies the name that is passed to the form processing script.

Hidden

When you select Insert⇨Forms⇨Hidden or click on Hidden in the Control Toolbox, Word defines an invisible input field whose value will be sent along with the other form values when the form is submitted. This tag is used to pass state information from one script or form to another:

```
TYPE="HIDDEN"
```

Password

When you select Insert⇨Forms⇨Password or click on Password in the Control Toolbox, Word inserts this tag to display a text box that accepts character data but hides input by displaying asterisks instead of the entered characters.

```
<INPUT TYPE=PASSWORD>
```

PASSWORD attributes are as follows:

```
SIZE="value"
```

This attribute determines the number of characters displayed for the password text box.

```
MAXLENGTH="value"
```

This attribute defines the maximum number of characters allowed in the password text box.

```
NAME="string"
```

This attribute specifies the name to be passed to the script processing the form.

Scrolling text

When you select Insert⇨Scrolling text, Word adds the MARQUEE tags. The MARQUEE tag is Microsoft Internet Explorer specific. It doesn't work with Netscape Navigator:

```
<MARQUEE> . . . </MARQUEE>
```

<MARQUEE> tag attributes are as follows:

```
ALIGN="TOP | MIDDLE | BOTTOM"
```

This attribute aligns the marquee to the top middle or bottom of text surrounding the marquee.

```
BEHAVIOR="SCROLL | SLIDE | ALTERNATE"
```

This attribute determines how the marquee presents text.

```
BGCOLOR = "color | #rrggbb"
```

The BGCOLOR attribute sets the background color for the marquee.

```
DIRECTION="LEFT | RIGHT"
```

The DIRECTION attribute defines the direction for the text to scroll.

```
HEIGHT="value"
```

The HEIGHT attribute specifies the height of the marquee in pixels.

```
HSPACE="value"
```

The HSPACE attribute sets the amount of horizontal space in pixels to appear to the left and right of the marquee.

```
LOOP="value | infinite"
```

The LOOP attribute sets the number of times to display the marquee text. Infinite causes the marquee to continuously loop.

```
SCROLLAMOUNT
```

The SCROLLAMOUNT attribute sets the number of pixels to move the marquee text.

```
SCROLLDELAY="value"
```

The SCROLLDELAY attribute specifies the number of milliseconds to delay between the next iteration of the marquee.

```
VSPACE="value"
```

The VSPACE attribute defines the vertical space in pixels to appear above and below the marquee.

```
WIDTH="value"
```

The WIDTH attribute defines the width of the marquee area in pixels.

Background sound

This tag defines an audio file to play when the document is loaded in Microsoft Internet Explorer. The BGSOUND tag is an extension that doesn't work with Netscape Navigator:

<BGSOUND>

<BGSOUND> tag attributes are as follows:

```
SRC="URL | file "
```

This attribute specifies the URL or the file to play when the document is loaded.

```
LOOP="value | infinite"
```

This attribute sets the number of times to play the audio file. If set to infinite, the sound file will loop continuously.

Field codes

Field results are converted to text; field codes are removed. For example, if you insert a DATE field, the text of the date converts, but the date will not continue to update.

Tables of contents, tables of authorities, and index information is converted, but indexes and tables of contents, figures, and authorities can't be updated automatically after conversion because they are based on field codes. The table of contents displays asterisks in place of the page numbers; these asterisks are hyperlinks that the reader can click to navigate through the Web page. You can replace the asterisks with text that you want to have displayed for the hyperlinks. Because an HTML document is considered a single page, page numbering is removed.

✦   ✦   ✦

Index

Numbers

` (accent grave) sequence value, 838, 841

+ (addition)
  mathematical operator, 675
  operator in expressions for field instructions, 829

+ (plus sign), field result, 838

& (ampersand)
  with command names, 809
  in HTML forms, 565
  repositioning for shortcut keys, 809
  search operator, 165

* (asterisks)
  in Password field, 252
  place holders for field codes, 646
  search operator, 102, 103, 165

, (comma), search operator, 165

/ (division)
  mathematical operator, 675
  operator in expressions for field instructions, 829

- (minus sign)
  field result, 837
  in front of header or footer margin measurement, 289

- (subtraction)

mathematical operator, 675
operator in expressions for field instructions, 829

* (multiplication)
  mathematical operator, 675
  operator in expressions for field instructions, 829

(number sign) placeholder, 673, 837

% (percent)
  mathematical operator, 675
  operator in expressions for field instructions, 829

"" (quotation marks), search operator, 165

' (single quotation marks) literal text, 838, 841

~ (tilde)
  search operator, 165
  temporary files, 170, 173

~$ (tilde+dollar sign), temporary files, 170

/ (forward slash) on the numeric keypad (show or hide character formatting), 694

/a (access) startup switch, 10

/l (load add-in) switch, 9–10

/m (macro) switch, 7, 8

/mGoBack shortcut, 7, 8

/n (no default document) switch, 7

/t (template) switch, 9

; (semicolon)
  field result, 838

on the numeric keypad (forwarding separator), 673

< (less than)
  mathematical operator, 675

operator in expressions for field instructions, 829

< search operator, 104

<= (less than or equal to)
  mathematical operator, 675

operator in expressions for field instructions, 829

<> (not equal to)
  mathematical operator, 675
  operator in expressions for field instructions, 829

= (equal to)
  mathematical operator, 675
  operator in expressions for field instructions, 829

> (greater than)
  mathematical operator, 675
  operator in expressions for field instructions, 829

> search operator, 104

>= (greater than or equal to)
  mathematical operator, 675
  operator in expressions for field instructions, 829

? (question mark)
  button control setting, 15

B

P

IDG BOOKS WORLDWIDE REGISTRATION CARD

Visit our Web site at http://www.idgbooks.com

Title of this book: **Word 97 Bible**

My overall rating of this book: ❑ Very good [1] ❑ Good [2] ❑ Satisfactory [3] ❑ Fair [4] ❑ Poor [5]

How I first heard about this book:

❑ Found in bookstore; name: [6] _____

❑ Advertisement: [8] _____

❑ Word of mouth; heard about book from friend, co-worker, etc.: [10] _____

❑ Book review: [7] _____

❑ Catalog: [9] _____

❑ Other: [11] _____

What I liked most about this book:

_____

_____

What I would change, add, delete, etc., in future editions of this book:

_____

_____

Other comments: _____

Number of computer books I purchase in a year: ❑ 1 [12] ❑ 2-5 [13] ❑ 6-10 [14] ❑ More than 10 [15]

I would characterize my computer skills as: ❑ Beginner [16] ❑ Intermediate [17] ❑ Advanced [18] ❑ Professional [19]

I use ❑ DOS [20] ❑ Windows [21] ❑ OS/2 [22] ❑ Unix [23] ❑ Macintosh [24] ❑ Other: [25]_____

(please specify)

I would be interested in new books on the following subjects:

(please check all that apply, and use the spaces provided to identify specific software)

❑ Word processing: [26] _____

❑ Data bases: [28] _____

❑ File Utilities: [30] _____

❑ Networking: [32] _____

❑ Other: [34] _____

❑ Spreadsheets: [27] _____

❑ Desktop publishing: [29] _____

❑ Money management: [31] _____

❑ Programming languages: [33] _____

I use a PC at (please check all that apply): ❑ home [35] ❑ work [36] ❑ school [37] ❑ other: [38] _____

The disks I prefer to use are ❑ 5.25 [39] ❑ 3.5 [40] ❑ other: [41]_____

I have a CD ROM: ❑ yes [42] ❑ no [43]

I plan to buy or upgrade computer hardware this year: ❑ yes [44] ❑ no [45]

I plan to buy or upgrade computer software this year: ❑ yes [46] ❑ no [47]

Name: _____ Business title: [48] _____ Type of Business: [49] _____

Address (❑ home [50] ❑ work [51]/Company name: _____)

Street/Suite# _____

City [52]/State [53]/Zipcode [54]: _____ Country [55] _____

❑ **I liked this book!** You may quote me by name in future
IDG Books Worldwide promotional materials.

My daytime phone number is _____

IDG BOOKS WORLDWIDE

THE WORLD OF COMPUTER KNOWLEDGE®

☐ YES!

Please keep me informed about IDG Books Worldwide's World of Computer Knowledge. Send me your latest catalog.

INFO WORLD
TECHNICAL BOOKS

...SECRETS®

...FOR DUMMIES™

BESTSELLING BOOK SERIES FROM IDG

3-D Visual™

Macworld® Books